American Dissidents

American Dissidents

AN ENCYCLOPEDIA OF ACTIVISTS, SUBVERSIVES, AND PRISONERS OF CONSCIENCE

VOLUME 2: K–Z

Kathlyn Gay, Editor

HARTNESS LIBRARY SYSTEM
Vermont Technical College/CCV
Randolph Center, VT 05061

ABC-CLIO

Santa Barbara, California • Denver, Colorado • Oxford, England

Copyright 2012 by ABC-CLIO, LLC

All rights reserved. No part of this publication may be reproduced, stored in a retrieval system, or transmitted, in any form or by any means, electronic, mechanical, photocopying, recording, or otherwise, except for the inclusion of brief quotations in a review, without prior permission in writing from the publisher.

Library of Congress Cataloging-in-Publication Data

American dissidents : an encyclopedia of activists, subversives, and prisoners of conscience / Kathlyn Gay, editor.
   p. cm.
   Includes bibliographical references and index.
   ISBN 978–1–59884–764–2 (hardcopy : alk. paper) — ISBN 978–1–59884–765–9 (ebook)
1. Dissenters—United States—Biography—Encyclopedias. 2. Political activists—United States—Biography—Encyclopedias. 3. Social reformers—United States—Biography—Encyclopedias. 4. Civil rights workers—United States—Biography—Encyclopedias. 5. United States—Politics and government—20th century—Encyclopedias. 6. United States—Politics and government—21st century—Encyclopedias. 7. Political culture—United States—History—20th century—Encyclopedias. 8. Political culture—United States—History—21st century—Encyclopedias. I. Gay, Kathlyn.
E747.A678 2012
303.48′4—dc23   2011042833

ISBN: 978–1–59884–764–2
EISBN: 978–1–59884–765–9

16 15 14 13 12   1 2 3 4 5

This book is also available on the World Wide Web as an eBook.
Visit www.abc-clio.com for details.

ABC-CLIO, LLC
130 Cremona Drive, P.O. Box 1911
Santa Barbara, California 93116-1911

This book is printed on acid-free paper ∞

Manufactured in the United States of America

Contents

List of Entries by Broad Topic, ix

Chronological List of Entries, xiii

Introduction, xvii

Abbey, Edward, 1

Abu-Jamal, Mumia, 4

Abzug, Bella, 9

Addams, Jane, 13

Al-Arian, Sami, 17

Ali, Muhammad, 22

Asner, Ed, 26

Ayers, William, 29

Balch, Emily Greene, 35

Baldwin, James, 39

Banks, Dennis, 43

Bari, Judi, 47

Beck, Glenn, 51

Benitez, Lucas, 55

Benjamin, Medea, 59

Berrigan, Daniel, and Berrigan, Philip, 63

Bethune, Mary McLeod, 67

Boggs, Grace Lee, 71

Bowe, Frank G., 75

Brown, Ruth, 78

Brownmiller, Susan, 82

Bullard, Robert, 86

Burroughs, William, 90

Cammermeyer, Grethe, 97

Carlin, George, 100

Carmichael, Stokely/Ture, Kwame, 105

Carson, Rachel, 109

Catt, Carrie Chapman, 113

Chávez, César, 117

Chavis, Benjamin Franklin, 121

Choi, Daniel, 125

Chomsky, Noam, 129

Clark, Ramsey, 134

Coffin, William Sloane, 137

Collier, John, 141

Commoner, Barry, 145

Corbett, Jim, 149

Corrie, Rachel, 152

Coughlin, Charles E., 156

Darrow, Clarence, 161

Dart, Justin, Jr., 165

Davis, Angela, 169
Day, Dorothy, 173
Debs, Eugene V., 177
Dees, Morris, 181
Dellinger, David, 185
Deloria, Vine, Jr., 189
Dennett, Mary Ware, 193
Douglas, Marjory Stoneman, 197
Dowie, John Alexander, 201
Du Bois, W. E. B., 205
Ellsberg, Daniel, 211
Farrakhan, Louis, 215
Flynn, Elizabeth Gurley, 219
Frank, Barney, 223
Franken, Al, 227
Friedan, Betty, 231
Gaskin, Stephen, 237
Gibbs, Lois, 240
Gilman, Charlotte Perkins, 244
Giovanni, Nikki, 248
Goldman, Emma, 253
Goodman, Paul, 256
Gregory, Dick, 260
Hall, Gus, 267
Hamer, Fannie Lou, 271
Hampton, Fred, 275
Hayden, Tom, 278
Height, Dorothy, 282
Herrick, William, 286
Hill, Joe, 290

Hill, Julia "Butterfly," 294
Hoffman, Abbie, 298
Horowitz, David, 302
Horton, Myles, 307
Hubbard, Walter, Jr., 311
Humphry, Derek, 315
Hurston, Zora Neale, 319
Johnson, Harriet McBryde, 325
Jones, Mary Harris, 329
Kelley, Florence, 333
Kelly, Kathy, 337
Kernaghan, Charles, 341
Kevorkian, Jack, 345
King, Martin Luther, Jr., 350
Kochiyama, Yuri, 354
Kovic, Ron, 358
Kuhn, Margaret, 363
Kunstler, William, 366
LaDuke, Winona, 373
LaRouche, Lyndon, 377
Leopold, Aldo, 380
Limbaugh, Rush, 384
Malcolm X, 389
Mankiller, Wilma, 393
Manning, Bradley, 397
McCarthy, Joseph, 401
McCorvey, Norma, 406
Means, Russell, 409
Michelman, Kate, 414
Milk, Harvey, 419

Moore, Harry, 423

Moore, Michael, 427

Murie, Margaret, 431

Nader, Ralph, 437

Norman, Mildred, 441

Ochs, Phil, 447

O'Hair, Madalyn Murray, 451

O'Keefe, James, 455

Oppenheimer, J. Robert, 460

Palin, Sarah, 465

Parks, Rosa, 469

Parsons, Lucy, 473

Paul, Alice, 477

Peltier, Leonard, 481

Perkins, Frances, 485

Rand, Ayn, 491

Randolph, A. Philip, 496

Rankin, Jeannette, 500

Robeson, Paul, 503

Roosevelt, Eleanor, 507

Rosenberg, Ethel and Rosenberg, Julius, 511

Rudd, Mark, 516

Rustin, Bayard, 520

Sacco, Ferdinando Nicola, and Vanzetti, Bartolomeo, 525

Sanger, Margaret, 529

Schlafly, Phyllis, 534

Schneiderman, Rose, 538

Seale, Bobby, 542

Seeger, Pete, 546

Sheehan, Cindy, 550

Sheen, Martin, 555

Silkwood, Karen Gay, 559

Simkins, Modjeska Monteith, 563

Sinclair, Upton, 567

Sontag, Susan, 571

Steinmetz, Charles, 576

Strong, Anna Louise, 581

Tall, JoAnn, 585

Tarbell, Ida, 589

Tiller, George, 593

Vera Cruz, Philip, 599

Vogler, Joe, 602

Walker, Alice, 607

Wallis, Jim, 611

Wiesel, Elie, 615

Wolf, Hazel, 619

Woodhull, Victoria, 623

Wright, Ann, 627

Yasui, Minoru, 633

Yeshitela, Omali, 637

Zappa, Frank, 643

Zinn, Howard, 647

Selected Bibliography, 651

About the Editor and Contributors, 671

Index, 673

List of Entries by Broad Topic

Civil Rights Activists

Abzug, Bella
Ali, Muhammad
Baldwin, James
Benjamin, Medea
Bethune, Mary McLeod
Boggs, Grace Lee
Brown, Ruth
Carmichael, Stokely/Ture, Kwame
Chavis, Benjamin Franklin
Coffin, William Sloane
Collier, John
Corbett, Jim
Darrow, Clarence
Dees, Morris
Du Bois, W. E. B.
Giovanni, Nikki
Hamer, Fannie Lou
Hampton, Fred
Height, Dorothy
Hoffman, Abbie
Horton, Myles
Hubbard, Walter, Jr.
Kelley, Florence
King, Martin Luther, Jr.
Kochiyama, Yuri
Kuhn, Margaret
Kunstler, William
Moore, Harry
Parks, Rosa
Parsons, Lucy

Randolph, A. Philip
Robeson, Paul
Rudd, Mark
Rustin, Bayard
Seale, Bobby
Sheen, Martin
Simkins, Modjeska Monteith
Walker, Alice
Wiesel, Elie
Yasui, Minoru
Zappa, Frank

Disability Rights Activists

Bowe, Frank G.
Dart, Justin, Jr.
Johnson, Harriet McBryde

End-of-Life Issues Activists

Humphry, Derek
Kevorkian, Jack

Environmentalists

Abbey, Edward
Bari, Judi
Bullard, Robert
Carson, Rachel
Commoner, Barry
Douglas, Marjory Stoneman
Gaskin, Stephen
Gibbs, Lois
Hill, Julia "Butterfly"

x | List of Entries by Broad Topic

Leopold, Aldo
Murie, Margaret

Labor Activists

Benitez, Lucas
Chávez, César
Day, Dorothy
Debs, Eugene V.
Flynn, Elizabeth Gurley
Hall, Gus
Herrick, William
Hill, Joe
Jones, Mary Harris
Kernaghan, Charles
Perkins, Frances
Randolph, A. Philip
Schneiderman, Rose
Silkwood, Karen Gay
Tarbell, Ida
Vera Cruz, Philip

LGBT Rights Activists

Cammermeyer, Grethe
Choi, Daniel
Frank, Barney
Milk, Harvey
Rustin, Bayard

Native American Rights Activists

Banks, Dennis
Deloria, Vine, Jr.
LaDuke, Winona
Mankiller, Wilma
Means, Russell
Tall, JoAnn

Peace Activists

Asner, Ed
Balch, Emily Greene
Berrigan, Daniel, and Berrigan, Philip
Corrie, Rachel
Day, Dorothy

Goodman, Paul
Hayden, Tom
Kelly, Kathy
Kovic, Ron
Norman, Mildred
Ochs, Phil
Rankin, Jeannette
Seeger, Pete
Sheehan, Cindy
Strong, Anna Louise
Wright, Ann

Political Activists

Abzug, Bella
Ayers, William
Beck, Glenn
Boggs, Grace Lee
Burroughs, William
Carlin, George
Chomsky, Noam
Coughlin, Charles E.
Davis, Angela
Dellinger, David
Ellsberg, Daniel
Franken, Al
Goldman, Emma
Horowitz, David
LaRouche, Lyndon
Limbaugh, Rush
McCarthy, Joseph
McCorvey, Norma
Moore, Michael
Nader, Ralph
Oppenheimer, J. Robert
Palin, Sarah
Rustin, Bayard
Schlafly, Phyllis
Sinclair, Upton
Sontag, Susan
Steinmetz, Charles
Vogler, Joe
Yeshitela, Omali
Zinn, Howard

Political Prisoners

Abu-Jamal, Mumia
Al-Arian, Sami
Peltier, Leonard
Rosenberg, Ethel, and Rosenberg, Julius
Sacco, Ferdinando Nicola, and Vanzetti, Bartolomeo

Religious Dissidents and Activists

Dowie, John Alexander
Farrakhan, Louis
Malcolm X
O'Hair, Madalyn Murray
Wallis, Jim

Social Justice Activists

Addams, Jane
Asner, Ed
Boggs, Grace Lee
Bullard, Robert
Perkins, Frances
Roosevelt, Eleanor

Women's Rights Activists

Abzug, Bella
Brownmiller, Susan
Catt, Carrie Chapman
Dennett, Mary Ware
Friedan, Betty
Gilman, Charlotte Perkins
Hurston, Zora Neale
Michelman, Kate
Paul, Alice
Perkins, Frances
Sanger, Margaret
Tiller, George
Wolf, Hazel
Woodhull, Victoria

Chronological List of Entries

Below are the people profiled in this book, listed in order by birth date.

Jones, Mary Harris (1830–1930)
Woodhull, Victoria (1838–1927)
Dowie, John Alexander (1847–1907)
Parsons, Lucy (1853–1942)
Debs, Eugene V. (1855–1926)
Darrow, Clarence (1857–1938)
Tarbell, Ida (1857–1944)
Kelley, Florence (1859–1932)
Catt, Carrie Chapman (1859–1947)
Addams, Jane (1860–1935)
Gilman, Charlotte Perkins (1860–1935)
Steinmetz, Charles (1865–1923)
Balch, Emily Greene (1867–1961)
Du Bois, W. E. B. (1868–1963)
Goldman, Emma (1869–1940)
Dennett, Mary Ware (1872–1947)
Bethune, Mary McLeod (1875–1955)
Sinclair, Upton (1878–1968)
Hill, Joe (1879–1915)
Sanger, Margaret (1879–1966)
Perkins, Frances (1880–1965)
Rankin, Jeannette (1880–1973)
Schneiderman, Rose (1882–1972)
Collier, John (1884–1968)
Roosevelt, Eleanor (1884–1962)
Paul, Alice (1885–1977)
Strong, Anna Louise (1885–1970)
Leopold, Aldo (1887–1948)
Randolph, A. Philip (1889–1979)

Douglas, Marjory Stoneman (1890–1998)
Flynn, Elizabeth Gurley (1890–1964)
Brown, Ruth (1891–1975)
Coughlin, Charles E. (1891–1979)
Hurston, Zora Neale (1891–1960)
Sacco, Ferdinando Nicola and Vanzetti, Bartolomeo (1891–1927) and (1888–1927)
Day, Dorothy (1897–1980)
Robeson, Paul (1898–1976)
Wolf, Hazel (1898–2000)
Simkins, Modjeska Monteith (1899–1992)
Murie, Margaret (1902–2003)
Oppenheimer, J. Robert (1904–1967)
Vera Cruz, Philip (1904–1994)
Horton, Myles (1905–1990)
Kuhn, Margaret (1905–1995)
Moore, Harry (1905–1951)
Rand, Ayn (1905–1982)
Carson, Rachel (1907–1964)
McCarthy, Joseph (1908–1957)
Norman, Mildred (1908–1981)
Hall, Gus (1910–2000)
Goodman, Paul (1911–1972)
Height, Dorothy (1912–2010)
Rustin, Bayard (1912–1987)
Parks, Rosa (1913–2005)
Vogler, Joe (1913–1993)
Burroughs, William (1914–1997)
Boggs, Grace Lee (1915–)
Rosenberg, Ethel, and Rosenberg, Julius (1915–1953) and (1918–1953)
Dellinger, David (1915–2004)

Herrick, William (1915–2004)
Yasui, Minoru (1916–1986)
Commoner, Barry (1917–)
Hamer, Fannie Lou (1917–1977)
Seeger, Pete (1919–)
Kunstler, William (1919–1995)
O'Hair, Madalyn Murray (1919–1995)
Abzug, Bella (1920–1998)
Berrigan, Daniel, and Berrigan, Philip (1921–) and (1923–2002)
Kochiyama, Yuri (1921–)
Friedan, Betty (1921–2006)
LaRouche, Lyndon (1922–)
Zinn, Howard (1922–2010)
Schlafly, Phyllis (1924–)
Baldwin, James (1924–1987)
Coffin, William Sloane (1924–2006)
Hubbard, Walter, Jr. (1924–2007)
Malcolm X (1925–1965)
Clark, Ramsey (1927–)
Abbey, Edward (1927–1989)
Chávez, César (1927–1993)
Chomsky, Noam (1928–)
Kevorkian, Jack (1928–2011)
Wiesel, Elie (1928–)
Asner, Ed (1929–)
King, Martin Luther, Jr. (1929–1968)
Humphry, Derek (1930–)
Milk, Harvey (1930–1978)
Dart, Justin, Jr. (1930–2002)
Ellsberg, Daniel (1931–)
Gregory, Dick (1932–)
Sontag, Susan (1933–2004)
Farrakhan, Louis (1933–)
Corbett, Jim (1933–2001)
Deloria, Vine, Jr. (1933–2005)
Nader, Ralph (1934–)
Brownmiller, Susan (1935–)
Gaskin, Stephen (1935–)
Dees, Morris (1936–)
Seale, Bobby (1936–)
Hoffman, Abbie (1936–1989)
Banks, Dennis (1937–)
Carlin, George (1937–2008)

Hayden, Tom (1939–)
Horowitz, David (1939–)
Means, Russell (1939–)
Ochs, Phil (1940–1976)
Frank, Barney (1940–)
Sheen, Martin (1940–)
Yeshitela, Omali (1941–)
Zappa, Frank (1941–1993)
Carmichael, Stokely/Ture, Kwame (1941–1998)
Tiller, George (1941–2009)
Ali, Muhammad (1942–)
Cammermeyer, Grethe (1942–)
Michelman, Kate (1942–)
Giovanni, Nikki (1943–)
Ayers, William (1944–)
Davis, Angela (1944–)
Peltier, Leonard (1944–)
Walker, Alice (1944–)
Mankiller, Wilma (1945–2010)
Bullard, Robert (1946–)
Kovic, Ron (1946–)
Silkwood, Karen Gay (1946–1974)
McCorvey, Norma (1947–)
Rudd, Mark (1947–)
Wright, Ann (1947–)
Bowe, Frank G. (1947–2007)
Chavis, Benjamin Franklin (1948–)
Kernaghan, Charles (1948–)
Wallis, Jim (1948–)
Bari, Judi (1949–1997)
Hampton, Fred (1948–1969)
Franken, Al (1951–)
Gibbs, Lois (1951–)
Limbaugh, Rush (1951–)
Benjamin, Medea (1952–)
Kelly, Kathy (1953–)
Tall, JoAnn (1953–)
Abu-Jamal, Mumia (1954–)
Moore, Michael (1954–)
Sheehan, Cindy (1957–)
Johnson, Harriet McBryde (1957–2008)
Al-Arian, Sami (1958–)
LaDuke, Winona (1959–)

Beck, Glenn (1964–)
Palin, Sarah (1964–)
Hill, Julia "Butterfly" (1974–)
Benitez, Lucas (1976–)

Corrie, Rachel (1979–2003)
Choi, Daniel (1981–)
O'Keefe, James (1984–)
Manning, Bradley (1987–)

Introduction

They march. They rally. They carry banners and handwritten signs. They stand on street corners or in front of government buildings. They sneak into offices to spy on politicians or corporate officials. They leak documents online. They write letters. They lobby and deliver messages of protest to government officials or seek support for numerous causes. They commit acts of civil disobedience—defying laws to bring about social justice or to further their particular cause. *They* are American dissidents and activists.

Scope

The focus of *American Dissidents: An Encyclopedia of Activists, Subversives, and Prisoners of Conscience*, a two-volume biographical encyclopedia, is on twentieth- and twenty-first-century Americans. In a few cases, the individuals profiled lived most of their lives in the late 1800s, but their activities carried over to the 1900s and influenced later generations. Birthdates of people featured in this encyclopedia span from 1830 to 1987, and a great many are active today. The 152 Americans featured are meant to represent diverse ethnic, racial, and religious backgrounds as well as various movements and ideologies. Included are authors, anarchists, civil rights advocates, communists, entertainers, environmentalists, government officials, labor organizers, libertarians, military personnel, muckrakers, pacifists, political activists on the left and right, religious leaders, and women suffragists. Some of them have been labeled subversives, and others have been jailed and are known as political prisoners or prisoners of conscience. Some have been executed for activities considered subversive. Others have been murdered by their opponents. Still others are current activists, deeply committed to the causes they espouse. The entries have been written primarily by longtime reference book author and editor Kathlyn Gay. Those entries are not signed. Seven other contributors have written other entries, and their names appear at the bottom of the entry.

The book is arranged in A–Z order, by individuals' names. At the beginning of the book, there are two helpful lists to help readers learn more about the people featured in this encyclopedia, including the list of entries arranged by broad topic, such as "Civil Rights Activists," "Environmentalists," and "Political Activists"; and a list of the people profiled arranged in chronological order by birth date. Each entry concludes with a list of references, and a selected bibliography provides resources such as books, articles, web sites, and videos for further research and reading on America's dissidents, subversives, and political prisoners. A comprehensive index completes the work.

A Long Tradition of Dissent

The dissidents and radicals of recent times have followed a long tradition. Dissent and challenges to the economy, social order, and government have been part of the American scene since colonial times. Rebels, reformers, and dissenters of the past laid the groundwork for social, economic, and political change in the United States.

Some of the earliest dissenters in American history were Christians such as Anne Marbury Hutchinson (1591–1643). She emigrated from England to the Massachusetts Bay Colony and believed in the right of individuals to determine their own lives. Hutchinson did not recognize civil authority or formal religious laws and doctrines. She and her family were continually harassed and eventually were banished from the colony in 1638. They were forced to move to a small island off of Rhode Island.

Another historic leader banished from the Massachusetts colony was Roger Williams (1603–1683), who disagreed with Puritans and their belief in governing by biblical codes. Puritans persecuted anyone who did not abide by their strict church rules. Williams established a settlement in 1638 that was a refuge for those who believed in religious liberty; the colony became the state of Rhode Island.

William Penn (1644–1718) was another dissident who was adamant about the right of every person to worship as she or he believed. A member of the Religious Society of Friends (or Quakers), Penn founded the Pennsylvania colony that welcomed people of diverse beliefs and those who had no religious affiliation.

The concepts of religious freedom and civil liberty lived on and inspired many rebels who protested British rule of the American colonies. Patrick Henry (1736–1799) was just such a person and loudly proclaimed "give me liberty or give me death." Thomas Paine (1737–1809) was well known for his 1776 pamphlet *Common Sense*, in which he asserts that government at its best is a "necessary evil" and government "in its worst state is intolerable." His words encouraged American rebels to fight for independence from the repressive British government during the Revolutionary War. That radical dissent brought about the United States of America.

Native American Dissent

As colonists from Europe fought for their right to dissent and establish their own form of government, the indigenous people of North America went to war to maintain their "rights of occupancy" of their homelands where they had lived for centuries. From the 1600s to the late 1800s, so-called Indian Wars between tribal groups and white militia and soldiers erupted intermittently. Frequently, tribes lost their battles and their lands. In some instances, tribes signed treaties with the U.S. government, agreeing to exchange their territories for annual payments that would allow Indians to buy food and other necessities. During the 1820s, tribal chiefs agreed to sell their land for as little as 53 cents per acre.

In 1830, the U.S. Congress passed the Indian Removal Act, which was designed to force thousands of Cherokee, Chickasaw, Choctaw, Creek, and Seminole in the Southeast to move to what is present-day Oklahoma. The Cherokees, who believed in nonviolent resistance, fought the removal laws in the U.S. Supreme Court, which ruled in favor of the Cherokee. Chief Justice John Marshall declared that the Cherokee Nation was sovereign and the removal laws invalid. However, President Andrew Jackson, who was elected in 1828, wanted Indian territory and believed that Indians should be sent as far west of the Mississippi River as possible. Jackson defied the High Court's decision. Thousands of Cherokee were forced into concentration camps where contagious diseases killed many, and many others died during the march west with little clothing, food, or shelter from freezing weather. The march became known as the Trail of Tears.

By the middle of twentieth century, Native American groups were rising up to challenge oppression and demand social justice. The American Indian Movement was formed in 1968, and other Indian rights organizations began agitating for their civil rights. Those efforts continue to the present time.

Early Abolitionists and Civil Rights Activists

Important dissenters of the past who risked and sometimes lost their lives in efforts to abolish slavery were individuals such as David Walker (1785–1830), a militant black man who wrote "Walker's Appeal," urging slaves to resort to violence when necessary to win their freedom. Although abolitionist William Lloyd Garrison thought emancipation could be accomplished through persuasion, he ran large portions of Walker's Appeal, together with a review, in his paper, the *Liberator*.

Elijah Lovejoy (1802–1837) was a publisher of an antislavery newspaper, the *Saint Louis Observer*. He was killed by a proslavery mob.

Sojourner Truth (1797–1883) was born a slave named Isabella. She walked to freedom when her owner refused to release her as was required by a New York law. She became a traveling preacher, taking the name Sojourner Truth. Though she could not read or write, she was a powerful orator and was committed to abolition and women's rights. She was often harassed and sometimes brutally attacked when she spoke, but continued her mission until the end of her life.

Sisters Sarah Grimké (1792–1873) and Angelina Grimké Weld (1805–1879), who were from a slaveholding family in South Carolina, became strong abolitionists. They moved to Philadelphia, joined the Quakers, and spoke out loud and clear about their firsthand experiences with the evils of slavery.

Escaped slave Frederick Douglass (1818–1895) was one of the leaders of the abolitionist movement who is still venerated today. He became famous when his autobiography was published in 1845. He was a strong advocate for black voting rights and civil liberties.

Henry David Thoreau (1817–1862) was an activist and dissident who watched over the underground railroad in Concord, Massachusetts, and delivered speeches attacking slavery. He is better known, however, for his essay *On Civil Disobedience*, in which he explained how he refused to pay the Massachusetts poll tax that the U.S. government implemented to fund a war in Mexico and to enforce the Fugitive Slave Law. The essay, in fact, has inspired many Americans to dissent, including Dr. Martin Luther King Jr., who wrote: "During my freshman days in 1944 at Atlanta's Morehouse College I read Henry David Thoreau's essay *On Civil Disobedience* for the first time. Here, in this courageous New Englander's refusal to pay his taxes and his choice of jail rather than support a war that would spread slavery's territory into Mexico, I made my first contact with the theory of nonviolent resistance. Fascinated by Thoreau's idea of refusing to cooperate with an evil system, I was so deeply moved that I reread the work several times" (Katz 1995, 468).

In more recent times, civil disobedience also has been at the core of some antiwar

Separation as Dissent

In their dissent, some Americans separated themselves from established society and founded utopian communities, or communes, in the 1800s. Josiah Warren (1798–1874), for example, founded the colonies Equity and Utopia in Ohio; and Modern Times in New York during the 1830s. None survived for long periods.

One group of German immigrant dissenters began an experiment in southern Indiana. Known as Harmonie, it was founded by George Rapp and his adopted son Frederick, who had emigrated from Wurtemberg (or Wurttemburg), Germany, in 1803. At least 600 people joined Rapp in setting up a colony in Pennsylvania. Members of the community agreed that all their cash and property would be used for the benefit of the community. In turn, they were provided with all the "necessaries of life." In 1824, Rapp sold his utopian experiment to Robert Owen (1771–1858).

Renaming the village New Harmony, Owen formed the Preliminary Society of New Harmony with the stated purpose of promoting worldwide happiness. He hoped to set up an "empire of peace and goodwill." But within two years, New Harmony failed, although Owen's ideas were the basis for other communities, including the Blue Spring Community near Bloomington, Indiana, an experiment called Maxwell in Ontario, Canada, and one in Yellow Springs, Ohio, now the site of Antioch College. But by 1830, all of the Owenite communities had disintegrated.

From about 1885 through the first decade of the 1900s, a number of communal experiments began in the Far West, in northern California, Oregon, and Washington. Some of these experiments were founded by religious groups; others were prompted by socialist and labor movement leaders.

At least six communitarian experiments established in western Washington were based on the ideal of sharing social and economic activities—dissents against the established capitalist system. One of the first was the Puget Sound Co-Operative Colony initiated in 1887, partly as a protest against the Chinese, who had been encouraged by business leaders to immigrate to Seattle and work for low wages. Several white labor organizations in Seattle agitated against the Chinese workers, causing riots and eventually bringing about the deportation of hundreds of Chinese.

Early Protests by Workers and Suffragists

While some of the individuals profiled in this encyclopedia were involved in advocacy for labor during the 1900s, long before that time, working people were fighting for a living wage and shorter workdays, and against deplorable working conditions and oppressive corporations and their wealthy executives. Before the Civil War (1861–1865), labor strikes were common. In 1828, for example, women mill workers struck in Dover, New Hampshire. "They shot off gunpowder, in protest against new factory rules, which charged fines for coming late, forbade talking on the job, and required church attendance," wrote Howard Zinn in his *People's History* (Zinn 2003, 228). In another example, Zinn points out that in 1835, "fifty different trades organized unions in Philadelphia, and there was a successful general strike of laborers, factory workers, bookbinders, jewelers, coal heavers, butchers, cabinet workers—for the ten-hour [work] day.... Weavers in Philadelphia in the early 1840s—mostly Irish immigrants working at home for employers—struck for higher wages, attacked the homes of those refusing to strike, and destroyed their work. A sheriff's posse tried to arrest some strikers, but it was broken up by four hundred weavers armed with muskets and sticks" (Zinn 2003, 225–26).

One of the most outspoken advocates for female and male workers in the early 1800s was Sarah Bagley (1806–1847?), one of the "mill girls" (as they referred to themselves) at the textile mills in Lowell, Massachusetts. Bagley became a powerful speaker and writer seeking the 10-hour workday. At the time, workers toiled for 12 to 14 hours per day in the textile mills that 10 corporations had established in Lowell. There, the textile corporations were all powerful. "Most pronounced was the control corporations exerted over the lives of their workers. The men who ran the corporations and managed the mills sought to regulate the moral conduct and social behavior of their workforce. Within the factory, overseers were responsible for maintaining work discipline and meeting production schedules. . . . Male and female workers were expected to observe the Sabbath, and temperance was strongly encouraged. The clanging factory bell summoned operatives to and from the mill, constantly reminding them that their days were structured around work (Lowell National Historic Park).

Bagley with five other women formed the Lowell Female Labor Reform Association in 1847. They petitioned the state legislature to pass a law requiring a 10-hour workday, but the lawmakers refused to act. Nevertheless, Lowell textile corporations gave in to the political pressure and shortened the workday to 11 hours.

In mills and other industries, workers achieved few if any reforms in spite of protests and strikes. Many striking workers were arrested and found guilty of criminal conspiracy, or they were injured or killed in confrontations with local police and state militia. Their sacrifices paved the way for the labor movement of the next century.

Along with workers, suffragists and women's rights advocates were making their presence felt in the 1800s. Individuals like Lucretia Mott (1793–1880), Elizabeth Cady Stanton (1815–1902) and Lucy Stone (1818–1893) were ardent suffragists (as well as abolitionists). Men who publicly supported women's rights included Lucretia Mott's husband James and Lucy Stone's husband Henry Blackwell. Anna Howard Shaw (1847–1919), an ordained Methodist minister and physician, was a forceful orator, and she used her skills to campaign for women's right to vote.

In 1848, suffragists organized the Seneca Falls Convention in upstate New York, which was attended by both women and men. The convention adopted a Declaration of Rights and Sentiments modeled after the Declaration of Independence. It declared "We hold these truths to be self-evident: that all men and women are created equal; that they are endowed by their Creator with certain inalienable rights" and pointed out that "The history of mankind is a history of repeated injuries and usurpations on the part of man toward woman, having in direct object the establishment of an absolute tyranny over her." After listing all the many "injuries and usurpations," the declaration concluded that "because women do feel themselves aggrieved, oppressed, and fraudulently deprived of their most sacred rights, we insist that they have immediate admission to all the rights and privileges which belong to them as citizens of the United States." Sixty-eight women and 32 men signed the declaration, which, when released to the public, generated widespread interest—and controversy—but ultimately paved the way for passage of the Nineteenth Amendment granting women the right to vote.

As American history demonstrates, dissent has been part of the nation's makeup for centuries. It has not stopped. And with all the many forms of communication available currently—from blogs to Facebook to Twitter to YouTube—dissent appears to have accelerated. The challenge often is to determine whether the people dissenting are pursuing social justice or seeking self promotion. Still, the pages following illustrate the ongoing struggles for social and economic justice, religious tolerance, and democratic government, as well as preservation of the natural environment that supports all Americans.

Kathlyn Gay

References

Katz, William Loren. *Eyewitness: A Living Documentary of the African American Contribution to American History.* Revised and updated. New York: Touchstone/Simon and Schuster, 1995.

Zinn, Howard. *A People's History of the United States: 1942–Present.* New York: HarperCollins, 2003.

Kelley, Florence (1859–1932)

Florence Kelley "was not afraid of truth, she was not afraid of life, she was not afraid of death, she was not afraid of enemies." This tribute by fellow social reformer Lillian Wald was given at a memorial service for Kelley in 1932. During her life, Kelley did indeed have enemies—some of whom condemned her for being a follower of Karl Marx and Friedrich Engels, who argued that in a socialist system no one would own private property and everyone would share the benefits of industrialization. (The two later advocated communism and wrote *The Communist Manifesto*.) In spite of critics, Kelley persevered as a social dissident, an impatient rebel who worked to prevent child-labor practices and to regulate factory working hours for women and children.

Born on September 12, 1859, in Philadelphia, Pennsylvania, to a Quaker-Unitarian family, Florence Kelley was the daughter of Republican congressman William Darrah Kelley, who represented a working-class community, and Caroline Kelley, who was from a family of distinguished Quakers. The Kelley family included five more girls, all of whom died in early childhood, and two boys. The deaths of the five Kelley girls left Caroline with a deep sadness and a fear that others in the family would be lost, although she tried to hide such feelings from her surviving children.

Florence was sickly as a child and was unable to attend school, so her father taught her to read. Her father's extensive library at home provided her with books for her self-education. During her childhood, her father took her on midnight tours of industries where she saw the deplorable conditions of factories that employed young boys in steel and glass manufacturing. This type of experience influenced her decision later in life to work for laws banning child labor. She also was influenced by her parents and relatives who were abolitionists and frequently at risk for their activism.

Kelley received her high school education at Miss Longreth's School, a highly respected Quaker institution in Philadelphia. In 1876, at age 17 and with encouragement from her father, Kelley enrolled at Cornell University in New York. At the time, most universities did not admit females, but Cornell had been accepting women since 1873. Because of illness, Kelley attended sporadically, graduating in 1882. She attempted to continue her graduate study at the University of Pennsylvania, but the school denied her admittance. She also was denied entrance to Oxford University. So, accompanied by her mother and younger brother, she traveled to Switzerland to study government and law at the University of Zurich, the only European university to admit women for graduate work.

During her studies in political economy, she met a group of Russian socialists and with them "began to attend political meetings led by exiled German socialists." In 1884, "she joined the German Social Democratic Party, a membership she retained through much of her life," according to Kathryn Sklar

Florence Kelley was a consumer movement leader and labor reformer during the late 1800s and early 1900s who devoted her life to securing laws protecting children and women in the workplace. (Library of Congress)

and Beverly Palmer, who compiled and edited a selection of Kelley's letters (Sklar and Palmer 2009, 2).

One of the socialists Kelley met in Zurich was a Russian-Polish medical student, Lazare Wischnewetzky. After about eight months of courtship, the two married in the fall of 1884, shocking friends and family. The couple eventually had three children.

While in Europe, Florence Kelley Wischnewetzky read the works of socialists Marx and Engels and developed a friendship with Engels. She translated Engels's book *The Condition of the Working Class in England in 1884* into English, and it is still studied by scholars. By this time, she was fluent in five languages and also was an accomplished speaker and activist in campaigns to reform factory working conditions.

The Wischnewetzkys moved to New York City in 1886 and joined the local Socialist Labor Party. Dr. Wischnewetzky was unable to establish a profitable medical practice, and the couple had to borrow money from friends and relatives to survive. Financial problems and the doctor's unstable mental health were factors in the couple's deteriorating relationship. Their marriage was "shattered early in 1891 when he began beating her" (Sklar and Palmer 2009, 4).

The verbal and physical abuse continued, and by the end of 1891, Kelley borrowed enough money to secretly leave New York with her three children and travel by train to Chicago. As soon as she arrived, she dropped her married name and called herself Mrs. Florence Kelley, although she did not have the legal right to change her name since she was not yet divorced. (Her divorce did not take place until 1899, when she also obtained custody of her children.) In Chicago, she took her children, ages six, five, and four, to the Woman's Christian Temperance Union (WCTU) headquarters, which consisted of offices, a hotel, a day nursery, a low-cost restaurant, and other facilities. Kelley had written articles for the WCTU's national newspaper and was familiar with their worldwide work.

Her next stop was 335 Halsted Street in the middle of Chicago's worst slum with its crowded tenements and factories, where Jane Addams had founded Hull House and provided social services. Years later, Kelley described her first visit:

On a snowy morning between Christmas 1891 and New Year's 1892, I arrived at Hull House, Chicago, a little before breakfast time, and found there Henry Standing Bear, a Kickapoo Indian, waiting for the front door to be opened. It was Miss Addams who opened it, holding on her left arm a singularly unattractive, fat, pudgy baby belonging to the cook, who was behind-hand with breakfast. Miss Addams was a little hindered in her movements by a super-energetic kindergarten child, left by its mother while she went to a sweatshop for a bundle of cloaks to be finished.

We were welcomed as though we had been invited. We stayed, Henry Standing Bear as helper to the engineer several months, when he returned to his tribe; and I as a resident seven happy, active years until May 1, 1899. (Sklar 1986, 77)

Addams provided Kelley with a room, board, and a job at Hull House. Addams also introduced Kelley to social reformer Henry Demarest Lloyd. He and his wife Jessie lived with their children in Winnetka, a wealthy Chicago suburb. The Lloyds arranged to take Kelley's children to board at their home. For Kelley, it was the beginning of a long friendship with the family.

Kelley's work at Hull House was helping immigrant women find employment. She also was active in campaigns to outlaw sweatshops in homes and factories, places that used young children in garment manufacturing. Kelley often spoke at protest meetings against sweatshops and wrote a report that led to a state law banning sweatshops and the employment of children under age 14. The law also mandated an eight-hour work day for females and a limit of 48 hours per week. In addition, the law required the governor to appoint factory inspectors. On the recommendation of Henry Lloyd, Illinois governor John Peter Altgeld appointed Kelley to the position of chief factory inspector for the state in 1893.

Chief Inspector Kelley was a strict enforcer of the law. For example, in 1894, she wrote to Rand McNally and Company reminding the Chicago publisher that work hours for women and girls should be posted and that they should be limited to eight hours per day. Kelley sent the letter demanding compliance with the law because she had received complaints from female employees.

One of Kelley's tasks was to obtain statistics on Chicago sweatshops—their locations and conditions. The result was *Hull House Maps and Papers: A Presentation of Nationalities and Wages in a Congested District of Chicago* (1895). The book included essays and statistics collected over a three-year period by Kelley and others at Hull House who went to tenements and sweatshops and gathered information about people's national origins and their employment. Maps included in the book showed where immigrant groups had settled near Hull House and the wages they earned.

While she was factory inspector, Kelley studied law at the Northwestern University School of Law, graduating in June 1895. She was admitted to the bar on June 12, 1895. That year the Illinois Manufacturers Association won a lawsuit that reached the Illinois Supreme Court. The justices declared in *Ritchie v. People* (1895) that limiting women's wage labor to eight hours per day was unconstitutional. Other provisions in the law such as banning child labor remained intact.

In 1899, Kelley left Chicago and moved to New York City, where she lived at the Henry Street settlement house. She became the first general secretary of the National Consumers League (NCL) that had just been organized by a group of Hull House women. In her position, Kelley toured the United States and lectured on the nation's working conditions. She emphasized the NCL's founding principles: "That the working conditions we accept for our fellow citizens should be reflected by our purchases, and that consumers should demand safety and reliability from the goods and services they buy" (National Consumers League n.d.). During one of her lectures at a college campus, Frances Perkins was a student in the audience. Years later, Perkins became U.S. secretary of labor and helped bring an end to child labor in the United States.

Among her numerous accomplishments during her leadership of the NCL, Kelley led efforts to establish a White Label to certify that garments were not manufactured with child labor or under illegal working conditions. She also worked on the landmark case *Muller v. Oregon* (1908) with Louis Brandeis (who later became a U.S. Supreme Court justice). The case dealt with an Oregon state law that prohibited women from working more than 10 hours in laundries or factories. Brandeis argued that the law was constitutional. He presented what has become known as the "Brandeis Brief," which at the time was an innovative approach. Working pro bono for the NCL and with Kelley, Brandeis compiled data to show that long working hours were harmful to women, rather than relying on legal facts alone. The brief's "emphasis on the human implications of the legislation at stake rather than legal and constitutional considerations, profoundly affected the course of later legislation directed towards social needs. It is well to recall a fact too often forgotten—that without the vision and fighting spirit of Mrs. Kelley and the organization she built up, the [Brandeis] Brief might not have been written," wrote historian Eleanor Flexner (1974, 215). The High Court found the Oregon law constitutional, and in effect reversed the *Ritchie v. People* decision.

With all of her work for just labor laws, Kelley still had energy to join an interracial group that helped organize the National Association for the Advancement of Colored People (NAACP) in 1909. Founding members included Jane Addams and other women from Hull House, and Kelley's friend W. E. B. Du Bois, who edited and published the NAACP newspaper, the Crisis. Du Bois was also on NAACP's board along with Kelley and others. Kelley served on the board for 20 years.

When World War I began in Europe in 1914, Kelley, a dedicated pacifist, opposed the war and in 1915 joined the Women's Peace Party and the Women's International League for Peace and Freedom in 1919.

Kelley remained director of NCL until her death on February 17, 1932, in Germantown, Pennsylvania. At her funeral, relatives, friends, and colleagues praised her in eulogies for her devotion to social justice and inspiring others to work on behalf of the powerless in society.

Karen L. Hamilton

See also Addams, Jane; Du Bois, W. E. B.; Perkins, Frances

References

Flexner, Eleanor. *Century of Struggle: The Woman's Rights Movement in the United States.* New York: Atheneum, 1974. Reprint of 1959 ed., Cambridge, MA: Harvard University Press.

Goldmark, Josephine. *Impatient Crusader: Florence Kelley's Life Story.* Urbana: University of Illinois Press, 1953.

National Consumers League. "A Brief Look Back on 100+ Years of Advocacy." n.d. http://www.nclnet.org/about-ncl/history (accessed October 10, 2010).

Sklar, Kathryn Kish. *Florence Kelley and the Nation's Work.* New Haven, CT: Yale University Press, 1995.

Sklar, Kathryn Kish. "Hull House in the 1890s: A Community of Women Reformers," Chap. 7 in *American Vistas: 1877 to the Present*, edited by Leonard Dinnerstein and Kenneth T. Jackson. New York: Oxford University Press, 1995.

Sklar, Kathryn Kish, ed. *Notes of 60 Years: The Autobiography of Florence Kelley.*

Chicago: Charles H. Kerr Publishing Company, 1986.

Sklar, Kathryn Kish, and Beverly Wilson Palmer, eds. *The Selected Letters of Florence Kelley, 1869–1931*. Urbana: University of Illinois Press, 2009.

Stebner, Eleanor. *The Women of Hull House: A Study In Spirituality, Vocation, and Friendship*. Albany: State University of New York Press, 1997.

Kelly, Kathy (1953–)

"If jailbirds were listed in an avian guide, Kathy Kelly would rate a special entry for 'Dove.' She has been arrested more than 60 times at home and abroad in her remarkable journey from St. Daniel the Prophet parish on [Chicago's] Southwest Side to the forefront of the American peace movement," wrote Don Terry in 2004 for the *Chicago Tribune*. He added that Kelly "has been willing to go anywhere in the world—Bosnia, Haiti, the West Bank—to do whatever she can to help victims of violence and demonstrate for peace" (Terry 2004, 7). A three-time Nobel Peace Prize nominee, Kathy Kelly is one of the most respected leaders in the American peace movement.

Kelly was born on December 10, 1953, to Frank and Catherine Kelly. She was the third of six children in a traditional Irish-Catholic family, who lived on the south side of Chicago, Illinois, in the Garfield Ridge neighborhood near Midway Airport. Kelly described herself as a "pious child, capable of great awe when genuflecting before the candle lit altar in our neighborhood church" (Kelly, "The Illness of Victors").

During the late 1960s, she attended St. Paul Kennedy High School, considered a shared-time high school. Kelly spent half her days at a Catholic school, where she studied the writings of Catholic priest and peace activist Daniel Berrigan as well as civil rights leader Martin Luther King Jr. She also attended a desegregated public school where she witnessed several incidents of racial violence.

While attending high school, she began reading about the Holocaust and continued learning about this Nazi slaughter perpetrated during World War II when she entered Loyola University in Chicago. She was moved by the documentary *Night and Fog*, a 1955 short film that depicted the lives of prisoners in Nazi concentration camps. She was also impressed by the writings of American lay theologian and activist Frank William Stringfellow and Deacon Tom Cornell, cofounder of the Catholic Peace Fellowship and leader of one of the first protests against the Vietnam War.

Kelly graduated from Loyola in 1974 and became a graduate student at Chicago Theological Seminary, working on her master's degree in religious education. During this time, she volunteered at a soup kitchen set up according to the Catholic Worker tradition, a movement cofounded by Dorothy Day and Frank Maurin in 1933. At that time, Day, a devout Catholic, was praised for her pacifism and her civil disobedience, and many called her a saint. She and others in the Catholic Worker movement shared a belief in the dignity of every person.

Kelly as a graduate student worked beside future activists such as Roy Bourgeois, founder of the School of the Americas Watch (SOA Watch), a grassroots movement committed to changing U.S. foreign policy in Latin America by educating the public, lobbying Congress, and participating in creative, nonviolent resistance. This experience allowed her to put her studies into action.

In 1980, Kelly began teaching religion at St. Ignatius College Preparatory School, where she strengthened her commitment to activism, focusing on poverty issues. In 1982, she married Catholic worker and activist Karl Meyer. The two engaged in "war tax resistance," a form of conscientious objection in which they refused to pay income tax in protest of government spending on war and preparations of war. She continues to refuse to pay federal income taxes.

In 1985, Kelly received a Jesuit professional grant, allowing her to travel to Nicaragua. Inspired by the works of priests Jay Mulligan and Bernie Survil, both of SOA Watch and prisoners of conscience, Kelly traveled to San Juan de Limay, Nicaragua. She participated in a fast led by Foreign Minister Miguel D'Escoto in protest of the U.S. financial backing of the Nicaraguan Resistance (Contras) against the Sandinista government. The Human Rights Watch reported that the Contras violated the basic laws governing armed conflict, including attacking and murdering civilians and mistreating prisoners. In 1986, she left her teaching job at St. Ignatius in order to focus on a career in activism. For two years, she taught low-income youth at Prologue High School in Chicago's Uptown district.

In August 1988, Kelly participated with 13 fellow activists in a Peace Planting, a nonviolent public stand against the nuclear missile silos. In a symbolic move demonstrating the peaceful use of land, she planted corn in the soil surrounding the silos. Cited for trespassing on government property, she and the others were arrested by military police and taken to a warehouse for questioning. She described what followed:

> [A] woman soldier began shouting at me to look straight ahead and spread my legs.... She then began an aggressive body search. When ordered to raise one leg a second time, I temporarily lost my balance while still being roughly searched and, in my view, "woman-handled." I decided that I shouldn't go along with this dehumanizing action any longer. When I lowered my arms and said, quietly, "I'm sorry, but I can't any longer cooperate with this," I was instantly pushed to the floor. Five soldiers squatted around me, one of them referring to me with an expletive ... and began to cuff my wrists and ankles and then bind my wrists and ankles together. Then one soldier leaned on me, with his or her knee in my back. Unable to get a full breath, I gasped and moaned, "I can't breathe." I repeated this many times and then began begging for help. When I said, "Please, I've had four lung collapses before," the pressure on my back eased. Four soldiers then carried me, hogtied, to the next processing station for interrogation and propped me in a kneeling position. The soldier standing to my left, who had been assigned to "escort" me, gently told me that soon the ankle and wrist cuffs, which were very tight, would be cut off. He politely let me know that he would have to move my hair, which was hanging in front of my face, so that my picture could be taken. I told him I'd appreciate that. (Kelly, "Hog-Tied and Abused at Fort Benning")

Kelly was sentenced to one year, but served nine months in the maximum security federal prison in Lexington, Kentucky.

In 1990, Kelly joined the Gulf Peace Team (GPT), an initiative organized out of Britain in response to the threat of war in the Persian Gulf. The group hoped to place themselves between the forces in the desert to stop a battle. A team of a little over 70 people, representing many countries, gathered on short notice. Although criticized for its lack of preparation, a peace camp was eventually established on the Saudi/Iraq border. Kelly spent 14 days encamped at the border. In February 1991, the team was evacuated to Amman, Jordan, where they stayed for the next months, coordinating medical relief convoys and study teams.

Over the following years, Kelly organized and participated in several nonviolent direct action teams, including teams for Haiti (1994) and Bosnia (December 1992 and August 1993). In April 2002, Kelly was one of the first internationals to visit the Jenin Palestinian refugee camp, established in 1953 on the occupied West Bank. In April 2002, just days before her arrival, the camp had been targeted by the Israeli Defense Forces (IDF) for being a launch site for terrorist groups attacking surrounding Israeli villages. The IDF had destroyed over 100 civilian homes.

In 1994, Kelly divorced Karl Meyer, although they remained good friends, and the next year, Kelly and several activists from the GPT founded Voices in the Wilderness (VITW), an organization that follows the traditions of Mohandas Gandhi, advocating nonviolent civil disobedience in opposition to the U.S. and UN economic sanctions and war effort in Iraq. In 1996, the VITW notified then attorney general Janet Reno of their intention to violate the sanctions against Iraq in order to transport medical and other supplies to civilians. Reno responded by warning them that they put themselves at risk for up to 12 years in prison and $1 million in fines. Participants refused to pay fines, and between 1996 and March 2003, VITW organized over 70 delegations to visit Iraq. Kelly worked on 26 of these delegations.

In October 2002, the VITW declared their intent to remain in Baghdad with Iraqi civilians. They still clung to hope that their efforts would stop the war. In March 2003, Kelly and fellow members of VITW witnessed a bombardment called Operation Shock and Awe, a doctrine of rapid dominance used by U.S. forces as the Second Gulf War began. After the bombardment, Kelly visited hospitals and was particularly moved by the plight of the burned victims, especially the children. She noted: "I feel passionately prepared to insist that war is never an answer. But nothing can prepare me or anyone else for what we could possibly say to the children who will suffer in the days and nights ahead. What can you say to a child who is traumatized, or maimed, or orphaned, or dying?" (Kelly, "The Illness of Victors").

Kelly joined 43 other activists in a 2003 School of the Americas (SOA) Watch demonstration, protesting a military combat training at the School of the Americas/Western Hemisphere Institute for Security at Fort Benning, Georgia. She was again convicted of trespassing federal property. In the spring of 2004, Kelly served a three-month sentence at Pekin federal prison.

In 2003, the U.S. government fined Voices in the Wilderness $20,000, but the organization refused to pay. Kelly coordinated the Voices for Creative Nonviolence (VCNV) in 2005 to continue challenging U.S. military and economic sanctions against Iraq and other countries.

In the summer of 2006, Kelly and three companions from VCNV visited Beirut, Lebanon, during the final days of the Israel-Hezbollah war. The war had begun in July 2006, when guerillas from the Islamic Lebanese group, Hezbollah (Arabic for "Party of God") crossed into Israel and attacked an IDF patrol, killing two and taking three prisoners. The Israel military retaliated by launching air, naval, and ground attacks. While both sides exchanged rocket, missile, and artillery fire, ending on August 14, 2006, most of the damage was done to civilian targets on both sides of the border. Israel had argued that Hezbollah brought death and destruction to their country because of its actions; however, many Lebanese Muslims, and even Lebanese Christians who were not sympathetic to Islamic parties or militias, blamed Israel for attacking civilians as an act of punishment.

The VCNV has organized many fasts, walks, and campaigns for peace. One program included an Arabic-language study. Believing fluency is a central component to forming peace teams, VCNV members study in Syria and Jordan to learn the language. In 2007, the VCNV also launched the Occupation Project, a campaign of sustained nonviolent civil disobedience aimed at ending funding for the U.S. war in and occupation of Iraq. The effort was joined by other organizations, including Declaration of Peace, Veterans for Peace, and CODEPINK, led by Medea Benjamin, considered a highly committed peace movement leader.

In 2007, Kelly returned to Amman, Jordan, where she lived for five months among the Iraqi refugees who had fled Baghdad and sought resettlement. In 2008, she helped organize a 19-day winter vigil two blocks from the Chicago home of then president-elect Barack Obama. The demonstration, called "Camp Hope: Countdown to Change," was joined by other organizations, and the vigil was a reminder to Obama of his campaign promises to take action for policy changes in areas such as the war in Iraq, global climate change, nuclear weapons, and more. However, Kelly did not remain for the entire vigil. In January 2009, she visited Gaza during Israel's three-week armed conflict, the Gaza War. She and a fellow activist stayed in Rafah, a Palestinian refugee city in the southern Gaza Strip just outside the evacuation zone and close to the war zone. She could hear the bombs falling and the helicopters firing upon the neighborhoods. Once the bombing stopped, and a ceasefire declared, Kelly visited the burn units at Shifa Hospital in Gaza before visiting other hospitals in Beit Lahiya and Tufa.

In January 2010, Kelly participated in a memorial vigil for Guantanamo prisoners who many believed had been tortured to death. Organized by Witness Against Torture, Kelly joined two dozen demonstrators in a 12-day fast on the Capitol steps and in the Rotunda of the U.S. Capitol building. On January 21, the final day of the campaign, Kelly and the others were arrested for unlawful entry. In June, the activists appeared in court wearing black shirts; the judge dropped the charges and granted a motion for acquittal.

Kelly continues to coordinate the Voices for Creative Nonviolence. She travels frequently to speak at schools, churches, and festivals of her experiences on peace teams and in prison. She has won many awards, including the Peace Abbey Courage of Conscience Award as well as the Consortium on Peace Research and Development Social Courage Award in 1999; nomination for the Nobel Peace Prize in 2000, 2001, and 2003; the Peace Seeker of the Year Award in 2005 by the Montana Peace Seekers Network; the Bradford-O'Neill Medallion for Social Justice, given by Dominican University in 2007; the Oscar Romero Award presented by the Pax Christi of Maine in 2007; and the 2010 Peace Award by the War Resisters League.

In December 2010, Kelly returned to Afghanistan to be with the Afghan Youth Peace Volunteers, a group of about one dozen young people who are interested in being practitioners of nonviolence. They hope to create a peace resource center.

Bobbi Miller

See also Benjamin, Medea; Berrigan, Daniel, and Berrigan, Philip; Day, Dorothy; King, Martin Luther, Jr.

References

Associated Press. "Torture Activists Arrested at the US Capitol Acquitted." *Witness against Torture*, June 14, 2010. http://www.witnesstorture.org/node/109 (accessed November 19, 2010).

Goodman, Amy. "Worse than the Earthquake: Peace Activist Kathy Kelly on the Destruction in Gaza." *Democracy Now!* January 27, 2009. http://www.democracynow.org/2009/1/27/peace_activist_kathy_kelly_returns_from (accessed November 21, 2010).

Kelly, Kathy. "Hog-Tied and Abused at Fort Benning." Antiwar.com, November 27, 2003. http://antiwar.com/orig/kelly.php?articleid=1713 (accessed November 21, 2010).

Kelly, Kathy. "The Illness of Victors." *CommonDreams.org*, March 19, 2003. http://www.commondreams.org/views03/0319-09.htm (accessed November 21, 2010).

Kelly, Kathy. "Iraq Activist Kathy Kelly Sentenced to Federal Prison." Antiwar.com, January 28, 2004. http://antiwar.com/orig/kelly.php?articleid=1799 (accessed November 19, 2010).

Kelly, Kathy. *Other Lands Have Dreams: From Baghdad to Pekin Prison*. Petrolia, CA: Counterpunch Press, 2005.

Kelly, Kathy. "Witnessing against Torture: Why We Must Act!" *Huffington Post*, June 22, 2010. http://www.huffingtonpost.com/kathy-kelly/witnessing-against-tortur_b_621038.html (accessed November 19, 2010).

Shetterly, Robert. *Americans Who Tell the Truth*. New York: Puffin, 2008.

Terry, Don, "The Peace Warrior." *Chicago Tribune Magazine*, October 17, 2004.

Kernaghan, Charles (1948–)

Some manufacturers have called Charles Kernaghan an "economic terrorist." Others have labeled him a "hammer" who is ready "to nail" corporations that are involved in unfair and inhumane labor practices (Duke 2005). Since the late 1980s, Kernaghan has exposed major U.S. retailers such as Nike, Gap, Sears, Kohls, Kmart, and Walmart that sell goods made by workers (some of them young children) who have no rights and labor for 14 to 20 hours per day for little pay—and sometimes for no pay at all. To human rights activists, Charles Kernaghan has been and is a heroic dissident, fighting against the practice of exploiting poor workers in countries like China, Bangladesh, Indonesia, Honduras, and Mexico as well as sweatshops in the United States to make goods for U.S. consumers.

Born in Brooklyn, New York, in 1948, Charles Kernaghan is one of three children. He grew up in a working-class family, proud of their labors. His father, a Scottish immigrant, worked in construction. In an interview, Kernaghan noted that his Catholic parents "were very religious, very devoted to education. Not political at all. We didn't even have newspapers in our house. They had a deep sense of justice. My parents always took in foster kids so they wouldn't have to stay in a hospital while waiting for homes. My mother had about 20 kids in a row, where they would live with us for a year before they were fully adopted" (DeFreitas 1999, 16).

Kernaghan attended a Catholic high school and after graduation, he enrolled at Loyola University, a Jesuit university, in Chicago. He intended to become a priest, but instead studied psychology. After earning a bachelor's degree in psychology, he went on to the New School of Social Research in New York and earned another bachelor's degree. He taught psychology for a short time at Duquesne University in Pittsburgh and at the State University of New York's Harry Van Arsdale Labor College. But he was soon out of the classroom and into the real world. He

In 1996, Charles Kernaghan, director of the National Labor Committee based in New York City, holds Jaclyn Smith Sport clothing made in Honduras. Kernaghan has fought against the practice of exploiting poor workers in countries like China, Bangladesh, Indonesia, Honduras, and Mexico as well as the United States. He uncovered abuses at the Honduran factory that made Kathie Lee Gifford's line for Wal-Mart, and found similar conditions at the Honduran plant that produces Jaclyn Smith clothes for Kmart. (AP Photo/Kathy Willens)

had to find a place to live and settled in Ohiopile (or Ohiopyle), population 47, in western Pennsylvania on the Youghiogheny River. "It was beautiful," Kernaghan reported. "I found a house where I could live there for $6 a week. . . . I sat in the backyard and read and read and read" (DeFreitas 1999, 15). His reading material included works by Russian writer Fyodor Dostoyevsky, Danish philosopher Søren Kierkegaard, French philosopher and political activist Jean-Paul Sartre, and German novelist Franz Kafka.

After staying for eight months in Ohiopyle, Kernaghan returned to New York and tried photography as a livelihood. But he could not earn enough to survive, so he took a variety of jobs from construction work to driving a cab. He still hoped to become a professional photographer.

He was able to use his photography skills in 1985 when he joined a group of Americans on a peace march in El Salvador, which was in the middle of a civil war between the military government and rebels who wanted social and economic reforms in their country. While in El Salvador, Kernaghan learned about horrible tortures that the military inflicted on anyone associated with reform, particularly efforts to organize workers and form unions. He returned to the United States ready to advocate for labor causes in El Salvador. He joined the National Labor Committee (NLC), which was originally founded in 1981 to combat sweatshops in countries like El Salvador and Honduras. Based in New York, NLC's stated mission "is to help defend the human rights of workers in the global economy" (Institute for Global Labour and Human Rights). Kernaghan soon became director of the NLC, which had only a few staff members. Because of its small budget, the NLC concentrated at first on contractors in Central America and the Caribbean making apparel for U.S. retailers.

In 1986, Kernaghan met Barbara Briggs, a University of Massachusetts graduate, who was on her way to Central America. When Kernaghan made trips to Central America, he and Briggs would date. In 1988, she returned to New York to help Kernaghan at the NLC. Ever since, they have lived and worked together; she attends academic meetings to gain support for NLC, and he devises tactics and gives speeches to publicize the abysmal labor practices of manufacturers in developing countries.

Throughout the 1990s, Kernaghan and his NLC campaigns have attacked numerous retailers who sell goods made in sweatshops. The term *sweatshop* has been used since the 1800s when immigrants in the United States with few skills were hired to sew clothing and were paid by the piece. Most worked in unsafe, unventilated factories, but some families worked where they lived—in crowded, filthy tenements. By the mid-1900s, labor reforms helped eliminate many sweatshops, but they began to reappear again in the 1960s, primarily because of globalization with goods made around the globe for American consumption and also because of a large immigrant labor force in the United States (Liebhold and Rubenstein 1998).

Across the United States, people began to pay attention to sweatshop issues after Charles Kernaghan testified in 1996 before a congressional committee; he described conditions at a Honduran factory that made clothing with the "Kathie Lee" label, a line of clothing sold under the name of television personality Kathie Lee Gifford. According to Kernaghan's testimony:

In 1995, Kathie Lee clothing was produced at the Global Fashion plant in Choloma, Honduras. The clothing was exported to the U.S. for sale exclusively at Wal-Mart. At the time the Kathie Lee clothing was being produced, I estimate that over ten percent—approximately 100—of the workers employed at Global Fashion were young teenaged girls, thirteen, fourteen and fifteen years old.

Conditions at the Global Fashion factory were not good. Thirteen year old girls were forced—along with everyone else—to work extraordinarily long overtime hours, most frequently from 7:30 in the morning to 9:00 at night, Monday through Friday. Occasionally, these young women were obligated to work, sewing Kathie Lee clothing, straight through the night until 5:00 a.m. the next morning. A 75-hour work week was not uncommon. (Kernaghan 1996)

Kernaghan in his testimony pointed out that the girls and women who worked at Global Fashion had no health care, were watched by armed guards, earned a base wage of 31 cents per hour, and frequently were cheated of their overtime pay. A 15-year-old worker from Honduras who had worked at Global Fashion since she was 13 noted:

The treatment at Global Fashion is very bad. The supervisors insult us and yell at us to work faster. Sometimes they throw the garment in your face, or grab and shove you. They make you work very fast, and if you make the production quota one day then they just increase it the next day.

The plant is hot, like an oven. They keep the bathroom locked, and you need permission and can only use it twice a day. We are not allowed to talk at work; if they see us talking, they punish us. (Kernaghan 1996)

The news media spread the story about Global Fashions. After reading the testimony, Gifford broke out in tears on her television show, *Live with Regis and Kathie Lee*. From then on, Kernaghan became known "as the activist who made Kathie Lee Gifford cry" (Duke 2005). Gifford vowed that factories making clothing with her label would reform. Gifford and NLC signed an agreement that allowed independent local human rights groups to monitor Honduran factories.

By 1998, labor groups and U.S. college students who organized as United Students Against Sweatshops (USAS) were protesting sweatshops. So were activists like Medea Benjamin and Global Exchange who have played key roles in the anti-sweatshop movement. Their efforts as well as those of NLC have prompted numerous multinational businesses to establish codes of conduct that recognize workers' right to organize and work in a healthy, safe environment. The code prohibits child labor, limits the work week to 60 hours, and sets a minimum wage.

Nevertheless, NLC investigations have continued. In 2005, Kernaghan with a hidden camera and NBC's *Dateline* investigators were in Bangladesh to examine several factories where workers labor from early morning to late at night and earn from 10 cents to 19 cents per hour to sew stripes on sports pants. Because of low labor costs, the pants are sold at bargain prices in the United States. Some retailers and their customers contend that the low pay and long hours of work in a country like Bangladesh are better than no job and no income at all—which is the case for the majority of the population.

In 2010, Kernaghan and NLC issued a report, *China's Youth Meet Microsoft*, which begins with a photograph of young Chinese teenagers asleep at their desks while on a break during a 15-hour work day making technology products for Microsoft and other companies such as Hewlett Packard and Samsung. Kernaghan's introduction to the report states that photographs of workers "were smuggled out of the KYE Systems factory in the south of China." The teenagers shown in the photographs make products like an optical mouse and laser mouse, which "are not necessarily ones the American people would associate with Microsoft. Unfortunately these are Microsoft products, and Microsoft has been outsourcing production to the KYE factory since at least 2003" (Kernaghan 2010, 4).

The Kernaghan report details factory and living conditions for the Chinese workers. The young women live in "primitive" dormitories that house 14 workers in each room. They sleep on two-level bunk beds and must supply their own mattresses. Each floor of the dormitory has two public bathrooms. To wash up, the young women must "fetch hot water in a small plastic bucket to take a sponge bath." At the factory, the teenagers "are prohibited from talking, listening to music or using the bathroom during working hours." They are also required to stay on the property (Kernaghan 2010, 16).

Microsoft responded to the NLC report by sending independent auditors to the KYE factory. On its official blog, Microsoft said "If we find that the factory is not adhering to our standards, we will take appropriate action." The company noted that "an independent auditor has been inspecting the KYE factory annually. In addition, Microsoft personnel conduct quarterly on-site assessments, and receive weekly reports from KYE on key labor and safety criteria that we monitor. . . . Over the past two years, we have required documentation and verification of worker age, and no incidence of child labor has been detected. Worker overtime has been significantly reduced, and worker compensation is in line with the Electronic Industry Citizenship Coalition standards for the Dongguan area [in South China]." Microsoft said it would conduct a "comprehensive on-site audit of the facility . . . with a specific goal of investigating the allegations raised in the NLC report" (Toby 2010).

In some instances, manufacturers, economists, and government officials have argued that working conditions that NLC have reported are rare and that in developing countries, people choose to take sweatshop-type jobs because other sources of income are not available. Closing down a factory would hurt the very workers who reformers are trying to help. However, NLC and such groups as Benjamin's Global Exchange and USAS do not advocate closing factories. Rather, they continue to press for better working conditions in poor countries and for multinational companies to establish codes of conduct regarding their employees.

See also Benjamin, Medea

References

Bowden, Charles. "Keeper of the Fire." *Mother Jones*, July–August 2003.

DeFreitas, Gregory. "Human Rights, Foreign Workers, and American Unions: A Conversation with Charles Kernaghan." *Regional Labor Review*, Fall 1999.

Duke, Lynne. "The Man Who Made Kathie Lee Cry." *Washington Post*, July 31, 2005. http://www.washingtonpost.com/wp-dyn/content/article/2005/07/30/AR2005073001413.html (accessed December 2, 2010).

Hansen, Chris, and Richard Greenberg. "Human Cost behind Bargain Shopping." *Dateline NBC*, June 17, 2005. http://www.msnbc.msn.com/id/8243331/page/4/# (accessed December 4, 2010).

Institute for Global Labour and Human Rights (formerly National Labor Committee). "About Us." n.d. http://www.globallabourrights.org/about (accessed August 22, 2011).

Kernaghan, Charles. "Children Exploited by Kathie Lee/Wal-Mart." Testimony before Democratic Policy Committee Congressional Hearings, April 29, 1996. http://www.globallabourrights.org/alerts?id=0246 (accessed December 4, 2010).

Kernaghan, Charles. *China's Youth Meet Microsoft*. New York: National Labor Committee, April 2010. http://www.globallabourrights.org/admin/reports/files/Chinas_Youth_Meet_Micro.pdf (accessed December 4, 2010).

Liebhold, Peter, and Harry Rubenstein. "Between a Rock and a Hard Place: A History of American Sweatshops, 1820–Present." *History Matters*, July 1998. http://historymatters.gmu.edu/d/145 (accessed December 5, 2010).

Toby, Brian. "Working to Ensure the Fair Treatment of Workers in Our Manufacturing and Supply Chain." The Official Microsoft Blog, April 15, 2010. http://blogs.technet.com/b/microsoft_blog/archive/2010/04/15/working-to-ensure-the-fair-treatment-of-workers-in-our-manufacturing-and-supply-chain.aspx (accessed December 4, 2010).

Kevorkian, Jack (1928–2011)

A widely publicized dissident, Dr. Jack Kevorkian, known as "Dr. Death," became prisoner #284797. He was released on parole in 2007 after serving eight years for second-degree murder. The *New York Times* reported that Kevorkian was "as deluded and unrepentant as ever" for his assisted-suicide methods (*New York Times* 2007). At the same time, Derek Humphry, founder of the Hemlock Society, which supports assisted suicide but did not support Kevorkian's methods, declared that Kevorkian's "euthanasia campaign in the 1990s [made] the general public aware of the unrecognized suffering of many dying people, and that physician-assisted suicide was often times their choice of dealing with it" (Humphry 2007). Kevorkian has spent his entire adult life fighting for people's right to choose how they will die and has assisted more than 100 people who wanted to take their own lives.

Jack Kevorkian, born on May 26, 1928, in Pontiac, Michigan, was the only son of Levon Kevorkian and Satenik Kechigian, refugees who fled to the United States to escape the Turkish genocide of Armenians. Jack's mother named him Mourad after a village hero in her country, but his birth certificate shows his American name.

The Kevorkian family included two other children: Flora, Jack's older sister who is now deceased, and a younger sister, Margo. They lived in a working-class neighborhood of Armenians, Bulgarians, and Greeks in Pontiac.

Very little is known about Kevorkian's early years, but he reportedly took part in common childhood activities—playing "kick the can," touch football, and other games after school. He quit Sunday school because he thought the Armenian Orthodox teachings were fraudulent—he could not believe in miracles and supernatural events. He was an avid reader, and his classmates praised his intelligence and wit. Kevorkian also liked to draw and later in life created oil paintings that now hang in the Ariana Gallery in Royal Oak, Michigan.

Jack loved baseball, and his dream was to be a radio sports announcer, but his parents discouraged that type of career. Later in life, he considered engineering as a profession or possibly becoming a lawyer. He eventually decided on a medical career. Kevorkian attended Pontiac High School, graduating at age 17 with honors. While he was in high school, World War II was underway, which prompted him to learn German and Japanese. He received his higher education from the University of Michigan's medical school, graduating in 1952 with a specialty in pathology. He served as an intern at Henry Ford Hospital in Detroit, where he first began to think seriously about euthanasia—helping someone die. In his book on assisted suicide written much later, he explained what happened when he saw a woman dying of cancer:

The patient was a helplessly immobile woman of middle age, her entire body jaundiced to an intense yellow-brown, skin stretched paper-thin over a fluid-filled abdomen swollen to four or five times normal size. The rest of her was an emaciated skeleton: sagging, discolored skin covered her bones like a cheap, wrinkled frock.

The poor wretch stared up at me with yellow eyeballs sunken in their atrophic sockets. Her yellow teeth were ringed by chapping and parched lips to form an involuntary, almost sardonic "smile" of death. It seemed as though she was pleading for help and death at the same time. Out of sheer empathy alone I could have helped her die with satisfaction. From that moment on, I was sure that doctor-assisted euthanasia and suicide are and always were ethical, no matter what anyone says or thinks. (Kevorkian 1991, 188)

Jack Kevorkian, a retired pathologist and advocate of physician-assisted suicide, poses with his "suicide machine," February 6, 1991. Kevorkian was convicted of murder and imprisoned, but was paroled in 2007. He died in 2011. (AP Photo)

Kevorkian received his license to practice medicine in 1953, but his career was put on hold because of the Korean War. He served in Korea as an army medical officer for 15 months and completed his service in Colorado where he learned to read and play music, teaching himself when he was off duty. After his discharge, he completed residencies at Pontiac General Hospital, Detroit Receiving, and the University of Michigan Medical Center. While he was training at Detroit Receiving, he developed an intense interest in terminal patients and took photographs of their eyes to record changes as they were dying, a practice that earned him the moniker "Dr. Death." Later in 1956, he published a medical journal article on the experiment, "The Fundus Oculi and the Determination of Death."

In 1958, Kevorkian began his quest to legalize doctor-assisted suicide when he went to Columbus, Ohio, and spoke to a condemned prisoner about the possibility of being given irreversible anesthesia so the medical experts could perform various experiments or retrieve organs before injecting lethal drugs to carry out the prisoner's death sentence. Among the benefits Kevorkian advocated was saving human organs so that they could be used for research or for donation. Criminologists could even study, in a very literal sense, the criminal mind during an autopsy. Shortly after visiting the prison, one prisoner wrote to let Kevorkian know that since he must die, he would like to see a more humane method of execution. Also, the prisoner felt that if he could help someone, somewhere, by being an organ donor, maybe his life would not have been a total waste.

The Ohio prisoner's request was denied, and as Kevorkian pointed out in his book *Prescription: Medicide* (1991), seven other people died because they were denied the organs the condemned man wanted to donate. The incident turned out to be pivotal in Kevorkian's life. While he stressed his neutrality on his views of the death penalty, he insisted that there were far more humane, rational, and beneficial ways to accomplish executions.

In late 1958, Kevorkian attended a medical meeting in Washington, D.C., and presented a paper advocating medical experimentation on consenting convicts during executions. Many people condemned his proposals, comparing it to the infamous Nazi experiments and the Holocaust. Kevorkian called this comparison "outrageously absurd," writing: "The Nazis condemned people on the basis of highly prejudicial statutes.... They were enacted by an impotent puppet 'legislature' in a totalitarian state at the mercy of a brutal and fanatical autocrat. And the resultant experiments were *wartime* atrocities beyond any hope of civilized control" (Kevorkian 1991, 37).

During the 1970s, Kevorkian left his position as chief pathologist for a Detroit hospital and moved to California to begin a new endeavor in movie production. He based the film on Handel's "Messiah," but could not find anyone to distribute it. The project was a failure. Over the next decade, he wrote numerous articles about the ethics of assisted suicide that were published in the journal *Medicine and Law*.

Kevorkian received widespread public attention in the 1990s for helping terminally ill patients control their own deaths. The first was Janet Adkins of Portland, Oregon, who was suffering with Alzheimer's disease.

Adkins chose not to let the disease take its course, which would have left her physically and mentally helpless. She had indicated to her husband, other family members, and friends that she wanted to plan her death while she was still mentally competent. The Adkins were members of the Hemlock Society, which espouses the right of a terminally ill patient to take his or her own life. After reading about Dr. Kevorkian and the machine he had invented to help a person voluntarily commit suicide, Adkins called Kevorkian to ask for assistance. Kevorkian refused at first and advised Adkins to take prescription drugs for the treatment of Alzheimer's.

After six months, the treatment had no effect, and Janet Adkins contacted Kevorkian again. Her husband Ron and her physician also talked to Kevorkian, explaining Janet's wishes. Kevorkian agreed to help, and Janet and Ron Adkins flew to Michigan so she could end her life with what later became known as the "suicide machine." The device called a thanatron (for the Greek meaning death machine) included three bottles: one of saline solution, the second a sedative, and the third a lethal potion of potassium chloride. The bottles were connected to an intravenous tube to be inserted into a patient's arm. It was designed so that the patient would go into a deep sleep and die quickly and painlessly. Janet Adkins pushed a button to activate the solutions that soon caused her death.

As soon as Adkins's death was reported publicly, Kevorkian was arrested, jailed, and placed on trial for murder. The judge dismissed the case on the grounds that Michigan had no law against physician-assisted suicide. It was not a crime in Michigan to provide information about suicide. However, public reaction—both pro and con—was swift and explosive. The controversy became more intense in 1991 when Kevorkian assisted in the deaths of two other seriously ill women: Sherry Miller, who suffered from multiple sclerosis, and Marjorie Wantz, who had a painful pelvic disease. Both women wanted to die. Kevorkian provided Miller with carbon monoxide, a lethal gas, which she inhaled through a mask. Wantz used a version of the suicide machine. Kevorkian reported the women's deaths immediately after they occurred. Not long afterward, the state board of medicine revoked Kevorkian's medical license, and state lawmakers began attempts to pass legislation that either would make assisted suicide a felony or would legalize the practice of euthanasia.

In March 1993, Michigan passed a temporary law making it a felony to assist a suicide, but the law expired in late 1994. Kevorkian continued with his assistance. Since his medical license had been revoked, drugs were no longer available to him. Therefore, as he had done in the Miller case, he used carbon monoxide. Arrests and court cases against Kevorkian persisted from 1995 to 1999 as Kevorkian repeatedly helped people end their lives. By March 1998, he had assisted in 100 suicides. In his view, legislators should stay out of the process and allow the medical profession to help patients who want to die because of a terminal or agonizing illness. "I will help a suffering human being at the right time when the patient's condition warrants it, despite anything else," Kevorkian said in an interview. "That's what a doctor should do" (Morganthau 1993, 46).

The state legislature and much of Michigan's population disagreed. In September 1998, a state law went into effect outlawing physician-assisted suicide. Nevertheless, that same month, Kevorkian helped Thomas Youk commit suicide. Youk suffered from amyotrophic lateral sclerosis, also known as Lou Gehrig's disease, a disorder of the nerves that control voluntary muscle movement. Youk was unable physically to administer lethal drugs by himself, so Kevorkian injected the fatal dose. He videotaped the process, and to challenge the law prohibiting assisted suicide, he submitted the tape to CBS's *60 Minutes* for airing in November 1998. The state immediately charged Kevorkian with murder and, in April 1999, sentenced him to 10 to 25 years in prison for murder and three to seven years' imprisonment for delivery of a controlled substance.

Over the next six years, Kevorkian appealed his conviction several times and requested a new trial, but was denied. He also was denied parole. However, after promising that he would no longer help patients die, he was paroled on June 1, 2007, and released from prison. Since that time, he has attempted to run as an independent for the U.S. House of Representatives but garnered less than 9,000 votes against the 183,000 tally of the winner, Gary Peters. Kevorkian also has lectured at several universities, appeared on TV talk shows, and is the subject of a made-for-TV movie, *You Don't Know Jack*, released in 2010. Al Pacino plays the role of Dr. Death.

As he promised, Kevorkian no longer attempted to practice assisted suicide, but he helped focus on the ethics of euthanasia or mercy killing and the right to choose how one dies. Few experts dispute that physicians can ethically halt certain types of medication or treatment to allow death to take its course, but many contend that Kevorkian's efforts violated the Hippocratic Oath—to help the sick and never cause harm. Kevorkian has rattled the establishment by his proactive role, and generated a widespread debate on euthanasia issues. However, he could not end his own life after he became seriously ill with pulmonary and kidney problems. After being hospitalized in 2011, he was too weak to go home to choose his own methods for dying. He died in the William Beaumont Hospital in Royal Oak, Michigan, on June 3, 2011, at the age of 83.

See also Humphry, Derek

References

Azodian, Edmond Y., Agop J. Hacikyan, and Edward S. Franchuk. *History on the Move: Views, Interviews and Essays on Armenian Issues.* Detroit, MI: Wayne State University Press, 2000.

Betzold, Michael. *Appointment with Dr. Death.* Royal Oak, MI: Momentum Books, 1993. Portions of this book are online at http://www.pbs.org/wgbh/pages/frontline/kevorkian/aboutk/drdeathchapters.html (accessed March 23, 2010).

Brown, David Jay. *Mavericks of Medicine: Exploring the Future of Medicine with Andrew Weil, Jack Kevorkian, Bernie Siegel, Ray Kurzweil, and Others.* Petaluma, CA: Smart Publications, 2007.

"Dr. Kevorkian's Wrong Way" (editorial). *New York Times*, June 5, 2007.

Humphry, Derek. "Dr. Jack Kevorkian Free at Last." Euthanasia Research and Guidance Organization, May 27, 2007. http://www.finalexit.org/dr.k.html (accessed March 22, 2010).

Kevorkian, Jack. *Prescription: Medicide the Goodness of Planned Death.* Buffalo, NY: Prometheus Books, 1991.

Morganthau, Tom, with Todd Barrett and Frank Washington. "Dr. Kevorkian's Death Wish." *Newsweek*, March 8, 1993.

King, Martin Luther, Jr. (1929–1968)

On an April Saturday in 2011, thousands filled Chicago's downtown Daley Plaza, chanting, "We are one," supporting Wisconsin union workers and those in other states where political leaders were trying to limit collective bargaining rights. The rally was tied into the anniversary of the assassination of Rev. Martin Luther King Jr.—killed in 1968 after marching in solidarity with sanitation workers. Demonstrators said working-class people were again being deprived of civil rights. Clips from King's speeches played on giant video screens at the rally, interspersed with recent footage of Midwestern protesters. "It's time to reclaim our moral outrage and our sense of indignation," William Lucy, a labor and civil rights leader who marched with King, told a reporter. Another rally attendee, a member of the Coalition of Black Trade Unionists of Chicago, "was moved to see people of all races standing up for rights for which King fought." She said, "I'd been in rallies before, but I think this one was more emotional. [King] might not have been here with us, but he's here watching us" (Healy 2010).

King was born in Atlanta, Georgia, on January 15, 1929. His mother, Alberta, was the daughter of A. D. Williams, a Baptist minister from whom Martin Sr. "inherited" his pastorate, Ebenezer Baptist Church. Both parents played big roles in Martin's character development and career path.

King said of his father, "I have rarely ever met a person more fearsome and courageous than my father... He never feared the autocratic and brutal person in the white community... The thing I admire most about my dad is his genuine Christian character. He is a man of real integrity, deeply committed to moral and ethical principles... his motives and actions are sincere. He never hesitates to tell the truth and speak his mind" (King 1998, 4). Martin Sr. was also a civil rights proponent, president of the Atlanta National Association for the Advancement of Colored People (NAACP) and a community activist for social reform.

Alberta had the task of teaching her son about discrimination and segregation:

> She taught me that I should feel a sense of "somebodiness" but that on the other hand I had to go out and face a system that stared me in the face every day

saying you are "less than," you are "not equal to."...She tried to explain the divided system of the South...as a social condition rather than a natural order. She made it clear...that I must never let it make me feel inferior...she said the words that almost every Negro hears before he can yet understand the injustice that makes them necessary: "You are just as good as anyone." (King 1998, 3–4)

King felt it almost his birthright to develop abhorrence for segregation, to find it irrational and immoral.

Martin Jr. finally settled on a career in the ministry himself and was ordained in the National Baptist Church prior to obtaining his 1948 bachelor's degree from Morehouse College. In 1951, he earned his master's at Crozer Theological Seminary—where he heard the nonviolent philosophies espoused by Mahatma Gandhi that would greatly influence his own thinking. Next, he attended Boston University, completing his PhD and meeting Coretta Scott, whom he married two years later. He became pastor of the Dexter Avenue Baptist Church in Montgomery, Alabama, in 1954.

As a NAACP member and serving on the Alabama Council on Human Relations, King had his hands full learning the ropes of being a new preacher and becoming a

Reverend Martin Luther King Jr. at a press conference in Birmingham, Alabama, on May 16, 1963. King led the African American struggle to achieve full rights of U.S. citizenship and eloquently voiced the hopes and grievances of African Americans and the poor before he was assassinated in 1968. King was a strong opponent of U.S. involvement in Vietnam. (Library of Congress)

father, with Coretta giving birth to the first of his three children. At that point in time, King was not seeking to become the leader of any cause; rather, the cause sought him out. As he would soon state, "I want you to know that if M. L. King had never been born this movement would have taken place. I just happened to be here. You know there comes a time when time itself is ready for a change. That time has come in Montgomery, and I had nothing to do with it" (King 1998, 78).

The impetus of his rise to influence: the arrest of an otherwise-nondescript black woman, Rosa Parks, who late on the day of December 1, 1955, refused to give up her seat to a white passenger on a Montgomery bus and move to assigned Negro seating as required. King led the community-organized Montgomery Improvement Association (MIA), which responded with an organized bus boycott. King worked with other leaders, including Ralph Abernathy—King's lifelong second-in-command and largely unheralded compatriot in his civil rights struggles. During the 381-day boycott, King, his family, and others were subjected to threats, harassment, and arrest. King's home was firebombed while the family was inside. All the while, he urged nonviolence (Branch 1988, 164–65).

Ultimately, the U.S. Supreme Court ruled against segregation of the buses. But MIA had obtained a larger victory. "the boycotters . . . had proven to themselves, the community, and the world that Negroes could join in concert and sustain collective action against segregation, carrying it through until the desired objective was achieved. The Montgomery Negro had acquired a new sense of somebodiness and self-respect, and had a new determination to achieve freedom and human dignity no matter what the cost" (King 1998, 99). King's *Stride toward Freedom* (1958) discussed the boycott as well as the role of nonviolent confrontation.

Early in 1957, King and other black leaders formed the Southern Christian Leadership Conference (SCLC). As its president, he traveled across the country, making appearances and giving speeches. He delivered his first major speech after leading a Prayer Pilgrimage to Washington, D.C., emphasizing the goal of black voting rights (King 1998, 100). He interacted with politicians, such as Vice President Richard Nixon, whom he met at Ghana's 1958 independence celebration, and President Dwight Eisenhower in 1959. Earlier that year, he organized an SCLC-sponsored Crusade for Citizenship, with mass meetings in 21 key southern cities. King's message was consistent: he urged direct, proactive, but always nonviolent means to attain African Americans' civil rights. His tactics, though in and of themselves peaceable, often had the opposite effect. In the South, they elicited almost rabid reactions even from those acting in official capacities.

In order to devote more time to SCLC, King resigned as Dexter Avenue Baptist Church pastor, becoming co-pastor in Atlanta of Ebenezer Baptist Church in 1960. Georgia governor Vandiver announced, "Wherever M. L. King has been there has followed in his wake a wave of crimes including stabbings, bombings, and inciting of riots, barratry, destruction of property and many others. For these reasons he is not welcome to Georgia. Until now, we have had good relations between the races" (Branch 1988, 267). As the decade began, "sit-ins" were being employed as a tactic, especially in the South. They were seen as useful tools in the fight to desegregate lunch counters and other public facilities and also used to emphasize voter registration issues and place economic burdens on employers in order to gain benefits for African Americans. SCLC called an April meeting to coordinate sit-in organizers; King urged continued nonviolence. From this, the Student Nonviolent Coordinating Committee (SNCC) was formed; for some time, the two groups worked closely together, eventually parting ways.

In one coordinated Atlanta lunch counter sit-in, King and dozens of students were arrested. The others were released, but King was held on a prior charge, although he too was released. SCLC then allied with SNCC and the Congress of Racial Equality (CORE), teaming black and white "Freedom Riders" on interstate buses throughout the South to desegregate public transportation facilities. Stores, buses, and public access areas were eventually desegregated. However, King's 1961 desegregation efforts in Albany, Georgia, were futile and resulted in widespread criticism.

SCLC went to deal with segregation in Birmingham, Alabama, in the spring of 1963. Leading massive protests there, King was imprisoned and penned his famous "Letter from a Birmingham Jail." Freed, he rejoined the protesters, who were assaulted by club-wielding police, using dogs and fire hoses. The nation watched the scenes on television, shocked at the brutality exerted on unarmed and noncombative black men, women, and children. Businesses soon caved to the negative publicity; President John F. Kennedy responded with federal troops to quell attacks.

SCLC, NAACP, CORE, SNCC, the Urban League, the Negro American Labor Council, and other groups organized a mixed-race march on Washington, D.C., drawing over a quarter million participants. King was the last to speak on August 28, 1963. He harkened back to President Lincoln's 1863 Emancipation Proclamation and mourned the lack of progress achieved in securing rights for America's black citizens. He delivered the "Let Freedom Ring" speech for which he is most famously known: "So I say to you today my friends, that even though we must face the difficulties of today and tomorrow, I still have a dream. It is a dream deeply rooted in the American dream that one day this nation will rise up and live out the true meaning of its creed—we hold these truths to be self-evident, that all men are created equal" (King 1991, 219).

Ever the preacher, King soared to oratorical heights, concluding his speech: "When we allow freedom to ring, when we let it ring from every village and hamlet, from every state and every city, we will be able to speed up that day when all of God's children—black men and white men, Jews and Gentiles, Protestants and Catholics—will be able to join hands and to sing in the words of the old Negro spiritual, 'Free at last, free at last; thank God Almighty, we are free at last' " (King 1991, 220).

King was present at President Lyndon Johnson's signing of the 1964 Civil Rights Act on July 2 (King 1998, 239), which guaranteed equal access for all U.S. citizens to public accommodations and facilities, employment, and education. That year, *Time* magazine named King Man of the Year, and in December, he became the youngest person to receive the Nobel Peace Prize.

Even though the Civil Rights Act had ended *de jure* segregation (forced by law), it still existed in a *de facto* sense. In 1965, King continued the battle. He organized a peaceful march in Selma, Alabama, and despite the positive recognition he had been receiving, he garnered criticism for not standing up to state troopers. More and more, King found himself and his philosophy of nonviolent confrontation challenged, especially by Malcolm X and Stokely Carmichael of the Black Power movement. Still his efforts aided in passage of the 1965 Voting Rights Act, granting the federal government authority to curtail voter literacy tests, poll taxes, and the ability to monitor elections. Soon after, the Watts Riots occurred in Los Angeles, California, diminishing King's message and influence, particularly in the North. King broadened his scope, addressing concerns of downtrodden people of all races. He also spoke against Vietnam, although this served to brand him as a communist by some and earn him the disfavor of the Johnson administration. It later came to light that this activism intensified FBI director J. Edgar Hoover's efforts to discredit King.

In March 1968, King went to Memphis, Tennessee, to support sanitation workers striking over working conditions. After riots broke out, he left, returning on April 3. Speaking at the Bishop Charles J. Mason Temple, he began by acknowledging the presence of his best friend, Ralph Abernathy. He prophetically addressed the crowd gathered that night, "Like anybody, I would like to live a long life. Longevity has its place. But I'm not concerned about that now. I just want to do God's will. And he's allowed me to go up to the mountain, and I've looked over, and I've seen the promised land. I may not get there with you. But I want you to know tonight that we as a people will get to the promised land" (King 1991, 286). The next day, standing on the balcony of the Lorraine Motel, King was shot to death, assassinated by James Earl Ray, who was convicted and serving a 99-year prison term at the time of his death at the age of 70 in 1998.

King was posthumously awarded the Presidential Medal of Freedom in 1977. The U.S. Congress took the rare step of establishing a national holiday in his honor in 1986, celebrated annually on the third Monday each January. In 2004, another posthumous award honored King: the Congressional Gold Medal.

Margaret Gay

See also Carmichael, Stokely/Ture, Kwame; Malcolm X; Parks, Rosa

References

Abernathy, Ralph David. *And the Walls Came Tumbling Down: An Autobiography*. Chicago: Lawrence Hill Books, 2010.

Branch, Taylor. *Parting the Waters: America in the King Years: 1854–1963*. New York: Simon and Schuster, 1988.

King, Martin Luther, Jr. *The Autobiography of Martin Luther King, Jr.* Edited by Clarence Clayborne. New York: Warner Books, 1998.

King, Martin Luther, Jr. *Stride toward Freedom: The Montgomery Story*. Boston: Beacon Press, 2010.

King, Martin Luther, Jr. *A Testament of Hope: The Essential Writings of Martin Luther King, Jr.* Edited by James M. Washington. New York: HarperCollins, 1991.

Ortiz-Healy, Vikki. "Union Workers Rally Here for Labor Rights." *Chicago Tribune*, April 10, 2011.

Kochiyama, Yuri (1921–)

Agents from the Federal Bureau of Investigation (FBI) knocked on the door of Yuri's home. It was only hours after the Japanese attack on the U.S. naval base in Pearl Harbor, Hawaii, on December 7, 1941, and President Franklin D. Roosevelt had declared war on Japan. The agents quickly took away Yuri's father, who had just returned from the hospital after having surgery. Her father's crime? He was a Japanese immigrant and a man in contact with Japanese fishermen who knew the waters of the Pacific Ocean, so without any evidence, he, like other Issei (first-generation Japanese), was accused of spying for Japan. Not long afterward, in February 1942, Roosevelt signed an executive order to forcefully relocate more than 120,000 men, women, and children of

Japanese descent (among them 70,000 American citizens) into prison camps, euphemistically called internment canters. Yuri, her brother, and mother soon were hauled away, eventually restrained in a concentration camp in Arkansas. It was here that Yuri, a Nisei (second-generation Japanese American), began to "see the world and America with entirely new eyes—Japanese American eyes" (Kochiyama 2004, xxiii), which put her on the path toward radicalization and dissident protests of later years.

On May 19, 1921, Mary Yuriko Nakahara and her twin brother Peter were born in San Pedro, California, a coastal town near Los Angeles. An older brother, Arthur, was born in 1918. Their parents, Seiichi and Tsuyako Nakahara, had immigrated from Iwate-ken, Japan. They were both well educated, and Seiichi owned and operated a market that sold fish, meat, and other supplies to the U.S. Navy and Japanese passenger ships that sailed between Japan and the West Coast of the United States.

Seiichi was able to provide a comfortable living for his family. His wife did not have to work, unlike many other Japanese immigrants who settled across the bay from San Pedro on Terminal Island, a community of fishermen. The Nakahara family lived in a neighborhood that included many European immigrants. Mary, who later changed her name to Yuri, wrote "Our home life was traditional in that we spoke Japanese and ate Japanese food and were expected to behave as proper Japanese children. Outside our home though I was very much an 'all-American' girl" (Kochiyama 2004, xxiii).

As an "all-American girl," Kochiyama was an unabashed patriot, a member of the Girl Scouts and YWCA volunteer, with no knowledge of discriminatory acts against people of color or religions other than Christianity. To her, the United States was a wonderful

Yuri Kochiyama, who was detained with her family in an internment camp during World War II, looks at a memorial erected for the inhabitants of a Japanese American internment camp, in Rohwer, Arkansas, September 26, 2004. The memorials and a cemetery is all that is left of the Rohwer Relocation Center. (AP Photo/Mike Wintroath)

country. She was unaware of worldwide events of the 1930s and early 1940s and the beginning years of World War II in Europe. In other words, she lived in a protected middle-class world.

She loved sports and, while a teenager, was a volunteer reporter covering high school sports for the *San Pedro News Pilot*. She also "loved reading and writing poetry, riding bikes, and hiking" (Kochiyama 2004, 10). After high school, she attended Compton Junior College, where she majored in journalism.

Yuri's interests included religion and the Christian faith; she taught Sunday school at a Presbyterian church. On the day Pearl

Harbor was bombed, she had returned home from church, arriving a few hours before the FBI took her ill father away. He was incarcerated at the federal prison on Terminal Island, where he was denied the medication he needed for diabetes. He was not allowed to have visitors except for his son Peter, who had been drafted into the U.S. Army. He became so ill that he had to be hospitalized and then was sent home in such poor condition that he died on January 21, 1942. The family learned later that FBI agents had been spying for years on her father.

Hysteria swept across the United States after war was declared on Japan. On February 19, 1942, President Roosevelt issued the infamous Executive Order 9066, which in part declared:

> [B]y virtue of the authority vested in me as President of the United States, and Commander in Chief of the Army and Navy, I hereby authorize and direct the Secretary of War, and the Military Commanders whom he may from time to time designate, whenever he or any designated Commander deems such action necessary or desirable, to prescribe military areas in such places and of such extent as he or the appropriate Military Commander may determine, from which any or all persons may be excluded, and with respect to which, the right of any person to enter, remain in, or leave shall be subject to whatever restrictions the Secretary of War or the appropriate Military Commander may impose in his discretion. (Our Documents)

Some members of Congress and First Lady Eleanor Roosevelt had objected strongly to the order as unconstitutional, but it was quickly enforced and changed the lives of tens of thousands of people of Japanese descent. Many homeowners and businessmen had to sell their properties quickly, resulting in an estimated loss of $1.3 billion, and net income loss at $2.7 billion in 1983 dollars (Our Documents).

In April 1942, Yuri, her older brother Arthur, and her mother were taken to one of the assembly centers, set up hastily in fairgrounds and race tracks while relocation camps in remote areas of western states and Arkansas were being built. "My family was billeted in horse stalls at the Santa Anita (California) Racetrack," Yuri reported. "The smell of the manure made many Issei sick." But they and others did the best they could to make their small spaces livable, creating furniture out of boxes and making curtains "for privacy in the latrines" (Kochiyama 2004, 12).

Eventually, Yuri and her family were assigned to a concentration camp in Jerome, Arkansas. Nearby was Camp Shelby, Mississippi, where ironically, many soldiers of Japanese descent were trained and became part of the 442nd Regimental Combat Battalion, which during the war was the most highly decorated of any battalion for its size and length of service. Bill Kochiyama and some of his friends in the battalion visited Jerome to see family and friends. When Yuri met Bill, "it must have been love at first sight," she noted. After a few visits they decided to marry (Kochiyama 2004, 15).

Yuri and Bill married after the war in 1946, in New York City, Bill's hometown, where they lived in Amsterdam Houses, a low-income housing complex. The couple's first child was born in 1947, and they eventually had six children, Billy, Audee, Aichi, Eddie, Jimmy, and Tommy. Two of the children, Billy and Aichi, died as young adults in tragic accidents.

In the housing complex where the Kochiyama family lived, residents were primarily black and Puerto Rican, and Kochiyama learned about the struggles and prejudice that her neighbors had endured. She began to take an interest in the civil rights movement that was gaining strength in the South during the 1950s and early 1960s.

In 1960 the Kochiyama family moved to Harlem, which she called "a university without walls" (Kochiyama 2005, 65). And Yuri's political life began. She and her husband were active in community improvement projects and education committees demanding improvements in schools. The Kochiyama home was the center for numerous community gatherings of revolutionaries and civil rights workers, such as the Freedom Riders from New York who traveled to the South to protest segregated interstate public transportation. The couple and their children took part in demonstrations advocating for construction jobs for blacks and Puerto Ricans in New York City. Whatever forms her activism took, Kochiyama believed that social justice could be achieved through political means and integration with the white mainstream as suggested by civil rights leader Martin Luther King Jr. But that changed when she met Malcolm X, who was once a member of the Nation of Islam (NOI), a black Muslim religious organization. Malcolm X left the NOI and formed the Muslim Mosque Incorporated and the Organization of Afro-American Unity (OAAU), which advocated African American self-determination. As he once told a press conference. "There can be no black-white unity until there is first black unity. There can be no workers' solidarity until there is first some racial solidarity. We cannot think of uniting with others, until after we have first united among ourselves" (Katz 1995, 493).

Kochiyama joined the OAAU, and she and her family enjoyed the friendship of Malcolm X. In February 1965, Yuri Kochiyama was in the audience when Malcolm spoke to OAAU members and black Muslims at a gathering in the Audubon Ballroom in New York City. While he was speaking, three black men in the crowd approached and shot Malcolm to death. Kochiyama reported that she "immediately ran on stage as soon as he fell to the floor. Cradling his head in my hands, I was shocked. Only one of his killers was apprehended. Two others were arrested, but there was controversy over their arrest" (Kochiyama 2004, 72).

From the late 1960s throughout most of her life, Kochiyama has been active in various causes. She worked with anti–Vietnam War groups, Native American organizations seeking sovereignty, and numerous Asian and Third World coalitions. She was involved with Puerto Rican movement for independence and, in 1977, took part in taking over the Statue of Liberty for nine hours to call attention to the struggle. She was arrested and imprisoned, an experience that underscored her dedication to freeing political prisoners who had little legal help. For example, she has worked for years to free Mumia Abu-Jamal, who was sentenced to death for the murder of a police officer, a conviction that supporters claim was based on a biased trial and faulty evidence.

During the 1980s, Yuri and Bill Kochiyama were active in Japanese American Redress and Reparations Committees—efforts to win reparations to Japanese Americans for the losses they incurred while in concentration camps during World War II. Some Japanese Americans already had received payment for property that had been confiscated. In 1988, the U.S. government allocated $20,000 each to 60,000 Japanese Americans.

In 1993, Bill Kochiyama died, and in 1997, Yuri suffered a stroke and moved to California to live with her daughter. In failing health, she "slipped into a depression" (Kochiyama 2004, 182); but with time in a nursing home and the help of family and friends, she improved. In early 2011, she was still speaking out on the many issues that she has been concerned about during her lifetime.

Over the years she has received many awards, such as the New York State Governor's award for Outstanding Asian American in 1994; 100 Most Influential Asian Americans of the Decade in 1999; Asian American Law Students Association Award in 2002; National Women's History Award in 2003; a Gustavus Myers Outstanding Book Award for her book *Passing It On* in 2004; and a nomination for the Nobel Peace Prize in 2005. In 2010, California State University, East Bay honored Kochiyama with a doctorate for "her life to community service by helping people of all ethnicities and those underserved by society in this country and around the world," said Mo Qayoumi, president of the university. "Ms. Kochiyama has championed freedom and a quality way of life for all people in the United States and around the world. She has served as a uniting force for civil rights and an outspoken proponent of education for all people" (Zepel 2010).

See also Abu-Jamal, Mumia; King, Martin Luther, Jr.; Malcolm X; Roosevelt, Eleanor; Yasui, Minoru

References

Fujino, Diane. *The Revolutionary Life of Yuri Kochiyama: Heartbeat of Struggle*. Minneapolis: University of Minnesota Press, 2005.

Hung, Melissa. "Yuri Kochiyama: The Last Revolutionary." ModelMinority.com, March 13, 2002. http://www.modelminority.com/joomla/index.php?option=com_content&view=article&id=390:yuri-kochiyama-the-last-revolutionary-&catid=43:leaders&Itemid=56 (accessed March 10, 2011).

Katagiri, Yasuhiro. "A Passion for Life, Liberty, and the Pursuit of Happiness Review of Fujino, Diane C., *Heartbeat of Struggle: The Revolutionary Life of Yuri Kochiyama*." H-Net Reviews, May 2006. http://www.h-net.org/reviews/showrev.php?id=11765 (accessed March 15, 2011).

Katz, William Loren. *Eyewitness: A Living Documentary of the African American Contribution to American History*. Revised and updated ed. New York: Touchstone/Simon and Schuster, 1995.

Kochiyama, Yuri. *Passing It On*. Los Angeles: UCLA Asian American Studies Center Press, 2004.

Roosevelt, Franklin D. "Executive Order 9066: Resulting in the Relocation of Japanese (1942)" Our Documents, http://www.ourdocuments.gov/doc.php?flash=old&doc=74# (accessed March 15, 2011).

Zepel, Barry. "Civil Rights Leader to Receive Honorary Doctorate from CSUEB." California State University, East Bay, May 6, 2010. http://www20.csueastbay.edu/news/2010/05/kochiyama-050610.html (accessed March 15, 2011).

Kovic, Ron (1946–)

Ron Kovic believed that he was preordained to a life in the U.S. military and service to his country. But after serving as a U.S. Marine during the Vietnam War, coming home wounded and receiving poor medical care, he became disillusioned and a bitter dissident—an avid antiwar activist.

Born on July 4, 1946, in Ladysmith, Wisconsin, Kovic was the first child in his family, which eventually included five more children. They grew up in Massapequa, Long Island, where Ron's father worked at a local supermarket and his mother was a homemaker. Ron's parents thought their son was destined to be a patriot because of his birth date. Both his father and uncle had served as Marines in Korea, and they often discussed the part Ron would play in the nation's defense. Raised an unquestioning Roman Catholic, Ron finished high school a clean-cut, straight-arrow wrestler and gymnast (Nicosia 2004, 235).

Following graduation in September 1964, Kovic enlisted in the Marines and began his 12-week basic training at Parris Island in South Carolina. Assigned the rank of private first class out of boot camp, Kovic went to the Infantry Training Regiment at Camp Lejeune in North Carolina for advanced combat training. He spent Christmas holidays visiting his family in Massapequa, New York, before returning to a new assignment at Norfolk, Virginia, where he attended radio school. Then it was back to Camp Lejeune and the Second Field Artillery Battalion.

Eager to serve his country in a more substantial way, Kovic volunteered for Vietnam and shipped out in December 1965. Once in the country, he participated in dangerous reconnaissance patrols behind enemy lines. He was returned stateside after a 13-month tour of duty, on January 15, 1967. Within several months, he volunteered to return to Vietnam. During this second tour, on January 20, 1968, "an enemy bullet severed his spinal cord, paralyzing his spinal cord, and depriving him of any sensation from his mid-chest down" (Nicosia 2004, 235).

Kovic spent a week in intensive care, and then was flown to St. Albans Naval Hospital in New York. American Legion members, with their wives and daughters, visited, calling him a "hero" and saying how proud his hometown of Massapequa was of him (Kovic 2005, 42–43). One day, a man delivered an envelope with a citation signed by Governor Rockefeller and a Conspicuous Service to the State of New York Medal (Kovic 2005, 43). Kovic also received a Bronze Star for his actions during combat. He was discharged from the Marines and released from the hospital—an overcrowded, unhygienic facility that provided substandard care.

Kovic was disgusted with the U.S. military and its treatment of him and his fellow soldiers. He also was discouraged about his lot in life and what the future held—or more aptly, did not hold. He soon headed west. "I had been in California for about a month when one day there was a big photo on the front page of the *L.A. Times*—a group of vets had gone to Washington and thrown away their medals. It had been one of the most moving war demonstrations there had been.... I knew it was time for me to join forces with other vets. I went home and called a couple people I knew. One of them told me there was going to be a meeting of Vietnam Veterans Against the War [VVAW] that night... All of the sudden, everything seemed to change." He was eager to get to work, saying at that first meeting, "Give me a speech. Give me a place to show this wheelchair" (Kovic 2005, 147–48).

Kovic gave a speech at a rally in Pasadena the very next day. Soon, he was a frequent VVAW speaker and also started appearing on television. Sometimes his handicap worked to his advantage and drew attention; other times, it repelled reporters, who thought viewers wanted something attractive on their TV screens. No matter; over time, his persistence and outspokenness was turning him into one of the most prominent antiwar activists of the day and, certainly, a leader of veterans against the war. At a rally, he listened to actor Donald Sutherland read from a book about a severely injured vet, *Johnny Get Your Gun*. Deeply moved, Kovic asked to be lifted to

Antiwar activist and decorated Vietnam war hero Ron Kovic holds a sidewalk news conference in 1981 in Los Angeles to express dismay at the reception offered to freed American hostages compared to the disrespectful homecoming vets received when they returned from the Vietnam War. (AP/Wide World Photos)

the stage where he read a poem he had written about the vets who had thrown away their medals (Kovic 2005, 149).

Going forward, he was totally dedicated to speaking and working against the war. In the course of his activism, Kovic wrote in 2005, "I had been beaten by the police and arrested twelve times for protesting the war and I had spent many nights in jail in my wheelchair. I had been called a Communist and a traitor, simply for trying to tell the truth about what had happened in that war, but I refused to be intimidated" (Kovic 2005, 16). At one demonstration outside presidential candidate Richard Nixon's headquarters, there was a confrontation between protesters and Los Angeles police. Officers deliberately dumped Kovic, caught up in the confusion, from his wheelchair. Arrested with others, he was taken into the station. There, officers realized Kovic was a wounded war veteran. Their manner began to soften until he defiantly responded to a query about his name with, "Ron Kovic, Occupation, Vietnam veteran against the War." Then came the mocking response. "You should have died over there . . . I'd like to take this guy and throw him off the roof" (Kovic 2005, 155–56).

Kovic took part in "The Last Patrol" in Miami, Florida, in August 1972, concurrent with the Republican Convention. He marched with the VVAW where the National Guard was bivouacked. "Ron delivered a speech to the Guard . . . 'They sent us to Vietnam to fight against the people. We found we were on the wrong side. And if they ever make us fight again, we'll fight with the people, and it will be the people's army.' One of the National Guardsmen, a black, put his rifle down and raised his fist. It was electric...the thing was starting to turn...so the officers pushed the Guard back...so they couldn't...hear Ron speak" (Nicosia 2004, 239). Kovic and two others also managed to crash the convention, where Nixon was accepting the presidential nomination. That night was later called "The Battle of Miami Beach" (Nicosia 2004, 244).

Over 1,000 arrests were made, but the media kept their cameras focused in the Convention Hall, largely ignoring what transpired outside. Inside, Kovic told anyone he came in contact with about the veterans' hospitals and how they treated returning soldiers and "that man that's going to accept that nomination tonight has been lying to all of us and spending the money on war that should have been on healing and helping the wounded. That's the biggest lie and hypocrisy of all that we had to go over there and fight and come home to a government and leaders who care less about the same boys they sent over" (Kovic 2005, 176). Just as Nixon stepped on stage, Kovic and his two conspirators began shouting, "Stop the bombing, stop the war" as loud as they could, continuing to interrupt Nixon until the Secret Service pulled them out of the hall (Nicosia 2004, 246).

In 1973, Kovic spent about three months in a California veterans' hospital. He was shocked to find it " 'just as bad, if not worse' as when he had come home from the war in 1968" (Nicosia 2004, 317). He noted that most of the patients "were there not to get well but to die. They were not getting the care they needed" (Nicosia 2004, 317). Kovic started the Patient's/Workers' Rights Committee that led to formation of the American Veterans Movement, or AVM (Nicosia 2004, 323). One of its first acts was to hold a multiple-week hunger strike in the office of Senator Alan Cranston, who chaired the subcommittee on Veteran's Health and Hospitals. Coupled with a brief takeover of the Washington Monument, AVM got a promised inquiry into the "national veterans crisis" and the VA director's resignation (Nicosia 2004, 327–35).

Problems undermined AVM—staffing, its tax status, fund-raising, and internal disputes about its aims. Kovic was charismatic but disorganized and polarizing. "Many blamed his ego for AVM's demise but...it became clear that what had happened...was a paradigm of the repeated collapses within the Vietnam veterans movement...in the end he had touched a nation's conscience chiefly as a wounded veteran, better able than most to articulate the abuses he and thousands of others like him had to endure—not from the Vietnamese, but from the U.S. government" (Nicosia 2004, 346).

In 1974, Kovic memorialized his story:

> I wrote *Born on the Fourth of July*...It was like an explosion...I worked... with an...almost obsessive feeling that I would not live past my thirtieth birthday...I struggled to leave something of meaning behind, to rise above the darkness and despair. I wanted people to understand. I wanted to share with them...what I had gone through, what I had endured. I wanted them to know what it really meant to be in a war—to be shot and wounded, to be fighting for my life on the intensive care ward—not the myth we had grown up believing. I wanted people to know about the hospitals and the enema room, about why I had become opposed to the war, why I had grown more and more committed to peace and nonviolence. (Kovic 2005, 16–17)

Kovic was again in the national spotlight in 1979. A parade was scheduled for returning Iranian hostages—most of whom, in the minds of many veterans, "were State Department employees, who had taken high-risk assignment for the pay, prestige, and possible advancement it brought" whereas they [veterans] "had laid their life on the line solely from a sense of duty, with little money and less glamour, and sometimes not even a 'thank you,' to reward them for it." Kovic held a press conference at Patriotic Hall in Los Angeles, speaking "eloquently about the 'cold shoulder' Vietnam vets had been given when they returned from the war.... He said there was no indication that the nation remembered the existence of its several millions of Vietnam veterans... Please don't forget us" (Nicosia 2004, 396–97).

For the next several years, Kovic—and other veterans—advocated for veterans, full-throttle. In the spring of 1981, both *Time* and *Newsweek* had major stories on Vietnam vets' readjustment problems and, in July, *Time*'s cover read, "Fighting for Their Rights: The Forgotten Warriors" (Nicosia 2004, 402).

In 1989, *Born on the Fourth of July* was made into an Academy Award–winning movie directed by Oliver Stone and starring Tom Cruise. Kovic received a Golden Globe in 1990 for Best Screenplay.

Kovic continues his activism, as much pro-peace as antiwar. From 1990 to 1991, he participated in several demonstrations against the first Gulf War. He protested prior to the invasion of Iraq, relentlessly speaking out as part of a promise he made years ago: "[W]e would never allow what happened to us in Vietnam to happen again. We had an obligation, an obligation as citizens, as Americans, as human beings, to raise our voices in protest" (Kovic 2005, 22). In the introduction to the 2005 edition of his book, Kovic writes about U.S. involvement in "a tragic and senseless war in Iraq... I have watched in horror the mirror image of another Vietnam unfolding... Refusing to learn from our experiences... our government continues to pursue a policy of deception, distortion, manipulation, and denial, doing everything it can to hide from the American people their true intentions and agenda in Iraq" (Kovic 2005, 19–20).

When he attended the 2008 Democratic National Convention in Denver, Colorado, Kovic spoke and led a march against the war. In April 2010, as a member of the Council for Dignity, Forgiveness, and Reconciliation, he flew to Rome to explore nonviolent alternatives to solve the world's conflicts. Kovic has spent more than four decades dealing with the physical and psychic injuries inflicted upon him during his service as a U.S. Marine. The damage done by the latter should not be understated. He "later obtained his own personnel file of surveillance documents from the FBI." That surveillance, he said, was "a 'grievous assault on the rights' he had fought for and had been wounded for in Vietnam, and it 'wounded him a second time'" (Nicosia 2004, xvi).

But for all of those body blows, literal and figurative, Ron Kovic remains true to his birthright, although today he serves in a fashion different from what he originally envisioned. He advocates for peace, not the military and war. In fact, in Los Angeles on March 19, 2011, he led a mass march that he sponsored along with Martin Sheen and many others to protest war. An estimated 4,000 people took part in a procession that included veterans and mock coffins draped with Iraqi, Afghani, and U.S. flags to represent deaths caused by U.S. wars and militarism.

Margaret Gay

See also Sheen, Martin

References

Kovic, Ron. *Born on the Fourth of July*. New York: Akashic Books, 1976, 2005.

Nicosia, Gerald. *Home to War: A History of the Vietnam Veterans' Movement*. New York: Carroll & Graf Publishers, 2004.

Trumbo, Dalton. *Johnny Got His Gun*. With an Introduction by Ron Kovic. New York: Carol Publishing Group, 1994.

Kuhn, Margaret (1905–1995)

She preferred that people call her "Maggie," and labeled herself a "wrinkled radical." Others said that Margaret Kuhn "blazed many paths to become many role models" (Nader.org 1991). During the 1960s, when Kuhn faced mandatory retirement from her job at the age of 65, she did not go peacefully or willingly from the workforce. She hated the idea of being "sent out to pasture" and decided to fight back. She began efforts to change public attitudes about older people and to lobby against ageism. She believed that the old should not be separated from the young—a common practice in much of U.S. society—and she spent decades educating the public on the concept that old age is a triumph, not a "disease" as many are prone to believe.

Kuhn was born August 3, 1905, in Buffalo, New York, into a middle-class family. She was the older of two children of Minnie Louise Kooman and Samuel Fredrick Kuhn. The family moved to Memphis, Tennessee, shortly after Margaret was born. Her father worked for the Bradstreet Companies (which eventually became Dun & Bradstreet) and was steadily promoted. He was transferred several times, and by Maggie's teenage years, the family was living in Cleveland, Ohio, where she attended West High School. She dated a classmate, but he was not welcome in the Kuhn home. In fact, her father, who was very strict about his daughter's social life, gave all Margaret's boyfriends "the cold shoulder" (Kuhn 1991, 33).

Kuhn attended Case Western Reserve's Flora Stone Mathew College for Women in Cleveland, and while there, she met and fell in love with the son of her church's pastor. They decided to marry, but at the last minute, she backed out. "Above all," she wrote, "I realized I loved school and wanted an education more than anything" (Kuhn 1991, 44).

After graduating from college, Kuhn began working for the Young Women's Christian Association (YWCA) in 1927. She continued work with the YWCA when she and her family moved to Philadelphia, Pennsylvania, in 1930. She taught classes on women's issues, unionizing, and human sexuality that included instructions on birth control, pregnancy, and the social pressure on women to marry even if they preferred to remain single. She encouraged women to really study their own lives and their world. She once wrote to companies for samples of their products and initiated a discussion of the products' "truth in advertising," the profits made from cosmetics and drugs, the conditions under which they were made, and the role of women as purchasing agents.

The YWCA sent her to New York in 1941 to be the association's project coordinator for the United Service Organization (USO), helping women who worked in defense plants. She also studied at Columbia University and Union Theological Seminary. She joined the national office of the United Presbyterian Church in the 1940s and became involved in a variety of social causes over the next two decades, from the desegregation movement, to affordable housing and national health care, to peace and antipoverty efforts. She edited and wrote for the church's magazine *Social Progress* and wrote a handbook titled *You Can't Be Human Alone* on group procedures for the local church. She was one of only two whites who worked in the Presbyterian Church's civil rights department.

In the 1950s, she moved back to Philadelphia to be with her aging and frail parents and took a job as "assistant secretary of the church's Social Education and Action Program. It was an executive position, and just the kind of job I was looking for," Kuhn wrote (Kuhn 1991, 97).

During her time in Philadelphia, Kuhn met a minister, a married man, with whom she had a 15-year affair. She firmly believed that sexuality is part of life and to deny it whether old or young is to deny life itself. She pointed out "Our affair was illicit and highly secretive. Exposure would have ruined our careers and his marriage." Kuhn stated frankly: "The issue of fidelity is a complicated one. Many women, who become involved with married men, sicken themselves with guilt. I did not. I considered his marriage to be his affair. I was troubled occasionally by the thought of his wife, but probably not enough" (Kuhn 1991, 106–7).

One of Kuhn's major issues during the 1960s was health care for the elderly and establishing Medicare, a program that was passed in 1965 after years of public and political wrangling. Another major issue was U.S. involvement in the Vietnam War. Kuhn joined with five other women who shared her views. In 1968, she took part in the Jeanette Rankin Brigade, a peaceful march on Washington, D.C., to protest the war. The march was named for the first woman elected to the U.S. Congress and the only congressional member to vote against U.S. entry into World War I.

In 1970, Kuhn turned 65 years old, which was the Presbyterian Church's mandated retirement age. Being forced out of a job prompted Kuhn to seek out friends who had undergone the same experience. They decided to organize to work on and publicize issues of the elderly. In addition, the group hoped to champion other social causes and protest the Vietnam War that was underway.

To bring old and young peace activists together, Kuhn and her friends formed the Consultation of Older and Younger Adults for Social Change with Philadelphia college students. Their motto was "Age and Youth in Action." The group soon advocated for social causes such as universal health care, nursing home reform, affordable and accessible housing, defense of Social Security, and elimination of nuclear weapons, which brought public condemnation upon them but did not deter their activities. Once a television producer called the group the Gray Panthers, after the militant civil rights group the Black Panthers, and the term stuck. The Gray Panthers came to widespread national attention in 1971 when they protested the fact that no African American representatives were included at the first White House Conference on Aging.

When Kuhn spoke publicly about social issues, she was well informed, and the media took notice. The popularity of the Gray Panthers rose rapidly as a result and grew steadily throughout the 1970s and 1980s to become a national organization with numerous local chapters. In 1985, the organization opened its first public policy office in Washington, D.C., and established headquarters there in 1990.

Kuhn's advocacy for seniors included public criticism of those who stereotyped seniors. She once reproached Johnny Carson for his "Aunt Blabby" skit that made fun of the elderly. She also demanded that older people be a part of the community and that mandatory retirement be abolished because, as she noted "it is socially wasteful and often personally devastating." She declared that "an institution that forces older people out of their work roles requires perpetuation of an agist (sic) belief system. This system requires that all groups buy into the concept that old people are less able than young and ought to enjoy leisure time, even if they don't want it" (Hessel 1977, 66, 70). Successful lobbying by the Gray Panthers eventually helped raise the age limit on mandatory retirement.

Maggie Kuhn refused to live in a housing complex for the elderly, calling such facilities "glorified playpens," a categorization that she admitted was exaggerated. In her view, even though retirement communities kept seniors safe, they also somewhat isolated them from the rest of society. Throughout her 25 years as a Gray Panthers activist, she lived in her own home in Philadelphia, Pennsylvania, sharing it with younger housemates. She called them her family of choice. They provided companionship and helped with chores in exchange for a place to live at a reasonable rent. She made clear that she had not established a commune, rather calling the arrangement shared housing. She also encouraged others to create group homes shared by people of various ages and set up the Shared Housing Resources Center on the ground floor of her home, which actually included two joined stone houses.

In spite of poor health (she suffered from severe arthritis and osteoporosis) and public criticism of her outspoken liberal views as well as hostile attitudes of government during the administration of President Ronald Reagan, she constantly fought discrimination against seniors. Kuhn and the Gray Panthers were involved in numerous lawsuits on behalf of older people. An editorial in the *Nation* explained: "What distinguishes the Gray Panthers from conventional advocacy groups for older people is their refusal to pit the interests of the old against those of the young. While well-funded senior citizens' lobbying groups like the American Association of Retired Persons battle for a bigger piece of a shrinking pie, the Panthers, with their smaller numbers and minuscule budget, fight for everyone's place at the table" (*Nation* 1990).

For years the Gray Panthers also have advocated for living wills, so that terminally ill people could decide for themselves whether they wanted to prolong their lives by artificial means, and they have fought against funeral practices that exploit survivors. Derogatory media images of the elderly were also targets of the Gray Panthers.

Because of efforts by the Gray Panthers as well as other advocates, the Older Americans Act of 1965 established the federal Administration on Aging and a network of area agencies on aging. In 1967, the Age Discrimination in Employment Act became law, protecting applicants and employees age 40 and over from discrimination. By 1978, workers no longer had to relinquish their jobs at age 65—the mandatory retirement age was 70 for many workers. Currently, most workers do not face mandatory retirement, although older people in dangerous jobs (police, firefighters, and airline pilots, for example) may be forced to retire if they cannot pass physical and mental examinations.

During her lifetime, Kuhn traveled hundreds of thousands of miles for speaking engagements and organizing events. In one instance, she participated as a panel member in a weeklong course on aging conducted by the Presbyterian Church. She made the case for combating "dehumanizing images of old age." In her words: "We are not 'senior citizens' or 'golden agers.' We are the elders; the experienced ones; we are maturing, growing adults responsible for the survival of our society. We are not 'wrinkled babies,' succumbing to trivial, purposeless waste of our years and our time" (Hessel 1977, 14).

Her autobiography, which she wrote with two collaborators, was published in 1991. It tells about her many years of outspoken advocacy for the empowerment of women and for a dignified old age. At the end of the book, she wrote: "I would like my gravestone inscribed with the words, 'Here lies Maggie Kuhn under the only stone she left unturned' " (Kuhn 1991, 232). She often expressed the hope that she would die before she turned 90, and her wish was fulfilled on April 22, 1995, in Philadelphia, when she died in her sleep at the age of 89. Part of her legacy includes two documentary films, *Aging in America* and *Maggie Kuhn: Wrinkled Radical*, which detail much of her fight for social justice. The Gray Panthers organization still survives, but its numbers are declining. Some pundits suggest that is because middle-age people are in denial over aging, thus they are likely to join organizations that stress youthful activities rather than those that advocate for serious causes. Whether or not the Gray Panthers continue, the issues that face an aging population will have to be addressed in some organized fashion in the future.

See also Rankin, Jeannette

References

Callimachi, Rukmini. "Group Still Champions Senior Rights, but Ranks Thin." *Capper's*, April 13, 2004.

Doehrman, Marylou. "Avoiding a Big Chill as Baby Boomers Retire." *Colorado Springs Business Journal*, March 11, 2005.

"Gray Power" (editorial). *Nation*, May 28, 1990.

Hessel, Dieter T., ed., and Margaret E. Kuhn. *Maggie Kuhn on Aging*. Philadelphia: Westminster Press, 1977.

Kuhn, Maggie. *Get Out There and Do Something about Injustice*. New York: Friendship Press, 1972.

Kuhn, Maggie, with Christina Long and Laura Quinn. *No Stone Unturned: The Life and Times of Maggie Kuhn*. New York: Ballantine Books, 1991.

"No Stone Unturned: Maggie Kuhn." Nader.org, September 12, 1991. http://www.nader.org/index.php?/archives/1771-No-Stone-Unturned-Maggie-Kuhn.html (accessed May 2, 2010).

Sanjek, Roger. *Gray Panthers*. Philadelphia: University of Pennsylvania Press, 2009.

Shapiro, Bruce. "Corliss and Maggie." *Nation*, May 29, 1995.

Kunstler, William (1919–1995)

He called himself a radical lawyer, as did others who knew William Kunstler. His detractors called him sanctimonious and often accused him of "showboating," or being a wild-haired, flamboyant trial lawyer. Others assailed him for defending some of the most despised persons in the United States. His biographer David Langum put it succinctly in the title of his book, *William M. Kunstler: The Most Hated Lawyer in America* (1999). Yet Langum and other writers also described Kunstler's many admirers, who praised him for standing up to the power of wealth and oppressive government. Courageous, brilliant, and skillful are some of the terms used to portray him. He was a foremost dissenter, fighting for social justice and arguing passionately for black civil rights, anti–Vietnam War activists, political prisoners, and others with little or no representation in the courts.

Born on July 7, 1919, in New York City, Kunstler was the firstborn child of Monroe Bradford Kunstler, a doctor, and Frances Mandelbaum Kunstler, daughter of a prominent physician. Kunstler's parents were of German-Jewish descent, which was a matter of special pride for his mother. The Kunstler family eventually included two more children, Michael and Mary. Although they moved several times, the family stayed within the Upper West Side of Manhattan between the Hudson River and Central Park. Monroe Kunstler had his doctor's office in part of their nine-room apartment. Frances Kunstler never worked outside the home, and was "family-oriented." But she did none of the housework, which was "done by maids and the children were overseen by governesses.... She was snobbish and treated the maids and governesses as her inferiors," wrote Kunstler in his autobiography (Kunstler 1994, 55)

Throughout their childhood, Billy or Bill, as William was known, and his younger brother Michael were good "buddies," although they had different personalities. Billy was not a good student and was rebellious in school, while Michael was studious and "a paragon of virtue" (Kunstler 1994, 59). When he was 13 years old, Billy joined a gang of blacks and Hispanics. He was the only Jew, as Kunstler wrote: "Although I ran with the gang, I never became close friends with any one boy. We broke windows, stole from penny gum machines, busted into warehouses, and attacked other kids. I rebelled hanging out with middle-class Jewish kids in the fancy high-rise apartment house where my family lived, and I reveled in my gang. There was no reason for it; I simply found the mixed gang more stimulating and exciting than the other group of kids—who were all like me" (Kunstler 1994, 58).

In high school, Kunstler changed completely. He realized that his previous misbehavior had hurt his parents, and he became determined to make them proud of him. He had been an avid reader since elementary school, so he had no problem becoming a serious student—a scholar—earning top grades and graduating with honors in 1937.

Kunstler was accepted at Yale University, and following the expectations of his family, he enrolled in premed courses. But his science grades were so low that his adviser convinced him and his physician father that Kunstler would do best with courses in humanities. The adviser was correct; Kunstler loved his studies of English poets and authors of the Romantic era of the late eighteenth and early nineteenth centuries. William Wordsworth (1770–1850), John Keats (1795–1821), and Percy Shelley (1792–1822) were among the poets Kunstler studied. He also wrote poetry and collaborated with another student on a book of poetry. And as a French major, Kunstler read French authors while learning the language, which he hardly used later in his life.

Kunstler enjoyed his time at Yale for the most part. One of the negative aspects was the anti-Semitism of many students. "Rooms were decorated with Nazi flags, and Jews were not admitted into certain clubs and societies.... The message given by anti-Semitic Yalies was that it was not okay to be different. I ended up feeling uncomfortable and sometimes ashamed of being Jewish," Kunstler wrote (Kunstler 1994, 67).

While he was still at Yale in 1940, the U.S. Army was expanding due to the outbreak of war in Europe in 1939. In September 1940, the U.S. Congress passed the first peacetime draft in U.S. history. Kunstler registered for the draft, but was not called when the United States entered World

War II in 1941. That year, he graduated from Yale and decided to enlist in the Navy, but was turned down because of health issues. So he joined the Army Signal Corps as a cryptographer.

In 1943, Kunstler married Lotte Rosenberger, a young woman he had known when Kunstler was a teenager and she was 11 years old. When they married, she was 17 and Kunstler was 23. In due course they had two children, Karen and Jane. But the couple divorced in the 1970s.

During World War II, Kunstler was deployed to the Pacific theater, and he saw combat briefly in the Philippines—in Leyte and Manila. In Manila he had an unexpected and emotional meeting with his brother, Michael, who had followed in William's footsteps to Yale and then into the military. Michael was discharged before his older brother.

While in the Pacific, Bill Kunstler began writing about his experiences and sent articles to the *Patterson* (New Jersey) *Evening News*. Publication of his pieces in the newspaper were an incentive (along with his love for writing) to study journalism, which he hoped to do after he was discharged. Kunstler rose to the rank of major in the army and, in 1944, was awarded a Bronze Star for his service.

After the war, Kunstler attended Columbia University Law School, although he had no intention of practicing law. But Michael also enrolled at Columbia and encouraged his brother to work toward a law degree. Bill Kunstler took the required courses, but he did not do well at first. He found more satisfaction in writing book reviews for major newspapers and national magazines. While in law school, he was offered a writing job with a travel magazine, but he realized that if he accepted the position and dropped out of school, Michael

William Kunstler rose to notoriety as an attorney who defended controversial and often unpopular clients. His most famous clients ranged from civil rights leader Martin Luther King Jr. to Shaykh Omar Abdel-Rahman (charged with the bombing of the World Trade Center). (AP/Wide World Photos)

would have a law degree and he would not. Since the two had been affable rivals since childhood, Bill Kunstler decided to take his studies seriously. He earned his degree and passed the bar in December 1948. He and Michael formed a partnership and, in 1949, set up a practice in New York City.

Their cases were fairly routine during the 1950s, and Bill Kunstler found the work monotonous, so he sought other outlets. He taught law at the New York Law School and hosted a radio program that discussed noted trials. He even wrote radio scripts for fictional trials of such figures as Jesus and radical abolitionist John Brown, who planned to arm slaves for an insurrection.

Kunstler's first civil rights cases occurred in the mid-1950s. He successfully defended a black man who was denied housing because of his skin color. He also represented a black journalist, Bill Worthy, whose passport was taken away because he had violated a U.S. ban on travel to Cuba; when Worthy returned to the United States, he was arrested because he had no passport. On appeal, Kunstler succeeded in overturning the archaic law that had convicted Worthy. The court decision "stated that the government could not make it a crime under the Constitution for an American citizen to return home without a passport." From that decision forward "no citizen who returned to the United States without a valid passport could be prosecuted," Kunstler wrote (Kunstler 1994, 97).

The Worthy case set Kunstler on the path toward prominence as a defender of civil rights activists, political dissidents, and political prisoners. As he put it: "The sixties was my time of transformation. During this period and into the 1970s I changed from a liberal into a radical" (Kunstler 1994, 165). Kunstler, with his exuberant style and penchant for using poetry in his summary remarks, defended numerous clients including civil rights leader Martin Luther King Jr.

In 1961, the American Civil Liberties Union (ACLU) asked Kunstler to represent the Freedom Riders, groups of black and white young people who rode interstate buses from the North to the South and attempted to integrate segregated public facilities like bus stations. When the riders were arrested and jailed, Kunstler won their release. Kunstler became director of the ACLU in 1964, serving at that post until 1972.

The latter part of the 1960s was a time of intense legal activity for Kunstler. He was cofounder of the Center for Constitutional Rights (CCR). Established in 1966, the CCR has worked on behalf of civil and human rights cases, with Kunstler taking a major lead.

In 1967, Kunstler and associates petitioned a judge to overturn the conviction of Morton Sobell, a codefendant in the widely publicized case of Ethel and Julius Rosenberg in 1951. The three were found guilty of conspiracy to commit espionage and transferring atomic bomb secrets to the Union of Soviet Socialist Republics (USSR) during World War II. The Rosenbergs were executed, and Sobell was sentenced to 30 years in prison. Kunstler was not successful in the Sobell petition, but after much research, he was convinced that the jury in the Rosenberg and Sobell case had not received the "real facts." In Kunstler's view, "the Rosenbergs and Sobell were selected as scapegoats by J. Edgar Hoover, then head of the FBI" (Kunstler 1994, 93). Over the years, other legal experts have reached similar conclusions.

A highly charged case in 1969 was that of the "Chicago Seven," originally the "Chicago Eight." The term derived from the group that Kunstler defended: eight activists who protested the Vietnam War at the 1968 Democratic Convention in Chicago, Illinois. They were arrested for conspiracy to foment a riot and tried. Among the eight who became well known during the trial were Black Panther cofounder Bobby Seale; Tom Hayden, leader of the Students for a Democratic Society who later became a state senator; and longtime antiwar activist David Dellinger. Seale had no respect for the proceedings and became so disruptive at the trial that the judge ordered him bound and gagged, which prompted a seething protest from Kunstler. The judge declared a mistrial and severed Seale's case from that of the other defendants; he spent four years in jail. The other seven defendants and Kunstler were charged with contempt of court, but an appeals court later reversed all contempt convictions.

For Kunstler, the 1970s brought more contentious cases. In 1971, he was involved in attempts to negotiate with prisoners who had taken over the Attica Correctional Facility, a state prison in New York. Prisoners had demanded improvements in their inhumane living conditions. When negotiations broke down, a riot ensued, resulting in the deaths of 29 prisoners and 10 corrections officers who had been taken hostage. Kunstler defended one of the prisoners, John Hill, and former attorney general Ramsey Clark defended another prisoner called Charlie Joe. Both prisoners were charged with the murder of a prison guard in a trial that began in 1975. By this time, Kunstler was married for a second time, and his attorney wife, Margaret Ratner, often assisted him. Kunstler and Clark worked together closely for several years on the prisoner cases. Charlie Joe was not convicted, but Hill was found guilty of murder. However, Hill's sentence was commuted and he was freed on parole in 1977.

Before the Attica prisoner trial, Kunstler defended members of the American Indian Movement (AIM). In February 1973, AIM occupied Wounded Knee, a small community in the Pine Ridge Indian reservation in South Dakota, and the place where Oglala Sioux were massacred by U.S. government forces in the 1890s. The 1973 occupation was a protest against a corrupt tribal leader who had been appointed by the U.S. Bureau of Indian Affairs (BIA). The BIA, which was responsible for overseeing government policies toward Indians, had done little to ease the extreme poverty and poor living conditions at Wounded Knee and had not honored the treaty rights of Native Americans. The AIM siege of Wounded Knee lasted until May, when armed government forces overpowered the protesters. When the confrontation ended, AIM leaders, including Dennis Banks and Russell Means, were arrested and tried by the federal government more than a year later. Kunstler defended them, and eventually charges were dropped against Banks and Means.

In Kunstler's fight for civil rights, his clients in the 1980s and 1990s included some notorious and reviled figures such as gangster John Gotti, an Islamic fundamentalist charged with assassinating Rabbi Meir Kahane, and terrorists accused of bombing the World Trade Center in New York City. Many friends and family members criticized him for taking these cases, but Kunstler firmly believed in equal justice for all and representation in court for everyone.

Over the years, Kunstler not only maintained a hectic legal practice, but also continued his writing. He was the author of a dozen books, such as *Beyond a Reasonable Doubt? The Original Trial of Caryl Chessman* (1961); *The Case for Courage: The Stories of Ten Famous American Attorneys Who Risked Their Careers in the Cause of Justice* (1962); *Politics On Trial* (1963); and his memoir, *My Life as a Radical Lawyer* (1994). Kunstler died on September 4, 1995, of heart failure in a Manhattan hospital.

Kunstler's two daughters Emily and Sarah, products of his second marriage, developed a documentary of their father titled *William Kunstler: Disturbing the Universe* (2009) that explores the effects his life had on them and others.

See also Clark, Ramsey; Dellinger, David; King, Martin Luther, Jr.; Means, Russell; Rosenberg, Ethel, and Rosenberg, Julius; Seale, Bobby

References

Kunstler, William M., with Sheila Isenberg. *My Life as a Radical Lawyer*. New York: Birch Lane Press, 1994.

Langum, David J. *William M. Kunstler: The Most Hated Lawyer in America.* New York: New York University Press, 1999.

McCabe, Scott. "Crime History—Attica Prison Riot Begins, Ending with 39 Killed." *Washington Examiner*, September 9, 2009. http://washingtonexaminer.com/crime-and-punishment/2009/09/crime-history-attica-prison-riot-beginsending-39-killed (accessed February 21, 2011).

Public Broadcasting Service. "William Kunstler: Disturbing the Universe." *POV*, June 10, 2010; updated June 20, 2010. http://www.pbs.org/pov/disturbingtheuniverse/background.php (accessed February 18, 2011).

Stout, David. "William Kunstler, 76, Dies; Lawyer for Social Outcasts." *New York Times*, September 5, 1995. http://www.nytimes.com/1995/09/05/obituaries/william-kunstler-76-dies-lawyer-for-social-outcasts.html (accessed February 21, 2011).

L

LaDuke, Winona (1959–)

Winona LaDuke has lived several lifetimes during her adult years. She speaks out against pollution of Native American lands in Minnesota and elsewhere in the United States and worldwide. She fights poverty on Indian reservations. She ran twice with Ralph Nader as a vice presidential candidate. She served as a director of the environmental organization Greenpeace. She defended Native lands from corporations that were clear-cutting forests for paper production. And she lectures before hundreds of groups about Indian culture and sustainable communities.

Winona was born on August 18, 1959, in East Los Angeles, California, to Vincent and Betty Bernstein LaDuke. Her father, a member of the Anishinaabeg (Ojibwe) White Earth tribe, was an activist advocating for indigenous (Indian) rights. Her mother of Russian/Polish Jewish descent was an artist from New York City, where the couple met. After Vincent and Betty married, they moved to California, where he worked in Hollywood as an extra in Western movies. When Winona was born, Vincent enrolled her, according to indigenous custom, as a member of his Bear clan, Mississippi band, Anishinaabeg of the White Earth Reservation. An enrolled member is recognized legally as part of a tribe. Both parents taught Winona to respect Indian culture and traditions and took her to visit Indian reservations and share in pow-wows and other ceremonies.

However, Winona's parents developed different interests, and they divorced in 1964. That year, Betty and Winona moved to Ashland, Oregon, where Betty took a position as art instructor at a local college. She also met and married Peter Westigard, an entomologist who was working at the time on a scientific project to save fruit trees from predatory insects without using chemical pesticides. The couple soon had a son, Jason—and Winona had a half-brother whom she loved and helped care for.

Winona grew up in a predominately white community, giving her the feeling that she was an "outsider" with her darker skin and "funny hair," as she called it. She said in an interview that "she was always the one passed over at dances and never picked for sports teams" (Paul and Perkinson 1998, 52). However, after she joined the debate team in high school, her attitude changed. She was naturally competitive and curious, and debated on political topics of worldwide interest.

After graduating from high school, LaDuke was accepted at Harvard, where her real political activism began. As she explained:

A great bunch of Indian students came and found me, and I was politicized pretty quickly. I was also very fortunate to have excellent role models. One of the first events I attended was a speech by Jimmie Durham of the International Indian Treaty Council. He talked about how there was no such thing as the "Indian Problem." He said that it was a problem with America. As a college student, I was trying

A leading Native American activist, environmentalist, and author, Winona LaDuke works to defend the social, political, economic, and environmental rights of Native Americans. She also ran for vice president in 1996 and 2000 on the Green Party ticket with Ralph Nader. (AP/Wide World Photos)

to understand the world, and all of a sudden I just got it. His message of decolonization resonated with me entirely. So I asked him if I could go to work for him. From that point forward, at the age of eighteen, I worked on Native environmental campaigns all over the West and learned from people on the front lines. They laid the foundation of my political thinking. (Paul and Perkinson 1998, 52–53)

LaDuke majored in Rural Economic Development at Harvard, and graduated with a bachelor's degree in 1982. After graduating from Harvard, she moved to the White Earth reservation in northern Minnesota, where she took a position as principal of the high school. Living on the reservation, she conducted research on its economy, which contributed to her thesis and master's degree at Antioch College. She left the school to become involved full time in efforts to reclaim White Earth Indian land, which once had included 837,000 acres when the federal government signed a treaty in 1867 establishing the reservation. Most of the land had been taken away by an allotment system established by a federal treaty in 1887. That system divided the White Earth Reservation into parcels, each one assigned to an individual Indian who was expected to farm the land and, in the government's view, become "civilized." But land in the Indian tradition was held in common, and people traveled from place to place during appropriate seasons to gather berries, harvest wild rice, hunt and fish, pick medicinal plants, and tap for maple syrup. Over the years, whites bought land or cheated individuals out of their land parcels; much of it was taken over by lumber companies, which benefited from clear-cutting Minnesota's vast pine forests on the reservation. Other land—some 250,000 acres—was allotted to the state of Minnesota as payment for taxes, which a court found to be illegal. But the government has returned only about 10,000 acres of what they acquired.

Indians have filed one lawsuit after another in attempts to reclaim land from local, state, and federal governments that hold most of the reservation land. But Indians have had little success. So LaDuke began lecturing and writing about Indian issues. She attended a 1986 Native American conference in Toronto, Canada, where she met Randy Kapashesit, who represented the Cree tribe from Moose Factory, Ontario. Winona and Randy married in 1988, but they separated in 1990 because of Winona's commitment to White Earth and Randy's dedication to his tribe. Their two children, Waseyabin and Ajuawak, have been raised on the White Earth Reservation, but as often as possible they visit their father in Moose Factory 26 hours away by public transportation.

In 1988, Winona received a Reebok Human Rights Award, a prize of $20,000. She used the funds to found the White Earth Land Recovery Project (WELRP) in 1989. One of the project's purposes is to buy back land that once was part of the reservation. Another aspect of its mission is preserving traditional Indian spiritual and cultural practices as well as protecting environmental diversity. As director of WELRP, LaDuke "also supervises maple-sugar and wild-rice processing operations, a stable of horses, an international network of indigenous women, an Ojibwe language program, a brand-new wind-energy project, and a herd of buffalo," wrote Peter Ritter in 2000. "All of this with a small volunteer staff and an annual budget of a half-million dollars. The WELRP's modus operandi is simple and ingenious: Develop a self-sustaining economy and local land ownership" (Ritter 2000).

As if operating WELRP is not enough for any one person to tackle, LaDuke is also the executive director of Honor the Earth, which raises funds for indigenous environmental groups. She also operates Native Harvest, which raises and sells natural indigenous products. In addition, she is cochair for the Indigenous Women's Network, a North American and Pacific indigenous women's group focused on increasing the visibility of indigenous women in political, social and cultural processes. She served on the board of the environmental group Greenpeace. She has found time as well to be a guest speaker at national and international events such as the 1995 United Nations Fourth World Conference on Women in Beijing, China. There she spoke about the lack of indigenous representation at the United Nations; the fact that transnational corporations make most of the decisions that affect people worldwide; the "predatory-prey relationship industrial society has developed with the Earth"; the rain forests that have been decimated by multinational companies in numerous countries; the dumping of toxic waste on indigenous lands; and the "human rights of self-determination." She called on women at the international conference "to support the struggle of Indigenous peoples of the world for recognition, and to recognize that until all peoples have self-determination, no one will truly be free" (LaDuke 1995).

In some respects, LaDuke echoes the views of a past sage, Aldo Leopold (1887–1948), who believed that people needed to discard the idea that land and its products were mere commodities. He declared people should see themselves and the land as part of an integral and inseparable community; then and only then would they start treating their environment with the love and respect it deserved.

LaDuke has written numerous articles for national magazines and newspapers on topics such as the lack of food access for millions of people worldwide and alternative energy (wind power, for example). In addition, she has written several books. The first, a novel, *Last Standing Woman* (1997), was followed by a nonfiction book on Native environmental struggles, *All Our Relations: Native Struggles for Land and Life* (1999); *The Winona LaDuke Reader: A Collection of Essential Writings* (2002); and *Recovering the Sacred: The Power of Naming and Claiming* (2005). She has also written a children's book with her daughter Waseyabin Kapashesit, titled *Sugar Bush* (1999); it describes how sap is collected from maple trees and turned into syrup.

In 1994, she was honored by *Time* magazine as one of the United States' 50 most promising leaders under 40 years of age. She received the Thomas Merton Award in 1996, the BIHA Community Service Award in 1997 and the Ann Bancroft Award for Women's Leadership Fellowship, and *Ms.* magazine named her Woman of the Year in 1998 for her work with Honor the Earth. She received the International Slow Food Award in 2003 for efforts to preserve wild rice from genetic engineering. She was inducted into the National Women's Hall of Fame in 2007.

With all of her accomplishments and emphasis on environmental issues, she is often introduced in articles, at lectures, and television interviews as the woman who ran in 1996 and 2000 for vice president of the United States on the Green Party ticket with Ralph Nader seeking the presidency. Nader was impressed with LaDuke's efforts to achieve social justice. Nader and LaDuke did poorly in 1996, but in 2000, they received 2,883,105 popular votes; they won no electoral votes. In the 2000 election, Al Gore ran as the Democrat nominee for president and George W. Bush was the Republican presidential candidate. Bush won the election, and many critics of Nader and LaDuke accused them of siphoning votes away from Gore (who lost by only 537 popular votes), in effect giving the election to Bush. Both Nader and LaDuke deny that was the case.

While campaigning, LaDuke championed Native American rights and called attention to environmental pollution. She also focused on her role as a mother—her third child, infant daughter Gwekaanimid, accompanied her on the campaign trail. In her home, where she handled the paperwork involved in any campaign, she also managed to care for the needs of her children and a niece and nephew. Her partner/significant other Kevin Gasco was by her side helping with multiple tasks, such as dealing with e-mail and phone calls. For more than a decade after the election campaign, LaDuke has continued to lecture at universities on such topics as climate change, renewable (nonnuclear) energy, and environmental justice for indigenous communities. Her major concern is sustainable living—in brief, to encourage industrial societies whose economies depend on consumption to consume less in order to sustain the environment. Future survival, she believes, depends on sustainability.

See also Leopold, Aldo; Nader, Ralph

References

LaDuke, Winona. "The Indigenous Women's Network: Our Future, Our Responsibility: Statement of Winona LaDuke." Presented at the United Nations Fourth World Conference on Women, Beijing, China, August 31, 1995. http://www.ratical.org/co-globalize/Winona LaDuke/Beijing95.html (accessed April 4, 2011).

Paul, Sonya, and Robert Perkinson. "Winona LaDuke." Chap. 4 of *No Middle Ground: Women and Radical Protest*, edited by Kathleen M. Blee. New York: New York University Press, 1998.

Paul, Sonya, and Robert Perkinson. "Winona LaDuke—Native American Ecological Activist—Interview." *Progressive*, October 1995. http://findarticles.com/p/articles/mi_m1295/is_n10_v59/ai_17598385/?tag =content;col (accessed April 4, 2011).

Ritter, Peter. "The Party Crasher." City Pages, October 11, 2000. http://www.citypages.com/2000-10-11/news/the-party-crasher/ (accessed April 1, 2011).

Rosen, Marjorie. "Friend of the Earth: Indian Activist Winona LaDuke Fights to Return Tribal Lands to Her People." *People*, November 28, 1994. http://www.people.com/people/archive/article/0,,20104531,00.html (accessed March 31, 2011).

Van Gelder, Sarah. "An Interview with Winona LaDuke." *Yes! Magazine*, Summer

2008. http://www.yesmagazine.org/issues/a-just-foreign-policy/an-interview-with-winona-laduke (accessed April 5, 2011).

LaRouche, Lyndon (1922–)

Lyndon LaRouche calls himself "the leading economist, in performance, in the world today. My influence is fairly described as 'world-wide,' in one fashion, or another. I am, for example, the most successful forecaster on record since 1956–57" (Appenzell Daily Bell 2010). He has been a controversial candidate for U.S. president and has gained enemies on both the political left and right. He is head of an organization that some have called a fascist movement. His supporters see him as a bright, original thinker. Yet, no one has been able to determine exactly what he and his organization represent. About the only certain assessment is that LaRouche is a dissident who attacks multiple targets ranging from Ayn Rand (1905–1982) and her philosophy of objectivism, to the U.S. government and its economic system, to his hatred for Queen Elizabeth and anything British.

Born on September 8, 1922, in Rochester, New Hampshire, he was named Lyndon Hermyle LaRouche Jr. His father, Lyndon Sr., worked for the United Shoe Machinery Corporation and was a member of the Society of Friends (Quakers) as was his mother, Jesse Weir LaRouche. Lyndon Jr. was the oldest of three children. He and his two sisters attended elementary school in Rochester. Those early school years were not pleasant for Lyndon Jr., whose classmates thought he acted superior because he was able to read at five years old. In addition, he was the target of bullies—his parents, in the pacifist tradition of Friends, would not allow him to fight even in self-defense when he was attacked. He noted in his autobiography: "Among my age-peers I was caught between slow-speaking farm boys and quick, restive youngsters, quick of speech and short of attention-span. I was dubbed 'Big Head,' and was a semi-outcast, the latter because I didn't fight and had different interests than either the farm boys or what passed locally for the city boys" (LaRouche 1979, 39).

When Lyndon's father retired from the shoe company, the family moved in 1932 to Lynn, Massachusetts, where the senior LaRouche set up his own business. In Lynn, Lyndon found his secondary schooling boring. But on his own, he was an avid reader of works by well-known philosophers as well as German mathematicians such as Gottfried Leibnitz, Bernard Riemann, and Johannes Kepler. His reading was relieved somewhat in the summers when he went to work in a shoe factory.

As an adolescent, Lyndon found his home life "unsatisfactory" and his social life a "total failure." He had few friends, often spent time alone in his room reading, or took long walks through the woods and explored nature. "Intellectually I never 'felt myself' with persons of my age group during childhood," he wrote. "I was much more at ease with adults. The few friends I acquired during high-school years I met across the chess board" (LaRouche 1979, 57).

In Lyndon's view, his schooling was influenced by the "poisonous influence of John Dewey on educational policy." Dewey argued that schools should teach students how to be problem solvers and how to think rather than simply learn by rote. Wrote LaRouche: "I had read some Dewey and I was enraged by his doctrines" (LaRouche 1979, 47). To Lyndon, Dewey was too pragmatic and not given to reason and finding the answer to "What is truth?" as put forward by LaRouche's favorite philosophers. LaRouche often refers to his philosophical understanding of epistemology, as espoused by Leibnitz, stressing the nature of knowledge—what is the relationship between truth and reality rather than practical how-to learning.

Other conflicts in Lyndon's life occurred because of his parents' religious views, and their insistence that he should be a minister. He had no intention of choosing that as his life's work. But he did agree with his parents when an issue arose concerning the American Friends Service Committee (AFSC), founded in 1917 and dedicated to social justice, peace, and humanitarian service. AFSC had received a grant from a trust fund set up by Jesse LaRouche's wealthy uncle. Lyndon's Orthodox Quaker parents objected strenuously to the grant, claiming that the AFSC was an ungodly, pro-communist, liberal organization and that AFSC was using the money for social work instead of for religious education, which was the purpose of the trust fund. The fight between the LaRouches and the AFSC became so bitter that Lyndon Sr. was rejected by the Quaker group in Lynn. Lyndon Jr. joined his parents in resigning from the group.

After graduating from high school in 1940, LaRouche enrolled at Northeastern University in Boston. He received poor grades and was disgusted with his instructors, claiming they were incompetent. He left the university in 1942 and joined an AFSC public service camp for conscientious objectors. There he quickly became part of a group opposed to the camp, but soon left to enlist in the U.S. Army. He has given two versions of his reason for enlistment: (1) he was fed up with camp people whom he described as socialists and ex-communists; and (2) he had always planned to enlist but did not do so when the United States entered World War II because of his father's objections. As LaRouche wrote: "My father was close to tears at the thought of my breaking with *his* conscience. Months later, having served his conscience, I presented my entrance into military service as a fait accompli" (LaRouche 1979, 59).

LaRouche served in the China-Burma-India theater and, during his time there, attempted to organize communists in India to rise up against British colonial rule. While in Calcutta, India, where he was stationed, he developed a hatred for the British, which has not diminished over the years. He often refers disdainfully to British imperialism (and others that he calls imperialists). His efforts to organize against British rule failed, and years later when he was running for U.S. president, he denied working with communists. Yet, in 1949 he became a member of the Socialist Workers Party (SWP), considered a subversive organization by U.S. senator Joseph McCarthy and the Federal Bureau of Investigation, who were investigating people accused or suspected of being communists or communist sympathizers. In order to avoid suspicion, he took the name Lyn Marcus and worked with the SWP in Massachusetts. In 1954, he moved to New York City, where the SWP's national center was located, and married fellow SWP member Janice Neuberger. Their son Daniel, an only child, was born in 1956. The couple separated in 1963.

During the 1960s, LaRouche opposed the Vietnam War, and numerous college students supported his protest efforts. At the time, he preached that U.S. military industries could be converted to a peaceful reindustrialization process.

LaRouche's first of eight bids for the U.S. presidency was in 1976, which failed, and in 1977, he was in Germany where he married Helga Zepp, an international political activist and a leading authority on Friedrich Schiller (1759–1805), a poet and essayist who developed aesthetic theories that focused on the creative powers of humanity. In 1984, Helga founded the international Schiller Institute, which still operates. Its web site posts numerous articles by Lyndon and Helga LaRouche and supporters of the LaRouche Youth Movement.

During the 1970s and 1980s, LaRouche attacked Jews, people of color, the British, the environmental movement, and even jazz and rock groups and video games. He developed numerous conspiracy theories, claiming, as *Washington Post* journalist April Witt pointed out, that "People are out to get him. Powerful people—Zionists, bankers, the British. People who control the Republican and Democratic parties and ensure his votes aren't counted. People, according to LaRouche and his followers, who have plotted to send brainwashed zombies to assassinate him" (Witt 2004, W12).

After his third presidential campaign in 1984, federal and Massachusetts state authorities began investigating LaRouche, his associates, and his various organizations. In 1986, the investigators raided LaRouche headquarters in Leesburg, Virginia, and arrested him and others on charges of conspiracy to commit mail fraud, and illegal and manipulative fund-raising practices, as well as tax evasion. At his trial, he was represented by Ramsey Clark, former U.S. attorney general who had protested the Vietnam War and later founded an organization to impeach President George W. Bush. Clark argued that the U.S. government persecuted LaRouche. But LaRouche was convicted and sentenced to prison. According to Witt, "LaRouche maintained that the convictions were engineered to silence him politically and set him up to be murdered in prison. He survived. One of his cellmates was disgraced televangelist Jim Bakker, who later described LaRouche as amusing, erudite and convinced their cell was bugged. 'To say that Lyndon was slightly paranoid,' Bakker wrote in his autobiography, 'would be like saying the Titanic had a bit of a leak' " (Witt 2004, W12).

In 1992, LaRouche campaigned for U.S. president from prison. His campaign was the second time in U.S. history that someone had run for president from jail—labor leader and socialist Eugene V. Debs (1885–1926) was the first. However, LaRouche never won more than 80,000 votes in any election and was not considered a serious candidate, while Debs was widely respected in the labor and antiwar movements and received nearly one million votes during his imprisonment.

Released from prison on parole in 1994, LaRouche continued his organizational activities and writing. His published works since 1970 include *Dialectical Economics* (1973), *The Power of Reason: A Kind of an Autobiography* (1979), *Basic Economics for Conservative Democrats* (1980), *What Every Conservative Should Know about Communism* (1980), *There Are No Limits to Growth* (1983), *Imperialism: The Final Stage of Bolshevism* (1984), *In Defense of Common Sense* (1989), and *The Science of Christian Economy, and Other Prison Writings* (1991); plus hundreds of articles and speeches in publications supportive of LaRouche: *Executive Intelligence Review, Fidelio Magazine*, and *21st Century Science and Technology*.

During the 2000s, LaRouche and his followers have persisted in their attacks on people who disagree with them, calling their opponents drug addicts, terrorists, and communists. They argue among other things that Jews and Jewish organizations are responsible for the international financial crisis, that people with AIDS should be quarantined, that bankers and other financial interests plunder the U.S. economy, and that global warming is a fake. LaRouche has opposed the economic and domestic policies of many U.S. presidents, although consistently he has supported President Franklin D. Roosevelt (1933–1945) and his policies, which he claims were destroyed by his successor Harry Truman (1945–1953). LaRouche has been especially critical of George W. Bush (2001–2009) and Barack Obama, whom he accuses of being like Hitler.

LaRouche supporters often set up displays in cities and towns across the nation displaying posters of Obama with a Hitler-like mustache, and signs that call for Obama's impeachment. They also harass members of the U.S. Congress who conduct town hall meetings, such as one that U.S. representative Barney Frank arranged in Dartmouth, Massachusetts, in 2009. A LaRouche supporter, holding up a picture of Obama with a Hitler-like mustache, asked Frank why he supported a German Nazi health care policy. Frank's response: "You stand there with a picture of the president defaced to look like Hitler and compare the effort to increase health care to the Nazis," Frank said. "Trying to have a conversation with you would be like trying to argue with a dining room table" (Franke-Ruta and Lovenheim 2009).

In March 2009, LaRouche gave a speech in which he recalled his warning on July 25, 2007, that the world was "on the verge of the beginning of a general breakdown crisis of the [global] financial systems. And in three days after that, the process which I had forecast began to occur." In his rambling speech, printed in *EIR Strategy*, LaRouche made his familiar charges: the British and the U.S. financial institutions are fascists, and only a return to Franklin Roosevelt's policies will save the United States and the world from collapse (LaRouche 2009, 52–57). In 2010, at age 88, LaRouche was still giving similar speeches and continuing his call for impeachment of Obama.

See also Debs, Eugene V.; Clark, Ramsey; Frank, Barney; McCarthy, Joseph; Rand, Ayn

References

Ambinder, Marc. "The Town Halls, Independents, and Lyndon LaRouche." *Atlantic*, August 13, 2009.

Appenzell Daily Bell with Scott Smith. "Lyndon LaRouche Explains the Collapsing Western Economy and How the World Really Works." *Gold Speculator*, June 20, 2010. http://www.gold-speculator.com/appenzell-daily-bell/31907-lyndon-larouche-explains-collapsing-western-economy-how-world-really-works.html (accessed August 14, 2010).

Berlet, Chip, and Matthew N. Lyons. *Right-Wing Populism in America: Too Close for Comfort*. New York: Guilford Press, 2000.

Franke-Ruta, Garance, and Sarah Lovenheim. "Frank Blasts Nazi Comparisons From LaRouche Backers," *Washington Post*, August 20, 2009. http://voices.washingtonpost.com/capitol-briefing/2009/08/town_hall_talk_frank_grills_op.html (accessed August 15, 2010).

King, Dennis. *Lyndon LaRouche and the New American Fascism*. New York: Doubleday, 1989.

LaRouche, Lyndon, Jr. *The Power of Reason: A Kind of an Autobiography*. New York: The New Benjamin Franklin House Publishing Company, 1979.

LaRouche, Lyndon, Jr. "LaRouche: We Must Return to FDR's 1944 Intention." *EIR Strategy*, March 27, 2009. http://www.larouchepub.com/eiw/public/2009/2009_10-19/2009-12/pdf/52-57_3612.pdf (accessed August 16, 2010).

Witt, April. "No Joke." *Washington Post Magazine*, October 24, 2004.

Leopold, Aldo (1887–1948)

The name Aldo Leopold is hardly a familiar one to most Americans. Yet U.S. life would be much the worst—in numerous respects—had Leopold not contributed as he did to the literal landscape of the nation. Leopold was a U.S. ecologist and environmentalist who approached those topics as they had never been dealt with previously, viewing them through a novel ethical periscope. He was a dissident voice in environmental politics, and led the charge in the wilderness conservation movement. If not for Leopold, it can be argued that Americans' appreciation for and access to its natural resources might not be where they are today.

Born on January 11, 1887, in Burlington, Iowa, at his birth he was named Rand Aldo Leopold, after two of his father's business partners. He came to be called solely by his middle name. His father Carl and mother Clara had three other children: Mary Luize, Carl Starker, and Frederic. They were raised with German as their first language but taught English as well. They learned to appreciate nature, spending much time outdoors.

Young Leopold enjoyed hunting, hiking, and fishing with his father. He also took an interest in ornithology, spending countless hours cataloging birds. Annually each August, the Leopolds vacationed in the heavily forested Les Cheneaux (French for "The Channels") Islands, found along 12 miles of Lake Huron coastline on the southeastern tip of the Upper Peninsula of Michigan. These trips allowed the Leopold siblings to explore this group of 36 islands (some of which remain uninhabited to this day) and gain exposure to the wonders of nature. From his earliest days, Leopold was drawn to all things having to do with the environment. His sister recalled, "He was very much an outdoorsman, even in his extreme youth. He was always out climbing around the bluffs, or going down to the river, or going across the river into the woods" (Lorbiecki 2005, 9).

Leopold was an excellent student, both at Prospect Hill Elementary School and then at Burlington High School. His parents were supportive of his desire to attend what was at that time the nation's fledgling forestry school at Yale University. Leopold first enrolled at the preparatory Lawrenceville School in New Jersey in January 1904. "Leopold's true genius, even then, lay not inside the school, but in the fields around it ... Within days of his arrival, he was off on daily 'tramps' into the winter countryside and soon after was being introduced as the 'naturalist.' Within a month, he had acquainted himself with the area for ten miles around, drawn a map and applied his own labels: Big Woods, Fern Woods, Cat Woods, Owl Woods, Ash Swamp, the Boulders, Grove Country" (Meine 1988, 35). In September 1905, Leopold moved on to New Haven. However, he did not immediately enter Yale's Forestry School, as it was solely for graduate studies. Instead, he enrolled in the Sheffield Scientific School's forestry program (Meine 1988, 51). His time at Yale was more challenging and took up increased time socially as well. Still, he made space each week for his "tramps." "He drew a new map, and applied new labels: Marvelwood, Queer Valley, Junniper Hill, The Castle" (Meine 1988, 52).

Educational credentials in hand, in 1909, Leopold accepted employment with the U.S. Forest Service. He was assigned to District 3, comprising the Arizona and New Mexico territories. His first posting was that of a forest assistant at the Apache National Forest in Arizona. With him, "Leopold brought his notion of the West as a wild wonderland, as well as a set of acute senses, a restless curiosity, and an ample young ego ... His training as a progressive forester gave him a new idea to impress on the landscape" (Meine 1988, 97). Soon thereafter—true to form—he was again drawing maps: "etched onto his paper

Leopold, Aldo (1887–1948)

The influential writings of 20th-century environmentalist Aldo Leopold changed the way that many Americans viewed nature. An employee of the U.S. Forest Service, Leopold was instrumental in the creation of Gila National Forest, the nation's first protected wilderness area. (Library of Congress)

was a land of stunning diversity and beauty" (Meine 1988, 88). In 1911, he transferred to the Carson National Forest in northern New Mexico where, as part of his duties, he hunted and killed bears, mountain lions, and wolves—all animals that preyed on ranchers' livestock. An avid hunter himself, Leopold came to regard these predators in a new light, developing a new way of thinking, an "ecological ethic" that rejected the idea of human dominance over the environment. Over time, Leopold would change many others' thinking about the role "predators" played in the balance of nature, and policy changes would result in the return of bears, mountain lions, and wolves to wilderness areas.

In 1915, Leopold started working on the first comprehensive management plan ever for the Grand Canyon. In September of that year, he also put together the U.S. Forest Service's first *Game and Fish Handbook*. Leopold's radical views were championed by some but not all. He left the public sector and went to work for the U.S. Chamber of Commerce for a short period. He returned to the Forest Service as Assistant District Forester in Charge of Operations in 1919 where he was responsible for overseeing 20 million acres of land and evaluating such functions as personnel, construction, fire control, roads and trails, other permanent improvements, public relations, recreation, timber management, land acquisition and exchange, supplies and equipment, grazing and watershed maintenance. Leopold would stay in New Mexico through 1924. During this time, he became increasingly concerned with the changes he saw taking place in the American West he had come to know and love. Americans were taking to the roads in ever-increasing numbers. He perceived that their love of automobiles and the related expansion of thoroughfares on which to drive them posed a grave threat. If there were not some sort of immediate intervention, there would be risk of irreparable loss. Leopold began formulating ways to preserve the national forests and the country's "wilderness" areas. With time, his thinking would evolve to include arguments that additionally were ethically and scientifically, rather than merely emotionally, based.

In 1924, Leopold achieved designation of the first official national wilderness area in the country's Forest Service system, the Gila Wilderness Area in New Mexico—a monumental accomplishment, particularly when viewed in light of the fact that it would take another 40 years before the U.S. Wilderness Act was signed into law, creating the national Wilderness Preservation System. That same year, Leopold was appointed associate director to the U.S. Forest Products Laboratory in Madison, Wisconsin, where he worked for four years before leaving the employment of the U.S. government for the final time.

Leopold spent the next four years of his career working for the Sporting Arms and Ammunition Manufacturers' Institute. He had been hired to conduct a game survey that would investigate on-the-ground conditions in the United States. His end report described game conservation efforts, made recommendations, and suggested research. Because he was from "the other side," he was exactly who the group wanted to project objectivity. From 1932 to 1933, he worked on publication of *Game Management*, which was published in 1933. That same year, Leopold achieved another first when he was appointed professor of game management in the Agricultural Economics Department at the University of Wisconsin–Madison, the first of its kind in wildlife management. His approach was unique: "Conservation is not merely a thing to be enshrined in outdoor museums, but a way of living on land" (Meine 1988, 310). He interacted with the community, preaching that wildlife management was not just a means of game restoration, but also a means to enhance the quality of rural life.

In 1934, President Franklin Delano Roosevelt appointed Leopold to serve on the Committee on Wildlife Restoration and, in the following year, along with forester Robert Marshall, Leopold helped found the Wilderness Society, dedicated to expanding and protecting the nation's wilderness areas. Since its founding, the society has helped protect nearly 110 million acres of wilderness in 44 states. Long-time conservationist Olaus Murie became president of the society in 1945; his wife, Margaret, was secretary. Both worked tirelessly to preserve the Alaska wilderness. Margaret Murie became known as the grandmother of the conservation movement.

In 1935, Leopold bought his own plot of sandy land in central Wisconsin where he tested his theories, ultimately resulting in his best-known work, *A Sand Country Almanac*. It called for the harmony and preservation of ecosystems. Published in 1949 after his passing, the book is credited with spurring on the then-burgeoning environmental movement.

Leopold underwent a radical metamorphosis during his life. He came to advocate a "land ethic" in which humans viewed themselves as a mere component of a larger natural community. He believed that man's abuse of land occurred because he viewed it as a commodity that belonged to him. Leopold felt that people needed to see themselves and the land as part of an integral and inseparable community; then and only then would they start treating their environment with the love and respect it deserved. He wrote about the need for "a revision of the national attitude toward land, its life, and its products. The basic assumption that land is merely an economic commodity, and that land-use is governed wholly by economic forces, must be definitely discarded. . . . The ways and means to conservation, then, must deal primarily with arresting these pathological tendencies, and with the removal of economic obstacles to better land-use" (Meine 1988, 363).

In *A Sand Country Almanac*, Leopold wrote:

> This sounds simple: do we not already sing our love for and obligation to the land of the free and the home of the brave? Yes, but just what and whom do

we love? Certainly not the soil, which we are sending helter-skelter down river. Certainly not the waters, which we assume have no function except to turn turbines, float barges, and carry off sewage. Certainly not the plants, of which we exterminate whole communities without batting an eye. Certainly not the animals, of which we have already extirpated many of the largest and most beautiful species. A land ethic of course cannot prevent the alteration, management, and use of these "resources," but it does affirm their right to continued existence, and, at least in spots, their continued existence in a natural state. In short, a land ethic changes the role of Homo sapiens from conqueror of the land-community to plain member and citizen of it. It implies respect for his fellow-members, and also respect for the community as such. (Leopold 2001, 171)

When Leopold first began speaking about the concept of "the wilderness," it was in the context of a place to camp, fish, and hunt. By the end of his life, Leopold viewed it in a much more philosophical manner, almost as a resource to which "civilization could turn to assess not only its ecological health, but even its social and psychological well-being" (Meine 1988, 504–5).

Leopold had a fatal heart attack on April 21, 1948, near Madison, Wisconsin, while helping to put out a fire on a neighbor's property. At the time, his wife, Estella and five children survived him. Leopold's followers continue to hoist the banner of his causes. In 2009, newly elected president Barack Obama signed into law the Omnibus Public Land Management Act on March 30 of that year. As the president noted: "This landmark bill will protect millions of acres of Federal land as wilderness, protect more than 1,000 miles of rivers through the National Wild and Scenic River System, and designate thousands of miles of trails for the National Trails System. It also will authorize the 26 million–acre National Landscape Conservation System within the Department of the Interior. Among other provisions, [the law] designates three new units in our National Park System, enlarges the boundaries of several existing parks, and designates a number of National Heritage Areas" (Obama 2009).

Margaret Gay

See also Murie, Margaret

References

Leopold, Aldo. *Game Management*. New Delhi, India: Natraj Publishers, 1996.

Leopold, Aldo. *A Sand Country Almanac, with Essays on Conservation*. New York: Oxford University Press, 2001.

Lorbiecki, Marybeth. *Aldo Leopold: A Fierce Green Fire*. Helena, MT: Falcon Press, 2005.

Meine, Curt D. *Aldo Leopold: His Life and Work*. Madison: University of Wisconsin Press, 1988.

Obama, Barack. "Statement by the President." Office of the Press Secretary, March 30, 2009. http://www.whitehouse.gov/the_press_office/Statement-from-the-Presidents-signing-statements-on-HR-146-the-Omnibus-Public-Lands-Management-Act/ (accessed March 26, 2011).

Limbaugh, Rush (1951–)

He is popular, and he is polarizing. That is the consensus of American listeners across the United States who hear Rush Limbaugh on his radio show as he insults, makes satirical remarks, and presents ultraconservative views on politics, politicians, celebrities, and other newsmakers. Rush, as he is usually called, is a boisterous dissenter of anything and anyone he labels as "liberal." People either seem to be devoted followers of the talk-show host, or they hate him. He has been called "a serial liar and a moral philosopher, a partisan hack and a public intellectual, nothing more than a radio windbag and nothing less than the heart of the Republican Party," according to Zev Chafets in a Limbaugh profile for the *New York Times Magazine* (Chafets 2008).

Born January 12, 1951, in Cape Girardeau, Missouri, Rush Hudson Limbaugh III is the son of Mildred Carolyn (Millie) Armstrong and Rush Hudson Limbaugh Jr. There are numerous lawyers in the extended family, and they have a long history of political activism for the Republican Party. In fact, Rush's grandfather, Rush Limbaugh Sr., was a Republican representative in the Missouri legislature, and the federal courthouse in Cape Girardeau is named for him. Big Rush, as Rush Jr. was called, was a lawyer who represented primarily Republican clients. He also was a popular orator at patriotic events and an outspoken foe of communism and liberalism.

Young Rush, who became known as Rusty, "had the standard upbringing of a well-born kid of his time and place," according to his biographer Chafets. "He played ball . . . mowed the family lawn, took piano lessons . . . joined the Cub Scouts . . . and attended the Methodist Sunday School. From the very beginning he dreaded school, which he considered a prison" (Chafets 2010, 20).

Big Rush wanted Rusty to study and someday enter college and become a lawyer like others in his family, but from an early age Rusty dreamt of being on the radio and gaining celebrity status. He got his start with a local station while he was in high school. At age 16, he was a disc jockey for his *Rusty Sharpe Show* that aired daily. Although loath to do so, Big Rush paid Rusty's fee for a summer course in radio electronics, and during his last year in high school, Rusty continued to insist that he wanted a career in radio. His father was adamant about his son attending college, and won the argument—for a time.

Rusty enrolled at Southeast Missouri State University, but left after two semesters. At the time—1970—the Vietnam War was still under way. Although some U.S. troops were being withdrawn, men without a deferment still could be drafted. Limbaugh was disqualified because of a health problem—a cyst on the tailbone. Later on, when he became a national figure, his draft status and lack of service were issues for some of his critics. But Limbaugh turned that criticism around to target prominent individuals who, he declared, were "draft dodgers."

Limbaugh's next step toward his intended occupation was in 1972. He had a job as a disc jockey, using the name Jeff Christie, at WIXZ in McKeesport, Pennsylvania, near Pittsburgh. He made his next move in 1973 to Pittsburgh as an evening disc jockey. That job lasted about a year, and unable to find comparable work, he returned to his hometown to live with his parents again. After seven months at his parents' home, he found another radio job in Kansas City, Missouri. He lived in suburban Overland Park, where he met Roxy McNeely, whom he married in 1977. The marriage lasted only two years. His job in Kansas City did not last as long—he was fired in 1978. "Limbaugh had personality conflicts with superiors, who found him argumentative," according to his biographer (Chafets 2010, 39).

For five years, Limbaugh was employed in another line of work: ticket sales and promotion for the Kansas City Royals baseball team. While at that job, he met Michelle Sixta, who would be his second wife. He was back on the radio again in 1984 as a talk show host in Sacramento, California, where he was "encouraged" to present his "highly personal right-wing monologues" (Chafets 2010, 42). Limbaugh quickly gained a large audience, although not a national one.

However, in 1988, he caught the attention of ABC Radio and was invited to New York City, where he began his national broadcast. Two years after the initiation of *The Rush Limbaugh Show*, he reportedly had more listeners than any other U.S. talk-show host. As journalist Lewis Grossberger described it at the time: "His subject is politics. His stance: conservative. His persona: comic blowhard. His style: a schizoid spritz, bouncing between earnest lecturer and political vaudevillian." Explaining his outrageous behavior on the air, Limbaugh said, "I demonstrate absurdity by being absurd" (Grossberger 1990, 58).

Biographer Chafets says that Limbaugh patterned his character after boxing great Muhammad Ali, "whose big mouth, braggadocio, and sheer raw nerve enabled him to draw and keep a crowd. . . . [Ali] invented disparaging nicknames for his opponents . . . and arrogantly predicted the round of his victories" (Chafets 2010, 7). In spite of criticism that he was nothing but a showman, Ali proved otherwise and became a boxing legend.

Through the 1990s, Limbaugh's popularity increased and his many supporters—"dittoheads," as they call themselves—repeated his opinions as "gospel." He appeared as a guest on numerous TV talk shows and, from 1992 through 1996, he had his own television show. Two of his books were published also: *The Way Things Ought to Be* (1992) and *See, I Told You So* (1993). In addition, he founded a monthly publication *The Limbaugh Letter*. He admired and was admired by conservative dignitaries; he was especially honored that President Ronald Reagan (Limbaugh called him "Ronaldus Maximus") was a fan. But his personal life was not so successful—his second marriage to Michelle Sixta ended in divorce. In 1994, he married Marta Fitzgerald, a marriage that lasted until 2004.

Politics and personal responsibility are main topics on Limbaugh's shows. He attacks liberals, the "liberal media," Democrats and the Democratic Party, and big government. During his show, he consistently claims that the mainstream media are biased. He also has been accused of distorting facts, has used name-calling to ridicule opponents and opposing views, challenges the patriotism of various individuals, and blasts political candidates who do not fit his criteria for a "true conservative."

For their part, some liberals attack Limbaugh with as much vitriol and derision as that exhibited by the talk-show host. One of the most severe critics is political satirist Al Franken (now U.S. Democratic senator from Minnesota), who wrote *Rush Limbaugh Is a Big Fat Idiot and Other Observations* (1996). Other liberals such as Keith Olbermann on his *Countdown* television show often ridiculed Limbaugh and his bombastic pronouncements.

The decade of 2000 to 2010 saw Limbaugh's fame spread, but he also faced a series of problems. In 2001, he had severe hearing loss that had been developing over many months. He had no hearing in his left ear and began to lose hearing in the other ear. He was almost totally deaf, but continued his show by answering questions that had been typed into his computer and by having a series of guest hosts while he was off for medical tests. His hearing was restored with a device called a cochlear implant, and he was able to return to his show full time in 2003.

That triumph was soon overshadowed by a scandal that erupted when his former housekeeper, Wilma Cline, turned over e-mail and phone messages to police authorities showing that Limbaugh allegedly had been getting different doctors to write prescriptions for hydrocodone, OxyContin, Xanax, and morphine pills. Cline and her husband had been helping Limbaugh obtain the prescription drugs. When the story appeared in the press, Limbaugh told his audience that he was addicted to painkiller medication, a disturbing revelation to his listeners. An investigation into his abuse of drugs began, and Limbaugh took a leave from his show to enter a drug treatment center. Authorities in Palm Beach County, Florida, where Limbaugh has a home, seized his medical records, which Limbaugh's lawyer declared violated his patient privacy rights.

The state attorney's office was looking for evidence to charge Limbaugh with "doctor shopping"—that is, obtaining multiple overlapping prescriptions from several doctors for pain medication. After three years of probing, the state attorney's office issued a warrant for Limbaugh's arrest for fraud. He turned himself in and prosecutors and Limbaugh reached an agreement: charges against him would be dropped if he continued drug rehabilitation and paid $30,000 to cover the costs of the investigation. He also agreed to relinquish gun ownership for 18 months.

The drug scandal did not diminish Limbaugh's popularity with his fans. By some estimates, his audience each week is more than 20 million. In 2008, he signed a contract for $400 million to continue his show through 2016.

In 2010, Limbaugh married again. His fourth wife, Kathryn Rogers, is a long-time friend. The couple lives in a Palm Beach mansion where they entertain friends and relatives. Limbaugh has no children.

Over the years, Limbaugh has received numerous awards. The National Association of Broadcasters honored him four times with the Marconi Radio Award as Personality of the Year. The award is named for Guglielmo Marconi, inventor of the radio telegraph system. Other honors include Limbaugh's induction into the Radio Hall of Fame in 1993, the Media Research Center's Award for Media Excellence in 2007, and a 2007 Man of the Year Award by *Human Events* magazine presented in 2008.

Limbaugh continues with his popular and controversial show from a Palm Beach studio. His supporters and detractors also continue their arguments over Limbaugh's influence and popularity. In some cases, there is a division along partisan political lines. Opinion polls often show that Republicans give Limbaugh a high approval rating. In fact, Limbaugh frequently is called the true head of the Republican Party.

On the other hand, a high percentage of Democrats disapprove of Limbaugh. In addition, many people who consider themselves liberals object to Limbaugh's conservative arguments that oppose gays in the military, environmentalism, feminism, women's right to choose abortion, and scientific opinions on global warming.

Two political experts at the University of Pennsylvania, Kathleen Hall Jamieson and Joseph N. Cappella, analyzed Limbaugh and the conservative media. Their findings were published in *Echo Chamber: Rush Limbaugh and the Conservative Media Establishment* (2010). In this heavily researched study, the authors show how Limbaugh, Fox News, and the opinion pages of the *Wall Street Journal* form an echo chamber that enhances conservative views and promotes negative judgments of opponents. One of the methods Limbaugh and other conservative talk show hosts use to persuade their listeners and create loyal followers is "moral outrage by engaging emotion," which, the authors say, "produces one advantage and one disadvantage; emotional involvement invites action and engagement rather than distancing and lethargy. On the downside, a steady diet of moral outrage feeds the assumption that the opponent is the enemy" (Jamieson and Cappella 2010, 245). The authors point out that as conservatives listen to talk shows like Limbaugh's, people of the opposite view are drawn to shows considered liberal, which could result in a "liberal media echo chamber." It is unclear at this time where such partisanship will lead, the authors conclude (Jamieson and Cappella 2010, 248).

See also Ali, Muhammad; Franken, Al

References

Chafets, Zev. "Late Period Limbaugh." *New York Times Magazine*, July 6, 2008. http://www.nytimes.com/2008/07/06/magazine/06Limbaugh-t.html?_r=2&pagewanted=1&hp (accessed July 22, 2010).

Chafets, Zev. *Rush Limbaugh: An Army of One*. New York: Centinel HC/Penguin, 2010.

Colford, Paul D. *The Rush Limbaugh Story: Talent on Loan from God: An Unauthorized Biography*. New York: St. Martin's Press, 1993.

Franken, Al. *Rush Limbaugh Is a Big Fat Idiot and Other Observations*. New York: Delacorte, 1996.

Grossberger, Lewis. "The Rush Hours." *New York Times Magazine*, December 16, 1990.

Jamieson, Kathleen Hall, and Joseph N. Cappella. *Echo Chamber: Rush Limbaugh and the Conservative Media Establishment*. New York: Oxford University Press, 2008.

Limbaugh, Rush. *The Way Things Ought to Be*. New York: Simon and Schuster, 1992.

Limbaugh, Rush. *See, I Told You So*. New York: Pocket Books, 1993.

M

Malcolm X (1925–1965)

Malcolm X was one of the most polarizing figures of the 1960s civil rights era. An African American, he underwent multiple emotional, political, and spiritual conversions during his lifetime. This made it difficult for others to easily define who he was, although that did not stop them from trying to do so. For example, Louis Lomax wrote: "Malcolm X is the St. Paul of the Black Muslim movement. Not only was he knocked to the ground by the bright light of truth when he was on an evil journey, but he also rose from the dust stunned, with a new name a burning zeal to travel in the opposite direction and carry America's twenty million Negroes with him" (Lomax 1965, 15).

He was named Malcolm Little when born in Omaha, Nebraska, on May 19, 1925. His father, Earl Little, played a large role in forming young Malcolm's beliefs. Baptist minister Little was a follower of Marcus Garvey, founder of the United Negro Improvement Association and 1920s Black Nationalist leader who advocated a "back-to-Africa" movement. The reverend was an outspoken, fiery preacher. The family's home burned down, and the resulting move in 1929 to the outskirts of Lansing, Michigan, was thought prudent as suspicion for the fire fell on the Black Legion, a white supremacist group.

In 1932, Malcolm's father died under suspicious circumstances, either mangled horribly in a streetcar accident, from suicide, or at the hands of anti-black vigilantes in reaction to his preaching. Five years later, Malcolm's mother Louise was committed to a state mental hospital. Malcolm and his siblings became separated, living largely in foster care. While a good student, his academic pursuits were discouraged by a teacher who told him, that he could not be a lawyer because "that's no realistic goal for a nigger. You need to think about something you *can* be . . . Why don't you plan on carpentry?" (Malcolm X 1964, 38).

In 1941, Malcolm moved to Boston. His first legitimate job was as a shoeshine boy at the Roseland State Ballroom. He also spent time in Flint, Michigan, and Harlem, New York. He supported himself with a succession of menial jobs and increasing involvement in a variety of criminal endeavors—dealing in bootleg liquor, gambling, selling drugs, general hustling, and burglary. He was in Boston in 1946 when he was arrested, convicted, and sentenced to an 8- to 10-year term for armed robbery.

While in prison, Malcolm was introduced to the teachings of the Honorable Elijah Muhammad, leader of the African American sect of the Black Muslims, also known as the Lost-Found Nation of Islam (NOI), headquartered in Chicago, Illinois. Malcolm began daily correspondence with Muhammad and soon underwent a transformation—both spiritual and intellectual in nature. Regarding the latter, he started a meticulous self-education program, copying every dictionary page in order to improve his vocabulary and penmanship. He schooled himself in the teachings of NOI, learning about blacks' role in history

Malcolm X was important in shaping a Black Muslim and black power movement that challenged the nonviolent and integrationist struggle for African American equality favored by Martin Luther King Jr.'s civil rights movement. (Library of Congress)

and how whites had claimed those accomplishments as their own.

Malcolm was enticed by NOI's position that whites were "devils," doomed to destruction by Allah; its advocacy of black separatism (removal from whites in every way—politically, culturally, physically, and psychologically); and its rejection of Martin Luther King Jr.'s principles of change through nonviolence. He had no problem adopting other NOI strictures, such as keeping oneself immaculately clean and impeccably groomed, foreswearing the use of alcohol and tobacco, and following certain dietary restrictions, such as not eating pork along with other traditional Muslim food limitations. Malcolm decided to convert while in prison. Upon his release in 1952, after serving six years of his sentence, he went to Chicago to meet with his mentor, Elijah Muhammad. He took a new name: "Malcolm X"—the "X" representing his unknown black heritage, the uncertain names of his ancestors, and all that had been lost to him due to their enslavement by whites.

Within a year, Malcolm X had made his presence known. In March 1953, the Federal Bureau of Investigation (FBI) was informed that Malcolm X had described himself as a communist, and the agency opened its file on him. But in the 1960s, the FBI was more interested in Malcolm's role as a NOI leader (Carson 1995, 95).

Malcolm rose very quickly in the NOI ranks. He started as an assistant minister of the Detroit mosque. In 1953, he started a new mosque in Boston, followed by yet another in Philadelphia in March 1954. In May of that year, he was sent to lead the Harlem congregation. During his association with NOI, Malcolm X helped NOI to become a major force in black America. He was a natural-born orator with an eloquent and fiery way of speaking. Malcolm railed against white exploitation of blacks. But even further, he called out the civil rights movement and, in particular, denounced what he saw as the ineffectual, moderate integrationist strategies of Martin Luther King Jr. and others. Malcolm's incendiary verbiage frightened much of white America. Even though he typically employed violent language to draw attention and raise others' awareness, Malcolm X did make a conscientious effort not to advocate violence except in self-defense, similar to what was espoused by Black Power leader Stokely Carmichael. These leaders, instead, called for black separatism and black pride. Malcolm's daughter, Attallah Sabazz, in the foreword to the revised edition of *The Autobiography of Malcolm X, as Told to Alex Haley* (1999), wrote:

> Malcolm never advocated violence. He was an advocate of cultural and social reconstruction—until a balance of equality was shared, "by any means necessary." Generally, this phrase of his was misused, even by those of us who were his supporters. But the statement was intended to encourage a paralyzed constituent of American culture to consider the range of options to which they were entitled. . . . "By any means necessary" meant examine the obstacles, determine the vision, find the resolve, and explore the alternatives towards dissolving the obstacles. Anyone truly familiar with my father's ideology, autobiography, and speeches sincerely understands the significance of the now-famous phrase. (Malcolm X 1964, xiii)

Malcolm's effectiveness as a recruiter for NOI was both a blessing and a curse. He singlehandedly was responsible for dramatically increasing the organization's membership roster, acting as spiritual advisers for prominent African American figures of the day, such as boxer Cassius Clay—soon to be known as Muhammad Ali (Ali 2004, 76). He became viewed, over time, as NOI's central spokesperson, and in some ways was indeed a more popular public figure than Elijah Muhammad himself. The media often sought him out knowing that he would give them something interesting to write about or a good sound bite; he was never reluctant to offer an opinion.

Those who were jealous of Malcolm's position in NOI played upon his increasing celebrity to foster divisiveness between him and Muhammad. There was also growing friction between the two men when Malcolm X learned of rumors that his mentor had broken NOI's strict moral code against adultery and possibly fathered children out of wedlock—sins he had excommunicated others for committing.

On December 1, 1963, following the assassination of President John F. Kennedy, Malcolm X made the comment that, "Being an old farm boy myself, chickens coming home to roost never did make me sad; they've always made me glad." In a later interview with Louis Lomax, he elaborated, "I meant that the death of Kennedy was the result of a long line of violent acts, the culmination of hate and suspicion and doubt in this country. You see, Lomax, this country has allowed white people to kill and brutalize those they don't like. The assassination of Kennedy is a result of that way of life and thinking. The chickens came home to roost; that's all there is to it. America—at the death of the President—just reaped what it had been sowing." The *New York Times* ran his "chickens remark" the next day: "Malcolm X Scores U.S. and Kennedy; Likens Slaying to 'Chickens Coming Home to Roost.'" Elijah Muhammad immediately suspended Malcolm X and ordered him not to speak on behalf of the organization publicly for 90 days (*New York Times* 1963, 21).

About the time that his suspension was lifted, on March 8, 1964, Malcolm X announced he was leaving NOI. He formed a new group in New York, the Moslem Mosque, Inc. (MMI) that would be a broad-based black nationalist organization for the purpose of advancing the spiritual, economic, and political interests of African Americans. In the immediate months to follow, Malcolm X traveled abroad, journeying to Europe, various Middle Eastern countries, and Africa. He made a pilgrimage to Mecca in April 1964. These travels caused a dramatic shift in his thinking and belief system. He met Muslims who were, to his surprise, Caucasian, and they embraced him as a brother. Praise was heaped upon him as a great warrior in the fight for the rights of American blacks. He began to believe in the possibility of a world in which men of all skin colors could unite, and he now began to embrace the orthodox interpretation of Islam. He saw past his prior belief in separatism and decided that he could now work with other groups, including whites, as long as their efforts to secure basic civil rights and freedoms for African Americans were sincere. Malcolm X commemorated his holy pilgrimage by taking the name El-Hajj Malik El-Shabazz. A "hajj" is a pilgrimage to Mecca, Saudi Arabia, the hallowed birthplace of the Prophet Muhammad; "Malik" is similar to Malcolm; "Shabazz" is a family name.

El-Shabazz returned to the United States with a new approach, believing that blacks should straightforwardly demand their rights, not beg for them. He recanted some of his more strident statements, softening his stance that all whites were evil devils. He declared that he was willing to work with black and white organizations on issues such as voter registration, on building black control of community public institutions such as schools and police, and on civil and political rights for black people. In June 1964, he started a second, secular organization, the Organization of Afro-American Unity (OAAU). El-Shabazz argued that the struggle for civil rights should be changed to one for human rights. He felt that as long as it remained the former, it would remain a domestic concern; by positioning it as a human rights issue, it would become an issue of international dimension; thus, it could be brought as a complaint before the United Nations. There, the emerging nations of the world could add their support to the cause of African Americans. El-Shabazz stressed that there was a connection between African Americans' civil rights struggles and Third World countries' liberation struggles. To him, African Americans needed to change their thinking: they were not a minority; in the global context, blacks were the majority.

Malcolm X's split with the NOI had not been amicable. He continued to speak out against the group's direction, and they did not like what he was now espousing. Their newsletter, *Muhammad Speaks*, ran a cartoon showing El-Shabazz's severed head. In another, Louis X (now known as Louis Farrakhan), wrote, "Such a man as Malcolm is worthy of death, and would have met with death if it had not been for Muhammad's confidence in Allah for victory over the enemies" (Gardell 1996, 82). The Shabazz home was firebombed on February 14, 1965. The family escaped without injury, but the residence was destroyed.

A week later, Malcolm X was assassinated—shot to death—on February 21, 1965. He was giving a speech at a rally in New York. His four daughters and his wife, Betty, pregnant with what would be twin girls, were present. One of three convicted shooters admitted guilt, and all had ties to NOI.

Today, Malcolm, his ideas, and his ideals live on in many forms. His writings and speeches have been issued and reissued. There are movies, plays, poems, posters, and songs created in tribute to his passionate, albeit brief life. Multiple academic institutions bear his name, as do scholarships and awards. Even the country that he advocated against saw fit to pay him homage when it released a U.S. postal stamp bearing his likeness in 1999. He left an imprint upon the United States; the task of defining the man remains as difficult today as it was when he was alive.

Margaret Gay

See also Ali, Muhammad; Carmichael, Stokely/Ture, Kwame; Farrakhan, Louis; King, Martin Luther, Jr.

References

Ali, Muhammad, and Hana Yasmeen Ali. *The Soul of a Butterfly: Reflections on Life's Journey.* New York: Simon and Schuster, 2004.

Carson, Clayborne. *Malcolm X: The FBI Files.* New York: Ballantine Books, 1995.

Gardell, Mattias. *The Name of Elijah Mohammad: Louis Farrakhan and the Nation of Islam.* Durham, NC: Duke University Press, 1996.

Lomax, Louis E. *When the Word Is Given: A Report on Elijah Muhammad, Malcolm X and the Black Muslim World.* New York: New American Library, 1963.

Malcolm X. *Malcolm X Speaks: Selected Speeches and Statements.* Edited by George Breitman. New York: Grove Press, 1994.

Malcolm X and Alex Haley. *Autobiography of Malcolm X: As Told to Alex Haley.* New York: Ballantine Books, 1964, 1999.

"Malcolm X Scores U.S. and Kennedy." *New York Times*, December 2, 1963.

Mankiller, Wilma (1945–2010)

I experienced my own Trail of Tears when I was a young girl.... the United States government, through the Bureau of Indian Affairs, was again trying to settle the "Indian problem" by removal. I learned through this ordeal about the fear and anguish that occur when you give up your home, your community, and everything you have ever known to move far away to a strange place. I cried for days, not unlike the children who had stumbled down the Trail of Tears so many years before. I wept tears—tears from my history, from my tribe's past. They were Cherokee tears. (Mankiller and Wallis 1999, 62)

This statement by Wilma Mankiller reflects the long struggle of not only Cherokee, but of many Native American tribes who have become dissidents and engaged in political activism to obtain their civil and land rights. Mankiller also represents the many strong Indian women who have fought to protect their culture.

Wilma Pearl Mankiller was born on November 18, 1945, in Tahlequah, Oklahoma. She was the sixth of 11 children (six boys and five girls) born to Charlie and Irene Mankiller. Her father was Cherokee and her mother of Irish-Dutch descent. Charlie Mankiller was active in Indian affairs and enjoyed engaging in political discussions with Wilma when she was a child. Mankiller's great-grandfather took part in the forced migration of Native Americans from the Southeast to what is now Oklahoma. The Cherokee gave up all they owned and their ancestral lands to live in unknown territory. President Andrew Jackson (1767–1845) ordered the confiscation of Indian lands and the march that became known as the Trail of Tears. It resulted in the deaths of thousands of Native Americans as well as the deaths of some African slaves who were also expelled.

The Mankiller family was very poor, living on land the U.S. government had allotted to their grandfather, John Mankiller, in 1907. It was difficult to eke out a living for such a large family on 160 acres, not all of them tillable. There was no electricity on

Wilma Mankiller, the first woman to become chief of the Cherokee Nation in modern times, poses in front of the tribal emblem at the Cherokee Nation in Oklahoma on July 19, 1985. (AP Photo)

Mankiller Flats, as the area was known, and the farm had no indoor plumbing. Yet, the family was happy. The children worked hard, but also enjoyed many hours of play in a nearby spring, walks in nature, horseback riding, and wonderful evenings spent in the outdoors under the stars. They grew corn and other vegetables and strawberries.

After two years of drought, the family could no longer survive on the farm, and they moved to San Francisco under a 1950s U.S. government program designed to "mainstream" Indians into general urban populations. The government promised the Native Americans better housing and jobs and access to educational opportunities. But as in years past, promises were not kept, and the people were most often moved into inner cities in high crime areas, where there was little opportunity for jobs and the housing was deplorable. Mankiller remembers watching from her upstairs window as rival gangs fought it out on the street below. Hunter's Point, located in southeastern San Francisco, saw clashes between black and Samoan youth. Mankiller notes, "I was taught invaluable lessons on those mean streets. They were part of our continuing education in the world of urban poverty and violence" (Mankiller and Wallis 1999, 109).

Due to the high crime rate, it was also a dangerous place to bring up children. Parents not only struggled financially, but also had to keep their children from drugs and from joining gangs. Law enforcement kept its distance, and people were forced to protect themselves. But the family eventually adapted, and the children attended schools and were educated. Only Mankiller's oldest brother had to drop out of school in order to help support the family.

During Mankiller's early adolescent years, she experienced prejudice and ridicule because of her last name, even though her parents taught her that the name had a very proud history among her people. Historically, Mankiller (*Asgaya-dihi* in Cherokee) was a person of high rank who protected the Cherokee community. She hated school and often ran away from home to be with her maternal grandmother Pearl Sitton. Sitton lived with her son and his family on a farm outside Riverside, California. Patiently, her parents repeatedly brought her back home. After being allowed to spend summers at the country home of a cousin, she gradually became less self-conscious and gained self-esteem.

Living in the ghetto taught Mankiller that the welfare of families depended largely on strong women, who provided for their children despite the odds against them and while living below the poverty level in areas forgotten by mainstream Americans. But there was one place where the Indians could find peace and some semblance of comfort—the Indian Center. There, children could play and learn about their culture, and adults could mix with others who shared their concerns.

Wilma Mankiller graduated from high school and attended San Francisco State University, where she studied sociology and Native American issues. At college, Mankiller met and married Hector Hugo Olaya de Bardi, a businessman from Ecuador. They had two daughters, Felicia and Gina.

In the 1960s, she empathized with people who had been and were oppressed by police, by the court system, and by nearly all whites. She was impressed by such groups as the Black Panthers and Hispanics who were beginning to rebel against poverty and prejudice, and men like César Chávez and his efforts to improve the lives of farm workers.

At the time, San Francisco was at the very hub of the 1960s counterculture. With blacks, farm workers, and college students demanding an end to the Vietnam War, she saw activists all around her. In 1968, she was deeply affected by the My Lai Massacre, which reminded her of the 1890 massacre at Wounded Knee. She admired the idealism of Robert Kennedy and believed that his interest in Native American issues was genuine. She credits his campaign for the presidency with awakening her interest in national politics.

Mankiller's social conscience became focused in 1969 when a group of young American university students, members of 20 tribes, and supporters occupied Alcatraz (a former federal prison) in order to bring attention to the government's systematic mistreatment of Natives and to claim rights to the land where the prison was located. By treaty, federal lands not used or abandoned were to revert to any male 18 years of age or older who filed a claim and whose ancestors had been a party to the treaty. The Alcatraz takeover also called attention to the 1870s, when many Natives had been executed or imprisoned there under horrific conditions and had been subjected to sadistic behavior of the whites in charge. Native men, women, and children from across the United States camped on Alcatraz for 19 months. Sometimes as many as 1,000 people stayed, many camping out in the open air. Mankiller decided that she, too, wanted to work on behalf of her people, and she became an activist for Indian rights. She took more courses at college to prepare. She worked with the Pit River Tribe on treaty-rights issues as they were attempting to reclaim ancestral lands.

The Alcatraz occupation was the springboard for other Indian activism, such as the 1973 Wounded Knee resistance that included protester JoAnn Tall of the Pine Ridge Reservation in South Dakota. Many Native Americans who were at Alcatraz followed with protests and occupations to demand Indian rights.

Mankiller's newfound activism and sense of independence led to the end of her marriage. Hugo Olaya was a businessman, and he expected Mankiller to concentrate on homemaking, the family, and his social agenda. When she refused to conform and continued her activism, he reluctantly agreed to divorce.

Soon afterward, she returned to Oklahoma with her daughters. Her father, who had died of kidney disease, had been buried there, and her mother had returned to be near other Cherokees. At first, they lived a very rugged existence. Living mostly outdoors, cooking food on a Coleman stove, and washing in a nearby spring-fed stream, she felt a strong spiritual awakening. Friends in the community loaned them an old house that had stood empty and was without indoor plumbing. But the three were happy. Before too long, all of Mankiller's siblings had also moved back to Oklahoma.

During the 1970s, she developed severe kidney problems and survived due to the gift of a kidney from her brother Don. Mankiller also survived a horrific automobile accident in which the driver of the other car, one of her dearest friends, died. Many operations were needed to repair and save Mankiller's legs and to repair damage to her face. She later developed a chronic neuromuscular disease called myasthenia gravis. Nevertheless, she was determined to continue to work for her people. She not only became a community organizer, but also wrote grants to fund various Indian projects, encouraging people to revitalize their own communities and to not simply rely on help from the U.S. government. In one small rural community, people constructed a 16-mile water line, repaired their own homes, and built a few new ones using tribal materials. Mankiller and her staff worked as facilitators and funding brokers for the Bell Community Revitalization Project, which soon gained national attention. She became recognized as an expert in community development not only by the Cherokee, but also by other tribes. She became tribal planner and program development specialist for the Cherokee Nation. The emphasis was always on Cherokees helping themselves. All aspects of Indian life were important to her, from preschool projects to adult education.

In 1983, Ross Swimmer, principal chief of the Cherokee Nation of Oklahoma, asked Mankiller to be his deputy chief in the upcoming election. She accepted and they won the election, even though people objected to a woman as a leader. This was especially shocking since, prior to the coming of the white man to the continent, Cherokee women had been on an equal footing with men and took an equal part in governing.

As deputy chief, she worked to end domestic violence toward Native women, and to establish health clinics, job training centers and new schools. But staff members did not want her to succeed and attempted to derail her projects. Meeting with so much opposition, she sought out a Cherokee medicine man to help her through this period. "He arranged a beautiful ceremony at dawn, which helped cleanse my mind, put the actions of my opponents in perspective and enabled me to continue to work with them in a good way," she wrote (Mankiller 2004, 17).

In 1985, Ross Swimmer was appointed head of the Bureau of Indian Affairs in Washington, D.C. According to tribal law, the deputy chief then becomes principal chief, making Wilma Mankiller the first Native American in modern times to obtain the title of chief of the Cherokee Nation. The Cherokee Nation is the second-largest tribe in the United States with between 120,000 and 140,000 members and a multimillion-dollar budget. About 7,000 square miles make up the tribal lands.

In 1986, Mankiller married longtime friend Charlie Soap, who was a former director of tribal development and who shares her passion for bettering the lives of the Cherokee peoples. They live on Mankiller land in Oklahoma.

As chief, Mankiller gained much respect throughout the Native American culture and she was reelected principal chief of the Cherokee Nation in her own right in 1991. She continued to work for the betterment of her people.

In 1995, Mankiller declined to seek another term as principal chief of the Cherokee Nation due to many health problems. But she continued to make public appearances, deliver lectures, and write numerous books and articles. Among the many honors she has received are the Presidential Medal of Freedom and honorary degrees from more than a dozen colleges and universities. She has been on the cover of *Parade*, and was named Woman of the Year in 1980 by *Ms.* magazine.

In early March 2010, her husband confirmed and announced through the Cherokee Nation that Mankiller was gravely ill with stage IV pancreatic cancer. Mankiller issued a statement saying that she could not deliver her message personally, but assured friends and family: "I am mentally and spiritually prepared for this journey; a journey that all human beings will take at one time or another. I learned a long time ago that I can't control the challenges the Creator sends my way but I can control the way I think about them and deal with them. On balance, I have been blessed with an extraordinarily rich and wonderful life, filled with incredible experiences" (Muchmore 2010). Mankiller died at her home near Tahlequah, Oklahoma, on April 6, 2010.

Anni Margrethe Callaghan

See also Chávez, César; Tall, JoAnn

References

Johnson, Troy. "The American Indian Occupation of Alcatraz Island 1969–1971." September 29, 1975. http://www.csulb.edu/~gcampus/libarts/am-indian/alcatraz/ (accessed May 12, 2010).

Mankiller, Wilma, and Michael Wallis. *Mankiller: A Chief and Her People*. New York: St. Martin's Griffin, 1999.

Mankiller, Wilma P. *Every Day Is a Good Day: Reflections by Contemporary Indigenous Women*. Golden, CO: Fulcrum Publishing, 2004.

Muchmore, Shannon. "Former Cherokee Chief Wilma Mankiller Gravely Ill, Husband Says." *Tulsa World*, March 2, 2010. http://www.tulsaworld.com/news/article.aspx?subjectid=11&articleid=20100302_11_0_WilmaM514814 (accessed March 31, 2010).

"People Expect Me to Be More Warlike" (interview). *U.S. News and World Report*, February 17, 1986.

Smith, Barbara, Gloria Steinem, Gwendolyn Mink, Marysa Navarro, and Wilma Mankiller, eds. *A Reader's Companion to the History of Women in the U.S.* Boston: Mariner Books, 1999.

Wood, Shelby Oppel. "Luminary of Native Life Shines at Univ. of Oregon." *Indian Life*, November–December 2005.

Manning, Bradley (1987–)

Private First Class Bradley Manning is a U.S. Army intelligence analyst responsible for the largest and most controversial leak of classified military data since Daniel Ellsberg's release of the Pentagon Papers in 1971. In a high-profile breach of intelligence security, Manning obtained and released thousands of classified diplomacy cables and Afghanistan and Iraq War reports, as well as two incendiary videos, to Julian Assange, who published it on his whistle-blowing web site WikiLeaks. The U.S. government's subsequent arrest and detention of Manning reignited an international storm over the government's policies regarding transparency, national security, and the use and definition of torture—issues that had become increasingly controversial since the George W. Bush administration.

Bradley E. Manning was born on December 17, 1987, in the small Midwest town of Crescent, Oklahoma, the second child of American father Brian Manning and Welsh mother Susan Manning. Brian had met Susan during his five-year tenure with the U.S. Navy in the late 1970s, where he worked with the navy's technology systems and as an intelligence analyst. The couple married and moved to Crescent together in 1979, where they raised their daughter Casey and son Bradley in a country farmhouse. Brian Manning worked as an information technology manager for the rental car company Hertz during Bradley's childhood.

Interviews with Bradley's father, neighbors, and teachers from his childhood community indicate that Manning was a precocious youth who was unusually opinionated for his age. He surprised teachers by refusing to recite the "one nation under God" phrase of the Pledge of Allegiance or to do homework assignments involving the Bible, and would sometimes act out if challenged on his views, even occasionally slamming books on his desk. This appeared to be more of an anti-religious attitude, as his parents report that he was unusually patriotic in his youth and proud of the freedoms that the United States offered. At an early age, Manning also showed an aptitude for computers and science. During middle school, he excelled in science fairs and the quiz bowl team. However, his academic performance began to suffer after his father moved out, and around this time, close friends also report he began to divulge to them his homosexual identity.

In 2001, the Mannings divorced, and Susan moved back to Haverfordwest, Wales, with Bradley, where he attended high school and reportedly was teased for being both effeminate and interested in computers. Manning returned to the United States to live with his father after graduating and began to work for a software company. However, he lost his job at the company and moved out in March 2006 due to conflict with both his father and stepmother; Bradley claims he was kicked out for being a homosexual, but others attribute it to a disrespectful attitude.

Manning then moved around quite a bit, from Tulsa to Chicago to Maryland, working several low-wage jobs along the way and attending community college. In the summer of 2007, he joined the U.S. Army. His basic training occurred at Fort Leonard Wood, Missouri. Afterwards, he was sent to Fort Huachuca, Arizona, where the army used his computer programming abilities, giving him a security clearance and training him as an intelligence analyst. During the training, he was mildly reprimanded after fellow soldiers reported that he revealed somewhat sensitive army material on YouTube videos; however, the incident was minor enough that he retained his security clearance. Manning was subsequently sent to Fort Drum, New York, to work in the Second Brigade 10th Mountain Division.

While stationed in New York, Manning met and formed a relationship with Brandeis University student Tyler Watkins in 2008. Through Watkins, Manning was introduced to several individuals in the Cambridge-area hacker community, including Massachusetts Institute of Technology researcher and computer scientist David House, who would later become an outspoken defender of Manning. The Cambridge hacking network was well-known for harboring a philosophy in favor of freedom of information. According to the *New York Times*, friends of Manning say he felt very comfortable and accepted in this community, which espoused liberal views that he could relate to, as opposed to the more conservative atmosphere of the army (Star 2011). By this time, his frustration with the army's policies, coupled with feeling underappreciated professionally by his superiors, had already been unleashed in two incidents that resulted in formal reprimands; one of the incidents involved Manning assaulting another officer.

During this time, Manning was also greatly affected by the political atmosphere of the country, as the 2008 presidential election was under way, and, in California, Proposition 8—the controversial proposal to ban same-sex marriage in the state—passed on the November ballot. Days after the measure's passage, Manning joined other Proposition 8 protesters at a rally in front of city hall in Syracuse, New York. At the rally, he was interviewed by a local high school journalist, who quoted him on Syracuse.com as saying "I was kicked out of my home, and I once lost my job [because I am gay]. The world is not moving fast enough for us at home, work, or the battlefield." He went on to describe the difficulty he had with being a homosexual in the military under the "Don't Ask, Don't Tell" policy and was outspoken for its repeal.

Despite army commanders being warned not to deploy Manning to Iraq due to the disciplinary action taken against him, the military was short on intelligence analysts, and Manning was sent in October 2009 to the Forward Operating Base Hammer, 40 miles east of Baghdad. In Iraq, he received a specialist rank with top secret/SCI clearance, giving him access to classified army networks.

In May 2010, Manning began chatting online with former computer hacker Adrian Lamo. He had initiated contact with Lamo after reading an article about the hacker in *Wired* magazine. In the chats, Manning confessed to Lamo that he had circumvented the army's security network to illegally download hundreds of thousands of classified, sensitive documents—about a quarter million State Department cables and a half million classified field reports from the wars in Iraq and Afghanistan—which he had burned to discs disguised as music by the recording artist Lady Gaga. Throughout his time in Iraq, Manning had become increasingly disillusioned with the military agenda of the United States, and the classified information he accessed only served to increase that skepticism. Manning told Lamo that the cables contained "incredible things, awful things . . . that belonged in the public domain and not on some server stored in a dark room in Washington DC." He reiterated in another chat, "I want people to see the truth. . . . regardless of who they are. . . . because without information, you cannot make informed decisions as a public" (Poulsen and Zetter 2010).

The chat logs specify that Manning had first contacted WikiLeaks founder Julian Assange in late November 2009, after the site had disclosed hundreds of thousands of pager messages from September 11, 2001. He also admitted to Lamo that he had leaked

260,000 cables to WikiLeaks, as well as two videos. One video, published on WikiLeaks in April 2010 and entitled "Collateral Murder," became notorious for its contents: footage of a 2007 incident in which two U.S. Apache helicopters fired at several individuals in a Baghdad suburb, which resulted in the deaths of three innocent civilians, two of them Reuters journalists, and the serious injury of two children. Critics of the incident reproached the U.S. soldiers for gunning at people who they contend clearly looked like civilians; the U.S. military, however, has defended the actions of the soldiers, saying their assessments followed military procedure for war zones.

Shortly after Manning confided in Lamo, the former hacker contacted the FBI and U.S. Army investigators with the information. The army then arrested Manning on May 26, 2010, detained him in Kuwait for two months, and then transported him to the U.S. Marine Corps Brig in Quantico, Virginia. On July 5, 2010, the army charged Manning under the Uniform Code of Military Justice. They filed 22 additional charges against the private on March 2, 2011, including aiding the enemy, violating the Espionage Act by transferring defense information, and violating army computer security law, among others. The government also argued that Manning's actions endangered other U.S. soldiers and Afghan allies by revealing their names when the cables went public. Although a count of aiding the enemy can amount to a capital offense, the U.S. government said it would not seek the death penalty. If convicted, however, Manning could face life in prison.

Many who support a more transparent government applauded Manning for his actions. Daniel Ellsberg, the former Department of Defense official who leaked the Vietnam War research reports known as the Pentagon Papers, has publicly defended Manning, stating in an April 2011 teleconference with the Bradley Manning Advocacy Fund that "Bradley Manning is acting in the interest of the United States." Ellsberg serves on the advisory board of the Bradley Manning Support Network, which was founded in 2010 by Manning's computer scientist friend House and antiwar activist Mike Gogulski. Notable dissidents who also serve on the organization's advisory board include filmmaker Michael Moore, who also contributed funds to the cause; former CIA intelligence official Ray McGovern; and former colonel Ann Wright, who quit her service in protest of the Iraq War.

Others have focused their protest specifically on the conditions of Manning's detention. Held under maximum security and prevention-of-injury watch at Quantico, Manning has been subjected to solitary confinement, only one hour of exercise a day, and routine nude inspections. In early April 2011, in a move that became controversial on an international scale, the Barack Obama administration blocked the United Nations Special Rapporteur on Torture, Juan Mendez, from a private visit with the imprisoned Manning. U.S. representative Dennis Kucinich of Ohio was also repeatedly denied visits with Manning. Hundreds of prominent constitutional and legal scholars, in addition to human rights organizations and anti–government secrecy protesters, denounced Manning's imprisonment conditions as amounting to torture or "enhanced interrogation techniques," especially in the context of being detained in such a manner without a formal conviction. These scholars, including Laurence Tribe, a law professor who taught Obama while he attended Harvard Law School, wrote and signed a formal letter published April 28, 2011, in the *New York Review of Books* in which they stated:

> Private Manning has been designated as an appropriate subject for both Maximum Security and Prevention of Injury (POI) detention. But he asserts that his administrative reports consistently describe him as a well-behaved prisoner who does not fit the requirements for Maximum Security detention. The Brig psychiatrist began recommending his removal from Prevention of Injury months ago. These claims have not been publicly contested. In an Orwellian twist, the spokesman for the brig commander refused to explain the forced nudity "because to discuss the details would be a violation of Manning's privacy.
>
> The [Obama] Administration has provided no evidence that Manning's treatment reflects a concern for his own safety or that of other inmates. Unless and until it does so, there is only one reasonable inference: this pattern of degrading treatment aims either to deter future whistle-blowers, or to force Manning to implicate Wikileaks founder Julian Assange in a conspiracy, or both. (Ackerman 2011)

Criticisms of President Obama's lack of action in the case reflect a disappointment among some constituents that the president may not be adhering to his campaign promises of increased government transparency and fairness, elements of the Bush administration that Obama had so highly critiqued. At a press conference, Obama addressed the complaints against Manning's detention: "I have actually asked the Pentagon whether or not the procedures that have been taken in terms of his confinement are appropriate and are meeting our basic standards. They assured me that they are." As of late 2011, Manning's confinement persists as he awaits determination on whether there is enough evidence in his case to proceed to a trial by court-martial. Manning's fate has major implications for future U.S. policy on matters of national security, prisoner detention, and the protections and punishments of whistle-blowers.

ABC-CLIO

See also Ellsberg, Daniel; Moore, Michael; Wright, Ann

References

Ackerman, Bruce, and Yochai Benkler. "Private Manning's Humiliation." *New York Review of Books*, April 28, 2011. http://www.nybooks.com/articles/archives/2011/apr/28/private-mannings-humiliation/ (accessed August 28, 2011).

"Bradley Manning." *Wired*, July 28, 2011. http://www.wired.com/threatlevel/tag/bradley-manning/ (accessed August 28, 2011).

"Collateral Murder." WikiLeaks. 2011. http://wikileaks.ch (accessed August 28, 2011).

Leigh, David, and Luke Harding. *WikiLeaks: Inside Julian Assange's War on Secrecy.* New York: Public Affairs, 2011.

Nicks, Denver. "Private Manning and the Making of Wikileaks." *This Land*, September 23, 2010. http://thislandpress.com/09/23/2010/private-manning-and-the-making-of-wikileaks-2/ (accessed August 28, 2011).

Poulsen, Kevin, and Kim Zetter. " 'I Can't Believe What I'm Confessing to You': The Wikileaks Chats." *Wired*, June 10, 2010. http://www.wired.com/threatlevel/2010/06/wikileaks-chat/ (accessed August 28, 2011).

Star, Alexander, ed. *Open Secrets: WikiLeaks, War and American Diplomacy.* New York: The New York Times, 2011.

McCarthy, Joseph (1908–1957)

"While I cannot take the time to name all of the men in the State Department who have been named as members of the Communist Party and members of a spy ring. I have here in my hand a list of 205 that were known to the Secretary of State as being members of the Communist Party and who, nevertheless, are still working and shaping the policy of the State Department" (Johnson 2005, 14). U.S. senator Joseph McCarthy made that charge while speaking at a meeting of the Republican Women's Club in Wheeling, West Virginia. It was just one of his many dissident pronouncements against the U.S. government, celebrities, and others during the 1950s. However, McCarthy failed to substantiate any of his allegations. "Indeed, almost 90 days after the Wheeling speech, not one of Joe's allegations of treason in the State Department could be judged by reasonable men as documented or even persuasive, and the fraudulence of most of them was already obvious," wrote biographer Thomas Reeves (1982, 283).

Joseph Raymond McCarthy was born on November 14, 1908, on a farm in Grand Chute Township, Wisconsin, near Appleton. He was the fifth of seven children born to Bridget Tierney and Timothy McCarthy. His mother was born in Ireland; his father was born in the United States to an Irish father and German mother. Bridget and Tim were married in 1901 and settled into a log cabin on their 142-acre farm. The first four of their children were born in the log cabin. Joseph Raymond was born in the new house that replaced the cabin. To neighbors, the devout Roman Catholic family appeared to be happy, and they fit in well in the community.

Joseph attended a one-room schoolhouse, where he did well and earned the respect of his teachers. He was an extrovert who liked joking around and performing stunts. Handsome and powerfully built, Joseph could intimidate neighborhood boys who shied away from his home after his father taught him how to box.

Because of poor economic times, Joseph left school at the age of 14 to help the family on the farm. He began to raise chickens, selling the eggs to local stores and later selling broilers to the Chicago poultry market. After becoming ill with influenza, he lost everything. Seeing little chance to prosper on a farm, he left for town where he worked as a grocery store clerk. He did well and was promoted to manager of a store in a neighboring town. He amazed the customers by his ability to remember their names. Although handsome with a certain Irish charm, he was sometimes awkward, especially around more affluent or sophisticated teens. He was shy with girls his own age, but flattered older women with compliments.

Working at the store, he realized that he needed an education; so at the age of 20, he decided to go back to school, but he had to convince the principal, Leo Hershberger, to let him attend. Hershberger was impressed with McCarthy and allowed him to enroll in Little Wolf High School in Manawa, Wisconsin. He studied independently and completed four years' worth of schooling in about nine months, graduating in 1930. He then attended the Jesuit Marquette University in Milwaukee, where he studied engineering for two years, but switched to law after his friends talked about the possibilities that lay ahead with a law degree.

McCarthy's classmates recall that he did not study much and seldom went to the library. He bluffed his way through courses and made jokes when he did not know answers to questions in class. Nights before exams, he attended study sessions and sat and listened while the other students discussed exams from previous years. His grades were not good, but they were sufficient enough for him to graduate.

Wisconsin senator Joseph McCarthy speaks in front of a television camera in 1953. McCarthy falsely accused numerous U.S. government officials of being members of the Communist Party or being communist sympathizers. (Library of Congress)

McCarthy was well liked by other students and was known to be jovial and happy-go-lucky. He had no respect for money, and even though he had to work hard to pay for college, he threw money around, gave it away, or gambled it away. He borrowed from friends and family and showed no concern about paying anyone back. Because women seemed to like him and he always had a beautiful woman on his arm, he became known as a womanizer. Despite his lack of money, he made sure he had a car to drive on campus.

Despite having graduated from law school, McCarthy was ill prepared to be a lawyer. He knew little about the law as he did not study, did no research, and cared little about knowing the facts. He just touched the surface of a topic and never looked deeply into anything. But he was an expert at bluffing his way through a course. Therefore, it is not surprising that McCarthy did not do well as an attorney and that he supplemented his earnings by gambling. His first law office was in Waupaca, Wisconsin, a small community with several well-established attorneys. He proceeded to ingratiate himself into the community, joining clubs and working on some social causes. He accepted a paid job with another attorney, Mike G. Eberlein, in Shawano in 1936. He did not do well there, but Eberlein had become his friend.

Failure as an attorney did not phase McCarthy, as his ultimate goal was political office. In 1936, at the age of 28, he ran for district attorney of Shawano County as a Democrat. He lost the election, but when he ran for circuit judge in 1939 as a Republican, he won. He knew at the time that his friend Eberlein had hoped to run for judge, but that did not deter McCarthy. To win, he employed vicious tactics and succeeded in destroying the credibility of Edgar V. Werner, a long-term judge, by implying that the judge's age was an issue. McCarthy's win was a shock to many. He was the youngest person ever to be elected circuit judge in Wisconsin.

After he was sworn in as a judge, McCarthy began tackling the backlog of cases he had inherited. True to his workaholic nature, he kept his office open hours longer than his predecessors. His courtroom was unorthodox, and he was accused of "making sly remarks in the presence of a jury to influence the outcome of a case" (Reeves 1982, 35). But others admired him and considered him a good judge. He was known for dispatching his cases quickly, but few of his cases were overturned.

In 1941, McCarthy began talking about running for the U.S. Senate as a Democrat, even though he lacked qualifications and money, was an unknown, and a state statute barred judges from running. Friends advised him that a stint in the military, especially in the Marines, would be to his political advantage and add to his electability. So, based on his college degree, he applied for a commission, and became a second lieutenant in the Marine Corps. He went on to claim that he had enlisted as a private and earned his promotions to lieutenant. He was extremely popular with his fellow Marines, who enjoyed his sense of humor and his boisterous ways. While in training, he injured his leg, and when the cast was removed he received a small burn, which left a scar. He would later apply for a medal, claiming a war wound and combat heroism. He forged his commanding officer's name on a letter recommending a citation.

When stationed in the Solomon Islands, McCarthy met Jack Kennedy, and they became friends. When McCarthy left the military (as a captain), he greatly embellished his service record as a gunner-observer on some combat missions. He later inflated the number of missions in order to receive the Distinguished Flying Cross. He wrote a letter of commendation for himself and signed his commanding officer's name, Admiral Chester W. Nimitz, chief of naval operations. It was known by many in the military hierarchy that the award was based on falsification of records.

While still in the military, McCarthy sought the Republican nomination to run for the Senate in his native Wisconsin. But he did not achieve this goal. After resigning his commission in April 1945, he ran for his former post as circuit judge, winning that election.

Still hoping to win the Senate seat for Wisconsin, McCarthy began a campaign to destroy his opponent, three-term senator Robert M. La Follette Jr. La Follette, of the Progressive Party, was an icon in Wisconsin politics. McCarthy questioned his opponent's patriotism and even suggested La Follette was a war profiteer. Though unfounded, the ploy worked, and along with his sterling and mostly made-up military record, McCarthy defeated La Follette in the primary election. He then went on to win the Senate seat by defeating his Democratic rival.

He arrived in Washington, D.C., in December 1946 and was a welcome guest at cocktail parties, where he was known to be witty and well liked. As a senator, he was considered unremarkable. He was not well liked by his fellow senators due to his volatile temper and inflexibility. He was despised by some as he falsified their records publicly and made wild accusations against them. Soon he found himself isolated in the capital. He was further ostracized by being voted the worst U.S. senator by the Senate press corps.

McCarthy was up for reelection in 1952, but his prospects were slim as his Wisconsin constituents had lost faith in him. His fortunes changed, however, after he began accusing U.S. State Department employees of being known communists or having affiliations with known communists. He claimed these persons posed a serious security risk for the United States. During the 1950s, fear of communism by Americans had reached a fever pitch bordering on paranoia. After McCarthy voiced his unsubstantiated rumors, Frank Desmond of the *Intelligencer* newspaper wrote about them without checking on facts, and a once-obscure senator had an issue he could utilize to become known.

Like the "Radio Priest" Father Charles Coughlin of the 1930s, McCarthy was obsessed with communism. In Senate hearings headed by Senator Millard Tydings, McCarthy claimed that he had a long list of persons who were communists and that he had thoroughly investigated them. When giving testimony, he lied and bluffed his way while his associates attempted to dig up information to prove his allegations. Even as he was accusing government employees of being communists, he had no knowledge of what communism stood for. He knew nothing of communist theory and had no idea of its history or objectives. But the American public knew only what they read in the incomplete stories in newspapers, and many believed that McCarthy had actually uncovered a cell of communists operating in the State Department.

With the complicity of mostly Republican senators, McCarthy and his McCarthyism, as his crusade was called, caused great harm to the U.S. government and divided the country. When the Tydings Committee wrote its report, it concluded that McCarthy "had perpetrated a 'fraud and a hoax ... on the Senate' " (Haynes 2005, 184). But the divisiveness and wrangling did not end there. Republicans called the report a "whitewash of communism," and not a single Republican voted to approve the Tydings report. McCarthy was hailed as a hero by many and sought out for speeches and endorsements. But he was also feared, and many, especially Democrats, would not speak out against him. Those who dared had their reputations smeared, and long productive careers were destroyed. At the 1952 Republican Convention, where Dwight David Eisenhower was nominated for president, McCarthy was treated as a hero.

The paranoia that gripped the government also gripped the nation, as McCarthyism spread to businesses and the movie industry. Friends turned on each other and suspicion reigned. Just being under suspicion of associating with a communist was enough to destroy a life or a life's work.

McCarthy's powers increased, and it was not until he accused Secretary of the Army Robert Stevens of misconduct that senators began to call for curbing his powers. Finally, senators began to speak openly against him and he was falling in the polls. He was removed from his leadership role on the investigation committee. His drinking increased dramatically, and it was evident that he suffered physically and mentally due to alcohol consumption.

In 1953, McCarthy married Jean Kerr, a researcher in his office. The couple adopted a baby girl, Tierney Elizabeth, in 1957, just a few months before McCarthy died.

By the spring of 1954, the army had compiled a list of 29 charges against McCarthy, and the Army-McCarthy hearings with witnesses were held between April 22, 1954, and June 17, 1954. During the hearings, army attorney Joseph Welch became so exasperated with McCarthy's unsubstantiated accusations that he asked a question that has been famous ever since: "Have you no sense of decency, sir, at long last? Have you left no sense of decency?"

Soon a select committee of the Senate began to work on censuring McCarthy. The Senate voted overwhelmingly for censure, and the great power McCarthy had wielded was gone. He did not give up but continued to give speeches in the Senate, most of which were ignored. He was no longer quoted by the press.

In the end, McCarthy seemed totally "demoralized, sometimes almost dazed, often disheveled, wandering aimlessly about Washington" (Wicker 2006, 185). His wife Jean stood by him until the end and would never acknowledge his alcoholism. He died of acute hepatitis, forsaken by most of his former friends and colleagues, on May 2, 1957, at Bethesda Naval Hospital outside Washington, D.C.

Anni Margrethe Callaghan

See also Coughlin, Charles E.

References

Cohn, Roy. *McCarthy*. New American Library, 1968.

Herman, Arthur. *Joseph McCarthy: Reexamining the Life and Legacy of America's Most Hated Senator*. New York: Free Press/Simon and Schuster, 2000.

Johnson, Haynes. *Age of Anxiety: McCarthyism to Terrorism*. Orlando, FL: Harcourt, Inc., 2005.

Reeves, Thomas C. *The Life and Times of Joe McCarthy: A Biography*. Briarcliff Manor, NY: Stein and Day, 1982.

Thomas, Lately. *When Even Angels Wept: The Senator Joseph McCarthy Affair—a Story without a Hero*. New York: William Morrow, 1973.

Wicker, Tom. *Shooting Star: The Brief Arc of Joe McCarthy*. Orlando, FL: Houghton Mifflin Harcourt, 2006.

McCorvey, Norma (1947–)

Most Americans did not know her real name, because Norma McCorvey used a pseudonym when she was lead plaintiff in the class-action lawsuit *Roe v. Wade* (1973), which was filed to challenge the strict antiabortion laws in Texas. The case was named for McCorvey's fictitious name "Jane Roe" and Texas attorney general Henry Wade. When the class-action began in 1970, McCorvey was single and pregnant. She wanted an abortion, but a Texas law made abortions illegal except to save the life of a pregnant woman. Attorney Wade defended that law. In its decision, the Supreme Court struck down state laws that severely restricted abortion. At the time, McCorvey believed that a woman had a right to choose abortion to end a pregnancy. But in 1995, she became an antiabortion activist and since then has been a political dissident, protesting abortion at a variety of public events.

Norma Leah Nelson was born on September 22, 1947, in the small town of Lettesworth, Louisiana, where people spoke both French and English. Her father, Olin Nelson, was a radio and television repair man and a Jehovah's Witness who "gave speeches in the local Kingdom Hall . . . usually talking about the wages of sin and so forth" (McCorvey and Meisler 1994, 14). Her mother, Mary Mildred Gautreaux, was of part Cajun and Cherokee ancestry and a beautiful woman who worked as a waitress in Baton Rouge south of Lettesworth. While her mother worked, Norma and her older brother Jimmy were in the care of a black lady whom Norma loved. She did not have the same feeling for her mother.

While she was growing up, Norma was often the target of her mother's wrath. "She called me stupid, and an idiot, and when she was angry, which was just about every time she saw me, she smacked me so hard my head hurt," Norma wrote (McCorvey and Meisler 1994, 15).

When Norma was nine years old, she and her family moved to Houston, Texas, where her father became a partner with a fellow Jehovah's Witness in a repair shop business. Her parents often fought and her father left for a time, but returned to move the family to Dallas, Texas, where he opened his own repair shop. Norma's mother seldom was home and when she was not working often was at a bar drinking or out with a variety of men. Anger began to build within Norma, and when she was 10 years old, she stole money from a gas station where she worked on occasion and ran away with a school friend to Oklahoma City. Police found her, and after going to family court in Dallas, she became a ward of the state. At age 11, she was sent to the State School for Girls, living there until she was released at the age of 15.

Norma returned to Dallas, where her mother found her a place to rent—a room in a relative's house. She had never met the male relative, whom she described as big and powerful. Every night while she was there, the man raped her. After three weeks, she finally told her mother about the abuse, and as Norma explained, "Completely to my surprise, she didn't blame me for what happened" (McCorvey and Meisler 1994, 41). Norma stayed with her mother and her boyfriend and found a job at a drive-in restaurant, where she met Woody McCorvey. The two dated for a short time, and at Norma's insistence, they married in 1965, when she had just turned 16. The couple moved to California to live with Woody's parents.

The marriage disintegrated soon after Norma learned she was pregnant. Woody angrily denied he could be the father. In her autobiography, she describes being beaten by Woody and left unconscious. With the help of a friend, she returned to Dallas and again stayed with her mother and found a job as a waitress. After her baby was born—a daughter named Melissa—Norma revealed that she had met several women who were lesbians and that she, too, had a sexual preference for women. That revelation incensed her mother who, Norma claims, kidnapped Melissa and adopted her.

Norma's life thereafter was more tumultuous than ever. She worked at a variety of jobs, including as a carnival vendor. She had another child, which she signed over for adoption. And when she became pregnant again in 1969, she sought an abortion, but was unable to terminate her pregnancy because of a highly restrictive Texas law that banned abortions except to save a pregnant woman's life. In 1970, friends suggested that she get in touch with two lawyers, Sarah Weddington and Linda Coffee, who were trying to overturn the Texas law.

McCorvey agreed to be part of a lawsuit filed on March 3, 1970, in the Dallas federal court house, declaring that the Texas law was unconstitutional. The defendant was Texas district attorney Henry B. Wade, who was responsible for enforcing the abortion law. To protect McCorvey's privacy, the lawyers used the alias Jane Roe as plaintiff. The fifth circuit found the law unconstitutional but did not stop enforcement of the law. As a result, Weddington and Coffee took the case, which then was a class-action suit, to the U.S. Supreme Court in December 1971. The case was reargued in 1972. By that time, McCorvey had delivered a child and had placed it for adoption. Nevertheless, the High Court in *Roe v. Wade* disallowed state laws that severely restricted abortion, declaring them unconstitutional because they did not protect a woman's right of privacy.

The Court based its decision in part on an earlier ruling, *Griswold v. Connecticut* (1965). In that case, the justices struck down a Connecticut law that prohibited distribution of contraceptive information to married couples. The Court ruled that marital privacy was a fundamental right guaranteed by the Constitution, and government could not interfere with that privacy.

In addition to establishing a woman's right of privacy, the *Roe* ruling set up a framework regarding abortion. During the first trimester (three months) of pregnancy, a woman has the right to an abortion for any reason. During the second trimester, the state may pass laws that protect the health of the woman. During the third trimester, the state may regulate or prohibit abortion to protect the fetus, except where abortion is necessary to preserve the life or health of the pregnant woman.

At the same time that *Roe* was decided, the Court issued its decision on *Doe v. Bolton* (1973). That ruling defined health as more than physical well-being. The Court determined that health also involved emotional and psychological conditions, family situations, and age as relevant to a pregnant woman's health.

McCorvey reports in her autobiography that she first learned of the Court's decision in *Roe* by reading about it in a newspaper. She was living then with her lesbian lover, in her partner's home. The two had set up their own business, cleaning apartments and later doing construction repair work. During a six-month period, McCorvey's daughter Melissa (Missy), who was 10 years old at the time, lived with the couple. Although McCorvey's mother Mary Mildred had insisted on the arrangement, Mary demanded that the child be returned to her. As McCorvey wrote: "The years rolled on. My mother moved from house to house, city to city, just as often as before. Missy became a voice on the phone" (McCorvey and Meisler 1994, 163).

In 1989, McCorvey revealed to a newspaper reporter that she was "Roe." After she was publicly identified, McCorvey received death threats and attacks on the house where she lived. She also was the subject of a television movie shown on NBC in 1989, and took part in a pro-choice rally in Washington, D.C.

During the early 1990s, she worked for various abortion clinics and confronted numerous antiabortion protesters. Her book *I Am Roe: My Life, Roe v. Wade, and Freedom of Choice* (1994) was published and detailed her chaotic background and efforts to obtain an abortion. Antiabortionists protested at her book signings, carrying signs and blaming her for the deaths of millions of unborn babies because she worked at an abortion clinic.

When the antiabortion or pro-life group Operation Rescue rented a house next to the abortion clinic where McCorvey worked, she began talking to some of the Operation Rescue members, who treated her kindly and talked to her about their beliefs. Her opinions about abortion slowly changed. In 1995, she converted to Christianity, was baptized, and, three years later, became a member of the Roman Catholic Church and an antiabortion activist. She also declared that she could no longer be in a lesbian relationship. Her book *Won by Love* (1997) tells about her work in abortion clinics that ultimately led her to drugs and suicide attempts, and describes her religious conversion.

In 1997, with the help of a friend, McCorvey started her own ministry, which she calls Roe No More Ministry. According to the web site for the ministry, her focus is on two main areas: (1) speaking out publicly on the abortion issue from a Christian/pro-life perspective; and (2) working as a catalyst to assist other pro-life organizations in their particular areas of expertise. As part of her ministry, "she has traveled to three countries and more than forty states to share her story with church congregations, civic organizations, university students, clergy, and rallies. She also has appeared on various major television news shows including NBC, ABC, CBS, Larry King Live, and FOX's Hannity and Colmes, in addition to testifying before various Congressional committees" (Roe No More).

During the 2000s, McCorvey's antiabortion activities have been diverse and well publicized. For example, she petitioned the Supreme Court to overturn the 1973 *Roe* decision, but the Court denied the petition. In 2009, she appeared at the campus of the University of Notre Dame, a Catholic university in South Bend, Indiana. She was with groups who were there to protest President Barack Obama's commencement address to graduates. The protesters demonstrated because Obama's views on abortion differ from those of the Catholic Church. Notre Dame police asked protesters to leave—the university only allows protests by those who are part of the university community. When the group refused to disperse, more than 20 of them were arrested, McCorvey among them. Later, all were released.

In 2009, McCorvey attended the hearing for the nomination of Sonia Sotomayor for the Supreme Court. When Senator Al Franken of Minnesota was giving his opening statement, McCorvey began screaming that Sotomayor was "wrong" about abortion. Police escorted her and three other protesters out of the Senate hearing room.

Some observers contend that McCorvey will continue her protest activities whenever there is an opportunity so that she can be in the spotlight. As she has often stated, her goal is to completely overturn *Roe v. Wade*, and she wants that view publicized. While the pro-life movement shares McCorvey's goals, pro-choice advocates do not. At times, some leaders of both groups have tried to find common ground, but they often raise more question than they find solutions. Some issues that continually arise are: Who should determine what kind of reproductive health care a woman will receive? How will continued advances in medical technology and knowledge about the fetus affect abortion decisions? How can violence associated with abortion debates be reduced? How can people on both sides of the abortion debate respectfully disagree? The answers are elusive.

Karen L. Hamilton

See also Franken, Al

References

Gay, Kathlyn. *Abortion: Understanding the Debate*. Berkeley Heights, NJ: Enslow Publishers, 2004.

McCorvey, Norma, and Gary Thomas. *Won by Love*. Nashville, TN: Thomas Nelson Publishers, 1997.

McCorvey, Norma, with Andy Meisler. *I Am Roe: My Life*, Roe v. Wade, *and Freedom of Choice*. New York: HarperCollins, 1994.

Roe No More Ministry. n.d. http://www.leaderu.com/norma/ (accessed October 27, 2010).

Means, Russell (1939–)

"I hope to be remembered as a fighter and as a patriot who never feared controversy—and not just for Indians. When I fight for my people's rights, when I stand up for our treaties, when I protest government lies and illegal seizures and unlawful acts, I defend all Americans, even the bigoted and misguided" (Means 1995, 535). Those are the words of adamant dissident Russell Means, a Lakota Sioux.

Means was born in Greenwood, South Dakota, on the Yankton Sioux reservation on November 10, 1939. Like the Haudenosaunee Confederacy (Iroquois) in the Northeast, the Sioux were a unity of seven tribes with the same essential language and culture who migrated to the West on the North American continent, where they became a horse-mounted people. When the related Sioux tribes gathered, each of them would assemble their lodges in a tremendous circle. The Yankton, a grammatical corruption by whites of their true name Ihanktonwan, means "People of the End Village," as this tribe was given the honor of guarding the southern side of the entrance to the great Sioux Nation encampment. Before the arrival of the white Europeans, their territory stretched from the woodlands of Wisconsin to the mountains and plains of Montana and central Canada.

According to Vine Deloria Jr. (as quoted by Peter Matthiessen):

> The Sioux, my own people, have a great tradition of conflict. We were the only nation ever to annihilate the United States Cavalry three times in succession. And when we find no one else to quarrel with, we often fight each other. The Sioux problem is excessive leadership. During one twenty-year period in the last century the Sioux fought over an area from LaCrosse, Wisconsin, to Sheridan, Wyoming, against the Crow, Arapaho, Cheyenne, Mandan, Arikara, Hidatsa, Ponca, Iowa, Pawnee, Otoe, Omaha, Winnebago, Chippewa, Cree, Assiniboine, Sac and Fox, Potawatomi, Ute, and Gros Ventre. This was, of course, in addition to fighting the U.S. Cavalry continually throughout that period. (Matthiessen 1991, 39)

The term "Sioux," as with many Indian nations, is a word with derogatory connotations, often given by an enemy, and bears no resemblance to the name used by the Indian nations among themselves. Just as the name "Apache" was the vicious name given by the Pueblo they encountered, the name "Sioux" described the way the Ojibwa (Chippewa) nation described their neighbors to the French—"Nadewisou" or "cutthroats," which the French shortened to the final syllable, Sioux. The Seven Council Fires included the Teton Sioux, four Santee nations, and two Yankton nations.

Russell was raised in the traditional way, with grandparents telling him stories of Sioux history and biography, and describing dances and songs. From his Grandma Twinkle Star, who heard it from her father and mother, he learned that at the Battle of the Little Bighorn, General George Armstrong Custer committed suicide when the attacking warriors of the Sioux, Cheyenne, and Arapaho spared his life while women and children rushed toward him. Russell's father, Walter "Hank" Means, was an Oglala whose great-grandfather broke horses for the U.S. Army. That man's name was "Trains His Horses Well," but when it was translated to "Mean to His Horses," Means became Russell's last name (Means 1995, 17).

Walter Means was taken away from his family at age eight and sent to a boarding school far from home. In efforts to assimilate Native Americans into the dominant culture, the U.S. government set up various boarding schools where Indian children were forbidden to speak their languages, or secretly practice their cultural heritage of songs, stories, dress, and religion. They were harshly punished for breaking the many rules.

When he returned to the Pine Ridge reservation, Walter married Theodora, who was the first Indian secretary to a reservation superintendent, also an Indian. In 1942, the Means family moved to Vallejo, California where Walter—turned down for the draft because of a deaf ear—found work as a welder. The end of the war sent the family back to South Dakota to live with Grandma Twinkle Star (Means 1995, 22).

Over the next years, the family moved many times seeking employment. In 1964, Russell's father Walter invited his son to participate in an action to claim Alcatraz Island, which was no longer a federal prison. An 1868 treaty gave the Lakota the right to claim any federal facility when the government ceased providing it with appropriations. Boatloads of U.S. marshals quickly ended the effort without bloodshed.

Russell's first contact with the American Indian Movement (AIM) came when he attended a meeting of the National Urban Indian Organization (NUIO) in San Francisco in late 1969. Among the final speakers were Dennis Banks and Clyde Bellecourt from Minneapolis, founding members of AIM. They took issue with NUIO, and threatened to destroy it if it did not accede to their demands, one of which was that NUIO move its headquarters to their hometown.

Several weeks later, Dennis Banks invited Russell to accompany him and Clyde to

Russell Means testifies before a special investigative committee of the Senate Select Committee on Capitol Hill, January 31, 1989. Means is one of the most important Native American activists to emerge from the militant 1960s American Indian Movement. During the 1980s, Means fought for environmental protection of Native American lands and, in 1987, supported by a constituency of the Libertarian Party, became the first Native American to run for president of the United States. (AP/Wide World Photos)

Detroit, Michigan, for a confrontation with the National Council of Churches, an organization of more than 30 large Protestant denominations, at their convention. There they took over the microphone during a plenary session with thousands of delegates and made their demands that funds donated to Indian causes be given to Indians, not outsiders. Their demands were accepted, and millions of dollars were so given.

Russell returned to Cleveland, where he had been working for the Council for Economic Opportunity and its community action programs. He resigned from the council and opened the Cleveland branch of AIM, the first chapter outside of Minneapolis. One of Russell's first targets was the Indian caricature of a mascot for the Cleveland Indians baseball team, Chief Wahoo. The caricature is offensive to many Indians, but it still appears on some baseball caps and other team materials.

By 1973, the AIM center operated around the clock, helping Indians with social work, referrals, collecting pension and Social Security benefits, and doing the paperwork for federal help programs like food stamps. There were also cultural programs, including Indian singing. If an Indian was arrested, the Cleveland police contacted AIM.

AIM also participated in the occupation of Mount Rushmore, the sacred Black Hills mountain carved with the faces of American presidents, many of whom were involved in acts that destroyed American Indian nations, stealing their lands. AIM's policy was to defend any and all Indians, singly or as nations, but only if invited to do so (Means 1995, 178). Another well-publicized AIM event was interrupting the traditional Thanksgiving Day celebration at Plymouth Rock. The event ignored the fact that pilgrims and their descendants stole Indian lands and eventually exterminated entire Indian nations in New England.

In November 1972, Russell Means led a car caravan through Indian Country to Washington, D.C., with more than a thousand people in cars and buses (Means 1995, 230). They took over the Bureau of Indian Affairs (BIA) headquarters, only leaving after trashing the entire building. As Means said, "We had confiscated tons of documents, had been paid to leave town—and no one had been arrested. I felt the growing force of our convictions and knew that spiritual power was our greatest strength" (Means 1995, 235).

In January 1973, a young Indian named Wesley Bad Heart Bull was stabbed to death in a South Dakota bar by a white businessman named Darold Schmidt, who reportedly bragged he intended to kill an Indian. When Schmidt was charged with involuntary manslaughter, more than 200 Indians came to the courthouse in Custer, South Dakota, demanding to speak with officials. Means and a handful of other leaders were permitted to enter the building, but when the mother of Bad Heart Bull was beaten by police on the courthouse steps, a riot broke out in which two police cars were destroyed and a nearby Chamber of Commerce building burned down. According to Peter Matthiessen, it was "the first outbreak of violence between white men and Lakota since the massacre of Wounded Knee in 1890" (Matthiessen 1991, 63).

In February 1973, AIM began its most spectacular action: occupying Wounded Knee, a place where Sioux were viciously massacred in the 1890s. The occupation was a protest against a corrupt tribal government led by Richard Wilson. By March 6, a number of AIM supporters slipped in, including black comedian and civil rights activist Dick Gregory. Reverend Ralph Abernathy of the Southern Christian Leadership Conference (SCLC) was escorted through the roadblocks, as was Reverend John Adams of the National Council of Churches. They sought to find some way to resolve the standoff.

AIM and its supporters had a handful of weapons including shotguns, a few pistols, and some hunting rifles. From February to May, when the siege ended, the federal force including marshals and FBI agents fired small arms as well as .50-caliber weapons night and day, with Air Force jets roaring overhead. When the confrontation ended, AIM leaders, including Dennis Banks and Russell Means, were arrested and put on trial by the federal government about a year and a half later. They were defended by the famed civil rights lawyer William Kunstler, and eventually charges were dropped against AIM leaders.

During the 1970s, Means was shot and seriously wounded in two separate incidents. On June 8, 1973, Means was shot in the back, the bullet piercing his kidney, by a Bureau of Indian Affairs officer. According to Matthiessen, Means "when he recovered, was charged with assaulting the officer who shot him" (Matthiessen 1991, 146). He was convicted and sentenced to four years in prison. On July 27, 1978, Means reported to the South Dakota State Penitentiary in Sioux Falls to begin serving his sentence. There, he began a fast lasting more than 35 days in which Means lost almost 70 pounds. The purpose of the fast was to obtain the right to practice his religion in prison. Soon after his fast, while walking through the prison yard with a Sisseton Sioux named Sidney Kitto, a man ran up and hit Kitto in the head with a big pipe wrench while another man stabbed Means in the chest. This man was a member of the Aryan Brotherhood, a white supremacist prison gang. The knife hit a rib, so Means recovered quickly from his wound.

After his release from prison, Means went to the Pine Ridge reservation and resumed his AIM duties, finding the organization in disarray. In 1981, after undergoing several spiritual revitalizations, Means decided to try to reclaim the Black Hills, which under a treaty with the United States had been set aside for the Sioux. Between 1876 and 1890, the Black Hills had been opened to gold mining through the efforts of Lt. Colonel George Armstrong Custer, and an estimated $1 billion worth of gold was removed from the Black Hills. For decades, the U.S. government had set aside a sum of money to buy the Black Hills from the Sioux, but the Indians refused to sell. They chose the anniversary of civil rights icon Dr. Martin Luther King Jr.'s death, April 4, as the day to begin the occupation. For the next eight months, Means spent every night in a tent with a communal kitchen. Though four of the poorest seven counties in the United States could benefit from the estimated $300 million for selling the Black Hills, the Sioux declined the funds and demanded return of the Black Hills to Native Americans.

In 1982, the first Sun Dance, an important Lakota religious ceremony, was held at the Yellow Thunder camp. When forest rangers interfered, claiming the ceremony would create a fire hazard, the officers began building a heavy-gauge wire-mesh fence around the dance site, despite the anger of the ceremony participants. When a ceremonial fire was lighted, its pitch-pine was so hot and full of huge floating sparks that it melted the wire mesh, leaving just the frame and shocking the forest rangers, according to Means (1995, 430).

In January 1984, as the Pine Ridge Indian reservation scheduled its election, Means registered to run for president against Richard Wilson. Means used as his platform the acronym TREATY, meaning "True Revolution for the Elders, Ancestors, Treaties and

Youth." Days before the election, the Executive Committee of the Oglala Sioux Tribe met in closed session and voted to exclude Means from the ballot because of a felony conviction. Eventually, the U.S. Commission on Civil Rights declared the election of Wilson invalid, saying one-third of the ballots were tainted (Matthiessen 1991, 128).

In November 1985, Means was asked to investigate how Nicaragua's Muskito Indians were being treated by the newly victorious Sandinistas under Daniel Ortega. The Sandinistas had promised the indigenous peoples self-determination. However, the Sandinistan government demanded that the Muskitos relocate. The Indians declared war and began a guerilla campaign against their socialist government. While Means was among the Muskitos, they were attacked, and Means suffered a slash from shrapnel across his abdomen. In that attack, three were wounded, and three killed. Means narrowly escaped capture and witnessed numerous attacks on innocent, unarmed civilians, including murder and rape.

In 1992, Means costarred in the film *The Last of the Mohicans*. In the film and in real life, Means is an imposing figure. In a 2008 story for the *Washington Post Magazine*, Bill Donahue writes: "Means is 6-foot-1, with a powerful broad-boned physique ... Arguably the most famous living Indian activist, he performs his role with panache.... Means's life has been something like a Johnny Cash song. He has done prison time for inciting a riot, and has been stabbed, accused of murder, hit by two bullets and divorced four times. Long ago, he was a fancy dance champion and a rodeo star. Even now, at age 68, he remains a forceful presence—a warrior" (Donahue 2008).

Currently, that summary of Russell Means still stands.

Daniel Callaghan

See also Deloria, Vine, Jr.; Gregory, Dick; King, Martin Luther, Jr.; Kunstler, William

References

Deloria, Vine, Jr. *Custer Died for Your Sins*. New York: Macmillan, 1969.

Donahue, Bill. "Ways and Means." *Washington Post Magazine* (cover story), June 29, 2008.

Matthiessen, Peter. *In the Spirit of Crazy Horse*. New York: Viking Penguin, 1991. First published by Viking, 1983.

Means, Russell, with Marvin J. Wolf. *Where White Men Fear to Tread: The Autobiography of Russell Means*. New York: St. Martin's Press, 1995.

Michelman, Kate (1942–)

"[Not] every issue has a male and female component," Kate Michelman said in an interview for *Salon*. "But I do think there are issues [that] women approach with a different perspective, often a very personal perspective. Men approach reproductive rights from a policy perspective, and women think about it from a personal point of view ... So we start with the personal and build out to policy" (Traister 2007). Michelman has always been serious about personal issues, which many times have prompted controversy. As a *Washington Post* reporter noted, she "has been at the forefront of one of this country's thorniest debates"—that is, abortion rights (Weeks 2006).

Born on August 4, 1942, Michelman grew up in Ohio as a practicing Catholic. She was introduced to social activism during the civil rights movement. But it was her marriage to her childhood sweetheart, at age 20, that provided a turning point in her life, driving her toward the zealousness for privacy rights that went "beyond the women's movement" (Weeks 2006).

Kate Michelman, president of the National Abortion and Reproductive Rights Action League (NARAL), now known as NARAL Pro-Choice America, testifies on Capitol Hill before the joint House-Senate Judiciary Committee hearing on partial birth abortions, March 11, 1997. The hearing was to focus on legislation the Republicans were pushing to outlaw a certain kind of late-term abortion. In 2004, Michelman retired as executive director of NARAL Pro-Choice and began working as a political consultant. (AP Photo/Joe Marquette)

When she married, Michelman accepted the Church's teachings prohibiting birth control. As a Catholic homemaker during the late 1960s, she believed that starting a family should take priority over a career. She also practiced the "natural" means of contraception (the rhythm method), and believed that breast-feeding prevented pregnancy. As a result, she had three daughters in three years (Weeks 2006). But in 1969, her husband (whom she does not name in her book) abandoned her and her daughters. Not long after the abandonment, and living on welfare, Michelman discovered she was pregnant with her fourth child and considered an abortion.

In 1970, she could not legally have an abortion unless her health or life was at risk. Michelman decided to have an abortion, recognizing that doing so challenged every religious, moral, ethical, and philosophical belief she held dear (Sober and Reardon 2000). She felt she had no choice. At the time, Pennsylvania, like most states, radically restricted access to the procedure. She had to appear before an all-male hospital review board to obtain permission on the grounds that she was unstable and incapable of raising another child. She had to answer questions that included whether she could dress her children in the morning, and if she satisfied her husband sexually. The board granted permission on one condition: she had to obtain permission from the very man who abandoned her, her ex-husband. This experience sparked a lifetime of activism that took her to the forefront of the pro-choice movement (Michelman 2009).

Michelman's early professional career focused on early childhood development with an emphasis on developmentally disabled children. She built on her work with special-needs children in rural Pennsylvania, developing a multidisciplinary diagnostic treatment program that serves as a model across the nation.

Michelman worked as executive director of Planned Parenthood in Harrisburg, Pennsylvania, where she expanded the range of reproductive health services available in the communities. She also worked as a clinical assistant professor in the Department of Psychiatry at Pennsylvania State University School of Medicine, where she trained medical students and residents in child development.

In 1985, Michelman became the national executive director for NARAL Pro-Choice America. Originally called the National Association for the Repeal of Abortion Laws, NARAL was established in February 1969. The organization worked with other groups to repeal state abortion laws and to oversee implementation of abortion policies. After the U.S. Supreme Court struck down restrictive abortion laws in *Roe v. Wade* (1973), the organization changed its name to the National Abortion and Reproductive Rights Action League. *Roe v. Wade* was named for a pregnant single woman named Norma McCorvey, who used the fictitious name Jane Roe, and Texas attorney general Henry Wade. Wade defended a Texas law that made abortions illegal except to save the life of the pregnant woman. (In 1995, McCorvey announced that she had converted to Catholicism and had begun an antiabortion ministry called Roe No More.)

In the *Roe* decision, the U.S. Supreme Court ruled that a woman's decision to have an abortion is protected by the constitutional right to privacy. Michelman later described the decision as "the promise that emerged from darkness to light. From despair to hope" (Michelman 1998).

In 2003, the organization simplified its title to NARAL Pro-Choice America to signal its focus on mobilizing pro-choice activists. As its executive director, Michelman ushered the organization into prominence to position a woman's freedom to choose as a fundamental American liberty. The organization sponsors public sex education as well as tracks state and national legislation affecting laws regarding women's health issues.

Michelman assumed her role as executive director just as Ronald Reagan was reelected as president with the support of the religious right. Reagan nominated Robert Bork for the Supreme Court, which created a crisis in the pro-choice movement. Bork questioned the reasoning underlying the Court's decision in *Roe*. His nomination threatened a reversal of the Court's decision. As one of her first tasks as president, Michelman lobbied against the confirmation of Bork. In 1987, NARAL and other pro-choice organizations were instrumental in defeating the nomination of Bork to the U.S. Supreme Court.

In 1989, NARAL Pro-Choice America cosponsored a demonstration in Washington D.C. in response to the Supreme Court's announcement to hear the case of *Webster v. Reproductive Health Services*. The case threatened the protections covered in *Roe*.

Over 500,000 pro-choice advocates marched on the Capitol. Michelman developed the now-famous catch-phrase "Who Decides?" featured in NARAL's campaign to counter the opposition's message, "Life!"

In 1991, Michelman testified before the U.S. Senate during the confirmation hearings for Clarence Thomas. For the first time, she publicly told her story. Michelman spoke before a television audience of millions, underscoring the humiliation and betrayal of her own abortion experience. In opposing Thomas, she said: "The record shows that, if confirmed, Judge Thomas would vote to take away this fundamental right—to take this nation back to the days when women had no alternative but the back alleys for health care. What happens in the halls of Congress must reflect what is in the hearts of the American people. This may be one of the last opportunities you have to stand up for a woman's fundamental right to choose before Roe versus Wade is ultimately overturned. I urge you to refuse to confirm Judge Thomas" (Michelman 1991).

In 1993, Michelman became a close adviser to then president-elect Bill Clinton. Under her leadership, she mobilized thousands of pro-choice Americans to help elect Clinton to office. Clinton is considered the first fully pro-choice president. Michelman and NARAL Pro-Choice, and other women's groups, began intense lobbying for the Family and Medical Leave Act, which President Clinton signed into law on February 5, 1993.

Michelman continued to work with the Clinton administration to reverse policies passed by the Reagan and George H. W. Bush administrations. Her organization helped to remove bans on the testing of RU-486 (also known as mifepristone, a non-surgical abortion method) and on the use of fetal tissue in scientific research. In addition, the organization helped to establish provisions for abortion services at military hospitals. NARAL Pro-Choice also played a significant role in passing the Freedom of Access to Clinic Entrances Act (1964). This act placed certain restrictions on protesters' ability to obstruct or hinder persons seeking access to abortion services (NARAL Pro-Choice America).

In 1996, Michelman gave the first speech for an abortion plank at the Chicago Democratic National Convention. That same year, Congress enacted a bill banning the practice of partial-birth abortions. By definition, a partial-birth abortion is a late-term abortion in which a viable fetus is partially delivered through the cervix before being extracted. Although President Clinton vetoed the bill, many states have since passed laws banning the procedure. Congress continues to debate the issue. NARAL Pro-Choice continues to be at the forefront of the debate. In 1997, Michelman testified before a joint House-Senate Committee on the dangers of legislation outlawing abortion procedures (NARAL Pro-Choice America).

During her sojourn as executive director of NARAL, Michelman earned many awards. *Washingtonian* magazine named her one of the capital's 100 most powerful women. *The Hill* named her as one of the top grassroots/non-profit lobbyists. *Vanity Fair Magazine* named her as one of America's 200 Women Legends and Leaders. And *Fortune Magazine* named NARAL Pro-Choice America as one of the top advocacy groups in America. In 2003, Michelman was named one of Pennsylvania's Most Politically Powerful Women by PoliticsPA.

In 2004, Michelman retired as executive director of NARAL Pro-Choice and began working as a political consultant. In 2007, she became senior adviser for the John

Edwards campaign for president. When Edwards withdrew from the campaign, she endorsed Barack Obama. Many critics, including Chris Matthews of *Hardball*, accused Michelman of abandoning her cause when she endorsed Obama rather than endorsing friend and fellow feminist Hillary Clinton, also running for president. As Michelman wrote in response, "The women's movement is about free choice, self-determination and challenging a status quo that fails a lot of Americans, not just women. And it is not about going along. It's about transcending, about having the freedom to follow one's heart, about creating and pursuing new opportunities, and about the American dream being for all Americans" (Michelman, "Why I'm Endorsing Barack Obama," 2008).

Another family crisis became the impetus that forced Michelman into a new direction in her political activism. In 2001, Michelman's daughter worked as a horse trainer in upstate New York, and suffered an accident that crushed three of her vertebrae. Paralyzed for life, she required full-time care. To take care of her daughter, who did not have health insurance, Michelman used her life's savings and eventually cashed in her Individual Retirement Account (IRA) to pay for the extensive care. A year later, just as her daughter's condition was stabilizing, Michelman's second husband, whom she had married in 1972, was diagnosed with Parkinson's disease. A retired college professor, his benefits included generous health care coverage. He had even planned ahead, purchasing long-term care insurance. But Michelman discovered it was not enough.

For seven years, Michelman coped, "if barely," with the financial strains of rising medical costs. In 2009, her husband collapsed while getting out of the car. He suffered a shattered hip, a broken femur, and internal bleeding. His medical insurance covered "most" of the emergency costs related to the fall. But as Michelman was reviewing the unpaid bills, she discovered her monthly costs reached into the thousands. As her husband's discharge date approached, Michelman felt caught in a trap. She explained, "We needed my income, but the kind of political consulting work that was my forte was incompatible with the demands of caring for him. It was simply not possible for me to be available for him 24/7 and simultaneously work overtime." While doctors advised that her husband be placed in an assisted living facility, Michelman made the difficult choice to bring her husband home. "This was a financial decision," explains Michelman, "not a medical one." The experience turned Michelman into "a fanatic about the need for comprehensive health insurance reform" (Michelman 2010).

According to Michelman, the debate over the health care brought a "traumatic unity" to her life. As Michelman wrote, "Pro-choice activists are torn between celebrating the passage of health care legislation and confusion, if not anger, at the price paid to obtain it. Millions of Americans, including a disproportionate number of women, will have access to health care . . . But the victory was achieved through a fundamental change in the way we treat reproductive rights" (2010). As Michelman prophesied in a 2006 interview, her life has been devoted to expanding "people's understanding of what it means to be pro-choice. And it doesn't mean to be pro-abortion." According to Michelman, the right to privacy is a fundamental American value, whether it involves a woman's body or governmental wiretapping (Weeks 2006).

Michelman currently works at the Women's Law Project in Pennsylvania. The project was founded by a group of feminist attorneys devoted to equality and justice, becoming a leading organization in the field of women's rights.

Bobbi Miller

See also McCorvey, Norma

References

"Famed Feminist Faces Medical Tragedies." National Public Radio, April 18, 2009. http://www.npr.org/templates/story/story.php?storyId=103250580 (accessed September 14, 2010).

Michelman, Kate. "Speech to the Commonwealth Club of California, San Francisco." NARAL, 1998.

Michelman, Kate. "Statement of Ms. K. Michelman, Executive Director, National Abortion Rights Action League." *Thomas Hearings*, September 19, 1991. http://cti.itc.virginia.edu/~ybf2u/Thomas-Hill/0919a02.html (accessed September 11, 2011).

Michelman, Kate. "A System from Hell: How Medical Crises Have Taken My Family to Financial Ruin." *Huffington Post*, April 13, 2009. http://www.huffingtonpost.com/kate-michelman/a-system-from-hell-how-me_b_186177.html (accessed September 14, 2010).

Michelman, Kate. "Victory's Cost: Healthcare and Abortion Rights." RealClearPolitics, March 28, 2010. http://www.realclearpolitics.com/articles/2010/03/28/the_cost_of_victory_abortion_and_health_care_104957.html (accessed September 17, 2010).

Michelman, Kate. "What I Really Wanted to Say to Chris Matthews." *Salon*, February 8, 2008. http://www.salon.com/news/opinion/feature/2008/02/08/chris_matthews (accessed September 17, 2010).

Michelman, Kate. *With Liberty and Justice for All: A Life Spent Protecting the Right to Choose*. New York: Hudson Street Press, 2005.

Michelman, Kate. "Why I'm Endorsing Barack Obama." *Huffington Post*, February 3, 2008. http://www.huffingtonpost.com/kate-michelman/why-im-endorsing-barack-o_b_84658.html (accessed September 17, 2010).

NARAL Pro-Choice America. Free Dictionary.com, n.d. http://legal-dictionary.thefreedictionary.com/National+Abortion+and+Reproductive+Rights+Action+League (accessed December 11, 2010).

Sobie, Amy, and David Reardon. "The Benediction of Kate Michelman: A Case Study on Coping with Post-Abortion Trauma." *Post Abortion Review*, Elliot Institute, 2000. http://www.afterabortion.org/PAR/V7/n1/michelman.htm (accessed September 14, 2010).

Traister, Rebecca. "The Ladies Man: Kate Michelman, Lifelong Feminist and Former head of NARAL, Talked about Why She's Signed Up to Work with John Edwards." *Salon*, January 29, 2007. http://www.salon.com/life/feature/2007/01/29/michelman (accessed September 14, 2010).

Weeks, Linton. "Kate Michelman, the Public Face of a Woman's Right to Privacy." *Washington Post*, January 12, 2006. http://www.washingtonpost.com/wp-dyn/content/article/2006/01/11/AR2006011102806.html (accessed September 14, 2010).

Milk, Harvey (1930–1978)

During the 1970s, Harvey Milk was a leading gay activist in San Francisco, California. He led efforts to help lesbian, gay, bisexual, and transgender (LGBT) citizens live their lives openly. His dissident political actions to prevent discrimination on the basis of sexual orientation brought on the ire of politicians, police, and the general public—and eventually his death. After he was assassinated, he was called "a martyr for gay rights."

Harvey Bernard Milk was the second son of William Milk and Minerva Eleanor Karns of Lithuanian Jewish heritage. He was born in Woodmere, New York, on May 22, 1930. His grandfather Morris owned a department store, where Harvey's father worked for a time, and later was in the retail clothing business. Morris was one of the organizing members of the first synagogue in the largely Jewish hamlet, and he had a strong influence on his grandson, even though Harvey rejected religion when he got older. It was his grandfather's inclusiveness and social activism that inspired Harvey.

When they were growing up, Harvey and his older brother Robert were mischievous youngsters. A cousin described one incident when the boys' mother had to leave them alone for a short time. "In those days there were no frozen foods. It was canned goods.... The two of them got together. I don't know whose idea it was, but they joined in and took all the labels off the cans. When [their mother] needed a can, it was always a surprise" (Chan 2009).

Harvey's sense of humor stayed with him throughout his life. When he attended Bay Shore High School in Bay Shore, New York, he was considered the class clown. He graduated from the school in 1947 and enrolled at New York State College for Teachers in Albany, which became the State University of New York at Albany. Harvey majored in mathematics and also wrote for the college newspaper. He graduated from college in 1951 and enlisted in the U.S. Navy, serving during the Korean War. He attained the rank of lieutenant, junior grade, and was discharged in 1954.

Although Harvey knew during his teenage years that he was homosexual, he did not acknowledge that publicly. During the 1950s, it was not prudent to reveal a preference for same-gender or bisexual relationships. The majority of Americans believed that homosexual men and women and bisexuals were mentally ill and engaging in criminal acts. In 1953, President Dwight Eisenhower by executive order commanded that all federal employees who were homosexual should be dismissed. In 1954, at the height of U.S. senator Joseph McCarthy's investigations, homosexuals as well as communists were targets of the senator's attacks.

After his military service, Harvey Milk taught for two years at George W. Hewlett High School in Long Island. He also became involved with his first lover, Joe Campbell. The two lived together for almost six years, moving for a time to Dallas, Texas, but soon returning to New York, where Milk worked for an insurance company.

Throughout the 1960s, Milk had several partners, one of whom was Craig Rodwell, a gay activist with the New York Mattachine Society. The organization's name was taken from a character in Italian theater, *mattachino*, a court jester who dared to tell the truth to the king. The members used aggressive tactics while demonstrating for gay rights. Rodwell was arrested during a protest and jailed, which alarmed Milk, and he ended their relationship.

Another lover was Jack McKinley, who worked in theater. The two moved to San Francisco, California, where McKinley was stage director for the traveling troupe production of the musical *Hair*, and Milk took a job in an investment firm. When McKinley returned to New York City, Milk stayed in San Francisco.

In the spring of 1970, during the Vietnam War, Milk was involved in a demonstration against U.S. president Richard Nixon (1913–1994) and his announcement that U.S. troops were invading Cambodia, a country west of Vietnam. The incursion was meant to prevent the communist Vietcong from obtaining supplies and to destroy their bases in Cambodia. But the campaign angered many Americans because Nixon had promised to cut back U.S. involvement in the Vietnam War. Protests erupted across the United States. In San Francisco, Milk's protest cost him his job, and once again he moved back to New York City. But he stayed only two years.

In 1972, Milk returned to San Francisco, this time with a new partner, Scott Smith. Together they opened a camera store and lived in an apartment above the shop on Castro Street, the main thoroughfare through a business district. Castro is also the name of the surrounding neighborhood, which had become known as an openly gay and lesbian community.

Milk began his political activities in Castro, although that had not been his intent when he first arrived there. He became incensed as the Watergate scandal unfolded. Burglaries had taken place in the Watergate complex of buildings in Washington, D.C. One of the break-ins was at the Democratic National Committee offices in 1972 as part of a Republican campaign of political spying and sabotage conducted to reelect Nixon. A U.S. Senate committee investigated in 1973, and hearings revealed Nixon's role in and cover-up of the scandal. He was faced with impeachment and forced to resign in 1974.

As the events became public, Milk made a decision to run for political office—a position on San Francisco's Board of Supervisors (city council). In 1973, he ran as a populist, bringing together various ethnic groups as well as the homosexual community. He focused on the needs of all, not just the few. With humor and excellent oratory skills, he often gave his Hope Speech, in which he noted that gays "must be judged by our leaders and by those who are themselves gay, those who are visible. For invisible, we remain in limbo—a myth, a person with no parents, no brothers, no sisters, no friends who are straight, no important positions in employment. ... we must give people the chance to judge us by our leaders and legislators. A gay person in office can set a tone, can command respect not only from the larger community, but from the young people in our own community who need both examples and hope" (Shilts 1982, 362).

As a public official in San Francisco, Harvey Milk not only worked to protect gay rights, but championed many social causes. In 1978, he was murdered by a former city supervisor. (San Francisco Public Library)

Milk lost the election but won enough votes to instill confidence that he should try again. While he was preparing for the next campaign, he conducted voter registration drives and initiated a Castro Street Fair in 1974, which is still held the first Sunday in October each year with local artists, vendors, craftspeople, and organizations celebrating the diversity of the neighborhood. For his activism, he was hailed as the "Mayor of Castro."

Milk's second attempt to win elected office was for the state assembly, or the house of the California legislature. He did not succeed, but on his third try in 1977, he ran again for the Board of Supervisors and won, becoming the first openly homosexual elected to public office in California. On a national level, however, U.S. representative Gerry Studds (1937–2006) was the first politician to publicly acknowledge his homosexuality.

In 1977, Milk led a march from the Castro district to San Francisco's Union Square to protest a successful campaign by fundamentalist Christians led by gospel singer Anita Bryant to repeal a gay rights ordinance in Miami, Florida, where Bryant lived. Bryant also led an effort to prohibit homosexuals from teaching in public schools in California by supporting an anti-gay bill known as Proposition 6. News of the fundamentalists' crusade spread quickly to gay communities across the United States. The Castro community rose up against Bryant's message of hate and bigotry directed at homosexuals. According to Rebecca Spence writing for the Jewish weekly *Forward*, "dozens of activist gay Jews, worked within the Jewish community [in San Francisco] to drum up opposition to the initiative." And Milk was largely responsible for defeating Proposition 6 (Spence 2008).

Milk also helped pass a San Francisco ordinance banning housing and job discrimination based on sexual orientation. In addition, during his short time in office, he called attention to the needs of urban neighborhoods, from the lack of child care to poor public transportation systems. Before he could tackle other human rights issues, which were part of his broad agenda, he and Mayor George Moscone were murdered. Not long before his death, Harvey Milk had made a tape recording, which was to be read only if he was assassinated. In it, he said: "if a bullet should enter my brain, let that bullet destroy every closet door."

On November 27, 1978, a former city supervisor, Dan White, stealthily entered city hall and shot Milk and the mayor to death. White was apprehended, tried, and convicted of voluntary manslaughter, not murder, even though he confessed to the intentional killings. White's attorneys argued that their client suffered from depression, which prevented him from differentiating between right and wrong. A psychiatrist testified that White had switched from a healthy diet to junk food, citing this as evidence of his depression. That argument became known as the "Twinkie Defense," even though White had not included the sugary snack cake in the junk food he had eaten. White received the lightest possible sentence.

After the verdict was delivered on May 21, 1979, the news spread quickly, and most of San Francisco's residents were in shock. A crowd gathered on Castro Street, and with no apparent destination, began to move toward City Hall. Clashes known as the "White Night Riots" ensued. Some in the crowd broke windows in City Hall; others set fire inside the building or torched police cars. When the crowd began to return to Castro, police and the marchers battled. Police in retaliation raided the Elephant Walk Bar, a gay establishment on Castro Street. All of the rioting cost the city hundreds of thousands of dollars and many police officers and rioters were injured.

The next night, May 22, thousands gathered again on Castro Street to celebrate what would have been Harvey Milk's 49th birthday. Although the city had issued a permit to close the street for the party, the police were on hand but not visible. In spite of tensions, the celebration took place without violence.

Since Milk's murder, a number of institutions have been named for him. There is the Harvey Milk branch of the San Francisco Library in Eureka, California. Others include the Harvey Milk Civil Rights Academy and the Harvey Milk Plaza in the Castro District, and the Harvey Milk High School in New York City.

Milk has been the subject of numerous books and films, including a documentary, *The Times of Harvey Milk* (1985); and a major motion picture, *Milk* (2008), starring Sean Penn, who won an Academy Award for the role. An opera titled *Harvey Milk* (1995) was performed in Houston, Texas. In 2009, President Barack Obama awarded Milk, along with others, the Medal of Freedom. Before presenting the medal to Stuart Milk on behalf of his uncle, Obama noted that Harvey Milk "stirred the aspirations of millions of people. He would become, after several attempts, one of the first openly gay Americans elected to public office. And his message of hope—hope unashamed, hope unafraid—could not ever be silenced. It was Harvey who said it best: 'You gotta give 'em hope.' "

See also McCarthy, Joseph

References

Chan, Sewell. "Film Evokes Memories for Milk's Relatives." *New York Times*, February 20, 2009. http://cityroom.blogs.nytimes.com/2009/02/20/film-evokes-memories-for-harvey-milks-relatives/ (accessed September 13, 2010).

Krakow, Kari. *The Harvey Milk Story*. Ridley Park, PA: Two Lives Publishers, 2002.

Marcus, Eric. *Making History: The Struggle for Gay and Lesbian Equal Rights*. New York: HarperCollins, 1992.

Miller, Neil. *Out of the Past, Gay and Lesbian History from 1869 to the Present*. New York: Vintage Books, 1995.

Shilts, Randy. *The Mayor of Castro Street*. New York: St. Martin's Press, 1982.

Spence, Rebecca. "Harvey Milk, in Life and on Film, Typified the Proud Jew as Outsider." *Forward*, December 19, 2008. http://www.forward.com/articles/14715/ (accessed September 17, 2010).

Weiss, Mike. *Double Play: The San Francisco City Hall Killings*. Reading, MA: Addison-Wesley, 1984.

Moore, Harry (1905–1951)

Years before the assassinations of such civil rights leaders as Martin Luther King Jr. and Malcolm X, Floridian Harry T. Moore and his wife Harriette were martyrs of the modern civil rights movement; although before their assassination, many African Americans had been murdered by members of the Ku Klux Klan and other racist groups. Moore was murdered on Christmas Day, 1951, when a bomb placed beneath his home exploded, killing him a short while later on the way to the hospital; his wife Harriette suffered serious injuries that caused her death nine days later.

As the twentieth century began, Florida contained about 530,000 people, some 44 percent of them African Americans. The construction of railroads and resorts in the late nineteenth century had brought tens of thousands of new settlers into Florida, so there were many nonagricultural and business opportunities for all seeking work (Saunders 2000, 3). Florida during the days of slavery became associated with freedom in the minds of southern slaves. Many slaves fled to Florida under Spanish and British rule, often living and fighting at the side of Seminole Indians, who, in turn, had come to Florida from largely Creek tribes decimated by fighting throughout the South. After the Civil War, and by the 1890s,

Florida had become one of the worst states for lynchings and other forms of racially motivated violence toward blacks (Saunders 2000, 4).

Moore was born on November 18, 1905, in Houston, Florida in Suwannee County in the Florida panhandle, a region that remains largely rural and much more conservative than the rest of the state. His parents were Johnny and Rosa Moore, and Harry was their only child. Johnny Moore tended water tanks for the Seaboard Air Line Railroad, and he and Rosa ran a small store in front of their home. When Harry was nine years old, his father died. His mother Rosa worked in the cotton fields, a job that leaves one with an aching back and hands cut by the sharp edges of the wispy cotton. After working in the fields, Rosa ran the store.

Harry was sent to live with one of Rosa's sisters in Daytona Beach along the east coast, and the next year, Harry moved in with three other aunts in Jacksonville, staying there for the next three years. By 1915, Jacksonville was Florida's largest city with an estimated 67,000 residents (Saunders 2000, 3). Jacksonville was a city predominantly African American at the time, with a large and vibrant black community, though the Ku Klux Klan was very active there as well. His three aunts were well-educated women (two were teachers, one a nurse), and they encouraged Harry to take education seriously.

When Harry returned to Suwannee County in 1919, he enrolled in a high school, then attended Florida Memorial College, where he excelled in his studies, receiving only one B+ among all his As. He was nicknamed "Doc" by his fellow students (Public Broadcasting Service 2001). In May 1925, Harry graduated and accepted a teaching position in Cocoa, Florida, in Brevard County.

Harry spent the next four years teaching fourth grade in Cocoa's only black elementary school. There he met Harriette Vyda Sims, who was then selling insurance for Atlantic Life Insurance Company. Her family lived in Mims, a small town near Miami, just outside of Titusville. The newly married couple moved in with Harriette's parents until they completed building their own home nearby. Harry became the principal at the Titusville Colored School, where he taught ninth grade and supervised a staff of six teachers. In March 1928, their first child was born, Annie Rosalea, whom they called Peaches. When Peaches was six months old, Harriette began teaching at the Mims Colored School. In September 1930, their daughter Juanita Evangeline was born (NAACP n.d.).

Florida was the first state to organize a state conference of the National Association for the Advancement of Colored People (NAACP). Moore and his friend John Gilbert had proposed the idea as early as 1934, but action came in 1946, the year that U.S. president Franklin Delano Roosevelt signed the famous Executive Order 8802 barring discrimination in defense industries and in government hiring (Saunders 2000, 18).

In 1934, Moore began his public work for civil rights, starting the Brevard County chapter of the NAACP. Three years later, with the involvement of the all-black Florida State Teachers Association backed by the NAACP's most famous attorney, Thurgood Marshall (who later became a U.S. Supreme Court justice), Moore filed the first lawsuit in the Deep South to equalize the salaries of white and black teachers. Eventually, the lawsuit was lost in state court, but many federal lawsuits that followed succeeded (NAACP n.d.).

In 1941, Moore became the NAACP's unpaid executive secretary for the state of

Florida. The first annual conference of the NAACP met at Bethel Metropolitan Baptist Church in 1941 in St. Petersburg, and Moore became their first elected president (Saunders 2000, 18). By 1943, Moore was publicly challenging violence toward African Americans, especially lynchings, leading investigations into every single one that occurred in Florida.

Then Thurgood Marshall won a major victory before the U.S. Supreme Court in the case *Smith v. Allwright* (1944). This decision said that all-white Democratic primary political races were unconstitutional. The decision struck down the Democratic white primary and opened that party to African American voters. Floridians quickly organized a separate entity called the Progressive Voters League with the goals of an open primary, registering and voting for more African Americans, and seeking candidates. In 1944, only 20,000 blacks were registered to vote, about 5.5 percent of the black population eligible to vote (Saunders 2000, 18–19).

In November 1945, Moore and the NAACP issued a ringing call: "Who are more directly responsible for the inequalities in educational opportunities, the lynchings, the police brutality, and other injustices suffered by Negroes—our state and county officials or the Administration in Washington? All of these evils can be traced directly to the prejudiced attitude of local officials ... In order to help select these officials, Negroes must vote in the Democratic primaries" (Saunders 2000, 20).

In January 1946, the Florida Democratic Party dropped its formal bar to black participation. In March, two African Americans ran for the Dade County school board. That same month, Moore's home NAACP county branch sued for access to the ballot for blacks. By the Fall, blacks voted in many urban counties and some rural ones. In 1947, the (Tampa) *Florida Sentinel* observed, "In 1947 the Negro participated freely for the first time in years, in the municipal election of Tampa," and in 1949 in the State and County elections in most cities and towns in Florida" (Saunders 2000, 20).

Over the next six years, 116,000 African Americans registered to vote in Florida, and even though that total only represented 31 percent of all those blacks eligible to vote, it was 51 percent higher than any other southern state (Public Broadcasting Service 2001). By the end of 1944, the Florida state conference contained 34 branches with almost 3,000 members (Saunders 2000, 18).

Following the end of World War II, "race leaders committed themselves to bringing real advancements out of the world conflict. Their symbol was the 'Double-V' standing for victory over the enemy abroad and victory over racism at home" (Saunders 2000, 18).

Because of their involvement in bettering the lives of African Americans in Florida, in 1946, both Harry and Harriette were fired from their teaching jobs. Harry soon became the first full-time paid organizer for Florida's NAACP. During his first two years, Moore built the Florida NAACP to a peak of over 10,000 members in 63 branches. By January 1949, the national NAACP doubled annual dues from $1 to $2, and membership fell drastically all over the country (NAACP n.d.).

In 1949, a horrifying incident of racial violence toward African Americans occurred in Groveland, Florida, a rural area near the middle of the state. A white woman said she was kidnapped and raped by several black men. A mob gathered at the Tavares Jail but was turned away by Sheriff Willis McCall of Lake County, considered the most violent sheriff in the country. The mob left Tavares and went to Groveland, burning several black homes and firing bullets into them as well.

Moore discovered that three African Americans arrested were severely beaten by McCall. Later that year, three men were convicted of the alleged crime, and two, Walter Irvin and Sammy Shepherd, were sentenced to death. A 16-year-old, Charles Greenlee, was spared the death sentence. The involvement of the NAACP in Groveland grew, and its attorney, Franklin Williams of its Legal Defense Fund, gathered evidence showing that the allegations of kidnapping and rape were highly suspect (Saunders 2000, 23). In April 1951, the convictions were overturned by the U.S. Supreme Court, and as the two older men were being driven back from a court hearing, Sheriff McCall stopped his vehicle, ordered the two men out, and opened fire on them, claiming later that they attacked him, although both men were shackled together. Shepherd was killed at the scene, and Irvin critically wounded. Moore demanded that the sheriff be arrested and removed from office by the governor. That did not happen.

Ironically, Moore found himself in trouble with the national headquarters of the NAACP in 1950. They accused Moore of not giving sufficient time to administration, and associating the NAACP too closely with state and local political matters, as well as concentrating NAACP efforts in rural areas rather than cities. In retaliation for these failings, the NAACP ceased paying a salary to Moore. Despite this, Moore attempted to block the appointment of former segregationist and governor Millard Caldwell to head a federal agency, led calls for the full integration of all public facilities in Florida, demanded civil rights legislation for Florida's congressional delegation, and charged a "whitewash" of the Groveland investigation. In 1951, the NAACP Florida conference began scheduling "Groveland Sundays," a technique to keep the Groveland incident in the public's eye and to build up defense funds (Saunders 2000, 23).

Six weeks later, on Christmas Day at 10:15 that night, also the Moores' wedding anniversary, a three-pound bomb of dynamite was placed beneath the floor joists of Harry and Harriette's bedroom at their home in Mims, and detonated. Moore had returned home tired and dejected from his struggles with the national NAACP and the difficulties of getting any action on the Groveland incident (Saunders 2000, 23). Harry and Harriette Moore were both killed in the explosion.

The national NAACP under the leadership of Walter White demanded state action to find and punish those guilty of killing Harry and Harriette Moore. Florida governor Fuller Warren reacted by accusing White and NAACP investigators of being Harlem (a predominantly black section of New York City) agitators trying to stir up problems for Floridians, white and black (Saunders 2000, 59). "In the meantime, the Florida State NAACP remained rudderless, African American residents feared for their lives, and NAACP membership and activities in Florida declined significant" (Saunders 2000, 59). In mid-September 1952, the *Florida Sentinel* newspaper announced "A Tampa son, Robert W. Saunders, has been appointed as the new secretary of the Florida NAACP" (Saunders 2000, 59). So, 10 months after the assassination of the Moores, a new leader began his work to ensure equal rights for all the citizens of Florida.

Despite several investigations over the next half-century, no one was ever charged or convicted of their murders. However, on August 6, 2006, Attorney General (and later governor) Charlie Crist released the results of a 20-month investigation into the assassinations of Harry and Harriette Moore by the Attorney General's Office of Civil Rights in conjunction with the Florida Department of Law Enforcement, who conducted more than 100 interviews and did the most detailed excavation of the crime scene ever undertaken. Their investigation concluded that four individuals were directly involved in these murders, three of whom were: Earl J. Brooklyn, who had floor plans of the bombed Moore house; Tillman H. Belvin, a friend and fellow Ku Klux Klan member; and Joseph N. Cox, who committed suicide shortly after being interviewed for the second time in 1952 by the FBI. Cox was implicated by the deathbed confession of the fourth individual, Edward Spivey, believed to have been there that night. The first two men died of natural causes, and the last died in 1978 soon after confessing. During this investigation, despite its being conducted in 2005 and 2006, the investigators found many people still reluctant to speak about the assassinations, fearing reprisals.

Daniel Callaghan

See also King, Martin Luther, Jr.; Malcolm X

References

Green, Ben. *Before His Time: The Untold Story of Harry T. Moore, America's First Civil Rights Martyr.* Gainesville: University Press of Florida, 2005. First published 1999 by Free Press.

Kennedy, David. "The Man, The Martyr, The Mystery: Harry T. Moore." *Florida Monthly*, 2004.

Kennedy, Stetson. *I Rode with the Ku Klux Klan*. London: Arco, 1954.

NAACP. "NAACP History: Harry T. and Harriette Moore." n.d. http://www.naacp.org/pages/naacp-history-Harry-T.-and-Harriette-Moore/ (accessed February 10, 2011).

Public Broadcasting Service. "Freedom Never Dies: The Legacy of Harry T. Moore." PBS.org, 2001. http://www.pbs.org/harrymoore/harry/mbio.html (accessed February 10, 2011).

Saunders, Robert W., Sr. *Bridging the Gap: Continuing the Florida NAACP Legacy of Harry T. Moore*. Tampa, FL: University of Tampa Press, 2000.

Moore, Michael (1954–)

Few people are neutral in their opinions about author and filmmaker Michael Moore. Some praise the award-winning provocateur who uses satire in his dissident attacks on many American business institutions, capitalism, and government officials. Others dismiss Moore as a hypocrite and at worst a liar, who has earned millions of dollars from the very corporations he criticizes and that he pretends in his style of dress and manner that he is a working-class citizen.

Michael Francis Moore was born on April 23, 1954, in Flint, Michigan, although his hometown is suburban Davison, east of Flint. Davison had no hospital. His parents, Frank and Veronica Moore, raised him along with two younger sisters in Davison. His father worked on the assembly line for AC Spark Plugs and his mother was a secretary for General Motors (GM). Flint was known as a company town because a majority of families worked for GM. His Irish American Catholic parents sent Michael to Catholic elementary and high schools in Davison. When he was 14 years old, he enrolled in a youth seminary in Saginaw, Michigan, about 35 miles (56.32 kilometers) from Flint. He thought he might escape working in a factory by becoming a priest, but he discovered that seminary life was not for him, and he returned to public school where he was active in drama and debate. However, he was bored with school and the conformity that was expected.

Before he graduated, Moore at age 18 ran for and was elected to the school board of Davison High School. According to biographer Emily Schultz, "He had one main goal: to remove the principal and assistant principal from the school he was still attending.... Moore also fought for student rights and supported the teacher union. He sued the school board to secure the right to tape-record public meetings. When the school board attempted to find ways to meet without Moore present, he reported them to the Michigan Attorney General, who sent the issue to court" (Schultz 2005, 21).

After graduating from high school, Moore enrolled at the University of Michigan–Flint, but he stayed only a year. He tried to work at a GM factory, but gave up the job after one day and embarked on a journalism career. Moore set up shop in a house in Burton, Michigan, a suburb of Flint. The house was home for the "Hotline," an intervention and advocacy service for teenagers that Moore had established and a hotline publication called *Free to Be* in 1976 and in 1977 named the *Flint Voice*. After the circulation of the *Flint Voice* grew and was distributed statewide in 1983, it became the *Michigan Voice* with Moore as editor. To keep his alternative newspaper in print, Moore had to find funding and persuaded music celebrities to hold benefit concerts on his publication's behalf.

In 1986, Moore accepted the position as editor of *Mother Jones*, a liberal political magazine named for the labor organizer of the late 1800s and early 1900s, Mary Harris "Mother" Jones. Moore shut down the *Michigan Voice* and moved to San Francisco, California, where *Mother Jones* was published. But his stint at the magazine was short-lived. He and the magazine's cofounder did not agree on content, and Moore was fired after four months on the job. He sued the magazine for breach of contract, but settled out of court with the magazine's insurance company for $58,000.

Moore, his longtime friend and movie producer Kathleen Glynn, and her daughter Natalie, who had moved to San Francisco with Moore, returned to Flint. (Moore and Glynn married in 1991, and Natalie became Moore's adopted daughter.)

In Flint, Moore was shocked one day to hear and see Roger Smith, the chief executive officer (CEO) of GM, announce on television that additional GM plants in Flint would shut down and operations would move to Mexico. Some plants had closed already. As a result, tens of thousands of workers lost their jobs. The closed plants wreaked havoc on Flint's economy. Since the late 1930s, when GM workers staged a historic sit-down strike to gain union representation and collective bargaining for higher wages and shorter work weeks until the plant closings in the 1980s, Flint had prospered. Flint's damaged economy was evident in closed businesses, lost homes, an increase in the high school dropout rate, a rise in crime, and an overall negative impression of the town. In fact, it became known as the worst place to live in the United States.

Moore's reaction to GM and its CEO was to form a production company called Dog Eat Dog Films in 1986. He was determined to make a documentary about GM's role in Flint's economic devastation even though he had no experience making films and no funds for such a venture. He sought help from professional filmmakers and he and his "coproducer Glynn drew on earlier fundraising skills and were able to organize a Tuesday night bingo, with the film as their own charity. Moore sold his house and held two garage sales. They solicited funds where they could, including from actor [and social activist] Ed Asner," according to biographer Schultz (2005, 68).

The film *Roger and Me* was completed in 1989 and was the beginning of Moore's particular type of documentary, using sardonic humor and injecting his scruffy self in on-screen interviews as well as historical film footage to tell a serious story. In the film, Moore and his crew are on a mission to try to get CEO Smith to see what his decisions have cost working-class families in Flint. After the film was shown and well received at film festivals, Warner Brothers acquired *Roger and Me* for $3 million and agreed to show it in more than 1,000 theaters and "to pay housing for two years for evicted families shown in the film" (Schultz 2005, 74).

Moore's first documentary brought him success and set him on a path for subsequent films as well as TV shows. For example, in 1994, he created and directed NBC's *TV Nation*, which won an Emmy Award. His book *Downsize This! Random Threats from an Unarmed American* (1996) takes aim at corporations and their greed. He then directed *The Big One* (1998), a documentary satire of corporate America based on interviews and observations he made while making a book tour for *Downsize This!*

An especially productive and lucrative year for Moore was 2002. His award-winning documentary *Bowling for Columbine* (2002), depicting America's gun mania, was released. The title reflects the fact that before the massacre of 12 Columbine (Colorado) High School students and a teacher in 1999, the killers went to a bowling class then went on a shooting spree. *Bowling for Columbine* won the 2002 Oscar for best documentary, and at the Academy Award presentation, Moore aimed his comments at President Bush and the invasion of Iraq. He said:

> I have invited my fellow documentary nominees on the stage with us . . . They're here in solidarity with me because we like nonfiction. We like nonfiction and we live in fictitious times. We live in the time where we have fictitious election results that elect a fictitious president. We live in a time where we have a man sending us to war for fictitious reasons. Whether it's the fiction of duct tape or fiction of orange alerts, we are against this war, Mr. Bush. Shame on you, Mr. Bush, shame on you. And any time you've got the Pope and the Dixie Chicks against you, your time is up. Thank you very much. (Jenkins 2011)

Some members of the audience booed while most cheered Moore. He was not alone in his criticism of the war; other award winners and directors delivered antiwar remarks as well.

Moore also saw publication of his book *Stupid White Men . . . and Other Sorry Excuses for the State of the Nation!* (2002), a biting satire of President George W. Bush's administration. The book became a best seller. But before publication, the book almost was cancelled. HarperCollins, the publisher, wanted Moore to rewrite parts of the book and eliminate negative references to Bush. Moore refused, and the publisher would not release the book. So Moore decided to read sections of his book to a small group in New Jersey. When a librarian in the group heard that the publisher was going to ban Moore's book, she contacted other librarians across the United States, and they in turn sent protests to HarperCollins. Shortly thereafter, Moore's book appeared.

Moore's documentary *Fahrenheit 9/11* (2004) is also a highly critical look at the Bush administration and its reaction to the September 11, 2001, Al Qaeda terrorist attacks—planes crashing into the twin towers of the New York World Trade Center and the Pentagon in Arlington, Virginia, and the planned plane attack on Washington, D.C., that was thwarted by passengers, causing the plane to crash in Shanksville, Pennsylvania. The film discusses the Bush family connection with the Saudi royal family and the bin Laden clan, whose foremost terrorist relative Osama bin Laden headed Al Qaeda. The film received top honors at the Cannes Film Festival.

Other Moore films include *Sicko* (2007), a documentary about the poor quality of the U.S. health care system. In *Capitalism: A Love Story* (2009), Moore continues to examine the disastrous impact of corporate dominance on the everyday lives of Americans. He sends the message that "An economic system founded on private profit is inhuman, immoral, and unsustainable, and alternatives exist," according to Danny Collum writing for *Sojourner Magazine* (Collum 2009, 46). Yet Moore does not embrace socialism as early 1900s reformers such as Dorothy Day, Eugene Debs, Florence Kelley, and others advocated. Instead Moore's "solutions to capitalism are essentially electoral ones, backed by struggle and popular resistance. This leaves a big gulf between him and revolutionary socialism. But, for all that, he is one of the good guys. We who stand in the revolutionary tradition are all the better for having him and his films as weapons against all that's rotten in the world," wrote socialist Pat Stack in *Socialist Review* (Stack 2010).

Documentary filmmaker Michael Moore talks about the state of the U.S. health care system, joined by Los Angeles Mayor Antonio Villaraigosa, left, and actress Yvette Freeman, right front, who played a nurse on the TV series *ER*, at a news conference outside Los Angeles City Hall, June 26, 2007. Moore's documentary film *Sicko* premiered that evening in Los Angeles. (AP Photo/Reed Saxon)

In spite of praise, awards, and great financial return from his films and books, Moore has numerous critics. One is Daniel Radosh, a New York freelance writer. In his view, Moore is "loudmouthed, self-serving and not funny." Radosh also criticized Moore for acting as though he is still the working-class guy from Flint, when in reality the filmmaker and author is very wealthy (Radosh 1997). He has been criticized for being obsessed with money, for having a bad temper, and making fun of working-class people. The book *Michael Moore Is a Big Fat Stupid White Man* (2004), as its title suggests, is a collection of negative critiques of Moore, some contending that he is a manipulator and liar.

Others argue that Moore stages preposterous confrontations with powerful people in order to humiliate them. Critics accuse him of editing his films to reach the conclusion he wants rather than sticking to the facts and to chronological order. Still others say Moore's documentaries are about him rather than the social and political issues he purports to advocate and that his humor is so broad that it overshadows all else.

In a *Time* magazine interview, Moore was asked: "How do you entertain people at the same time you're trying to get them to think about hard things?" Moore responded: "When I'm shooting a movie, I'm always in an invisible theater seat. I respect the fact that people have worked hard all week and want to go to the movies on the weekend and be entertained. But the struggle for me does not come between politics and entertainment, because I know that if I succeed in making an entertaining and funny or sad film, that the things I want to say politically will come through very strong. If there ever is a struggle, making a good movie will always supersede the need to be noble" (Kluger 2007).

In 2011, Moore participated in numerous Occupy Wall Street movement protests against social and economic inequality and corporate greed. It is uncertain whether Moore will base a documentary on those protests.

See also Asner, Ed; Day, Dorothy; Debs, Eugene V.; Kelley, Florence

References

Collum, Danny Duncan. "Fat Cats and Failed Systems." *Sojourners Magazine*, December 2009.

Hardy, David, and Jason Clarke. *Michael Moore Is a Big Fat Stupid White Man*. New York: HarperCollins, 2004.

Jenkins, Beverly. "10 Memorable Oscar Acceptance Speeches." Listverse, February 24, 2011. http://listverse.com/2011/02/24/10-memorable-oscar-acceptance-speeches/ (accessed September 11, 2011).

Kluger, Jeffrey. "Michael Moore's New Diagnosis." *Time*, May 17, 2007. http://www.time.com/time/magazine/article/0,9171,1622592,00.html (accessed November 10, 2010).

Moore, Michael. *Stupid White Men . . . and Other Sorry Excuses for the State of the Nation*. New York: HarperCollins, 2001.

Radosh, Daniel. "Moore Is Less." *Salon*, June 6, 1997. http://www.salon.com/june97/media/media970606.html (accessed November 10, 2010).

Schultz, Emily. *Michael Moore: A Biography*. Toronto, Ontario, Canada: ECW Press, 2005.

Stack, Pat. "Capitalism: A Love Story." *Socialist Review*, March 2010. http://www.socialistreview.org.uk/article.php?articlenumber=11209 (accessed November 10, 2010).

Murie, Margaret (1902–2003)

In congressional testimony prior to passage of the Alaska Lands Act of 1960, Margaret Murie, known as the Grandmother of the

Conservation Movement, said: "I am testifying as an emotional woman and I would like to ask you, gentlemen, what's wrong with emotion? Beauty is a resource in and of itself. Alaska must be allowed to be Alaska, that is her greatest economy. I hope the United States of America is not so rich that she can afford to let these wildernesses pass by, or so poor she cannot afford to keep them." There was vociferous political opposition from miners, loggers, and others who wanted to continue developing their industries in what was called the "Last Great Wilderness." But Murie and her husband Olaus Murie, a distinguished biologist, were adamant in their defense of the Alaska wilderness. They helped convince President Dwight D. Eisenhower's administration to designate a northeastern Alaska area of eight million acres as a refuge in 1960.

Eisenhower issued an executive order "to preserve unique wildlife, wilderness, and recreational values" in the far northeast corner of Alaska. The area was first called the Arctic National Wildlife Range and in 1980 renamed the Arctic National Wildlife Refuge (ANWR). Currently it consists of more than 19 million acres between the Beaufort Sea and the Brooks Range. It is the largest refuge in the National Wildlife Refuge system. Since the designation, a section of ANWR has been a battlefield between those who want all of ANWR preserved and those like former Alaska governor Sarah Palin and petroleum companies who say parts of ANWR should be open for oil drilling.

Named Margaret Elizabeth Thomas when she was born on August 18, 1902, in Seattle, Washington, Margaret grew up primarily in Fairbanks, Alaska. Her mother, Minnie, and father, Ashton Thomas, divorced when she was about five years old. Minnie remarried Louis R. Gillette. When Margaret (called Mardy) was nine years old, her stepfather, who had just taken the position of assistant U.S. attorney for the territory of Alaska, sent for Mardy and her mother to join him in Fairbanks. The two had only three days in September to prepare for the three-week trip from Seattle to Fairbanks. They had to travel before the rivers froze over and the last steamship could make its way on the Yukon. "In 1911 the river steamer was queen," wrote Margaret years later in her memoir (Murie 1978, 10). From Dawson, where Louis met Mardy and Minnie, the family traveled on the steamers *Sarah* and the *Schwatka* on their way to Fairbanks.

In Fairbanks, they made their home in a log cabin of four rooms with an addition of another room constructed of wood slabs. Although water was available, it was rusty and smelled of iron, so spring water was brought in. A wood-fed range and stove provided heat for warmth and cooking. Some food provisions were kept in a cellar, and an outdoor cupboard held frozen caribou, moose, and whitefish. "We did have some helpful things: electric lights . . . and a telephone," Mardy wrote (Murie 1978, 19).

The Fairbanks where Mardy and her younger siblings Louis, Louise, and Carol grew up was an isolated community. It was far from any other town—"eight days by horse sleigh or ten days by river steamer," she wrote (Murie 1978, 21). It was inhabited by people of varied backgrounds: gold miners, merchants selling groceries and dry goods, saloon keepers, lawyers, gamblers, and prostitutes. She ventured beyond Fairbanks in 1919 when she attended Reed College, a liberal arts college in Portland, Oregon, and studied to be a teacher. But two years later, she returned to Fairbanks and enrolled at the University of Alaska, earning her degree in 1924, the first woman to do so at that institution.

On her return to Fairbanks in 1921, Mardy met Olaus Murie, a field biologist

Margaret Murie is known as the "grandmother of the conservation movement." She and her husband Olaus Murie (right), a distinguished biologist, were adamant in their defense of the Alaska wilderness. They helped convince President Dwight D. Eisenhower's administration to designate a northeastern Alaska area of eight million acres as a refuge in 1960. (Wilderness Society)

with the U.S. Bureau of Biological Survey (now the U.S. Fish and Wildlife Service). Mardy and Olaus soon established a romantic relationship, and in 1924, they married in a small Episcopal mission at Anvik. Their honeymoon trip was on a steamship up the Yukon to the Koyukuk River, where they waited for the freezeup that would enable them to travel by dogsled to the north country, where Olaus would continue his study of migrating caribou, which he had begun in 1920.

The Muries' first child, Martin, was born in 1925 in Washington State, where Mardy was staying with her parents while Olaus was on an expedition studying Alaska brown bears. Olaus did not see his son until he was three months old. That convinced the couple that they would not be separated that long again, and when Olaus was assigned to another Alaska mission to band geese, the rest of the family went along. Like their previous trip, they traveled by river, this time in a motorboat and with a scow loaded with supplies. In the motorboat, Martin, who was less than a year old, traveled in a little box built especially for him. As Mardy explained: "In the bottom of this box we had a thick pad, a rubber sheet, and a baby sized eiderdown sleeping bag.... Here he sat, or jumped up and down, or slept, clad in khaki coveralls.... He also wore a baby harness, and whenever he was aboard, the leather leash attached to it was hooked to a stout screw eye in the bottom corner of his box. The boat was open, and the rushing relentless water was right there beside us" (Murie 1978, 213). In subsequent years, the two other Murie children, Joanne and Donald, made many trips to the Alaska wilderness with their parents and also to the mountain areas surrounding Jackson Hole, Wyoming, where Olaus was sent in 1926 to study the North American elk.

The Muries moved to Jackson Hole, and because the place reminded them of Alaska, they built a permanent home there. When they were not traveling, they were active in the community. During the years of World War II (1939–1945), the U.S. government held the entire North Slope of Alaska for military purposes. In Jackson, Mardy did wartime volunteer work in the town's hospital where Olaus served as superintendent.

In 1945, Olaus resigned from the Biological Survey to become director (and later president) of the Wilderness Society, founded in 1935. Since that time, the society has led the effort to permanently protect U.S. wilderness areas that range from forests to deserts to the Alaska tundra. Olaus worked for 17 years for the society, and Mardy was his secretary.

The couple, in a partnership with Mardy's sister and her husband, bought a dude ranch in 1945 at the southern end of the Grand Teton National Park near Moose, Wyoming. In 1946, a log cabin on the ranch became the Muries' home and headquarters of the Wilderness Society. The ranch was surrounded by wilderness and wildlife. "Their first summer there, sons Martin and Donald built a footbridge across one of the streams, deciding next that a dam would create a fine swimming hole," wrote Pattie Layser in *Life in the Tetons*. Friends and guests at the ranch helped carry rocks and build part of the dam, but darkness prevented them from completing the job. Two days later, Olaus discovered that beavers had finished the dam for them (Layser 2009).

In 1956, the Muries led an expedition to the Sheenjek River Valley in Alaska's far north to draw attention to the wilderness area that would be preserved in 1960 as the Arctic Wildlife Range, home to a great diversity of wildlife. Their experiences and observations helped establish the concept of preserving an entire ecological system and became the foundation for creating large natural parks. According to the U.S. Fish and Wildlife Service, the refuge "is inhabited by 45 species of land and marine mammals, ranging from the pygmy shrew to the bowhead whale. Best known are the polar, grizzly, and black bear; wolf, wolverine, Dall sheep, moose, muskox, and the animal that has come to symbolize the area's wildness, the free-roaming caribou. Thirty-six species of fish occur in Arctic Refuge waters, and 180 species of birds have been observed on the refuge" (U.S. Fish and Wildlife Service).

In several chapters of her book *Two in the Far North* (1978), Murie described the experiences and observations of participants in the 1956 expedition to the Arctic refuge, where the sun never set. She wrote:

> In this day and age it is a rare experience to be able to live in an environment wholly nature's own, where the only sounds are those of the natural world.... The scratch of the muskrat diving off the edge of the ice; ptarmigan were crowing, clucking, talking, and calling all around us; tree sparrows and white-crowned sparrows sang continually—their voices were almost constant background to all the other sounds.... The sights and sounds of our days and daylight nights were not of our making or doing; we were

simply the visiting observers of spring in the Arctic's natural world. (Murie 1978, 271–73)

Murie's book prompted countless people to advocate for preservation of the Arctic wilderness and also for a Wilderness Act, while long-time colleague Howard Zahniser, director of the Wilderness Society, and Olaus and Mardy campaigned diligently to get the bill through Congress. The Wilderness Act of 1964 established a "National Wilderness Preservation System to be composed of federally owned areas designated by Congress as 'wilderness areas,' and these shall be administered for the use and enjoyment of the American people in such manner as will leave them unimpaired for future use as wilderness."

Unfortunately, Olaus Murie and Howard Zahniser died before U.S. president Lyndon Johnson signed the act into law. But Mardy Murie and Zahniser's wife Alice were able to attend the signing ceremony in the Rose Garden of the White House.

Following the death of her husband, Mardy Murie continued her efforts to conserve wilderness areas from her home at the Moose ranch, writing letters and articles. She also made speeches, testified regarding conservation legislation at congressional hearings, and traveled regularly to the Alaska wilderness to call attention to development projects that could damage wildlife.

Since the 1970s, there has been a constant debate over whether to drill for oil in the coastal plain of ANWR, which is where the Porcupine caribou give birth to their calves. Oil drilling proponents claim that modern technology would prevent damage to the coastal environment and that the oil found would help reduce the United States' high oil prices. Conservationists contend that drilling and oil spills would endanger wildlife, as was evident with the 1999 oil spill from the Exxon Valdez in Prince William Sound, Alaska. The controversy over drilling in ANWR has continued long after Murie's death in 2003, and both sides will no doubt debate in the future.

During her lifetime, Murie received numerous awards and honors. She was awarded the Audubon Medal, the John Muir Award, and the Robert Marshall Conservation Award in the 1980s. The National Park Service made her an Honorary Park Ranger, and the University of Alaska bestowed an honorary doctorate. She received the prestigious Presidential Medal of Freedom from President Bill Clinton in 1998. In 2002, she received the National Wildlife Federation's highest honor for conservationist of the year. The following year, Murie, who had been confined to a wheelchair for several years, died on October 19, 2003, at her log cabin near Moose, Wyoming.

Her legacy includes the Murie Ranch, which is a National Historic District and is the home of the Murie Center, a nonprofit organization that strives to carry on the legacy of the Muries. A film *Arctic Dance: The Mardy Murie Story* (2000) commemorates her life and work.

See also Palin, Sarah

References

Kaye, Roger. "Celebrating a Wilderness Legacy: The Arctic National Wildlife Refuge." *International Wildlife Journal*, April 2010.

Layser, Pattie. "A Candle in the Wind." *Teton Home and Living*, Fall–Winter 2009. http://www.lifeinthetetons.com/Teton-Home-and-Living/Fall-Winter-2009/A-Candle-in-the

-Wind/index.php?cparticle=2&siarticle=1 (accessed November 22, 2010).

Murie, M. E. Testimony, Senate Committee on Interstate and Foreign Commerce.

Hearings, S. 1899. *A Bill to Authorize the Establishment of the Arctic Wildlife*, July 1, 1959. Washington, DC: Government Printing Office, 1960.

Murie, Margaret E. *Two in the Far North*. 2nd ed. Anchorage: Alaska Northwest Publishing Company, 1978.

U.S. Fish and Wildlife Service. "Arctic National Wildlife Refuge." n.d. http://www.fws.gov/refuges/profiles/index.cfm?id=75600 (accessed November 23, 2010).

N

Nader, Ralph (1934–)

Ralph Nader "has been busy since 1968 being the most vigilant citizen in America," wrote Karen Croft in *Salon.com*. "He works harder than any president or member of Congress. He has affected your life as a consumer more than any man, but you didn't elect him and you can't make him go away. . . . Nader's accomplishments have become part of the fabric of American public life" (Croft 1999). Nader has engendered both fans and foes during his nearly eight decades on earth. Yet no one can deny that his presence will be felt after he is no longer around to share his views and opinions.

Ralph's parents emigrated from Lebanon, settling in Winsted, Connecticut, where their five children were raised speaking both Arabic and English. Ralph, the youngest, was born on February 27, 1934. His parent owned a bakery-restaurant. Early on, Ralph's interests were fostered by political dinner-time discussions.

Ralph attended Princeton University on scholarship, challenging authorities even then about policy. He graduated magna cum laude and Phi Beta Kappa from the Woodrow Wilson's School of Public and International Affairs in 1955. Harvard Law School was his next endeavor. While there, he wrote for the *Harvard Law Record* and studied vehicle-related injury cases. He thought undue emphasis was placed on driver error, ignoring the role of car design. He earned his law degree in 1958 and served briefly in the U.S. Army. After traveling through Latin America, Europe, and Africa, Nader practiced law in Connecticut and lectured at the University of Hartford, while continuing to work locally on auto safety.

In 1963, Nader got a job in Washington, D.C., as a Labor Department consultant, in which he prepared a paper that called for the federal government to take responsibility for auto safety. Thus began what the media came to call his "David and Goliath battle" with the car industry. Nader campaigned for safety design changes (for example, seat belts, collapsible steering columns, stronger windshields, and padded dashboards) by writing articles and speaking before civic groups. He provided auto accident data to the Senate Government Operations Subcommittee.

Nader quit his job to write *Unsafe at Any Speed: The Designed-In Dangers of the American Automobile* (1965). This book indicted the automobile industry for choosing profits and styling over people and safety. Its dual-pronged appeal requested federal auto safety standards that would *prevent* accidents from happening and *protect* passengers when accidents did happen. The title came from the first chapter, "The Sporty Corvair: The One-Car Accident." Manufactured by General Motors' (GM) Chevrolet division, the Corvair was "unsafe at any speed," according to Nader. *Unsafe* set forth Nader's beliefs concerning public regulation of technology that would be his impetus to take on numerous other issues in decades to come. "A great problem of contemporary life," he wrote, "is how to control the power of economic interests which ignore the

Consumer advocate Ralph Nader speaks during an interview on September 10, 1975. Nader ran for U.S. president on the Green Party ticket in 1996 and 2000. (Library of Congress)

harmful effects of their applied science and technology" (Croft 1999).

Publicity generated by Nader's best seller assured passage of the National Traffic and Motor Vehicle Safety Act of 1966. National auto standards and the National Traffic Safety Administration (NTSA) were established. During Nader's crusade, GM harassed him with phone calls, hired a private detective to investigate him, and tried to lure him into a "compromising situation." GM's president eventually apologized when testifying at televised congressional hearings; Nader successfully sued GM for invasion of privacy and later used some of the $425,000 award to seed his other ventures.

Nader, now well known nationally, became larger than life; he was proof of an individual's ability to effect change. In August 1966, the *Washington Post* said of this feat, "The auto safety bill that the Congress will probably send to the President this week is a remarkable achievement... [A] one-man lobby for the public prevailed over the nation's most powerful industry" (*Washington Post* 1966, A18).

He helped pass the 1966 Freedom of Information Act. Next, his focus was on the 1967 Whole Meat Act, setting meatpacking plant guidelines. He helped establish the Occupational Safety and Heath Administration (OSHA) in 1970, which develops and enforces workplace safety and health regulations; that same year, he also supported creation of the Environmental Protection Agency (EPA).

In June 1968, Nader had recruited seven law students (all volunteers) to examine the Federal Trade Commission (FTC), charged with protecting consumers from dangerous and defective products, fraudulent business practices, and misleading advertising. They trolled the FTC's halls, discovering an agency "fat with cronyism, torpid through an inbreeding unusual even for Washington, manipulated by the agents of commercial predators, impervious to governmental and citizen monitoring." Their January 1969 report generated praise from Senator Albert Ribicoff: "Bureaucracy being what it is, I am fascinated by your ability to get in so deep, and get so much information. I am sure that you gentlemen are the envy of the large number of reporters here" (Center for the Study of Responsive Law web site).

In 1969, Nader set up an operational base, the Center for Study of Responsive Law, to expose corporate irresponsibility and government failure to regulate business. Two hundred new Raiders were chosen from a pool of 30,000 applicants in the second summer. Focus in succeeding years turned to corruption and incompetence at the Interstate Commerce Commission, health hazards of air pollution, and the Food and Drug Administration's lax oversight of the food industry. By the end of 1972, they had compiled 17 reports. Nader wanted the work to be inspirational examples of citizenship, asking rhetorically, "Can we diminish or lose our rights if we do not use them with some degree of constancy?" Nader thought his task forces were "a social innovation that will produce just and lasting benefits for the country as these young people generate new values and create new roles for their professions." Reinforcing the belief that a single person *could* make a difference in the world, he declared, "Almost every significant breakthrough has come from the spark, the drive, the initiative of one person. You must believe this" (Center for the Study of Responsive Law web site).

In 1971, Nader cofounded with fellow public interest lawyer Alan Morrison the organization Public Citizen, designed to protect consumers and to investigate corporations, Congress, and health, environmental, economic, and other issues. That year, he also founded the U.S. Public Interest Research Group (PIRG), an umbrella organization. The first PIRG was a D.C. law firm; other state PIRGs emerged in the early 1970s on college campuses across the country. Nader was influential in creating the Consumer Product Safety Commission (CPSC) in 1972. The next year, his books, *Consumer and Corporate Accountability* and *Corporate Power in America* (1973) were published.

He spent considerable time throughout the 1970s on ecology education. Often to great skepticism, he preached that American waterways were dangerously contaminated; yet, today, most of his "overly dire" predictions have proven true. He held "Critical Mass" conferences in 1974 and 1975 on atomic power, using the phrase "a technological Vietnam," helping to start a movement to shape global energy policy. In the 1970s and 1980s, Nader was prominent in the antinuclear movement. He organized a march on Washington, D.C., after the 1979 Three Mile Island nuclear reactor meltdown incident in Pennsylvania (Croft 1999).

His other accomplishments and involvements during these time periods include the creation of Nader-inspired groups such as s Congress Watch, the Center for Auto Safety, the National Insurance Consumer Organization, and the Health Research Group. He also published *Working on the System: A Comprehensive Manual for Citizen Access to Federal Agencies* (1974) and *Government Regulation: What Kind of Reform?* (1976).

The Reagan administration, which lasted from 1981 to 1989, viewed most government regulations as red tape that strangled business and damaged the economy. As a result, Nader's influence ebbed, although his efforts did not—he just did not receive much press coverage. However, as Jason Deparle wrote, "In 1988, [Nader] successfully campaigned to roll back California car insurance rates, then ignited public opinion to block a proposed 50 percent pay hike for members of Congress. Last year, Mr. Nader played a central role in passing a California initiative that rolled back the cost of auto insurance. He also led a successful, though bitter, fight against a proposal to raise Congressional pay by 51 percent; when he stepped up to the battered lectern this week, he was seeking the repeal of a smaller increase approved by the House of Representatives" (Deparle 1990).

In the 1980s and 1990s, he spoke up about the bank bailouts, objected to chlorinated fluorocarbons because of the danger they pose to the ozone layer, and worked against caps placed on damages consumers may recover from corporations. The latter was the first real chink in Nader's white-knight armor. He was the cover story of a September 1990 *Forbes* magazine accusing him of working with trial lawyers supporting Americans' right to sue. The article "derided him as 'Ralph Nader, Inc.,' a hypocritical and paranoid empire-builder" and charged that Nader received "an inordinate amount of his money from rich trial lawyers," according to Deparle. "Mr. Nader disputes those accusations ... He said the I.R.S. forms are on file ... contributions from trial lawyers represent less than one percent of his fund raising" (Deparle 1990).

In that same article, Deparle summed up Nader's life work, stating, "he has tried not just to reinvent the automobile but also to reinvent the nation's idea of democracy. Being interviewed for the article, Nader said, 'I want people to spend more time as public citizens. Otherwise they won't be able to enjoy their time as private citizens.' " A few years later, Nader's book *Collision Course: The Truth About Airline Safety* (1994), written with Wesley J. Smith, was released to criticism about the manner in which statistics were employed. In 1993, his efforts to stop the North American Free Trade Agreement failed. That fall, his name had a better association when his group, Public Citizen, offered $10,000 to any member of Congress who would read and answer 10 simple questions about the 500-page World Trade Organization (WTO) treaty. Colorado senator Hank Brown, a WTO supporter, took the bet and aced the quiz, donating his winnings to charity. He then announced that, having read the treaty, he was now compelled to vote against it (Mickey Z. 2005, 136).

Nader's name first arose as a potential presidential candidate in 1971, when he declined a bid from the New Party, a progressive Democratic Party split-off. He ran unsuccessfully in 1996 as a candidate for the Green Party, with Native American advocate and environmentalist Winona LaDuke as his vice presidential running mate. The Green Party emphasized environmentalism, nonhierarchical participatory democracy, social justice, respect for diversity, peace, and nonviolence. Nader and LaDuke ran again in 2000 with the campaign slogan "Not for Sale." His run was contentious, with Democrats accusing him of denying their candidate, Al Gore, of critical votes needed to beat Republican George W. Bush, who ultimately was awarded the title of president by the U.S. Supreme Court.

In the documentary *An Unreasonable Man* (2006), which traces his career, Nader explained that one of the main reasons he ran an active race in 2000 was due to his increasing inability to get his interests groups heard. He threw his hat in the presidential ring a third and fourth time in 2004 and 2008 as an independent to challenge the "two-party duopoly," which he sees as damaging democracy because in order to get on the ballot in 50 states, third parties must undergo time-consuming and expensive processes.

In 1990, *Life* magazine named Nader one of the 100 most influential Americans of the twentieth century (Deparle 1990). And, in 1999, a New York University panel of journalists ranked *Unsafe at Any Speed* 38th among the top 100 pieces of journalism of the twentieth century.

Asked in 1999 how he wanted to be remembered, Nader replied, "For helping strengthen democracy, for making raw power accountable and enhancing justice and the fulfillment of human possibilities" (Mickey Z. 2005, 89). Ever the activist, he had similarly said years earlier, "I just think that the striving for justice, when you spell it out, has to be seen as a source of pleasure" (Deparle 1990).

Margaret Gay

See also LaDuke, Winona

References

Barringer, Felicity. "MEDIA: Journalism's Greatest Hits: Two Lists of a Century's Top Stories." *New York Times*, March 1, 1999.

Croft, Karen. "Brilliant Careers: Citizen Nader." *Salon*, January 26, 1999. http://www.salon.com/bc/1999/01/26bc.html (accessed April 22, 2011).

Deparle, Jason. "Washington at Work: Eclipsed in the Reagan Decade, Ralph Nader Again Feels Glare of the Public." *New York Times*, September 21, 1990.

"History of the Center for Study of Responsive Law." *Center for the Study of Responsive Law Website*, 2009. http://www.csrl.org/about (accessed April 20, 2011).

Nader, Ralph. *Unsafe at Any Speed: The Designed-in Dangers of the American Automobile*. New York: Grossman Publishers, 1965.

Nader, Ralph, and Theodore Jacobs. "Do Third Parties Have a Chance? Ballot Access and Minority Parties." *Harvard Law Record*, October 9, 1958. http://www.facebook.com/topic.php?uid=2208102184&topic=1948 (accessed April 22, 2011).

Z., Mickey. *50 American Revolutions You're Not Supposed to Know: Reclaiming American Patriotism*. New York: The Disinformation Company, Ltd., 2005.

Norman, Mildred (1908–1981)

In the fall of 1952, Mildred Norman accomplished a significant milestone: she became the first women to ever hike the entire Appalachian Trail. She spent an entire five-month period living outdoors, while walking the 2,050 miles necessary to complete her journey. The experience gave her a sense of inner peace and inspired her to move on to what she felt was her ultimate purpose in life. Norman adopted the name "Peace Pilgrim" and began a 28-year walk across the United States, leaving behind all claims to any kind of personal identification. She was a dissident who rejected materialism and militarism, vowing to wander until humankind had learned the way of peace.

Mildred Lisette Norman was the oldest of three children born to Josephine and Ernest Norman on July 18, 1908, in Egg Harbor, New Jersey. She was raised on a poultry farm. Her father made his living as a carpenter, while her mother earned extra money as a tailor. The family was relatively poor, despite both parents' efforts. But the Normans were well regarded in the community of German immigrants. Their relatives had settled in the area, leaving Germany in 1855 to escape conflict and militarism. Mildred's parents subscribed to no particular religion but "instilled a strong peace ethic in their children, encouraging discussion of social, political, and moral questions" (Ware 2005, 564). Norman received no formal religious training as a child; in fact, her first view inside of a church was when she was 12 and peeked in to watch the janitors cleaning a Catholic cathedral. Four years later, she took her first steps inside a church to attend a wedding.

In high school, Norman began to ponder the question of God. On long walks with her dog, she contemplated the uncertainties of who and what God was. She observed trees, plants, stars, and nature around her. This communion helped her arrive at a belief in a "sustaining power.... When I reached confirmation from within I knew beyond all doubt that I had touched my highest light. Intellectually I touched God many times as truth and emotionally I touched God as love.... It came to me that God is a creative force, a motivating power, an over-all intelligence, an ever-present, all pervading spirit—which binds everything in the universe together and gives life to everything" (Peace Pilgrim 1992, 2).

At the same time, Norman also began to question many things that had been presented as accepted "givens" in her life. She had been led to believe that money and possessions would ensure a life of happiness and peace of mind. But, with personal experience, she learned that earning money and spending it foolishly was meaningless—she did not see much purpose in a life of making money just to spend it with little to show in return. Norman had also been raised to believe that, on one hand, she should be kind to others. On the other hand, she was also taught that it was honorable to maim and kill in war, if so ordered—indeed, people were even awarded medals for doing so. Such contradictory stances were confusing. Norman could never reconcile them, nor could she ever, at any time, believe there could ever be acceptable justification for hurting someone. Similarly, after being taught that unselfishness was a virtue, again it seemed contradictory to be expected to aggressively compete for one's share of worldly goods in order to be considered successful. Norman wrestled with these types of opposing ideologies for some time, eventually arriving at a personal moral stance.

In *Peace Pilgrim: Her Life and Work in Her Own Words*, a collection of her writings and recorded words, Norman recounts her life-turning point that took place during an all-night walk in the woods.

> I came to a moonlit glade and prayed. I felt a complete willingness, without any reservations, to give my life—to dedicate my life—to service. "Please use me!" I prayed to God. And a great peace came over me. I tell you it's a point of no return.... I began to live to give what I could, instead of to get what I could, and I entered a new and wonderful world. My life began to be meaningful. From that time on, I have known that my life work would be for peace—that it would cover the *whole peace picture*: peace among nations, peace among groups, peace among individuals, and the very, very important inner peace. However, there's a great deal of difference between being *willing* to give your life and actually *giving* your life, and for me fifteen years of preparation and inner seeking lay between. (Peace Pilgrim 1992, 7)

Norman's views on God and religion continued to deepen over her lifetime and are further elaborated upon in *Peace Pilgrim*. She explains that she is deeply religious but follows no specific doctrine. "One can become so attached to the outward symbols and structure of religion that one forgets its original intent—to bring one closer to God. We can only gain access to the Kingdom of God by realizing it dwells within us as well as in all humanity. Know that we are all cells in the ocean of infinity, each contributing to the others' welfare" (Peace Pilgrim 1992, 85). Through her words, she offered guidance and direction to those seeking spiritual, if not religious, growth and serenity, as well as a means of instilling a sense of meaning and purpose in their lives.

After her night in the woods, Norman began to adopt a life of austerity and simplicity, what she would call her 15-year period of preparation, not then aware of the purpose for which she was preparing. She did an assortment of volunteer work, assisting peace groups and helping individuals with physical, emotional, and mental problems. As the years passed, Norman says she found inner peace and, ultimately, her calling to be a "peace pilgrim." As defined by Norman:

A peace pilgrim prays and works for peace within and without. A peace pilgrim accepts the way of love as the way of peace, and to depart from the way of love is to depart from the way of a peace pilgrim. A peace pilgrim obeys God's laws and seeks God's guidance for one's life by being receptively silent. A peace pilgrim faces life squarely, solves its problems, and delves beneath its surface to discover its verities and realities. A peace pilgrim seeks not a multiplicity of material things, but a simplification of material well-being, with need level as the ultimate goal. A peace pilgrim purifies the bodily temple, the thoughts, the desires, the motives. A peace pilgrim relinquishes as quickly as possible self-will, the feeling of separateness, all attachments, all negative feelings. (Peace Pilgrim 1992, 125)

In 1952, Norman made plans to begin her journey. In her view, it was the right time. The United States was involved in a war in Korea, and U.S. senator Joseph McCarthy was in the midst of his campaign to expose communists who he claimed were infiltrating government, the military, and other institutions. Many Americans who were labeled as communists or communist sympathizers lost their careers, and some committed suicide.

Norman's pilgrimage began on January 1, 1953, in Pasadena, California, at the Tournament of Roses Parade. Her only possessions were the clothes on her back and the few items she carried in the pockets of her blue tunic: a comb, a folding toothbrush, a ballpoint pen, copies of her message, and her current correspondence. Her tunic read "PEACE PILGRIM" on the front and "Walking Coast to Coast for Peace" on the back. (Later on, the latter message would be switched out to read, "Walking 10,000 Miles for World Disarmament," "Walking 25,000 Miles for Peace," and finally, "25,000 On Foot for Peace.") Peace Pilgrim, as she was now calling herself, had no organizational backing. She carried no money and, from that day forward, would not ask for food or shelter—although she would accept it when offered. At the start of this pilgrimage, she took a vow to "remain a wanderer until mankind has learned the way of peace, walking until given shelter and fasting until given food" (Peace Pilgrim 1992, 181).

On that fateful first day of her long trek across the United States, with the courage of her convictions and without hesitation, the 44-year-old Norman joined the Tournament of Roses Parade. "I walked ahead along the line of march, talking to people and handing out peace messages, and noticing that the holiday spirit did not lessen the genuine interest in peace. When I had gone about half way a policeman put his hand on my shoulder and I thought he was going to tell me to get off the line of march. Instead he said, 'What we need is thousands like you' " (Peace Pilgrim 1992, 27).

In her early years as a pilgrim, few knew who she was, but she usually received food and shelter from strangers along the way. When no one took her in, she slept in wheat fields, haystacks, cemeteries, drainage ditches, and under bridges and by roadsides. Although many people thought she subjected herself to dangerous situations, she believed they were tests. She was arrested twice for vagrancy, but behind bars she found a receptive audience for her philosophy and songs.

On her trek, Peace Pilgrim carried three petitions. The first was a simple call to stop the killing in Korea. The second was a plea for a Peace Department in the U.S. government. The third appealed to the United Nations and world leaders, "to free us all from the crushing burden of armaments, to free us from hatred and fear, so that we may feed our hungry ones, mend our broken cities, and experience a richness of life which can only come in a world that is unarmed and fed" (Peace Pilgrim 1992, 28).

Along with being a walking messenger, Peace Pilgrim took on what would become her frequent role as a speaker. She spoke at universities and in alleyways, at truck stops and in ghettos, on city streets and on dusty roads. She addressed churches, radio audiences, high school assemblies, and reporters. If crowds did not seek her out, then she went looking for them. She had a message that she believed needed to be heard: "When enough of us find inner peace, our institutions will become more peaceful and there will be no more occasion for war" (Peace Pilgrim 1992, xi).

Peace Pilgrim reached her 25,000-mile goal in 1964. At that point, she stopped counting. She then made speaking engagements her top priority, although she continued to walk daily. Because of her increased speaking schedule, in the interest of expediency, Peace Pilgrim began to accept rides to get from one engagement to the next. And so it was—in a somewhat ironic twist of fate—that on July 7, 1981, while traveling near Knox, Indiana, Peace Pilgrim was killed in an auto accident.

At the time of her death, Peace Pilgrim was crossing the United States for the seventh time, having visited all 50 states at least once, even Alaska and Hawaii. She had been flown to the latter two states courtesy of a gentleman who had been eager to have her meet his children. Peace Pilgrim had also visited the 10 provinces in Canada as well as parts of Mexico.

After her death, Peace Pilgrim was cremated and her ashes were interred in a family plot near the city of her birth. Friends of Peace Pilgrim, a volunteer, nonprofit group, was formed to keep Peace Pilgrim's message alive. The organization is dedicated to making information about her life and words available to all who are interested. Five friends gathered after her death to organize a collection of her written and recorded words. *Peace Pilgrim: Her Life and Work in Her Own Words* has sold nearly half a million copies and is also available for free download on the Peace Pilgrim website. It can also be ordered there free of charge. The Friends have also put together an equally popular booklet, *Steps Toward Inner Peace: Harmonious Principles for Human Living*. The two publications have been distributed to more than 100 countries, with the former having been translated into 12 languages and the latter into over 20.

Peace Pilgrim was awarded the Peace Abbey Courage of Conscience Award posthumously in 1992. Her own words are a fitting tribute to Mildred Norman, who became Peace Pilgrim: "We must walk according to the highest light we have, encountering lovingly those who are out of harmony, and trying to inspire them toward a better way. Whenever you bring harmony into any unpeaceful situation, you contribute to the cause of peace. When you do something for world peace, peace among groups, peace among individuals, or your own inner peace, you improve the total peace picture" (Peace Pilgrim 1992, 109).

See also McCarthy, Joseph

References

Cousineau, Phil. *The Art of the Pilgrimage: The Seeker's Guide to Making Travel Sacred*. Berkeley, CA: Conari Press, 2000.

Friends of Peace Pilgrim. *Peace Pilgrim*. n.d. http://www.peacepilgrim.org (accessed October 11, 2010).

Peace Pilgrim. *Peace Pilgrim: Her Life and Work in Her Own Words*. Santa Fe, NM: Ocean Tree Books, 1992.

Peace Pilgrim, *Steps toward Inner Peace: Harmonious Principles for Human Living*. Santa Fe, NM: Ocean Tree Books, 1992.

Ware, Susan, and Stacy Brauhman, eds. *Notable American Women: A Biographical Dictionary, Volume 5: Completing the Twentieth Century*, Entry on Mildred Norman Ryder. Boston: Harvard University Press, 2005.

Ochs, Phil (1940–1976)

Folksinger and political activist Phil Ochs of the turbulent 1960s was described by John Poses as "the uncompromising patriot, the rebel with causes" (Rubiner 2006). When Ochs wrote and performed his signature protest song, *I Ain't Marching Anymore* (1965), American involvement in the Vietnam War was growing. Ochs pointed out in the lyrics that elders send the young to die in America's wars and wondered if any of it was worth it.

Philip David Ochs was born on December 19, 1940, in El Paso, Texas. He was the second child of Jacob (Jack) and Gertrude Phin Ochs. Phil's father was a New York–born doctor educated at the University of Edinburgh in Scotland. While in Scotland, he married Gertrude Phin, and the couple's daughter, Sonia (Sonny), was born in 1937. By the time they returned to New York City, the United States had entered World War II. Jacob was drafted into the army and served on the medical staff at army bases in New Mexico and Texas. After Phil's brother Michael was born in 1943, Jacob received his overseas orders and was shipped to England for additional training. He was then shipped to the front lines, taking part in the Battle of the Bulge. The major German defensive, taking place December 1944 to January 1945, was the largest and bloodiest battle of the war. The U.S. military suffered 70,000 to 89,000 casualties, including 19,000 killed in action. The experience left Jacob mentally compromised. Given an honorable discharge, Jacob was diagnosed with manic depression and spent the next two years in a mental institution. When he finally returned to his family, Jacob remained emotionally distant and at times displayed erratic behavior (Schumacher 1997). He was thereafter unable to maintain a medical practice.

Phil's childhood was defined by his father's mental disorder and chaotic behavior. His mother remained the one constant and became the primary support of her three children. In 1951, the family moved to upstate New York. Ochs found escape from the emotional upheaval of his home life in the movie theater. Because his mother worked, Ochs and his younger brother were often sent to see movies, as many as nine a week. His early childhood heroes became John Wayne and World War II hero-turned-actor Audie Murphy. Phil was drawn to books that featured strong heroes, and he enjoyed romantic tales. During this time, he was introduced to the dramatic elements of storytelling and the powerful use of imagery to convey a message, all of which would influence his music making in later years (Unterberger and Eder n.d.).

It was also during this time that Ochs was introduced to the clarinet, and was determined to have "an exceptional musical feeling" (Schumacher 1997, 24). By 1954, the family had moved to Columbus, Ohio, where Ochs continued to excel at the clarinet. By age 15, he was playing with the college orchestra, and at age 16, he was lead soloist at the Capital University Conservatory of Music.

Following a teenage prank, in which he shot himself in the foot, Ochs was sent to the Columbus Academy. However, the academy did not have a band, so in 1956, Ochs entered Staunton Military Academy in Virginia. During this time, he developed an interest in country music, which would later lead to his interest in folk music (Unterberger and Eder n.d.). Graduating in 1958, Ochs entered Ohio State University, deciding upon a career in journalism. His college roommate was Jim Glover, future peace activist and folksinger. The two became immediate friends. Glover introduced him to the protest tradition found in folksingers such as Woody Guthrie, Lee Hays, Pete Seeger, and the Weavers.

It was during this time that Ochs formed his political stance and began accompanying Glover to campus political rallies. Glover introduced Ochs to his father, the socialist Hugh Glover. The elder Glover proved influential to both young Ochs and Glover as the three often discussed politics. In fact, Ochs became very close to Hugh Glover, as noted by biographer Marc Elliot. Ochs looked to the elder Glover as the father he never had (Eliot 1989, 23).

Ochs soon began leading protests against mandatory Reserve Officers' Training Corps (ROTC). He became interested in the Cuban Revolution of 1959 and considered Fidel Castro and Latin American revolutionary leader Che Guevara as heroic as his childhood movie heroes. Ochs started writing for the college publication, the *Lantern*. His writings focused on radical themes. When school authorities blocked him from submitting further articles because of his leftist sentiments, he began publishing his own radical newspaper called the *Word*.

Glover also taught Ochs how to play the guitar. During the 1960 John Kennedy–Richard Nixon presidential election, the two friends made a bet as to who would win the election. Ochs won the bet, and the prize was Glover's guitar. The two formed a musical duo, calling themselves the Singing Socialists. Soon thereafter they changed their name to the Sundowners, playing in area clubs. The team was short-lived, however, as Glover moved to New York City to build a singing career on his own. Ochs and Glover remained longtime friends.

While still in college, Ochs continued playing in Cleveland area clubs, establishing his own singing career. He became the opening act for many musicians, including the Smothers Brothers and Bob Gibson. Gibson was a leading musician during the folk music revival in the late 1950s and early 1960s, and known for recognizing musical talent.

In 1961, Ochs became bitter when he was turned down as editor-in-chief at the college newspaper for being too controversial. He left college during his last semester, and followed Glover to New York City. Living with his friend in Greenwich Village, Ochs thrived in the bohemian setting. During the 1960s, the village was a leading center in the folk music scene. Ochs began writing songs for left-wing luminaries such as Tom Paxton, Joan Baez, and Dave Van Ronk. Rather than calling them protest songs, Ochs called them "topical" songs, and wrote about timely social issues that included segregation and civil rights, labor struggles, and antiwar songs. In fact, he wrote many of his songs based on stories he read in *Newsweek* (Schumacher 1997, 54).

In 1962, Ochs married Alice Skinner; Glover was his best man. Ochs started to display sharp mood swings, reminiscent of his father's disorder. Hinckley noted in his tribute, "When he was up, he was a force of nature. When he was down, he became a black hole" (Hinckley 1992). In a time when

Folk singer Phil Ochs poses in this undated 1960s publicity photo. Ochs led protests against the Vietnam War, and his album *I Ain't Marching Anymore* helped to establish Ochs as a leading protest singer/composer of the 1960s. (AP Photo)

little was understood about manic depression, the mood swings were dismissed as artistic temperament. Alice was unable, or unwilling, to cope with the mood swings. In 1965, Alice left Ochs and moved to California, taking with her their young daughter Meegan. While the couple remained separated, they never divorced. Already a heavy drinker, Ochs began taking an antidepressant medication to help him cope with the emotional duress.

By 1963, Ochs had become a contributing editor to *Broadside Magazine*, a topical song magazine, where he also published many of his political essays as well as his songs. Ochs also developed a friendly rivalry with Bob Dylan. As Mervis notes in his tribute, Ochs had once said, "I went to New York to become the best songwriter in the country and then I met Dylan and I decided I'd be the second best" (Mervis 2011). Dylan was considered the star of the folk scene (Rubiner 2006). Ochs, compared to Dylan, "was as bold and piercing in his use of language or song structure as Dylan, but his words sung in a voice that might've belonged to the boy next door, if you will, in middle America, had a quiet anger, outrage and irony that drove home their message as surely as Dylan's rough-hewn raspy declarations" (Unterberger and Eder n.d.).

The rivalry was exemplified by an incident in which Dylan threw Ochs out of his limousine after Ochs criticized Dylan's non-political song "Can I Please Crawl out Your Window?" Dylan is noted as telling Ochs, "You're not a folksinger. You're a journalist" (Schumacher 1997, 106).

Also in 1963, Ochs was invited to sing at the Newport Folk Festival in Rhode Island. He performed with fellow folk singers Joan Baez, Tom Paxton, and Bob Dylan. His patriotic anthem "Power and Glory" was received with a standing ovation. Ochs returned the following year. By this time, Ochs was achieving widespread attention. He released his first album, *All the News That's Fit to Sing* in 1964. *Rolling Stone* called the album "a manifesto of social urgency" (Rubiner 2006). His next album, *I Ain't Marching Anymore* helped to establish Ochs as the leading protest singer/composer of the 1960s. The lead song became the anthem for the anti–Vietnam War movement. Ochs described the song as bordering "between pacifism and treason, combining the best qualities of both" (Ochs 1965).

From 1965 to 1968, Ochs was at his peak. His third album, *Phil Ochs in Concert*, was his strongest success. Joan Baez's recording of his song "There but for Fortune" (1989), was nominated for a Grammy Award for Best Folk Recording. Following this, Ochs played to a sold-out audience at Carnegie Hall.

Ochs continued his involvement in the anti–Vietnam War movement. He organized two "War Is Over" rallies and toured folk festivals throughout the United States. He also continued to write and record songs on social commentary. His song "Outside a Small Circle of Friends" (1966), inspired by the murder of Kitty Genovese, became one of his most popular songs despite attempts by the Federal Communication Commission to ban the song because of references to smoking marijuana.

In 1968, Ochs supported Eugene McCarthy's bid for the Democratic presidential nomination. At the same time, he became involved in the Youth International Party (Yippies), a countercultural offshoot of the free speech and antiwar movements founded by Abbie Hoffman, Jerry Rubin, and others. Noted members of the Yippies included Allen Ginsberg, poet and leading figure of the Beat Generation, and Ed Saunders, social activist and environmentalist.

In 1968, Ochs accompanied the Yippies to the Democratic National Convention in Chicago. The Yippies joined other organizations, such as Students for a Democratic Society, to protest against the war. Denied permits to demonstrate legally, Ochs, Rubin, and others held their own presidential nominations, using a live pig named Pigasus as the satiric candidate for president. The demonstration turned violent as 10,000 protesters clashed with 23,000 policemen and National Guardsmen. After the riot, Rubin and others, together known as the Chicago Eight (and later the Chicago Seven), were charged with conspiracy and incitement to riot. Ochs testified for their defense at their trial.

Following the Chicago riot, Ochs became disillusioned, and his mood swings deepened. He struggled with intense writer's block. While he continued to perform live, he did not make more recordings. His mental capacity continued to deteriorate over the next few years. In 1972, Ochs was mugged while traveling in Tanzania. His vocal chords were severely and irreparably damaged. The experience intensified his growing depression. In one of his last appearances, Ochs celebrated the end of the Vietnam War in 1975, performing in a final War Is Over rally. Ochs and Baez sang a duet of "There But For Fortune." He closed the rally with his song "The War Is Over." In 1976, Ochs moved in with his sister Sonny in New York, where he was diagnosed with bipolar disorder. On April 9, 1976, Ochs hanged himself.

On April 29, 1976, congresswoman and activist Bella Abzug, who had spoken at the final War Is Over rally, entered a statement into the *Congressional Record*. As quoted in Schumacher, Abzug noted: "Phil Ochs' poetic pronouncements were part of a larger effort to galvanize his generation into taking action to prevent war, racism, and poverty. He left us a legacy of important songs that continue to be relevant" (Schumacher 1977, 355).

Bobbi Miller

See also Abzug, Bella; Hoffman, Abbie; Seeger, Pete

References

Baker, Bob. "Tracing the Arc of a Tragic Folk Singer." *New York Times*, December 22, 2010. http://www.nytimes.com/2010/12/26/movies/26ochs.html?_r=1 (accessed March 10, 2011).

Eliot, Marc. *Death of a Rebel: A Biography of Phil Ochs*. New York: Franklin Watts, 1989. First published 1979.

Hinckley, David. "Phil Ochs: Green Leaves of Summer." *New York Daily News*, December 13, 1992. http://www.nydailynews.com/archives/news/1999/12/13/1999-12-13_phi_ochs_green_leaves_of_su.html (accessed March 10, 2011).

Mervis, Scott. "Documentary Traces Troubled Life of Committed Protest Singer Phil Ochs." *Pittsburgh Post-Gazette*, March 3, 2011. http://www.post-gazette.com/pg/11062/1129118-388.stm (accessed March 10, 2011).

Ochs, Phil. Album Notes for *I Ain't Marching Anymore*. Elektra, 1965.

"Phil Ochs: The Life and Legacy of a Legendary American Folk Singer" (transcript). *Democracy Now!* January 6, 2011. http://www.democracynow.org/2011/1/6/phil_ochs_the_life_and_legacy (accessed March 10, 2011).

Rubiner, Megan, and Michael L. LaBlanc, eds. "Ochs, Phil." *Contemporary Musicians*. Gale Cengage, 1992. *eNotes.com*, 2006. http://www.enotes.com/contemporary-musicians/ochs-phil-biography (accessed March 8, 2011).

Schumacher, Michael. *There but for Fortune: The Life of Phil Ochs*. New York: Hyperion Books, 1997.

Unterberger, Richie, and Bruce Eder. "Phil Ochs on MSN Music." *All Music Guide*, n.d. http://music.msn.com/music/artist-biography/phil-ochs/ (accessed March 9, 2011).

Wilton, Tim. "Here's to the Life of Phil Ochs." *Special Stories*, Texas Heritage Music Foundation, n.d. http://www.texasheritagemusic.org/special_stories/Texas_Stories/Phil%20Ochs.pdf (accessed March 8, 2011).

O'Hair, Madalyn Murray (1919–1995)

It may be hard to imagine that the "most hated woman in America" celebrated her headline-grabbing status on a 1964 cover of *Life* magazine. Madalyn Murray O'Hair had loudly maintained her truth in the news, in the courts, and in your face if someone had the audacity to challenge her on the righteousness of her path. By the time her picture appeared on the cover of *Life*, she had achieved the goal of an almost single-handed effort over three years to end prayer in public schools. In a country where 90 percent of the citizens claim a belief in a supreme being, her victory in the U.S. Supreme Court case known as *Murray v. Curtlett* (1963) shocked the nation and restructured the daily religious landscape. That anyone would have the power to end a practice and deny a belief system so engrained in the American psyche since before its founding was simply abhorrent.

Madalyn Murray (later O'Hair) knew that the U.S. founders had called for separation of church and state, and she would simply not be silenced about the value of atheism and her distain for the hypocritical morality that gave the holier-than-thou their power. She called them Christers, and she made fun of religious belief and practice wherever and whenever she could. She complained bitterly about the reprisal she experienced at the hands of true believers, but she would spend the next 30 years of her life never giving an inch.

It is important to recall just how basic the idea of God was to the political and social fabric of the United States in these days of intense Cold War hysteria. The Soviet Union was the "evil empire" that banned religion and purported to be an atheist state. Communists were around every corner, hiding in plain sight, ready to spread their godless credo to the unsuspecting. Attitudes about God in the United States in the 1950s could be summed up generally as "God is on our side. Communists can only win if Americans lose their faith."

O'Hair's crusade incurred the wrath of a great swath of the American public by challenging the tradition of honoring God in public school classrooms. After all, the U.S. Congress had adopted the motto In God We Trust in 1956 and required all U.S.

Madalyn Murray O'Hair, of Austin, Texas, was head of the Society of Separationists and the American Atheist Corporation. She appears here on a radio talk show in Dallas, Texas, on February 1, 1975. (AP Photo)

coins to include the statement in 1955. The Pledge of Allegiance saw the addition of the phrase, "under God," a year earlier than that. But this woman could simply not allow her truth to rest.

Madalyn Mays was born on April 13, 1919, in Pittsburgh, Pennsylvania. Her parents Lena Scholle and John "Irv" Mays baptized her in the Presbyterian faith. The family moved to Rossfield, Ohio, and that is where the young Madalyn graduated from high school in 1937. She was bright and outgoing. But because of her family's hardscrabble economic condition, there were only two books in her household: the Bible and a dictionary. She did not even have access to a library. When she was 12 or 13, she explained that she reached the "age of intellectual discretion" with the help of one of the resources she could lay her hands on: the Bible. She noted in an interview:

> I picked up the Bible and read it from cover to cover one weekend—just as if it were a novel—very rapidly, and I've never gotten over the shock of it. The miracles, the inconsistencies, the improbabilities, the impossibilities, the wretched history, the sordid sex, the sadism in it—the whole thing shocked me profoundly. I remember I looked in the kitchen at my mother and father and I thought: Can they really believe in all that? ... Later, when I started going to church, my first memories are of the minister getting up and accusing us of being full of sin, though he didn't say why; then they would pass the collection plate, and I got it in my mind that this had to do with purification of the soul, that we were being invited to buy expiation from our sins. So I gave it all up. It was too nonsensical. (Tregaskis 1965)

She completed her bachelor's degree at Ashland University, a religiously oriented Brethren College that required two years of Bible study for graduation. She told about how she relished the opportunity to study the Old Testament one year and then the New Testament the next, even though she believed almost nothing of the text. She was proud of her ability to score, because, through these studies, she understood a simple fact of religious dogma. If they were teaching that the devil was a guy in red suit with a pitchfork and forked tail, then that is what she wrote on the test. A perfect score would come from parroting even the most absurd ideas.

Her goal was to keep up with the narratives and the particulars of religious thought so that she would be in better position to repudiate the thinking. She remained inquisitive about the use of the gospels in American society and continued to study the Bible and religious doctrine for many years after her graduation from Ashland University.

In the beginning, and especially at college, Madalyn was always hard-pressed to find any writings that supported, or even spoke to an antireligious point of view. She had read about the famed lawyer Clarence Darrow (1857–1938), who was a nonbeliever. But she did not even know the word *atheist* until she was 24 years old. She was having a philosophical discussion with friends when someone called her an atheist. This was a revelation that thrilled her. She eventually came to understand that there was a substantial body of work in humanist philosophy and that a nonbeliever reality was a well-defined alternative view in some parts of the world since the beginning of history.

Madalyn joined the military after the United States entered the Second World War. Even though she had married a man named John Roth in 1941, they had both decided to separate to join the war effort. He went into the Marines, and she left for a cryptography posting in Italy as a WAC—the Women's Army Corps. In a very short time, Madalyn Mays had developed a romantic relationship with a married officer assigned to the same area, William "Bill" Murray. She became pregnant, but he was a practicing Catholic and would not divorce his wife. Madalyn did, however, divorce her husband John, took the last name Murray regardless of the father's situation, and named her son Bill Murray.

By the early 1950s Murray was living in Baltimore, raising her son, and chafing at the confinement of gender-driven expectations and puritanical hypocrisy. She found herself "fighting for a place in an oppressively conventional age." With her level of education and the expectations raised from her European experiences, she was hard-pressed to find her next act in conservative America. She drifted into the study of law and received a degree from South Texas School of Law in 1952. She never practiced as an attorney, however, as she failed the bar exam.

In the meantime, she worked at a variety of jobs in Baltimore, lasting no more than a month or two at any one firm before she had alienated coworkers, management, and ownership. She was fired often during this time period. She also became pregnant once again as a result of a relationship with boyfriend Michael Fiorillo. Her second son, John Garth Murray, was born in November 1954.

Living with her parents was an added pressure, and they fought all of the time. She became very dissatisfied with her life and her future prospects, as professor Bryan Le Beau, an expert on religion in the United States, says of Madalyn at this time: "Things begin to fall apart for her and she begins to write in her diary about, very honestly, about her failings; having two children out of wedlock, unable to keep a job. She says I've just made some bad choices, bad decisions and I'm paying the price for it" (*Godless in America*).

Madalyn became so depressed that she wrote about the possibility of suicide in that diary. And she eventually developed the idea that maybe she should defect to the Soviet Union. She packed up her two boys and boarded a ship for Europe. She arrived at the Soviet embassy in Paris, France, and asked for asylum for her and her family. The Soviets refused her request, and in 1960, she was back living with her parents in Baltimore once again. She went to work for the Baltimore public welfare department as a supervising psychiatric social worker. But this was not the career that would come to define her life.

She had enrolled her son Bill in a public school upon her return to the United States, and one day in the autumn of 1960, she came upon a classroom where students were reciting a prayer, en masse, as part of their daily routine. Madalyn Murray became incensed by the manner in which religion was being institutionalized in the school and many aspects of American life. She took the establishment clause (interpreted as the separation of church and state) of the First Amendment of the U.S. Constitution seriously and decided to make the elimination of prayer in schools her crusade. But that decision was hardly a simple one. She was, in fact, motivated by her son, who as a teenager had declared himself an atheist and did not understand why he was forced to say prayers. He challenged his mother to stand up for her beliefs as well as his, and Murray began the lawsuit that resulted in the Supreme Court ruling that banned prayer in public schools.

That decision rocketed Madalyn Murray O'Hair into the public sphere. She saw an opportunity to leverage her work against school prayer by following up with the establishment of American Atheists. Based in Austin, Texas, the national organization and movement defended the civil rights of nonbelievers. Madalyn used this platform to publish the first of her 25 books on atheism. She also acted as the chief executive officer of the nonprofit group, and for the first time in her life, she was able to accumulate some wealth. By all accounts, she was an almost tyrannical leader of the organization, excommunicating (her term) members for perceived slights or petty disagreements. Yet she married again, this time to Richard O'Hair. The couple separated, but Madalyn remained married until Richard died in 1978.

The 1960s and early 1970s were a time of upheaval in the United States, and O'Hair caught that wave. She went on talk shows and spoke on college campuses or wherever people would provide her with a forum for her views. She took on the role of what she herself called "*The* Atheist" so that others could learn that there were alternatives to the Christian-centered point of view that was the de facto structure for the country she saw around her. She continued to fight the legislative battle as well, filing suits to have the motto In God We Trust from coins. She championed abortion and masturbation. She took every opportunity to be as outrageous and unapologetic as possible. In the end, she lived every minute of her public persona as the most hated woman in America for decades.

O'Hair's enemies in government, in the public arena, in the churches, and even within the atheist movement were legion. She was arrested or under threat of arrest often. Her life was threatened, and the safety of her children was always in question. And in the end, August 27, 1995, the 76-year-old O'Hair, her son John Garth, and her granddaughter Robin met an almost predictable fate. Unknown to anyone at the time, a former employee of the organization abducted the family from their offices at American Atheists. After extorting hundreds of thousands of dollars from O'Hair, he killed them all and buried their remains in the desert near Austin, Texas. For years, the public was left to speculate about the whereabouts of the famous rabble-rouser. Many were certain that the three had conspired to make off with the funds of the nonprofit.

Law enforcement did not spend a great deal of time on the disappearances until a reporter started looking into the case. Eventually, it was discovered that O'Hair had written a very scathing criticism of this former employee, David Waters, in the American Atheist newsletter. She had just discovered that Waters was a convicted felon and had stolen $54,000 from the American Atheists.

The investigation turned on Waters, who eventually admitted to killing the O'Hair family. He led them to the shallow grave in January 2001.

O'Hair's legacy is an important turning point in the way the United States of a particular generation came to see itself. Her effort on behalf of the Constitution over the beliefs of nearly everyone in the country was a remarkable feat and a most disruptive influence in a very disruptive era. It is hard not to conclude that O'Hair was happy in her role. She was asked in a 1966 interview by *The Freedom Writer* how she would like to be remembered. O'Hair responded: "I just want three words on my tombstone, if I have one. I'll probably be cremated. One is 'woman.' I'm very comfortable in that role. I've loved being a woman, I've loved being a mother, I've loved being a grandmother. I want three words: Woman, Atheist, Anarchist. That's me."

Martin K. Gay

See also Darrow, Clarence

References

Godless in America (documentary), dir. Leslie Woodhead, 2006.

Le Beau, Bryan F. *The Atheist: Madalyn Murray O'Hair.* New York and London: New York University Press, 2003.

"O'Hair on Church and State." *The Freedom Writer*, March–April–May 1989. http://www.publiceye.org/ifas/fw/8903/ohair.html (accessed January 11, 2011).

Tregaskis, Richard. "Madalyn Murray Interview." *Playboy*, October 1965. http://www.positiveatheism.org/hist/madplay.htm (accessed January 11, 2011).

O'Keefe, James (1984–)

James O'Keefe is a politically conservative activist and videographer, infamous for his controversial undercover videos that have injured the public relations of left-leaning, publicly funded organizations such as ACORN, Planned Parenthood, and National Public Radio. A self-described citizen journalist muckraker, O'Keefe's subversive methods have captured extensive media coverage and have garnered praise from admirers who think he plays an important role in unearthing institutionalized corruption, and censure from critics who admonish his methods as deceitful and at times fabricated.

James O'Keefe III was born on June 28, 1984, and grew up in Bergen County, New Jersey. His father, James O'Keefe Jr., works as a materials engineer, and his mother, Deborah O'Keefe, a physical therapist. The couple has one other child, James's younger sister, who is a painter and sculptor. James's father described the household environment that James and his sister grew up in as moderately conservative. O'Keefe attended Westwood High School in New Jersey, where he was involved in theater, Eagle Scouts, and journalism. He went to college at Rutgers University, where he earned a degree in philosophy. He also participated in journalistic endeavors, contributing a biweekly column for one student newspaper, the *Daily Targum*, until he founded his own conservative student newspaper in 2004, called the *Rutgers Centurion*.

O'Keefe described the *Rutgers Centurion* as the "Journal of Conservative thought at Rutgers University," with the purpose of counterbalancing the liberalism of the Rutgers academic atmosphere. His efforts were sponsored both financially and influentially by the Leadership Institute (LI), a nonprofit devoted to training and instilling conservative activists in the realms of media, politics, and public policy. In the inaugural issue, published on November 1, 2004,

O'Keefe addressed his complaints about what he saw as a lack of political balance in the U.S. academic community and the intended purpose of the newspaper to close that gap:

> Why, in a country that is at least half conservative, do we not have this ratio represented in higher learning? ... There is nothing academic about an ideological majority. There is nothing liberal about a monopoly of thought, nothing enlightening about blatant partisan endorsement, and nothing equitable about discriminating against conservative students and professors because their beliefs are different than your own. Rutgers is a diverse research university with a goal not only to represent the citizens of New Jersey, but views and theories from all over the country and the world. ... Let us rock the foundations of academia and challenge the thrones that have for too long indoctrinated us about our world and the context in which we live. (O'Keefe 2004)

Much of O'Keefe's frustration stemmed directly from seeing political endorsements tacked onto Rutgers professors' office doors. In fact, this frustration inspired his first act of video journalism, in which he video interviewed a professor on the propriety of his political advertising.

O'Keefe's next video escapade, this time with a hidden camera, occurred months later. In a satirical ploy to poke fun at what O'Keefe saw as hyper-political correctness on the campus, the journalist posed with three other *Centurion* staff members pretending to be from the fictional Irish Heritage Foundation and taking offense to the Rutgers cafeteria's inventory of Lucky Charms cereal, claiming the branding of the cereal stereotyped Irish Americans. In the video with a university official, which is posted on YouTube, O'Keefe declares that the leprechaun depicted on the cereal box is "portrayed as a little green-cladded gnome ... and we think this undermines the importance and sincerity of St. Patrick's day" ("Banning Lucky Charms at Rutgers" 2009). Although the university representative assured the students their concerns would be considered, Lucky Charms remained.

After graduating from Rutgers in 2006, O'Keefe went to work for the LI in Arlington, Virginia. His duties entailed visiting colleges throughout the United States to recruit and train students about establishing student newspapers, much as the LI had done with him. However, the LI's founder, Morton Blackwell, asked O'Keefe to leave after about a year, citing that his growing enthusiasm for exposing liberals via hidden cameras and identity disguises could potentially threaten the nonprofit status of the organization, which could not be linked to influencing legislation in order to retain tax exemption.

Although espousing antigovernment, free-market views that are typically viewed as principal tenets of conservatism, O'Keefe asserted himself to the *New York Times* as a "progressive radical" who wants to change the status quo. He attributed British writer G. K. Chesterton as one of his primary intellectual influences. O'Keefe was also persuaded by leftist leader Saul Alinsky's "Rules for Radicals," taking its rule "make the enemy live up to its own book of rules" as his cornerstone to use back at the very ideology that propagated it.

O'Keefe's next muckraking hustle captured intensive media attention nationwide. While attending a year of law school at the University of California, Los Angeles (UCLA) from 2006 to 2007, O'Keefe joined with fellow UCLA student Lila Rose in an exposé of Planned Parenthood. O'Keefe planned the operation, which involved Rose, a pro-life activist, posing as an underage pregnant teenager needing an abortion and visiting various Planned Parenthood clinics for advice. They filmed seven of the meetings at different Planned Parenthood branches across the country. In several of the meetings, the organization's workers failed to report the statutory rape involved after Rose claimed the father of her child was over 18 years of age, some of them even suggesting that Rose lie about her and the father's age so she could legally secure an abortion. O'Keefe also recorded some questionable tactics by Planned Parenthood employees over telephone calls. Pretending to be interested in contributing a donation to the organization, O'Keefe requested if he could specify that his funds be applied only to abortions of minority patients, and in seven states, the clinics said they would accept his funds.

The videos and recordings, posted on YouTube and Rose's organization's web site Live Action, quickly spread through the news cycle, adding even more controversy to the already heated debate over the federally funded organization that applies tax dollars to abortions. The organization apologized for its employees accepting racially motivated donations and ensured the public that such actions violated company policies. However, many antiabortion and African American organizations demanded that Congress reconsider funding the organization as a result of the video footage, and some even claimed that Planned Parenthood was participating in genocide against minorities.

Two years later, in 2009, O'Keefe, in what became his most notorious sting operation, unearthed corruption in the Association of Community Organizations for Reform Now (ACORN), a semipublicly funded collection of nonprofit organizations that sought to address community issues—such as housing, discrimination, and government aid—for low- to moderate-income people through local means. Undercover as a pimp with one of his prostitutes, O'Keefe and conservative cohort Hannah Giles secretly filmed meetings with ACORN counselors in eight different U.S. cities in which they asked for advice on certain illegal activities, including tax evasion, human trafficking, and child prostitution. In September 2009, the duo published edited versions of the videos, which depicted some ACORN employees giving advice on how to succeed in these illegal ventures. A Washington, D.C., ACORN counselor, who was subsequently fired after the video was released, was recorded encouraging the faux prostitute and pimp to conceal the former's profession on her house application and tax returns: "She's not going to put [on the loan application] that she's doing prostitution ... she doesn't have to. You don't have to sit back and tell people what you do" (Beh 2009). Another employee in San Diego offered assistance in smuggling in child sex slaves from El Salvador.

The videos were widely disseminated through conservative news outlets, originating at Fox News and BigGovernment.com. They sparked public outrage, especially among Republicans and other conservatives who had previously accused the organization of fraud and vote-mongering. They also significantly damaged ACORN's reputation. Shortly after their release, Congress voted to eliminate any funding for the organization, and the U.S. Census Bureau cut its working ties with the group.

ACORN responded by firing the employees who engaged in advising the illegal motives of the posing muckrakers and also suspended some of its advising operations while it conducted an internal investigation.

Several other investigations of ACORN were initiated by state attorneys general and the U.S. Government Accountability Office. All the investigations uniformly concluded that the videos had been substantially edited to the point of misconstruing the remarks of the ACORN employees; therefore, no criminal charges were sought after, and ACORN was simply reprimanded for poor management of some of its low-level employees. However, the videos' damage to ACORN's credibility wrecked the organization's funding, and it filed for bankruptcy on November 2010.

O'Keefe quickly made headlines again in January 2010, after getting arrested on charges of entering a federal building on false pretenses. Along with three other conservative activists, O'Keefe pretended to be a telephone repairman in order to get into the federal building housing Louisiana Democratic senator Mary Landrieu's office. In an interview with Fox News's Sean Hannity, O'Keefe related his motives for the incident, saying that the senator's constituents had complained about not being able to reach her by phone after she voted in favor of President Barack Obama's health care reform bill. Although Landrieu insisted her phone lines were jammed, O'Keefe said that this excuse was "troubling" because he believed the senator had received millions of dollars for her health care vote and that he and his associates "wanted to get to the bottom of the fact—of the claim that she was not answering her phones or phones were jammed" ("James O'Keefe Gives First Interview Since Arrest" 2010).

Many news reports suggested that O'Keefe had intentions of tapping the senator's phones, which would be a felony. O'Keefe, however, denied having any such intentions but did admit that in the future that "while I continue to do sort of undercover videos I have to be a little more careful, a little more thoughtful" ("James O'Keefe Gives First Interview Since Arrest" 2010). In court, a district judge eventually reduced O'Keefe's charges to a single misdemeanor count, and he was sentenced to probation, community service hours, and a $1,500 fine.

The somewhat negative publicity surrounding O'Keefe's attempt to target Senator Landrieu—as many began to more outspokenly critique his methods following his arrest—did not stop him from performing two other major controversial stunts, one involving the New Jersey Teachers Union, and the other National Public Radio (NPR). The former stunt occurred in late 2010, at a time when the nation was in heightened debate over public pensions and other benefits of government employees. In October of that year, O'Keefe posted a series of videos he titled "Teachers Unions Gone Wild" on his BigGovernment.com web site. The videos focused on members of the New Jersey Education Association (NJEA). O'Keefe and other undercover journalists recorded teachers bragging about tenure, a superintendent admitting that a teacher who had supposedly racially slurred a student would not get fired but only demoted, and NJEA associate director Wayne Dibofsky flippantly discussing voter fraud in a 1997 mayoral election in the state, stoking preexisting suspicions about much-ingrained voting corruption in the state. The videos angered New Jersey governor Chris Christie and added more fuel to his efforts to reform education in the state, but many in the teachers union decried the footage as staged and heavily edited.

In the other incident with NPR, O'Keefe published a video on March 8, 2011, in which two of his cohorts, purporting to be affiliated with the Muslim Brotherhood, met with NPR's senior vice president for development Ron Schiller to discuss their desire to donate millions to the public radio organization. The edited video quotes Schiller as saying "The current Republican Party is not really the Republican Party. It's been hijacked by this group [the Tea Party movement] ... that is Islamaphobic, but really xenophobic ... they're seriously racist, racist people" (Rovzar 2011). Schiller also made remarks that NPR would be better off without funding from the government in the long run. Congressional Republicans, already pressing for the defunding of NPR in order to reduce the national debt and deficit, pointed to Schiller's comments as additional proof that the organization should not be paid for with any taxpayer dollars.

NPR quickly publicly apologized for Schiller's comments and sent him on administrative leave. In addition, the incident provoked the resignation of president and CEO Vivian Schiller (no relation to Ron Schiller) in a company effort to show accountability to the public. However, much like many of his other interviews, after more extensive review of O'Keefe's edited video compared to the raw footage, some political activists and journalists decried his work as a setup, misconstrued to make a political stab.

Despite the controversy over his work, O'Keefe remains a staunch defender of his journalistic methods. In an April 2011 address to a crowd of Tea Party pundits, O'Keefe encouraged the attendees to participate in similar investigations: "Anyone who is abusing the trust of our people needs to be investigated ... It's a movement to expose hypocrisy" (Gibson 2011). He continues to promote investigative journalism to expose misconduct in both public and private entities through his company and web site, Project Veritas.

ABC-CLIO

References

"Banning Lucky Charms at Rutgers." YouTube video, 3:40, posted by "RUCenturion," May 3, 2009. http://www.youtube.com/watch?v=Qh3WUnFiEJ4.

Beh, Asha. " 'Pimp Sting' Taints ACORN, Obama Supporters." NBC Washington, September 11, 2009. http://www.nbcwashington.com/news/local/Pimp-Sting-Taints-ACORN-Obama-Supporters-59069402.html (accessed August 24, 2011).

Big Government.com [Andrew Breitbart Presents Big Government]. 2011. http://biggovernment.com/author/jokeefe/ (accessed August 24, 2011).

Gibson, Ginger. "N.J. Activist James O'Keefe Encourages Tea Party Members in East Windsor to Conduct Investigations." NJ.com, April 16, 2011. http://www.nj.com/news/index.ssf/2011/04/nj_activist_james_okeefe_tells.html (accessed August 24, 2011).

"James O'Keefe Gives First Interview Since Arrest" (transcript). Fox News, February 2, 2010. http://www.foxnews.com/story/0,2933,584563,00.html (accessed August 24, 2011).

O'Keefe, James. "Inaugural Issue: What Is Conservatism?" *Rutgers Centurion*, November 1, 2004. http://rucenturion.com/archive/centurion_inaugural.pdf (accessed September 18, 2011).

Project Veritas. http://theprojectveritas.com (accessed August 24, 2011).

Rovzar, Chris. "The Inevitable Backlash against James O'Keefe's Heavily Edited NPR 'Sting' Begins." *New York*, March 14, 2011. http://nymag.com/daily/intel/2011/03/the_inevitable_backlash_agains.html (accessed August 24, 2011).

Shepard, Alicia. "On the Media Interviews: James O'Keefe III." National Public Radio, March 24, 2011. http://www.npr.org/blogs/ombudsman/2011/03/24/134808849/on-the-media-interviews-james-okeefe-iii (accessed August 24, 2011).

"Times Topics: James O'Keefe." *New York Times*, updated May 27, 2011. http://topics.nytimes.com/top/reference/timestopics/people/o/james_okeefe/index.html (accessed August 24, 2011).

"UCLA Student Sting Exposes Racism at Planned Parenthood." Catholic News Agency, February 28, 2008. http://www.catholicnewsagency.com/news/ucla_student_sting_exposes_racism_at_planned_parenthood (accessed August 24, 2011).

U.S. Department of Justice. "Four Men Arrested for Entering Government Property Under False Pretenses for the Purpose of Committing a Felony." News release, January 26, 2010. http://neworleans.fbi.gov/dojpressrel/pressrel10/no012610.htm (accessed August 24, 2011).

Zamost, Scott. "Fake Pimp from ACORN Videos Tries to 'Punk' CNN Correspondent." CNN, September 29, 2010. http://www.cnn.com/2010/US/09/29/okeefe.cnn.prank/index.html (accessed August 24, 2011).

Oppenheimer, J. Robert (1904–1967)

The United States tested its first atomic bomb in a desert near Alamogordo, New Mexico, on July 16, 1945. Upon seeing the huge explosion and the massive mushroom cloud it created, J. Robert Oppenheimer, the developer of the bomb, remarked: "I am become death, the shatterer of worlds." He was quoting from the *Bhagavad Gita* (Bird and Sherwin 2006, 309).

J. Robert Oppenheimer was born April 22, 1904, in New York City into a family of German Jewish descent. His father, Julius, was a German immigrant who arrived in New York City in 1888. He was penniless, but because several relatives had preceded him and already had established businesses in the men's clothing industry, he was given immediate employment. He soon acquired what was great wealth for that era.

Robert's mother was Ella Friedman, a woman of Bavarian Jewish descent and a painter who taught art. She and Julius had another son, Lewis Frank, born in 1908, but he died soon after birth from a congenital abnormality. After the death of Lewis, Ella feared germs and illnesses and became very protective of Robert. She kept him close and severely restricted his life.

As he grew up, Robert became absorbed with his interest in science, and his parents encouraged him to pursue anything that interested him. He also enjoyed reading and writing poetry. The activities of children his own age had little appeal, and he appeared shy and introverted.

In 1912, when Robert was eight years old, his brother Frank Friedman, was born. Both children were pampered by their parents and had only to ask and they would be given what they wanted. The family had several maids and a chauffeur to cater to their wishes. In later years, Robert admitted that he was not easy to get along with as he developed a huge ego.

The Oppenheimers did not follow the Jewish religion. Instead they belonged to "an offshoot of Judaism—the Ethical Cultural Society—that celebrated rationalism and a progressive brand of secular humanism" (Bird and Sherwin 2006, 9). The society sought to foster social justice and humanitarianism and ran a private school at New York's Central Park West, where Robert received his elementary and secondary educations, instilling in him the knowledge that he had a responsibility to help reform the world and to live ethically.

From an early age, Robert was a brilliant student. By the age of 10, he was studying physics and chemistry. He skipped several grades and found it difficult to have conversations with children his own age as they had little in common. His knowledge was way beyond them, and they bored him. He met with a lot of bullying and was brutally mistreated the one time his parents sent him to a summer camp.

Several of Robert's teachers were in awe of his intellect and became his personal friends and tutors. In his junior year of high school, he took physics and became a close friend of the teacher, Augustus Klock, who taught him chemistry and opened up the fascinating world of science to Robert.

In September 1922, Robert entered Harvard University. He is remembered as being shy, studious, awkward, and eccentric. A few old friends from the Cultural Society also attended at the same time, but he made few new friends. He was depressed at times and would shut everyone out or just pass out. He took an electric heating pad to bed each night at college. At times, he walked for miles talking all the while about some physics problem. Friends said he appeared to be "wrestling in these years with inner demons" (Bird and Sherwin 2006, 36). He also was found "lying on the floor, groaning and rolling from side to side" (Bird and Sherwin 2006, 43). His family arranged for counseling but to no avail, as he was more intelligent than the counselors. In spite of his "inner demons," he graduated from Harvard summa cum laude in 1925, after three years of study, with a bachelor's degree in chemistry.

After graduation, Oppenheimer decided that his future lay in physics, and he wanted to go to Cambridge in England to study under the renowned physicist Ernest Rutherford. Rutherford, however, declined to become his tutor. Later, J. J. Thomson, former director of Cavendish Laboratory at Cambridge and semiretired, agreed to supervise his studies. He met the leading physicists of the day, among them Patrick Blackett (Nobel Prize winner for physics in 1948), who became one of his tutors.

After Cambridge, Oppenheimer studied at Göttingen in Germany. He felt much more comfortable there as it was considered the home of theoretical physics. Oppenheimer had never been any good in the laboratory doing experiments and when required to do so, he became distressed. However, he wrote papers that were highly regarded by other physicists. He graduated with a doctorate from Göttingen.

Oppenheimer taught physics at the California Institute of Technology and the University of California, Berkeley, from 1929 to 1947. He had a relaxed teaching style and socialized with his students who admired him. He also lectured at the University of Michigan.

Most famous for his close involvement with the development of the atomic bomb, J. Robert Oppenheimer was also a major influence on the quantum physics of his day. He was director of the prestigious Institute for Advanced Study for two decades. Oppenheimer's brilliant career was marred by government allegations regarding his political affiliations and patriotic loyalty, although his name was later cleared. (Library of Congress)

While Oppenheimer took little interest in politics, he surrounded himself with people who did. In 1936, he met Jean Tatlock, a vibrant young woman with whom he became romantically involved. She was an on-again, off-again communist, and Oppenheimer contributed to some of their causes. He did not become a card-carrying member of the party but associated with many who did. Their turbulent affair came to an end in 1939. He later met Katherine "Kitty" Puening Harrison, and they married in 1940. Robert and Kitty had a son, Peter, and a daughter, Katherine.

As early as 1939, Oppenheimer and other physicists knew that an atomic bomb would be developed. On September 18, 1942, an army officer, Col. Leslie R. Groves, took charge of the Manhattan Project, the code name for a highly secret research program to develop a nuclear weapon. He chose Oppenheimer as director of the research team in Los Alamos, New Mexico.

The work at Los Alamos was fraught with conflicts. Oppenheimer was watched closely by agents of the Federal Bureau of Investigation (FBI). The FBI made no secret of the fact that Oppenheimer was under investigation due to his past associations with known communists, and they believed that, despite his claims to the contrary, he had been a member of the Communist Party. The FBI also watched everyone associated with the project. Despite this, secrets were leaked to the Soviet Union.

Niels Bohr, the renowned Danish physicist who had become a very good friend of Oppenheimer's, was often present at Los Alamos and was credited with lifting the spirits of the team. Some were having misgivings about this powerful and deadly weapon they were building, and never wanted the bomb used. But the work went on, and an atomic bomb was successfully tested July 16, 1945, in a desert site named Trinity by Oppenheimer. The site was located 60 miles northwest of Alamogordo, New Mexico.

Bohr feared the proliferation of atomic weapons unless all the great powers were made aware of the research that had been done, and unless rules were put in place to insure openness and inspections. Oppenheimer agreed with this. But the U.S. government, greatly influenced by U.S. Air Force officials, adamantly disagreed, wanting to be in control of all atomic power.

The Los Alamos scientists had assumed that the bomb would be used in World War II against the German dictator Adolf Hitler and his Nazi forces. But with Hitler's suicide on April 30, 1945, a new target was sought—Japan, the U.S. enemy in the Pacific. One suggestion was to conduct a demonstration to show the Japanese government what the bomb could do. But some scientists, with Oppenheimer among them, wanted a populated area to be bombed so that the effect would be more powerful. "Oppenheimer voiced no disagreement with the choice of the defined target. Instead, he seems to have initiated a discussion on whether several such strikes could be mounted simultaneously" (Bird and Sherwin 2006, 296). At that time, he was a member of the Interim Committee, which had been formed to help the government plan for the use of the bomb.

Oppenheimer and his fellow scientists were "unaware that military intelligence in Washington had intercepted and decoded messages from Japan indicating that the Japanese government understood the war was lost and was seeking acceptable surrender terms" (Bird and Sherwin 2006, 300). Bombs were dropped on Hiroshima and Nagasaki on August 6, 1945, and August 9, 1945, respectively.

Six days after the bombing, Japan surrendered and World War II ended. Americans were jubilant. But euphoria turned to horror and guilt for some of the scientists. Oppenheimer delivered a letter to the U.S. War Department stating that the scientific community wanted the bomb declared illegal as there was no defense against it. But the government was not interested. Oppenheimer became increasingly depressed. He resigned from the Los Alamos directorship in October 1945. He said, "If atomic bombs are to be added as new weapons to the arsenals of a warring world, or to the arsenals of nations preparing for war, then the time will come when mankind will curse the names of Los Alamos and Hiroshima" (Bird and Sherwin 2006, 323).

In 1947, Oppenheimer was appointed chairman of the General Advisory Committee to the Atomic Energy Commission (AEC), serving until 1952. He also served as director of Princeton's Institute for Advanced Study from 1947 to 1966.

As chairman of the AEC, Oppenheimer expressed strong opposition to the development of the hydrogen bomb (H-bomb), and resisted the building of another atomic laboratory, which was highly sought by the air force. He spoke out against a nuclear-powered aircraft and opposed the secrecy surrounding nuclear data. The forces working against him were powerful, and a new laboratory was built at Livermore, California, in 1952.

During the 12 years he worked for the U.S. government, Oppenheimer had made many powerful enemies, who now came together to destroy his reputation. When he began to voice his opposition to building even more powerful nuclear weapons such as the H-bomb, he ran afoul of the government and especially of J. Edgar Hoover, director of the FBI. It also was the time of a "Red Scare"—there were widespread anticommunist sentiments in the United States, and U.S. senator Joseph McCarthy was falsely accusing government officials and others of being communists.

A security hearing of the AEC board was held beginning April 12, 1954, at a secret location in a rundown building in Washington, D.C. The proceedings were a sham, with the defense being denied access to documents, and the rules of the proceedings changing constantly and without notification. At stake was Oppenheimer's reputation. His past associations with the Communist Party were dredged up, and the man who was known as "the father of the atomic bomb" was now looked upon as being disloyal to the United States. The charges against him included opposition to the H-bomb, disloyalty, spying for the Soviet Union, and giving false information to the government in an effort to slow down the development of the H-bomb. Behind the scenes, government officials knew he was not disloyal. But they insisted the bomb program must go on, and they feared the popularity that Oppenheimer enjoyed among other scientists could derail their plans for increased nuclear development. Also, the powerful enemies he had made over the years wanted their revenge.

The security hearing ended on May 6, 1954. The AEC found Oppenheimer guilty of left-wing leanings, and of slowing the development of the H-bomb. His security clearance was not reinstated. There was no evidence of disloyalty. Ward Evans, a chemistry professor from Chicago, offered the one dissenting opinion of the AEC board. "Of Oppenheimer, Evans wrote in his opinion that 'to damn him now and ruin his career and his service, I cannot do.' 'I personally think that our failure to clear Dr. Oppenheimer will be a black mark on... our country'" (McMillan 2005, 227).

The Oppenheimer family was devastated by the outcome. Katherine, who had always been a drinker, now drank even more. Oppenheimer returned to Princeton and the Institute for Advanced Study. He transformed it into a world-class center for physics. His character and his loyalty to his country were so strong that even with the verdict against him, he never said anything against the government. Knowing his character, almost to the soul of the man, "the government counted on his loyalty even as it tried to destroy him" (McMillan 2005, 254). The AEC selected him for the 1963 Enrico Fermi Prize for his contributions to theoretical physics.

Oppenheimer died in Princeton, New Jersey, on February 18, 1967, from throat cancer. He was 62 years old.

Anni Margrethe Callaghan

See also McCarthy, Joseph

References

Alperovitz, Gar. *The Decision to Use the Atomic Bomb.* New York: Vintage Books/Random House, 1996.

Bird, Kai, and Martin J. Sherwin. *American Prometheus, the Triumph and Tragedy of J. Robert Oppenheimer.* New York: Vintage Books/Random House, 2006.

Feis, Herbert. *Japan Subdued: The Atomic Bomb and the End of the War in the Pacific.* Princeton, NJ: Princeton University Press, 1961.

McMillan, Priscilla J. *The Ruin of J. Robert Oppenheimer and the Birth of the Modern Arms Race.* New York: Viking, 2005.

P

Palin, Sarah (1964–)

When presidential candidate Senator John McCain announced his running mate in August 2008, he surprised countless political pundits and the public with his choice: the little-known, 44-year-old Alaska governor Sarah Palin, the first female vice presidential candidate of the Republican Party. McCain-Palin created an interesting team on that first stage appearance in Dayton, Ohio, and the media seemed to sit bolt upright. The presence of a bright, youthful, down-to-earth reformer with very little national exposure but with obvious energy and presence immediately changed the political landscape. Palin was a natural communicator, a "hockey mom," as she called herself, who loved her family and the spotlight and projected a populist demeanor that was impossible to ignore.

When McCain introduced his running mate, he gladdened the hearts of liberal politicians who were certain that it would be easy to dismiss Palin's candidacy because of her relative inexperience on the national stage and her mostly unsophisticated message of making the government more responsive to the values of the typical U.S. citizen. During the 2008 presidential campaign, Palin was linked to Joe Vogler, who founded the Alaska Independent Party (AIP) and declared on his web site that he had no use for America. In news reports, Palin was said to support Vogler's AIP, and her husband Todd was a member of the party. However, the connection to Vogler seemed to have little or no impact on the presidential campaign.

Palin's greatest strength has come from what she learned growing up in an unforgiving part of the country where what you do and how you do it can mean the difference between merely surviving and thriving. Palin appears to have always found a way to thrive. Her presence on the 2008 Republican ticket energized the McCain effort, but fell short of victory. Barack Obama was elected and became the first African American president of the United States. However, in many ways, Palin remained a challenge to the political system in the United States—a dissident against the status quo.

Sarah Louise Heath was born in Sandpoint, Idaho, to Sarah (Sally) and Charles (Chuck) Heath on February 11, 1964. Both her parents worked in the local school district, where her father was a science teacher and track coach while her mother served as the school secretary. But Chuck Heath had a love for the outdoors that served as the impetus to seek employment in Alaska, where the wages were much higher and adventure seemed to be much more likely. He convinced Sarah's mother to try it for a year, and they moved the family to the great northwest; he took an elementary school teaching position in Skagway, just weeks after the earthquake that caused incredible devastation across the state.

In Skagway, Chuck Heath also served as the high school basketball coach and began to hone his hunting, fishing, and trapping skills throughout the local bush. Like many of his new neighbors in the relatively wild region of the country, hunting for game was not merely a hobby. The goal was to provide food for the growing family. Moose, caribou, seal, mountain goat, rabbit, fish, and the occasional brown bear were all fair game for the table; and his children, including the young Sarah, embraced this value. By the time the family had located to the small town of Wasilla, just north of Anchorage, all of the children were imbued with an independent spirit of self-reliance and making do. "Sarah shot her first rabbit at age ten not far from the back porch. In her teens, she hunted caribou with her father. The family's freezer was always full of fish and game. . . . Gardening helped fill the family larder," her biographer Johnson reported (2008, 17). Game as the main protein source was so common in the Heath household that Sarah's oldest brother, Chuck Jr., had not even tasted beefsteak until he was in high school.

At Wasilla High School, Sarah succeeded as an athlete through participation on the girls' cross country and basketball teams. She served as the high school's president of a chapter of the national Christian evangelical organization known as the Fellowship of Christian Athletes. By the time she reached her senior year, she was cocaptain of the Wasilla Warriors basketball squad that went on to win the Alaska Class 4A championship tournament. Many reports say that it was during this time that she was given the moniker of "Sarah Barracuda," because her peers were impressed with her tenacity and competitive spirit and the fact that she had played in the tournament with a stress fracture in her ankle. However, her coach at the time, Don Teeguarden, believes that the nickname must have come from a stint at basketball camp. Regardless, the competitiveness of high school sports had a profound influence on Palin, and she has said that the tournament changed her life. An *Anchorage Daily News* article quotes her former coach: "I've heard her say that 'Everything I needed to learn, I learned on a basketball court,'" Teeguarden said. "I say, I'm glad she feels that way. But my perspective is Sarah was going to be Sarah if we won that game or not. It's all about opportunities for growth. Wherever you can find them, they're beneficial. For a lot of people, Sarah being one of them, it was the athletic arena."

There were other accomplishments besides athletics for Sarah Heath subsequent to her high school years, however. She was interested in a college degree in journalism and the possibility that she would eventually find a career in broadcast news. As her biographer Johnson noted:

> Sarah had two childhood traits that her family says played pivotal roles in her life. From the time she was in elementary school, she consumed newspapers with a passion. "She read the paper from the very top left-hand corner to the bottom right corner to the very last page . . . She didn't just read it—she knew every word she had read and analyzed it . . . "
>
> Sarah's other trait is what her father calls an unbending, unapologetic streak of stubbornness. "The rest of the kids, I could force them to do something," Chuck Sr. said. "But with Sarah, there is no way. From a young age she had a mind of her own. Once she made up her mind, she didn't change it." (Johnson 2008, 21–22)

Sarah has always surprised people who thought they could tell what she was planning to do. That was never more evident in her early years than when she made the decision to enter the Miss Wasilla beauty pageant as a prelude to the Miss Alaska competition in

1984. She shocked her brothers and sisters by winning the local event and then reaching second runner-up status in the state competition. She played flute in the event and paraded (somewhat embarrassed) in a bathing suit for her prizes: the Miss Congeniality Award and a college scholarship.

Sarah Heath attended several colleges starting in 1982, and was eventually successful in obtaining a bachelor of arts degree in communication with an emphasis in journalism from the University of Idaho in 1987. Soon after graduation, she found work as a sportscaster on two TV stations in the Anchorage market. She also spent time as a sports reporter for the *Mat-Su Valley Frontiersman*, the local paper of Wasilla.

It was not long before Sarah Heath made her next big move. Her boyfriend at the time was a man she had known and dated from her high school days when the girls' squad often traveled with the boys' team to away games. Todd Palin, a regular on the boys' squad in high school, eloped with Sarah in August 1988, and the young bride joined her new husband in his commercial fishing enterprise. Months later, the couple began to grow a family: their first son Track was born in 1989, followed by daughter Bristol (1991), daughter Willow (1995), daughter Piper (2001), and son Trig (2008). It was her involvement with her children's schooling that started her political career. At least, this is the narrative she used to introduce herself to the nation when she made her first speech as John McCain's running mate in 2008: "I was just your average hockey mom in Alaska . . . we were busy raising our kids . . . got involved in the PTA and then was elected to the city council and then elected mayor of my home town where my agenda was to stop wasteful spending and cut property taxes and put the people first" (CBS 2009).

By the time she made this speech, Palin had indeed served on the Wasilla City Council from 1992 to 1996. In that year, she decided to run against the incumbent mayor John Stein, whom she defeated by talking about the issues of spending and high taxes, but also by injecting abortion and gun rights concerns into the race. By 1999, when she ran for reelection, she was able to handily defeat Stein once more.

During her tenure as mayor, Palin drove many infrastructure expansion projects and won the admiration of many of Wasilla's residents. The economy was on an upswing at the time, and the mayor was able to take advantage of earmarked federal dollars that flowed to Wasilla with the aid of a lobbying firm, which won nearly $8 million in grants for the small town. It was during her terms as Wasilla's mayor that Sarah Palin first demonstrated an uncompromising style of leadership. In her first year on the job, the city experienced a great deal of upheaval. As a *Seattle Times* article noted in September 2008:

> Her first months also exposed threads that would later become patterns—friends become enemies, enemies become friends and questions get raised about why she fired this person or that person.
>
> But the situation calmed, and rather than being recalled, Palin was re-elected. She later acknowledged, "I grew tremendously in my early months as mayor." (Armstrong and Bernton 2008)

Term limit laws meant that Palin would have to leave office in 2002, and that year she ran in the five-person Republican primary to pick a lieutenant governor candidate to run with the popular Senator Frank Murkowski, who had resigned that seat to run for governor. Palin came in second to the eventual winner Loren Leman, but she campaigned hard for the Republican ticket. When Murkowski-Lehman won the race, Palin had some hope that she would be named by the new governor to fill his vacated term as U.S. senator. Instead, after a very long public process, Murkowski appointed his daughter, state senator Lisa Murkowski. Many Alaskans saw this as nepotism. The governor eventually offered Palin a position as the "public representative" on the Alaska Oil and Gas Conservation Commission. She quickly was elevated to chair of the commission and also served as its ethics supervisor.

She made a name for herself on that board when she conducted a very public investigation of another Murkowski appointee and state Republican Party chair, Randy Ruedrich. Palin received almost no cooperation from the governor or the attorney general during the ethics investigation, and many Republicans accused her of working for and with Democrats in a purely political ploy for power. She denied the charges and was eventually vindicated months after she resigned the commission in frustration: Ruedrich was found to be in violation of state ethics rules. He admitted wrongdoing and paid a record fine of $12,000.

Subsequent to the Ruedrich investigation, Palin also joined state representative Eric Croft, a Democrat, to file a formal complaint to the state personnel board over the activities of Attorney General Gregg Renkes. It was alleged that Renkes owned stock in a Colorado company that would benefit from trade negotiations he was conducting with a firm from Taiwan. Governor Murkowski was angered by the complaint as he had earlier attempted to squash the controversy with an independent investigation. As a result, the governor had reprimanded Renkes, but allowed him to remain at his post. After the Palin filing, Renkes soon resigned.

The atmosphere of political corruption in Alaska state government was the perfect platform for Palin to leverage her newfound status as reformer and fearless fighter for the people when she ran for the governor's race in 2006. The incumbent's fatal error of naming his daughter to fill his Senate seat also played well for Palin, and she ousted Murkowski in the Republican primary in which he actually came in third. Days later, the FBI raided offices of six Republican legislators on corruption and bribery warrants, and Palin cruised to victory. She became the first woman and the youngest person to fill the office of Alaska's governor.

After the 2008 presidential contest that saw the historic election of the first African American president, Palin returned to her duties as governor. But just one half year later, Palin made another radical move. Announcing at a televised news conference that she had made a decision to save the state of Alaska millions of dollars from possible litigation and to work for positive change for all of the nation's children, she resigned from Alaska's top office. Weeks later, she announced a deal with HarperCollins to publish a memoir for which she was reportedly paid a $7 million advance. *Going Rogue: An American Life* (2009) made the best seller list before it was shipped. On the book tour to promote, Palin used the media focus to extend and expand her views on smaller government, less taxation, and the necessity for the United States to cleave to Constitutional values. She began speaking on behalf the Tea Party movement, whose members also espoused those views. The tour lasted for months and she was in virtually every news cycle during that time. Another book, *America by Heart: Reflections on Family, Faith, and Flag*, was published in late 2010.

Often criticized by liberals and many in the more traditional political establishment, she nonetheless has found a comfortable niche as a spokesperson for conservatives and independents who are fearful the country they grew up in has changed for the worst. They consider Palin to be their most effective advocate. As for Palin herself, she is very confident in her ability to make a difference in or out of mainstream political action.

Martin K. Gay

See also Vogler, Joe

References

"America: Meet Sarah Palin." YouTube video, 19:20, posted by CBS, August 29, 2009. http://www.youtube.com/watch?v=Gg0darQB7r4 (accessed November 7, 2010).

Armstrong, Ken, and Hal Bernton. "Sarah Palin Had Turbulent First Year as Mayor of Alaska Town." *Seattle Times*, September 7, 2008. http://seattletimes.nwsource.com/html/politics/2008163431_palin070.html (accessed September 10, 2011).

Benet, Lorenzo. *Trailblazer: An Intimate Biography of Sarah Palin*. New York: Threshold Editions, 2009.

James, G. Robert. *Sarah Palin: The Real Deal*. Lakeland, FL: White Stone Books, 2008.

Johnson, Kaylene, *Sarah: How a Hockey Mom Turned Alaska's Political Establishment Upside Down*. Kenmore, WA: Epicenter Press, 2008.

Palin, Sarah. *Going Rogue: An American Life*. New York: HarperCollins, 2009.

Wilmot, Ron. "True or False: Hoops Title Changed Palin's Life, but What about That Nickname?" *Anchorage Daily News*, September 14, 2008. http://www.adn.com/2008/09/14/525556/sarah-barracuda-tidbits.html#ixzz14QnjF39b (accessed November 7, 2010).

Parks, Rosa (1913–2005)

The U.S. Congress in May 1999 honored Rosa Parks as the "first lady of civil rights" and described her as the "mother of the freedom movement" when they enacted Public Law 106-26. It authorized President Bill Clinton to award a gold medal on behalf of the Congress to Parks in recognition of her contributions to the nation. The law proclaimed that Parks's "quiet dignity ignited the most significant social movement in the history of the United States" and that she symbolized "all that is vital about nonviolent protest, as she endured threats of death." By refusing to give up her seat on a bus to a white person, Rosa Louise Parks on December 1, 1955, in Montgomery, Alabama, helped launch the modern-day civil rights movement. The repercussions of such a seemingly simple act of defiance, wrought by such a seemingly simple woman, would be nothing but stupendous.

Born in Tuskegee, Alabama, on February 4, 1913, Rosa was the eldest of James and Leona McCauley's two children. Her father was a carpenter, and her mother was a teacher. Although considered African American, she also shared Cherokee-Creek and Scots-Irish ancestry bloodlines with her brother Sylvester. When her parents separated, the children moved with their mother to her parents' farm in Pine Level, Alabama, just outside Montgomery. There, Rosa attended the local, rural schools until age 11, when she went to a private school for blacks, the Montgomery Industrial School, founded and staffed by white northerners. Because there were no high schools in the area for blacks, she attended the Alabama State Teachers College for Negroes during 10th and 11th grades. However, she was forced to drop out when her grandmother, and then her mother, took ill.

From a young age, Rosa realized that her lot in life as a black person was second-class. Her childhood was filled with recollections of the Ku Klux Klan terrorizing the black community, burning its churches and beating and killing its members.

In 1932, Rosa married Raymond Parks. Although he was a self-educated man himself, he supported Rosa's desire to complete her formal education, and soon after their marriage, she earned her high school diploma. A barber by trade, Raymond was active in the National Association for the Advancement of Colored People (NAACP), and Rosa soon became a member herself, taking on responsibilities such as local chapter secretary and, later on, a youth adviser. She also worked to bring in additional income, largely employing her considerable talents as a seamstress. Raymond's activism increased when he and Rosa accepted work at Maxwell Air Force Base, a federal facility where segregation was not allowed. For the first time, Rosa was free of many of the restrictions that had defined her day-to-day activities.

In the summer of 1955, Rosa spent time at the Highlander Folk School founded by Myles Horton in Monteagle, Tennessee, a center for workers' rights and racial equality. During her 10-day stay, she attended several workshops, one entitled "Racial Desegregation: Implementing the Supreme Court Decision" or *Brown v. Board of Education* (1954). Rosa recalled, "One of my greatest pleasures there was enjoying the smell of the bacon frying and coffee brewing and knowing that white folks were doing the preparing instead of me ... It was hard to leave, knowing what I had to go back to ... where you had to be smiling and polite, no matter how rudely you were treated. And back to city buses, with their segregation rules" (Parks 1999, 101–7). By the end of the year, Rosa would feel compelled to take a stand against those rules.

Hers would not be the first protest of its kind—nor even her own such objection. More than a decade before, she had refused to enter a Montgomery bus by a rear door as was required of blacks at the time. Driver James E. Blake made her exit to reenter "properly." He then sped off before she could do so (Parks 1999, 79).

In 1946, the NAACP had successfully brought a case involving Irene Morgan—who had staged a protest similar to the one Rosa Parks would nine years later—before the U.S. Supreme Court. However, the suit dealt only with segregation laws applicable to interstate commerce, such as interstate bus travel. Southern bus companies immediately created a loophole around the Morgan decision, setting up their own Jim Crow regulations. This loophole was finally

When Rosa Parks refused to give her bus seat to a white passenger in 1955, she sparked a boycott of the Montgomery, Alabama, bus system, which in turn activated the larger civil rights movement throughout the United States. Martin Luther King Jr. stands behind her. (National Archives)

addressed in another important legal case by the Interstate Commerce Commission, *Keys v. Carolina Coach* (1955) which determined that carriers imposing segregation violated the antidiscrimination provision of the Interstate Commerce Act. But, as critical as both the Morgan and Keys rulings were, neither one spoke to Jim Crow (anti-black laws) within individual states. And that is where Rosa Parks would play her pivotal role.

In March 1955, a 15-year-old girl named Claudette Colvin had refused to give up her seat to a white man on the same bus line that Rosa would use later. Colvin was forcibly removed and arrested. Parks was among those raising money for Colvin's defense. However, Colvin's reputation as a "bad girl" swayed opinions to seek another more suitable symbol for their cause (Parks 1999, 111–12). Nine months later, no such aspersions would be cast upon Parks, a lifelong member of the African Methodist Episcopal (AME) Church, married and gainfully employed, with a calm and quite civil demeanor and altogether respectable reputation.

Thus, on December 1, 1955, after a full day working at the Montgomery Fair department store, Parks boarded the Cleveland Avenue bus in downtown Montgomery. She paid her fare and took a seat in the first row of seats reserved for blacks in the designated "colored section," near the middle of the bus, behind the seats reserved for whites. James F. Blake was the bus driver—the same person who had evicted her previously.

Before long, the seats reserved for whites filled up. Per local ordinance, drivers could assign seats to segregate passengers by race but riders were not required to move nor give up their seats and stand if the bus was crowded and no other seats were available; in practice, drivers made blacks move regardless. On this day, Blake—seeing that the white section was full and white male passengers standing—moved the "colored section" sign behind Parks and told the blacks now in front of it that they had to relocate. All but Parks complied. "I only knew that, as I was being arrested, that it was the very last time that I would ever ride in humiliation of this kind," she reported (CNN 2005).

Some years later, when asked why she acted as she did, Parks replied, "I had been pushed as far as I could stand to be pushed and decided that I would have to know once and for all what rights I had as a human being and a citizen" (Burns 1997, 9). "When I sat down on the bus . . . All I felt was tired. Tired of being pushed around. Tired of seeing bad treatment and disrespect of children, women, and men just because of the color of their skin" (Parks 1994, 16–17). "People always say that I didn't give up my seat because I was tired, but that isn't true. I was not tired physically, or no more tired than I usually was at the end of a working day. I was not old, although some people have an image of me as being old then. I was forty-two. No, the only tired I was, was tired of giving in" (Parks 1999, 116).

Parks's trial was set for December 5, 1955. The Women's Political Council (WPC) decided that this was the chance for which it had been waiting. Led by Jo Ann Robinson, who herself had once been ordered out of the "whites only" section of a bus, WPC members distributed 35,000 leaflets calling for a black bus boycott on the day of Parks's trial. Despite the fact that it rained that day and that blacks typically made up 75 percent of the riders, the community united, and the one-day day boycott was a success. That night at the Mt. Zion AME Church, a group met and formed under the name of the Montgomery Improvement Association (MIA). They chose a young Baptist minister new to Montgomery as their leader—Martin Luther

King Jr. These local civil rights activists decided to initiate a long-term boycott of the Montgomery bus system to financially damage the bus company as well as challenge the white social structure in the city. The boycott lasted for 381 days, ending in December 1956 when the U.S. Supreme Court overturned the law segregating public transportation, and the Montgomery buses were finally integrated. Ultimately, the Montgomery bus boycott was one of the largest and most successful stands against racial segregation. It led to many other protests, ushering in an era of nonviolent demonstrations, and notably brought Martin Luther King Jr. to national prominence in the civil rights movement.

Parks did not come out of her ordeal unscathed. As a result of her protest, she lost her job as a seamstress at the department store where she had worked. Raymond quit his job after his employer forbade him to talk about Rosa and the lawsuit. In 1957, the Parks relocated to Hampton, Virginia, for a short while and then later settled in Detroit, Michigan. Rosa became an icon of the civil rights movement and, as such, traveled and spoke frequently throughout the years. She also continued to work as a seamstress until 1965, when African American U.S. representative John Conyers hired her as a secretary for his Detroit office.

In 1977, she lost both her husband and brother to cancer; her mother died two years later. Parks renewed her passion for civil rights, cofounding the Rosa L. Parks Scholarship Foundation for college-bound high school seniors in 1980. In 1987, she cofounded the Rosa and Raymond Parks Institute for Self Development which runs Pathways to Freedom bus tours, introducing young people to civil rights and Underground Railroad sites across the United States. She retired from her secretarial job with Conyers in 1988.

During the 1990s, her autobiography *Rosa Parks: My Story* (1992, 1999) and *Quiet Strength* (1994) were published. In 1994, Parks was again the subject of national news. In August, she was attacked and robbed in her home by an African American drug addict. Not surprisingly, the press made much of her attacker's race. Parks went on record stating, "I pray for this young man and the conditions in our country that have made him this way. I urge people not to read too much into the attack. I regret that some people, regardless of race, are in such a mental state that they would want to harm an older woman... Despite the violence and crime in our society, we should not let fear overwhelm us. We must remain strong. We must not give up hope; we can overcome" (Parks 1994, 37). Also that year, the Ku Klux Klan made headlines when it applied to sponsor part of U.S. Interstate 55 entitling it to signs stating that part of the road was maintained by the KKK. An uproar ensued because the state could not legally refuse the application, so the state legislature cleverly acted to rename the roadway section the Rosa Parks Highway.

Parks again was the subject of much media attention in 1999 when she filed suit against popular hip-hop artists OutKast and LaFace Records alleging they had used her name without her permission in the song "Rosa Parks." The parties settled and agreed to work together to create programs about Parks's life for the Rosa and Raymond Parks Institute for Self Development. She made the news once more for even sadder reasons in 2002. She was in danger of being evicted from her apartment because she was unable to manage her affairs due to declining physical and mental capacities. A local church paid her rent, but two years later, she was again facing homelessness. The notoriety of the situation prompted the building owners to grant her rent amnesty for the remainder of her life. Parks was 91 at the time and died the following year, on October 24, 2005, amid controversy about her affairs and estate.

Parks received numerous accolades and honors. Among them were the NAACP Springarn Medal; the Martin Luther King Jr. Award; induction into the Michigan Women's Hall of Fame; the Peace Abbey Courage of Conscience Award; the Presidential Medal of Freedom; the International Freedom Conductor Award from the National Underground Railroad Freedom Center; the Congressional Gold Medal; and her being named by *Time* magazine as one of the 20 most influential and iconic figures of the twentieth century.

Parks was not forgotten after she died. Both Detroit and Montgomery proclaimed that the front seats of their city buses would be marked off with black ribbons while her casket was flown to Montgomery and taken to the St. Paul AME Church. Parks lay in repose there until her memorial on October 30, at which time her casket was transported to Washington, D.C., to lie in state at the U.S. Capitol. Parks was the first female and the second black person to lie in state at the Capitol Rotunda. Approximately 50,000 people viewed her casket in person, and millions more witnessed the event on television. On October 30, President George W. Bush ordered all flags on U.S. public areas, both within the country and abroad, be flown at half-staff on the day of Parks's funeral. A second memorial was held at the St. Paul AME church in Washington, D.C., on October 31, 2005.

To commemorate the 50th anniversary of Rosa Parks's arrest, the American Public Transportation Association declared December 1, 2005, to be a National Transit Tribute to Rosa Parks Day. A statue of Parks was placed in the U.S. Capitol's National Statuary Hall. In authorizing the placement, President Bush stated: "By placing her statue in the heart of the nation's Capitol, we commemorate her work for a more perfect union, and we commit ourselves to continue to struggle for justice for every American" (Bush 2005).

Margaret Gay

See also Horton, Myles; King, Martin Luther, Jr.

References

Burns, Stewart, ed. *Daybreak of Freedom: The Montgomery Bus Boycott*. Chapel Hill: University of North Carolina Press, 1997.

Bush, George W. "President Signs H.R. 4145 to Place Statue of Rosa Parks in U.S. Capitol." White House Archives, December 1, 2005. http://georgewbush-whitehouse.archives.gov/news/releases/2005/12/20051201-1.html (accessed November 21, 2010).

"Civil Rights Icon Rosa Parks Dies at 92." CNN.com, October 25, 2005. http://articles.cnn.com/2005-10-24/us/parks.obit_1_raymond-parks-institute-rosa-parks-civil-rights-act?_s=PM:US (accessed November 16, 2010).

Parks, Rosa, with James Haskins. *Rosa Parks: My Story*. New York: Penguin Group, 1999. First published by Dial, 1992.

Parks, Rosa, and Gregory J. Reed, *Quiet Strength*. Grand Rapids, MI: Zondervan Publishing House, 1994.

"The Story behind the Bus." Henry Ford web site, n.d. http://www.thehenryford.org/exhibits/rosaparks/story.asp (accessed November 21, 2010).

Parsons, Lucy (1853–1942)

Lucy Gonzalez Parsons often stands in the shadows of her husband's notoriety. Of the pair, Albert Parsons is typically more readily recognized for the impact the couple made on American history—both together and separately. This is largely because of the infamy involved in the Haymarket Affair in Chicago when Albert and others were hanged in 1877 because of their anarchist activities. However, Lucy, who was a contemporary of better-known female radicals such as Emma Goldman and Mary Harris "Mother" Jones, was a "formidable figure in labour and radical movements and an able and effective defender of the rights of working people" (Meyers 1987, 35). The sexism that stood in her way when she was alive continues to somewhat deny her a full and rightful place of prominence in the history books today. Nevertheless, now or then, such an obstacle would never deter her from causes. "For almost 70 years, Lucy Parsons fought for the rights of the poor and disenfranchised in the face of an increasingly oppressive industrial economic system. Lucy's radical activism challenged the racist and sexist sentiment in a time when even radical Americans believed that a woman's place was in the home" (Industrial Workers of the World).

There is no record of Parsons's early life. Contrary to her lifelong denials, Lucy is believed to have been born into slavery on a plantation in Hill County, Texas, in 1853. She asserted that she had been orphaned at age three but that her mother Maria del Gather, was Mexican, and her father, John Waller, was a Creek Indian. She claimed to have been raised by an uncle on a Texas ranch. It is also widely believed that she lived with a former slave of African descent, Oliver Gathing, for a period of time. Around 1870, she met Albert Parsons. They were wed in 1871 or 1872, although whether or not they were ever legally married is questionable, given the fact that he was white and such a mixed marriage would have been against the law (Lowndes 1995).

Albert had served in the Confederate army prior to meeting Lucy and was radical in his Republican-leaning political beliefs. The latter, along with his marriage to Lucy, compelled the couple to leave Texas for a more hospitable place to begin their lives together. So, in 1873, they made their way to Chicago, Illinois. While they left the antagonism of the Ku Klux Klan behind them in Texas, they found a different sort of hostility fomenting in the Midwestern city they would now call home.

The Parsons were taking their place among an impoverished, working-class community. It was a militant environment, one in which there were often clashes between workers, whose material conditions had eroded drastically, and capitalists, who did not hesitate to use arms to enforce their dictates. These were tough times, particularly in industrial cities like Chicago. The United States was in a depression, with millions out of work. The passage of the 1864 Contract Labor Law made things worse, letting companies bring in masses of cheap immigrant laborers. As the pool of unskilled workers in Chicago grew larger and larger, wages decreased proportionately. While all of this was going on, the working class was getting its first introduction to the radical ideas of socialism and anarchist ideology. Parsons took up his printing trade with the *Chicago Times*, but it was against the backdrop of the aforementioned circumstances that the Parsons' political activism transformed into radicalism.

In 1876, the couple became members of the Social Democratic Party and the First International, both founded by Karl Marx and Friedrich Engels. This was their first contact with leftist groups. However, these associations were short-lived as both organizations disbanded in that same year. They soon found a kinship with the Chicago Chapter of Workingmen's Party of the United States (WPUSA). In 1877, representing the group, Albert ran for ward alderman.

This was an historic year as well, marking the first general strike in the United States—the railroad strike. And WPUSA played a big role with its support. Across the nation, rail workers picketed in protest of the Baltimore and Ohio Railroad's wage cuts. Strikers in Chicago derailed an engine and baggage cars, and they engaged physically with police trying to disperse them and break the strike. Albert made a name for himself in the anarchist movement at this time, promoting peaceful negotiation when addressing crowds of up to 25,000 people. Albert was dismissed from his job at the *Times* due to his organizing efforts and considered untrustworthy in the printing trade. So, in 1877, Lucy opened a dress shop to support her family's financial needs. This led to her involvement with the International Ladies' Garment Workers Union and her exposure to the unique challenges that women found in the work world.

At the end of 1877, political divisions within the WPUSA resulted in creation of another group, the Socialistic Labor Party (SLP), which was renamed the Socialist Labor Party in 1892. Lucy was a frequent writer for the SLP *Socialist*, opining on the struggles of the working class. She did so through poetry, as well as through articles in which she denounced capitalism. Drawing on her experiences as a working woman, she was also a voice for the Working Women's Union that was established in the mid-1870s. She often brought women's issues to the attention of SLP. For example, she demanded women's suffrage as a party platform item, as well as equal pay for men and women. She also focused on concerns of mothers, to which she could speak personally after she bore two children of her own—a son, Albert Richard, in 1879, and a daughter, Lula Eda, in 1881.

Lucy helped found the International Working People's Association (IWPA) in 1883, having left SLP. Not only was Parsons dissatisfied with SLP's lack of attention to the plight of blacks, but she also was fundamentally opposed to "its peaceful approach to transforming capitalist social relations." IWPA was an anarchist-influenced labor organization. It was adamant on its stance on the equality of blacks and women and equally as fervent in promoting revolutionary action toward a stateless and cooperative society (McClendon 1995, 515).

Lucy again put pen to paper, her words appearing often in IPWA's weekly paper the *Alarm* in 1884. Her most famous piece, "To Tramps," urged a violent uprising of the common man against his oppressors.

Though she denied her own racial identity, Parsons strongly advocated for the rights of African Americans. She wrote frequent condemnations of racist attacks and killings. "The Negro: Let Him Leave Politics to the Politician and Prayer to the Preacher" appeared in *Alarm* on April 3, 1886, and was a response to the lynching of 13 blacks in Carrollton, Mississippi. Her position was that blacks were only victimized because they were poor and, therefore, racism would disappear when capitalism ceased to exist. "But your course in future, if you really value freedom, is to leave politics to the politicians, and prayer to those who can show wherein it has done them more good than it has ever done for you, and join hands with those who are striving for economic freedom" (Ahrens 2003, 54). Her position was unlike most other blacks of her day, who were taking a more conciliatory, compromising path toward acceptance in white society (McClendon 1995, 515–16).

For Parsons, who had lived a life of uncharacteristic independence and strength for a woman of her day, the years 1876 and 1877 would test her courage greatly. On

May 1, 1886, she and others began a strike against McCormick Harvest Works lobbying for an eight-hour workday. A few days later, violence broke out when police fired into a crowd of unarmed workers, killing four and wounding many more. When radicals gathered in Haymarket Square, police arrived. Someone tossed a bomb, killing one officer. Over the course of the next several days, police swept through the town, hunting down all reputed anarchists and radicals. Albert Parsons and seven others were taken into custody. Although Lucy was looked upon with suspicion, she was never charged with conspiracy in the bombing. Authorities deemed the chances of convicting a woman of murder—a crime punishable with the death penalty—too slim; they also thought that if she stood trial with the eight men, it might diminish the odds of winning a harsh verdict. How could a woman be capable of such radical and militant action?

The men went on trial in October 1887, and seven were sentenced to death by hanging. Eventually, one committed suicide (or was murdered) in jail and three of the men's sentences were commuted to life in prison. Lucy spoke in defense of the "Haymarket Eight," touring the United States on their behalf, seeking clemency for her husband. Much to her dismay, the Knights of Labor, to whom she belonged for 10 years, failed to offer her support. To the contrary, the group's leader, Terrence Powderly, took a strong stand against the Haymarket activists. He opposed the militant tactics of the anarchists. Even worse, Powderly believed the government should make an example of the Haymarket Eight. Lucy's efforts proved for naught. Four of the men were executed, including Albert Parsons, on November 11, 1887 (Meyers 1987, 38–39, 41–44).

The following year, Parsons traveled abroad to speak before the Socialist League of England. On her return home, she found the United States repressive in comparison to the freedom of speech that had been available to her in London. She was continually fined and arrested for her pronouncements and for peddling her pamphlet *Anarchism* on city streets. Embattled though she was, and even struck with another personal tragedy—the death of her daughter Lula Eda in 1889 from lymphadenoma—she did not back down from her radical causes.

In 1891, Parsons began editing *Freedom: A Revolutionary Anarchist-Communist Monthly*. In it, she heralded the coming of revolution, documenting various labor struggles such as the ones at the Carnegie steel mills in Pennsylvania and silver mines of Coeur d'Alene, Idaho, and even the failed 1894 boycott by Pullman workers led by the famous labor leader Eugene V. Debs. She also started publishing *Freedom* in 1892, which covered lynchings and servitude of black sharecroppers.

In June of 1905, a Continental Congress was held in Chicago. It was a call to action by the labor movement and was the founding meeting of the Industrial Workers of the World (IWW). Parsons was the second woman to join the organization, one that espoused a well-organized working-class movement that planned to seize the methods of production. IWW believed in militant strikes and direct action—exactly in accord with Lucy's own philosophies. She took on the role of editor of IWW's *The Liberator*, speaking out on variety of women's issues, such as the right to divorce, remarry, and have access to birth control. In 1907 and 1908, at a time when the country was facing huge challenges, she devoted her efforts to hunger and joblessness. She continued in these efforts, organizing the homeless and unemployed to great success in 1914 and 1915 in San Francisco and Chicago.

To Parsons's way of thinking, the anarchist movement no longer actively moved toward revolution. She began to explore the Communist Party in 1925, formally joining in 1939. She worked with political prisoners in the South with one of the party's subgroups, the Coalition for International Labor Defense, sitting on its national committee in 1927.

A fire broke out in Lucy Parsons's home in 1942, resulting in her death. Controversy exists over the disappearance of her books, papers, and other belongings from her residence at the time of the fire. However, there is no doubt as to the legacy that she left behind. Not only was Parsons one of the first minority activists to associate openly with leftist, radical social movements, but she was also a leader in those same organizations, ones that almost exclusively were composed of white males. As an avowed anarchist, socialist, and communist—depending upon the stage of her life—Parsons shouldered and fought to ease the burdens of workers, of women, of minorities, of the homeless, and the unemployed. There is no doubt that she left her mark on history.

Margaret Gay

See also Debs, Eugene V.; Goldman, Emma; Jones, Mary Harris

References

Ahrens, Gale, ed. *Lucy Parsons: Freedom, Equality and Solidarity.* Chicago: Charles H. Kerr, 2003.

Industrial Workers of the World. "Lucy Parsons: Woman of Will," n.d. http://www.iww.org/en/culture/biography/LucyParsons1.shtml (cited October 25, 2010).

Lowndes, Joe. "Lucy Parsons (1853–1942): The Life of an Anarchist Labor Organizer," The Lucy Parsons Project, 1995. http://www.lucyparsonsproject.org/aboutlucy/lowndes_life_of_parsons.html (accessed August 29, 2011).

McClendon, John, III. "Lucy Parsons (1853–1942), Anarchist, Socialist, Communist, Journalist, Poet." In *Notable American Black Women, Book II*, edited by Jessie Carney Smith. Farmington Hills, MI: Thomson Gale, 1995.

Meyers, Arlene, ed. *The Radical Papers, the Haymarket Affair and Lucy Parsons: 100th Anniversary.* Montreal, Quebec, Canada: Black Rose Books, Ltd, 1987.

Parsons, Lucy. "To Tramps: The Unemployed, the Disinherited, and Miserable." *Alarm*, October 4, 1984. http://courses.washington.edu/spcmu/speeches/lucyparsons.htm (accessed October 22, 2010).

Paul, Alice (1885–1977)

Alice Paul became a political prisoner after she was arrested in 1917 for demonstrations in front of the U.S. White House in support of woman suffrage. While in jail, she went on a hunger strike, was taken to the prison's psychiatric ward, and was finally released from prison after seven months. She was a controversial woman who had a great influence on the women's suffrage debate in the United States during the early 1900s.

Paul was born on January 11, 1885, to Quaker parents William and Tacie Paul in Mount Laurel, New Jersey. Her siblings William (called Billy), Helen, and Parry were born between 1886 and 1895. William Paul was president of a trust company and provided a comfortable living for his family. The Paul family made their home outside Moorestown, New Jersey, on a 265-acre farm known as Paulsdale, where hired farmworkers provided most of the labor. However, the Pauls believed in simple living and staying close to nature, as their religion stressed, and the children often helped out with farm chores.

The Pauls followed the traditions of Hicksite Quakers, a liberal group that broke away from the traditional Society of Friends and believed that men and women were equal and that women should be educated. They also were committed to social justice and service. Alice's mother was a member of the National American Woman Suffrage Association and often took Alice along to suffrage meetings, introducing her early in her life to the struggle for women's rights.

Alice received her education at a Hicksite Quaker school, graduating in 1901 as the top student in her class. She went on to Swarthmore College, which her mother had attended, graduating in 1905 with a bachelor's degree in biology. She received a one-year fellowship to continue her education at the New York College Settlement School of Philanthropy, and while there made plans to study social work in England. In 1907, she studied at the Woodbrooke Settlement in Birmingham, England, and met radical activists in the British women's suffragist movement. To raise awareness of their issues, suffragists addressed crowds in the streets and took part in such direct actions as throwing rocks and breaking windows. Paul joined some of these demonstrations and was arrested along with others and jailed in Halloway Prison. The women protested their imprisonment by refusing to eat and were forcibly fed.

In 1910, Paul returned to the United States and continued her education at the University of Pennsylvania in Philadelphia, where she earned a master's degree in sociology and, in 1912, a PhD in economics. While she was working toward her degrees, she joined the National American Women's Suffrage Association (NAWSA) led by Carrie Chapman Catt, and participated in suffragist street meetings in Philadelphia. A friend, Lucy Burns, an American suffragist she had met in a London police station, joined her in suffragist activities. The two met with Jane Addams in Chicago, where Addams had established Hull House, to discuss the possibility of working for the amendment to the U.S. Constitution that would enfranchise women. In January 1913, Paul and Burns went to Washington, D.C., to develop a campaign for a suffrage amendment, and within two months, they organized a march along Pennsylvania Avenue that took place on March 3, a day before President Woodrow Wilson was inaugurated. That day was selected because many visitors were expected to be in Washington.

The parade of an estimated 5,000 to 8,000 women drew large crowds, but groups of men and boys soon attacked the marchers with obscenities and by breaking into the parade. No police arrived to help the women. But members of the Pennsylvania National Guard came to assist, as did college students who formed a guard to protect the marchers. In the end, the march was a success—it generated newspaper headlines across the United States and public outrage over the treatment of the suffragists. Grassroots organizers in numerous states gathered 200,000 signatures on petitions calling for an amendment to franchise women, delivering them to members of Congress and President Wilson's office.

Building on their success, Paul and Burns formed a group known as the Congressional Union, chaired by Paul to work directly for a federal suffrage amendment by holding the federal government responsible for women's disenfranchisement. But Catt and the NAWSA disagreed with this approach. They argued that it was more effective to concentrate on campaigns to enfranchise women on a state-by-state basis, which would then lead to a federal amendment. Because of these differences in policy, Paul's group left the NAWSA and, in 1916, formed the National Woman's Party (NWP).

Alice Paul was a feminist and suffragist during the early 1900s. Although she was raised in a Quaker family, she favored the use of militant tactics and devoted her life to fighting for women's rights. She also wrote the Equal Rights Amendment and worked hard, though unsuccessfully, to secure its passage. (Library of Congress)

In early 1917, organization members volunteered to picket in front of the White House. They called themselves "silent sentinels" that brought forth a patronizing reaction—a tip of the hat—from President Wilson when he passed by. However, when the United States entered World War I in April 1917, Wilson's response and the public's attitude changed. Protests before the White House were deemed unpatriotic or, at worst, a threat to national security because the pickets carried signs calling the U.S. president "Kaiser Wilson," equating him to the wartime enemy, German emperor Wilhelm II. Some of the picket signs also reminded the public that England and Germany had enfranchised women even though they were at war.

Police soon arrested pickets, including Paul, on false charges of obstructing sidewalk traffic. They, in fact, were not violating any law. When the women refused to pay the fines, they were sent to Occoquan Workhouse, a notoriously filthy Virginia prison where the women were fed vermin-infested food and suffered beatings. They demanded that they be treated as political prisoners, being jailed illegally on false charges. They were not allowed legal representation and protested with hunger strikes. Like the suffragists in England, Paul and others were forcibly fed. When the brutal conditions in the prison finally became known publicly, many government officials and the press demanded that the suffragists be released. They were freed in November 1917. According to author Eleanor Flexner, "on March 4th, 1918, the District of Columbia Court of Appeals invalidated every single one of the prison sentences and the original arrests as well" (Flexner 1974, 287).

Paul went on with her campaign, and NWP began a speaking tour with suffragists released from jail dressed like prisoners. They traveled on a train called the Prison Special. Some suffragists drove across the nation, stopping along the way to get signatures on petitions for the federal amendment. Still other suffragists publicized the fact that while the United States was fighting for worldwide democracy, the nation denied justice to millions of American women. That argument finally convinced Wilson that he should support a federal amendment, but the U.S. Senate did not agree. Opposition came from legislators who believed in states' rights and also from lobbyists representing businesses that objected to higher wages for women and groups that claimed the amendment would threaten the family. After much wrangling and the vote of one senator who switched from "no" to "yes," the Senate finally passed the Nineteenth Amendment on June 4, 1919.

However, 36 states had to ratify the amendment, which did not happen until August 18, 1920. The amendment reads: "The right of citizens of the United States to vote shall not be denied or abridged by the United States or by any State on account of sex. Congress shall have power to enforce this article by appropriate legislation."

In spite of this long-awaited victory, Paul wanted to go beyond American women's voting rights to providing equal rights for women in employment, pay, and other areas where they faced discrimination. She began to work for a federal Equal Rights Amendment (ERA) that stated: "Men and women shall have equal rights throughout the United States and every place subject to its jurisdiction." The amendment was introduced in 1923 and in every Congressional session until 1972, when it passed. (However, it has not been ratified by the states to date due to anti-ERA political activists such as Phyllis Schlafly who organized STOP-ERA soon after the amendment's passage.)

Meantime, while working on the ERA, Alice Paul earned a law degree from Washington College of Law in 1922 and one from American University in 1927. She received a doctorate in law from American University in 1928.

During the 1930s, Paul was active in efforts to organize an international committee of the NWP. In 1938, she established the World Women's Party (WWP) for Equal Rights with headquarters in Geneva, Switzerland. The WWP worked with the League of Nations, established at the end of World War I to ensure peace and the precursor of the United Nations founded in 1945. WWP's efforts were designed to promote global equality for women, and in 1946, the United Nations established the UN Commission on the Status of Women, which is dedicated to gender equality and advancement of women.

When World War II (1939–1945) was underway, Paul and WWP assisted people driven from their homes by German Nazi invaders. A villa near the WWP's headquarters sheltered the refugees. WWP also helped the refugees find safe passage to the United States. In 1941, the WWP moved to the United States and began work for American women's equality issues.

During the 1960s, women were pressing for their rights and equality. For example, author Betty Friedan's book *The Feminine Mystique* (1963) exposed the sense of discontent and frustration that millions of women felt due to their lack of choices other than caring for the home and children. About the same time, Paul was instrumental in convincing the U.S. Congress to include provisions that prohibit gender discrimination in the Civil Rights Act of 1964. Requirements of Title VII of the act, for example, make it unlawful for an employer:

1. to fail or refuse to hire or to discharge any individual, or otherwise to discriminate against any individual with respect to his compensation, terms, conditions, or privileges of employment, because of such individual's race, color, religion, sex, or national origin; or

2. to limit, segregate, or classify his employees or applicants for employment in any way which would deprive or tend to deprive any individual of employment opportunities or otherwise adversely affect his status as an employee, because of such individual's race, color, religion, sex, or national origin.

Other lengthy provisions in Title VII that outlaw gender discrimination include employment agency practices, work training programs, discriminatory use of test scores, and duties of the Equal Employment Opportunity Commission.

During the early 1970s, Paul continued to lobby for states to ratify the ERA, but she suffered a mild stroke in 1974 and was hospitalized in New York. Since she was disabled, she was transferred to the Quaker Greenleaf Extension Home in Moorestown, New Jersey, near Paulsdale, her family home. She died of heart failure on July 9, 1977, in Moorestown.

Much of Paul's legacy is preserved at the Alice Paul Institute in Mount Laurel, New Jersey, which has maintained Paulsdale and obtained its designation as a National Historic Landmark. She is also remembered by Swarthmore College and Montclair State University in New Jersey which have named buildings in her honor. The NWP, which Paul founded, continues its efforts on behalf of the ERA and other women's rights issues.

See also Addams, Jane; Catt, Carrie Chapman; Friedan, Betty; Schlafly, Phyllis

References

Adams, Katherine H., and Michael L. Keene. *Alice Paul and the American Suffrage Campaign.* Urbana and Chicago: University of Illinois Press, 2008.

Butler, Amy E. *Two Paths to Equality: Alice Paul and Ethel M. Smith in the ERA Debate, 1921–1929.* Albany: State University of New York Press, 2002.

Flexner, Eleanor. *Century of Struggle: The Woman's Rights Movement in the United States.* New York: Atheneum, 1974. Reprint of 1959 ed. published by Harvard University Press.

Gillmore, Inez Haynes. *The Story of the Woman's Party.* New York: Kraus Reprints, 1971. First published 1921.

Lunardini, Christine A. *From Equal Suffrage to Equal Rights: Alice Paul and the National Woman's Party: 1910–1928.* New York: New York University Press, 1988.

Walton, Mary. *A Woman's Crusade: Alice Paul and the Battle for the Ballot.* New York: Palgrave Macmillan, 2010.

Peltier, Leonard (1944–)

The web site of the United States Federal Bureau of Prisons lists American Indian rights activist Leonard Peltier as a prisoner at its penitentiary in Lewisburg, Pennsylvania. His original sentence—handed down in April 1977—of two consecutive life terms for killing two Federal Bureau of Investigation (FBI) agents currently translates into a release date of October 21, 2040, barring any change made at his next scheduled parole hearing set for July 2024. At his last hearing, held in July 2009, a federal prosecutor said, "authorities decided that releasing him would diminish the seriousness of his crime" (Nicholson 2009). However, Peltier's "crime" has been surrounded by controversy and debate. Some doubt that Peltier committed the deeds of which he was accused. Others feel that, regardless of his guilt or innocence, he was convicted by an unfair legal system. Still others believe that if guilty, Peltier had a legitimate claim of self-defense. Another segment argues that he and his comrades were justifiably "at war" and, therefore, mere soldiers innocent of wrongdoing; instead, they were defending their homes and people.

Born in Grand Forks, North Dakota, on September 12, 1944, Leonard was the 11th of 13 children in the Peltier family. His father, Leo, was three-quarters Chippewa and one-quarter French, while his mother, Alvina Peltier, was half Dakota-Sioux and half Chippewa. When Peltier was four, his parents divorced. He and his sister were sent to the Turtle Mountain Indian Reservation to be raised by their paternal grandparents, Alex and Mary Dubois-Peltier.

When he turned nine in 1953, Peltier was sent to a boarding school in Wahperen, run by the Bureau of Indian Affairs (BIA). During his time there, his experiences were similar to those of most Indian children enrolled in such facilities: they were removed not only from their families, but also from all aspects of their culture, made to speak only English and to live in the "White man's world," while continually being reminded that they were inferior Indians. Upon leaving in 1957, he attended Flandreau Indian School in South Dakota but dropped out before earning his high school diploma. He worked a variety of jobs, eventually moving to Seattle, Washington. In his 20s, he opened an auto body repair shop. Before long, he realized that he was more interested in Indian rights issues than in his career and became of member of the American Indian Movement (AIM), forever changing his life.

AIM was founded in 1968 by Dennis Banks, an Ojibwa, Russell Means of the Oglala Dakota Nation, and others. AIM's purpose was to deal with a variety of Native American issues, such as poverty, housing, and treaty concerns. In 1972, Peltier joined Banks and Means in the Trail of Broken Treaties, a march to Washington, D.C., to protest the U.S. government's broken agreements with Native Americans.

In 1973, AIM was involved in the 71-day siege at Wounded Knee at the Pine Ridge Indian Reservation, home to the Lakota (or Dakota) Nation. During the siege, both sides traded gunfire repeatedly. Two AIM members were killed. The siege officially ended in May 1973. But the next three years were ones of great retribution against the traditionalists, with over 60 unsolved murders. Hundreds were harassed and beaten. More than 500 were arrested without cause, with few convictions resulting. There was a bitter divide on the reservation between traditionalists, those who adhered to traditional Lakota cultural ways and wanted greater freedom from the federal government, and progressives who did not. The traditionalists believed that the tribal leaders had been co-opted and were working against the tribe's interests and, instead, were mere puppets of the BIA and the U.S. government.

From the start of the Wounded Knee siege, AIM had protested the leadership role of Richard "Dick" Wilson, ensconced as tribal chairman, president of the tribal council. He had developed a militia of sorts, the Guardians of the Oglala Nation, nicknamed by his opposition as the GOON squad that he employed ruthlessly to maintain his grasp on tribal funds and power. When he was reelected to the position in 1974, "the U.S. Commission on Civil Rights declared Wilson's election 'invalid.'" However, "The Justice Department took no action, and Richard Wilson, restored to office, dismissed the Civil Rights Commission as 'a bunch of hoodlums.' Without noticeable protest from U.S. authorities ... his goons embarked on a new reign of terror; increasingly, the AIM supporters, their families, and their friends were attacked, beaten and run off the road in an ongoing series of 'accidents,' many of them fatal. Despite the open lawlessness and violence he encouraged, Wilson seemed entirely confident of state and federal support" (Matthiessen 1991, 128).

Although Peltier was not at Wounded Knee, he was one of many AIM members who traveled to nearby Pine Ridge Reservation to support the cause. Some of them encamped at the Jumping Bull Ranch and were armed with rifles to protect the traditionalists from Wilson and his GOON

Leonard Peltier (shown here in prison in 1986) remains perhaps the most controversial figure of the American Indian Movement. Serving two life sentences for killing two FBI agents, he contends that his conviction was political and not criminal in nature. (AP/Wide World Photos)

Squad. Wilson was employing every means he could to maintain control, and covertly (and, sometimes, even overtly), local, state, and federal government employees were trying to help him succeed in his efforts. About the same time, two FBI agents, driving in separate, unmarked cars, drove onto the Pine Ridge Reservation on June 26, 1975. They had observed and were following a red pickup truck that fit the description of one belonging to an Indian youth, Jimmy Eagle, who was wanted for questioning.

The first indication of any trouble came swiftly when Agent Ronald A. Williams announced over his radio that he and fellow agent Jack R. Coler had come under attack from the truck they had been pursuing. He indicated they were unable to return fire with their .38-caliber pistols and were virtually defenseless against the high-powered rifles being used against them. A subsequent panic-stricken message conveyed his fear that they would be killed if help did not arrive. A further communication indicated he had been wounded.

Reinforcements arrived, supported by BIA members and local police. Hours passed, as they were pinned down under heavy fire. A BIA rifleman fatally wounded tribal member Joseph Stuntz. Records noted that at least two more hours passed before authorities were able to make their way to the agents' bullet-ridden vehicles, where their lifeless bodies were found. Near dusk, aided by tear gas, the Jumping Bull compound was stormed. However, all inside had escaped across the southern hills, setting off an extensive manhunt.

In the fall of 1975, two AIM members, Darrelle Brown and Robert Robideau, were arrested and charged in connection with the deaths of Williams and Coler. In late December, Peltier was put on the FBI's 10 Most Wanted Fugitives List. He was eventually tracked down in Canada, where he, too, was arrested and charged in the shootings. The trial of the first two men proceeded without Peltier, since the FBI had to first clear the hurdle of justifying the case for his extradition back to the United States. Brown and Robideau's trial, held in Cedar Rapids, Iowa, resulted in a jury acquittal on the grounds of self-defense. The U.S. government, in the meantime, based its extradition request on testimony from Myrtle Poor Bear, who claimed to be Peltier's girlfriend and a witness to the killings. She later recanted these statements, but the trial judge would not allow her to testify to this in court, saying she was not mentally competent and calling into question whether her extradition affidavit ever should have been allowed in the first place.

Peltier was returned to the United States in February 1976; his trial was not held until the following year and took place in Fargo, North Dakota. The prosecution of his case was significantly more aggressive than that of Brown and Robideau. The jury was presented with repeated verbal and visual evidence of the manner in which the agents were killed, that is, by being shot—after already being incapacitated—at close range, in the head, execution style.

Since 1977, there have been numerous attempts to challenge Peltier's conviction in the Eighth Circuit Court of Appeals. A veritable laundry list of reasons to overturn the verdict have included some of the following: (1) three witnesses who placed Brown, Robideau, and Peltier at the shootings later recanted and said their statements had been coerced by the FBI, with varied degrees of emotional and physical threat; (2) the description of the vehicle the agents pursued changed at trial from a "red pickup truck" to a "red and white station wagon/panel van," coincidentally matching what Peltier drove; (3) years later, a Freedom of Information request revealed that an FBI expert had performed a forensics test of the firing pin from the rifle Peltier was alleged to have used and had determined that the crime scene cartridge case could not have come from that gun; this information had not only been withheld from the defense and the jury, but during the trial, the FBI had one of its experts testify that a shell casing found near the agents' bodies had in fact matched Peltier's rifle—contrary to their own report; (4) additionally, more ballistic and other crime scene evidence was inadequately investigated and processed; (5) the defense was not allowed to inform the jury that the FBI previously had been rebuked for tampering with both evidence and witnesses, even though there was precedent for doing so; (6) Peltier was convicted and sentenced on the basis of a first-degree murder charge; at the trial, the prosecutor stated, "We proved that he went down to the bodies and executed those two young men at point blank range," but later on appeals, the government's position changed to, "We had a murder. We had numerous shooters. We do not know who specifically fired what killing shots ... we do not know, quote-unquote, who shot the agents" (Goodman 2000).

It is not surprising that AIM members consider Peltier to be a political prisoner. However, his cause also has been taken up by a broad base of supporters around the globe. They have included Nelson Mandela; Amnesty International; the United Nations Commission for Human Rights; the National Council of Churches; the Dalai Lama; the parliaments of Europe, Belgium, and Italy; the Kennedy Memorial Center for Human

Rights; Archbishop Desmond Tutu; and Reverend Jesse Jackson. Peltier was the subject of the 1992 documentary *Incident at Oglala*, and the movie *Thunderheart* was partly based on Peltier. A petition containing over 500,000 names was delivered to the White House in December 1993 on his behalf. Six months later, thousands demonstrated in Washington, D.C., for Peltier's freedom, and the next month, an equal number participated in a Walk for Justice, then lobbied their senators for his release.

Efforts continued unabated, taking on greater momentum in 1999, toward the end of President Bill Clinton's tenure. In response to a rumor that Peltier might be pardoned, then FBI director Louis Freeh expressed opposition to clemency via a much-publicized letter. More than 500 FBI agents and their families joined his protest, demonstrating outside the White House. No pardon was issued. The succeeding president, George W. Bush, also declined to act on Peltier's behalf. To date, Peltier's petition for clemency remains inactive and ignored at the Department of Justice.

Peltier maintains that he did not shoot the two agents. In an interview with Amy Goodman, he said "I was defending myself. I was defending women and children. We were under attack" (Goodman 2000). He continues to pursue legal recourse for his freedom, not expecting parole. His supporters, meanwhile, continue to do battle with the government, attempting to obtain documentary evidence that has been withheld to date.

Margaret Gay

See also Banks, Dennis; Means, Russell; Tall, JoAnn

References

Federal Bureau of Prisons. "Statement from the Federal Bureau of Prisons Regarding the Current Status of Inmate Leonard Peltier (89637-132).'' Press Release, February 1999. http://www.bop.gov/news/press/press_releases/ipapelt.jsp (accessed September 10, 2011).

Goodman, Amy (interviewer). "Leonard Peltier Speaks from Prison." *Democracy Now!* June 12, 2000. http://www.democracynow.org/2000/6/12/leonard_peltier_speaks_from_prison (accessed March 20, 2011).

Grossman, Mark. *The ABC-CLIO Companion to the Native American Rights Movement*. Santa Barbara, CA: ABC-CLIO, 1996.

Matthiessen, Peter. *In the Spirit of Crazy Horse*. New York: Penguin Books, 1991.

Nicholson, Blake, Associated Press. "American Indian Activist Peltier Denied Parole." *Newsday*, August 21, 2009. http://www.newsday.com/american-indian-activist-peltier-denied-parole-1.1385273 (accessed March 15, 2011).

Thompson, Carolyn, Associated Press. "Judge Allows FBI to Withhold Some Peltier Documents." Leonard Peltier Defense Committee, February 27, 2006. http://lpdctexas.blogspot.com/2006_02_01_lpdctexas_archive.html (accessed September 10, 2011).

Perkins, Frances (1880–1965)

Frances Perkins was a labor reformer, a social worker, an advocate for the powerless, an antiwar activist, and a champion of women's rights. She became the first woman to serve in a U.S. presidential cabinet as secretary of labor. But she was not admired by American conservatives, who considered her a dissident who did not comply with mainstream values; some even labeled her a subversive for her pacifist stance.

At her birth on April 10, 1880, in Boston, Massachusetts, Perkins was named Fannie Coralie. In later years, she legally changed her given name to Frances. When Fannie was two years old, her parents, Frederick and Susan (Bean) Perkins, moved their family to Worcester, Massachusetts, a Republican stronghold west of Boston, where Frederick and a partner opened an office supply store. The business soon became profitable and provided a comfortable middle-class income for the Perkins family. Frederick and Susan were Congregationalists, devout believers in doing good works in God's name, which included helping the impoverished. However, they were inclined to believe that poverty was a weakness of individuals and had nothing to do with social injustice.

In 1884, Fannie's younger sister Ethel was born. Ethel was not especially bright, according to biographer Kirstin Downey. On the other hand, "Fannie was an exceptional child, unusually verbal and articulate, and she discovered she had more in common with her father than with other members of her immediate family." At a young age, she learned Greek and under her father's guidance began to prepare for college, even though at the time only a small percentage of females received an education beyond high school (Downey 2009, 8).

Fannie attended Worcester Classical High School. She was one of the few female students enrolled in this public college preparatory school. After graduating in 1898, she attended Mount Holyoke, a women's college. While there, she took a class on the elements of political economy, which turned out to be a revelation; her professor "sent her students into the local mills and had them write a report on the lives of workers." Fannie's experience demonstrated to her that people were not poor because of some moral failing, as her parents believed, but "that people could fall into poverty due to harsh circumstances" (Cohen 2009, 163).

At Mount Holyoke, Fannie met Florence Kelley, executive secretary of the National Consumers League, which has operated since 1899 on the principle that consumers should demand reliable goods and services and safe working conditions for people who produce those goods and services. Kelley was on a speaking tour, traveling across the United States and lecturing on unhealthy and dangerous working conditions in factories and mills, advocating for a minimum wage for workers, and condemning child labor. Fannie was greatly influenced by Kelley and the league's work; Kelley, in fact, became a mentor and friend.

As a young adult, Fannie also read books by Jacob A. Riis, a reporter who investigated and wrote about New York City's crowded tenements with their appalling living conditions and about the children abandoned on the streets. His book *How the Other Half Lives: Studies among the Tenements of New York* (1890) was especially revealing to Fannie.

By the time Fannie graduated from Mount Holyoke in 1902, she was certain that she wanted to be a social worker. She considered returning to her home, which was customary for young women. Instead, she chose to go to New York City and find work. Her application with a social work agency was turned down because of her lack of experience dealing with impoverished people. She was forced to return to Worcester and take teaching jobs. But she longed to get away and, in 2004, went to Lake Forest, Illinois, a Chicago suburb, to teach science at a women's college. As a faculty member of Ferry Hall, she changed her name to Frances Perkins and became a part of the strict campus life required for females—faculty and students alike. She also joined the local Episcopal church, whose parishioners were primarily affluent Lake Forest residents.

Through a classmate, Perkins learned about Hull House, a settlement house, or "sanctuary," in the poorest neighborhood in

Chicago. Founded by Jane Addams, Hull House offered food, housing, health and child care, education, and other social services for the impoverished working class and newly arrived Eastern European immigrants. During her free time, Perkins traveled the short distance from Lake Forest to work on social welfare projects at Hull House. There she met author Upton Sinclair, who wrote *The Jungle* (1906), a muckraking story of the abominable conditions in Chicago's meatpacking industry and the plight of the working class in the city. In her social work, Perkins was able to help some meatpackers as well as other needy workers living near Hull House.

Even though Perkins was involved in the type of work she long had wanted to do, she also had to earn a living. She accepted a social work position in Philadelphia, Pennsylvania, and moved there in 1907. She worked with immigrant women and southern black women who had been lured into prostitution with deceptive offers of good jobs. She found ways to put out of business some of the criminals who solicited women for sex.

While in Philadelphia, Perkins enrolled at the University of Pennsylvania's Wharton School of Finance. One of her professors was impressed with her abilities and helped her obtain a fellowship at Columbia University in New York City. She moved there in 1908 and lived in Greenwich House, a settlement house in Greenwich Village. She earned a master's degree at Columbia in 1910. That year, she took a job as secretary of the New York office of the Consumers League. As she worked on campaigns and lobbied legislators to improve working conditions in factories and to abolish child labor, she received guidance from Florence Kelley who by then was well known for her leadership of the National Consumers League. Perkins also was active in the women's suffrage movement, giving speeches on street corners and marching with other advocates for women's right to vote.

In 1911, a tragedy occurred in Greenwich Village. She witnessed the terrible fire at the Triangle Shirtwaist factory, which was on the 8th, 9th, and 10th floors of an industrial building off Washington Square. Hundreds of immigrant women and girls were employed at the factory, working under crowded, unsanitary conditions. When the fire broke out, workers tried to get out of the locked building that had no working fire escapes. Many in panic jumped from windows, falling to their deaths. As the fire raged, 146 people died.

The tragedy deeply affected Perkins, who resolved to fight the inhumane conditions that led to the disaster. A week after the fire, she heard a speech by Rose Schneiderman, head of the Women's Trade Union League (WTUL), who exhorted her audience to take action to help pass protective legislation for workers. Perkins took heed and became politically active, not only lobbying legislators, but also seeking help from friends and acquaintances with political connections. One of her first major successes came when former U.S. president Theodore Roosevelt in 1912 appointed Perkins executive secretary of an industrial reform organization called the Committee on Safety. The committee convinced state legislators to establish a panel to investigate working conditions statewide and to find ways to improve them.

By 1913, Perkins was ready to marry a man she had seen off and on from about 1910. He was handsome, affluent Paul Caldwell Wilson, who was one of the New York mayor's personal secretaries. Wilson and Perkins were deeply in love. Yet Perkins was unsure about a permanent relationship;

she liked being independent. When they married in September 1913, Perkins insisted on keeping her own name. The couple had one daughter, Susanna; prior to her daughter's birth in 1916, Perkins suffered a miscarriage and in a second pregnancy, a child was stillborn. By 1918, Wilson had lost his job and a great deal of money in bad investments. He became emotionally unstable, and as his mental health deteriorated, he was eventually placed in an institution for the mentally ill. (He died in 1952.)

Perkins had to find a way to support the family. Because of her political connections, she was appointed in 1918 to the New York State Industrial Commission, a position that paid a good salary. She was the first woman to hold that post, and headed the commission as chairperson from 1926 to 1928, when she became industrial commissioner of New York State. New York's governor Franklin D. Roosevelt (1882–1945), who had known Perkins professionally and socially for many years, reappointed Perkins to that position in 1929. She also had the support of the president's wife, Eleanor Roosevelt.

When Franklin Roosevelt became president in 1933, he appointed Perkins secretary of labor; she was the first female to serve in a cabinet position and stayed throughout Roosevelt's presidency. During the Great Depression, Perkins led the President's Committee on Economic Security and convinced Roosevelt to set up programs to help the unemployed. She wrote *People at Work* (1934) and also helped draft the Social Security Act (officially the federal Old-Age, Survivors, and Disability Insurance program), which became law in 1935.

In addition, Perkins was able to steer legislators to pass the National Labor Relations Act of 1935, which protected workers' rights to organize, and the Fair Labor Standards Act of 1938, which established a minimum wage and banned most child labor. These laws and programs were part of Roosevelt's "New Deal," which also included the Agricultural Adjustment Act to pay farmers to set up camps for migrant workers; the Public Works Administration that hired workers to construct roads, bridges, and other infrastructure; the Civilian Conservation Corps that sent young men to stem erosion, plant trees, and prevent destruction of the nation's natural resources; and the Tennessee Valley Authority that provided electrical power and flood controls in the Tennessee River Valley, a poor, undeveloped region.

In spite of these accomplishments, Perkins seldom received credit. Also, she had acquired enemies, some of whom resented a woman at the helm of the Department of Labor. In addition, some members of Congress railed against her for supporting Harry Bridges, leader of the longshoremen's union and their strike in 1934 on the West Coast. Because President Roosevelt was on vacation aboard a ship, Secretary of State Cornell Hull was acting president. Hull wanted to send the army to stop the strike. But Perkins was opposed, saying it was a local issue; she cabled Roosevelt, who agreed and ordered Hull not to send the army. This infuriated Perkins's congressional enemies, who sought to impeach her. They believed that Perkins should have deported Bridges, who was from Australia, because, they argued, he had allowed communists to infiltrate the union and he was an undesirable alien. There was no evidence to support such a contention, and Bridges was not deported. But for months after her impeachment hearings, Perkins received hate mail. Still, she persevered with her many tasks.

Roosevelt died of a stroke in 1945, and Perkins left the Department of Labor. Vice President Harry Truman (1884–1972) became president and appointed Perkins to the U.S. Civil Service Commission. She also wrote a book, *The Roosevelt I Knew* (1946).

From 1953 to 1956, Perkins lectured at the University of Illinois, and from 1956 to 1965, she was on the faculty of Cornell University School of Industrial and Labor Relations. She also continued her public speaking tours. On May 14, 1965, she died at the age of 85 in New York. In 1980, on what would have been her 100th birthday, the building housing the U.S. Department of Labor in Washington, D.C., was named in her honor. She was inducted into the National Women's Hall of Fame in 1982 and the Labor Hall of Fame in 1988.

See also Addams, Jane; Kelley, Florence; Roosevelt, Eleanor; Schneiderman, Rose; Sinclair, Upton

References

Cohen, Adam. *Nothing to Fear: FDR's Inner Circle and the Hundred Days that Created Modern America*. New York: Penguin Press, 2009.

Downey, Kirstin. *The Woman behind the New Deal: The Life of Frances Perkins, FDR's Secretary of Labor and His Moral Conscience*. New York: Nan A. Talese/Doubleday, 2009.

Pasachoff, Naomi E. *Frances Perkins: Champion of the New Deal*. Oxford and New York: Oxford University Press, 1999.

R

Rand, Ayn (1905–1982)

"You will see that man is not a helpless monster by nature, but he becomes one when he discards that faculty: his mind. And if you ask me, what is greatness? I will answer: it is the capacity to live by the three fundamental values of John Galt: reason, purpose, self-esteem" (Toffler 1964). Ayn Rand was speaking of a fictional character in her novel *Atlas Shrugged* (1957) in an interview with Alvin Toffler. Toffler described Rand as one of the most important and outspoken intellectuals in twentieth-century America. Often considered fringe by critics and philosophers because of her "explosively unpopular ideas," Rand rejected the criticism "with unblinking immodesty" (Toffler 1964). As Rand stated, her intent was to challenge the cultural tradition of 2,500 years.

Rand was born Alisa (sometimes written as Alissa or Alyssa) Zinovievna Rosenbaum on February 2, 1905, in St. Petersburg, Russia, which biographer Heller described as "the capital city of the most anti-Semitic and politically divided nation on the European continent" (Heller 2009, 2). Rand was born just three weeks following the 1905 revolution, in which Czar Nicholas II's cavalrymen fired upon 30,000 striking factory workers, labor organizers, students, and families who marched in protest of political, social, and labor conditions. The massacre became known as Bloody Sunday.

Ayn's mother, Anna Borisovna, was a religiously observant Jew who had worked as a dentist prior to having children. Ayn's father, Zinovy Zakharvich, was a successful pharmacist who owned his own shop. He was tolerant of his wife's religious practices, although he was a nonobservant Jew. Rand had two younger sisters, Natasha (born 1907) and Eleanora, known as Nora (born 1910). Considered a difficult child by her mother, Rand was intelligent and solitary. Nicknamed Ayinotchka, her father sometimes called her Ayin. Rand loved storytelling and was an ardent reader. An avid reader himself, Rand's father admired her proud spirit and encouraged her to write stories (Heller 2009, 9).

In the summer of 1914, when Rand was nine years old, the Rosenbaums went on a six-week vacation through Europe. When they reached Paris, the family learned that Archduke Franz Ferdinand of Austria-Hungary had been assassinated in Sarajevo. Austria-Hungary and Germany had declared war on Serbia. Those countries allied with Serbia, including Russia, France, and England, retaliated. World War I had begun, and the family returned to Russia.

As the Russian army marched to war, Rand entered school. Considered "the brain" of her class, Rand spent much of her time writing and reading stories about "unflinching heroes." One of her heroes was Joan of Arc, because "she stood alone against everyone, even to the point of death." By age 10, Rand was determined to be a writer. As her mother wrote to her years later, "You [always] planned to be greater than Columbus" (Heller 2009, 21).

By 1917, six million Russians had been killed as the world war entered its third year. Acts of anti-Semitism increased. Czar Nicholas abdicated his throne in February 1917 in the first of two revolutions occurring that year. Rand's father followed the politics of Alexander Kerensky, vice chairman and dominant figure of the newly formed socialist-liberal coalition government. In October 1917, Vladimir Lenin and the Russian Social Democratic Labor Party, called the Bolsheviks, overthrew the provisional government. Rand was 12 years old as the second revolution broke out, and the Russian Civil War began. When the Bolsheviks confiscated her father's pharmacy in the fall of 1918, not long before the end of World War I in November, the family fled to the Ukraine. In the spring of 1919, the family found refuge in Yevpatoria, Crimea.

Now living in Crimea, Rand attended high school. During these years, she was introduced to the works of Aristotle and his emphasis on metaphysical naturalism, reason, and self-realization. These values would later provide the cornerstone for her philosophy in objectivism. She also announced that she was an atheist. She disregarded faith, as she later explained, "in the sense of blind belief, belief unsupported by, or contrary to, the facts of reality and the conclusions of reason. Faith, as such, is extremely detrimental to human life: It is the negation of reason" (Toffler 1964).

In high school, she was also introduced to American history, and became convinced that it provided a model for what a nation of free men could be. A witness and survivor to the brutality of the Russian revolutions, she admired the ideals of the U.S. founding fathers. As she would write later, "All previous systems had regarded man as a sacrificial means to the ends of others, and society as an end in itself. The United States regarded man as an end in himself, and society as a means to the peaceful, orderly, voluntary coexistence of individuals" (Rand, April 1963).

American writer Ayn Rand used her fictional characters to express the philosophy of objectivism. Rand is best known for her novel *Atlas Shrugged* (1957), which was met with negative reviews but became a best seller. (Library of Congress)

In 1921, Rand graduated from high school. Not long after, Rand and her family returned to St. Petersburg, now called Petrograd, where Rand entered the Petrograd State University to study philosophy and history. She graduated from the university in October 1924. An admirer of the cinema, she then enrolled in the State Institute of Cinema Arts in Leningrad to study screenwriting. Abbreviating her Russian surname to Rand, she adopted the professional penname Ayn Rand, and wrote her first published works, a booklet on the Polish silent film actress *Pola Negri* (1925) and another titled *Hollywood: American Movie City* (1926).

In January 1926, Rand obtained a visa and left Russia to visit relatives living in Chicago, Illinois. While her visit was to be brief, she was determined never to return to her homeland. Arriving in the United States on February 19 on a ship that anchored in New York harbor, she welcomed the Manhattan skyline with "tears of splendor" (Heller 2009, 53). While staying with her relatives, she perfected her English as she continued to study films. She also wrote her first short story in English, "The Husband I Bought." Receiving an extension for her visa, she moved to Hollywood, California, intent on becoming a screenwriter.

Not long after arriving in Hollywood, she met Cecil B. DeMille, one of the leading Hollywood directors of the time. DeMille hired her as an extra for his film, *The King of Kings*. While on set, she met the aspiring actor, Frank O'Connor. The two were married on April 15, 1929. On March 13, 1931, Rand became an American citizen.

Eventually becoming one of DeMille's script readers, Rand also worked at other jobs to support her writing, including in the RKO wardrobe department. In 1932, she sold her first screenplay, *Red Pawn*, to Universal Studios. The project featured several anti-Soviet themes and proved unsuccessful. This was the beginning of Hollywood's "Red Decade" (1936–1946) in which many American intellectuals were pro-Communist and respected the Soviet experiment.

After Rand finished her first significant novel, *We The Living* (1936), she called it "as near to an autobiography as I will ever write ... but only in the intellectual sense" (Rand 1995, xviii). The book was Rand's first political statement against communism, reflecting the brutality of life in postrevolutionary Russia. It explored Rand's ideas of individualism versus collectivism. As with *Red Pawn*, the anticommunist theme proved unpopular. Several publishers rejected the novel until Macmillan published it in the United States. The book was not a commercial success and quickly went out of print. However, it was reprinted in 1959, following the success of *Atlas Shrugged*.

In 1935, Rand began her next significant work, *The Fountainhead*. Rand investigated the more ethical themes of individual independence and integrity. As Stephen Cox explained, the book is a metaphysical statement on the American experience, and the ideas were regarded as dangerous. Cox stated, "Rand's courageous challenge to accepted ideas was rendered still more courageous by her willingness to state her individualist premises in the clearest terms and to defend the most radical implications that could be drawn from them" (Cox 2006).

As with her previous work, Rand had difficulty in finding a publisher. Bobbs-Merrill Company finally published it in 1943. Although intellectuals and reviewers dismissed the book, it became a best seller, offering Rand both financial security and fame. The book was made into a movie, starring Gary Cooper and Patricia Neal in 1949, for which Rand wrote the screenplay.

In 1940, Rand became involved in political activism. She and her husband volunteered full time for the presidential campaign of Republican Wendell Willkie. A member of the liberal wing of the Republican GOP, Willkie crusaded against Franklin Roosevelt's policies of the New Deal. The United States had yet to enter World War II. Unlike the leading Republican candidates, including Robert Taft and Thomas Dewey, Willkie supported the need to aid Britain in its fight against Germany.

During this time, Rand met many intellectuals who supported free-market capitalism.

She also developed a friendship with libertarian writer Isabel Paterson. Paterson's book, *The God of the Machine* (1943), was published the same year as Rand's *The Fountainhead*. Over the next few years, the two promoted each other's work. Rand, an atheist, enjoyed discussing at length her ideas on religion and philosophy with Paterson, a deist.

Rand also became involved with the Motion Picture Alliance for the Preservation of American Ideals (MPA). Formed in the early 1940s, the politically conservative organization was cofounded by Walt Disney, and included many leading actors of the day. Following World War II, the Second Red Scare (1947–1957) targeted national and foreign communists who allegedly influenced society and infiltrated the government. In 1947, the House Un-American Activities Committee (HUAC) held nine days of hearings into alleged communist propaganda and influence on the Hollywood motion picture industry. The first systematic Hollywood blacklist was created, citing 10 writers and directors who refused to give testimony. Rand testified as one of the "friendly" witnesses.

In 1951, Rand and her husband moved to New York City. She began working full time on her next project, considered her most ambitious novel, *Atlas Shrugged* (1957). Several admirers often gathered at her apartment, including economist Alan Greenspan, future Federal Reserve chairman, as well as psychologist Nathanial Branden and his wife Barbara, and Leonard Peikoff. Branden in particular became a prominent figure in Rand's life. In 1954, despite the 25-year age difference, Rand and the younger Branden entered into a romantic affair with the consent of their spouses. Branden would later found the Nathanial Branden Institute, the leading objectivist institution during the 1960s.

When *Atlas Shrugged* was published, David Kelley called the book a capitalist manifesto, stating that "Rand's great achievement was to offer a vision of capitalism as a moral ideal... the meaning of these events is put into words, in speeches by various characters that lay out a new philosophy and moral code of individualism. In its characters, its plot and its philosophical themes, *Atlas* is about a new revolution, a capitalist revolution" (Kelley 2009). The book became an international best seller. It was also Rand's last work of fiction.

Throughout the 1960s and 1970s, Rand wrote and lectured on her philosophy, now called objectivism. Rand's philosophy advocated such virtues as independence, productiveness, integrity, and justice. Grounded in reason and metaphysics, the basic principles included the rejection of mysticism (an acceptance of faith or emotion as a means of knowledge), skepticism (the claim that certainty is impossible), and determinism (that man is a victim of forces beyond his control). The most significant of her publications included *The Virtue of Selfishness* (1964), *Capitalism: The Unknown Ideal* (1966), the *Romantic Manifesto* (1969), and *Introduction to Objectivist Epistemology* (1979). Interest in the objectivist movement began to wane in 1968 when Rand and Branden parted ways for personal and professional reasons. Rand's own involvement in the movement began to decline following the death of her husband in 1979.

Rand died of heart failure in her New York City home on March 6, 1982. Writer Sam Anderson reflected on the life of Rand, stating "She was proud, grouchy, vindictive, insulting, dismissive, and rash. (One former associate called her 'the Evel Knievel of leaping to conclusions.') But she was also idealistic, yearning, candid, worshipful, precise, and improbably charming... an irresistible force, a machine of pure reason, a free-market Spock who converted doubters left, right, and center" (Anderson 2009).

Rand's influence is apparent currently with such talk show hosts as Glenn Beck and Rush Limbaugh and various conservative politicians who discuss or recommend Rand's ideas. U.S. Supreme Court justice Clarence Thomas also has acknowledged that Rand's works have had substantial influence on his life, as has Representative Paul Ryan from Wisconsin, a rising star in the Republican Party. And there is little doubt that Rand and her ideas are still of interest, since two biographies about her—*Ayn Rand and the World She Made* and *Goddess of the Market: Ayn Rand and the American Right*—were published in 2009 and since then have been circulating widely. A film of *Atlas Shrugged* was released in 2011, receiving mostly negative reviews for the poor quality of the movie.

Bobbi Miller

See also Beck, Glenn; Limbaugh, Rush

References

Anderson, Sam. "Mrs. Logic." *New York*, October 18, 2009. http://nymag.com/arts/books/features/60120/ (accessed December 26, 2010).

Cox, Stephen. "The Literary Achievement of the Fountainhead." Reprinted from *The Fountainhead: A Fiftieth Anniversary Celebration*, 1933. The Atlas Society, June 2006. http://ayn-rand.info/cth—1706-The_Literary_Achievement_of_The_Fountainhead.aspx (accessed December 27, 2010).

"Frequently Asked Questions about Ayn Rand." Ayn Rand Lexicon, Ayn Rand Institute, 2010. http://aynrandlexicon.com/about-ayn-rand/faq.html (accessed December 24, 2010).

Heller, Ann Conover. *Ayn Rand and the World She Made*. New York: Anchor Books, 2009.

Kelley, David. "The Capitalist Ideal: The Moral Vision of *Atlas Shrugged*." The Atlas Society, March 2009. http://ayn-rand.info/cth—2165-Capitalist_ideal.aspx (accessed December 27, 2010).

Kirsch, Adam. "Ayn Rand's Revenge." *New York Times*, October, 29, 2009. http://www.nytimes.com/2009/11/01/books/review/Kirsch-t.html (accessed December 26, 2010).

Lawrence, Richard. "Ayn Rand Biographical FAQ." Objectivism Reference Center, 1999–2009. http://www.noblesoul.com/orc/bio/biofaq.html#Q4 (accessed December 26, 2010).

Murray, Charles. "Who Is Ayn Rand?" *Claremont Review of Books*, Claremont Institute, June 1, 2010. http://www.claremont.org/publications/crb/id.1708/article_detail.asp (accessed December 26, 2010).

Peikoff, Leonard. "Introduction." Ayn Rand Lexicon, Ayn Rand Institute, 1986. http://aynrandlexicon.com/book/intro.html (accessed December 24, 2010).

Rand, Ayn. "Foreword" (1936). In *We the Living*. 60th anniversary ed. New York: Dutton, 1995.

Rand, Ayn. "Racism." *Objectivist Newsletter*, September 1963. http://FreedomKeys.com/ar-racism.htm#individualism (accessed December 26, 2010).

Rand, Ayn. *Capitalism: The Unknown Ideal*. New York: Signet/Penguin Group, 1967.

Rand, Ayn. "Man's Rights." Ayn Rand Center for Individual Rights, April 1963. http://www.aynrand.org/site/PageServer?pagename=arc_ayn_rand_man_rights (accessed December 26, 2010).

Rand, Ayn. "Ninety-Three." *Ayn Rand Column: Written for the* Los Angeles Times. New York: Second Renaissance Books (2nd ed.), October 1998.

Toffler, Alvin. "Playboy Interview: Ayn Rand: A Candid Conversation with the Fountainhead of 'Objectivism.'" *Playboy*, March 1964. http://www.campaignforliberty.com/blog.php?view=17265 (accessed September 9, 2011).

Randolph, A. Philip (1889–1979)

The administration of President Woodrow Wilson, in office from 1913 to 1921, called A. Philip Randolph "the most dangerous Negro in America" (*Time* 1979). The U.S. Department of Justice in 1919 declared that the socialist publication the *Messenger*, which Randolph cofounded, was subversive and "the most dangerous of all the Negro publications." But Bayard Rustin, a civil rights leader, said that: "No individual did more to help the poor, the dispossessed and the working class in the United States and around the world than A. Philip Randolph" (Associated Press 1979).

The second son of Reverend James Randolph, a minister of the African Methodist Episcopal (AME) church, and Elizabeth (Robinson) Randolph, Asa Philip was born in Crescent City, Florida, on April 15, 1889. Asa's father named his son for a biblical king. Rev. Randolph was a proud man who refused to be subservient to anyone. He studied world history and often in his sermons described black contributions to civilization.

In 1891, the family moved to Jacksonville, Florida, where Asa grew up, attending a local primary school and then industrial school operated by the AME church. Later he enrolled in the Cookman Institute in Jacksonville, a boy's school that became a coeducational high school when the Bethune Education and Industrial Training School for Negro Girls merged with Cookman in 1923. (Currently, it is the Bethune-Cookman University in Daytona.) At Cookman, Randolph was a popular student, a top player on the baseball team, and a member of the choir. He was an excellent student, reading the works of Karl Marx, a German philosopher who with Friedrich Engels wrote the *Communist Manifesto* (1848), which presented the principles of communism. His reading also included the ideas of W. E. B. Du Bois, who wrote about the need for black political representation and a black elite to work for African American progress.

In high school, Randolph gained a reputation as a persuasive speaker, an attribute that served him well later in life. He was valedictorian of his class, and at graduation in 1907, he gave a speech on racial pride. His father wanted him to use his deep baritone voice to preach. But Randolph had other ambitions, such as running for political office, becoming a lawyer, or acting in Shakespearean plays—he memorized and liked to recite speeches that Shakespeare wrote for his leading characters.

After graduation, Randolph worked for several years at a variety of menial jobs, hoping to earn enough money to go to New York and begin a career in theater. In 1911, he got a job on a ship sailing to New York City, and after his arrival there settled in Harlem. In 1912, he began taking classes at the City College of New York, where he studied literature and sociology and was first exposed to socialism and the concept of labor organizations. To support himself, he worked wherever he could find a job and was frequently fired for trying to organize black workers.

At City College, he met Lucille Campbell Green, a wealthy widow whom he married in 1914. Lucille introduced Randolph to Chandler Owen, a law student at Columbia University and a socialist. The two had many interests in common and became close friends. They joined the Socialist Party of America led by Eugene V. Debs, a labor leader who ran five times as the party's candidate for U.S. president. Randolph and Owen often touted socialist views as soapbox orators on Harlem streets. Randolph became known as Trotsky (Leon Trotsky, 1879–1940, who devised tactics for a

A. Philip Randolph won respect for his quiet dignity and his firmness in a lifelong committment to racial justice. A union organizer and socialist early in life, he became the country's best-known African American trade unionist and a nationally prominent leader in the struggle for civil rights during the early to mid-20th century. (Library of Congress)

Bolshevik armed takeover of the Russian government); Owen was dubbed Lenin (Vladimir Lenin, 1870–1924, a major Russian revolutionary and political leader). The two friends started a small employment bureau for southern blacks who had moved north looking for work but were untrained.

In 1917, Randolph and Owen began a monthly magazine called the *Hotel Messenger*, which supported organized black workers in the Headwaiters' and Sidewaiters' Society. Later known as simply the *Messenger*, the magazine became an advocacy publication for socialism and trade unions, particularly the Industrial Workers of the World (IWW). Editorials in the *Messenger* argued against U.S. participation in World War I, and encouraged blacks to forcefully resist attacks by white mobs that wanted to ban black membership in labor unions. The magazine was too radical for black waiters, who soon severed their relationship with the editors and their views.

Randolph and Owen went separate ways in the 1920s—Owen to Chicago, where he became managing editor of the *Chicago Bee*, an African American newspaper; and Randolph continuing his union efforts in New York. In 1925, members of the sleeping-car porters of the Pullman Railroad Company met with Randolph, asking him for help in organizing a union. At the time, the Pullman Company was the largest single employer of blacks in the United States, and porters worked 400 hours per month, earning $67.50. Pullman opposed unions and fired porters who tried to organize for better pay and working conditions. After Randolph took leadership of the Brotherhood of Sleeping Car Porters, membership in the brotherhood increased, with chapters in major cities from New York to Seattle and from Los Angeles to Boston. Pullman hired spies to gather information about members, and some lost their jobs or were beaten. It took more than a decade before the black union won the right to make an agreement with Pullman and create a contract that reduced work hours to 240 per month and raised wages.

In 1941, Randolph worked with black leaders Bayard Rustin and A. J. Muste on a proposal for a march on Washington in efforts to convince President Franklin D. Roosevelt to integrate the armed forces and defense industries, which were gearing up as U.S. involvement in World War II became more imminent. But Roosevelt refused, and Randolph announced that he would organize thousands of blacks for a protest march in

Washington, D.C., declaring that masses needed to gather on the White House lawn in order to convince the government that justice for blacks was a priority. Although Roosevelt did not integrate the military, he signed Executive Order 8802 in 1941 that prohibited discrimination in defense industries and established the Fair Employment Practices Committee, which was supposed to investigate discrimination complaints and correct grievances. As a result, Randolph called off the March on Washington, which met with criticism from some blacks who felt that the nation needed to see a show of black power.

In spite of the president's order, little progress was made in terms of halting discriminatory practices nationwide. Randolph continued his fight for equal rights for blacks with his March on Washington Movement. Speaking about the initiative in 1942, Randolph addressed a Policy Conference meeting in Detroit, Michigan: "[O]ur nearer goals include the abolition of discrimination, segregation, and jim crow in the Government, the Army, Navy, Air Corps, U.S. Marine, Coast Guard, Women's Auxiliary Army Corps and the Waves, and defense industries; the elimination of discriminations in hotels, restaurants, on public transportation conveyances, in educational, recreational, cultural, and amusement and entertainment places such as theatres, beaches, and so forth. We want the full works of citizenship with no reservations. We will accept nothing less" (Randolph 1942, 488).

By 1945, the segregated practices in the military had changed little, and black soldiers were often harassed even as they prepared to fight in World War II. Just before the end of the war, President Roosevelt died, and Vice President Harry Truman became president. In 1947, Truman called for a peacetime draft, and Randolph saw an opportunity to pressure Truman to issue an executive order to end segregation in the military. When Truman refused, Randolph and an associate began a civil disobedience campaign, urging young black men not to register for the draft. Randolph was willing to go to jail for his convictions. Although Truman was furious, he began the process of desegregating the military. On July 26, 1948, he issued Executive Order 9981, stating that "there shall be equality of treatment and opportunity for all persons in the armed forces without regard to race, color, religion, or national origin." The military resisted the executive order, but by the end of the Korean conflict, almost all the armed forces were integrated.

Throughout the 1950s and 1960s, Randolph continued his work for equal employment opportunities for blacks. In 1955, he was elected to the executive council of the American Federation of Labor and Congress of Industrial Organizations (AFL-CIO) and helped set up a civil rights committee. In 1957, he became vice president of the AFL-CIO.

In 1960, Randolph took part in a protest outside the Democratic convention in Los Angeles. He and other black leaders, including Martin Luther King Jr., demanded that the Democratic Party, as part of its platform, write a plank guaranteeing black civil rights and expelling segregationists from party leadership. Delegates approved the inclusion of the civil rights plank, although southerners were adamantly opposed. When a reporter asked an Alabama delegate for his reaction, he "replied with thunder in his voice: 'no comment, suh! Go to hell! No comment'" (Travis 1987, 273). Black dissident leaders also organized protests at the 1960 Republican convention in Chicago. They demanded civil rights from both political parties.

After years of protests, marches, acts of civil disobedience, and other dissents against segregation and discrimination, the lives of most black Americans had not improved much in 1963. Unemployment for blacks was more than double that of white workers, and black family income per year was half the amount that white families earned. Violence against blacks had increased, and one of the most publicized incidents was aired on television in May 1963, when police in Birmingham, Alabama, used dogs and high-pressure fire hoses against civil rights demonstrators.

In the summer of 1963, Lucille Randolph died, and Randolph, who was 74 years old, suffered from heart disease. But he and black leader Bayard Rustin planned a March on Washington to demand passage of a Civil Rights Act, fair employment practices, public school integration, and job training programs. In a mass demonstration on August 28, 1963, an integrated rally of more than 250,000 people gathered in front of the Lincoln Memorial in Washington, D.C. In opening remarks, Randolph said "We are gathered here in the largest demonstration in the history of this nation. Let the nation and the world know the meaning of our numbers. We are not a pressure group, we are not an organization or a group of organizations, we are not a mob. We are the advance guard of a massive moral revolution for jobs and freedom" (Williams 1987, 200). At the rally, Martin Luther King Jr. delivered his now-famous "I Have a Dream" speech. His words brought hope that blacks in the United States would be free and live in "a symphony of brotherhood" one day.

However, acts of violence did not stop. Within a short time, four young people were killed in a church bombing in Birmingham, and two teenagers were murdered on the streets. But in 1964, President Lyndon Johnson signed the Civil Rights Act, which outlawed segregation in businesses such as theaters, restaurants, and hotels; banned discriminatory practices in employment; and ended segregation in public places such as swimming pools, libraries, and public schools.

As Randolph aged, younger men and women took over as civil rights leaders. But Randolph remained highly respected for his courage, convictions, and perseverance. Although he was often criticized by more militant blacks for being old-fashioned, he consistently advised young people to get an education and to work in a positive, peaceful manner for reforms. He spent his last years writing his autobiography and a history of the union he founded, although his poor health forced him to give up those efforts. He died in his New York City apartment on May 16, 1979.

Memorials to Randolph abound, ranging from schools, libraries, museums, and streets named in his honor, to photo displays and a postage stamp (1989) with his portrait, to the A. Philip Randolph Institute headquarters in Washington, D.C.

See also Bethune, Mary McLeod; Debs, Eugene V.; King, Martin Luther, Jr.; Rustin, Bayard

References

A. Philip Randolph Institute (web site). http://www.apri.org/ht/d/sp/i/225/pid/225 (accessed May 11, 2011).

Andersen, Jervis. *A. Philip Randolph: A Biographical Portrait*. Berkeley: University of California Press, 1986.

Associated Press. "A. Philip Randolph Is Dead; Pioneer in Rights and Labor." *New York Times*, May 17, 1979. http://www.nytimes.com/learning/general/onthisday/bday/0415.html (accessed June 4, 2010).

Bynum, Cornelius L. *A. Philip Randolph and the Struggle for Civil Rights*. Urbana: University of Illinois Press, 2010.

Kersten, Andrew Edmund. *A. Philip Randolph: A Life in the Vanguard*. Lanham, MD: Rowman and Littlefield Publishers, 2006.

Miller, Calvin Craig. *A. Philip Randolph and the African-American Labor Movement*. Greensboro, NC: Morgan Reynolds, 2005.

"Nation: The Most Dangerous Negro." *Time*, May 28, 1979. http://www.time.com/time/printout/0,8816,947299,00.html (accessed June 4, 2010).

Randolph, A. Philip. "The March on Washington Movement." *Survey Graphic*, November 1942. http://www.bsos.umd.edu/aasp/chateauvert/mowmcall.htm (accessed June 6, 2010).

Travis, Dempsey J. *An Autobiography of Black Politics*. Chicago: Urban Research Press, 1987.

Williams, Juan, with the Eyes on the Prize production team. *Eyes on the Prize: America's Civil Rights Years, 1945–1965*. New York: Viking Penguin, 1987.

Rankin, Jeannette (1880–1973)

"This woman from the land of cowboys and Indians never touched a gun; Jeannette Rankin was a pacifist. Acclaimed for her unique feminine achievement of election to Congress, she was almost immediately derided for her 'unmanly' vote against the First World War" (Smith 2002, 26). Rankin's antiwar position subjected her to charges of subversive and disloyal activities.

Jeannette Rankin was born on a ranch six miles from Missoula, Montana, on June 11, 1880. She was the first of seven children (six girls and one boy) in the affluent family of John and Olive Pickering Rankin. Her siblings were named Philena, Hattie, Wellington, Mary, Grace, and Edna. John Rankin was a Canadian immigrant who with his brother moved to Montana to search for gold. In addition to the land that the Rankins acquired for prospecting, John Rankin also claimed acreage under the U.S. Homestead Act passed by Congress in 1862. The act provided 160 acres (65 hectares) of unoccupied public land to U.S. citizens who paid a filing fee of $10 and lived on the land for at least five years. The law was designed to encourage people to settle vast stretches of territory in the Midwest and West and, in the case of immigrants, to encourage them to become citizens.

Jeannette's mother, Olive Pickering, was an elementary school teacher from New Hampshire who moved to Missoula in 1878. In 1879, she met and married John Rankin, who built the house that would eventually be home for his large family. Olive Rankin cared for the home and her children and taught her girls how to do household tasks. While growing up, Jeannette also learned to do many of the ranching chores, from chopping wood to caring for the farm animals.

Jeannette attended school in Missoula, where the family home was located, but she was bored with formal education. She loved to read and often talked over with her parents the ideas she learned about in books. She also accompanied her father, one of the town's leaders, when he met with other influential men and discussed politics and business.

During her teenage years, Jeannette longed to find a satisfying career; but she had no desire to teach, one of the few professions that were open to women at that time, and she had no plans for marriage and raising a family. After obtaining her degree from the University of Montana, she taught for a year, but still longed for another way of life. In 1904, while visiting her only brother who was attending Harvard Law School in Boston, Jeannette Rankin observed for the first time the terrible living conditions of the

Rankin, Jeannette (1880–1973)

Jeannette Rankin was the first woman ever elected to the U.S. House of Representatives and the only member of Congress to vote against U.S. entry into both World War I and World War II. (Library of Congress)

urban poor and began to read about reformers such as Jane Addams and her settlement house in Chicago, Illinois. She was inspired to work for social change and take up social work. For four months, she was a resident in a San Francisco settlement house, and then entered the New York School of Philanthropy (later becoming the Columbia School of Social Work). She took a position as a social worker in Spokane, Washington, for a time.

In 1910, Rankin joined the woman suffrage movement and took part in the campaign to pass a state law giving women the right to vote. Some states and territories already had passed legislation allowing women to vote. Beginning with Wyoming, which provided voting rights to women in 1869, Western territories such as Colorado, Utah, and California followed Wyoming's example in the years from 1869 to 1911.

Rankin became a professional lobbyist for the National American Woman Suffrage Association (NAWSA), whose efforts helped Montana women win the right to vote in 1914. Rankin's successful campaigning prompted her to run for the U.S. House of Representatives in 1916. Although she was the first woman to campaign for a seat in the U.S. Congress, she had become well known as a suffragist. She also had the financial backing of her brother Wellington, a lawyer who had political connections in the Republican Party. (Wellington later was elected Montana attorney general and in the 1920s was appointed U.S. district attorney.)

When Rankin won the nomination for a U.S. House seat, she promised to work for a suffrage amendment to the U.S. Constitution, providing voting rights to women nationwide. She traveled across Montana talking to people on street corners, at mines, and in their homes and meeting houses, emphasizing not only suffrage, but also social welfare issues such as child labor. She also explained to voters her opposition to possible U.S. participation in the European war that had been ongoing since 1914. In her view, the United States should send old men to fight and let the young stay home to help produce the next generation. In 1915, she joined Jane Addams when she formed the Women's Peace Party in Washington, D.C. Several years later, Rankin and Addams traveled along with a group of women to a peace conference in Switzerland.

After Rankin won election and was seated in the 65th Congress in November 1916, she attended a congratulatory luncheon sponsored by suffragist groups. She sat between two suffragist leaders, Carrie Chapman Catt and Alice Paul. The two leaders had opposing views: Catt had been fighting for women's voting rights at both the state and federal level, while Paul had been emphasizing the need for a constitutional amendment by lobbying Congress. Nevertheless, the luncheon did not stir up controversy—participants were united in their best wishes for their guest of honor.

In Congress, Rankin continued to speak out in opposition to the war, a view that many Americans shared. President Woodrow Wilson had promised to keep the United States out of the war, but in April 1917, after Germany launched submarine attacks on American shipping vessels, Wilson appeared before Congress in a special session to ask members to protect democracy and vote for a war resolution. As a pacifist, Rankin could not vote for war, and her suffragist colleagues, especially Catt, were concerned that her nay vote would jeopardize voting rights efforts. Rankin did not take part in the congressional debate, but when she did cast her vote, she said she wanted to stand by her country, but she could not vote for war. Later when asked about her nay vote, she had no regrets, saying "I felt that the first time the first woman in Congress had a chance to say no to war, she should say it" (Davidson 1994, 45–46).

Because of her antiwar stance, Rankin was subjected to a great deal of abuse; some representatives called her a coward and a traitor for not supporting the war. A Montana newspaper called her a German propagandist and likened her to a naive schoolgirl. And the NAWSA did not want the organization associated with Rankin's views. Yet in Congress, she lobbied successfully for a Committee on Woman Suffrage and became a member of it.

Rankin made a second bid for Congress in 1918, but she was unsuccessful because of her opposition to war and also because the state legislature through redistricting had made her district overwhelmingly Democratic. So she decided to organize a campaign for a U.S. Senate seat—she was the first woman to do so—but she was defeated in the Republican primary. Still, she did not give up and ran as a third-party candidate. Even though she was not successful, she enhanced the image of women in politics and changed negative attitudes about female congressional members.

For a time, running for political office was not at the top of Rankin's agenda. She worked for peace causes and social welfare programs. In 1919, she was a participant in the Women's International Conference for Permanent Peace held in Switzerland, and she joined the Women's International League for Peace and Freedom (WILPF), becoming field secretary for the organization and lobbying for peace. During the early 1920s, she was a field secretary for the National Consumers League. Her duties consisted of lobbying Congress to pass social welfare legislation and a constitutional amendment banning child labor.

After moving to a Georgia farm in 1923, she formed a Georgia Peace Society and was a paid lobbyist for the National Council for the Prevention of War, an organization consisting primarily of Quakers known for their pacifist views. Rankin left the council when members began to support President Franklin Roosevelt's position on increased funding for the War Department and support for the war efforts of the British and French, whose countries were being threatened by German dictator Adolf Hitler and his armies.

In 1939 at the age of 60, Rankin once again ran for Congress. This time, she won the election, but in 1941, the Japanese attacked the U.S. naval base at Pearl Harbor in Hawaii, killing more than 2,000 people, destroying planes, and damaging or destroying battleships. On December 8, 1941, Roosevelt, along with the British government, declared war on Japan.

Rankin still held to her antiwar stance, arguing that because she was a woman, she would not be allowed to go to war and she would not send anyone else in her place. Because of her opposition to U.S. participation in World War II, most members of Congress ignored her, and she had little influence for the rest of her term. The press showed little interest in covering her peace efforts. She decided not to run for reelection in 1942, and divided her time between Montana and Georgia.

After World War II, Rankin traveled worldwide, making seven trips to India where she studied the way of life of the common people and learned as much as she could about Mohandas Gandhi and his absolute pacifist views, which she shared. She also lived simply, with few material goods, preferring instead to use funds from an inheritance left by her brother, who died in 1966, to work for peace and women's rights. When the United States entered the war in Korea and later the war in Vietnam, Rankin spoke out. During the Vietnam War, she led 5,000 women in a protest march called the Jeannette Rankin Brigade in Washington in January 1968. She granted newspaper and magazine interviews and appeared on radio and TV shows to plea for world disarmament.

When she was 91 years old, Rankin spoke at a conference of southern women about organizing for political action. According to a *Life* magazine reporter, Rankin said "We have to make every woman count. That's the only way to get rid of all these men [in politics]" (Frappollo 1972, 65). She worked for the pacifist cause and women's rights almost to the time of her death. For example, during 1972, she gave major addresses to women's political groups in Atlanta, Georgia; Syracuse, New York; Little Rock, Arkansas; Helena, Montana; and Nashville, Tennessee.

She also was an advocate for veterans, believing they had been used by politicians for their war games. She championed the GI Bill, which provided educational and other benefits for veterans.

Jeannette Rankin died in her sleep at her home in Carmel, California, on May 18, 1973. She left a substantial legacy that includes funds for the Jeannette Rankin Foundation in Athens, Georgia, which helps unemployed female workers. The foundation also provides scholarships for women. In Missoula, Montana, the Jeannette Rankin Peace Center carries on Rankin's work for social justice and peace. A docudrama titled *Peace Is a Woman's Job* (2004) by Allyson Adams is a reenactment of Rankin's life.

See also Addams, Jane; Catt, Carrie Chapman; Paul, Alice

References

Berson, Robin Kadison. *Marching to a Different Drummer.* Westport, CT: Greenwood Press, 1994.

Chall, Malca, and Hannah Josephson (interviewers). "Jeannette Rankin: Activist for World Peace, Women's Rights, and Democratic Government." Suffragists Oral History Project. Berkeley: Regents of the University of California, 1974. http://content.cdlib.org/view?docId=kt758005dx&brand=calisphere&doc.view=entire_text (accessed May 21, 2010).

Frappollo, Elizabeth. "At 91, Jeannette Rankin is the Feminists' New Heroine." *Life*, March 3, 1972.

Josephson, Hannah. *Jeannette Rankin, First Lady in Congress: A Biography.* Indianapolis, IN: Bobbs-Merrill, 1974.

Smith, Norma. *Jeannette Rankin: America's Conscience.* Helena: Montana Historical Society Press, 2002.

Robeson, Paul (1898–1976)

In 1944, Paul Robeson was glowingly referred to as "America's No. 1 Negro." By decade's end, he was "the nation's most vilified black man" and "blacklisted as an artist in the United States" (Robeson Jr. 2001, xiii). In a preface to Robeson's autobiography, Lloyd L. Brown noted:

> [S]uddenly, the spotlight was switched off. In place of the glow of stardom, a thick smokescreen was spread around him ... the most famous Afro-American ... could no more be seen. The blackout was the result of a boycott ... by the Establishment ... meant both to silence him and to deny him any opportunity of making a living. All doors to stage, screen, concert hall, radio, TV, and recording studio were locked ... he was banished as a performing artist ... denied his rights as a citizen ... never charged with any illegal activity ... never arrested or put on trial. But his persecutors made no bones about why he was being punished: Robeson, they said, was a dangerous Red. Robeson, they said, was a dangerous Black. That made him twice as bad as anyone else in the "Fearful Fifties," when Communism at home and abroad was said to be a clear and present danger to the American Way of Life. (Robeson 1958, xxv).

Born in Princeton, New Jersey, on April 9, 1898, Robeson was the youngest of seven children (two died in infancy). His father, William, escaped slavery via the Underground Railroad and eventually became a Presbyterian preacher. Robeson's mother, Maria Louisa—of a prominent abolitionist Quaker family—taught school until health issues interfered (Robeson 1958, 6). When Paul was born, his family members were "pillars of Princeton's sizeable, tightly knit black community" (Robeson Jr. 2001, 4). However, white authorities, upset with Reverend Robeson, removed him from his pastorate in 1901 and he was forced to do menial labor until he returned to the pulpit.

When Paul was six, his mother was fatally burned in an accident. Yet, Robeson remembered a happy childhood, culminating in his 1915 graduation from high school. He entered Rutgers College (now University) on a full academic scholarship. He was one of two blacks during his four years on campus. He excelled in all areas but not without adversity. In football tryouts, "his teammates ... they ganged up on him. They broke his nose, dislocated his shoulder, and cleated his hand, tearing away all the fingernails" (Robeson 1958, xii). Yet he went on to be named Rutgers' first ever All-American player, consecutively chosen in 1917 and 1918. He lettered in four sports, did volunteer work, won debating prizes, was elected to honor societies, and sang in the Glee Club. Robeson said of his temperament, "when I was out on a football field or in a classroom or anywhere else, I wasn't just there on my own. I was the representative of a lot of Negro boys who wanted to play football, who wanted to go to college ... I had to show that I could take whatever they [whites] handed out" (*Freedomways* Editors 1978, 20).

He also credited his ability to get along with childhood lessons. "From an early age, I had come to accept and follow a certain protective tactic of Negro life in America, and did not fully break with this pattern until many years later ... Always show that you are *grateful*. (Even if what you have gained has been wrested from unwilling powers, be sure to be grateful lest 'they' take it all away.) Above all, *do nothing to give cause to fear you*" (Robeson 1958, 20). But when chosen valedictorian in 1919, his address, "Loyalty to Conviction," began a break from this pattern. It "gave serious consideration to the liberation of the masses of blacks, and argued that his loyalty to them was sacred." In

1918, Robeson said, "That I chose this topic was not accidental, for that was the text of my father's life—loyalty to one's conviction. ... From my youngest days I was imbued with that concept' " (Robeson 1958, xi–xii).

Robeson earned a law degree at Columbia in 1923. He paid his tuition by playing in the American Professional Football Association (now the National Football League), coaching at Lincoln University, and playing on the St. Christopher Club traveling basketball team. He accepted his first stage roles, playing Simon in *Simon the Cyrenian* at the Harlem YMCA in 1920 and Jim in *Taboo* in 1922. He toured London as Jim that summer, earning critical acclaim. Robeson worked as an attorney after graduation but quit when a white secretary refused to take his dictation. His wife Eslanda Cardozo Goode, whom he married in 1921, encouraged him to join the Provincetown Players, and he set his sights on a performing arts career. He soon gained world renown in days when African Americans were usually limited to comic or racially stereotyped roles. Breaking that mold, Robeson was considered a "serious actor" and cast in lead roles in productions such as Eugene O'Neill's *All God's Chillun Got Wings* (1924) and *The Emperor Jones* (1924). His bass-baritone brought down the house with his 1928 performances of "Ol' Man River" in *Show Boat*. He was the first to give an entire program of Negro spirituals, becoming one of the most popular concert singers of his time. He starred in other stage presentations, such as *Toussaint L'Ouverture* (1934) and *Stevedore* (1935), as well as productions of Shakespeare, hugely popular with everyday people and critics alike. He appeared in films, among them *Emperor Jones* (1933), *Show Boat* (1936), *Song of Freedom* (1936), and *Proud Valley* (1939).

Realizing his roles were limited, due both to his own acting range and the choice of roles available to blacks, Robeson turned to singing full time. This served as an outlet for his creative energies and provided a forum for his growing social convictions. As he toured and traveled, Robeson said he "learned that the essential character of a nation is determined not by the upper classes, but by the common people, and that the common people of all nations are truly brothers in the great family of mankind" (Robeson 1958, 48). While abroad, Robeson learned about his African ancestry. He met people who were politically left and African nationalists. He began to see himself and his talents as tools that could serve in the struggle for racial equality for nonwhites and economic justice for workers of the world. He began to believe in the principles of socialism. In 1934, he made his first of many visits to the Soviet Union and found it free of racial prejudice and segregation. "[I]n Russia I felt for the first time like a full human," he wrote (Robeson 1958, 48).

Robeson returned to the United States in 1939, after the start of World War II in Europe. He was once again America's top entertainer when he performed *Ballad for Americans* at the Hollywood Bowl. Although he supported the war, Robeson continued to advocate his politics. In 1942, he was involved in a trade union production that the FBI called a "Communist project." He took part in *Tales of Manhattan*, showing sharecropping living conditions; dissatisfied with how blacks were portrayed in the edited project, he unsuccessfully tried to buy up all copies. Afterward, he said he would no longer act in demeaning Hollywood films and turned down parts in *Moby Dick*, *Gone with the Wind*, *Song of the South*, and *Porgy and Bess* (Nollen 2010, 137).

In 1943, Robeson reprised the role of Othello on Broadway and toured North America with the play through 1945. For his portrayal, Robeson received the 1944 Donaldson Award for Best Performance; he was the first black with a white supporting cast on the Broadway stage. At his zenith, Robeson received the 1945 Springarm Medal from the National Association for the Advancement of Colored People (NAACP) for his artistic achievements and active concern for the human rights of every race, color, religion, and nationality.

With the advent of the Cold War, Robeson's advocacy for socialism brought him negative attention from the media and white establishment. His antiracism socialist positions did not sit well at a time when relations between the United States and the Soviet Union dissolved into virtual hysteria. But his interest in "radical politics" increased over the years, even though it limited his opportunities to perform. "He was the first American artist to refuse to sing before a segregated audience. He spoke out against lynching, segregated theatres and eating places a generation before the beginning of what is referred to as the Black Revolution," wrote Hunter College professor John Henrik Clarke (*Freedomways* Editors 1978, 191).

From 1946 through 1948, Robeson was part of campaigns to stop lynching, job discrimination, and other civil rights violations. The more he spoke out, the more his popularity plummeted. He was called before the U.S. Senate Judiciary Committee that was considering a bill (ultimately defeated) requiring registration of Communist Party members and questioned about his affiliation with the Communist Party. He refused to answer.

Late in 1948, Robeson learned his spring U.S. concert dates were canceled; the FBI threatened to brand booking agents as "pro-Communist." Robeson was without a concert audience for the first time; his recordings were banned from radio and stores. The entertainment industry was coerced into blacklisting him. He had to go overseas to work. While attending the Paris Peace Congress in April 1949, Robeson performed and spoke. His controversial words there contributed to his final downfall. According to the *New York Times*, he said, "It is unthinkable that American Negroes could go to war on behalf of those who have oppressed them for generations against the Soviet Union which in one generation has raised our people to full human dignity" (Robeson 1958, xvii).

After his return to the United States, those remarks led to one of the worst riots of the century. On August 27, 1949, Robeson was prevented from performing at a benefit concert for the Civil Rights Congress in Peekskill, New York. Local anticommunist, anti–civil rights residents and members of veteran groups attacked concertgoers with baseball bats and rocks. The event, rescheduled, was held on September 4. But afterward, a large mob, including state troopers, beat attendees, taunting them with racial epithets. The U.S. State Department made it known that it considered Robeson one of the world's most dangerous men; it revoked his passport in 1950. From then on, it seemed everyone was against him—even the black establishment, with the NAACP purging him from its list of Springarm recipients. Protests were launched in the United States, Canada, and Britain—the latter sponsored by members of Parliament as well as by writers, scholars, actors, lawyers, trade union leaders, and others. Labor unions organized concerts at the International Peace Arch on the U.S.-Canadian border; Robeson performed standing on the back of a flatbed truck from 1952 to 1955. At the time, W. E. B. Du Bois (considered by people of all races to be an intellectual black leader) said of Robeson, "He is without doubt today, as a person, the best known American on earth, to the largest number of human beings. His voice is known in Europe, Asia and Africa, in the West Indies and South America and in the islands of the seas. Children in the streets of Peking and Moscow, Calcutta and Jakarta greet him and send him their love. Only in his native land is he without honor and rights" (Robeson 1958, xxv).

Constrained from traveling, Robeson still spoke out. His son recounted the 1956 congressional hearings exchange when a U.S. representative asked, "Why do you not stay in Russia?" Robeson replied, "Because my father was a slave, and my people died to build this country, and I am going to stay here, and have a part of it just like you. And no fascist-minded people will drive me from it. Is that clear?" (Robeson Jr. 2010, 253). When his book *Here I Stand* (1958) was released, no mainstream newspaper or journal reviewed or mentioned it. African American publications generally criticized it (Robeson 1958, xviii).

When Robeson's passport was finally reinstated in 1958 as the result of a successful court case, he and his wife traveled again to Europe and Russia. However, he never regained the career or acclaim of his earlier days. The couple returned to the United States in 1963. After Eslanda died in 1965, Robeson lived with family members on the East Coast. His health had been declining, and he spent the remainder of his life largely away from the public. In 1976, Paul Robeson suffered a stroke and died on January 23, 1976, in Philadelphia, Pennsylvania.

In January 1995, *Sports Illustrated* reported, "The College Hall of Fame last week took a long-overdue step toward atonement ... By finally opening its doors to Paul Robeson, the Hall has most clearly shown that it's ready to live up to its name" (Scorecard 1995, 31–32). More and more efforts are being made to correct other omissions of Robeson's achievements and restore them to record books in the varied arenas of American history, performing arts, and sports so that Robeson's true legacy lives on.

Margaret Gay

See also Du Bois, W. E. B.

References

Freedomways Editors. *Paul Robeson: The Great Forerunner.* New York: Dodd, Mead, 1978.

Nollen, Scott Allen. *Paul Robeson: Film Pioneer.* Jefferson, NC: McFarland Publishing, 2010.

Robeson, Paul. *Here I Stand.* Boston: Beacon Press, 1958.

Robeson, Paul. *Paul Robeson: Tributes, Selected Writings.* New York: Paul Robeson Archives, Inc., 1976.

Robeson, Paul, Jr. *Paul Robeson: Quest for Freedom, 1939–1976.* New York: John Wiley & Sons, 2010.

Robeson, Paul, Jr. *The Undiscovered Paul Robeson: An Artist's Journey.* New York: John Wiley & Sons, 2001.

Scorecard. "Paul in the Hall." *Sports Illustrated*, January 30, 1995.

Roosevelt, Eleanor (1884–1962)

Eleanor Roosevelt served as first lady of the United States for the longest period of any woman ever to have that title—12 years. Her husband, Franklin Delano Roosevelt, held office from 1933 to 1945, before the Twenty-second Amendment to the U.S. Constitution in 1951 imposed a two-term limitation on the office. The impact the president's wife had in that role had more to do with the substance of her words and deeds during her tenure than it did with the accumulation of days in the White House. She was an independent woman, able to dissent from the president's opinions and to challenge his policies. One would be hard pressed to find another presidential spouse who was as or more active than she.

Born Anna Eleanor Roosevelt in New York City on October 11, 1884, she immediately became part of a world of immense wealth and privilege. Her mother, Anna Hall Roosevelt, "belonged to that New York City society that thought itself all-important . . . in that society you were kind to the poor, you did not neglect your philanthropic duties, you assisted hospitals and did something for the needy." This would be the basis for Eleanor's commitment to the less fortunate. Her mother also was raised to believe, and raised her own children to believe, "you conformed to the conventional pattern" (Roosevelt 1992, 4). Her father, Elliott Roosevelt, "dominated my life as long as he lived, and was the love of my life for many years after he died. With my father I was perfectly happy." That state of mind stands in contrast to her more typical demeanor; she described herself as "a shy, solemn child even at the age of two" (Roosevelt 1992, 5).

When Eleanor was five years old, the family traveled to France where her father, battling a drinking problem, entered a sanatorium. Her pregnant mother sent Eleanor to a convent to stay until her sibling was born. Recalling that time, Eleanor wrote, "I must have been very sensitive, with an inordinate desire for affection and praise, perhaps brought on by the fact that I was conscious of my plain looks and lack of manners. My mother was troubled by my lack of beauty, and I knew it as a child senses these things" (Roosevelt 1992, 5). The family returned home, and when Eleanor was eight, her mother contracted diphtheria and died. Less than two years later, her father's alcoholism took its toll. Eleanor, her two brothers, and one stepbrother were orphaned. Mary Ludlowe Hall, their maternal grandmother, finished raising them.

Eleanor was privately tutored until age 15. She then went to London, England, to attend the prestigious Allenswood Academy, a finishing school for girls. Headmistress Souvestre was a "feminist" who aimed to develop independent thinking. Eleanor learned to speak fluent French and gained self-assurance. Her sense of confidence was apparent when she returned home in 1902. As customary in her social circle, Roosevelt was presented at a debutante ball at the Waldorf Astoria in December; later she had her own coming-out party. She began performing the requisite social obligations and became a member of the New York Junior League, doing volunteer worker in the City's East Side slums.

She met her father's fifth cousin, Franklin Delano Roosevelt, and was stunned by the attentions of the handsome Harvard University student, two years younger than she, and seemingly smitten. Soon, they began courting. Early on, Eleanor took Franklin on a tour of the tenements where she volunteered. This was the first of many occasions on which Eleanor would draw Franklin's attention to a matter about which she felt he needed educating. The pair became engaged in late 1904. His mother, Sara, objected; she lobbied against the match until it took place. Sara did not bear any ill will; she merely felt that Eleanor was just not up to the task of being an adequate or appropriate wife for her son.

Eleanor and Franklin chose March 17, 1905, as their wedding date so that her uncle, then sitting president Theodore Roosevelt, could give the bride away—bringing much national attention to the event. They celebrated their nuptials with a one-week honeymoon in the New York area and, that

As First Lady from 1933 to 1945, Eleanor Roosevelt was known for her independence and efforts for social justice. Here, she looks at the Universal Declaration of Human Rights, circa 1950, which she helped draft. (Corel)

summer, went on a three-month European tour. Eleanor was a very wealthy woman, and the couple could have subsisted on her income. But Sara was determined to contribute to their income, purchasing their family estate in Hyde Park, New York.

The Roosevelts seemed to have everything necessary to ensure a wonderful life. In many respects, they projected a facade of an idyllic wedded couple. They would have six children (one of whom died in infancy). However, in 1918, Eleanor discovered that Franklin was having an affair with her social secretary, Lucy Mercer. Eleanor gave him an ultimatum: end the affair or face a divorce. His mother threatened to disinherit him. Franklin knew divorce would stain his social status and hamper his political ambitions. He agreed to Eleanor's demands, and they reconciled—or, at least, came to an agreement about their marriage.

But Franklin would start seeing Lucy again in the 1930s, their relationship continuing for the remainder of his life. Lucy, not Eleanor, would be with him when he died. Franklin also was reputed to have had a relationship with his secretary, Missy LeHand. There has been similar speculation about the identity of the person(s) to whom Eleanor gave her affections, ranging from Earl Miller, her onetime bodyguard, to a lesbian love affair with longtime friend Lorena Hickok.

The Roosevelts' relationship was "distant"—psychically (because of the emotional strains on their marriage) and physically (due to nature of their respective activities over the years). Regardless, in many respects, they were a uniquely close couple and supported each other's endeavors wholeheartedly. But they understood that they would never be able to provide for each other's personal happiness.

To find fulfillment, Eleanor began to seek independence and assert her individuality. An ironic twist of fate gave her that chance. In August 1921, the president contracted polio; his legs were permanently paralyzed. Eleanor's devotion to him during that time, and thereafter, was irreproachable. When feasible, she was the first to urge him to aspire to an active life. She committed herself to being his constant partner in order to compensate for his lack of mobility. Franklin rewarded her with effusive praise for her sacrifices, no matter their personal differences and distances. He was quick to make it known that he valued her assistance and counsel and considered them to be a team.

In the 1920s, with Franklin's blessings and his political adviser as her coach, Eleanor began to make a splash in New York state politics. She was on the board of the League of Women Voters and worked for the Women's Trade Union League. She advocated for women's rights and related causes such as suffrage, minimum wage, a 48-hour workweek, and abolition of child labor. She was an enthusiastic fund-raiser and campaigner for the Democratic Party. In 1928, she campaigned for her husband who ran—and won—as New York governor.

Eleanor was concerned that her role would be diminished once her husband took office, but he immediately found ways for Eleanor to use her creative abilities, often as a buffer to soften his own image in the process. They worked in tandem successfully, earning Franklin a second term as governor, and later the Democratic nomination to the presidency. Franklin was sworn into the first of his four terms as U.S. president on March 4, 1933, with Eleanor at his side.

The United States had never seen a first lady such as Eleanor Roosevelt. In her, the American people had a champion, a challenger, a cheerleader and above all, a constant communicator. She instituted weekly press conferences; by the end of her husband's time in office, she had held approximately 350. These were open only to female reporters, as she felt too many areas in life were off limits to women. In 1933, Eleanor began penning a monthly magazine column in *Women's Home Companion*. A year later, she began a radio program. In 1936, until 1962, she wrote a daily newspaper column called "My Day" that was syndicated nationally. In 1938, the first installment of her autobiography, *This Is My Story*, was released. She lectured and made public appearances, meeting face to face with the American people, and gathering knowledge to be a competent presidential adviser on the needs and wants of the American people.

Eleanor was a passionate advocate. She supported her husband's agenda but, independently, was a proponent of liberal causes. When Eleanor asked her husband whether he was bothered by her outspokenness, Franklin replied, "No, certainly not. You can say anything you want. I can always say, 'Well, that is my wife. I can't do anything about her'" (Goodwin 1994, 164).

Although Eleanor had been raised with a "southern perspective" and called the White House staff "darkies" and "pickannies," she began to change as she became more aware "of the Negro situation." It was "a gradual awakening" (Goodwin 1994, 162). Eleanor believed she could set an example for the American public through her actions. She made certain to be seen interacting with African Americans, inviting them to the White House and being photographed with them. She had established a friendship with Mary McLeod Bethune while attending an education conference, and she urged the president to appoint Bethune director of the Division of Negro Affairs of the National Youth Administration, a federal agency assisting young people. Bethune was the first African American woman to head a federal office.

Eleanor resigned from the Daughters of the American Revolution when black singer Marian Anderson was not allowed to perform at Constitution Hall (Goodwin 1994, 163). In 1940, she advocated for racial equality in the military as U.S. involvement in World War II became more imminent. Although President Roosevelt refused to integrate the military, he signed Executive Order 8802 in 1941 that prohibited discrimination in defense industries and established the Fair Employment Practices Committee, which was supposed to investigate discrimination complaints and correct grievances.

America's first lady made international news in 1943, during the height of World War II, when she traveled across the South Pacific in excess of 20,000 miles. She won over even her most vehement detractors with her unflappable, indefatigable attitude, as she visited American soldiers in field hospitals and on enemy lines.

Eleanor was in the nation's capital when her husband suffered a stroke and passed away in Warm Springs, Georgia, on April 12, 1945. She remained active following his death. President Truman, the vice president who succeeded her husband, appointed Eleanor as the first chair of the preliminary United Nations Commission on Human Rights. She helped draft the historic Universal Declaration of Human Rights and served as the nation's first representative to the commission until 1953. She joined the Brandeis University Board of Trustees and was a visiting lecturer in international relations at age 75. President John F. Kennedy appointed her to the National Advisory Committee to the Peace Corps and also chair of his Commission on the Status of Women (although she died just prior to the latter's report being issued).

Roosevelt received about four dozen honorary degrees during her lifetime. She was also received an honorary membership in Alpha Kappa Alpha Sorority, the world's first and oldest sorority for African American women.

President Kennedy ordered flags be lowered to half-mast when Eleanor Roosevelt died on November 7, 1962, in her Manhattan home. On November 9, UN ambasssdor Adlai Stevenson addressed the UN General Assembly, with these words: "The United States, the United Nations, the world, has lost one of its great citizens. Mrs. Eleanor Roosevelt is dead, and a cherished friend of all mankind is gone" (Stevenson 1962).

Margaret Gay

See also Bethune, Mary McLeod

References

Goodwin, Doris Kearns. *No Ordinary Time: Franklin and Eleanor Roosevelt*. New York: Simon and Schuster, 1994.

Lash, Joseph P. *Eleanor and Franklin: The Story of Their Relationship, based on Eleanor Roosevelt's Private Papers*. New York: W. W. Norton and Company, 1971.

Roosevelt, Eleanor. *The Autobiography of Eleanor Roosevelt*. New York: First Da Capo, 1992.

Stevenson, Adlai. "Memorial Address for Eleanor Roosevelt," *American Rhetoric*, November 9, 1962. http://www.americanrhetoric.com/speeches/adlaistevensonelean orroosevelteulogy.htm (accessed September 9, 2011).

Rosenberg, Ethel (1915–1953), and Rosenberg, Julius (1918–1953)

"It is now more than four decades," wrote historians Ronald Radosh and Joyce Milton in 1997, "since the deaths of Ethel and Julius

Rosenberg. Yet despite all the words written about their case, the mere mention of their names still elicits highly emotional reactions from partisans, pro and con" (Radosh and Milton 1997, ix).

On June 19, 1953, Ethel and Julius Rosenberg, a couple in their 30s with two small boys, were executed in the electric chair in New York State's Sing Sing Prison. They had been convicted of conspiracy to commit espionage and sentenced to death. According to the Federal Bureau of Investigation (FBI), the Rosenbergs were central figures in a spy ring responsible for obtaining secret information related to building the atomic bomb and conveying it to the Soviet Union.

What is remarkable about the Rosenbergs is how unremarkable they were. Both Ethel and Julius were first-generation Jewish Americans born to immigrant parents in New York City. Julius's father Harry was a skilled tailor. He worked in the garment industry as a sample maker. His mother, Sophie, was a housewife who stayed home to raise five children. She never learned to read or write English.

The Rosenbergs were a religious family. Julius received an excellent Jewish education at the Downtown Talmud Torah, a progressive religious and cultural school. At one time, he even considered becoming a rabbi. His family was fairly affluent according to the standards of the Depression years of the 1930s. Julius graduated from Seward Park High School in 1934. Unlike many of his friends, he never felt the need to quit school and find a job.

Ethel's family was less happy and less well off. The Greenglasses lived in an unheated tenement flat on New York's Lower East Side. Ethel was the oldest of four children. Her father Barnet eked out a meager living repairing sewing machines. Her mother Tessie, a dominating, fiercely religious woman, ran the household. She and Ethel often clashed. When Ethel, who dreamed of a musical career, would practice her singing, her mother would make a point of covering her ears. She teased Ethel for being plain and not having a boyfriend.

Ethel's determination to make something of herself won the respect of her friends, neighbors, and teachers, if not of her mother. Though not remarkably beautiful, intelligent, or talented, she succeeded through perseverance and hard work. An excellent student, she skipped several grades, graduating from Seward Park High School when she was only 15 years old.

Ethel went to work immediately. Within a month after graduation, she found a job as a shipping company clerk. As much as she needed the job, and as difficult as jobs were to find during the Depression, Ethel would not accept unfair working conditions. She organized a strike against her employer. Ethel and 150 women coworkers lay down in the middle of Manhattan's 36th Street to block the company's delivery trucks. Ethel was fired, but she filed a complaint with the Labor Relations Board and won.

During her free time, Ethel worked on her singing. She participated in amateur theater groups. She became the youngest member of a respected amateur chorus, the Schola Cantorum, which performed in Carnegie Hall. She entered amateur night contests in vaudeville theaters, usually winning first prize. Ethel was even a contestant on the popular radio show Major Bowes Amateur Hour. It was while performing at a New Year's Eve benefit for the International Seamen's Union that Ethel Greenglass met Julius Rosenberg.

By this time, Julius was attending New York's City College, with plans to become an electrical engineer. City College, known at the time as the Proletarian Harvard, was

Ethel (left) and Julius Rosenberg ride to separate prisons following their espionage convictions on March 29, 1951. The Rosenbergs' trial for conspiracy to commit espionage took place in New York City during the height of the Red Scare. (Library of Congress)

highly politicized. Julius had become a member of the Federation of Architects, Engineers, Chemists, and Technicians (FAECT), a white-collar union with a pro-communist leadership. He was also an active member of the Steinmetz Club, the City College branch of the Young Communist League, the junior branch of the Communist Party.

The Communist Party had a strong appeal for young Jewish Americans like the Rosenbergs during the 1930s. Anti-Semitism was blatant. Colleges, universities, and professional schools openly discriminated against Jewish students. Newspaper advertisements for jobs often carried the words "Christian Only." Immigration policies inaugurated after World War I effectively closed American doors to Jewish immigrants even as their situation overseas became more desperate. Meanwhile, public figures such as Father Charles Coughlin, who praised fascist leaders Benito Mussolini and Adolf Hitler, broadcast anti-Semitic propaganda over the air waves. The German-American Bund, an openly Nazi organization, held a massive rally in New York's Madison Square Garden as late as 1939, and 20,000 attendees heard Fritz Kuhn, the "American Führer," denounce President "Frank D. Rosenfeld" and the "Jew Deal."

The Communist Party appeared to offer solutions to counter the Depression and the growth of worldwide fascism. Communists condemned all forms of racial and religious discrimination. Joseph Stalin, the leader of the Soviet Union, appeared to be the only world leader to appreciate the danger of Hitler's Nazi movement.

Julius considered his political work more important than his studies. Ethel, however, insisted that he devote more attention to his books. While studying at the Greenglass apartment, Julius became friendly with Ethel's younger brother David and engaged him in political discussions, giving him books and pamphlets to read. David Greenglass joined the Young Communist League at Julius's urging.

Julius graduated from City College in 1939. He and Ethel were married a few months later. Despite Roosevelt's New Deal, the Depression lingered. The couple struggled to get by. However, as the United States moved closer to war, employment opportunities began to appear. Julius was hired as a civilian employee of the U.S. Army Signal Corps. In 1942, he received a promotion to become an engineer inspector. He traveled throughout New York and New Jersey, visiting factories in both states to inspect electronic parts being produced for the armed forces. The higher salary enabled Julius and

Ethel to move to a larger apartment. David Greenglass, meanwhile, had dropped out of high school to look for work. He married Ruth Printz, a fellow Young Communist, in 1942. Five months later he was drafted into the U.S. Army.

By this time, Julius and Ethel had become full members of the Communist Party. Julius even chaired one of its branches, which met in their apartment. However, by 1943, both Julius and Ethel had scaled back their political involvement. Ethel had just had a baby, their first son Robert. Julius's job and its constant traveling left little time for politics. In addition, a routine security check that revealed Julius's Communist Party membership came close to costing him his job. Only the fact that trained engineers were critical for the war effort saved him. By 1944, the Rosenbergs no longer appeared to be active party members.

At this point, David Greenglass was working as a machinist in an ordinance unit scheduled to go overseas when he was selected to work on the Manhattan Project, the top-secret effort that led to the first atomic bomb. Greenglass was transferred to Oak Ridge, Tennessee, and then to Los Alamos, New Mexico. His wife Ruth moved to Albuquerque, where she found a job as a secretary. According to Greenglass, Julius expressed considerable interest in the research going on in Los Alamos. He urged Greenglass to take notes and make drawings of the high explosive lens he was working on. This key device would be used to detonate the bomb.

On June 3, 1945, a man later identified as Harry Gold appeared at the Greenglass apartment in Albuquerque. Greenglass passed his notes and drawings to him. In return, he received an envelope from Gold containing $500. Greenglass also claimed to have passed additional information about the bomb to Julius on a later visit to New York.

Despite Julius's urging him to remain at Los Alamos as a civilian worker, Greenglass left the army in 1946 and returned to New York. By this time, with the war over and postwar tensions with the Soviet Union increasing, Julius's membership in the Communist Party was seen as a more serious security risk. He was fired from his Signal Corps job. He and Greenglass became partners in a machine shop. By 1949, the business failed. The brothers-in-law blamed each other. Julius claimed that Greenglass's work in the machine shop was substandard. For his part, Greenglass claimed that Julius never produced the high-paying contracts he promised to deliver.

By 1950, Greenglass was broke, out of work, and thoroughly disillusioned with Julius. At this time, he received a visit from two FBI agents. Soon afterward, Harry Gold was arrested on a charge of espionage. Julius urged Greenglass and his wife to leave the country as soon as possible. He supposedly gave them money to finance an escape to Europe. However, neither Ruth nor David Greenglass had passports. In addition, Ruth was severely burned in a household accident and hospitalized. Leaving the country was out of the question.

On June 15, four FBI agents appeared at the Greenglass apartment. Harry Gold had identified photos of Ruth and David Greenglass as his contacts in New Mexico. Desperate to save his wife and himself, Greenglass signed a confession. He and Ruth agreed to cooperate with the government. Greenglass identified his brother-in-law, Julius Rosenberg, and his sister Ethel as coconspirators. Julius was arrested on June 17, 1950; Ethel on August 11, 1950. Their two children, Robert (age seven) and Michael (age three), were removed to a Jewish orphanage after a brief and unsuccessful stay with their grandmother Tessie.

The government's goal was to get the Rosenbergs to "tip." It offered them reduced sentences in exchange for naming others. Greenglass had confessed after only a few hours of questioning. It was expected that the Rosenbergs would do the same. The Rosenbergs, however, refused to implicate anyone else and insisted that they had done nothing wrong. Throughout their trial, they maintained that they were never involved in any spy ring and that they had never urged David Greenglass to commit espionage. According to the Rosenbergs and their supporters, Greenglass, at the government's urging, had falsely accused the Rosenbergs to save himself. The Rosenbergs would not even admit that they had ever been communists. They pleaded the Fifth Amendment when asked the question.

The trial of the Rosenbergs began on March 6, 1951. It polarized the nation and the world, much as the Nicola Sacco and Bartolomeo Vanzetti case had done 30 years before. The two Italian immigrants were executed for crimes they consistently claimed they did not commit.

The Rosenberg trial lasted three weeks, and the jury delivered its verdict on March 29, 1951. Ethel and Julius Rosenberg, with their codefendant Morton Sobell, were found guilty of conspiracy to commit espionage. Sobell, who had once been a fugitive (and who had sought refuge with the parents of radical environmentalist Judi Bari when she was a young girl), received a 30-year sentence. The Rosenbergs were sentenced to death.

The verdict generated worldwide protests. The Rosenbergs' lawyers appealed to the U.S. Supreme Court. The Court initially refused to review the case. Then, surprisingly, Justice William O. Douglas issued a memorandum indicating that he had changed his mind and that the Rosenbergs deserved a hearing.

Justice Felix Frankfurter felt that Douglas simply wanted to avoid having to approve the death sentence. Frankfurter urged that the Court's decision on such an important case be unanimous. Chief Justice Robert Jackson offered to vote for a review with Douglas so that the case might be heard. At this point, Douglas withdrew his memorandum. He eventually ended up voting with the majority against a stay of execution.

Seven thousand people attending a rally in New York's Union Square received the news of Ethel and Julius's deaths on June 19, 1953, in silence. Eight thousand people attended their funeral on June 21, 1953.

Were the Rosenbergs guilty? Evidence from interviews with key figures in the United States and Russia, in addition to information from recently opened Soviet archives, appears to indicate that Julius was involved in middling levels of espionage, although the secrets obtained from a notorious spy ring known as Kim Philby/Klaus Fuchs played a much larger part in developing a Soviet bomb. While Ethel may have supported Julius in his activities, she was accused of only one concrete act: typing David Greenglass's notes. Whether these notes were typed at all, or by Ethel, cannot be determined.

Much of the prosecution's case against the Rosenbergs came from David Greenglass's testimony, with little corroborating evidence. The question for the jury was whom to believe: Greenglass, or the Rosenbergs. In the end, they believed Greenglass. Questions about Greenglass's reliability remain.

An equally important issue is whether or not the death penalty was justified. Nearly all scholars, researchers, and legal experts who have studied the case over the years agree that it was excessive. No other convicted spy—not even Rudolph Abel, the Soviet Union's chief spymaster in the United States—was executed by the United States during the entire Cold War. According to journalist I. F. Stone," By American standards the Rosenberg case is unsatisfactory ... The Supreme Court never reviewed the case; the way the Douglas stay was steamrollered was scandalous; the death sentence—even if they were guilty—was a crime" (Radosh and Milton 1997, 452–53).

Eric A. Kimmel

See also Bari, Judi; Coughlin, Charles E.; Sacco, Ferdinando Nicola, and Vanzetti, Bartolomeo

References

Feklisov, Alexander. *The Man behind the Rosenbergs.* New York: Enigma Books, 2003.

Meeropol, Robert. *An Execution in the Family.* New York: St. Martin's Griffin, 2004.

Radosh, Ronald, and Joyce Milton. *The Rosenberg File.* 2nd ed., with a new introduction containing revelations from National Security Agency and Soviet sources. New Haven, CT: Yale University Press, 1997.

Roberts, Sam. *The Brother: The Untold Story of the Rosenberg Case.* New York: Random House, 2003.

Rudd, Mark (1947–)

The Federal Bureau of Investigation (FBI) compiled a dossier on the activities of Weather Underground Organization (WUO), formed in the early 1970s for the purpose of bringing more direct action to the causes of antiwar activism and government resistance. Mark Rudd was one of the cofounders of WUO and was then a dissident political organizer and self-described socialist revolutionary. Many years later, after taking stock of his and the organization's role in the revolutionary cause for which he was so passionate, Rudd noted: "Trying to understand my motivation at the time, I think I wanted to hold a mirror up to this country, I wanted to tell people, 'Here's a little taste of what you dish out everyday.' Of course that's stupid, it never works. Underlying that was the despair of seeing what our country was doing in the world" (Rudd, "Frequently Asked Questions," n.d.).

Mark Rudd was born on June 2, 1947, in Maplewood, New Jersey. He spent his early years in Maplewood where his father, Jacob Rudd, worked as a real estate agent. His mother was Bertha Bass, a first-generation American born of Lithuanian parents. His brother David worked as an attorney. Mark graduated from his hometown Columbia High School, and in the fall of 1965, his parents dropped him off for his freshman year at Columbia University in New York City. In his 2009 autobiography, Rudd wrote:

> My mother tells this story about dropping me off at the dorm at West 114th Street and Broadway on the first day of Freshman Week. She and my father and I were unloading the car when a kid came up to me and handed me a blue and white beanie, the official headgear of the Columbia College freshman. He said, "We have to wear it all week."
>
> I replied, "That's stupid, I'm not gonna wear that thing!"
>
> Bertha, my mother, looked at Jake, my father, and said quietly, "We're in for trouble." (Rudd 2009, 1)

It was at Columbia University that Rudd became radicalized in his views about the conduct of the war in Vietnam, and it was also where he made his first dramatic moves toward revolutionary action against the militarism, racism, and imperialism that shamed him about his country. He joined the Students for a Democratic Society (SDS) almost immediately after entering college. SDS was the largest and arguably most influential of the groups aligning themselves in the larger New Left counterculture that had been catalyzed as a result of Vietnam and the elimination of student draft deferments in 1966. At its peak, almost 100,000 people had joined SDS across the nation.

Rudd was considered one of the leading figures of the movement given his position within the New York City group, and he was among the national SDS organizers who were invited to Fidel Castro's Cuba in 1968. The goal was to experience the results of the communist revolution that had toppled the decades-long, American-supported dictatorship on the island. There, he and other student leaders of SDS like Bernardine Dohrn met with delegates from Latin America, the USSR, and North Vietnam to discuss the tactics of anti-imperialism and the benefits of a socialist state. And it was in Cuba that Rudd became imbued with the ideals and philosophy of Ernesto "Che" Guevara, the ultimate revolutionary of the time: "From the first moment I heard about Che, Ernesto Guevara, he was my man, or, rather, I was his. Brilliant, young, idealistic, a daring commander of rebels, willing to risk his life to free the people of the world, I wanted to be like him. Who wouldn't fall for this rifle-toting poet who wrote, 'At the risk of sounding ridiculous, let me say that the true revolutionary is guided by great feelings of love'" (Rudd 2008).

Upon his return to Columbia, Rudd was chosen to be the president of the university's SDS chapter. In March 1967, the previous year, an SDS activist discovered that the university had established a covert connection with a Department of Defense initiative known as the Institute for Defense Analyses (IDA). Since that discovery, the SDS had made this relationship a priority, and it had continued to mount pressure against the institution to resign its membership in what the students considered a group in support of the worst war-mongering goals of the government they had come to hate.

By April 1968, events in and outside of the university aligned to bring the protest to a head. Black students and African American residents from the Harlem neighborhood that was adjacent to Columbia were upset about plans for a student athletic center in Morningside Park that the university was intent on constructing. Many of the minority community felt that the building perpetuated institutional racism by not taking into consideration the needs of the surrounding poor community. Rudd and the SDS were sympathetic to this notion, and the group decided to combine their own protest against the university's involvement with IDA and the effort to end the construction at Morningside Park.

The first demonstration was held eight days prior to the assassination of civil rights leader Martin Luther King Jr. Black and white students marched together. On April 23, a second protest march involved both Columbia and Barnard students, and the first goal was to occupy the Low Library on the Columbia campus. Security guards rebuffed this attempt, and most of the protesters then decided to march to the Morningside Park construction site. Confrontations with police there sent the crowd back to the campus. Led by Rudd, the students decided to take over Hamilton Hall, where the college administration offices were located.

At this point, black Columbia students decided to split from the SDS effort led by Rudd to concentrate on the athletic complex issue. In an agreement with Rudd and the other SDS leaders, the white students left Hamilton Hall to the black students and moved on to occupy the university president's office back at Low Library. For a week, the nation was captivated by the peaceful demonstration that was occurring at one of the United States' most prestigious institutions of higher learning, and Rudd was singled out as the charismatic leader of the action. He has noted that he was just one of many in the group who were taking part in a historic action that was not really controlled by any one individual: "The events of April 23rd, 1968 at Columbia were kind of adlibbed. There was no plan. I was in awe of what we were doing but in another way I was completely lost. At one point after having been up for forty-eight hours I walked over to the President's desk, picked up the phone and called my parents. I said we took a building. My father said, well give it back!" (Rudd, "Underground with Mark Rudd," 2009).

In the end, after five campus buildings were occupied over a period of a week, the administration at the university asked New York City's mayor, John Lindsay to intervene. A thousand police officers descended on the campus and violently extricated the protesters. Over 150 were injured in the action, and approximately 700 were arrested. Later, Columbia University suspended 30 students, including Rudd. It is worth noting here that the university did disassociate from the IDA, and the development of the controversial athletic complex at Morningside Park was abandoned.

Rudd was just at the beginning of his radicalization, however. By June 1969, he was elected to the post of national secretary of SDS, but by January of the next year, he and a group of national leaders of the organization, including Bernardine Dohrn and William Ayers, had effectively killed that organization.

Writing for the *Los Angeles Times* in a review of Rudd's memoir *Underground: My Life with SDS and the Weathermen* (2009), Jon Weiner explains that a rival leftist group within the SDS had challenged Rudd and the others by setting out a plan of direct action. "The Progressive Labor faction had a strategy for revolution: a 'worker-student alliance' to overthrow capitalism. The national leadership of SDS—Rudd and his friends—concluded that they needed one too. What they came up with was to call on young people to become urban guerrillas to fight 'Amerikka' " (Weiner 2009).

Most of the organization wanted to have nothing to do with the radical shift in focus. Rudd and the others, burning with the revolutionary fervor that now consumed their lives, had no intention of slowing down. They established the Revolutionary Youth Movement (RYM) that they would name the Weatherman after the line in the Bob Dylan song popular at the time: "You don't need a weatherman to know which way the wind blows." At the SDS national convention in 1969, everything came to a head. The RYM faction took control of the leadership in a contentious session that saw Rudd and others walk out of the convention, which effectively split the decade-old organization. The newly conceived Weatherman would go on to organize the Days of Rage in Chicago, lead demonstrations and actions throughout the United States in opposition to the war, militarism, and capitalism, and take responsibility for bombing scores of sites from California to Washington, D.C., in response to government action they deemed egregious. Their stated goal: "the violent overthrow of the government of the US in solidarity with the struggles of the people of the world" ("About Mark Rudd" n.d.).

No civilians were ever harmed by the Weather Underground Organization. But a tragedy did unfold in a Greenwich Village apartment in 1970 when three members of the group blew themselves up while constructing bombs that were designed to be used at an army dance in Fort Dix, New Jersey. The people killed were all colleagues of Rudd.

Rudd and the others were known to the FBI and other authorities before the explosion in Greenwich Village, of course. Many of the WUO were wanted for questioning or had actually been indicted for their efforts in the Days of Rage riots that took place during the trial of the Chicago Seven in 1969. Most were wanted for crossing state lines to incite a riot, for instance. But it was the incident in New York City that frightened Ayers, Dohrn, and Rudd to reconsider how they should proceed. These three leaders and others made the decision to go underground to avoid apprehension and prosecution for their crimes. While some would keep up the fight for a while, carrying on their activity as instigators and activists, Rudd made the decision to end participation in the organization he helped create just a year after it was born. He stayed hidden from 1970 until 1977, when he turned himself in to authorities.

All federal charges had been dropped by that time, because it was revealed that the government had acted illegally in their dealings with the WUO. The remaining state charges were plea-bargained to a few months in jail, and by 1978, Rudd was hired as a mathematics teacher at a community college in Albuquerque, New Mexico. He retired in 2007, wrote a successful memoir, and spends his time organizing and helping to grow the latest iteration of the Students for a Democratic Society.

Rudd has shown remorse for some of his actions and the decisions that were made in his passion to stop the immoral actions of his country. But he is most disappointed about his contribution to the elimination of SDS in 1969. As he says, "On the negative side, we destroyed SDS, the largest radical student group, at the height of the war (1969). We split the larger anti-war movement over the bogus issue of 'armed struggle.' We killed three of our own people in an accident.... Horrible stuff" (Rudd, "Frequently Asked Questions," n.d.).

Martin K. Gay

See also Ayers, William; King, Martin Luther, Jr.

References

Rudd, Mark. "About Mark Rudd." MarkRudd.com, n.d. http://www.markrudd.com/?/about-mark-rudd.html (accessed March 11, 2011).

Rudd, Mark. "Che and Me." A revised version of a talk given April 10, 2008, to the Peace Studies Program at Oregon State University, April 10, 2008. http://www.markrudd.com/?violence-and-non-violence/che-and-me.html (accessed March 11, 2011).

Rudd, Mark. "Frequently Asked Questions." MarkRudd.com, n.d. http://www.markrudd.com/?/faq.html (accessed March 11, 2011).

Rudd, Mark. *Underground: My Life with SDS and the Weathermen.* New York: HarperCollins, 2009.

Rudd, Mark. "Underground with Mark Rudd." YouTube video, 3:02, posted by "William Morrow1," April 6, 2009. http://www.youtube.com/watch?v=pxrL9iiDcSg (accessed March 11, 2011).

Weiner, Jon. "Underground by Mark Rudd." *Los Angeles Times*, March 29, 2009. http://www.latimes.com/entertainment/la-ca-mark

-rudd29-2009mar29,0,4098976.story (accessed March 11, 2011).

Rustin, Bayard (1912–1987)

"The role of the civil rights movement in the reorganization of American political life is programmatic as well as strategic. We are challenged now to broaden our social vision, to develop functional programs with concrete objectives... But we can agitate the right questions by probing at the contradictions which still stand in the way of the 'Great Society'" (Rustin 1965). In 1963, 250,000 people participated in the March on Washington for Jobs and Freedom. Martin Luther King Jr. was the leader of the demonstration, delivering his incomparable "I Have a Dream" speech. But it was Bayard Rustin who was the principal strategist of the coalition. In fact, he helped integrate nonviolent direct action into the civil rights movement. Although Rustin had directed the course of social protest for 30 years by the time of the march, few remembered his contribution. Openly gay, and concerned that his sexual orientation would undermine the credibility of the coalition, Rustin voluntarily remained the "quintessential outsider in black civil rights circles" (Carbado and Weise 2004).

Rustin was born on March 17, 1912, in West Chester, Pennsylvania. Because his mother was an unwed teenager, Rustin was adopted and raised by his grandparents, Julia and Janifer Rustin. Rustin's sense of social activism was developed at an early age. Julia and her family were members of the Religious Society of Friends, called Quakers by nonparticipants. Founded in 1652, the Friends were a sect of Protestant Christianity with a strong history of dissent and community service.

Rustin's first act of social activism began in high school at the West Chester Senior High School. At the time, state and local government imposed Jim Crow laws, which mandated *de jure* racial segregation. West Chester was the only integrated school in the county. An accomplished student, Rustin was also an accomplished school athlete. In his senior year, he carried the track team to the state mile championship. The same year, he played offensive lineman for the school football team, and was credited for the team's 10-game winning streak. Despite his success, he and fellow black team members were not allowed in the local YMCA or restaurants. They had to sit in the segregated balcony seats at the local movie theater. When the team played out-of-state games, the black team members were not allowed to stay at the same hotel with the rest of the team. At one point, Rustin organized the team into a protest squad, refusing to play unless they were allowed to stay in the same accommodations. The coach gave in to the demands, but later refused to give Rustin track awards that he had earned (Warren 2009). Rustin then organized protests at the local YMCA and local stores. When he sat in the white section of the movie theater, he was arrested, the first of many arrests in the years to come. Rustin graduated in 1932 as class valedictorian.

With his grandmother's help, Rustin received a scholarship to attend Wilberforce University, a historically black college in Ohio. By the time, Rustin had already acknowledged his homosexuality. He was also introduced to the philosophy of Mohandas Karamchand Gandhi, a young Indian lawyer who practiced total nonviolence as a form of civil disobedience. Gandhi's concept of nonviolent activism integrated well with the Friends' pacifism, and became Rustin's core approach to social and political activism.

In 1936, Rustin transferred to Cheyney State Teachers College in Pennsylvania. He left the college, however, before graduating. According to biographer John D'Emilio, he was pressured to leave after he was discovered having sexual relations with a white man (Kennedy 2003). He also joined the Young Communist League (YCL), attracted to its antiracism stance. Rustin did not graduate from this college either, moving to Harlem, New York, in 1937. Studying at the City College of New York, Rustin played a leading role in a "Communist takeover" of the student senate, campus newspaper, and the American Student Union (Steinberg 1997) and was involved in efforts to defend the Scottsboro Boys, a group of nine young men who were alleged to gang rape two white women in March 1931.

In 1941, Rustin was commissioned by the YCL to organize protests against the military's segregation policy. When Nazi dictator Adolf Hitler invaded the Soviet Union, the YCL directed its members to suspend protests for sake of wartime allegiance. Rustin did not agree with the direction and quit the YCL.

Rustin joined the emerging March on Washington Movement (MOWM), founded by union organizer and civil rights leader A Philip Randolph. Rustin was assigned as the movement's head of the youth arm. The two worked with Abraham Johannes (A. J.) Muste to organize a march on Washington D.C., protesting racial discrimination in war industries and segregation in the military. Pressured by the impending march, President Franklin D. Roosevelt issued the Fair Employment Act on June 25, 1941, prohibiting employment discrimination. As a result, the march was suspended.

Rustin also was involved in A. J. Muste's religious nonviolent organization, Fellowship of Reconciliation (FOR). Muste appointed Rustin as field secretary for youth and general affairs. He traveled to college campuses and addressed civic and religious groups, honing his skills as a political organizer.

In 1942, Rustin helped found the Congress of Racial Equality (CORE), which was dedicated to nonviolent direct action. Rustin continued to travel cross-country to organize demonstrations, sit-ins at public places, and other events.

As a conscientious objector, Rustin was exempt from the draft as long as he enlisted in the Civilian Public Service. Believing that the work camps supported the war effort, Rustin refused. In 1944, Rustin was sentenced to three years in Lewisburg Federal Penitentiary. During his incarceration, Rustin organized hunger strikes in the dining hall in protest of the segregated seating. Released in 1946, Rustin returned to work for FOR as race relations secretary.

In 1946, the Supreme Court delivered the Irene Morgan decision. Like the more famous Rosa Parks, who would 11 years later refuse to give up her seat, Morgan refused to give up her bus seat to a white person while traveling interstate. Morgan was arrested and punished. Federal law prohibited states from imposing segregation in interstate travel, but many state and local authorities still enforced Jim Crow segregation laws. In 1947, Rustin organized the first Freedom Ride, called the Journey of Reconciliation. A group of interracial volunteers rode a bus from the North to the South. Rustin and many of the volunteers were arrested, and Rustin spent 30 days on a chain gang. This protest became the precursor to the Freedom Rides of the 1960s.

By the 1950s, Rustin began creating a significant presence as a social activist. He traveled to England, Europe, Africa, and India, joining others in condemnation of the cold war and nuclear weaponry development. However, in 1953, Rustin was caught in a homosexual affair and arrested on charges of lewd vagrancy. He was sentenced to 60 days in jail. The humiliation of the arrest would prove pivotal in future work. He was forced to resign his post at FOR and was branded a sex offender (Kennedy 2003). A year after his resignation, Rustin was appointed executive secretary for the War Resisters League. He would hold that post for 12 years.

In 1955, Rosa Parks's arrest triggered the Montgomery bus boycott. The event was led by the young minister Martin Luther King Jr. Rustin traveled to Montgomery to meet King, and became one of King's key speechwriters and chief advisers. Rustin helped King organize the Southern Christian Leadership Conference (SCLC), drafting the founding documents. Rustin and the War Resisters League mobilized the Committee for Nonviolent Integration, and funneled aid to King. Rustin also helped organize such groups as In Friendship to raise funds for the Montgomery Improvement Association; the Prayer Pilgrimage, King's first major protest event outside the South; and the Youth March for Integrated Schools in 1958, in which 10,000 students marched on Washington, D.C.

Although open about his sexual orientation, Rustin was keenly aware that his homosexuality could be used by his critics to compromise the growing movement. As a result, Rustin tended to be low-key about his participation. Still, many of King's supporters were concerned, stating that "sensationalist reporting" because of Rustin's "Communist past and homosexual proclivities" would damage their efforts (Kennedy 2003). One such critic was Adam Clayton Powell Jr., U.S. representative and chief minister of Harlem's Abyssinian Baptist Church. Powell threatened to discuss Rustin's 1953 moral charges, and if need be, leak fraudulent claims that King and Rustin were having an affair, if Rustin was not removed. In 1960, Rustin publicly resigned from the SCLC, although he continued to work with King in the following years.

In 1963, Rustin joined Randolph to organize a march that focused on economic issues, particularly the need for jobs, higher wages, and improved work conditions. The march was sponsored by the Negro American Labor Council, the association of black unionists that Randolph formed within the AFL-CIO. However, King proposed that the focus be expanded to civil rights as well as economic issues. Rustin became the chief organizer and tactician for the 1963 March on Washington for Jobs and Freedom. "This required all kinds of things that you had to think through," he reported. "You had to think how many toilets you needed.... We had to consult doctors on exactly what people should bring to eat so that they wouldn't get sick ... We had to arrange for drinking water. We had to arrange what we would do if there was a terrible thunderstorm that day" (Williams 1987, 198–99). Rustin garnered support of major civil rights organizations, unions, religious leaders, and celebrities.

Critics continued to hound Rustin. U.S. senator Strom Thurmond of South Carolina, for example, hoped to discredit the civil rights movement by attacking Rustin, inserting into the *Congressional Record* the accounts of Rustin's 1953 arrest and calling him a "sexual pervert." But Randolph and others came to Rustin's defense, and Thurmond's hope to discredit the movement was abated (Kennedy 2003). The march took place on August 28, and is considered the epitome of protest politics. It was "the biggest, and surely the most diverse, demonstration in history of human rights" (Steinberg 1997).

The 1963 march marked a decisive turn in Rustin's politics. He began devoting more time to such issues as nonalignment and nuclear disarmament. As Rustin noted in Stephen Steinberg's account, his activism was rooted in his Quaker upbringing. Following Randolph's philosophy, Rustin as a socialist regarded the struggle for racial justice as secondary to class struggle. Critics saw his movement to the larger political agenda as a betrayal of civil rights to which he had devoted so much of his time (Steinberg 1997).

In 1964, Rustin founded the A Philip Randolph Institute and became a regular contributor to the AFL-CIO newspaper. In 1965, he published his influential essay, "From Protest to Politics: The Future of Civil Rights Movement," arguing that "the civil rights movement is evolving from a protest movement to a full-fledged social movement" in which economics played a more important role in undermining racial equality. He asserts "I fail to see how the movement can be victorious in the absence of radical programs for full employment, the abolition of slums, the reconstruction of our education system, new definitions of work and leisure" (Rustin 1965).

Rustin was an early supporter of President Lyndon B. Johnson's Vietnam policy. As the war escalated, however, Rustin withdrew his support. Following King's assassination in 1968, Rustin traveled to Ghana, Nigeria, Vietnam, Laos, and other countries, supporting native leaders in their freedom movements. In 1977, he became an advocate for the LGBT movement, testifying before the New York legislature.

Rustin died on August 24, 1987, of a ruptured appendix.

Bobbi Miller

See also King, Martin Luther, Jr.; Parks, Rosa; Randolph, A. Philip

References

Carbado, Devon, and Donald Weise. "The Civil Rights Identity of Bayard Rustin." *Texas Law Review*, April 2004, http://www.utexas.edu/law/journals/tlr/abstracts/82/82carbado.pdf (accessed September 9, 2011).

D'Emilio, John. "Chicago Gay History: 1951, Bayard Rustin in Chicago." *Windy City Times*, August 1, 2008. http://outhistory.org/wiki/John_D'Emilio,_%22Bayard_Rustin_in_Chicago,%22_1951 (accessed March 19, 2011).

D'Emilio, John. *Lost Prophet: The Life and Times of Bayard Rustin*. New York: Free Press, 2003.

Edwin, Ed (interviewer). "The First Freedom Ride: Bayard Rustin on His Work with CORE." Columbia University Oral History Collection, September 1985. http://historymatters.gmu.edu/d/6909 (accessed March 20, 2011).

Kennedy, Randall. "From Protest to Patronage." *Nation*, September 11, 2003. http://www.thenation.com/article/protest-patronage (accessed March 19, 2011).

Rustin, Bayard. *Down the Line: The Collected Writings of Bayard Rustin*. Chicago: Quadrangle Books, 1971.

Rustin, Bayard. "From Protest to Politics: The Future of the Civil Rights Movement." *Commentary*, February 1965. http://www.commentarymagazine.com/article/from-protest-to-politics-the-future-of-the-civil-rights-movement/ (accessed March 18, 2011).

Steinberg, Stephen. "Bayard Rustin and the Rise and Decline of the Black Protest Movement." *New Politics* 6, no. 3 (Summer 1997). http://www.hartford-hwp.com/archives/45a/128.html (accessed March 19, 2011).

Warren, Patricia Neil. "Bayard Rustin: Offensive Lineman For Freedom." Outspors.com, February 15, 2009. http://www.outsports.com/os/index.php/component/content/article/45-2009/170-bayard-rustin-offensive-lineman-for-freedom%20 (accessed March 19, 2011).

Williams, Juan, with the Eyes on the Prize Production Team. *Eyes on the Prize: America's Civil Rights Years, 1954–1965*. New York: Viking Penguin, 1987.

S

Sacco, Ferdinando Nicola (1891–1927), and Vanzetti, Bartolomeo (1888–1927)

"Some considered them demonic—murderers, anarchists, immigrants bent on savaging 'all the institutions that Americans hold dear.' Others saw them as 'shining lights,' gentle pacifists framed by a heartless judge and a ruthless prosecutor" (Watson 2004, 1). These are opening words of a book about the highly controversial trial and execution of Nicola Sacco and Bartolomeo Vanzetti, known as the shoemaker and the fish peddler, whose joint case resonated around the world and is still being debated.

Sacco was named Ferdinando Sacco at birth on April 22, 1891, in Torremaggiore, Foggia Province, in southern Italy, where his father was an olive oil dealer. His formal education was brief; accounts vary but Sacco claimed he dropped out of school at age 14.

Vanzetti was born on June 11, 1888, in Villafalletto, Cuneo Province, in northern Italy. His father was a farmer and also owner of a café. At the age of 13, Bartolomeo left school because his father had apprenticed him to the owner of a pastry shop, a seven-day-a-week job that he hated. He worked in the shop for seven years and developed pleurisy, causing difficulty in breathing. While recovering, he became an insatiable reader, devouring books on religion and philosophy. Soon after his recovery, Vanzetti's mother died of cancer. Devastated, he decided to immigrate to the United States.

Although the two did not know each other, Sacco and Vanzetti both came to the United States in the same year—1908—and settled in Massachusetts. Sacco worked as a shoe trimmer for a company in Milford and, in 1912, met and married Rosina Zambelli. The couple's first child, son Dante, was born in 1913. Ines, a daughter, was born in 1920. In 1913, Sacco began attending weekly meetings of an Italian anarchist group and subscribed to *Cronaca Sovversiva* (*Subversive Chronicle*), an anarchist newspaper published by Luigi Galleani. Sacco also wrote articles for the paper and solicited funds for anarchist activities.

Vanzetti, a bachelor, held a variety of menial jobs in the United States and frequently was unemployed, sometimes living on the streets and moving about to find work and a place to live. But he was still an avid reader, and political books and articles about anarchism roused his interests. He eventually found work in Plymouth, Massachusetts, and settled there.

Sacco and Vanzetti did not meet until about six weeks after the United States entered World War I in 1917; both were attending a meeting of Galleanist Anarchists in Boston. Luigi Galleani, the leader, was a foremost Italian anarchist-communist, a proponent of *propaganda by deed* (or *propaganda of the deed*), that is, taking action—sometimes violent action—against those who oppress the working class. Galleani urged men who were required to register for the draft not to do so. A federal law mandated that males between the ages of 21 and 30 register with their draft board, but those who were not citizens did not have to serve in the military. Both Sacco and Vanzetti were aliens, although Vanzetti had applied for citizenship. They could see no reason to register; they were convinced that the war was being fought by the poor and powerless for the rich. Such an attitude expressed publicly was not tolerated by most Americans and certainly not by the federal government.

To prevent opposition to U.S. entry into the world war, the U.S. Congress passed the Espionage Act of 1917, which required heavy penalties against those who refused military service or obstructed the draft. The nation also was experiencing the beginning of a "Red Scare," which was a reaction to the communist takeover of Russia and the fear that communists would infiltrate the United States and attempt to overthrow the government. People who called themselves "patriots" demanded that all Americans demonstrate their loyalty.

Galleani told his followers that there was no need to support warmongers and advised them to get out of the country. Sacco and Vanzetti joined about 60 Italian anarchists and fled to Mexico. Sacco changed his first name to Nicola and for a time used his mother's maiden name Mosmacotelli to avoid detection. Vanzetti grew a long, drooping mustache to shield his identity. For several months, the group lived communally on the edge of Monterrey, but they soon became short of funds. They received news from the United States that because of the war efforts, jobs were plentiful and that they could easily avoid registering for the draft. The group also "wearied of their exile. Nerves became frayed, tempers short, and quarrels occasionally broke out" (Avrich 1991, 66).

In September 1917, Sacco was one of the first to return to the United States to find work and to be with his family, whom he greatly missed. Sacco had difficulty finding a job as a shoe trimmer, and the family moved often as Sacco took low-paying work with various companies. Finally, he was hired as a shoe trimmer for a factory in Stoughton, Massachusetts, and the Sacco family settled there. Besides his trade, Sacco loved to tend his garden, which he cared for early in the morning before he left for the factory and after work until dark.

A short time after Sacco left Mexico, Vanzetti returned to the United States and worked at various jobs at different locations over a year's time. He eventually bought a cart, knives, and other equipment to become an outdoor fish vendor in Plymouth, Massachusetts. He peddled cod, swordfish, halibut, and eel—the latter was a favorite among Italians during the Christmas holidays. Along his routes, Vanzetti made numerous friends and frequently stopped to have coffee with them and tell stories. He was especially loved by the children he met along the way. When the weather turned cold, he had to resort to odd jobs to earn a living.

Both Sacco and Vanzetti kept in touch with other Italian radicals and took part in anarchist meetings on weekends. They also wrote articles for *Cronaca Sovversiva*. Law enforcement officials raided the newspaper office in early 1918, at the height of the Red Scare, looking for links to anarchists and subversives. Later that year, Congress passed the Sedition Act of 1918, virtually outlawing any criticism of or protests against U.S. government war policies.

In 1919, after the end of World War I, U.S. attorney general A. Mitchell Palmer initiated raids in cities nationwide to arrest thousands he claimed were subversives. Authorities held anarchists, communists, religious antiwar dissenters, and other

Bartolomeo Vanzetti (center left) and Nicola Sacco (center right), immigrant Italian anarchists convicted in a 1920 armed robbery and murder, enter the Dedham, Massachusetts, courthouse in handcuffs. The two were executed in 1927. Their conviction and execution were debated throughout the world and called into question the fairness of the American justice system, particularly during the post–World War I red scare. (Library of Congress)

pacifists. In one raid, officials discovered a bomb plot that involved dynamiting the homes of more than 30 people, including Palmer, business tycoons J. P. Morgan and John D. Rockefeller, and Justice Oliver Wendell Holmes. On June 2, 1919, a militant anarchist, Carlo Valdinoci, who had been in Mexico with Sacco and Vanzetti, did ignite a bomb in front of Palmer's home, and in the process, Valdinoci killed himself.

The country was in an uproar over the bombings and anarchist activities, a climate that prevailed in 1920 when two employees of a shoe company in Braintree, Massachusetts, were killed while being robbed of a payroll. A similar robbery had taken place a few months earlier, and a witness described the robbers as Italians, leading police to conclude that an Italian gang was responsible.

Three weeks after the Braintree murders, Sacco and Vanzetti were arrested as "suspicious characters." They both carried guns, but denied to police that they were armed. Officers also found an announcement for an anarchist meeting in Sacco's pocket—Vanzetti was the featured speaker. When asked about their anarchist connections, the men denied involvement. From that time on, authorities considered the men guilty, but others were convinced the men were concealing their anarchist views in order to protect themselves from the hysteria raging across the country.

Sacco and Vanzetti were charged and indicted for robbery and murder; they were put on trial on May 21, 1921, before Judge Webster Thayer, who showed contempt for the anarchists and openly criticized their lawyer from the American Civil Liberties Union. The trial lasted six weeks, and the men were convicted in spite of witnesses who testified to their whereabouts at the time of the crime. According to *Time* magazine, "20 Italians said they had purchased eels from Mr. Vanzetti at the hour of the crime, and the Italian consul in Boston swore that Mr. Sacco had been in his presence at that time" (*Time* 1927, 14). Actually, Sacco was in Boston to see about a passport to Italy because his mother had died and he wanted to be with his grieving father. In addition, no stolen money was ever found, and a convicted criminal confessed to the crime. But witnesses for the prosecution testified that they had seen Sacco and Vanzetti at the crime scene.

After the verdict, lawyers for Sacco and Vanzetti appealed and petitioned for a new trial. Felix Frankfurter, a Harvard law professor who later became a U.S. Supreme Court justice, worked on the case and also wrote news article claiming that Sacco and Vanzetti were victims of political and ethnic bias. Investigators found new evidence that they claimed would prove that Sacco and Vanzetti were innocent, but the judge refused to reopen the case. The Massachusetts Supreme Court denied appeals and Governor Alvan T. Fuller refused all petitions for clemency.

Many individuals and groups in the United States and Europe came to the men's defense and fought for their freedom, claiming the police had framed the anarchists because of their radical views and Italian origin. Protesters demonstrated in cities across the United States. When Sacco and Vanzetti were sentenced to death on April 9, 1927, more protests erupted, but to no avail. The two, who had proclaimed their innocence up to the time of their deaths, were executed on August 23, 1927, and their bodies cremated. But the Sacco and Vanzetti saga went on.

Over the years since the executions, books, film documentaries, plays, poetry, protest songs, paintings, newspaper editorials, magazine articles, and web sites have appeared in attempts to exonerate or to further condemn Sacco and Vanzetti. Upton Sinclair, known for his book *The Jungle*, was one author who publicly supported the anarchists. On August 23, 1977, Massachusetts governor Michael Dukakis issued a proclamation declaring the date was Nicola Sacco and Bartolomeo Vanzetti Memorial Day. He further stated that the trial of the two men "was permeated by prejudice against foreigners and hostility toward unorthodox political views.... the conduct of many of the officials involved in the case shed serious doubt on their willingness and ability to conduct the prosecution and trial ... fairly and impartially." Governor Dukakis proclaimed "any stigma and disgrace should be forever removed from the names of Nicola Sacco and Bartolomeo Vanzetti, from the names of their families and descendants" (Young and Kaiser 1985, 3–4).

In spite of the exoneration, the guilt of Sacco and Vanzetti continues to be the subject of debate.

See also Sinclair, Upton

References

Avrich, Paul. *Sacco and Vanzetti: The Anarchist Background*. Princeton, NJ: Princeton University Press, 1991.

Burnett, Paul. "The Sacco and Vanzetti Trial: Key Figures." n.d. http://www.law.umkc.edu/faculty/projects/ftrials/SaccoV/SaccoV.htm (accessed June 9, 2010).

Davis, John. *Sacco and Vanzetti*. Melbourne, Victoria, Australia: Ocean Press, 2004.

Frankfurter, Felix. "The Case of Sacco and Vanzetti." *Atlantic*, March 1927. http://www.theatlantic.com/past/docs/unbound/flashbks/oj/frankff.htm (accessed June 10, 2010).

Frankfurter, Felix. *The Case of Sacco and Vanzetti: A Critical Analysis for Lawyers and Laymen*. Boston: Little, Brown, 1927.

National Affairs. "Sacco and Vanzetti." *Time*, April 18, 1927.

Sacco, Nicola, and Bartolomeo Vanzetti. *The Letters of Sacco and Vanzetti*. New York: Penguin Group, 1997. First published by Viking, 1928.

Watson, Bruce. *Sacco and Vanzetti: The Men, the Murders, and the Judgment of Mankind*. New York: Viking, 2007.

Young, William, and David E. Kaiser. *Postmortem: New Evidence in the Case of Sacco and Vanzetti*. Amherst: University of Massachusetts Press, 1985.

Sanger, Margaret (1879–1966)

"Woman must have her freedom—the fundamental freedom of choosing whether or not she shall be a mother and how many children she will have. Regardless of what man's attitude may be, that problem is hers —and before it can be his, it is hers alone" (Sanger 1919). So wrote Margaret Sanger in her battle to legitimize contraception and improve conditions for women. She actively challenged religious, political, and social patriarchy that dominated the waning years of Victorian society to become one of the inspirations for the 1960s sexual revolution.

Margaret Louise Higgins was born on September 14, 1879, in Corning, New York. She was the sixth surviving child of 11 children. Her mother, Anne Purcell Higgins, was a devout Irish Catholic, and was pregnant 18 times in 22 years. Weakened from multiple pregnancies, Sanger's mother also suffered from tuberculosis. Her father, Michael Hennessy Higgins, was a stonecutter for the local Roman Catholic Church. He was also a political radical, and an activist in woman suffrage and free public education. He told his daughter to always think for herself. In 1894, Michael Higgins alienated the Catholic community by asking the atheist socialist Robert Green Ingersoll to speak at a public meeting.

Sanger attended the parish high school of St. Mary's Church until 1896, when she enrolled in a nursing program at Claverack College in Claverack, New York. Her studies were interrupted in 1896, when she returned home to tend to her dying mother, who wasted away from tuberculosis. Anne Purcell Higgins died on March 31, 1896, at age 50.

Determined to avoid her mother's fate, Sanger returned to school. After graduating from Claverack in 1900, Sanger enrolled in the rigorous nursing program at a hospital in the affluent New York City suburb of White Plains. Again, her studies were interrupted; she became ill with tuberculosis. Her physical condition deteriorated quickly, and the doctors twice predicted her impending death. In 1902, she left her studies permanently when she married aspiring architect and socialist William Sanger. Still weakened from her ordeal with tuberculosis, Sanger retreated into "tame domesticity." The Sangers moved to Saranac, New York, in order to give her time to heal. In 1903, she gave birth to her first child, Stuart. Over the next years, she gave birth to two more children, Grant and Peggy.

By 1910, the Sangers had returned to New York City, and were living in Greenwich Village, known as a bohemian gathering place where many avant-garde thinkers, socialists, and artists as well as activists lived. They became involved with many of the village's radical personalities, including author Upton Sinclair, whose book *The Jungle* (1906) exposed the appalling and unsanitary conditions in the meatpacking industry; and Emma Goldman, an anarchist known for her political activism. In fact, Goldman impressed Sanger and her influence underscored much of Sanger's own activism. She joined the Liberal Club and became a supporter of the anarchist Ferrer Center and Modern School.

To help with the family financial situation, Sanger worked as a midwife and nurse for the impoverished population on the Lower East Side. She saw destitute families trapped in poverty because their wages were too low to adequately support large numbers of children. She worked primarily with women suffering from the physical effects of frequent pregnancies and self-induced abortions. Already living in desperate conditions, women turned to home remedies to induce abortions. These included using laxatives and quinine, douching solutions using Lysol and other caustic chemicals, herb teas, or steaming. They also threw themselves downstairs, or inserted slippery eels, knitting needles or shoe hooks to induce an abortion. These methods caused severe bleeding, often leading to painful deaths.

Even if contraception had been available, it was not an option for these women because of the 1873 Comstock Law named after Anthony Comstock, a special agent for the U.S. Post Office Department. He was a zealous Christian who considered himself the moral guardian of the U.S. mails. The law banned "Every obscene, lewd, or lascivious, and every filthy book, pamphlet, picture, paper, letter, writing, print, or other publication of an indecent character" and declared these materials "to be nonmailable matter and shall not be conveyed in the mails or delivered from any post office or by any letter carrier." The law effectively banned contraceptives as well as the distribution of information on abortion for educational purposes.

In 1912, Sanger tended to Sadie Sachs, who was suffering from the lingering effects, possibly infection, of a self-induced abortion. Sachs begged the attending doctor for information on how to prevent pregnancies in the future. The doctor advised her to remain abstinent. A few months later, Sanger was called again to Sachs's apartment, where the woman had died from another self-induced abortion. The experience became a turning point in Sanger's life: "I went to bed, knowing that no matter what it might cost, I was finished with palliatives and superficial cures; I was resolved to seek out the root of evil, to do something to change the destiny of mothers whose miseries were vast as the sky" (Sanger 1938, 92).

Sanger began to openly challenge the Comstock Law. She was no stranger to political activism. She had joined the Industrial Workers of the World, and protested with the textile mill workers of Lawrence, Massachusetts, on strike in 1912 for higher wages. She also had testified before Congress about the strike. She began writing a column for a socialist newspaper, the *New York Call*. Entitled "What Every Girl Should Know," the column discussed sexual issues, including venereal disease. Deemed obscene under the Comstock Law, the column was banned. Sanger challenged the ban, and gained support from free-speech advocates. Eventually, she was able to continue writing the column.

In 1913, Sanger separated from her husband William as she became more involved in her activism. Sanger was influenced by anarchist Emma Goldman's publication *Mother Earth*, which focused on myriad socialist topics including a woman's right

Margaret Sanger dedicated her life to the birth-control movement in the United States, of which she was the founder and controversial leader. She actively challenged religious, political, and social patriarchy that dominated the waning years of Victorian society to become one of the inspirations for the 1960s sexual revolution. (Library of Congress)

to limit her family and to reject forced motherhood. In 1914, Sanger began her own publication, the *Woman's Rebel*. The feminist newspaper was written for the working-class woman, and used the motto: "No Gods. No Masters." The aim of the paper, wrote Sanger, "will be to stimulate working women to think for themselves and to build up a conscious fighting character." In addition, the paper promised "to advocate the prevention of conception and to impart such knowledge in the columns of this paper" (Sanger 1914).

After only six monthly issues of the paper, Sanger was indicted for nine charges of violating the 1873 Comstock Law. Like one of her contemporaries, Mary Ware Dennett, who championed sex education and advocated for birth-control information, Sanger faced a public trial and a possible 30-year prison term.

Without saying goodbye to her estranged husband or her children, Sanger fled to Canada. Using the alias of Bertha Wilson, Sanger obtained a visa and sailed to England. However, once the ship entered international waters, Sanger ordered 100,000 copies of *Family Limitation* to be distributed. The 16-page pamphlet contained information about sex education, abortion, and birth control, including types of contraceptive methods and instructions for their use.

Sanger lived in England for a year, and met several British radicals and feminists who supported the use of birth control. Among them was Havelock Ellis, a British sexologist and social reformer. His theories of female sexuality helped Sanger to expand her arguments for birth control, including her view that a woman should enjoy sexual relations without the worry of an unwanted pregnancy. During this time, Sanger visited a Dutch birth-control clinic where she learned about flexible contraceptive diaphragms. She decided these were more effective than the suppositories and douches she had been advocating and distributing. She would later smuggle the contraceptive into the United States, introducing the diaphragm to American audiences.

Anthony Comstock, Sanger's harshest critic, died in 1915. That same year, Sanger's estranged husband was handing out copies of Sanger's publication *Family Limitation*. He was arrested for distributing obscene material and jailed for 30 days. Sanger recognized the situation as an opportunity for publicity. In October 1915, Sanger returned to the United States to stand trial.

In November 1915, as Sanger prepared for trial, Sanger's four-year-old daughter Peggy died of pneumonia. Dressed in her black mourning gown, Sanger posed with her two sons for a portrait. The portrait garnered public sympathy. The government, already leery of further publicity on radical sex theories and birth control, dropped all charges against Sanger.

In October 1916, she opened the first U.S. family-planning and birth-control clinic, the Brownsville Clinic, in Brooklyn, New York. Doctors refused to become involved with the clinic, and Sanger and her sister Ethyl Byrne, a registered nurse, and two women made up the staff. Ten days after it opened, the police raided the clinic. Sanger, Byrne, and two women staffers were arrested, tried, and sentenced to 30 days in jail. Byrne, following the example of British suffragists, went on a hunger strike. Her brutal force-feeding made front-page headlines. The trial of the "birth control sisters" firmly established Sanger as a national figure. Sanger appealed her case, and in 1918, the New York Court of Appeals clarified the law that forbade distribution of birth control information, allowing doctors to prescribe contraception.

In 1916, the Catholic Church became one of Sanger's strongest opponents. Catholic groups tried to stop her public speaking as well as the distribution of materials. She often invoked the First Amendment, and in the process, cited the Church's willingness to ignore the constitutional separation of church and state. An avowed atheist, Sanger frequently opposed Christian leaders.

In August 1920, when women won the right to vote, many suffragists and feminist groups began to oppose Sanger. Some of her opponents found the legalization of birth control 'sordid,' regarding motherhood as the highest vocation and birth control an insult to their femininity. Others denounced marriage and sex entirely.

Sanger's views also were in direct conflict with those of Mary Ware Dennett, who founded the National Birth Control Movement in 1915. Dennett believed that information about birth control should be legalized and available to the public—at the time, such information was considered obscene and banned by federal law. Sanger disagreed and argued that only doctors should distribute contraceptive information.

Sanger founded the American Birth Control League (ABCL) in 1921, and planned to lecture on the morality of birth control in the New York City Town Hall. Pressured by Catholic monsignor Patrick J. Ryan, the police raided the meeting, arresting Sanger and others. While the charges were dropped the next morning, free speech activists, the media, and the American Civil Liberties Union remained outraged.

In 1921, William and Margaret Sanger were divorced. Sanger traveled and lectured around the world. In 1922, she traveled to Japan to work with Japanese feminist Kato Shidzue. She returned to Japan several times, becoming the first foreign woman to address the Japanese national legislature in 1954. In 1922, she met and married oil tycoon James Noah H. Slee.

In 1923, Sanger established the Birth Control Clinical Research Bureau (BCCRB). With the help of wealthy supporters, including a grant from wealthy oil industrialist John D. Rockefeller, Sanger opened the first legal birth-control clinic, staffed with female doctors and social workers.

In her zeal to promote access to birth control for all women, Sanger frequently aligned herself with controversial movements, such as eugenics, a social philosophy purporting that human hereditary traits should be improved through social intervention and supported the supremacy of the white Aryan race. In her book *The Pivot of Civilization* (1922), she described decreasing the birth rate of those who were mentally and physically defective. In 1926, she gave a lecture to the women's auxiliary of the Ku Klux Klan in Silver Lake, New Jersey, later describing it as one of her weirdest experiences.

When Franklin D. Roosevelt became president in 1932, Sanger lobbied to integrate birth control programs into Roosevelt's New Deal programs.

In 1937, Sanger became chairperson of the Birth Control Council of America, launching two publications, the *Birth Control Review* and the *Birth Control News*. In 1942, the ABCL and BCCRB fused into one organization, the Birth Control Federation of America, which later became Planned Parenthood. One of the more controversial campaigns of the organization was the Negro Project in 1939, focusing on the high birth rates and poor quality of life in the South. The concept of the project was controlling the number of black children born, which in current times would be seen as blatant racism or at worst black genocide. However, it was widely supported in the late 1930s by such black leaders as Mary McLeod Bethune and W. E. B. Du Bois.

Sanger lived long enough to see birth control finally legalized for married couples in a U.S. Supreme Court decision, *Griswold v. Connecticut* (1965). She died a year later on September 6, 1966, in a nursing home in Tucson, Arizona.

Bobbi Miller

See also Bethune, Mary McLeod; Dennett, Mary Ware; Du Bois, W. E. B.; Goldman, Emma; Sinclair, Upton

References

Brace, Robin. "Margaret Sanger; A New Appraisal." *UK Apologetics*, January 2010. http://www.ukapologetics.net/10/sanger.htm (accessed October 30, 2010).

Galvin, Rachel. "Margaret Sanger's 'Deeds of Terrible Virtue.'" *Humanities*, September–October 1998. http://www.neh.gov/news/humanities/1998-09/sanger.html (accessed October 30, 2010).

History Matters. "'No Gods, No Masters': Margaret Sanger on Birth Control." http://historymatters.gmu.edu/d/5084/ (accessed October 30, 2010).

Margaret Sanger Papers. "Birth Control or Race Control? Sanger and the Negro Project." *Margaret Sanger Papers Project #28*, Fall 2001. http://www.nyu.edu/projects/sanger/secure/newsletter/articles/bc_or_race_control.html (accessed October 28, 2010).

Margaret Sanger Papers. "Sanger, Censorship, and the Catholic Church—the Latest Battle in a Long War." *Margaret Sanger Papers Project #6*, Winter 1993–1994. Revised November 2002. http://www.nyu.edu/projects/sanger/secure/newsletter/articles/sanger_censorship_and_catholic_church.html (accessed October 28, 2010).

Sanger, Margaret. *Margaret Sanger: An Autobiography*. New York: W. W. Norton, 1938.

Sanger, Margaret. "Morality and Birth Control." *Margaret Sanger Project* (originally published in *Birth Control Review*, February–March 1918). http://www.nyu.edu/projects/sanger/secure/documents/speech_morality_and_bc.html (accessed October 30, 2010).

Sanger, Margaret. "A Parents' Problem or Woman's?" *Margaret Sanger Project* (originally published in *Birth Control Review*, March 1919). http://www.nyu.edu/projects/sanger/webedition/app/documents/show.php?sangerDoc=226268.xml (accessed October 30, 2010).

Sanger, Margaret H. *What Every Girl Should Know*. Springfield, IL: United Sales Co., 1920. http://archive.lib.msu.edu/DMC/AmRad/whateverygirl1920.pdf (accessed October 30, 2010).

United States History. "Margaret Sanger." http://www.u-s-history.com/pages/h1676.html (accessed October 30, 2010).

Schlafly, Phyllis (1924–)

"In the scale of liberal sins, hypocrisy is the greatest, and they have always considered me a hypocrite," Phyllis Schlafly stated in a 2006 interview. A staunch Republican, lawyer, and political activist, Schlafly has "passionately endorsed domestic life" as a woman's greatest achievement (Bellafante 2006). Schlafly played a critical role in one of the most important domestic political events of the twentieth century. She helped to defy the "seemingly unstoppable" Equal Rights Amendment (ERA) in 1972 (Allen 2005). Her endorsements infuriated the feminist movement. "I simply didn't believe we needed a constitutional amendment to protect women's rights... I know of only one law that was discriminatory toward women, a law in North Dakota stipulating that a wife had to have her husband's permission to make wine" (Bellafante 2006).

Born Phyllis Stewart on August 15, 1924, Schlafly grew up in a strict Catholic in St. Louis, Missouri. Her father, John Bruce Stewart, worked as a machinist and heavy-equipment salesman for Westinghouse. During the Depression, when Schlafly was in the fourth grade, her father lost his job. Her mother Odile Dodge Schlafly supported the family by working as a department store saleswoman, an elementary school teacher, and eventually as a librarian for an art museum. Despite these financial setbacks, Stewart "despised" Franklin Roosevelt's New Deal programs (Allen 2005). The New Deal was a series of economic programs implemented between 1933 and 1936. The programs focused on relief for the unemployed and impoverished, on economic recovery, and reform of the financial system. Stewart advocated self-reliance, family, and moral integrity (Allen 2005). "I grew up believing that I should support myself," says Schlafly (Bellafante 2006).

Graduating as valedictorian from the Academy of Sacred Heart, Schlafly won a full scholarship to a local Catholic women's college. In her first year, she decided the college was not challenging and transferred to Washington University in St. Louis. Because she had lost her scholarship, she paid for her tuition by working full time at the St. Louis Ordinance Plant as an ammunition tester and laboratory technician. Working the night shift, she fired rifles and machine guns, investigating misfires and photographing tracer bullets in flight. She graduated Phi Beta Kappa in three years, earning her BA in 1944. She won a fellowship to study politics at Radcliffe College in Cambridge, Massachusetts, earning her master's degree in government in 1945.

In 1946, Schlafly moved to Washington, D.C., to work as a researcher for the American Enterprise Association. Founded in 1938 by New York businessman Lew H. Brown, the AEA included executives from the leading business and financial firms of the day. It also included prominent policy intellectuals such as Roscoe Pound of the Harvard Law School, economic journalist Henry Hazlitt, and disillusioned New Dealer Raymond Moley. The AEA's purpose was to educate the public on the importance of maintaining a system of free, competitive enterprise. The organization prepared analyses of legislative proposals and published studies on many topics, including Social Security reform, government health insurance, and the effects of trade on domestic employment. In 1970, the AEA was renamed the American Enterprise Institute.

Schlafly worked for the AEA for a year, and was exposed to "anti-liberalism as a philosophical proposition" (Allen 2005).

Phyllis Schlafly is shown in 1977 as she spearheads a nationwide campaign to stop the Equal Rights Ammendment. She also has supported groups concerned about a communist takeover of the United States. (AP Photo)

Her experience at the AEA solidified her conservative philosophy as an advocate for free enterprise and the preservation of American liberty. She also worked in the successful election campaign of Republican Claude I. Blakewell to the House of Representatives.

On October 20, 1949, Phyllis married conservative Republican attorney John Fred Schlafly Jr. She was 25, and John Schlafly was 15 years her senior. Within a year, her first son, John, was born. In the following years, she had three additional sons and two daughters. The family moved to Alton, Illinois, where she joined several political and civic organizations, including the Illinois Federation of Republican Women, Daughters of the American Revolution, and the Radcliffe Club. Although she took pride in her homemaker status, Schlafly was quickly becoming a popular public speaker. As biographer Donald Critchlow notes, Schlafly encouraged Republican women to think of themselves as more than "envelope-stuffers and luncheon adornments" (Allen 2005). Schlafly considered it a time-honored tradition that women become involved in social and moral reform, just as they had done during the antislavery and temperance movements of the nineteenth century.

In 1952, and with her husband's endorsement, Schlafly ran for the U.S. Congress. She ran against five-term Democrat incumbent Melvin Price. Following World War II, and during the 1950s, the United States was experiencing a fear-driven movement known as the Second Red Scare. U.S. citizens feared that the Soviet Union wanted to spread communism all over the world, irradiating democracy and capitalism. Schlafly's campaign reflected this movement, as she attacked Price for championing "big government and big spending" and "coddling Communist sympathizers" (Kolbert 2005). Accusing the Truman administration of treason, stating that the New Deal Party was slow to realize the dangers of communism, she also announced that "Many government bureaus have developed extensive programs of brainwashing to push through social medicine and universal military training" (Kolbert 2005). Schlafly lost the election.

Retuning to private life, Schlafly and her husband continued their stance against what they believed to be the communist threat. They showed films to dinner quests, such as "Operation Abolition," portraying students protesting the House Un-American Activities Committee as 'violence-prone radicals,' and "Communism on the Map," showing red ink spreading across the globe (Kolbert 2005). In 1958, Schlafly and her husband were among the founding members of the Cardinal

Mindszenty Foundation, a Catholic organization whose goal is to reveal the harm of ideologies such as secularism and communism. Schlafly predicted communism would take over the United States by 1970 (Kolbert 2005).

Schlafly's strong views came into strong opposition with that of her own Republican Party. In 1958, as negotiations opened with the Soviet Union, President Dwight Eisenhower proposed a one-year ban on nuclear testing. Schlafly wrote that this was "a victory for appeasement-minded politicians" and such actions were useless in stopping the "Red aggression" (Kolbert 2005). She compiled a reading, "Inside the Communist Conspiracy," in which she stated that the United States failed to realize that it was already fully engaged in a war with the communists.

In 1960, Schlafly was president of the Illinois Federation of Republican Women. She opposed Vice President Richard Nixon as the Republican presidential nominee. Well liked among the party regulars, Nixon was considered the obvious heir to Eisenhower's presidency. Days before the 1960 convention, Nixon met with his opponent Nelson Rockefeller to create a platform policy. Called the "Pact of Fifth Avenue," the policy covered 14 crucial points in U.S. foreign and domestic policy. Schlafly considered the platform a "sell-out" (Kolbert 2005). Nixon lost the presidential election to John F. Kennedy.

In 1964, the Republican Party was divided between its conservatives and moderate liberal factions. Schlafly supported Barry Goldwater as Republican presidential nominee. His chief opponent was Nelson Rockefeller. To help Goldwater gain the 1964 nomination, Schlafly self-published *A Choice Not an Echo*. Considered by some critics to be of mixed truths and conspiracy theories, the book accused Rockefeller Republicans of corruption, detailing how Republican "kingmakers" influenced the nomination of presidential candidates. Incumbent Lyndon B. Johnson, who had been in office less than a year following Kennedy's assassination, won the election with an overwhelming 61.1 percent of the national popular vote and 486 electoral votes compared to Goldwater's 52 electoral votes. The landslide created panic in the Republican Party. The result was that many who supported Goldwater were "purged" from the national Republican establishment. Schlafly lost her own bid for presidency of the Illinois Federation of Republican Women in 1967.

During this time, Schlafly joined the John Birch Society, a right-wing political advocacy group. However, Schlafly soon left the organization because she believed the communist threat was external rather than internal. In 1970, Schlafly lost her run for a seat in the Illinois House of Representations to Democratic incumbent George Shipley.

In 1972, Schlafly turned her focus from defense issues to the Equal Rights Amendment (ERA). The ERA was first proposed in 1923 by Alice Paul, suffragist leader and founder of the National Woman's Party. The amendment states that rights shall not be denied or abridged to individuals because of their sex, and is considered the next step following the Nineteenth Amendment, which guarantees women's right to vote. By 1972, the ERA had passed through the Senate and the House of Representatives. On March 22, 1972, the proposed Twenty-seventh Amendment was sent to the states for ratification. It quickly found approval in 30 of the necessary 38 states required for ratification. Schlafly believed that the ERA would abolish many legal safeguards that protected a woman's place in the home, including Social Security benefits for widows and alimony and child support. She also claimed that supporting the ERA would lead to other social upheaval, including same-sex marriages, women drafted into the military, and taxpayer-funded abortions (Eagle Forum). Schlafly organized the Stop Taking Our Privileges (STOP ERA) campaign. As part of her campaign, Schlafly created the Eagle Forum, a conservative pro-family organization.

Ironically, many of Schlafly's claims have evolved to become public policy. By late 2011, same-sex marriages were recognized in six states and the District of Columbia. New York became the largest state to legalize same-sex marriages on June 24, 2011. The law went into effect 30 days later. Some states grant same-sex licenses, although they do not recognize the union. Other states have created "legal unions," in which same-sex couples are offered rights and responsibilities of marriage.

Initially drawing support from the those conservatives who had helped Schlafly with her Goldwater campaign, Schlafly's campaign quickly grew in 1973, when the ERA movement became entangled with the fight over abortion rights as the Supreme Court handed down its decision in *Roe v. Wade* (Kolbert 2005). Schlafly called the decision the worst "in the history of the U.S. Supreme Court," and said it "is responsible for the killing of millions of unborn babies" (*Washington Post* 2002).

Schlafly traveled extensively, appearing on talk shows, speaking before women's clubs, and testifying in state legislatures. She debated against several women's rights leaders, including Eleanor Smeal, Karen DeCrow, and Betty Friedan. In one heated debate with Friedan in Bloomington, Illinois, Friedan shouted, "I'd like to burn you at the stake . . . I consider you a traitor to your sex" (Kolbert 2005). Schlafly replied, "I'm glad you said that, because it just shows the intemperate nature of proponents of ERA" (Fields 2006). By the end of 1973, the momentum for the amendment slowed significantly.

In 1978, Schlafly earned her law degree from Washington University Law School. Her critics often pointed out the apparent hypocrisy of Schlafly's position. Schlafly's argument, the critics said, was that a woman's greatest satisfaction and achievement lay in caring for her family, yet Schlafly—with four children at home—spent much of her time working out of the home. Yet, as Elizabeth Kolbert suggested in the *New Yorker*, Schlafly's personal life could also be used as evidence to support her own argument: women had no need for the ERA. As Karen DeCrow, feminist attorney and president of NOW, had said, Schlafly was "everything you should raise a daughter to be . . . She's an extremely liberated woman" (Kolbert 2005).

In 1977, Indiana became the 35th and the last state to ratify the ERA. Alice Paul, the creator of the amendment, died the same year. In 1982, 10 years after Schlafly started her campaign to stop the ERA, the final deadline approached. The ratification of the ERA fell by three states. While it has been introduced into every Congress since then, it has yet to be ratified.

Schlafly has authored or edited 20 books, and numerous articles on many topics, including *Strike from Space* (1966), *The Power of the Positive Woman* (1983), *Who Will Rock the Cradle?* (1990), *Feminist Fantasies* (2003), and *The Supremacists: The Tyranny of Judges and How to Stop It* (2006).

Between 1985 and 1991, Schlafly served with late Chief Justice Warren Burger as a member of the Commission on the Bicentennial of the U.S. Constitution. *Ladies Home Journal* named Schlafly one of the 100 most important women of the twentieth century.

Bobbi Miller

See also Friedan, Betty; Paul, Alice

References

Allen, Charlotte. "The Great Woman Theory of History." *First Things*, November 2005. http://www.firstthings.com/article/2007/01/the-great-woman-theory-of-history-18 (accessed February 24, 2011).

"Anniversary: *Roe v. Wade* with Phyllis Schlafly." *Washington Post*, January 18, 2002. http://www.washingtonpost.com/wp-srv/liveonline/02/nation/nation_schlafly011802.htm (accessed September 9, 2011).

Bellafante, Ginia. "At Home with Phyllis Schlafly: A Feminine Mystique All Her Own." *New York Times*, March 30, 2006. http://www.nytimes.com/2006/03/30/garden/30phyllis.html?_r=1&pagewanted=all (accessed February 24, 2011).

Critchlow, Donald T. *Phyllis Schlafly and Grassroots Conservatism: A Woman's Crusade*. Princeton, NJ: Princeton University Press, 2005.

"Equal Rights Amendment." Alice Paul Institute, in collaboration with the ERA Task Force of the National Council of Women's Organization, last updated February 24, 2011. http://www.equalrightsamendment.org/overview.htm (accessed February 26, 2011).

Fields, Suzanne. "A Radical Who Wasn't Completely Wrong: Reconsidering Betty Friedan." *Jewish World Review*, February 9, 2006. http://www.jewishworldreview.com/cols/fields020906.php3 (accessed February 26, 2011).

"History of AEI." American Enterprise Institute for Public Policy Research. http://www.aei.org/history (accessed February 25, 2011).

Kolbert, Elizabeth. "Firebrand: Phyllis and the Conservative Revolution." *New Yorker*, November 7, 2005. http://www.newyorker.com/archive/2005/11/07/051107crbo_books (accessed February 25, 2011).

"Phyllis Schlafly Biography." Eagle Forum, n.d. http://www.eagleforum.org/misc/bio.html (accessed February 24, 2011).

"Phyllis Schlafly, President." Eagle Forum, n.d. http://www.eagleforum.org/misc/bio.html (accessed September 9, 2011).

"Women: Trouble for ERA." *Time*, February 19, 1973. http://www.time.com/time/magazine/article/0,9171,906864,00.html (accessed February 26, 2011).

Schneiderman, Rose (1882–1972)

Rose Schneiderman is said to have taught Eleanor Roosevelt, wife of President Franklin D. Roosevelt, everything she "knew about trade unionism" (Schneiderman and Goldthwaite 1967, 251). Throughout most of her adult life, Schneiderman, at the risk of her own health and safety, spent grueling hours organizing female workers and fighting for humane solutions to labor problems during the early 1900s. But police officers often forced workers to call off protests and return to unbearable working conditions, and when she first tried to organize workers, she received little if any help from male union members. During World War I, she campaigned to prevent the New York State Assembly from suspending labor laws that protected female workers, and conservative legislators called her "the Red Rose of Anarchy."

She was named Rachel Rose when she was born on April 6, 1882, in the village of Saven in Russian Poland, to Samuel and Deborah Schneiderman. She was the first of four children. Her father was a tailor, and according to history professor Annelise Orleck, Rose's mother "did a little bit of everything; she took in sewing, baked ritual breads, sewed uniforms for the Russian Army, treated the sick with herbal medicines, and even tended the bar at a local inn when the barkeep was too drunk to do it herself. Strong believers in education for girls,

[Rose's] parents bucked Jewish tradition to send her to school. When she was four, they enrolled her in a heder [Jewish elementary school]. At six, they moved to the city of Chelm so that [Rose] could attend a Russian public school" (Orleck n.d.).

As with many Eastern European Jews in the late 1800s, Rose's family immigrated to the United States in 1890. They settled in New York City, and two years later, in 1892, Rose's father died of meningitis, leaving a wife who was pregnant and three children.

Deborah Schneiderman tried to support her family as a seamstress and by taking in borders, but soon found she could not care for four children and maintain her job. She was forced to place Rose and her two brothers in separate Jewish orphanages for almost a year. When Rose's mother was able to reunite the family, she was earning a livelihood, but her pay was so meager that Rose had to quit school after ninth grade and go to work at the age of 13. With the help of a Jewish charity, Rose found a job as a department store clerk, a position thought to be more reputable than factory work. Rose worked 64 hours per week for $2.16, a wage that rose to $2.66 after three years.

Seeking better pay, she found a job with a cap maker, but she had to provide her own sewing machine and thread and, from the $6.00 per week she earned, pay for electricity that the machine used. Conditions in the factory where she worked were similar to most industries of the time—unsanitary, poorly lighted, and generally unsafe. Yet she managed to put in a full workday and still go to night school.

When she was 20, Rose spent a year in Montreal, Quebec, Canada, where she and the rest of her family stayed with relatives. From a neighboring family, who were socialists, she learned about socialism and trade unions; and in 1903, after returning to New York, she was spurred to help organize a trade union for women, who had no representation in the all-male unions. She would hand out union leaflets to workers and speak on street corners near factories. Since she was only four and a half feet tall, she climbed up on a ladder to be seen, and carried the ladder around for street meetings. Speaking passionately in Yiddish and in English, she exhorted young women in the garment trades to organize for better working conditions and wages. At the time, factories were increasing their demands on workers and cutting wages.

With the help of friends, Schneiderman signed up enough women to qualify for a charter membership in the Jewish Socialist United Cloth Hat and Cap Makers Union, and the local quickly grew so that it commanded enough strength to negotiate a half day rather than a full day of work on Saturdays. She was elected a delegate to the national Central Labor Union, and by the following year, was on the executive board, the first woman to hold such a high position in the cap makers union.

In 1905, the Women's Trade Union League (WTUL) helped Schneiderman organize a 13-week strike against cap makers, a dangerous activity at the time because women were often arrested, jailed, and abused by the police and courts. Schneiderman joined the union in 1906, although at first she had been suspicious of the group, which was dominated by upper middle-class and wealthy reformers and unionists who were not factory workers and believed their purpose was to educate working women about the importance of unions. Schneiderman became a dedicated member, and in 1907, the WTUL provided her a grant so that she could attend the Rand School of Social Science, where her studies enabled her to become an even more effective organizer and field worker. She was elected vice president of the New York chapter in 1908, and a generous Jewish donor paid her salary to work full time, organizing working women.

From that time on, she pursued her life's work as a union organizer and eloquent spokesperson for the women's labor movement, although this was often a discouraging as well as dangerous job. Organizing meant, in her words, "hours and hours of standing on corners in all sorts of weather to distribute handbills . . . calling an endless number of meetings and never knowing whether anyone will show up. On top of all this, you never have a life of your own, for there is no limit to the time you can put on this job." But she had deep faith in the trade union movement and believed "with every cell in [her] body" that urging women "to organize was absolutely right for them" (Schneiderman and Goldthwaite 1967, 111). She was partly responsible for spontaneous strikes called in late 1909 among garment workers who left their shops—some 20,000 women joined the walkout, creating a work stoppage that lasted until February 1910.

Although many of the workers' demands were met, the Triangle Shirtwaist Company, which made popular high-necked blouses known as shirtwaists, refused to go along with improvements in unsafe factory conditions, such as well-maintained fire escapes and open staircases. The company was located on the 8th, 9th, and 10th floors of the Asch Building in Greenwich Village. Locked doors prevented union organizers from coming in and kept workers on the job. Because of those conditions and the lack of other safety measures, a horrible disaster occurred. On March 25, 1911, a fire erupted, started by a careless smoker, and spread through the shirtwaist factory. The fire killed 146 young workers who were incinerated or jumped to their death, unable to use the only fire escape available—it collapsed with the weight of hundreds trying to flee the fire—or to escape by the two small passenger elevators. Ladders on fire trucks could reach only to the seventh floor.

A week after the fire, Schneiderman, as head of the WTUL, gave a speech at the Metropolitan Opera House, where hundreds from all walks of life gathered for a memorial service and civic leaders called for "industrial improvements." Schneiderman spoke about the realities of working conditions:

> I would be a traitor to these poor burned bodies if I came here to talk good fellowship. We have tried you good people of the public and we have found you wanting. This is not the first time girls have been burned alive in this city. Every week I must learn of the untimely death of one of my sister workers. Every year thousands of us are maimed. The life of men and women is so cheap and property is so sacred!
>
> We are trying you now . . . every time the workers come out in the only way they know to protest against conditions which are unbearable, the strong hand of the law is allowed to press down heavily upon us.
>
> Public officials have only words of warning for us—warning that we must be intensely orderly and must be intensely peaceable. . . . The strong hand of the law beats us back when we rise—back into the conditions that make life unbearable. . . . I can't talk fellowship to you who are gathered here. Too much blood has been spilled. I know from my own experience it is up to the working people to save themselves and the only

way is through a strong working-class movement. (Stein 1977, 196–97).

In the audience hearing that speech was Frances Perkins, who took heed. She later directed the New York Factory Investigating Commission, and eventually served as U.S. secretary of labor in the administration of President Franklin D. Roosevelt (1882–1945). Eleanor Roosevelt joined the WTUL in 1922, and Schneiderman and the Roosevelts became good friends. Schneiderman taught both the president and Eleanor about trade unions and the problems female workers faced. As a result, Eleanor Roosevelt became chair of the WTUL finance committee and promoted the union in speeches and newspaper columns.

Along with calling for labor to organize and strike, Schneiderman also worked for reform legislation and woman suffrage, speaking at countless rallies, often at makeshift sites because of the violent opposition to women gaining the right to vote. During one instance, Schneiderman spoke against a New York state senator who opposed suffrage for women because he feared that if women had the right to vote, they would lose their femininity. Schneiderman pointed out the absurdity of such reasoning by describing the way women had to work in foundries stripped to the waist because of the intense heat, a condition the senator had never censured. Schneiderman reminded him also that he had never been critical of the way women had to work in hot, steaming laundries for 13 and 14 hours a day. How, she challenged, could a woman lose more of her beauty and charm by voting than by working under sweatbox conditions?

During her more than 50 years of efforts on behalf of labor, Schneiderman's list of accomplishments grew. She organized the International Ladies' Garment Workers Union and helped organize laundry workers. She served as the president of the national WTLU from 1926 until 1950, when the organization disbanded. In the 1930s, President Franklin D. Roosevelt appointed her to the Labor Advisory Board of the National Recovery Act, which prompted some of her critics to brand her a communist. In 1937, she became secretary of the New York Department of Labor, serving until 1943. Schneiderman officially retired in the mid-1950s and began writing her book about the struggles of the labor movement. Summing up that work in the final chapter of *All for One*, she wrote: "Working women today have not the faintest inkling of what the conditions were before the terrific increase in trade-union organization, nor do they begin to realize what their predecessors went through in order to change those conditions.... Broken skulls, arrests, jail sentences, hunger—nothing stopped them" (Schneiderman and Goldthwaite 1967, 260).

Indeed, nothing stopped Schneiderman until 1967, when failing health forced her to enter the Jewish Home and Hospital for the Aged in New York. She died there on August 11, 1972, at the age of 90.

See also Perkins, Frances; Roosevelt, Eleanor

References

Berson, Robin Kadison. *Marching to a Different Drummer.* Westport, CT: Greenwood Press, 1994.

Copeland, Edith. *Notable American Women, Vol. 1.* New York: Belknap Press, 1971.

Foner, Philip S. *Women and the American Labor Movement: From Colonial Times to the Eve of World War I.* New York: Free Press/Macmillan, 1979.

Orleck, Annelise. "Rose Schneiderman." Jewish Women's Archive, n.d. http://jwa.org/encyclopedia/article/schneiderman-rose (accessed September 25, 2010).

Schneiderman, Rose, with Lucy Goldthwaite. *All for One*. New York: Paul S. Eriksson, 1967.

Stein, Leon. *The Triangle Fire*. New York: J. B. Lippincott Company, 1962.

Stein, Leon, ed. *Out of the Sweatshop: The Struggle for Industrial Democracy*. New York: Quadrangle/New York Times Book Company, 1977.

Whitman, Alden, ed. *American Reformers*. New York: H. W. Wilson Company, 1985.

Seale, Bobby (1936–)

Political pundits and commentators have found it difficult to pigeonhole Bobby Seale. He is known as a chef, a comic, a teacher, a community leader, or as a threat to U.S. domestic security. Seale has played numerous roles in his life, some of them contradictory to the popular image of the "angry black man" who cofounded the Black Panther Party for Self Defense in 1966. Reacting to what many ghetto residents believed were incessant incidents of police brutality, and following the death the year before of Malcolm X, the Black Panthers became one of the first radical community-based organizations to emerge out of the student protest movement of the 1960s. Chairman Seale and Defense Minister Huey P. Newton, along with a very small contingent of fellow African American men, adopted Malcolm X's motto "Freedom by any means necessary." They created a manifesto—a list of demands that included full equality and employment, education, and decent housing for blacks; an end to police brutality against black people; and exemption from military service for black men. At the time, the demands sent a chill through white communities across the nation.

Robert George Seale was born on October 22, 1936, in Dallas, Texas, to a carpenter named George Seale and his wife Thelma, whom Bobby has described simply as "a Christian." For the next 10 years, his family struggled to make a life for Bobby and his two siblings in the still-segregated Texas communities in and around Jasper County. When World War II employment opportunities beckoned in California, George packed up the family and relocated to the West Coast. But every summer the Seales made their way back to southeast Texas to rekindle familial connections that remained strong in Bobby throughout his life. It was this connection, and his tutelage under his Uncle Tom who operated the locally famous Turner's Bar B Que Pit restaurant in Liberty, Texas, that sparked an interest in good eating. It remained a constant through all his celebrated and more infamous activities over the next 65 years. As he describes the scene during those summer vacations in Texas: "Under enormous tents which sheltered us from the blazing Texas sun, we'd feast on dishes prepared by the sisters of the church. Sweet potato pie, fried chicken and fish, and barbeques of smoked beef and spareribs were prepared by the men and women at the pits. In the midst of happy greetings, praises to the Lord, and harmless gossip, I'd hear statements like: "This bobbyque sho' is good! But Lawd, it takes Tom Turner to really bobbyque some meat!" (Seale, online essay, n.d.).

The idealism of those summers could not supplant the difficult struggles of the poor, young African American student who grew up in the ghettos of Oakland. While he generally stayed under the radar of police and other authorities in his youth and received decent enough grades through his school career, he failed to graduate from high school when his attention to academics waned in his senior year. He joined the U.S. Air Force soon after his 18th birthday and was sent to Amarillo,

Texas, to be trained as a sheet-metal mechanic. After graduating with honors, he was posted to Ellsworth Air Force Base in Rapid City, South Dakota. He served honorably and without a major incident for over three years, but then was given a bad conduct discharge when corporal Seale disobeyed the order of a colonel at the base.

Seale developed a passion for his work in the Air Force, and when he came home to Oakland, he continued sheet-metal work at various jobs. Eventually, in 1961, he enrolled at Oakland's Merritt College to study engineering.

It was in his early days of college that he first heard Malcolm X speak about the need for black people to stop relying on the American government and the U.S. courts if they were to reach a more equitable life situation in the dominant white culture. In 1962, Seale met Huey P. Newton, a student and a fellow member of the Afro-American Association (AAA). The members were then known as young militants and had banned together to explore means to assert African American equality. They read the works of Malcolm X, Kwame Nkrumah, Mao Zedong, W. E. B. Du Bois, and Booker T. Washington. The AAA discussions and meetings proved to be less than satisfying for Seale or his new friend, the more cerebral Newton. Soon they left to form the Soul Students Advisory Council, whose purpose was to end the drafting of black men to fight in the Vietnam conflict. Newton and Seale were looking for action instead of talk, and they burned with a dedication to the black liberation movement as epitomized by Malcolm X. His assassination in 1965 was a turning point, and hit Seale very hard.

In his book, *Seize the Time: The Story of the Black Panther Party and Huey P. Newton* (1966), Seale explains what it was like to hear the news: "When Malcolm X was killed in 1965, I ran down the street. I went to my mother's house, and I got loose red bricks from the garden. I got to the corner, and broke the [bricks] in half. I wanted to have the most shots that I could have.... Every time I saw a paddy roll by in a car, I picked up one of the half-bricks, and threw it at the [police]. I threw about half the bricks, and then I cried like a baby" (Seale 1970, 3).

It was soon after this episode that Seale and Newton joined with other black activists to create the Black Panther Party for Self Defense. Later, the name was shortened to the Black Panther Party. The men were dedicated to the philosophy of Malcolm X and the call to militant self-defense of minority communities against the U.S. government. Marxist thought and organizing were also an important touchstone for these men. The undercurrent of violent action was often more than an implied threat of the Panthers, whose intent was to become one of the first groups in U.S. history to take a domestic military stance for minority and class emancipation. Almost immediately, their confrontational style and strategic use of the symbols of power made the party leadership targets of local police as well as federal government authorities.

FBI director J. Edgar Hoover established the Counterintelligence Program (COINTELPRO) to keep tabs on communists in the 1950s, and he expanded its mission to track and disrupt the Panthers and other revolutionary organizations gaining footholds in the late 1960s: the Peace and Freedom Party, Students for a Democratic Society, the Student Nonviolent Coordinating Committee, Southern Leadership Council, César Chávez and the United Farm Workers, and the American Indian Movement. Virtually every New Left group became targets; they were considered major

Bobby Seale was a political activist of the 1960s and cofounder of the Black Panther Party for Self-Defense, which advocated black power and opposed the Vietnam War. (AP/Wide World Photos)

threats to peace and security. As the Church Committee was to say a decade later in its final report out of the Senate Committee in 1976 on COINTELPRO, "the Bureau conducted a sophisticated vigilante operation aimed squarely at preventing the exercise of First Amendment rights of speech and association" (Political Research Associates n.d.).

The pushback took a toll on the Black Panthers and their affiliates. Within a year of the party's inception, Huey Newton was arrested for the killing of an Oakland police officer. In April 1968, an unarmed Bobby Hutton (then the 17-year-old treasurer of the Black Panthers) was killed in a 90-minute gun battle with Oakland police. He was shot 10 times as he fled his burning house. Fred Hampton, a 21-year-old Panther community organizer, was killed in his Chicago apartment along with 17-year-old Mark Clark when police raided the residence that served as a party headquarters.

Ninety shots were fired by Chicago police officers; one bullet was fired by a Black Panther. Survivors were charged with attempted murder, and no police officers were ever held to answer for their actions.

Seale escaped the most violent retribution experienced by his peers, and as other leaders fell, his role as organizational head and national spokesman gained stature. Under his guidance, the Panthers' reputation grew among African American neighborhoods from the West Coast to the East Coast. By establishing programs that worked regardless of gender or race, he hoped to see real economic, social, and political equality begin to rise across the nation,. One of the earliest and most successful programs was Free Breakfast for Children that started in Oakland in 1967. At St. Augustine's Church, Panthers cooked and served food before school to poor children. By the end of the year, 10,000 children across the country were receiving free breakfast in each city where the Black Panther Party had a chapter. It was actually the success of this program that caused FBI director Hoover to warn that the Panthers were "the greatest threat to the internal security" of the nation. Neither the guns nor the bullets were the biggest threat, in his mind; rather it was the propaganda value of the social programs that embarrassed the government and painted the activists in a positive light.

This was the first of what were called Survival Programs by the Black Panther Party and are the true legacy of the movement envisioned by Newton and Seale. At its peak, the party was running 35 different Survival Programs in many cities. However, the party successes did not mean that Seale would reach a state of immunity from persecution or prosecution by the authorities. He was jailed on multiple occasions for following through on his confrontational strategy and promise to do whatever it takes. For instance, in May 1967, Seale led a group of 30 armed Black Panthers to disrupt the California State Assembly when it was in session to discuss a bill to ban the carrying of weapons in public. Seale made this symbolic protest as a statement to the press and then led his men from the chamber. All were immediately arrested. Seale pleaded guilty to a charge of disrupting the legislature, and he was ordered to serve five months in prison.

While the action served to gain a greater recognition on the national level for the party and its goals, it also intensified the focus by authorities on Seale as an agitator and a dangerous man. This fact became apparent a year later, when Seale was arrested for his activities during protests outside the 1968 Democratic National Convention held in Chicago. Many believe that even though Seale had not met with any of the other indicted individuals (among them Youth International Party founders Jerry Rubin and Abbie Hoffman, and Tom Hayden and Rennie Davis, the founders of Students for a Democratic Society) prior to the protest and subsequent riots, his inclusion in the proceedings would help the prosecution's case by demonstrating that this violent black man was part of the conspiracy.

The eight men (identified in the press as the "Chicago Eight") went on trial on September 24, 1969. Seale's attorney was unable to attend the trial at the start because of recent surgery. Two weeks earlier, Seale had asked the presiding judge, Julius Hoffman, for a stay so that his lawyer would have adequate time to recover. Judge Hoffman declined that request and a subsequent Seale appeal to serve as his own lawyer. Seale was incensed and showed his displeasure with the judge by continually disrupting proceedings in the courtroom. He demanded repeatedly that it was his constitutional right to defend himself in court. He called Judge Hoffman names and refused to remain quiet. He showed no respect for the proceedings and turned normal court decorum into a spectacle that was reported across the globe.

Frustrated and angry, Hoffman ordered marshals to remove Seale to an anteroom off the court. They gagged his mouth with rags and tape, handcuffed his wrists to the legs of a folding chair, and looped chains around his ankles and secured them to the chair. Then they carried him back into the courtroom to await the jury. But even this did not keep Seale quiet. He cursed and protested through his gag and sought to make his point that he had the right to a defense. This went on for several days and created an amazing scene for the world to witness: a black man chained and gagged and denied his right to a fair trial in federal court.

The spectacle ended when Hoffman declared a mistrial and severed Seale's case from that of the other defendants. He then found Seale guilty of 16 counts of contempt and sentenced him to four years in prison. The trial of the now "Chicago Seven" went on without him as he was remanded to prison. In 1972, after serving two years for the contempt charges, Seale was released from custody. He was never recharged for the original offense.

By the 1970s, Seale was steering the Panthers away from confrontation in order to further develop the party's Survival Programs. As his local constituency increased, he even made a run for the office of Oakland's mayor in 1973, coming in second in a field of nine candidates.

In 1974, he made a decision to end his involvement with the Panthers and started an organization called Advocates Scene. He wanted to help underprivileged and the poor develop grassroots political power in their struggle for equal access and a better life. He eventually moved to Philadelphia and established a new organization known as Youth Employment Strategies to help black students become more successful in university doctorate programs. He has also served on the faculty of Temple University.

Martin K. Gay

See also Du Bois, W. E. B.; Hampton, Fred; Malcolm X

References

Political Research Associates. "The FBI COINTELPRO Operations." n.d. http://www.publiceye.org/liberty/Feds/cointelpro.html (accessed August 9, 2010).

Seale, Bobby. *Barbeque'n with Bobby Seale*. Berkeley, CA: Ten Speed, 1998.

Seale, Bobby. "Barbeque'n with Bobby Seale" (online essay). n.d. http://www.bobbyqueseale.com/bobbyqy.html (accessed August 9, 2010).

Seale, Bobby. *A Lonely Rage: The Autobiography of Bobby Seale*. New York: Times Books, 1978.

Seale, Bobby. *Seize the Time: The Story of the Black Panther Party and Huey P. Newton*. New York: Random House, 1970. First published 1968.

"What Ever Happened to Black Panther Bobby Seale?" *Journal of Blacks in Higher Education*, January 2006.

Seeger, Pete (1919–)

Until September 4, 1949, folk singer and activist Pete Seeger believed he "was fighting in the right way ... I was not getting angry, I was singing songs ... Robeson had the crowd singing 'America the Beautiful.' How could they be attacked for that?" Seeger's autobiographer says, on "that day, the observer in Seeger departed and the activist burst forth" (Dunaway 2001, 15–16). Seeger had just performed at a concert near his home in upstate New York headlined by Paul Robeson—an African American who was world-renowned for his acting and singing abilities but recently accused of anti-American sentiments. Originally scheduled for August, the event had been cancelled due to rioting. Confident that law enforcement would not allow a repeat occurrence, Seeger brought his family to watch him perform. All went well until it came time to leave. He recalled: "We hadn't gone a hundred yards from the gate when I saw glass on the road." Seeger's vehicle and others were attacked by a stone-throwing mob. Police did nothing to stop the mayhem that followed. But Seeger managed to drive his "terrified family through acres of blood and broken glass" to safety (Dunaway 2008, 12–13).

Peter Seeger was born on May 3, 1919, in New York City and initially lived with his parents and two brothers in Patterson, New York. His father greatly influenced him and was one of his favorite people. Charles Seeger introduced ethnomusicology, that is, the study of cultural and social aspects of nonclassical music, including folk music, in the 1920s (Dunaway 2008, 22). When Peter was young, his father was a professor at the University of California at Berkeley, but he was pushed out because of his stance as a conscientious objector to World War I. The family returned to New York, on a circuitous route through the South. Pete's mother had musical talents to share as well. Constance was a classical violinist who taught at Julliard. His parents divorced when Pete was seven, with his father remarrying Ruth Crawford, a composer. Charles was responsible for "radicalizing" Peter. He wrote a music column for the *Daily Worker* and worked for the Composers Collective, where Peter met his first communists (Dunaway 2008, 38–39).

Peter was sent to boarding schools at age four. There, as a teen, he was first exposed to the banjo; until then he had played the ukulele (Dunaway 2008, 32–33). Of the three Seeger sons, Peter was the only one who did not take piano or voice lessons. "Yet, he wasn't unmusical, just undisciplined: 'Whistles, anything that made music I banged on. I didn't want to study, I was just having fun ... The idea of reading notes was as boring to me as painting by numbers. Another problem was Peter's foot ... no matter what ... Peter couldn't keep his foot from tapping" (Dunaway 2008, 33).

After prep school, Seeger enrolled at Harvard. By this time, he had a subscription to the communist literary magazine, *New Masses*, and had joined the Young Communist League, although he had not been active. Seeger lost his partial scholarship in 1938, so, with dreams of being a *New York Times* journalist, he dropped out and headed for New York City. According to biographer Alec Wilkinson, at the time, his stepmother observed, "Peter, you have a talent for song leading. I think you should develop it." She saw what others would, as well:

[H]aving people sing with him was not merely a means of gratifying an audience's desire to be entertained ... He hoped that by making people feel themselves to be elements of a collective identity, he could intensify their experience ... During the most fractious periods of discourse in the 1960s, Seeger's earnest and unadorned desire to unite disparate people had a pacifying effect. It soothed the rougher edges of the hectoring. A song when he sang it and a crowd sang with him was a version of worldly benediction. ... He embraced as a young man the conviction that songs are a way as binding people to a cause. 'A piece of writing might be read once or twice,' he says, 'a song is sung over and over.' (Wilkinson 2010, 13–14)

After time spent on miscellaneous endeavors, Seeger realized that his true calling was music, and he began trying to earn a living as a performer. He got a summer job in 1939 touring with the Vagabond Puppeteers, already starting to combine his artistry with activism. After a show coinciding with a dairy farmer strike, the October 2, 1939, *Daily Worker* reported, "In the farmers' homes they talked about politics and the farmers' problems, about anti-Semitism and Unionism, about war and peace and social security." In the fall of 1939, Seeger worked briefly as an assistant in the Archive of Folk Music at the Library of Congress. Then, on March 3, 1940, he made his first professional appearance at the "Grapes of

Singer and environmental activist Pete Seeger plays the banjo on the banks of the Hudson River in New York in 1996. As a scholar, collector, organizer, and performer, Seeger was a prime mover in the rediscovery of American folk songs. (AP/Wide World Photos)

Wrath" benefit concert for migrant workers and met fellow folk singer Woody Guthrie.

Soon, Seeger, Guthrie, and Huddie "Lead Belly" Leadbetter were traveling the country. He learned his basic musicianship from these two (Dunaway 2008, 72). He practiced tirelessly on the five-string banjo and began amassing a collection of folk songs. These three formed the Almanacs, which also included at various times other performers. "They put their lives and politics into songs. Sometimes it costs jobs, sometimes their reputations" (Dunaway 2008, 91). Their popularity and pacifist position, as the United States was readying itself to enter World War II, did not sit well with the political powers-that-be. Their album *Songs for John Doe* (1941) was not well received by the establishment. A June 1941 *Atlantic Monthly* review called the album "strictly subversive and illegal . . . whether Communist or Nazi financed . . . a matter for the Attorney-General. But you can never handle situations of this kind democratically by mere suppression" (Friedrick 1941). Once Germany invaded Russia, however, the Almanacs were fully behind the Allies. Seeger even recorded a solo, expressing his patriotism.

The Almanacs lasted about a year, dwindling down to Guthrie and Seeger before disbanding altogether (Dunaway 2008, 96). In 1942, Seeger became a Communist Party member, although in 1949, when he learned of Joseph Stalin's atrocities in the Soviet Union, he began drifting away from communism. He was also drafted in 1942.

Although trained as an airplane mechanic, Seeger was reassigned and mostly entertained enlisted men in the South Pacific. He met and married Toshi-Aline Ōta in 1943, with whom he would have three children. Returning to the United States, Seeger became national director of Peoples Songs, creating, promoting, and distributing songs about labor and the American people. This job allowed him the time to get involved with the 1948 presidential campaign of Henry Wallace, who ran as a third-party progressive candidate. It was then Seeger drafted his classic *How to Play the Five-String Banjo*. In 1981, he told biographer David Dunaway, "My banjo book. . . . I wrote it in hotel rooms during Henry Wallace's campaign in 1948. 'What the heck,' I decided. 'I might as well publish it myself.' " Since then, it has sold many thousands of copies (Dunaway 2008, xxi).

With Lee Hays, Ronnie Gilbert, and Fred Hellerman, Seeger formed the group with whom he attained his first real stardom and his greatest popular success—the Weavers.

Later, others were also part of the group. Because of the Cold War atmosphere, the Weavers were less overt in their political messaging than the Almanacs. They had a succession of major hits, including "On Top of Old Smokey," "Goodnight, Irene," and "Kisses Sweeter than Wine." They appeared on national television and dominated radio play. But, their popularity came just when the U.S. House Un-American Activities Committee (HUAC) was focusing on the Weavers. An informant—Harvey Mantusow—made an accusation of communist affiliations within the group. Soon, their bookings were being cancelled. Stations refused to play their songs, and they were no longer desired TV guests. The Weavers were blacklisted as "Commie sympathizers." Seeger practiced what he called "guerilla cultural tactics" sending brochures to summer camps, colleges, schools, churches, offering to perform, teach, do whatever he could to earn an income. He would sneak into bookings, attempting to get out of town before anyone who objected to him knew he was there. Still, he often walked past picket signs reading "Moscow's Canary" and "Khrushchev's Songbird" (Wilkinson 2010, 4).

On August 18, 1955, Seeger testified before HUAC, and invoked his First Amendment rights of free speech. He was indicted for contempt and sentenced to a 10-year term. But, in 1962, an appeals court overturned his conviction. The informant who testified against him and 240 others in 1952 eventually recanted and was himself sentenced to a four-year jail term.

In 1955, the Weavers performed a sold-out concert at Carnegie Hall and then went on tour. By 1958, Seeger was a solo act, performing on college campuses and in coffee houses. The blacklist stigma followed him wherever he went. In 1960, he was scheduled to perform at a high school concert in San Diego, California. The San Diego school board wanted him to sign a statement stating that he would not promote a communist agenda or overthrow of the government. Seeger refused, and the American Civil Liberties Union had to get an injunction so that the concert could be held.

The 1960s brought about a change in politics and music. Seeger's simple, passionate songs spoke to the youth being awakened by current issues: civil rights, nuclear disarmament, and the Vietnam War. Seeger led the songs that would become the anthems of those times, like "Where Have All the Flowers Gone?" and "Turn, Turn, Turn." He also marched in protests and appeared at rallies. "Peter Seeger used to say 'It's not how good a song is that matters, it's how much good a song does' " (Dunaway 2008, 418). He helped organize the prestigious Newport Folk Festivals and was one of the most popular performers there in the early and mid-1960s. In 1963, he helped organize a concert at Carnegie Hall featuring the Freedom Singers to benefit the Highlander Folk School founded by Myles Horton in Tennessee. Horton was a champion of the oppressed in the South, and because he was active in the labor and civil rights movements, he was labeled a subversive, a rabble-rouser, and a threat to American values.

In 1963, Seeger also participated in Martin Luther King Jr.'s August "March on Washington" and made "We Shall Overcome," a song based on "I'll Overcome Someday" by African American hymn writer Philip Tindley (1856–1933), and a nineteenth-century spiritual "No More Auction Block for Me," the rallying cry for human equality. In 1964–1965, he made a world tour with his family, performing in 24 countries. In 1965 and 1966, he hosted 39 hour-long regionally broadcast, music television shows called *Rainbow Quest*.

Guests included Johnny Cash, the Stanley Brothers, the Mamou Cajun Band, Judy Collins, and Roscoe Holcomb. He created controversy again with an appearance on the *Smothers Brothers Comedy Hour* in 1967. His song, "Waist Deep in the Deep Muddy," was seen as an attack on President Lyndon Johnson's war policies; Seeger's performance was cut from the initial airing but included when the program was rerun the following January.

Seeger and his wife became involved in environmental causes in the mid-1960s. They launched the *Clearwater* on the Hudson River in 1969, a floating classroom, laboratory, stage, and speaker's forum. Seeger believes people should "think globally and act locally," as the saying goes, and that by individually cleaning up one's own corner of the world, all peoples' actions collectively will add up to make a significant difference.

Public perceptions about dissent and criticism of the U.S. government have changed since the 1960s and 1970s, and Seeger is now lauded by the people who once shunned him. In 1994, he received both the National Medal of the Arts and the Kennedy Center Lifetime Achievement Honor. In 1996, he was inducted into the Rock and Roll Hall of Fame. Seeger won a Lifetime Achievement Grammy in 1993 and, three years later, the Grammy for Best Traditional Folk Album (*Pete*). That year, Harvard honored him with its Arts Medal. In 2007, he spoke and performed at the American Folklife Center at the Library of Congress, where he had worked 67 years earlier. He made a rare television appearance in September 2008 on *Late Show with David Letterman*, singing "Take It from Dr. King." And, he joined Bruce Springsteen, his grandson Tao, and the crowd in singing Woody Guthrie's "This Land Is Your Land" at President Barack Obama's January 18, 2009, inaugural concert in Washington, D.C.

Contemporary rock icon Springsteen (often himself taken to task for being an activist) released an album of folk songs in April 2006 entitled *We Shall Overcome: The Seeger Sessions*. Why? "Because Pete's Library is so vast that the whole history of the country is there" (Wilkinson 2010, 6–7).

Margaret Gay

See also Horton, Myles; King, Martin Luther, Jr.; Robeson, Paul

References

Dunaway, David King. *How Can I Keep from Singing? The Ballad of Pete Seeger*. New York: Villard Books, 1982, 2008.

Friedrick, Carl Joachim, "The Poison in Our System." *Atlantic Monthly*, June 1941. http://www.peteseeger.net/poison.htm (accessed April 8, 2011).

Seeger, Pete. *How to Play the 5-String Banjo*. New York: Beacon Press, 1992. First published 1948.

Wilkinson, Alec. *The Protest Singer: An Intimate Portrait of Pete Seeger*. New York: Vintage Books, 2010.

Sheehan, Cindy (1957–)

After her son Casey's death in Iraq, Cindy Sheehan declared, "I went from being the mom who did everyone's laundry, packed lunches, kissed boo-boos, tucked in at night, cleaned up everyone's messes, to being someone who fights for all of humanity's children, not just her own" (Sheehan 2006, 128). Sheehan is best known for setting up a protest site called "Camp Casey" near the Texas ranch of U.S. president George W. Bush in 2005. That began a series of dissident actions that propelled her into the spotlight as one of the foremost American peace activists.

Cindy Lee Miller was born July 10, 1957, in Inglewood, California, to Shirley Huelin and Dennis Miller. Cindy's mother was a stay-at-home mom and her father worked for Lockheed Corporation. He was an electrician and he and Shirley Miller raised three children while living in Bellflower, California. Dennis Miller died at the age of 60.

Cindy received her education at May Thompson Elementary School, Washington Junior High School, and Bellflower High School. She attended Cerrito College and UCLA majoring in history. Cindy married Patrick Sheehan in 1977 and four children —Carly, Casey, Christy, and Scott—followed in quick succession. She became a very dedicated and family-oriented mother. Her husband was also a hands-on father. She speaks fondly of the children's childhood years. "One morning we decided we'd had enough pancakes, so we used them as frisbees.... We had a fun life, even if it sometimes approached total anarchy in our house" (Sheehan 2006, 10).

She and her family were heavily invested in the Catholic faith and the programs it offered to youth. She later became a highly respected youth leader, working with at-risk children and as a youth minister at St. Mary's Catholic Church in Vacaville. She considered it an ideal job as she was able to spend a lot of time with her own children who were all involved in the youth programs she ran. Cindy worked at the church for seven years and enjoyed a good relationship with the priest in charge. But when a new priest took over, he was hostile toward her and the youths she served. There were complaints about her appearance and her effectiveness as a teacher. Eventually, there were only a few children in her classes, and the new priest fired her.

The Sheehans were surprised when their 21-year-old son, Casey, announced he had enlisted in the U.S. Army and again later when he reenlisted. The U.S invasion of Iraq was underway, and Casey's decision to enlist was influenced by the promises made by the military recruiter. He was promised a $20,000 sign-on bonus and a free college degree, and he was led to believe that upon completion of training, he would become a chaplain's assistant and see no combat. The promises were not kept, and on April 4, 2004, five days after Casey arrived in the Iraq war zone, he was killed.

Cindy felt an overwhelming sense of guilt after Casey's death. She blamed herself for not paying attention to what had been going on in the world and in the U.S government. She had heard the drumbeats of war, but stood by silently. She had honestly believed that saner heads would prevail and that the nation would not invade countries that had done nothing to the United States.

After Casey's death, the Sheehan family, along with a number of other families that had lost children in the invasion, were flown at government expense to Seattle, Washington, and were taken by bus to Fort Lewis to meet with then U.S. president George W. Bush. She was shocked that President Bush showed little genuine interest in the family, and did not know Casey's name. The family received a Gold Star Pin. Cindy states, "I was going to fight against the idea that dying for a piece of cloth with stripes on it to spread a failed idea of freedom and democracy was worth it. A Gold Star is not a fair trade for a son's life" (Sheehan 2006, 14).

She made a promise to Casey and herself that she would oppose the war machine. So out of despair, she protested in Benicia, California. There, she met others who opposed the invasion and she was on her way to becoming a foremost antiwar protester. The thought of another mother having to grieve for a son or daughter lost in an illegal

Cindy Sheehan stands with other antiwar activists before leaving Camp Casey in Crawford, Texas, on July 10, 2007. Sheehan bid farewell to her former "peace camp" near President Bush's ranch and ever since has been demonstrating and speaking out against war and what she views as the imperialistic and aggressive actions of the U.S. government. (AP Photo/*Waco Tribune-Herald*, Duane A. Laverty)

invasion of a sovereign nation was more than she could bear. She was appalled by the Bush administration "Lying . . . and selling a war to the public based on fear and 'terrorism' " (Sheehan 2006, 69).

Cindy became very active in the 2004 presidential election campaign. She wanted to do all she could to make sure Bush did not get elected to another term. She and her daughter Carly made anti-Bush commercials for RealVoices.org. She campaigned for John Kerry mainly as a protest against Bush; she did not like Kerry's stance on the invasion.

The Sheehans became friends with the family of Sgt. Michael Mitchell, who was killed in an ambush just before Casey died. Together, they wanted to try to bring an end to the Iraq invasion. With Michael's father, Bill Mitchell, Cindy founded Gold Star Families for Peace. They wanted to be a support group for each other during the duration of the conflicts and be there for each other when peace was reached. Currently, the group includes members who have lost loved ones in earlier conflicts such as World War II. She, along with her daughter Carly also joined Military Families Speak Out (MFSO). In October 2004, MFSO marched for peace in Washington, D.C. The two groups were joined by Veterans for Peace (VFP) and Iraq Veterans Against the War (IVAW) in seeking an audience with Defense Secretary Donald Rumsfeld. But Rumsfeld refused to meet with them.

As she became increasingly active, Sheehan and her husband divorced in 2005. Many of Sheehan's relatives and friends were outraged that she would openly criticize the president. Many of the parents and families who lost relatives in the conflict believed their family members died as heroes in a great and noble cause. Sheehan's assertions that the soldiers died for lies and for oil were met with hostility and death threats.

Devastated by the reelection of George W. Bush, she vowed to redouble her efforts for peace. She held on to the hope that the administration would one day be held accountable for their actions. "I believe that Congress expediently abrogated their constitutional responsibility to declare war when they passed the War Powers Act, and they bear at least some responsibility for the needless heartache wrought on this world by our government," she said in an address to a congressional commission (Sheehan 2006, 119).

Sheehan became well known as the mother of a fallen soldier and was sought out for speeches and antiwar advertisements. Other peace groups such as Code Pink and Global Exchange founded by activist Medea Benjamin enlisted her help. She spoke in Washington, D.C., in January 2005 for the "Eyes Wide Open: The Human Cost of War" exhibit. The group responsible displayed military boots, which represent U.S. service personnel who have been killed. Casey Sheehan's boots are a part of this traveling exhibit.

But Sheehan became world famous when she set up Camp Casey outside President Bush's Prairie Chapel Ranch near Crawford, Texas. The camp was not the result of a plan; it happened spontaneously on August 23, 2005, and lasted until August 31, 2005. She wanted to ask Bush for what noble cause her son had died and she said she would stay outside the ranch until she got an answer from him. When she headed for Crawford, Texas, she was accompanied by members of VFP, IVAW, and Vietnam Veterans Against the War (VVAW). Code Pink members came, as did Daniel Ellsberg (who had leaked the Pentagon Papers to the *New York Times*). They were greeted by sheriff's vehicles that blocked their path. So they settled down at the edge of the road that first day.

At first the camp consisted of a couple of tents. But Hadi Jawad of Crawford Peace House lent his support and property to the cause. Fred Mattlage, a relative of a man who had threatened them, offered them the use of two acres of land he owned which was closer to Bush's ranch. Soon thousands of people came and went, and reporters and supporters from around the world took notice of Camp Casey. Sheehan was now the best-known antiwar activist in the world, and along with this came problems as others in the movement resented all the attention she was getting. She was accused of grabbing attention away from other peace organizations. Many turned against her, criticizing her methods and the language she used in speeches. She also received nasty phone calls and threats against her life, and was accused of aiding and abetting the enemy. In the media, conservatives such as Bill O'Reilly and Rush Limbaugh criticized her antiwar activities. When Sheehan stayed at Camp Casey, she was accused of pouring "gas on the debate over the war on terror in Iraq" (Moy 2006, 139). She did not give in to this treatment and was determined to have Casey's death and the deaths of so many others count for something by exposing the lies of the government.

On September 24, 2005, thousands of people joined the "Bring Them Home Now Tour" that traveled through 50 cities in several states before assembling in Washington, D.C. After reaching Washington, Sheehan and over 300 other protesters were arrested for demonstrating in front of the White House. Sheehan was released and has never been found guilty of any crime.

Well-known Hollywood celebrities have shared the stage with Sheehan at speeches, and others have marched with her at demonstrations. She counts Martin Sheen, Ed Asner, and the Reverend Jesse Jackson as people who share much of her antiwar philosophy. But associating with well-known personalities and her appearances on TV and in news articles have caused some former supporters to accuse her of being selfish or even a pawn in the hands of other antiwar movements. She has taken this in stride, contending that "the issue of peace and people dying for no reason is not a matter of 'right or left' but of 'right and wrong' " (Strong 2008, 260).

Sheehan's life since the death of her son has been a whirlwind of travel, speaking engagements, and article and book writings. She speaks out not only against the invasions of Iraq and Afghanistan, but about other actions by the U.S. government and its allies that disturb her. For example, she has expressed concern about the bombings of the tribal areas of Pakistan by U.S. drones, FBI raids of the homes and offices of social activists, U.S. imperialistic actions around the world, the uncontrolled power of U.S. and international corporations, and election abnormalities in the United States.

Around the world, she has been asked to give her message of peace and in the process has met with heads of state and important government officials. She laments that news reporters do not ask the tough questions, instead reporting the information they have been fed by the politicians and corporations, thus leaving much of the population ignorant of what is happening at home and abroad.

In 2008, Sheehan ran for Congress trying to unseat Nancy Pelosi in her California district. She did not win but received 15.3 percent of the vote.

Her Internet site "Cindy Sheehan's Soapbox" offers a weekly radio show with interesting and provocative guests. She reports on her activities and travels, new books, and demonstrations. She also writes for the Al Jazeera English web site. Her books include *Peace Mom* (2006); *Not One More Mother's Child* (2005); *Myth America: 10 Greatest Myths of the Robber Class and the Case for Revolution* (2009); and *Myth America II, 20 Greatest Myths of the Robber Class and the Case for Revolution* (2010). For the book *Myth America*, she toured all 50 states to bring her message to the people. She has worked on a documentary titled *Revolution, a Love Story*, which is about the changes that have swept Venezuela under Hugo Chavez and Bolivia under Evo Morales. She has become a supporter of both South American leaders. Many Hollywood activists and others have contributed to the project.

Much of Sheehan's activism now takes place on her Soapbox and blogs. Through these media, she is calling on people to fight what she calls "the robber class." She suggests forming Revolutionary Communities, somewhat socialist in nature, where people can for cooperatives and use peaceful means to fight the rich and their manipulation of the masses. By her actions, Sheehan has shown the world that one person can make a difference, but one of her greatest disappointments has been that people are not demonstrating in the streets and demanding an end to what she views as the imperialistic and aggressive actions of the U.S. government. She stated: "My mission isn't about breaking into the media, or having my 'fifteen minutes of fame.' It is about truth. It is about Democracy. It is about our essential human rights. It is about creating a paradigm of peace in our country and in our world. When all these issues are resolved, then I will go away. Not a minute before" (Sheehan 2006, 201).

Anni Margrethe Callaghan

See also Asner, Edward; Benjamin, Medea; Ellsberg, Daniel; Limbaugh, Rush; Sheen, Martin

References

Moy, Catherine, and Melanie Morgan. *America Mourning the Intimate Story of Two Families Joined by War, Torn by Beliefs*. Nashville, TN: WND Books, an imprint of Cumberland House Publishing, Inc., 2006.

Sheehan, Cindy. *Not One More Mother's Child*. Kihei, Maui, HI: Koa Books, 2005.

Sheehan, Cindy. *Peace Mom: A Mother's Journey through Heartache to Activism*. New York: Atria Books, 2006.

Strong, Shari MacDonald, ed. *The Maternal Is Political: Writers at the Intersection of Motherhood and Social Change*. Berkeley, CA: Seal Press, 2008.

Sheen, Martin (1940–)

Martin Sheen has been arrested dozens of times for protesting war and social injustice, a strange situation for a man who was president—that is, the fictional U.S. president Josiah Bartlet on the television show *The West Wing*, which aired from 1996 to 2006. In the show, Sheen played the role of a liberal Democrat, but in real life, he has been much more than a politician. He has been not only a highly successful film and TV actor, but also a peace and social justice activist and an outspoken civil rights champion. And because of his actions on and off screen, he has been heavily criticized, some of whom call him a traitor for not supporting U.S. wars.

Sheen was named Ramón Gerardo Antonio Estévez when he was born on August 3, 1940, in the Midwestern industrial-belt city of Dayton, Ohio. His father was Francisco Estévez, a skilled worker employed by National Cash Register Company and other manufacturers. He had emigrated from Spain. His mother Mary Ann Phelan was born in Tipperary, Ireland. She and Francisco met in citizenship classes in Dayton. Both parents were devout Catholics and raised their 10 children in the faith, including a traditional parochial education. His mother died when Sheen was just 10 years old; by then he was already developing a passion for acting.

His commitment to his faith has never been far from the actions he performs. A story about how he came to choose his name illustrates this. He has said that he adopted the stage name Martin Sheen in honor of Archbishop Fulton J. Sheen, a very prominent Catholic spokesman of the day who was one of the first successful televangelists. It should be noted that Sheen is very supportive of immigrant rights and is proud of his Irish as well as Hispanic heritage. And while the world knows him only by his stage name that he admits to taking as a hedge against producers' and casting directors' possible discrimination, he has never legally dropped his birth/family name. He answers to either Ramon or Martin.

Against his father's advice, he pursued his acting dream by making the trip to New York City with bus fare borrowed from a local priest. At age 19, he became a member of the Living Theater that had been founded in 1947 as an alternative to the traditional commercial theater by Judith Malina and Julian Beck, an abstract expressionist painter. The Living Theater and Beck, especially, influenced the young Sheen as he recalls in this interview answer: "It had a very profound effect on me. I started with them when I was nineteen and spent two-and-a-half years with them. Through them, I was introduced to Women's Strike for Peace, the ban the bomb movement. It was an avant-garde theater, filled with very liberal, progressive, intelligent, passionate, heroic people. Julian Beck was one of my mentors and heroes. He introduced me to the Catholic Workers' movement" (Kupfer 2003).

The connection was propitious. It was through Beck and his work as a member of the Catholic Worker Movement that Sheen made the acquaintance of the great journalist and urban social activist, Dorothy Day. She had started the Catholic Worker Movement in an effort to make laborers and the lower classes better aware of the social justice aspects of Catholic doctrine. This was especially important, she felt, as communism had become an appealing alternative to the workers who had gone through the Great Depression. Day and her followers highlighted and promulgated the progressive traditions of the Church and young Sheen became a committed member of the cause of social justice.

Many years later, both Day (1972) and Sheen (2008) would receive the prestigious Laetare Award given by the University of Notre Dame for recognition of a practicing Catholic in America who has made outstanding contributions to the faith and society. Rev. John I. Jenkins, C.S.C., University of Notre Dame president, said of Sheen at the ceremony when the award was presented: "As one of our nation's most recognizable and accomplished screen actors, Martin Sheen has achieved a level of celebrity that few Americans enjoy. He has used that celebrity to draw the attention of his fellow citizens to issues that cry out for redress, such as the plight of immigrant workers and homeless people, the waging of unjust war, the killing of the unborn and capital punishment. We welcome the opportunity to lift up his example for our Church, our country, and our students" (Garvey 2008).

Father Jenkins would likely not have presented the award to Sheen had he been a pro-choice supporter as many in Hollywood are purported to be. But it is a doctrine of the faith that abortion is a sin, and Sheen has stated that he is personally opposed to abortion. However, he is loath to make that decision for a woman, especially the poor or a woman of color. He also insists that he is pro-life in every avenue: he is against the death penalty and the use of war or any movement where people are sacrificed to justify some perceived end.

Sheen is known to several generations of audiences for seminal stage, television, and film roles that, in the year 2011, have spanned half a century. Driven to emulate his hero James Dean (whom he resembled slightly), his early career was marked by a rebellious private life that included drug and alcohol use, which ended his churchgoing days and threatened to disrupt his rise to celebrity status. He was in an apparent death spiral when he suffered a massive heart attack during the filming of *Apocalypse Now* (1979). A priest called to his bedside gave him the last rites. But he did survive the immediate crisis and the addiction. And through the inspiration and counsel of Terrence Malick, his director on the film *Badlands* (1973), he had an epiphany about himself and life and returned to active participation in his religion. He has not wavered since, and he has been married to the same woman, Janet Templeton, since 1961. They have four children: Emilio, Ramon, Carlos

(Charlie Sheen), and Renee, all of whom became actors.

Sheen's star rose quickly. It was certainly helped along when he triumphed in the Pulitzer Prize–winning play *The Subject Was Roses* (1968) in the role of Timmy Cleary for which he won a Tony Award. He reprised that role in the Hollywood film four years later. Worldwide fame would follow in 1979 when he was cast as army captain Benjamin L. Willard in Francis Ford Coppola's landmark film *Apocalypse Now*.

His list of important films includes: *Wall Street* (1987), the Academy Award-winning *Gandhi* (1982), Spielberg's *Catch Me if You Can* (2002), *The American President* (1995), and Martin Scorsese's *The Departed* (2006, which won the Academy Award for Best Picture). He is also credited with being the only actor to have played both John Kennedy and Robert Kennedy.

Sheen has said that one of his favorite roles was that of Kit Carruthers in the Terrence Malick film *Badlands*, which was released in 1973. At the time, it eclipsed Scorsese's *Mean Streets* on critics' lists. *Badlands* is a dramatization of the Charles Starkweather/Caril Ann Fugate saga of teenage murder and violence that took place in the 1950s. Sheen received rave reviews for his performance.

From 1996 through 2006, he was the choice of Aaron Sorkin to play President Josiah Bartlet on the critically acclaimed TV drama *The West Wing*. It is the role that comes closest to representing the actor's personal political sensibilities, but as it has become clear since Sheen's earliest days in the spotlight, the liberal President Bartlet was hardly the radical that Sheen is as an activist and dissident.

As Sheen explained to Bob Edwards in an interview on National Public Radio in 2003, the happy coincidence of this role dovetailed nicely with his life's work and his passion for humanity. "I'd often thought about doing a series over the years, but nothing ever came along that I really felt I could commit to for the long term, and this came at a time when I was getting towards the period in your life you start thinking about retiring. And I could not believe that it was coming at that time, and that it was what it was: a liberal Democratic progressive Catholic president. It just fell on me like a mighty blessing" (Edwards 2003).

For decades, Sheen has taken an interest in causes that he felt were crucial to making the world a more just place for all of its inhabitants. He was known to pick up beggars in India in 1981 when he was there making the movie *Gandhi*. He would just drive them around the town in his taxi to get to know them and better understand their plight. He later donated his $200,000 salary from that film to Mother Teresa and other nonviolent causes throughout the world. His direct action did not stop there, of course. He has been arrested more than 60 times for taking part in public protests and nonviolent actions wherever he thought his celebrity status might help a cause.

These causes are diverse. From the mundane parish work of youth groups, council meetings, and soup kitchens where he was a church member, to the high-risk, high-visibility world of political action, Sheen has a long history of personal involvement. Homelessness, workers' rights, government overreach, and peace are his key issues. He has come out against political repression in Central America, shined a light on the atrocities of the U.S.-supported Salvadoran death squads, studied the United States' political asylum policies and promoted a more liberal view, protested against nuclear testing, and marched against immigration reform legislation in 1993 and later to protect immigrant rights. He demonstrated against abuses by the Israeli army in the Occupied Territories in the late 1980s.

He was inspired by the life work of Father Philip Berrigan (1923–2002), the Jesuit priest who, with his brother Daniel Berrigan, frequently was arrested for civil disobedience during antiwar protests. Sheen was arrested along with the Berrigans when they demonstrated against President Ronald Reagan's "Star Wars" program, that is, the Strategic Defense Initiative (SDI) designed to construct a space-based antimissile system. It was part of Reagan's military buildup.

Also an inspiration was César Chávez, who became the most famous advocate for farm workers in California and fasted several times to call attention to farm workers' rights. Sheen along with other Hollywood stars demonstrated their support for Chávez in 1988 by fasting. In 2000, Sheen received the inaugural César E. Chávez Spirit Award.

At an antiwar rally in San Francisco in January 2003, during the lead-up to the Iraq War that would commence two months later, an interviewer asked Sheen why he was so active in social justice and peace issues. He responded:

> I do it because I can't seem to live with myself if I do not. I don't know any other way to be. It isn't something you can explain; it is just something that you do; it is something that you are ... It [nonviolent civil disobedience] is one of the only tools that is available to us where you can express a deeply personal, deeply moral opinion and be held accountable. You have to be prepared for the consequences. I honestly do not know if civil disobedience has any effect on the government. I can promise you it has a great effect on the person who chooses to do it. Once you follow a path of nonviolence and social justice, it won't take you long before you come into conflict with the culture, with the society. You can't know what is at stake or how much it is going to cost you until you get in the game. That's the only way, and the level of cost is equal to the level of involvement. (Kupfer 2003)

In February 2003, Sheen, along with other celebrities and church leaders, gathered for a press conference in Los Angeles to announce their "virtual anti-war march," in the form of advertisements against the pending Iraq war through local cable television outlets. National cable channels refused to air antiwar commercials.

Throughout the 2000s, Sheen has continued his protests against the U.S. invasion of Iraq as well as the war in Afghanistan. For example, Sheen and actor Edward Asner participated in an antiwar march protesting both Iraq and Afghanistan wars in Los Angeles in 2009.

In addition, Sheen has continued making movies. In 2010, he was in Detroit, Michigan, filming *The Double*. A devout Catholic, he also attended St. Aloysius Catholic Church on a regular basis while in Detroit and took part in the annual block party that the church sponsors. Fans and critics alike keep up with Sheen, whether in film or in social justice activities, on a great variety of web sites.

Martin K. Gay

See also Asner, Edward; Berrigan, Daniel, and Berrigan, Philip; Chávez, César; Day, Dorothy

References

Edwards, Bob. "Martin Sheen's 'West Wing' Fantasy." NPR, January 28, 2003. http://www.npr.org/templates/story/story.php?storyId=942641 (accessed September 9, 2011).

Garvey, Michael O. "Actor Martin Sheen to Receive Notre Dame's Laetare Medal." Notre Dame News, March 1, 2008. http://newsinfo.nd.edu/news/9310-actor-martin-sheen-to-receive-notre-damersquos-laetare-medal/ (accessed January 23, 2011).

Kupfer, David. "Martin Sheen Interview." *Progressive*, July 2003. http://www.progressive.org/mag_intvsheen (accessed January 23, 2011).

Rasmussen, Dana. *The Estevez/Sheen Family: Martin Sheen, Emilio Estevez, and Charlie Sheen*. Webster's Digital Services, 2011.

Silkwood, Karen Gay (1946–1974)

To many, the name Karen Silkwood—if at all familiar—may mean nothing more than a role played by Meryl Streep in the 1989 movie *Silkwood*. But Silkwood sparked broad public awareness in the United States about nuclear issues. In doing so, pressure was put on the industry to be more responsive to health and safety concerns. The agency responsible for industry oversight was completely overhauled, partly because of issues brought to light following Silkwood's death.

Karen was born on February 19, 1946, in Longview, Texas. The oldest of Bill and Merle Silkwood's three daughters, she had an ordinary childhood. She got good grades and was a member of the National Honor Society, earning her a scholarship to attend Lamar State College in Beaumont, Texas. She studied medical technology. After a year of college, she dropped out, marrying Bill Meadows, an oil pipeline worker. With Silkwood a stay-at-home mother to their three children, the family struggled financially and eventually declared bankruptcy. Matters worsened when Silkwood learned her husband was unfaithful. The couple divorced in 1972. Silkwood ceded custody of her children and moved to Oklahoma City, Oklahoma, where she briefly worked as a hospital clerk. She then found a job as a metallography laboratory technician, making plutonium pellets for nuclear fuel rods. The position was with Kerr-McGee at its Cimarron River plant in Crescent, about 30 miles north of Oklahoma City.

Silkwood joined the Oil, Chemical and Atomic Workers (OCAW) Union and, soon after, in 1972, OCAW went on strike. She joined the picket lines, demanding higher wages, better training, and safety policies. Nine weeks later, the strikers conceded. "Karen was back at work under a new, two-year contract written by Kerr-McGee. For the twenty OCAW members left in the battered local, it had been a total defeat, but for Silkwood, it had been an awakening. Taking a stand against Kerr-McGee, walking the line, living off part-time wages as a clerk in a building supply company, watching OCAW members one by one knuckle under to the pressure—all of this had forged her ties with the union. Her relationship with Kerr-McGee would never be the same" (Rashke 2000, 14).

Nevertheless, she was not really interested in becoming an activist. "But in the spring of 1974 ... Kerr-McGee speeded up production. There were twelve-hour shifts, seven-day workweeks, rotations from day to night shifts, and spills and contaminations. Karen became more and more worried about health and safety, about nineteen-year old farm boys with grease under their fingernails treating plutonium like fertilizer, and about a management that used them up and sent them back to plough the fields with plutonium in their bodies, unaware that they were hot." In one incident, five workers inhaled 400 times the weekly limit of insoluble plutonium permitted by the Atomic Energy Commission, or AEC (Rashke 2000, 14–15).

Karen Silkwood poses with her children in this undated photo. From left are Beverly, Dawn, and Michael. During the 1970s, Silkwood sparked broad public awareness in the United States about nuclear issues. (AP Photo)

Silkwood was the first female elected to the union's bargaining committee. Her first job was looking into plant health and safety issues; she discovered evidence of spills, leaks, and missing plutonium, including exposure of workers to contamination, faulty respiratory equipment, and improper storage of samples. She thought the lack of sufficient shower facilities increased employee contamination (Rashke 2000, 19–23). With their contract expiring on December 1, 1974, a campaign was launched to decertify the union, with a vote scheduled for October 16.

Hoping to gain support and the ability to prove to workers that the union made a difference, three union representatives, including Silkwood, traveled to Washington, D.C., where they first met with a national union representative Tony Mazzocchi. While preparing them for their meeting the next day with AEC, Mazzocchi explained the dangerous nature of their employment—much of which was news to them. Silkwood had never been told that the metals she worked with were carcinogenic (even exposure to pollen-sized grains of uranium is hazardous) and that she might develop cancer decades later. "It angered her, for she had been in a contaminated room without a respirator just two months before" (Rashke 2000, 20). The following day, the union representatives and Mazzocchi's assistant, Steve Wodka, met with AEC. They alleged that Kerr-McGee did not "keep levels of exposure to plutonium as low as practicable, provide proper hygiene facilities, educate and train workers adequately, and monitor worker exposure" and provided 39 examples to substantiate their charges. Silkwood also claimed that employees mishandled fuel rods and that inspection records were falsified (Rashke 2000, 22–23). AEC promised a confidential investigation. Silkwood agreed to obtain documentation to substantiate her charges. Returning to work, she began carrying a notebook, obsessively recording violations.

On November 5, Plutonium-239 was found on Silkwood's hands. She had been working in a "glovebox" in the metallography lab that night, grinding and polishing plutonium pellets. "Strangely, the gloves [she had been using] were found to have plutonium on the 'outside' surfaces that were in contact with Silkwood's hands; no leaks were found in the gloves. No plutonium was found in the surfaces of the room where she had been working and filter papers from the two air monitors in the room showed that there was no significant plutonium in the air." Silkwood was "cleaned up" and, as a precaution, her urine and feces were collected for five days. When she left the plant later that night, she checked herself and found nothing. The next day, she examined prints and did paperwork for an hour; monitoring detected alpha activity scattered over the right side of her body; she was again decontaminated. At her request, her locker and car were checked, but no activity was found.

On November 7, Silkwood turned in her urine and fecal samples to the Health Physics Office, and a nasal swipe was taken. That detected significant levels of activity in each nostril—particularly surprising since one had been completely blocked since childhood. Preliminary examination of her other samples showed "*extremely* high levels of activity." No activity was found when her car and locker were rechecked. Kerr-McGee physicists went with Silkwood to her apartment, where significant activity was found in the bathroom and kitchen, along with lower levels in other areas. Her roommate was escorted to the plant for decontamination. The alarming levels of plutonium discovered at the apartment compelled Kerr-McGee to send Silkwood, her roommate, and her boyfriend to Los Alamos for further testing on November 11. While the latter two showed insignificant traces of plutonium in their bodies, not so for Silkwood. However, she was reassured that she should not worry about developing cancer, dying from radiation poisoning, or bearing abnormal children. When they reported back to the plant on November 13, Silkwood and her roommate were restricted from radiation work (*Los Alamos Science* 1995, 252–55).

That evening, Silkwood attended a local union meeting at the Hub Café in Crescent. Afterward, she left, driving her white Honda, heading in the direction of Oklahoma City, where she was to meet her friend, Drew Stephens, *New York Times* reporter David Burnham, and Wodka. She was to deliver the documentation she had been collecting over the past seven weeks. Ten miles later, seven miles outside of Crescent, Silkwood was the victim of a one-car crash—her Honda had gone off the road, skidded for more than 100 yards, hit a guardrail, and plunged off the highway, down an embankment. The onsite police report was spotty, at best, and state police determined Silkwood had fallen asleep at the wheel, ruling the crash—and her death—accidental. Blood tests conducted at the time of her autopsy revealed a trace amount of alcohol in her system, along with a sedative, twice the amount prescribed to induce sleepiness; an additional undissolved amount of the sedative remained in her stomach. A private investigator put forth a contradictory hypothesis, positing that Silkwood had been forced off the road by another car. The Honda's rear bumper was freshly dented and contained metal, paint, and rubber fragments, as if Silkwood had been rammed from behind (Rashke 2000, 99–115).

In addition to questions about the accident's cause, there remained the unresolved matter of the disposition of the documentation that Silkwood had with her that evening. When Stephens arrived at the accident scene that night, he could not locate the materials even though Silkwood's other personal effects remained undisturbed in her car. Wanda Jean Jung, a friend also at the Hub that night, later testified about this matter. "Jung was an important witness ... she saw Karen's documents just minutes before Karen was killed ... Jung described in great detail the folder and notebook Karen had with her ... That was when she told me about having been contaminated so much that it could eventually kill her ... And she said, 'I have got all of my proof ready that I have been working on for quite some time.' ... She said she had proof of the falsification of records" (Rashke 2000, 346). A Los Alamos team assisted in Silkwood's November 14 autopsy. "The highest concentrations [of plutonium] were in the contents of the gastrointestinal tract... This demonstrated that she had ingested plutonium prior to her death." and showed "an indication that Silkwood had probably been exposed within 30 days prior to her death" (*Los Alamos Science* 1995, 255). The Justice Department closed its cursory investigation of Silkwood's death and the events leading up to it without making a formal report. However, congressional hearings on the matter raised additional questions and issues that remain unanswered to date, from possible FBI involvement, to wiretapping, to black market sales of nuclear materials and more.

In 1979, a jury awarded Silkwood's estate $10 million in punitive damages, finding Kerr-McGee negligent and clearing Silkwood of allegations that she had stolen plutonium. An appeals court overturned the decision, but the Supreme Court restored the original verdict. To avoid retrial, the parties settled out of court for $1.38 million (*Los Alamos Science* 1995, 255).

AEC found Kerr-McGee's plant in violation of safety regulations, and National Public Radio reported that 44 to 66 pounds of plutonium had been misplaced at Cimarron. The company shut down all of its plants in 1975 and was still decontaminating in Crescent City 25 years later (BBC h2g2, 2002). The Energy Reorganization Act of 1974 abolished AEC and created two new agencies, the Energy Research and Development Administration and the Nuclear Regulatory Commission. Critics claimed AEC failed in key areas, including radiation protection standards, nuclear reactor safety, plant siting, and environmental protection. Established by Congress in 1946, its broad powers were inherently conflicting, to both promote *and* regulate the nuclear industry. "The AEC had become an oligarchy controlling all facets of the military and civilian sides of nuclear energy, promoting them and at the same time attempting to regulate them, and it had fallen down on the regulatory side... a growing legion of critics saw too many inbuilt conflicts of interest" (Cooke 2009, 252).

Antinuclear activists say Silkwood and Cimarron should have been a clarion call. Since Silkwood's death, the debate over nuclear power safety has intensified due to accidents. On March 28, 1979, about half of the reactor core of the Pennsylvania Three Mile Island plant underwent a meltdown. Although widespread radioactive contamination was averted, the crisis underscored the need for increased training and the ever-looming possibility of equipment failure.

On April 26, 1986, a nuclear accident occurred at the Chernobyl Nuclear Power Plant in the Ukraine, spreading radioactive contamination over much of western Russia and Europe. At that time, it was considered the worst nuclear power plant accident ever, "classified a level 7 event" on the International Nuclear Event Scale. Chernobyl raised doubts about the Soviet nuclear industry and nuclear power in general. Mortality estimates resulting from the accident vary, ranging from the 31 deaths directly attributable to the accident to 985,000 additional deaths occurring between 1986 and 2004, as a result of radioactive contamination (Yablokov 2009, 210).

On March 11, 2011, a 9.0 magnitude earthquake struck the island of Japan, followed by a tsunami. These triggered a series of ongoing equipment failures and subsequent release of radioactive material at the Fukushima Nuclear Power Plant maintained by the Tokyo Electric Power Company (TEPCO). The disaster may well exceed that of Chernobyl. In the wake of the Japanese tragedy, the safety of nuclear power in the United States and elsewhere has been debated. And the awareness of nuclear dangers that Silkwood sparked decades ago has been carried on by such diverse antinuclear activists as JoAnn Tall of the Oglala Lakota Tribe in South Dakota and biologist and environmentalist Barry Commoner.

Margaret Gay

See also Commoner, Barry; Tall, JoAnn

References

Cooke, Stephanie. *In Mortal Hands: A Cautionary History of the Nuclear Age*. New York: Bloomsbury, USA, 2009.

"Karen Silkwood—Campaigner." BBC h2g2, January 8, 2002. http://www.bbc.co.uk/dna/h2g2/A634213 (accessed April 20, 2011).

"The Karen Silkwood Story." *Los Alamos Science*, November 23, 1995. http://library.lanl.gov/cgi-bin/getfile?23-14.pdf (accessed April 18, 2011).

Kleiner, Diana J. "Silkwood, Karen Gay." *Handbook of Texas Online*. Texas State Historical Association, n.d. http://www.tshaonline.org/handbook/online/articles/fsi35 (accessed April 19, 2011).

Rashke, Richard L. *The Killing of Karen Silkwood: The Story behind the Kerr-McGee Plutonium Case*. 2nd ed. New York: Cornell Paperbacks, 2000.

Yablokov, Alexey V., Vassily B. Nesternko, Alexey V. Nesterenko, and Janette D. Sherman-Nevinger, eds. *Chernobyl: Consequences of the Catastrophe for People and the Environment*. New York: Annals of the New York Academy of the Sciences, 2009. http://www.strahlentelex.de/Yablokov%20Chernobyl%20book.pdf (accessed April 18, 2011).

Simkins, Modjeska Monteith (1899–1992)

"I mean, history has repeated itself that you can't pressure the mass but so much before it revolts. I thought . . . things are a little easier now. But . . . we were moving toward a revolution in this country" (Hall 1976). Simkins, a leader in the early years of the civil rights movement and social reform, garnered a reputation of fearlessness as she challenged state and national authority. She became known as the mother of the civil rights movement in South Carolina.

Born Mary Modjeska Monteith on December 5, 1899, Modjeska, as she was usually called, was the eldest of eight children. From an early age, she learned the power of the individual and family, and how to stand up against social injustice. Her great-grandparents and grandparents had been enslaved. Of her great-grandmother, Simkins said, "Although she was a slave, she didn't fear anyone" (Hall 1976).

Modjeska's father, Henry Clarence Monteith, worked as a bricklayer. Her mother Rachel Evelyn Hall had been educated at the Howard Free School, the first public school for African Americans in South Carolina, and was employed as a teacher by the time she married Henry. Both parents grew up during Reconstruction, the turbulent years following the Civil War, a time for rebuilding the devastated Southern economy as well as providing freedmen with equal rights under the law. While some saw reconstruction as an opportunity to build a new nation, many in the southern states sought to protect their old way of life. As explained by historians, it was a time of chaos and violence, a war of terror in an effort to reestablish white supremacy (Smith 2003).

Determined to raise his daughters in a safe environment, Henry bought a farm and a substantial plot of land outside of Columbia, South Carolina. There, Simkins's parents emphasized self-sufficiency and education. The family grew most of their own food, selling the surplus in town. Simkins, as the eldest, was expected to help out on the farm when her father traveled for work.

Rachel Monteith taught her children how to read and write at an early age, and their education included "things as they were, no matter how cruel or atrocious they might be" (Hall 1976). Simkins read newspapers about the lynching and mutilations of African Americans. "My father was a fearless man," Modjeska said in a 1976 interview. At one point, while the family was in Huntsville, Alabama, a lyncher showed Henry the victim's finger. Rather than be intimidated, Henry took a stand, offering to fight him with his trowel and hammer (Hall 1976).

Modjeska's mother also instilled in her a strong sense of community service. Her mother and her aunts were members of the National Association for the Advancement of Colored People (NAACP), and they helped to organize care for black tubercular patients. As a teenager, Modjeska accompanied her mother and aunts to the NAACP meetings.

Modjeska attended Benedict College, a "practice" school in which students were trained to become teachers and ministers. She attributes her education at Benedict for influencing her racial identity in relationship to helping the disadvantaged. She did not have that "consciousness of color," either from her home or her education. As a result, "I have always been interested in the disadvantaged, no matter what their color was," she said (Hall 1974).

After graduating from Benedict College in 1921, Modjeska Monteith taught medieval history for a year at the college. In 1927, she began teaching elementary education at Booker T. Washington High School. Because she did not like the textbook, she refused to teach South Carolina history and challenged the school administration. Thereafter, she taught algebra until 1929, when she married widower and businessman Andrew Whitfield Simkins. At the time, married women were not allowed to work in the public school system, so she was forced to resign.

Andrew Simkins was a prominent businessman in real estate. He had five children from his previous marriages. The couple would eventually have three of their own children. Although he was not an activist, Andrew supported his wife's efforts in civil rights and social reforms. He used his connections to recommend his wife for a position with the South Carolina Tuberculosis Association. During the first decades of the twentieth century, poverty and southern racism spurred an alarming rise in African American mortality by tuberculosis, pellagra, and other diseases. In 1931, Simkins became director of the Negro Work for the South Carolina Tuberculosis Association, and was the only full-time statewide African American public health worker. The position required her to travel extensively across the state. Exposed to the extreme poverty of the African American community, she became an advocate for establishing TB-testing clinics. She taught health education classes at South Carolina State College, supervised clinics, and educated communities about good health practices.

In 1935, at the height of the Depression years, federal jobs were established through President Franklin D. Roosevelt's New Deal to help boost the national economy, promising that federal jobs did not discriminate in terms of salary or position. In South Carolina, officials from the federal relief agency Works Progression Administration (WPA) planned to offer the black community only low-skilled manual labor positions. Simkins joined other African American leaders to challenge the administration. As a result of their demands, the WPA hired African American teachers and professionals for a state history project.

During the Depression years, Simkins helped to organize the State Negro Citizens Committee, where she served as secretary. The organization lobbied for an antilynching bill. Southern democrats aggressively and successfully blocked the legislation. The bill proposed that should the state not act upon the crime, the federal government has authority to step in. While the bill failed to pass, the movement became more energized. African American students began to organize campus protests. Civil leaders organized the Columbia Civil Welfare League, in which Simkins also served as secretary. The organization protested police brutality.

In 1938, Simkins attended an antilynching hearing in Birmingham, where she met First Lady Eleanor Roosevelt, who was deeply involved in racial justice issues. While several antilynching bills were introduced into Congress during the 1930s and 1940s, and several were passed by the House of Representatives, none ever came to a vote in the Senate. The proposed antilynching laws were eventually subsumed by the Civil Rights Act in 1964.

A member of the NAACP since her teenage years, Simkins was by now a board member of the Columbia chapter. In 1939, she helped to organize a state chapter of NAACP, and became the first chair of the state programs committee. In 1941, she was elected state secretary, and the only woman to serve as an officer. She soon became a contributing writer for the NAACP publication the *Lighthouse and Informer*. In 1942, she became the director for the organization's publicity committee. However, because of her increased involvement in NAACP, she was released from her position with the South Carolina Tuberculosis Association.

Simkins continued to volunteer for the South Carolina NAACP, becoming instrumental in several civil rights lawsuits and movements. In 1943, she was involved in the NAACP teacher equalization lawsuits in Sumter and Columbia. During this time, state employees who became involved with NAACP litigation risked losing their jobs. In 1945, Simkins began working on a significant case with the Reverend Joseph DeLaine, president of the Clarendon County NAACP. Initially, *Briggs v. Elliot* was a request to provide bus transportation for black students, but in 1949, the case was rewritten as a request for equal educational opportunities. Once the Clarendon case reached the Supreme Court, it was combined with five other suits and included in the Supreme Court decision *Brown v Board of Education* (1954), challenging the "separate but equal" doctrine. NAACP lawyer Thurgood Marshall argued the case, and he became a close friend of Simkins.

Another central issue that Simkins worked on involved voting rights for African Americans. Despite the passage of the Fifteenth Amendment in 1870, African Americans had difficulty exercising their right to vote. In the 1920s, southern states began using tactics to limit the black community's involvement in the political process. The Democratic Party adopted the rule that political parties were private organizations and not part of the election process, calling them white primaries. Under the white primary, blacks were not allowed to vote. In the decades following, the U.S. Supreme Court reviewed several white primary cases, and in 1944, the High Court ruled that white primaries were a violation of the Fifteenth Amendment to the U.S. Constitution, which declares "The right of citizens of the United States to vote shall not be denied or abridged by the United States or by any state on account of race, color, or previous condition of servitude." However, South Carolina, still determined to exclude the black community from the voting process, dropped all of its primary voting laws, making the Democratic Party a private organization and outside state law.

The NAACP challenged the Democratic Party. Simkins helped plan the legal strategy, attending trials in Columbia and in Washington, D.C. While the NAACP won the lawsuit in 1948, it was not without its complications. The laws were changed, but the registration process became more challenging. Simkins traveled around the state, offering educational programs to African American communities on how to exercise their voting rights. In 1953, the Supreme Court ruled on the last of the "white primary" lawsuits, which prohibited private racial discrimination under the Fifteenth Amendment. It set the precedent for later legislation, including the Voting Rights Act of 1965.

At different times, Simkins was actively involved with both the Republican and the Democratic parties. However, Simkins considered herself a National Democrat, "independent in political philosophy" and "not married to any party" (Simkins 1981). Simkins joined the board of the Southern Negro Youth Conference as well as the Southern Conference for Human Welfare. Because members of the American Communist Party also belonged to these organizations, Simkins was often criticized as being a communist, and was accused of being engaged in subversive activities by the Federal Bureau of Investigation. The House Un-American Activities Committee (HUAC) maintained on file on her. In 1957, the South Carolina Conference of the NAACP did not reelect Simkins as secretary, in part because of governmental pressure to remove effective leaders (Aba-Mecha 1978). However, Simkins was also becoming disillusioned with the role of the NAACP in the civil rights movement. She challenged NAACP executive secretary Roy Wilkins, stating "sometimes they didn't seem interested in any movement unless they started it. That's one of the characteristics of NAACP: if they can't spearhead a movement they just don't like to bother with it much, because they want the credit for everything that's done" (Hall 1976).

Simkins was also critical of gender roles within the civil rights movement, stating that African American women were outspoken in their ideas for social justice, but it was often men who received public recognition as leaders of the movement (Hall 1976). In 1957, after 16 years, Simkins left her position in the NAACP. She maintained her membership, focusing her volunteer efforts at the local level. In 1960, she played host to the young minister and civil rights leader Martin Luther King Jr. when he addressed the African American community in Columbia.

In 1956, Simkins became public relations director for Victory Savings Bank, and remained very active as a community activist. She ran for political office four times, including for the city council twice, for the school board, and for the state House of Representatives. However, she did not win any election.

In 1990, Simkins was awarded the South Carolina Order of the Palmetto, honoring those who made contributions of statewide significance.

Simkins died on April 5, 1992, in Columbia. The Modjeska Monteith Simkins House in Columbia is listed on the National Register of Historic Places.

Bobbi Miller

See also King, Martin Luther, Jr.; Roosevelt, Eleanor

References

Aba-Mecha, Barbara W. "South Carolina Conference of NAACP: Origin and Major Accomplishments, 1939–1954," *Proceedings of the South Carolina Historical Association* (1981).

Botsch, Carol Sears. "Modjeska Monteith Simkins." South Caroliniana Library, University of South Carolina–Aiken, December 14, 2007. http://www.usca.edu/aasc/simkins.htm (accessed March 23, 2011).

Egerton, John. Oral History Interview with Modjeska Simkins, May 11, 1990. Southern Oral History Program Collection, Wilson Library, University of North Carolina at Chapel Hill. http://docsouth.unc.edu/sohp/A-0356/ (accessed March 24, 2011).

Eichel, Henry. "Civil Rights Pioneer Simkins Lauded as Mother of S.C. Efforts." *Charlotte Observer*, April 10, 1992.

Hall, Jacquelyn. "Oral History Interview with Modjeska Simkins, July 28, 1976." Southern Oral History Program Collection, Wilson Library, University of North Carolina at Chapel Hill. http://docsouth.unc.edu/sohp/G-0056-2/menu.html (accessed March 23, 2011).

Hall, Jacquelyn. "Oral History Interview with Modjeska Simkins, November 15, 1974." Southern Oral History Program Collection, Wilson Library, University of North Carolina at Chapel Hill. http://docsouth.unc.edu/sohp/G-0056-1/menu.html (accessed March 23, 2011).

Siegel, Robert. "Anti-Lynching Law in U.S. History." *All Things Considered*. National Public Radio, June 13, 2005. http://www.npr.org/templates/story/story.php?storyId=4701576 (accessed March 24, 2011).

Simkins, Modjeska Monteith. "Letter to Mr. W. J. Bryan Dorn. April 16, 1981." Modjeska Monteith Simkins Papers, South Caroliniana Library, University of South Carolina. http://www.usca.edu/aasc/simkins.htm (accessed March 27, 2011).

Smith, Llewellyn. "Reconstruction: The Second Civil War." *American Experience*, PBS Online, December 2003. http://www.pbs.org/wgbh/amex/reconstruction/filmmore/pt.html (accessed March 23, 2011).

Sinclair, Upton (1878–1968)

More than 100 years after publication of Upton Sinclair's *The Jungle* (1906), a novel about the appalling and unsanitary conditions in the meatpacking industry, the book is still read and is a topic of discussion in many schools. So is Sinclair himself. He was a prolific writer and a foremost muckraker, a term used by President Theodore Roosevelt (1858–1919), who disapproved of reporters "raking in the muck"—that is, writing stories about wrongdoings in big business and government. Among other well-known muckrakers was Ida Tarbell, who investigated and uncovered Standard Oil's illegal activities in the early 1900s.

Not only was Sinclair a muckraker, but he also was a socialist, believing that private property should be abolished and that all citizens, not just a few, should own the means of production. These views made him a target of industrialists, government officials, and other advocates of capitalism who labeled him a dissident, an enemy of the American mass production system, which implied that he was a communist.

In 1878, Upton Beall Sinclair Jr. was born in Baltimore, Maryland, to Upton Beall and

Priscilla Harden Sinclair. He was their only child. Upton's father was a salesman who had a drinking problem, which exacerbated the family's poverty. Yet being poor did not diminish Upton's precociousness. He taught himself to read by the time he was five years old.

When he was 10 years old, Upton and his family moved to New York City. There, at age 14, he enrolled in the College of the City of New York, graduating in 1897 and continuing his studies at Columbia University. He supported himself at both institutions by writing and selling a variety of works such as children's stories, poetry, and adventure sagas. While at Columbia, each week he wrote what he called "half-dime" novels, stories of 30,000 words that he produced under the pen names Lieutenant Garrison and Ensign Clarke Fitch.

Sinclair left Columbia in 1900 and moved to Quebec, Canada, renting a cabin on Lake Massawippi where he wrote *Springtime and Harvest* (1901). The following year, he married his first wife, Meta Fuller. They had a son, David. The marriage broke up in 1911 when Fuller left to live with a poet. In 1913, Sinclair married Mary Craig Kimbrough, a southern belle and writer from Greenville, Mississippi. Throughout their happy 48 years of marriage, Craig, as she was known, shared in many of Sinclair's political pursuits and supported his liberal causes.

Over several years from 1902, Sinclair wrote other novels, and occasionally contributed articles to *Appeal to Reason*, a socialist weekly. But not until 1906 when *The Jungle* was published did he have financial success. The story is an exposé of the filthy and dangerous meatpacking industry in Chicago. Against the slaughterhouse background, Sinclair wove his tale of an impoverished immigrant family that experiences the hard, dangerous life in their slum neighborhood near the stockyards. Jurgis, one of its members, tries to escape the miserable working conditions and his family life and in the process eventually joins the Socialist Party.

However, the socialist solutions for reform of the meatpacking industry suggested in the book did not impress the reading public as did the sensational descriptions of what went on in the slaughterhouse, such as poisoned rats ground up to become part of sausage meat. Sinclair through his protagonist Jurgis also called attention to the plight of the workers:

> Of the butchers and floorsmen, the beef-boners and trimmers, and all those who used knives, you could scarcely find a person who had the use of his thumb; time and time again the base of it had been slashed, till it was a mere lump of flesh against which the man pressed the knife to hold it. The hands of these men would be criss-crossed with cuts, until you could no longer pretend to count them or to trace them. They would have no nails—they had worn them off pulling hides; their knuckles were swollen so that their fingers spread out like a fan. . . . There were the wool-pluckers, whose hands went to pieces . . . for the pelts of the sheep had to be painted with acid to loosen the wool, and then the pluckers had to pull out this wool with their bare hands, till the acid had eaten their fingers off . . . as for the other men, who worked in tank rooms full of steam, and in some of which there were open vats near the level of the floor, their peculiar trouble was that they fell into the vats; and when they were fished out, there was never enough of them left to be worth exhibiting—sometimes they would be overlooked

for days, till all but the bones of them had gone out to the world as...Pure Leaf Lard! (Sinclair, Chapter 9, 1906)

When President Theodore Roosevelt read *The Jungle*, he asked Sinclair to meet with him in the White House to discuss the slaughterhouse conditions the author had researched. Soon afterward, Congress investigated meatpacking companies and passed two federal laws: the Meat Inspection Act, which empowers the U.S. Department of Agriculture to inspect all types of food animals that are slaughtered and processed into products for human consumption; and the Pure Food and Drug Act, which prevents "the manufacture, sale, or transportation of adulterated or misbranded or poisonous or deleterious foods, drugs, medicines, and liquors." President Roosevelt signed both acts into law in June 1906.

Reading *The Jungle* in later years, social worker Dorothy Day (1897–1980) was inspired while in Chicago to take long walks to the city's stockyard district in order to connect with the people in the area. Frances Perkins (1880–1965), who became the first woman to serve as U.S. secretary of labor, also was influenced by Sinclair's book while she was working on social welfare projects at Jane Addams's Hull House in Chicago. Perkins was able to help some meatpackers as well as other needy workers living near the slaughterhouse.

The Jungle became a best seller, and Sinclair used the earnings from his book to purchase a former boys' school on seven acres called Helicon Hall in 1906. He established Helicon Home Colony, a community based on socialist values near Englewood, New Jersey, where 12 families lived. He hoped to attract others that shared his views, but the building burned to the ground in 1907, destroying his dream utopia. He tried once more to form a colony with only two families in Bermuda, and during his time there, he wrote a health book and a play—the latter was never produced.

Upton Sinclair was a prominent novelist and socialist who pointed out the need for reform in many areas of American life. He is best known for *The Jungle* (1906), a novel about the appalling and unsanitary conditions in the meatpacking industry. The book is still read and is a topic of discussion in many schools. (Library of Congress)

While in New Jersey, Sinclair ran for U.S. representative from the state on the Socialist Party ticket. He had joined the party in 1902, and from that time on he attempted periodically to win political office as a socialist. After he moved to California in 1915, he continued to seek public office as a U.S. representative, as a senator, and as governor, but he was unsuccessful.

However, he continued writing on political subjects, underscoring his belief in socialism and the injustices of capitalism. Backed by thorough research, his novels such as *King Coal* (1917) and *Oil!* (1927) describe corruption in the coal mining and oil industries and focus on the exploitation of workers. His book *Boston* (1928) tells about the Nicola Sacco and Bartolomeo Vanzetti case—two Italian immigrants who were convicted of robbery and murder and executed in 1927. Many individuals and groups in the United States and Europe claimed the men were innocent and came to their defense, charging that police had framed them because of their anarchist views and Italian origin.

Always eager to explore new topics and ideas, Sinclair became interested in parapsychology. He knew that his wife Mary Craig had exhibited psychic powers, and they experimented with mental telepathy. In a book published as *Mental Radio* (1930), Sinclair describes a variety of experiments in which Craig "sees" in her mind what someone miles or yards away is drawing. In one incident, Craig's brother living in Pasadena, 40 miles from the Sinclair home, drew a picture of a fork, documenting the time and date and concentrating on the drawing for 15 minutes. At the same time, Craig in Long Beach created a drawing of a fork. Pairs of telepathic and original drawings are included in the book which can be read free online.

In 1931, Sinclair was nominated by a group of well-known authors and academicians for the Nobel Prize in Literature awarded in 1932. Despite an international petition on Sinclair's behalf signed by 770 prominent persons, including such luminaries as Bertrand Russell and Albert Einstein, Sinclair was defeated in the final voting. The prize went to John Galsworthy (1867–1933), a British author of the *Forsyte Saga*, a series of three novels published between 1906 and 1921.

Sinclair again turned his attention to politics in 1934, running for nomination as governor of California and registering as a Democrat rather than Socialist. Unemployment in the state was at a high level due to the Great Depression and the influx of many Midwesterners and others fleeing to the West Coast in search of jobs. His platform was called End Poverty in California (EPIC), which included a series of proposals. At the core was a socialist-like plan for a full employment program that would turn over idle land and factories to colonies of the unemployed. Hundreds of EPIC clubs formed to support Sinclair and his proposals. Sinclair attempted to gain President Franklin Roosevelt's endorsement, but Roosevelt and Democratic leaders refused to back EPIC. The Democratic establishment denounced Sinclair, calling him a communist or a "crackpot." They wanted him to drop out of the race. Many Democrats eventually backed a Republican for governor, and a smear campaign against Sinclair, lies about his background, and financial support for his opponent helped defeat him.

Nevertheless, Sinclair pursued numerous social justice causes through his writings. He wrote *The Flivver King: A Story of Ford-America* (1937), a fictionalized account of Henry Ford, the automobile manufacturer and his company, from the viewpoint of workers. In the 1940s, he wrote a series of 11 novels with antifascist hero Lanny Budd as protagonist. The stories are set against the background of world events since 1914. One of the series, *Dragon's Teeth* (1942), won a Pulitzer Prize.

In 1961, Mary Craig died of a stroke in Pasadena, and not long afterward, at the age of 83, Sinclair married Mary Elizabeth Willis (1882–1967). In 1962, he rewrote his autobiographical *American Outpost* (1932), which was published as *The Autobiography of Upton Sinclair* (1962).

Over the years, Sinclair's prolific writings included more than 90 books, 30 plays, and countless articles and pamphlets. His books were translated into dozens of languages. Some reviewers and publishers criticized him for lacking literary talent. But he did not write for the elite. He wrote for "ordinary" readers, the masses, and he wanted people to understand the plight of characters in his stories. Praise came from authors like Sir Arthur Conan Doyle, Jack London, Irving Stone, and Sinclair Lewis. There is little doubt that he was one of the most prominent muckrakers, and that his investigations and the novels he produced helped bring about industrial and institutional reforms that improved the lives of millions.

Upton Sinclair died on November 25, 1968, in a Bound Brook, New Jersey, nursing home. In an obituary in the *New York Times*, Alden Whitman wrote: "Upton Beall Sinclair was a rebel with a cause; indeed, a multitude of causes.... Mr. Sinclair's weapon was his pen, and few writers wielded it so tellingly in battles against the social and economic ills of the United States. Although he was not a memorable stylist, his books were graphic, pungent and direct, arousing strong emotions in their readers, many of whom felt impelled to join his struggle against the wrongs he portrayed" (Whitman 1968). Memorials to Sinclair include his home in Monrovia, California, where he did much of his writing. It is a National Historic Landmark.

See also Addams, Jane; Perkins, Frances; Sacco, Ferdinando Nicola, and Vanzetti, Bartolomeo; Tarbell, Ida

References

Bloodworth, William A. *Upton Sinclair*. Boston: Twayne Publishers, 1978.

Harris, Leon A. *Upton Sinclair, American Rebel*. New York: Crowell, 1975.

Scott, Ivan. *Upton Sinclair: The Forgotten Socialist*. Lanham, MD: University Press of America, 1996.

Sinclair, Upton. *Autobiography*. New York: Harcourt, Brace, & World, 1962.

Sinclair, Upton. *The Jungle*, 2006. (In the public domain.) Project Gutenberg e-book, released March 11, 2006.

Sinclair, Upton. *My Lifetime in Letters*. Columbia: University of Missouri Press, 1960.

Sinclair, Upton Beall. *Mental Radio*. Forgotten Books, 2008. http://www.forgottenbooks.org (accessed September 27, 2010). First published 1930 by Albert and Charles Boni.

Whitman, Alden. "Upton Sinclair, Author, Dead; Crusader for Social Justice, 90: Rebel with a Cause." *New York Times*, November 26, 1968. http://www.nytimes.com/learning/general/onthisday/bday/0920.html (accessed September 28, 2010).

Sontag, Susan (1933–2004)

"Politics, the politics of a democracy—which entails disagreement, which promotes candor—has been replaced by psychotherapy. Let's by all means grieve together. But let's not be stupid together. A few shreds of historical awareness might help us understand what has just happened, and what may continue to happen. 'Our country is strong,' we are told again and again. I for one don't find this entirely consoling. Who doubts that America is strong? But that's not all America has to be" (Sontag 2001). So wrote Susan Sontag on the U.S. reaction to the September 11, 2001, attacks on the World Trade Center. Her comments ignited widespread criticism, but writer and filmmaker Gary Indiana (born Hoisington), in his 2004 memorial of Sontag, defended her: "Certainly she felt the same revulsion and horror at the atrocity of 9-11 that any New Yorker, any citizen of the world, did. But she also had the moral scruple to connect the attacks to generally untelevised, lethal American actions abroad, to the indiscriminate carnage that has typified both state policy and terrorist violence in the new century" (Indiana 2004).

A second-generation Jewish American, Susan Sontag was born Susan Rosenblatt on January 16, 1933, in New York City to parents Jack Rosenblatt and Mildred Jacobsen. Because her father worked as a fur trader in Northern China, her parents experienced long separations. During the Japanese invasion in 1938, when Sontag was five, her father died of tuberculosis while overseas. Because her sister Judith suffered from asthma, Sontag's mother moved to Tucson, Arizona. In 1945, after moving to Los Angeles, Mildred met and married navy captain Nathan Sontag. While Nathan did not formally adopt Susan or her younger sister Judith, Susan took his surname.

Sontag learned to read at age three, so she was told. By the time she was six, she was reading profusely, including biographies and travel books. After reading the biography of Madame Curie, Sontag decided to become a chemist, then a physician. However, literature 'swamped' her. As Sontag explained to interviewer Edward Hirsch, "What I really wanted was every kind of life, and the writer's life seemed the most inclusive" (Hirsch 1995).

Because Sontag could already read and write, she was placed directly into the third grade. Later, she was skipped another semester. As a result, Sontag graduated from North Hollywood High School when she was 15. Soon thereafter, she enrolled at the University of California, Berkeley. After a semester, she transferred to the Hutchins College of the University of Chicago.

While at the University of Chicago, she studied with political philosopher Leo Strauss and the philosopher Richard McKeon. One of her most influential teachers was literary theorist and philosopher Kenneth Burke. Burke taught Sontag how to "unpack" a text "word by word, image by image." This process of deconstructing a text laid the foundation by which she would later write her explorations into art and modern culture. Burke's influence is also seen in *The Benefactor* (1963), Sontag's first novel (Hirsch 1995).

In her sophomore year, 17-year-old Sontag walked into the classroom of sociologist Philip Rieff, 10 years her senior. They married 10 days later. Her reasons for marrying at such a young age were complex. As she wrote in her diary, "I marry Philip with full consciousness [plus] fear of my will toward self-destructiveness." Married life, as Tuhus-Dubrow noted in a review of Sontag's diaries, "appears...as a grim series of claustrophobic quarrels, and her unmet needs haunt her dreams" (Tuhus-Dubrow 2009).

Graduating with a degree in philosophy in 1951, Sontag moved to Cambridge, Massachusetts, where she began her graduate studies at Harvard. In 1952, she bore her only child, David Rieff, the future political analyst and editor of his mother's works at Farrar Straus and Giroux. In 1954, Sontag received her master's degree in English literature, and a year later she received her MA in philosophy. She began her doctoral studies but did not complete her dissertation. During these years, she collaborated with her husband on the study *Freud: The Mind of a Moralist* (1959).

In 1957, Sontag received a fellowship from the Association of American University

Women for postgraduate study at Oxford. However, after one semester, she transferred to the University of Paris. Sontag enjoyed a bohemian circle of friends, expatriate artists and academics. She also resumed an affair with the woman she identifies only as H, "the brash libertine who had initiated her into sex years earlier." As Tuhus-Dubrow states, "[Sontag] never publicly asserted her lesbianism... But her sexuality, along with her intellect, formed, it seems, the core of who she conceived herself to be." Sontag and Rieff were divorced in 1958. She never remarried (Tuhus-Dubrow 2009).

In early 1959, Sontag returned to New York City, now as a single mother. For several years, she worked as an editor at *Commentary* as well as taught philosophy and religion at several colleges, including Sarah Lawrence and Columbia University. From 1959 through the 1960s, she frequently attended parties and other gatherings that included Paul Goodman (1911–1972), whose writing she admired, although she did not like him personally. In an essay "On Paul Goodman," she wrote: "It was his voice, that is to say, his intelligence and the poetry of his intelligence incarnated, which kept me a loyal and passionate" reader (Sontag 1972, 7). In 1964, she left teaching because she felt "academic life destroy[s] the best writers of my generation," and focused full time on her writing (Hirsch 1995). Between 1962 and 1965, Sontag published 26 essays and her first novel, *The Benefactor*. But it was her debut article for the *Partisan Review*, "Notes on Camp," published in 1964, that made her a literary sensation. She addressed gay popular culture through an academic lens, mainstreaming the cultural connotations of the word "camp." As art critic and professor Arthur Danto noted in a 2004 interview with Margalit Fox, Sontag's article "prepared the ground for the pop revolution, which was in many ways essentially a gay revolution. ... She didn't make that art, but she brought it to consciousness." The article earned her several titles, including "The Dark Lady of American Letters." When Sontag published her first essay collection, *Against Interpretation and Other Essays* (1966), her title essay argued that art should be "experienced viscerally rather that cerebrally," cementing her reputation as "a champion of style over content" (Fox 2004).

Her second novel, *Death Kit* (1967), was written in the shadow of the Vietnam War. Sontag describes it as "a book of grief" (Hirsch 1995). In 1968, Sontag embraced revolutionary communism after visiting North Vietnam for two weeks. She reflected on her experience in her book *Trip to Hanoi* (1968), stating that the United States is a "doomed country... founded on genocide" (McGrath 2004).

Sontag wrote many influential works that explored, and often challenged, contemporary culture. Her short-fiction "The Way We Live Now," published in 1986 in the *New Yorker*, addressed the AIDS epidemic. She gained additional success for her historical romance *The Volcano Lover* (1992). In 2000, Sontag won the National Book Award for her historical fiction *In America* (1999). In May 2000, she was accused of plagiarism. Sontag defended her lack of citations and footnotes, as Carvajal suggests, because "[s]he considers it 'a work of art' that belongs to a new genre that doesn't require the footnotes of traditional histories" (Carvajal 2000).

During the mid-1970s, Sontag was diagnosed with stage-four breast cancer that had spread to her lymphatic system. Given six months to live, Sontag had a breast as well as the muscles in her chest and part of an armpit removed. The experience

Susan Sontag burst onto the U.S. literary scene in the early 1960s when she stirred up both admiration and controversy for her creation of a new aesthetic that focused on sensation, immediacy, and style. (AP/Wide World Photos)

influenced her next book, *Illness as Metaphor* (1978). Sontag challenged the public stigma on cancer. As her son David Rieff reflected after her death, the book was a fervent, and somewhat defiant, plea to treat cancer as an illness and not as "the result of sexual inhibition, the repression of feeling, and ... that somehow people who got ill had brought it on themselves" (Rieff 2008).

Ten years later, Sontag expanded her argument in *AIDS and Its Metaphors* (1989), tackling the social stigmas and language surrounding Acquired Immune Deficiency Syndrome (AIDS). At the time, AIDS was still a relatively unknown disease. Little was known about how the disease was transmitted. Much of the community, including the medical community, thought it was linked to gay men. In fact, many referred to it as Gay Related Immune Deficiency (GRID), and "gay cancer."

Although Sontag recovered, she intermittently struggled with cancer the rest of her life. In 1998, Sontag was diagnosed with a uterine sarcoma.

Another of her most important works, *On Photography* (1977) is a collection of six essays that examined the philosophy and ethics of photography. Calling photography an "aggressive act," Sontag called photographers "war tourists and voyeurs," who choose "to record rather than to intervene in the suffering they witnessed," suggesting "that people who look at such photographs were spectators, who had depersonalized their relationship with the world" (Kakutan 2003). The collection won the National Book Critics' Circle Award in 1977.

Sontag continued to bear witness on the war front. In the wake of the 1973 Arab-Israeli War, she visited Israel to make her film *Promised Land* (1974). The documentary explored both the Palestinian and the Israeli perspective on the warfront.

In 1982, Sontag gave a speech during a demonstration for support of the Solidarity movement in Poland. She described European communism as "fascism with a human face" (Fox 2004). Including herself in her denouncement, she stated "much of what is said about politics by people on the so-called democratic left ... has been governed by the wish not to give comfort to 'reactionary' forces ... [as a result] people on the left have willingly or unwillingly told a lot of lies" (*New York Times* 1982). The remarks sparked a debate on the nature of communism.

In 1989, Sontag was president of PEN American Center, the U.S. branch of an international literary and human rights organization, International PEN. The program is also an advocate for writers who are persecuted because of their work. During this time, Ayatollah Ruhollah Khomeini, one of the highest-ranking religious and political authorities in Iran, issued a fatwa (a religious ruling) against British-Indian writer Ahmed Salman Rushdie for his novel *The Satanic Verses* (1988). Many in the Islamic faith, especially fundamentalist groups, claimed that the book gave an irreverent depiction of the Prophet Muhammad. The Ayatollah called the book blasphemous, and offered a bounty for Rushdie's death. Opposition turned violent as many stores that carried the book were bombed and translators were assassinated. The book was banned in many countries with a large Islamic following, including India, Sudan, and South Africa. The controversy led to a break in diplomatic relations between Britain and Iran. Many American writers were reluctant to support Rushdie. However, Sontag remained staunch, even aggressive, in support of literary freedom. As Christopher Hitchens later reflected, "Susan would have none of that, and shamed many more pants wetters whose names I still cannot reveal" (Hitchens 2009).

During the height of the Bosnian War in the early 1990s, Sontag visited Sarajevo more than a dozen times, as the Serb forces from the Republika Srpska and the Yugoslav People's Army besieged the city. While using flashlights and candles, Sontag staged Samuel Beckett's play, *Waiting for Godot*. She criticized Western European powers and the United States for refusing to intervene. As Sontag reflected, "[T]hat's my belief in righteous action ... just do something for other human beings out of a sense of solidarity" (Farnsworth 2001).

Her last book, *Regarding the Pain of Others* (2004), explored war imagery and disasters. She revisited, and at times revised, many of her opinions reflected in her seminal book, *On Photography*. Her May 2004 essay, "Regarding the Torture of Others," was written in response to the psychological and sexual abuse, as well as torture, of Iraqi prisoners by army military police personnel at the Abu Ghraib prison in Iraq.

In 2004, Sontag was diagnosed with myelodysplastic syndrome (MDS), a precursor of an aggressive form of leukemia. She died on December 28, 2004, in Manhattan. Sontag had a 15-year relationship with the celebrated photographer Annie Leibovitz from 1990 until her death. Leibovitz's book, *A Photographer's Life 1990–2005*, included many images of Sontag.

Writer Margalit Fox reflected in her 2004 obituary of Sontag that "public response to Ms. Sontag remained irreconcilably divided. She was described ... as explosive, anticlimactic, original, derivative, naïve, sophisticated, approachable, aloof, condescending, populist, puritanical, sybaritic, sincere, posturing, ascetic, voluptuary, right-wing, left-wing, profound, superficial, ardent, bloodless, dogmatic, ambivalent, lucid, inscrutable, visceral, reasoned, chilly, effusive, relevant, passé, ambivalent, tenacious, ecstatic, melancholic, humorous, humorless, deadpan, rhapsodic, cantankerous and clever. No one ever called her dull" (Fox 2004).

Bobbi Miller

See also Goodman, Paul

References

Carvajal, Doreen. "So Whose Words Are They?" *New York Times*, May 27, 2000. http://partners.nytimes.com/library/books/052700sontag-america.html (accessed January 14, 2011).

Farnsworth, Elizabeth. "Conversation: Susan Sontag." *Online NewsHour*, PBS.org, February 2, 2001. http://www.pbs.org/newshour/

conversation/jan-june01/sontag_02-02.html (accessed January 7, 2011).

Fox, Margalit. "Susan Sontag, Social Critic with Verve, Dies at 71." *New York Times*, December 29, 2004. http://www.nytimes.com/2004/12/28/books/28cnd-sont.html (accessed January 7, 2011).

Hirsch, Edward. "Susan Sontag, the Art of Fiction No. 143." *Paris Review*, Winter 1995. http://www.theparisreview.org/interviews/1505/the-art-of-fiction-no-143-susan-sontag (accessed January 14, 2011).

Hitchens, Christopher. "Assassins of the Mind." *Vanity Fair*, February 2009. http://www.vanityfair.com/politics/features/2009/02/hitchens200902 (accessed January 9, 2011).

Indiana, Gary. "Susan Sontag (1933–2004): Remembering the Voice of Moral Responsibility—and Unembarrassed Hedonism." *Village Voice*, December 28, 2004. http://www.villagevoice.com/2004-12-28/news/susan-sontag-1933-2004/ (accessed January 15, 2011).

Kakutam, Michiko. "Books of the Times: A Writer Who Begs to Differ . . . With Herself." *New York Times*, March 11, 2003.

McGrath, Charles. "A Rigorous Intellectual Dressed in Glamour." *New York Times*, December 29, 2004. http://www.nytimes.com/2004/12/29/books/29appr.html (accessed January 14, 2011).

Mitgang, Herbert. "Victory in the Ashes of Vietnam?" *New York Times*, February 4, 1969. http://www.nytimes.com/books/00/03/12/specials/sontag-vietnams.html (accessed January 14, 2011).

Movius, Geoffrey. "Interview with Susan Sontag." *Boston Review: A Political and Literary Forum*, June 1975. http://bostonreview.net/BR01.1/sontag.php (accessed January 14, 2011).

Rieff, David. "Why I Had to Lie to My Dying Mother." *Observer*, May 18, 2008. http://www.guardian.co.uk/books/2008/may/18/society (accessed January 9, 2011).

Sontag, Susan. *Against Interpretation and Other Essays*. New York: Farrar, Straus and Giroux, 1966.

Sontag, Susan. "Regarding the Torture of Others." *New York Times*, May 23, 2004. http://www.nytimes.com/2004/05/23/magazine/regarding-the-torture-of-others.html (accessed January 9, 2011).

Sontag, Susan. "The Talk of the Town." *New Yorker*, September 24, 2001. http://www.newyorker.com/archive/2001/09/24/010924ta_talk_wtc (accessed January 15, 2011).

Sontag, Susan. *Under the Sign of Saturn: Essays*. New York: Picador USA/Farrar, Straus, and Giroux, 2002. First published 1972.

"Susan Sontag Provokes Debate on Communism." *New York Times*, February 27, 1982. http://www.nytimes.com/books/00/03/12/specials/sontag-communism.html (accessed January 15, 2011).

Tuhus-Dubrow, Rebecca. "Self-Portrait: Susan Sontag's Early Years." *Dissent*, February 5, 2009. http://www.dissentmagazine.org/online.php?id=203 (accessed January 9, 2011).

Steinmetz, Charles (1865–1923)

The name Steinmetz is associated with a great variety of electrical engineering feats and inventions, and Charles Steinmetz, a German immigrant who came to the United States when he was 24 years old, was called an "electrical wizard." He also was an ardent socialist who publicly proclaimed his dissident views about capitalism in the late 1800s and early 1900s. He was especially concerned about unequal pay for workers and he advocated a four-hour workday. In addition, he believed that social insurance should be available for "the old, the sick,

[and] the unemployed," paid for by industries (Garlin 1991, 51). Yet, wealthy General Electric (GE) executives with whom he worked in the United States were among his friends, and in a humorous fashion, he chided them and other corporate executives about their high salaries.

When Charles Steinmetz was born on April 9, 1865, in Breslau, Germany, he was named Karl (or Carl) August Rudolph Steinmetz. His parents were Carl Heinrich and Carolyn Neubert Steinmetz. His mother died a year after his birth, and his father sent for Karl's grandmother to care for his children. Karl's fraternal grandmother, whom he called "grossmutter," became his substitute mother while he was growing up in Breslau, which is now Wroclaw, Poland. She had an affectionate nickname for him—Carluszek—and she adored her grandson. His aunt Julia, "Tante Julia," also was part of the household as were Karl's older sisters, Marie and Clara (Hammond 2008, 17).

The family lived in an apartment house in a primarily middle-class neighborhood; residents were Protestant and politically conservative. Karl had a pleasant childhood and from all accounts apparently was well accepted by most of his peers. However, he had to deal with kyphosis, a severe curvature of the spine, a handicap that he inherited from his father. He also was unusually short—a little more than four feet in adulthood. "Although this restricted his physical activity, it did not prevent him from enjoying canoeing, swimming, biking, and other outdoor pursuits, which he loved and engaged in throughout his life" (Union Notable).

In the early elementary grades, Carl showed little promise as a student, but that changed when he was 10 years old and he "became one of the school's brightest students" (Flynn). He studied and became proficient in five languages: Latin, French, Greek, Polish, and Hebrew. He went on to higher education at the University of Breslau, where he studied in diverse fields ranging from astronomy to mathematics to political science. Because he was proficient in so many academic fields, his fellow students nicknamed him "Proteus" after a Greek god in mythology who was able to change his form whenever he chose. Steinmetz wrote articles for German scientific journals, providing recognition among scientists in other parts of the world. He also was a member of the Socialist Party and editor of a socialist newspaper, *Volksstimme* (*People's Voice*). The kind of socialism he embraced was not that envisioned by Karl Marx, who saw socialism as the first step toward communism. Instead, Steinmetz and other party members believed in a socialism that would create a utopia without war, poverty, and inequality. However, being a socialist brought unwanted attention from the government.

German chancellor Otto von Bismarck had passed a law meant to counter the socialist and workers' movement and made the Social-Democratic Party of Germany illegal. The law also prohibited all party and mass workers' organizations, and the socialist and workers' press; socialist literature was confiscated, and Social-Democrats were subjected to reprisals.

About to be arrested in 1888 for his connections to socialism, Steinmetz quickly left for Zurich, Switzerland. There, "he enrolled as a student of mechanical engineering at the Federal Institute of Technology" and met a fellow socialist, Oscar Asmussen. The two became friends and in 1889, Asmussen offered to pay passage to the United States for Steinmetz, who was almost penniless (Garlin 1991, 53). The two traveled together across the Atlantic.

Upon arrival in New York, Steinmetz was shunted aside; officials took one look at his deformed body and disheveled appearance and were ready to deny him entry to the United States. But his friend Asmussen convinced authorities that Steinmetz was a rich genius, and the official allowed Steinmetz to immigrate.

Steinmetz had a letter of introduction addressed to Rudolph Eickenmeyer, an electrical engineer, who helped Steinmetz find a job in Yonkers, New York, at the Osterheld and Eickenmeyer Company. Eickenmeyer and Steinmetz found they had interests in common both in work and politics. For three years, Steinmetz worked in Eickenmeyer's factory, developing a number of electrical devices. About this time, he officially changed his given name and became Charles Proteus Steinmetz.

In 1892, at the age of 27, Steinmetz explained the complex Law of Hysteresis at a meeting of electrical engineers. "The law let engineers know before building an electrically powered machine just how much power loss would occur due to magnetism," wrote Doris Kilbane in *Electronic Design* (Kilbane 2006, 76).

When Thomas Edison, founder of General Electric (GE), tried to hire Steinmetz, the engineer would not leave Eickenmeyer's company. So Edison bought the firm and merged it, its patents, and Steinmetz into GE. From 1893 until his death, Steinmetz worked as chief consulting engineer at GE in Schenectady, New York, and also at a huge laboratory that GE built for him at his Schenectady home on Wendell Avenue.

Steinmetz shared his home with a large number of feathered and furry friends—pet crows, squirrels, cranes, raccoons, dogs, and even alligators. He obviously loved animals and also the outdoors. He built a campsite on the Mohawk River and in the summer entertained guests on weekends. He especially liked having children around as he never married, fearing that if he fathered children, they would inherit his deformity. In 1905, he legally adopted Joseph L. Hayden, a young engineer who had been his assistant for several years. When Hayden married Corinne Rost, Steinmetz shared his home with the couple. The Haydens had three children—Joseph, Margaret, William—and they became his foster grandchildren.

Some of Steinmetz's endeavors included the development of high-powered motors

Charles Proteus Steinmetz's theories of alternating current, worked out in complete mathematical detail, have been credited with facilitating the rapid expansion of the U.S. electric power industry at the start of the 1900s. After his arrival in this country, he worked for the General Electric Company (GE) for the rest of his short life. He had more than 200 patents to his name, one of which was a design for "man-made lightning" that made him a celebrity. (Library of Congress)

for elevators, generators for the power station at Niagara Falls, arc lights used to illuminate U.S. cities, the use of alternating current to run trolley cars, and a method to protect overhead wires and other electrical equipment during lightning strikes. As his biographer put it: "Steinmetz's inventions had none of the popular appeal of Edison's, [but] he nevertheless solved hundreds of problems that had puzzled engineers for years, in the designing of transformers, motors, and generators, and the distribution of electricity for greater distances at higher voltage" (Garlin 1991, 55–56).

One widely publicized accomplishment was a lightning generator, developed in 1916. Steinmetz created lightning in his laboratory and demonstrated it dramatically for the press.

> The newspapers loved it, with headlines calling him "Modern Jove" and "The Thunderer" after the ancient god of lightning and thunder.
>
> And General Electric's publicity machine loved it, too, but for more than the immediate good news value. GE used Steinmetz and his lightning generator to promote a massive advertising campaign to sell electrical consumer goods based on their utility, safety, and modernity. The universal electrification of America had begun. (*Union College News* 1998)

While at GE, Steinmetz registered nearly 200 patents for his inventions, all in GE's name. He had no misgivings about the ownership of the patents or the fact that his inventions did not bring him great wealth. In fact, he made clear that any invention he produced came about because of data and equipment provided by the corporation, and his pay from the company was all that was due him.

Along with his work for GE, Steinmetz also taught electrical engineering as a part-time professor at Union College in Schenectady. In addition, he renewed his interest in socialism when Socialist George P. Lunn was elected mayor of Schenectady in 1911. Lunn appointed Steinmetz to the city's board of education, which he served for six years, four of them as president. On the board, Steinmetz acted on his utopian socialist beliefs by initiating construction of more schools and establishing programs to feed undernourished children, teach English to immigrant children, set up special classes for disabled children, and provide free textbooks for elementary schools.

Steinmetz continued his association with the Socialist Party, and in 1913, he became president of the city's board of parks and city planning. According to a feature in *Union College News*: "He carried out his party's desire for more city parks accessible to Schenectady's working class by securing a bond issue and recommending the purchase of three properties for parks; oddly, one park had to be pushed through the process using the mayor's political clout because local party members felt it would benefit the middle and upper class more than the workers" (*Union College News* 1998).

In other socialist activities, Steinmetz served on the advisory council for the socialist weekly magazine the *New Review*. His colleagues on the council included his friend, Eugene V. Debs (1855–1926), who was the Socialist Party's candidate for president four times, and W. E. B. Du Bois (1868–1963), who strongly supported the Socialist Party as well as the communist Soviet Union.

Steinmetz was particularly interested in the electrification program of the Soviet Union and, in February 1922, sent a letter to Vladimir Lenin, leader of the Communist

Party, offering electrical engineering help. In April, Lenin responded with a letter to Steinmetz, thanking him for his offer of help and pointing out that Steinmetz's

> sympathies with Soviet Russia have been aroused, on the one hand, by your social and political views. On the other hand, as a representative of electrical engineering and particularly in one of the technically advanced countries, you have become convinced of the necessity and inevitability of the replacement of capitalism by a new social order, which will establish the planned regulation of economy and ensure the welfare of the entire mass of the people on the basis of the electrification of entire countries. In all the countries of the world there is growing—more slowly than one would like, but irresistibly and unswervingly—the number of representatives of science, technology, art, who are becoming convinced of the necessity of replacing capitalism by a different socio-economic system. (Lenin 1976)

Lenin declined the offer of help, citing the lack of official relations between Soviet Russia and the United States. Steinmetz and Lenin corresponded a few more times, although in mid-1922, Lenin had a stroke followed by several more strokes that year. (He died in 1924.)

Steinmetz continued following events in the Soviet Union and supported various Soviet causes such as food aid through the American Committee on Soviet Relief. His efforts alienated some Americans. As biographer Hammond noted, Steinmetz's support for the Soviet Union and Lenin "did not add to the prestige of Dr. Steinmetz in the opinion of many persons who fail to sympathize with the Soviet point of view" (Hammond 2006, 319).

Although GE, which employed Steinmetz, had little sympathy with the Soviets, they had no intention of releasing their famous and valuable scientist. He worked for the company until his death. Steinmetz died in his sleep at his Schenectady home on October 26, 1923.

See also Debs, Eugene V.; Du Bois, W. E. B.

References

Berardinis, Larry. "Chalk One Up for Math." *Motion System Design*, May 2004.

"Charles Steinmetz: Union's Electrical Wizard." *Union College News*, November 1, 1998. http://www.union.edu/N/DS/s.php?s=1512 (accessed March 29, 2011).

Flynn, Tom. "Charles Proteus Steinmetz, Inventor." YonkersHistory.org, n.d. http://www.yonkershistory.org/stein.html (accessed March 27, 2011).

Garlin, Sender. *Three American Radicals: John Swinton, Crusading Editor; Charles P. Steinmetz, Scientist and Socialist; William Dean Howells and the Haymarket Era*. Boulder, CO: Westview Press, 1991.

Hammond, John Winthrop. *Charles Proteus Steinmetz: A Biography*. Reprint ed. Kennsinger Publishing, 2006. First published by the Century Company, 1924.

Kilbane, Doris. "Charles Proteus Steinmetz: Genius, Freethinker." *Electronic Design*, October 20, 2006.

Lenin, V. I. *Lenin Collected Works*. Moscow: Progress Publishers, 1976. First published in *Pravda*, April 19, 1922. http://www.marxists.org/archive/lenin/works/1922/apr/10cps.htm (accessed March 29, 2011).

Steinmetz, Charles Proteus. *America and the New Epoch*. New York and London: Harper & Brothers, 1916.

"Union Notable—Charles Proteus Steinmetz." Mandeville Gallery, Union College, n.d. http://www.union.edu/Resources/Campus/mandeville/notables/profiles/steinmetz.php (accessed March 27, 2011).

Strong, Anna Louise (1885–1970)

Anna Louise Strong "was a press agent for some of this century's least attractive people," wrote a reporter for the *New York Times*. She "was an American radical who settled in the Soviet Union in 1921 and promptly fell in love with totalitarianism" (Corry 1986). Although not an actual paid publicist, Strong was a journalist and a socialist, who often depicted the Soviet Union and China and their Communist regimes in favorable terms. She was also a pacifist, outspoken in her opposition to World War I and the military draft. In addition, she supported labor unions, especially the Industrial Workers of the World (IWW) or "Wobblies," and was an advocate for child welfare.

The eldest of four children, Anna was born in Friend, Nebraska, on November 24, 1885, to Sydney and Ruth Tracy Strong. *Time* magazine reported that in tornado-prone Nebraska, Anna was once blown off a porch when a tornado hit, sending the youngster flying into a cow pasture. She recalled being more frightened by the cows than the whirlwind weather.

Sidney and Ruth Strong were devout Christians and were active in social justice and outreach programs, moving about the country as missionary activists. When Anna was two years old, the family moved to Ohio, where her mother began organizing clubs urging women to be independent. Strong encouraged her children's education by playing word games and reading to them at the dinner table. Anna was a highly intelligent child and at the age of six, she was writing poetry. She attended school in Ohio until 1896, when the family moved to Oak Park, Illinois, a western suburb of Chicago, and she enrolled in high school there, graduating at age 14.

She planned to attend highly progressive Oberlin College, in Oberlin, Ohio, her mother's alma mater, but she was not allowed to enroll until she was 16. Her parents sent her to Europe in the interim to study and learn languages. In 1902, she entered Oberlin and, in three years, earned a degree. After graduation, she returned to Oak Park to live with her father; her mother had died in 1902 while she was at Oberlin.

She took a job with the *Advance*, a religious newspaper in Chicago, and wrote news items for women's pages and some poetry. Strong lost her job after six months, which was a tremendous blow since her editor had praised her work. She subsequently learned that the newspaper routinely hired college graduates to take advantage of their talents to increase subscriptions, and then fired the rookies and repeated the process. The experience prompted her to continue her education and study at the University of Chicago for a doctorate in philosophy. Within a few months of her studies, she discovered that she hated "the dry philosophy" courses at the university. But she received a PhD magna cum laude in the field at the age of 23.

Two years later, Strong moved to Seattle, Washington, where her father had relocated to serve as a pastor. Seattle appealed to the Strongs because of its progressive politics and social programs. In Seattle, she organized "Know Your City" tours and discussion groups about civic affairs. These events were so popular and well publicized that Strong set up similar seminars in other cities and soon became well known for her educational and organizational skills.

In 1909, Strong moved to New York to take a job with the Russell Sage Foundation, a social science research center aimed at improving U.S. social and living conditions and developing social work as a profession.

It was a period in the nation's history known as the "Progressive Era," when numerous groups and individuals called for economic and social justice for the nation's poor and powerless. Many reform groups fought to establish compulsory education for children. Others agitated for a decent wage, shorter workdays, and better working conditions for laborers.

One nonpartisan and broad-based reform group was the National Child Labor Committee (NCLC), which Strong joined in 1910. The following year, she developed Child Welfare Exhibits for the U.S. Department of Labor Children's Bureau. A New York exhibit, for example, was designed to "show all the influences affecting the welfare of children in the city." It "gave rise to a series of similar exhibits in Chicago, Kansas City, Northampton, St. Louis, Buffalo, Montreal, Louisville, Providence, Knoxville, Rochester, New Britain, Peoria, Toledo, Seattle, Indianapolis, and Dublin (Ireland), and many smaller places," according to a brochure that Strong prepared (Strong 1915, 7). Exhibits varied in content, with some focusing on infant welfare, others on children's health, or still others presenting comprehensive educational materials about the entire well-being of a community's children, including health, recreation, education, and problems of delinquent young people.

While traveling for exhibits, Strong met and became engaged to Roger Baldwin of Kansas City, but the couple broke up within a year. When she was on the West Coast, Strong decided not to return to Washington, D.C., and instead made a home in Seattle. She established herself as part of the community, joining or founding several organizations. One example was the Washington Alpine Club (WAC), which she set up to encourage mountain camping and climbing. She was an avid mountaineer and led a Mount Hood climb and was a guide for Mount Rainier hikers. She ran for and won election to the Seattle school board. She also wrote for local newspapers. Her reporting for the *Seattle Daily Call*, a socialist weekly, set her on course for radical journalism as she covered the labor movement and the IWW, which was flourishing in the "Soviet of Washington," as the U.S. postmaster general called the state.

Strong was on hand to report on the infamous 1916 Everett Massacre, "a tragedy that horrified the world!" noted one newspaper headline. Members of the shingle workers union in Everett (north of Seattle) had been on strike for months and were demonstrating for better working conditions—their jobs consisted of cutting cedar blocks for shingles on rapidly moving circular saws that often took fingers and hands along with the wood. The IWW repeatedly sent supporters for the strikers, but they were accosted by sheriff deputies who beat and jailed or chased the Wobblies out of town. On November 5, 250 Wobblies sailed by ferry from Seattle to Everett, and at the dock, a mob of local police, hired company guards, and citizen deputies were ready to stop them. An all-out gun battle ensued, ending in seven dead—two deputies and five IWW members—and 50 wounded.

When the Wobblies returned to Seattle, 74 of them were arrested and tried for murder. All eventually were acquitted. Strong covered the trial, and her reporting in the *Daily Call* favored the IWW, which quickly prompted her recall from the Seattle school board. The trial and her board recall contributed to her increasing radicalism, which she soon demonstrated by joining the IWW and, after the *Daily Call* declared bankruptcy, accepting an editorial job with the *Seattle Union Record*, where she focused on labor, human rights, women's issues, and social change.

Another radicalizing event for Strong was the U.S. entry into World War I in April 1917. Like dissidents such as Emma Goldman and Eugene V. Debs, Strong spoke out fervently against the draft and military training in schools. With other radicals, including her former editors, she helped write a pamphlet "No Conscription! No Involuntary Servitude!" which led to the trial of all involved. Strong was not convicted, but her compatriots were sentenced to two years in prison.

After World War I ended, she concentrated on worker issues and was adamant in her support of labor during the events surrounding the General Strike of 1919, a strike of more than 65,000 workers in numerous industries across the city. The strike lasted only one week but set off reactions against the IWW and what opponents called a communist conspiracy; it was the beginning of a "Red Scare" in the country.

In 1921, Strong traveled to Poland and Russia to report on the relief services of the American Friends Service Committee and also to write articles for North American newspapers. Her observations increasingly led her to embrace socialism and the Union of the Soviet Socialist Republics (USSR), established in 1922 by the Communist Party.

During the decades of the 1920s and 1930s, Strong seemed in perpetual motion, not only visiting with Soviet leaders in Moscow, but also traveling to China, Mexico, Spain, and back to Soviet Central Asia to meet with revolutionaries. She became known as an expert on Soviet affairs, and when in the United States, she spoke to business leaders about investing in USSR industries.

By 1930, she was an ardent supporter of —some say an apologist for—the Soviet system and founded the *Moscow Daily News*, a Soviet-backed English-language newspaper that circulated within English-speaking countries. In 1932, she married Joel Shubin, an agronomist and socialist who was killed 10 years later in World War II.

Strong returned to the United States periodically to lecture and sometimes write features for major publications. She also wrote a number of books throughout the two decades, including *The First Time in History: Two Years of Russia's New Life* (1924), *Children of Revolution* (1925), *China's Millions* (1928), *Red Star in Samarkand* (1929), *The Soviets Conquer Wheat* (1931), *I Change Worlds* (1934), *This Soviet World* (1936), and *The Soviet Constitution* (1937); interspersed were books of poetry, drama, and stories as well as religious tracts. Although many of her books praised the USSR, she was disillusioned when Stalin initiated purges of dissidents and repression of opponents beginning in 1936. Nevertheless, she did not give up on her belief that a communist (lower "c") system could work to bring about social justice.

Her prolific writing continued for the next 30 years, with dozens of books as well as hundreds of articles published. Strong traveled extensively, visiting the USSR, Yugoslavia, Poland, and China as well as Mexico and Guatemala. The highlight of one trip to China was a long interview with Communist Party chairman Mao Zedong in 1946 at his headquarters, a room dug into a cave in the Yenen Mountains. Favorable accounts of the Chinese Communist Revolution followed in her articles and books, such as *The Chinese Conquer China* (1949), which included criticism of the USSR's communist leaders. When she returned to the USSR, officials arrested her, accusing her of spying for the United States, an unsubstantiated charge. In 1949, after six days in jail, she was expelled to Poland and then went on to the United States, where her passport was revoked because of the Soviet accusation; the charges eventually were withdrawn, and by 1956, she had regained her passport and was on her way to China once more.

In China, she met with Communist Party officials and Tibetan leaders. While in Asia, she traveled to Laos and Vietnam and interviewed Ho Chi-Minh. Chinese leaders honored Strong with an 80th birthday party in 1965. By this time, she was not in good health and was having difficulty writing. Yet in 1968, she began to write a second autobiography and planned to return to the United States to lecture about China. But those goals were not reached. She died in Beijing, China, on March 29, 1970, and was eulogized by newspapers worldwide as a foremost Asian journalist.

See also Debs, Eugene V.; Goldman, Emma

References

"Communists: Sentimental Journey." *Time*, February 28, 1949. http://www.time.com/time/magazine/article/0,9171,799831,00.html (accessed March 15, 2010).

Corry, John. "TV: 'Witness to Revolution,' Anna Louise Strong." *New York Times*, March 22, 1986. http://www.nytimes.com/1986/03/22/arts/tv-witness-to-revolution-anna-louise-strong.html (accessed April 26, 2010).

Nies, Judith. *Nine Women: Portraits from the American Radical Tradition*. Berkeley, Los Angeles, and London: University of California Press, 2002.

Strong, Anna Louise. *Child-Welfare Exhibits: Types and Preparation*. Washington, DC: U.S. Department of Labor Children's Bureau, 1915.

Strong, Anna Louise. *I Change Worlds*. New York: Henry Holt, 1935.

Strong, Anna Louise. *I Saw the New Poland*. Boston: Little, Brown and Company in Association with Atlantic Monthly Press, 1946.

Strong, Tracy B., and Keyssar, Helene. *Right in Her Soul: Life of Anna Louise Strong*. New York: Random House, 1983.

T

Tall, JoAnn (1953–)

"The whole focus that I've always worked on as a grassroots environmentalist is that you do not tear up Mother Earth." JoAnn Tall's words reflect her own beliefs, as well as an overarching Lakota philosophy of the Oglala Lakota Tribe of which she is a member. To this day, Tall lives on the Pine Ridge Reservation located in the Black Hills of South Dakota. In 1993, she was awarded the Goldman Environmental Prize for her protests against uranium mining and plans for testing nuclear weapons in the Black Hills. Each year, six grassroots environmental activists, one from each of six geographic areas (Africa, Asia, Europe, Islands and Island Nations, North America, and South and Central America), receive this honor. "The Prize seeks to inspire other ordinary people to take extraordinary actions to protect the natural world" (Goldman Environmental Prize web site).

Except for the year 1953, there is no exact date on record for Tall's birth. However, there is a record of the time when she was 12 years old and forced to leave the Pine Ridge Reservation to attend a Christian boarding school. Such schools were set up with the intent of assimilating Indians into the Anglo-Saxon culture, and children were required to speak English, worship as Christians, and often were abused physically, mentally, and sexually. In a YouTube presentation filmed in 2007, JoAnn recalled: "It was a school that was there, I guess, to set us on the right path.... They said that we had to get saved. From what I don't know.... The indoctrination part of it, we had church three times a day, breakfast, noon, and evening after our chores.... I started walking out; I wanted to go home" (Tall 2007).

JoAnn got as far as the entrance gate of the school, but the principal had followed her in a car and forced her to get in and return to the home where he and his wife lived. The couple told her she had to be punished for trying to run away. That punishment was severe. The principal made her kneel down and began "spanking" her with a board from her lower back to the back of her legs, saying all the time that God loved her. The beating went on "until I fell over," JoAnn said through tears. "It made me angry at the same time. I was just a little girl." There was no family to protect her and "when I look back to that time ... my spirit was almost broken." Yet, she recalled "because of the sacredness of the Black Hills, that was the Southern Black Hills, that somehow the spirits had to have their hands over me to make me survive that physical abuse, mental abuse that I went through during that time" (Tall 2007).

The Lakota hold a great reverence for the land and, in particular, believe in the sacredness of the Black Hills. To understand how Tall became involved in environmental activism, one first must know something of the history of her people. The Lakota is an Indian Nation consisting of seven subtribes, one of which is the Oglala. They were originally referred to as the Dakota when they lived in the Great Lakes region of the United States and are also known as the Sioux. Increasingly encroached upon by non-Indian settlers, the tribe eventually moved westward. Today, Oglala peoples live both on and off the Pine Ridge Reservation.

The continued westward expansion brought growing tension between Indian tribes and the United States, sometimes escalating into bloodshed. In the mid-nineteenth century, the United States constructed a garrison on Lakota land. Hoping to ensure safe passage of those traversing the Oregon Trail, the United States signed the Fort Laramie Treaty of 1951 with the Lakota and other tribes, giving the Indians sovereignty over the Great Plains. The Lakota took issue with the increasing presence of settlers in their territories, and ongoing attacks against settlers prompted repeated retaliation. Additionally, because they considered the Black Hills sacred, the Lakota objected to the increased mining taking place there. The Fort Laramie Treaty of 1868 exempted the Black Hills from white settlement for perpetuity, but the discovery of gold redefined "perpetuity" to mean four years. Hordes of prospectors flocked to the area. The Indians attacked the miners, and the U.S. military responded accordingly.

The Battle of the Little Bighorn involving the ignominious defeat of General George Custer took place during this time frame (the late 1870s). But the Indians' success was short-lived. Congress appropriated funds to strengthen the army's efforts, and soon the Lakota were living on reservations, unable to hunt buffalo and dependent upon the government for basic sustenance. Over time, restrictions were placed on Lakota customs and religious practices, and thereafter, occasional skirmishes occurred.

On December 15, 1890, Sitting Bull was killed at Standing Rock Reservation. He had been a major leader of Lakota resistance, commanding the forces that defeated Custer at Little Bighorn. The infamous Wounded Knee Massacre occurred two weeks later, resulting in the deaths of at least 150 Lakota men, women, and children, with dozens more wounded; at least two dozen armed officers died, with many more suffering injuries. In more recent times, conflict broke out again at Wounded Knee in 1973 when a 71-day siege ensued. Tall played a role in this modern-day protest, as did Lakota leader Russell Means and such supporters as black comedian Dick Gregory. In fact, this would be the germination of Tall's activism.

On February 27, 1973, a group of armed Native Indians reclaimed the infamous area of Wounded Knee in the name of the Lakota Nation. They were spurred on and supported by members of the American Indian Movement (AIM), an activist organization founded in 1968. Tall was a member of this group that sought to address Native American issues such as poverty, housing, treaty concerns, and harassment. Over 75 Indian nations joined the cause. The U.S. government sent federal marshals and National Guardsmen to the scene. Although they blocked all routes in and out of Wounded Knee, supporters found their way into the seized area. The Indians demanded investigations into the misuse of tribal funds and into alleged retribution against people who had spoken against the tribal council. They demanded a Senate hearing on the Bureau of Indian Affairs (BIA) and the Department of the Interior, as well as an investigation into all treaties between the Native nations and the U.S. government, which they said had been dishonored. Until their demands were met, the Indians said they would not end the siege. The government cut off the electricity and attempted to cut off all access to those at Wounded Knee, including delivery of basic supplies of food and medicine. Gunfire was exchanged on both sides on an ongoing basis; two AIM members died as a result. The standoff finally ended on May 8, 1973.

According to Tall, her participation in the siege was limited to delivering food and medicine. She was the sole female member from a group of two dozen from Pine Ridge to go to Wounded Knee in March 1973. This involvement—what she considered her first true protest effort—was a turning point. While the gunfire was going on at night, she:

> was just crawling on the ground, you know, and when the flares were going up, it just made me think ... why should I be crawling around like this? This is my land, you know, and I have every right to be here. It was dealing with that fear of losing your life and fear of the authority of the government that I had to come to terms with. But during that time going into Wounded Knee, I did come to terms with it. Once I had done that, then I was okay ... I would say that in my whole career, all my twenty-two years of being a leader and organizer on all kinds of issues, that was the one experience that strengthened me for all the other struggles.... It started there at Wounded Knee. I made a commitment in '73 at that time that I would always stand up for my people and do what I can, even if it is laying life on the line for my people. That is how much I believe in appreciating the identity that was given back to me, the identity that I got back in my growing spirituality. This is the Lakota way of thought. Our belief that when you are given something you always give back to the people. That's just how it is. (Prazniak 2001, 255–56)

After the siege ended, Tall went underground, fleeing to Canada. Despite her claims of carrying only food and medicine, the government believed she had supplied the resisters with weapons. In May 1974, she returned to the United States. The FBI soon found her and tried to get her to testify against some of those held responsible for the siege. She again fled, this time to the Mohawk Indian community in New York. She stayed there until 1975. By then, the Wounded Knee trials were over and all charges had been dropped, so she could safely return to her sacred hills. After a year attending the Red School, immersed in Indian tradition and lore, she went home to Pine Ridge in 1976.

Once back on the reservation, Tall helped found the Native Resource Coalition (NRC), dedicated to research and education for the Lakota people on issues of land, health, and the environment. Tall also became an active member of the Black Hills Alliance (BHA), which was formed in 1979 in response to escalating iron and uranium prospecting in the hills of South Dakota. This group was made up of Lakota Sioux, white environmentalists, Black Hills residents, farmers, and some off-reservation ranchers, all of whom shared the belief in protecting the land and water resources. They investigated and tracked the records of uranium companies looking to mine in the region. Businessmen in a nearby town were "fighting to bury up to 1 million cubic feet of low-level nuclear waste each year under the rolling grasslands of southwestern South Dakota. The businessmen say a nuclear waste dump could mean up to 300 new jobs in the area, almost doubling the employment in this community of 1,200 people" (Brokaw 1984). On the reservation, the opposition argument that BHA was positing could be an especially difficult one to make when the tribe was faced with so much poverty and unemployment. However, the Indians in BHA were particularly resistant to development schemes that would involve the sacrifice of either their land or their sovereignty. On July 7, 1979, BHA held a 25-mile protest march and drew about 11,000 from South Dakota and neighboring states, garnering national attention to its cause.

In early 1990, Amcor, a waste disposal firm in Connecticut, wanted to locate a landfill and incinerator at Pine Ridge. Tall was an uninvited guest at the tribal council's meeting with the company at the Rapid City Hilton on June 21. For years, Tall and some other members of the tribe had opposed council leaders who allowed strip mining on the reservation, accusing them of working against the best interests of their people and acting, instead, at the behest of the BIA, that is, the U.S. government. At the Rapid City meeting, Tall pointed out that the council members were not reading the disposal company's proposal and were being influenced by corporate wining and dining. Eventually, Amcor's proposal was rejected. Tall then turned her efforts to helping neighboring Rosebud Reservation defeat a similar proposition.

Tall was part of a notable protest that began on May 6, 1992. She was one of the original board members of KILI, the first-ever Indian-controlled, Indian-owned, and Indian-run radio station. Its mission was and is to keep the tradition of the Oglala Lakota alive. It broadcasts in both the tribe's native language as well as English and provides information that the tribal council (that to this day is supported by the BIA) might want suppressed. The station is known as "the voice of the Lakota Nation" and is located at Porcupine Butte, about 10 miles from Wounded Knee. The '92 protesters established a camp of tepees and demanded the resignation of the white station manager and for programming to reflect the tribe's culture, traditions, and tongue (Baum 1992).

Currently, Tall is on the board of directors for the Seventh Generation Fund for Indian Development. The organization promotes and maintains the uniqueness of Native peoples throughout the Americas; its name is derived from "a precept of the Great Law of Peace of the Haudenosaunee (Six Nations Iroquois Confederacy) which mandates that chiefs consider the impact of their decisions on the seventh generation yet to come" (Seventh Generation Fund web site). Tall is looked upon as an elder, educator, and adviser, someone who inspires "both native and non-native people around the world to protect the environment" (Goldman Prize web site).

Margaret Gay

See also Gregory, Dick; Means, Russell

References

Baum, Dan. "Protest Broadcasts Displeasure with KILI Radio—Activists Want 'Voice of the Lakota Nation' to Return to Programming Rooted in Oglala Sioux Traditions." *Los Angeles Times*, August 31, 1992. http://articles.latimes.com/1992-08-31/news/mn-5914_1_lakota-nation (accessed October 24, 2010).

Brokaw, Chet. "Town Wants Nuclear Dump." *Free Lance-Star*, January 10, 1984.

Brown, Dee, *Bury My Heart at Wounded Knee: An American History of the West*. New York: Henry Holt and Company, 1970.

The Goldman Environmental Prize web site. http://www.goldmanprize.org (cited October 12, 2010).

"Nuke Protest Walk Starts." *Spokane Daily Chronicle*, July 7, 1979.

Official web site of the Sioux tribe. http://www:oglalalakotanation.org (accessed October 23, 2010).

Ostler, Jeffrey, *The Plains Sioux and U.S. Colonialism from Lewis and Clark to Wounded Knee*. Cambridge: Cambridge University Press, 2004.

Prazniak, Roxann, and Arif Dirlik. *Places and Politics in an Age of Globalization*. Oxford: Rowman & Littlefield Publishers, 2001.

Reinhardt, Akim D. *Ruling Pine Ridge: Oglala Lakota Politics from the IRA to Wounded Knee (Plains Histories)*. Lubbock: Texas Tech University Press, 2007.

Seventh Generation Fund for Indian Development web site. http://www.7genfund.org/ (accessed October 20, 2010).

South Dakota Tribal Government Relations web site. http://www.state.sd.us/oia/ (accessed October 24, 2010).

Tall, JoAnn. "Indian Boarding School Abuse." YouTube video, 4:02, posted by "robertleokelly," July 24, 2007. http://www.youtube.com/watch?v=p1tiQB8gt5g (accessed October 24, 2010).

Tarbell, Ida (1857–1944)

Friends and family members warned Ida Tarbell that she would be investigated if she reported on the monopolistic practices of Standard Oil Company and its president, John D. Rockefeller. It was the early 1900s and a time of mergers with small businesses combining to form one huge corporation, which some said stifled competition and raised prices, benefiting only the company officials. Indeed, Tarbell's two-year investigation of Standard Oil revealed illegal price-fixing and corruption within the company, and her book *The History of Standard Oil* (1904) brought on the wrath of Rockefeller and U.S. president Theodore Roosevelt. She was the forerunner of writers like Upton Sinclair who revealed the corruption in the meatpacking industry. On April 14, 1906, President Roosevelt gave a speech that would lead to the creation of a new word "muckraker." He said:

> [Y]ou may recall the description of the Man with the Muck-rake, the man who could look no way but downward with the muck-rake in his hands; Who was offered a celestial crown for his muckrake, but who would neither look up nor regard the crown he was offered, but continued to rake to himself the filth of the floor... There are, in the body politic, economic and social, many and grave evils, and there is urgent necessity for the sternest war upon them. There should be relentless exposure of and attack upon every evil man whether politician or business man, every evil practice, whether in politics, in business, or in social life. I hail as a benefactor every writer or speaker, every man who, on the platform, or in book, magazine, or newspaper, with merciless severity makes such attack, provided always that he in his turn remembers that the attack is of use only if it is absolutely truthful. (Andrews 1958, 246–47)

In common parlance, the term muckraker came to describe—oftentimes derogatorily—investigative journalists who specialized in reporting on and exposing the seedy side of business and government, digging up instances of corruption, crime, fraud, graft, and waste, as well as dangers to public health and safety. At the turn of the twentieth century, exposés by muckrakers were quite successful at arousing and inflaming public opinion and helped bring about many Progressive Era reforms. Their best writings were filled with factual revelations about the nation's most powerful institutions. Many relied on lengthy investigative processes that were reported upon in serialized and firsthand fashion that dramatically captured readers' attention. Their worst examples were sensationalistic, earning the descriptor of "yellow journalism," lending credence to Roosevelt's rebuke. When examples of "classic" twentieth-century muckrakers are given, a few notables always make the list: Lincoln Steffens, Upton Sinclair, Ray Stannard Baker, Julius Chambers and—a lone female and, arguably, the first of all of the genre—Ida Tarbell (Filler 1950, 55).

Ester Ann McCullough Tarbell gave birth to a daughter, Ida Minerva, on November 5, 1857. At the time, she and her husband, Franklin, lived in the village of Hatch Hollow in Amity Township in Erie County, Pennsylvania, in a log cabin that was the home of Ida's maternal grandfather, Walter Raleigh McCullough, a Scots-Irish pioneer. The family moved to Rouseville and later to Titusville, in the western part of the state, where towns were dependent on oil. Franklin's work revolved around the petroleum industry. Before long, the Southern Improvement Company—an assortment of companies that would later became Standard Oil—controlled most of Titusville's businesses, including railroad transport. Local producers' rates doubled while Southern Improvement merited low freight costs for its own oil transport. As a child, Ida did not quite understand how Southern Improvement's monopoly affected her father's and others' businesses but, "she perceived that privilege, at least the version of it accorded to owners of expanding oil companies, badly upset her world" (Kochersberger 1996, xxix).

Ida became interested in science while attending high school and graduated at the head of her class. She majored in biology at Allegheny College in Meadville, Pennsylvania. In 1880, she was the only woman to graduate in her class. She then accepted a position at Poland Union Seminary in Poland, Ohio, teaching four language classes as well as geology, botany, geometry, and trigonometry. After two years, she decided teaching was not her calling and returned to Pennsylvania (Tarbell 2003, 1–48).

Shortly after her return, on a visit to her family's home, Dr. Theodore L. Flood, a preacher retired from the active ministry, recruited Tarbell to help out for a month or two with his new magazine, the *Chautauquan*, a teaching supplement for home study courses at Chautauqua, New York. She accepted eagerly. By 1886, she had become managing editor of the magazine, and her duties included proofreading, answering reader questions, providing proper pronunciation of certain words, translating foreign phrases, identifying characters, and defining words. After four years in that role, she resigned her position and moved to Paris in 1890. While there, she did postgraduate work, studying at the Sorbonne and the College de France for three years. She began writing feature articles about the city and about French revolutionaries for a variety of U.S.-based newspapers and magazines. Unlike the pieces she had produced for the *Chautauquan*, her new style of writing was more factual and less advocacy-based.

In 1894, *McClure's* magazine offered Tarbell a full-time position, so she returned to the States. *McClure's* was one of the foremost periodicals of the day that existed largely to expose political and industrial corruption and trumpet the need for reform. In time, Tarbell's talents earned her the title of associate editor. One of her most successful pieces at *McClure's* was a 20-part series on Abraham Lincoln that doubled the magazine's circulation. She gained national recognition as a major author when the series was published in book form, *The Life of Abraham Lincoln* (1900), and she was

Ida Tarbell's condemnation of the Standard Oil monopoly at the beginning of the 20th century placed her among the leading American muckrakers and brought her international fame as a journalist. (Library of Congress)

considered a leading authority on the slain president. Her meticulous research in the backwoods of Kentucky and Illinois uncovered previously unknown information about Lincoln's youth, and she offered a lively description of his ascent to the presidency (Serrin 2002, 154). Other works on Lincoln by Tarbell include *He Knew Lincoln* (1907); *Father Abraham* (1909); *In Lincoln's Chair* (1920); *Boy Scouts' Life of Lincoln* (1921); *He Knew Lincoln and Other Billy Brown Stories* (1922); *In the Footsteps of the Lincolns* (1924); and *A Reporter for Lincoln: Story of Henry E. Wing Soldier and Newspaper Man* (1926).

In the early 1900s, the editor of *McClure's* asked Tarbell to write a series of articles on the Standard Oil Company. With her assistant, John Siddall, she began her investigations, and the first article on Standard Oil, its monopoly, and the deliberate manner in which its president, John D. Rockefeller, set about eliminating his competition appeared in 1902. "The notes, archived with the rest of her papers at Allegheny College, reveal that the goal of the Standard Oil trust project was to give readers 'a clear and succinct notion of the processes by which a particular industry passes from the control of the many to that of the few' " (Weinberg 2008, 206). Moreover, "McClure believed that he, his reporters and his magazine were providing the evidence that would enable the citizenry to eradicate, or defray, the invasive and insidious efforts of the trusts" (Weinberg 2008, 237). Tarbell's investigation of Rockefeller and Standard Oil spanned two years, beginning in November 1902, and continuing for a total of 19 issues. Her research uncovered price-fixing practices and deep-seated corporate corruption.

Tarbell employed standard "muckraker" journalistic practices in her efforts to expose Standard Oil. She relentlessly tracked down public documents all over the country, piecing together the puzzle that, when united, formed a damning portrayal of the company and its ruthless pursuit of profit at the expense of all others in its path. She followed up the series with a profile of Rockefeller himself. Similar to her series on Lincoln, the popularity of this group of articles soon saw it published in book form, entitled *The History of the Standard Oil Company*. Ninety-five years later, in 1999, the *New York Times* listed it as number five of the top 100 works of twentieth-century American journalism, describing it as an example of the "windows on the passions that animated an era" (Barringer 1999).

Standard Oil and other like-minded business conglomerates attacked Tarbell and her methods. But her peers—other journalists of the day—admired her work, and it has since withstood the test of time. Tarbell did not enjoy being called a muckraker and, characteristically, took pen to paper and wrote an article entitled, "Muckraker or Historian."

[T]his classification of muckraker, which I did not like, helped fix my resolution to have done for good and all with the subject that had brought it on me. But events were stronger than I. All the radical element, and I numbered many friends among them, were begging me to join their movements. I soon found that most of them wanted attacks. They had little interest in balanced findings. Now I was convinced that in the long run the public they were trying to stir would weary of vituperation, that if you were to secure permanent results the mind must be convinced. (Tarbell 2003, 242)

Her approach was to use facts and figures—undeniable and reasoned findings—to make her case. Her research was the basis for charges being brought against Standard Oil in 1906, and the company was ultimately convicted of conspiracy to control interstate commerce in oil. Upon appeal to the U.S. Supreme Court, the conviction was upheld, and its monopoly was finally broken.

Ironically, the Supreme Court decision actually benefitted Rockefeller; its unintended consequences effectively quadrupled his net worth within a short period of time, creating the country's first billionaire. In response, President Roosevelt is quoted as saying, "No wonder that Wall Street's prayer now is 'O Merciful Providence, give us another dissolution'" (Weinberg 2008, 257).

Still, a man is more than his money, and Rockefeller's reputation suffered mightily. "If Ida M. Tarbell had never written her magazine serialization of Standard Oil's history and the articles that followed, John D. Rockefeller might be revered today instead of reviled by so many. Because of Tarbell's expose, however, the most admired during his lifetime ended up consigned forever to an infamous group of popular villains" (Weinberg 2008, 259).

Tarbell took a position as associate editor of the *American Magazine* in 1906, remaining in that job through 1915. For the remainder of her career, she pursued fraudulent business practices and worked to bring to light dangerous work conditions. She also continued on with corporate and executive biographies, many of them positive in nature. She was a frequent speaker on numerous subjects and continued to publish a wide variety of books, including her own autobiography. Even at the time of her death of pneumonia in Bethel, Connecticut, on January 6, 1944, she was working on yet another book, *Life after Eighty*.

In 1993, the Ida Tarbell House was declared a National Historic Landmark, and in October 2000, Tarbell was inducted into the National Women's Hall of Fame in Seneca Falls, New York. Two years later, the United States Postal Service issued a commemorative stamp honoring Tarbell as part of a series of four stamps honoring women journalists.

Margaret Gay

See also Sinclair, Upton

References

Andrews, Wayne, ed. *The Autobiography of Theodore Roosevelt, Condensed from the Original Edition, Supplemented by Letters, Speeches, and Other Writings (1st ed.).* New York: Charles Scribner's Sons, 1958.

Barringer, Felicity. "Journalism's Greatest Hits: Two Lists of a Century's Top Stories." *New York Times*, March 1, 1999.

Filler, Louis. *Crusaders for American Liberalism*. Yellow Springs, OH: Antioch Press, 1950.

Ida M. Tarbell web site. http://tarbell.allegheny.edu (accessed November 3, 2010).

Kochersberger, Robert C., Jr., ed. *More than a Muckraker: Ida Tarbell's Lifetime in Journalism*. Knoxville: University of Tennessee Press, 1996.

Serrin, Judith, and William Serrin. *Muckraking! The Journalism that Changed America*. New York: New York Press, 2002.

Tarbell, Ida M. *All in the Day's Work*. Urbana and Chicago: University of Illinois Press, 2003.

Tarbell, Ida M. *The History of the Standard Oil Company*. 2 vols. Gloucester, MA: Peter Smith, 1963.

Weinberg, Steve. *Taking on the Trust: How Ida Tarbell Brought Down John D. Rockefeller and Standard Oil*. New York: W. W. Norton and Company, 2009.

Tiller, George (1941–2009)

Many antiabortionists called Dr. George Tiller a murderer and baby killer—Tiller the Killer—because he legally performed late abortions. Some compared him to a Nazi, constantly harassed him, sent him death threats, or tried to kill him. When Dr. Tiller was assassinated in 2009, religious zealots declared that the doctor got what he deserved.

Tiller's friends and family, lawyers, and many of his patients have an entirely different view of the doctor. To them, Tiller was a genuine hero and a courageous defender of a woman's right to abortion. "George's colleagues who knew of his deep religious faith, generosity, kindness and love called him St. George when we spoke among ourselves, though we knew it embarrassed him to hear himself addressed this way," wrote his friend Dr. William F. Harrison, an abortion provider in Fayetteville, Alabama, who also was a frequent target of abortion protesters (Harrison 2009). Dr. Harrison died in 2010.

On August 8, 1941, George Richard Tiller was born in Wichita, Kansas, the son of Dr. Dean Jackson ("Jake"/"Jack") Tiller, a family physician, and Catherine Tiller. While George was growing up, he accompanied his father on house calls and was inspired by the rapport his father had with his patients, a motivating factor in his decision later to become a doctor.

George was educated at Alcott Elementary School, Robinson Junior High School, and Wichita East High School. After high school graduation in 1959, he enrolled at the University of Kansas and earned a degree in zoology in 1963. The following year he married Jeanne Guenther, a marriage that lasted for 45 years. The couple's family eventually included four children: son Maury and their daughters Jennifer, Rebecca, and Krista.

Tiller went on to study at the Kansas School of Medicine, graduating in 1967. He joined the U.S. Navy and was an intern at the U.S. Naval Hospital, Camp Pendleton, California. Later, he studied to become a U.S. Navy flight surgeon. He planned to continue his education and specialize in dermatology, but that changed in 1970 when his father, mother, sister, and brother-in-law were killed in a private plane crash, leaving an orphaned infant whom the Tillers adopted. The navy granted Tiller a hardship discharge, and he returned to Wichita to sell his father's practice and take care of family affairs. But he learned that his father's patients expected Dr. George Tiller to stay on as their physician.

Not long after taking over the family practice, Tiller learned that his father had provided abortions—safe abortions—for women who otherwise would have had no option except to go surreptitiously to untrained individuals and endure botched abortions, infections, injuries to internal organs, or death. Like his father, Tiller believed it was a matter of conscience to care for women seeking abortions, and after the U.S. Supreme Court ruling in *Roe v. Wade* (1973), Tiller provided abortion care as part of his obstetrics/gynecology practice.

The *Roe* case was named for Norma McCorvey, who used the alias Jane Roe as plaintiff and who was seeking the right to an abortion in Texas; and Texas district attorney Henry B. Wade, who was responsible for enforcing the strict abortion law in his state. The High Court ruled that state laws severely restricting abortion were unconstitutional because they did not protect a woman's right of privacy. The *Roe* ruling set up a framework regarding abortion. During the first trimester (about 13 weeks) of pregnancy, a woman has the right to an abortion for any reason. The state may pass laws to protect the health of the woman in the next trimester. During the third trimester (from 27 weeks to birth), the state may regulate or prohibit abortion, except where it is necessary to preserve the life or health of the pregnant woman.

By 1975, Tiller's abortion services overshadowed his family practice, and he opened Women's Health Care Services in Wichita. Over the years, he became one of only a few doctors who performed late abortions—that is, after the 20th or 21st week of gestation. Such abortions in some cases were due to medical complications of a pregnancy that threatened a woman's life, such as extremely high blood pressure that can cause a stroke, or carrying a dead fetus or one with a lethal fetal anomaly (a fatal abnormality). Or an abortion took place because a severely

Dr. George Tiller, a late-term abortion provider, speaks to a small group during a rally at Tiller's clinic in Wichita, Kansas, on January 19, 2002. Tiller was shot and killed at his church in Wichita on May 31, 2009. (AP Photo/Larry Smith)

disabled person had been raped and impregnated. Or a young teenager was ready to commit suicide because of a pregnancy. Or a child was a victim of incest and pregnant at age 10 or 11.

Tiller and other doctors who have provided abortions were subjected to strong opposition for their work by antiabortion groups who refer to themselves as "pro-life," many of whom cite religious beliefs to support their views. Most who oppose abortion are convinced that life begins at conception, the moment the female ovum is fertilized by the male sperm. According to this view, from conception on a human is developing, thus abortion at any point in a pregnancy is not only immoral, but akin to murder.

Another view, primarily held by groups known as "pro-choice," acknowledges that the egg and sperm have the potential to become a person, but that does not mean that the fetus is the same as a living human. Until the whole brain takes shape—about the seventh month of a pregnancy—a fetus is not a person, and does not exist as a person with legal rights until birth. According to this view, the morality of abortion takes into account a woman's circumstances and the quality of her life and that of the potential human.

For decades, from the late 1970s on, Tiller and his clinic staff were subjected to countless attacks by antiabortion groups, who believe that abortion whenever it occurs for whatever reason is murder. As his physician friend William Harrison explained, "physicians like Dr. George Tiller and me ... became the targets of large groups of people standing in front of our offices, screaming at us, our staff and our patients: 'Baby killer!' 'Abortion is murder!' 'Don't kill your baby!' They waved large pictures of electively aborted fetuses, more of large miscarried fetuses and sometimes of late-term stillbirths. . . . They attempted to terrorize us into ending a desperately needed service. Dr. George Tiller and I refused to be terrorized" (Harrison 2009).

Attacks on Tiller's clinic included much more than screaming protests. When women tried to enter the clinic, protesters with the antiabortion group Operation Rescue (now known as Operation Save America) and others confronted the women and shoved antiabortion pamphlets at them. Vendors who tried to deliver supplies were threatened with boycotts of their businesses. Even pizza deliveries were blocked. Protesters photographed patients and staff entering Women's Health Care Services and posted their pictures on web sites, which those pictured viewed as a form of intimidation. They used sit-ins to block entrances to the clinic, poured superglue into doors and locks, and parked a large truck with gory pictures of what were said to be aborted fetuses beside the clinic. They planted white crosses beside the sidewalk to represent "dead babies." In the mid-1980s, the Women's Health Care Services clinic was bombed.

As protests increased in intensity, Tiller's family urged him to turn down requests for public appearances; he often had spoken at medical conferences and various meetings on reproductive services. He wore a bulletproof vest and drove an armored car. A bodyguard accompanied him when he left his clinic, where he had installed protective measures such as metal detectors, bulletproof glass, and security cameras.

In spite of security measures, Tiller was shot in 1993 in both arms by Shelly Shannon, who followed the teachings of the Army of God, an antiabortion group that condones violence. She believed in using force and had spent a year in 1992 firebombing abortion clinics in three states. She was arrested, convicted of attempted murder, and sentenced to prison. A few days later, she was defiant and declared that shooting Tiller "was the most holy, most righteous thing I've ever done" (Bower 1996). Tiller, whose injuries were not serious, went back to work. Another doctor who performed abortions in Florida, David Gunn, did not fare as well. In 1993, he was shot and killed by a man who claimed he was acting in the name of God.

The killing of David Gunn and the attempted murder of Tiller as well as deaths of clinic workers and increasingly combative clinic blockades prompted a public backlash. In 1994, the Freedom of Access to Clinic Entrances (FACE) Act passed and was signed into law by President Bill Clinton. FACE prohibits anyone from using "force or threat of force or ... physical obstruction ... or attempts to injure, intimidate or interfere with any person ... from, obtaining or providing reproductive health services." Violation of the federal law can bring a prison sentence and fines up to $250,000.

Nevertheless, in 2001, antiabortion protesters appeared at Tiller's church, Reformation Lutheran, demanding "that the church excommunicate the Tiller family.... For at least two years, protesters showed up each Sunday, sometimes disrupting services from the pews. Protesters obtained a copy of the membership address book and sent all members postcards showing aborted fetuses," according to David Barstow of the *New York Times* (Barstow 2009).

The National Organization for Women (NOW) attempted to use another federal law to provide some protection for abortion providers: the Racketeer-Influenced and Corruptions Act of 1970. Known as RICO, the act enables people who have been injured financially because of extortion or seizure of property to seek amends in court. In a lawsuit, *NOW v. Scheidler* (1986), that finally went to trial in 1998, NOW charged that Joseph Scheidler, leader of the Pro-Life Action League, and other antiabortionists of racketeering activity that conspired to shut down abortion clinics. Scheidler and the other defendants were found guilty of racketeering, but the U.S. Supreme Court overturned that ruling in February 2003.

When Tiller's opponents could not close down his clinic, they tried other tactics: lawsuits against Tiller on various complex charges such as taking kickbacks from doctors who sent patients to him. Tiller was acquitted of all charges against him.

Opponents also attempted to influence the media with inflammatory stories against Tiller. Indeed, national talk show hosts such as Rush Limbaugh, Glenn Beck, and Bill O'Reilly quickly repeated fraudulent charges, with O'Reilly charging that Tiller performed abortions for women who were depressed and killed babies for a $5,000 fee. Some legal, religious, and civic leaders claim that such outrageous comments led to the tragedy that occurred in May 2009.

On May 31, 2009, Dr. Tiller and his wife, Jeanne, were attending services at the Reformation Lutheran church in Wichita. Jeanne Tiller was in the sanctuary while the doctor was in the foyer of the church handing out bulletins to late arrivals. His assassin, Scott Roeder, arrived and at close range shot Tiller through the eye. Tiller died in the foyer, and Roeder escaped but was apprehended three hours later, arrested, and charged with murder. He was convicted of premeditated murder in 2010 and sentenced to life in prison.

Reaction to Tiller's assassination came from people of many persuasions. Groups called pro-choice, such as the Feminist Majority Foundation, Physicians for Reproductive Choice and Health, the National Abortion Federation, NARAL: Pro-Choice America, NOW, Planned Parenthood, and the Religious Coalition for Reproductive Choice, were quick to condemn the heinous act, and some blamed antiabortionists' hateful talk and demonstrations for fueling such violence. Leaders of groups known as pro-life, such as American Life League, Americans United for Life, Family Research Council, Feminists for Life, National Coalition for Life and Peace, National Right-to-Life Committee, and Operation Rescue, also quickly denounced the killing. However, some took the opportunity to rail against Tiller. Randall Terry, founder of Operation Rescue, said "George Tiller was a mass-murderer. We grieve for him that he did not have time to properly prepare his soul to face God." Terry's statement was repeated numerous times in print and electronic media.

In a *Time* magazine article, Nancy Gibbs pointed out that "Mercifully, the abortion debate typically occurs within the boundaries a democracy sets, one of peaceful, if not always respectful, debate and advocacy on both sides. But what Tiller's murder reminds us is that in matters of life and death, the argument itself can become a matter of life and death" (Gibbs 2009).

See also Beck, Glenn; McCorvey, Norma; Limbaugh, Rush

References

Barstow, David. "An Abortion Battle, Fought to the Death." *New York Times*, July 26, 2009. http://www.nytimes.com/2009/07/26/us/26tiller.html?_r=2&pagewanted=1&ref=global-home (accessed November 26, 2010).

Bower, Ann. "Soldier in the Army of God." *Albion Monitor*, February 18, 1996. http://www.albionmonitor.com/abortion/abortionsoldier.html (accessed November 27, 2010).

Chaloupka, Maren Lynn. "TLC Methods in Practice." *The Warrior: Journal of the Trial Lawyers College*, Fall 2009.

Gibbs, Nancy. "Tiller's Murder: The Logic of Extremism on Abortion." *Time*, June 2, 2009. http://www.time.com/time/nation/article/0,8599,1902120,00.html (accessed November 27, 2010).

Harrison, Dr. William " 'Dr. Satan Come Out!' " *Arkansas Times*, June 11, 2009. http://www.arktimes.com/arkansas/ArticleArchives?author=933704 (accessed November 25, 2010).

V

Vera Cruz, Philip (1904–1994)

The name Philip Vera Cruz, a Filipino, is seldom associated with the first organized strike of agricultural workers in California. In the view of one scholar, Joaquin L. Gonzalez III, Vera Cruz was among "the many Filipino activists that changed the face of the agricultural labor movement in America. Because from the moment they arrived in Hawaii and California, Filipinos, as born revolutionaries for human equity and social justice, already began organizing for a non-violent struggle against the greed and abuse of capitalist America" (Gonzalez 2006, 59). Vera Cruz laid the groundwork for the United Farm Workers that eventually was led by César Chávez, of Mexican descent, who became famous for his advocacy for migrant farmworkers.

Filipinos "as born revolutionaries" have a long historic connection to the United States. After the Spanish-American War of 1898, which lasted only a few months, the United States defeated Spain, which brutally controlled its overseas colonies—Cuba, Puerto Rico, the Philippine islands, Guam, and other islands. After a decisive victory, the United States acquired Cuba and Puerto Rico as possessions and gained control of Wake Island, Guam, and the Philippines in the Pacific. Cuba won its independence by the end of 1898, but Spain had ceded the Philippines to the United States for a payment of $20 million, and then U.S. president William McKinley instructed the American occupying army to use force, as necessary, to impose American sovereignty over the Philippines. McKinley believed in what was known then as "manifest destiny"—the divine right of the United States to expand its territories. Many Filipinos had declared their independence and established a constitution for the Philippine Republic. But the United States refused to recognize the Philippine revolutionary government, and a rebel insurrection began in February 1899, ending with the rebels' defeat in July 1902.

Two and one-half years later, Philip Vera Cruz was born on December 26, 1904, in the small barrio of Saoag, Ilocos Sur Province, the Philippines. People of the province were "among the first to oppose foreign rule," according to Sid Valledor, Philip's comrade of later years (Valledor 2006, 48).

Philip's father, Andriano Sanchez Vera Cruz, and mother, Maria Villamin Vera Cruz, were "just simple folks" with very little education, but "both had a lot of common sense" (Sharlin and Villanueva 2006, 71). "I was born in a very poor family," Vera Cruz noted. "We used to have land . . . we were better off than a lot of people. Because my father got sick, then some of the land my father inherited was gone" (Valledor 2006, 55).

Philip lived with his grandmother from the time he was two years old until he was seven, a common practice among Filipino extended families (Scharlin and Villanueva 2000, 92–93). Four of Philip's younger brothers died shortly after their births. His family included two other siblings younger than Philip: sister Leonor, born when Philip was 17 years old; and a brother, Martin, born several years later.

Philip loved school, but his parents thought it was a waste of time. Regardless, without his parents' knowledge, Philip went to school anyway. During his teenage years he enrolled in high school in Vigan, capital of the province. He received an education in a public school system similar to that of the United States and established by American school teachers. His American teachers often spoke glowingly about the economic opportunities in the United States. So did young Filipinos who had been to the United States and returned to the Philippines to work at a higher pay than many Filipinos in the same jobs. Philip longed to go to the United States to pursue his education, but he believed he was too poor to make the trip. A teacher, however, persuaded him that he could work part time and attend school as well. When he told his mother about his dream of going to the United States, she was concerned because he did not know anyone there. As Vera Cruz explained: "In the Philippines, you see, when you moved you always moved to a place where you knew someone. So my mother couldn't understand that anyone would want to go to a place without friends or relatives living there. I didn't understand this myself back then, but this didn't stop me from dreaming about going to America anyway" (Scharlin and Villanueva 2000, 52–53).

To fulfill Philip's dream, his father with no resentment sold the last parcel of property that he owned, exacting a promise from Philip to send money home to his family, a vow Philip never forgot. In April 1926, Philip and three other young men left their homes for Manila, where they got their passports and sailed in the steerage section of a ship, *The Empress of Asia*, which took them across the Pacific Ocean to Vancouver, British Columbia, Canada. From there they traveled by ferry to Seattle, Washington, arriving in May 1926. At that time, the Philippines was a U.S. territory; so the Filipinos were technically U.S. nationals due to their colonial status, and they had a right to travel to the United States. As U.S. nationals, the federal exclusion laws that barred immigration of people of Asian descent, primarily Chinese and Japanese migrants, did not apply to Filipinos.

In 1934, the U.S. Congress passed the Tydings-McDuffie Act, named for the senator and representative who authored it. The act provided for the independence of the Philippines from the United States within 12 years. During the transitional period, the Philippines had commonwealth status. In addition, the act reclassified Filipinos as aliens and allowed only 50 Filipino immigrants into the United States each year. The quota was established during the Great Depression of the 1930s, when white Americans believed Filipino immigrants who worked for low wages were taking jobs away from whites. There was also a prejudicial belief that Filipinos brought disease to the United States. In truth, however, Filipino migrants as farm laborers often were subjected to disease-producing conditions; they were forced to live in sheds like chicken coops, drink contaminated water, use crude outdoor toilet facilities, and eat unhealthy food during their time as farmhands. They also were accused of luring white women away from their own race. But there were very few Filipino women in the rural areas, so white women were the choices for Filipino men. In addition, Filipino workers were condemned for their "immoral" activities, but they had little to do after work and gambled or engaged in cockfighting, an illegal game condoned by local politicians who encouraged Filipino participation.

Throughout the 1930s, Vera Cruz continued his education piecemeal while he worked at odd jobs—for example, building crates in a box factory, working at a restaurant as a bus boy and for a family as a house servant, and going to North Dakota for a short time to work in beet fields. In some cases, he found jobs (and places to live) through Filipino friends or relatives who had arrived in the United States earlier.

Back in Washington State, Philip completed his high school education and enrolled at the Catholic Jesuit school, Gonzaga University, in Spokane. But he had to drop out because after the death of his father in 1928, he had to work and send money to his mother, who was supporting his younger sister and brother. He took a job in a restaurant and went to night classes at an extension school of Washington State College. However, as he noted, "I went for only one semester and that was the end of my formal education" (Scharlin and Villanueva 2000, 83).

Vera Cruz and a friend decided to travel by train to Chicago, Illinois, where they hoped to find good jobs. But that did not happen, and they worked for "seven or eight years" as busboys or at the soda fountain of a restaurant. Vera Cruz also was active in Filipino literary and social clubs in Chicago until World War II began (Scharlin and Villanueva 2000, 85).

When the Japanese attacked the U.S. naval base at Pearl Harbor, Hawaii, on December 7, 1941, the United States declared war on Japan, and thousands of Filipinos petitioned to serve in the military. According to Alex S. Fabros of the California State Military Museum, "Although the Philippine Commonwealth Constitution permitted the United States to draft Filipinos in the Philippines to defend American interests there, Filipinos in the United States, quite ironically, were exempt from military service.... On January 2, 1942, President Franklin Delano Roosevelt signed a law revising the Selective Service Act. Filipinos in the United States could now join the U.S. Armed Forces" (Fabros).

Vera Cruz was drafted into the U.S. Army in August 1942, "and was immediately sent to San Luis Obispo, California, for basic training," he reported. "Those of us over 38 years old were then discharged and assigned to jobs on the farms in the San Joaquin Valley or in the shipyards up north in Vallejo or other defense-related industries" (Scharlin and Villanueva 2000, 7–8).

After his discharge, Vera Cruz went to work as a farm laborer in Delano, California. Since his brother and sister in the Philippines no longer needed his financial help, he was able because of his frugal ways to save enough money to buy land and build a house during the 1950s. He also joined various labor organizing efforts and became a member of the Agricultural Workers Organizing Committee (AWOC), established in 1959 by the AFL-CIO union. AWOC members primarily were Filipinos.

In September 1965, AWOC Filipinos working in vineyards went on strike against the grape growers in Delano, California, demanding wages equal to the federal pay standards for foreign workers. One of the oldest strikers was Vera Cruz, who was 60 years old. He and others were soon joined by predominantly Mexican members of the National Farm Workers Association led by César Chávez. The two organizations merged in 1966 to become the United Farm Workers (UFW), which organized rallies and support groups to champion their cause. The strike lasted until 1970, and through boycotts, protest demonstrations, and marches, the UFW won contracts with and concessions from grape growers and the right to advocate for workers.

Vera Cruz was one of the vice presidents of the UFW and sometimes disagreed with the decisions and authoritative character of Chávez, the UFW president. But Vera Cruz did not discuss his differences publicly, particularly when Chávez would not listen to the concerns of Filipinos. Vera Cruz opted instead to prevent friction within the union and quietly support the UFW.

One of the major differences occurred when Chávez supported the dictatorial president of the Philippines, Ferdinand Marcos, and his corrupt government. Vera Cruz was angered by the fact that Chávez did not recognize that Marcos and the Philippine government had declared martial law and imprisoned dissenters. Marcos also "made it illegal for workers to strike or organize their own unions." In spite of his dissent with Chávez, Vera Cruz appreciated the strong leadership of Chávez and his inclusion of all races within the UFW. Vera Cruz noted, "I liked [Chávez] and even with all of our differences I trusted him and defended him publicly for 12 years" (Scharlin and Villanueva 2000, 141–43).

Vera Cruz resigned from the UFW in 1977, and in 1988, Philippine president Corazon Aquino presented him an award for his advocacy for Filipinos in the United States. After his retirement from the UFW, he also was able to freely recount his experiences in the union and as a farm laborer with his oral autobiography, *Philip Vera Cruz: A Personal History of Filipino Immigrants and the Farmworkers Movement* (2000; originally published 1992). He maintained his interest in and advocacy for Filipino farmworkers until the end of his life. He died of emphysema in Bakersfield, California, on June 12, 1994.

See also Chávez, César

References

Bulosan, Carlos. *America Is in the Heart: A Personal History*. Seattle: University of Washington Press, 1976. First published 1946.

Fabros, Alex S. "A Short History of the 1st and 2nd Filipino Infantry Regiments of the U.S. Army in World War II." California State Military Museum, n.d. http://www.militarymuseum.org/Filipino.html (accessed March 4, 2011).

Gonzalez, Joaquin L., III. "Reflections on Philip Vera Cruz and the Filipino Diaspora." *Asia Pacific: Perspectives, an Electronic Journal* 6, no. 1 (May 15, 2006). http://www.pacificrim.usfca.edu/research/perspectives (accessed March 1, 2011).

San Juan, E., Jr. "Philip Vera Cruz: Narrating a Filipino Life in the Imperial Heartland." Philippines Matrix Project, October 3, 2008. http://philcsc.wordpress.com/2008/10/03/a-homage-to-philip-vera-cruz-founder-of-the-united-farmworkers-of-america/ (accessed March 3, 2011).

Scharlin, Craig, and Lilia Villanueva. *Philip Vera Cruz: A Personal History of Filipino Immigrants and the Farmworker Movement*. Seattle: University of Washington Press, 2000.

Valledor, Sid Amores. *Americans with a Philippine Heritage: The Original Writings of Philip Vera Cruz*. Indianapolis, IN: Dog Ear Publishing, 2006.

Vogler, Joe (1913–1993)

Joe Vogler disappeared under mysterious circumstances in 1993 and his body was found and identified in 1994, but his words have been quoted many times since and before his death. "My government is my worst enemy. I'm going to fight them with any means at hand," Vogler said. He also declared on the web site for the Alaska Independent Party (AIP), which he founded:

"I'm an Alaskan, not an American. I've got no use for America and her damned institutions." Although Joe Vogler was well known in Alaska for his incendiary statements, he was not readily recognized throughout the "lower 48," as Alaskans called the rest of the contiguous United States. However, during the 2008 presidential campaign, Vogler's name was cited frequently in connection with Sarah Palin, the Republican candidate for vice president of the United States. In news reports, Palin was said to support Vogler's AIP, and her husband Todd was a member of the party.

Born on April 24, 1913, in Barnes, Kansas, Vogler was one of five children—three boys and two girls—in a farm family who lived on land homesteaded by Joe's grandfather. Their farm was near the Little Blue River where Joe often went fishing during his childhood. He also helped farm the land and learned to be a hard worker. In one story about his childhood, he described the agitation of a guinea hen whose nest had been invaded by a snake. Joe "feared serpents, but he killed this one with his corn knife, and cut off its head," reported John McPhee in his book *Coming into the Country*. McPhee explained that the snake had bulges below its neck, and Vogler was able to squeeze 21 eggs out of its body. "He wiped each one with his handkerchief and returned it to the nest. The guinea hen eventually hatched twenty-one chicks" (McPhee 1991, 314–15).

Little else is known about Joe's childhood, except that he attended a one-room school. At the age of 16, he won a scholarship to the University of Kansas and graduated with a degree in constitutional law in 1934. "He passed the Kansas bar, but the Depression came along and limited Joe's chance of practicing law," wrote Alaskan author Dan O'Neill (2007, 202). The Depression also had a devastating effect on the Vogler farm, as did three years of drought that produced the Dust Bowl of the 1930s when tons of topsoil blew off dry farmland in Kansas and across the Plains. Wells went dry and crops were lost. When Joe could not find a job, he became embittered.

In 1941, Vogler went to Texas to look for work and found a job at Dow Chemical. He was fired from the job when he publicly called U.S. president Franklin D. Roosevelt (1882–1945) a communist and traitor. Vogler contended that the president had provoked Japan to attack the U.S. Navy ships in Pearl Harbor, Hawaii, on December 7, 1941. The Federal Bureau of Investigation (FBI) insisted that Vogler leave Dow Chemical, which was, after all, producing supplies for the U.S. military.

Vogler left not only his job, but also the state. In 1942, he moved to Kodiak, Alaska, and was a construction worker on a military base. Later he moved to Fairbanks and found construction work at Fort Wainright. In 1943, Vogler was drafted, but he let officers know that he would not pledge allegiance to President Roosevelt and would do as he pleased in the military. As a result, he was not inducted and was sent back to civilian life. By this time, Vogler was married and had two children, but his wife did not join him in Alaska until about 1945. She did not like rural living and, in 1948, left him, taking the children with her.

In 1951, Vogler began mining for gold and bought land around Fairbanks and across the Alaska interior. He filed for an 80-acre homestead near Homestead Creek and bought 320 acres on the north side of Fairbanks (Coppock 2008). He did not actually produce much gold himself, but instead he "made his money subdividing his land in Fairbanks," according to O'Neill. Vogler "was well known for the covenant he insisted every buyer accept: a legally binding agreement to cut down every aspen tree. Joe considered them 'arboreal weeds' and had no problem suing eight of his new neighbors to see that they obeyed the covenant" (O'Neill 2007, 203).

After Alaska achieved statehood in 1959, Vogler increasingly resented what he believed was intrusion of the federal government. He did not like the government regulating mining, logging, agriculture, and other activities on homestead land. The U.S. Congress passed the Homestead Act in 1862, which allowed men 21 years of age or older to buy 160 acres of land for $20 per acre, with the requirement that they live on the land and improve it over a five-year period, when they would obtain legal ownership. After the United States purchased Alaska from Russia in 1867, homesteaders began claiming land in Alaska. When the Homestead Act was repealed in 1976, Alaska was granted an extension until 1986.

Vogler's resentment of the U.S. government was based on his argument that Alaskans never had the opportunity to vote on independence, and in order to achieve another referendum on statehood that included a choice for independence, Alaska had to turn to the United Nations. He consistently referred to the UN Charter, the Declaration Regarding Non-Self Governing Territories. In Vogler's view, "Alaska statehood violated the U.N. Charter which the United States signed. That charter declared signatory's territories must be allowed self-determination and a vote on independence.... Alaska and Hawaii were denied this," wrote Michael Coppock. He added that in the late 1950s, Alaskans discussed the possibility of becoming a commonwealth like Puerto Rico is today; independence was not considered. Vogler believed this was because the U.S. government did not want to risk the possibility of losing its strategic military position (Coppock 2008). In fact, after World War II, the Soviet Union became a U.S. rival during a period known as the Cold War. If the Soviets should attack, the United States reasoned, they would take the shortest route, which would be over the North Pole, and Alaska was in a position to alert the rest of the United States of such a threat.

For the rest of his life, Vogler persisted in his efforts for an independent Alaska. "Joe Vogler considered himself an exile from an America that he believed was no longer worth loving," wrote columnist Bill Kauffman (2008). Vogler also continued his mining operations.

In 1964, Vogler married for a second time. His wife Doris often went with him to his placer mines—mines that involve mining gold that has been washed away from its source and deposited in small cracks, holes, or sandbars in the mainstream of a river. Vogler was proud of the fact that Doris was a great campsite cook as well as mining companion.

By the 1970s, Vogler and some of his miner friends were so angry with the U.S. government that they formed the Alaska Independent Party (AIP). According to Vogler, who was interviewed by author McPhee in the 1970s, "The United States has made a colony of Alaska. When they want something they come and get it.... We are a developing nation, like any developing nation in the world, and we cannot develop under American laws.... They have their independence from Britain. We do not have our independence from them." In other comments, Vogler declared: "In the federal government are the biggest liars in the United States, and I hate them with passion. They think they own this country. There comes a time when people will die with honor rather than live with dishonor. That time may be coming here. Our goal is ultimate independence by peaceful means under a minimal government fully responsive to the people" (McPhee 1991, 316–17).

In 1980, the U.S. Congress passed the Alaska National Interest Lands Conservation Act (ANILCA), which infuriated Vogler even more than he had been. ANILCA created a preserve in the area where Vogler had mine claims, and the act stipulated environmental regulations, some of which banned roadways into sensitive tundra areas. Vogler refused to comply. Several years after ANILCA passed, in mid-1984, the National Park Service closed a road leading to Vogler's mine, so with two other miners, Vogler drove his heavy-duty Caterpillar D-9 bulldozer down the road. But he was soon stopped. Armed park rangers in a helicopter circled overhead and landed to arrest Vogler for violating federal regulations. Vogler paid a fine and had to give up his bulldozer, which he left on the road to rust.

Vogler turned his attention to the AIP and politics. He had made two attempts—in 1974 and 1978—to run for governor of Alaska. He ran for the third time in 1986 as an AIP candidate. Alaska recognized the AIP as an official third political party in 1984. While campaigning, Vogler presented a pocket-sized version of the U.S. Constitution and argued that the federal government had gone far beyond what the Constitution allowed. Although Vogler's candidacies were not successful, he served as chairman of the AIP from 1986 until his death.

In 1991, Vogler withdrew from his stormy public life to care for his wife, who suffered from cancer and was bedridden. Doris died in January 1992, and Vogler buried her in Dawson City, Yukon, Canada. He refused to have her buried in the United States.

Vogler was scheduled to appear before the United Nations in 1993 to deliver his familiar denouncement of the United States. His sponsor was the government of Iran, a dictatorship and an avowed enemy of the United States. But he did not present his complaints. During the Memorial Day weekend of 1993 Vogler disappeared from his home. According to a report in the *Seattle Times*:

> On May 30, AIP member Al Rowe forced open the door to Vogler's cabin.
>
> Inside the cabin, Rowe found Vogler's wallet and heart medication on the kitchen table. All five of Vogler's dogs were inside and a blanket was draped over the cage of his pet goose. Missing were Vogler's .32-caliber "belly pistol" and gray fedora—things he wouldn't leave behind on a walk to the mailbox.
>
> Rowe called police, then party officials, and in no time people were tramping all over the place. Friends, volunteers, police, search-and-rescue teams, trained dogs, reporters and photographers. Planes with spotters circled overhead. (Williams 1993).

For months, the search for the missing man went on. There were numerous theories about what might have happened to Vogler. Some people thought the U.S. government had kidnapped him. Others were convinced that someone had robbed him of gold and then killed him. Still others believed Vogler had gone off to one of his mines to commit suicide.

Vogler's remains were not found until 17 months after his disappearance. In October 1994, fingerprint tests confirmed that the remains found in a gravel pit were that of Vogler. He had been buried there by Manfred West, who months earlier had confessed to killing Vogler during an argument over the price of dynamite used in mining. A jury convicted West of murder, and he was sentenced to 80 years in prison.

Vogler's hatred for the U.S. government followed him to his grave. He frequently had demanded that he not be buried under the American flag. According to Vogler's wishes, his body was sent to Dawson City, Yukon, Canada for burial beside his wife.

See also Palin, Sarah

References

Coppock, Michael. "On Vogler, an Independent Alaska." JuneauEmpire.com, March 14, 2008. http://www.juneauempire.com/stories/031408/nei_257857638.shtml (accessed February 6, 2011).

Kauffman, Bill. "Joe the Panner." *First Principles Web Journal*, October 31, 2008. http://www.firstprinciplesjournal.com/articles.aspx?article=1114&theme=home&page=1&loc=b&type=cttf (accessed February 7, 2011).

McPhee, John. *Coming into the Country*. New York: Farrar; Straus & Giroux, 1991. First published 1977.

O'Neill, Dan. *A Land Gone Lonesome: An Inland Voyage along the Yukon River*. New York: Counterpoint, 2007. First published 2006.

Williams, Marla. "Missing Myth—Alaska Buzzes with Theories on Maverick's Fate." *Seattle Times*, August 15, 1993. http://community.seattletimes.nwsource.com/archive/?date=19930805&slug=1714552 (accessed February 9, 2011).

Walker, Alice (1944–)

"As a poet and writer, I used to think being an activist and writing about it 'demoted' me to the level of 'mere journalist.' Now I know that . . . activism is often my muse" (Walker 1997, xxiv). So wrote Alice Walker on her role as civil rights and social activist and political dissident. Walker attributes her activist roots to the attitude and courage of her great-great-great-great grandmother, May Poole, who had been enslaved. Her parents were also engaged in activism, resisting white supremacy in Putnam County, Georgia.

Walker was born the last of eight children on February 9, 1944, in Putnam County. Her parents Minnie Lou (Tallulah) Grant Walker and Willie Lee Walker worked as sharecroppers, and they became concerned over their landlord's ruling that their children should pick cotton rather than go to school. In defiance of their landlords, Minnie and Willie enrolled Alice into East Putnam Consolidated, an elementary and middle school established by the community elders, and led by Willie Walker.

In 1952, when Alice was eight years old, she was playing with her older brothers and was shot accidentally with a BB gun. The accident left her blind in her right eye. Self-conscious about the disfiguring scar, Walker became shy and withdrawn. She attributes the event as the turning point in her life that fueled both her artistic career and her activism. From that moment, according to Walker, she "began to really see people and things, to really notice relationships and to learn to be patient enough to care about how they turned out" (Byrd 2010, 35).

As a student at Butler-Baker High School, Walker worked as a salad girl at the 4-H Center Rock Eagle in Eatonton, Georgia. While driving to work one day, Walker and her classmates began talking about how it was unfair that they had to walk to school while the white students could take a bus, and how they were paid less than their white counterparts for doing the same work. When one classmate stated that "we just had to accept it and there was no use complaining," Walker demanded they stop the car, whereby she walked the rest of the way. Before she left, however, she told her classmates that they should be ashamed of themselves. As classmate Porter Sanford recalled later, "Alice was always real serious about her issues" (Byrd 2010, 28). Walker went on to graduate as high school valedictorian and prom queen.

In 1961, Walker entered Spelman College as a scholarship student. When Walker left home, her mother gave her three special and symbolic gifts: a suitcase for traveling the world, a typewriter for creativity, and a sewing machine for self-sufficiency.

Walker became a student of historians and activists Howard Zinn and Staughton Lynd, both of whom became her strong advocates and mentors. It was during this time that Walker committed herself to the civil rights movement. She became involved in demonstrations organized by the Student Nonviolent

Coordinating Committee, as well as other civil rights organizations in the Atlanta University Center. In 1962, she represented Spellman College, and was sponsored by Coretta Scott King, as a delegate to the World Festival of Youth and Students in Helsinki, Finland. In August 1963, she attended the historic March on Washington, in which Dr. Martin Luther King Jr. delivered his now-famous "I Have a Dream" speech. Her commitment to the civil rights movement became the framework for her participation in social justice movements, including international women's rights, antinuclear and environmental causes.

While at Spelman College, Walker had to submit to a pelvic examination, a requirement for all students during their first and second years. The purpose of the exam was to determine if the student was pregnant. The experience left her feeling violated and humiliated. After Zinn was dismissed from the college for his participation in the civil rights movement, Walker also decided to leave the college.

In 1964, Walker began her studies at Sarah Lawrence in New York. She became a student of poets Jane Cooper and Muriel Rukeyser. Rukeyser, also a daughter of sharecroppers, taught her that she could live "in this world on your own terms" (Walker 1972). Walker also became a student of social philosopher Helen Lynd, mother of Spelman professor Staughton Lynd. Each of these teachers, like Zinn, influenced Walker's creative and activist spirit.

In 1965, while a senior at Sarah Lawrence, Walker experienced another major turning point when she learned she was pregnant. Despondent, Walker considered suicide. She received an abortion, an illegal procedure at the time, after which she became increasingly depressed. Walker found consolation in her poetry, which became the basis for her first collection, *Once*, published three years later. Recovering from the experience, as she describes in an interview with John O'Brien, "[writing the poems] clarified for me how very much I love being alive" (Byrd 2010, 39). As she spoke at the National March for Women's Equality and Women's Lives, held in Washington, D.C., in May 1989, "Abortion, for many women, is more than an experience of suffering beyond anything most men will ever know; it is an act of mercy, and an act of self-defense. To make abortion illegal again is to sentence millions of women and children to miserable lives and even more miserable deaths" (Walker 1989).

In 1966, Walker graduated from Sarah Lawrence and began working as a caseworker at the New York City's Department of Welfare. Shortly thereafter, she was awarded a Merrill Fellowship and was named a Bread Loaf Writers' Conference Scholar. However, she felt the strongest responsibility to the growing civil rights movement. Walker accepted an internship at the National Association for the Advancement People's (NAACP) Legal Defense and Educational Fund in Jackson, Mississippi. During this time, she wrote dispositions based upon the testimony of black sharecroppers who had been evicted from their homes because they had registered to vote. She worked with Jewish civil rights lawyer Melvyn R. Leventhal, with whom she fell in love. Although interracial marriages were illegal, Walker and Leventhal married in a civil ceremony on March 17, 1967. Three months later, the U.S. Supreme Court outlawed state laws banning interracial marriages. Walker and Leventhal were divorced in 1976.

In 1974, Walker became an editor at *Ms.* magazine and forged a lifelong friendship and fellowship with the magazine's cofounder Gloria Steinem. Walker's commitment to international women's rights propelled her to become an activist against the practice of clitoridectomy, or female genital mutilation (FGM). In 1993, she collaborated with British filmmaker and activist Pratibha Parmer, producing the film *Warrior Marks*, which brought the FGM practice to global attention.

Walker's literary works often reflected her social activism. In 1976, she published her second novel, *Meridan*, chronicling the struggles of a young woman during the civil rights movement. Her Pulitzer Prize–winning novel, *The Color Purple* (1982), is set in rural Georgia, and depicts the harsh realities and often violent struggles of black women during the 1930s. The novel is on the American Library Association list of the 100 Most Frequently Challenged Books of 2000–2009.

As a daughter of sharecroppers, and growing up in the segregated South, Walker felt solidarity with struggling peoples and by such revolutionaries as Che Guevara and Fidel Castro because, as she writes "[Fidel] was fighting the same greedy men we were also fighting . . . As we were beaten, battered by firehoses, thrown into jail for demanding the right to eat . . . and also the more important right to vote, the Cuban Revolution gave me hope" (Walker 1997, 201). In 1962, she participated in a student demonstration, led by her college professor Staughton Lynd, picketing the White House during a Hands off Cuba rally. In 1978, Walker traveled to Cuba for the first of three visits. In 1983, Walker travelled to Nicaragua, where she visited the controversial leader of the Sandinista National Liberation Front, Daniel Ortega.

In March 1996, Walker wrote to President Clinton, protesting the Cuban embargo as well as the Helms-Burton Bill. The bill

One of the best and most influential writers of her generation, Alice Walker (seen here in 1990) has affected modern American life not only through her brilliant poetry and novels, but through her actions as a black feminist ("womanist") and social activist. Her novel *The Color Purple* is perhaps her most popular work so far. It was made into a movie starring Oprah Winfrey in 1985. (AP/Wide World Photos)

made it possible for complainants to sue foreign companies, excluding U.S. executives. In the letter, she tells President Clinton: "I have seen how the embargo hurts everyone in Cuba, but especially Cuban children, infants in particular . . . The bill is wrong, the embargo is wrong, because it punishes people, some of them unborn, for being who they are" (Walker 1997, 213). She encouraged Clinton to have a "face to face" with Castro in hopes of coming to some understanding. In 1992, she finally had an audience with Fidel Castro.

Walker is a member of Code Pink: Women for Peace, cofounded by antiwar activist Medea Benjamin. The controversial antiwar group, criticized for vigorous publicity tactics, began in October 2002 as a women-initiated grassroots peace and social justice movement working to end the wars in Iraq and Afghanistan. On March 8, 2003, the eve of the Iraq War, Walker and fellow literary activists and Code Pink members Maxine Hong Kingston and Terry Tempest Williams were arrested with 24 other participants as they crossed a police line during an antiwar protest outside the White House.

In 2006, Walker, working with Women for Women International, visited Kigali in Rwanda, the largest city and center of the Hutu violence against the Tutsi and moderate Hutu by the Hutu militia. In *Overcoming Speechlessness*, Walker describes encountering the aftermath of genocide, where over one million persons were "hacked into sometimes quite small pieces by armed strangers, or by neighbors, or by acquaintances and 'friends' they knew" (Walker 2010, 7). She then visited the eastern Congo to pay homage to the survivors of the genocide. She writes, "Though the horror of what we are witnessing ... threatens our very ability to speak, we will speak" (Walker 2010, 72).

In November 2008, Walker wrote an open letter to the newly elected president, Barack Obama. Having been actively engaged in the civil rights movement decades before, it was monumental for Walker to celebrate the United States' first African American president. Addressing the letter to "Brother Obama," she writes "Seeing you take your rightful place, based solely on your wisdom, stamina and character, is a balm for the weary warriors of hope, previously only sung about" (Walker 2008).

In March 2009, just a few weeks following the controversial Israeli offensive in the 22-day Gaza War, Walker travelled to Palestine. She travelled with 60 others, including fellow Code Pink member and retired colonel Ann Wright, to review the devastation on the Gaza Strip, to deliver aid, to meet with the residents, and to persuade Israel and Egypt to open their borders into Gaza. Walker and the delegation received rare permission from Egypt to enter Gaza through the southern border. As Walker offers in her book *Overcoming Speechlessness*, there are different opinions over the Palestinian and Israel conflict, but her fundamental belief "is that when a country primarily instills fear in the minds and hearts of the people of the world, it is no longer useful in joining the dialogue we need for saving the planet" (Walker 2010, 66).

In December 2009, Walker participated in the Gaza Freedom March, which brought together 1,300 people from more than 43 countries in a nonviolent political march to end the blockade of the Gaza Strip. Notable participants included political and social activist Ann Wright, and her old friend and college professor Howard Zinn.

"My activism—cultural, political, spiritual—is rooted in my love of nature and my delight in human beings," Walker wrote in *Anything We Love Can Be Saved*. "I do not want fear of war or starvation or bodily mutilation to steal both my pleasure in them and their own birthright" (Walker 1997, xxii).

Bobbi Miller

See also Benjamin, Medea; King, Martin Luther, Jr.; Wright, Ann; Zinn, Howard

References

Byrd, Rudolph, ed. *The World Has Changed: Conversations with Alice Walker*. New York: New Press, 2010.

Nissenbaum, Dion. "Author Alice Walker in Gaza: A 'Catastrophe' Has Fallen." *Checkpoint Jerusalem*, March 11, 2009. http://washingtonbureau.typepad.com/jerusalem/2009/03/author-alice-walker-in-gaza-a-catastrophe-has-fallen.html (accessed August 30, 2010).

Tristam, Pierre. "Overcoming Speechlessness: Alice Walker in Gaza." Pierre's Middle East Issues Blog, July 28, 2009. http://middleeast.about.com/b/2009/07/28/overcoming-speechlessness-alice-walker-in-gaza.htm (accessed August 30, 2010).

Walker, Alice. "Alice Walker—an Open Letter to Barack Obama." NowPublic.com, November 7, 2008. http://www.nowpublic.com/world/alice-walker-open-letter-barack-obama-1 (accessed August 30, 2010).

Walker, Alice. *Anything We Love Can Be Saved: A Writer's Activism*. New York: Random House, 1997.

Walker, Alice. *Overcoming Speechlessness: A Poet Encounters the Horror in Rwanda, Eastern Congo and Palestine/Israel*. New York: Seven Stories Press, 2010.

Walker, Alice. "A Talk: Convocation 1972." *In Search of Our Mothers Gardens*. New York: Mariner Books, 2003; 38.

Walker, Alice. *We Are the Ones We Have Been Waiting For*. New York: New Press, 2006.

Walker, Alice. "What Can the White Man Say to the Black Woman?" Address in support of the National March for Women's Equality and Woman's Lives, Washington, DC. May 1989. http://www.hartford-hwp.com/archives/45a/584.html (accessed August 30, 2010).

Wallis, Jim (1948–)

In March 2010, Jim Wallis, an evangelical theologian and president and chief executive officer of Sojourners, a faith-based organization, found himself in an unprovoked controversy with radio and television talk show host Glenn Beck. Wallis, who is also editor of *Sojourners Magazine*, advocates for social and economic justice within Christian beliefs. Beck took issue with Jim Wallis for his advocacy. As Beck wrote on his ever-present chalkboard on his television show, "My definition of social justice is the forced redistribution of wealth, with a hostility to individual property, under the guise of charity and/or justice." Wallis responded by writing for *Huffington Post* that "virtually no church in America, or the world, would support anything close to that as a definition of social justice. Beck needs to hear some good church teaching—including from his own Mormon church members who fundamentally disagree with him and have said so."

The two carried on this argument off and on for much of the year. On one show, Beck urged Christians to leave their churches if they heard their preacher or priest talk about social justice, declaring that the clerics were on a slippery slope toward Marxism, meaning communism. Wallis retorted, with a tinge of sarcasm, that someone ought to tell Catholic Charities and the Salvation Army that they are supporting communism when they work with the public sector to serve people in need (Wallis 2010).

Wallis has been berated not only by Beck but also by fundamental Christians and political conservatives who adamantly disagree with Wallis's progressive views. For example, in summer 2010, local pastors and a radio station objected to Wallis being one of 58 speakers at Lifest, an annual Christian music festival held in Oshkosh, Wisconsin. Radio station Q90 FM declared that "After researching extensively the words and published positions of Jim Wallis and his organization . . . we believe the social justice message and agenda they promote is a seed of secular humanism, seeking an unholy alliance between the Church and Government" (Barrick 2010).

Wallis was born in Detroit, Michigan, on June 4, 1948, to conservative evangelical Christian parents. He was the eldest of five children. His father Jim Wallis was an engineer for Detroit Edison and the lay leader of Plymouth Brethren assembly; the group had no clergy. He explained in an interview for public radio that his father "got up every day at 5:00 in the morning to study his Bible for two hours, and then got us up for work and school." Both parents were committed church leaders. But his mother Phyllis Wallis was not allowed to be a public leader because women were barred from such positions. The church, Wallis said, was:

> very Evangelical in the usual ways back then. And I remember ... I was 6 years old and my parents were a little nervous, because, well, I wasn't saved yet. And I was getting up in years, I was 6, you know? So there's a fiery evangelist that was billed to be coming in a couple of weeks, and so I was kind of dreading the day because I heard he was pretty scary. And all unsaved kids had to sit in the first row. You know—we never wanted to sit in the first row, because I think the closer you are to a sermon, the more impact it will have in your life, you know? But he preached and he pointed his finger—it seemed right at me—and he says, "If Jesus came back tonight, your mommy and daddy would be taken to heaven, and you would be left all by yourself." (Tippett 2007).

Wallis often describes how his religious views differed from those of his parents. In another interview with Change.org, he noted the following when he was 14 years old:

> I realized life was so different in white Detroit where I lived, than in black Detroit just a few blocks away. That seemed wrong to me. But nobody in my school, neighborhood or church seemed to have given it a thought. Since I wasn't getting answers to my questions in my community, I went into the city, met the black churches and took jobs alongside young African-Americans, who while living in the same city had really grown up in a different country than I had. From there everything changed. I knew there had to be a better way and my life began to change. (Wallis, January 16, 2010)

Wallis wondered why his church never invited African American ministers to visit, such as Rev. Martin Luther King Jr., a civil rights leader whom he was just beginning to learn about. When Wallis questioned why his church did nothing about segregation, he was told that racism was a political issue and that members of the Plymouth Brethren were concerned foremost about personal faith. He left the church as an angry person, believing his church had betrayed him. He enrolled at Michigan State University, where he led the radical Students for a Democratic Society and participated in protests against the Vietnam War and the May 1970 killings of four Kent State University students in Kent, Ohio, by National Guardsmen. The Kent State students were protesting the invasion of Cambodia and the escalation of the Vietnam War. Wallis was arrested and jailed for his part in protests. In fact, as the years progressed, he was jailed more than 20 times for civil disobedience.

During the 1960s, he began reading works by American Black Muslim organizer Malcolm X (1925–1964), German philosopher and economist Karl Marx (1818–1883), Vietnamese revolutionary Ho Chi Minh (1890–1969), and Cuban revolutionary Che Guevara (1928–1969). However, Wallis soon decided that the Marxist views did not qualify as a solid foundation for his life. Like others before him, such as Dorothy Day (1897–1980), whom he met when she was in her 80s, he rejected Marxism and returned to a religious approach. Day, who was once a Marxist, converted to Catholicism and launched the Catholic Worker movement to aid the homeless and poor. Wallis began reading the biblical New Testament and concentrating on the Sermon on the Mount and the Beatitudes in the book of Matthew. He also went on to do graduate work at Trinity Evangelical Divinity School in Deerfield, Illinois. At the school, in the early 1970s, he and several other students started a small magazine called *Post-American* and a community with a Christian commitment to social justice, which later would become Sojourners, publishing a magazine by the same name.

Wallis and his fellow students lived off campus as a community that they first established in Chicago's poorest neighborhood. They appealed to alienated young people with rock-and-roll music and preaching the biblical basis for social justice. They soon had hundreds of participants.

In 1975 the community moved to Washington, D.C., to an area known as the "war zone," renamed itself Sojourners, and continued to publish *Sojourners Magazine*. Throughout the 1970s and 1980s, Sojourners also was a leader in the movement to abolish nuclear weapons. It was a time when Wallis, like many other antinuclear activists such as his friends Catholic Jesuit priests Daniel and Phillip Berrigan, was arrested and jailed because of protests.

In the early 1980s, when the religious right or Christian right became increasingly influential in public life, it appeared that the United States was headed for a nation ruled by religious conservatives. In Wallis's view, the religious right was extremely political and focused on "a narrow set of issues: abortion, homosexuality, and pornography. There was still no concern for the issues the Bible talks most about, like poverty, war and peace, and suffering. We wanted to press for Christians to concern themselves with those things," he told an interviewer for *Patheos* (Dalrymple 2010).

As Wallis and Sojourners made their case in the media, Wallis gained prominence and also numerous critics nationwide. His opponents were especially critical when Wallis opposed U.S. foreign policy and the Iraq invasion and the war in Afghanistan. Critics also condemned his earlier support of communist regimes. As one detractor wrote for DiscovertheNetwork.org, a web site sponsored by David Horowitz and his far-right Freedom Center: "Wallis remains fiercely opposed to capitalism and the free market system.... While Wallis ... concedes that Communism was not all that he and his Sojourners colleagues claimed it to be, he remains adamant in his insistence that capitalism is no improvement" (Laksin 2005).

In 1997, Wallis married Joy Carroll, one of the first women priests ordained in the Church of England. Both Jim and Joy Wallis are authors and lecturers, as well as pastors. Jim Wallis lectured at Harvard Divinity School during 1998–1999. They have two sons, Luke and Jack, and live about 10 blocks from the White House in Washington, D.C. Their son Jack was born just before the United States invaded Iraq in 2003, which both Jim and Joy had opposed. They had campaigned for alternatives to war, which Jim Wallis explains in detail in his best-selling book *God's Politics: Why the Right Gets It Wrong and the Left Doesn't Get It* (2005). In a 2008 interview for *Christianity Today*, he noted "The war in Iraq was not a just war. It didn't conform to the standards at all. And that's the view of the vast majority of evangelicals around the world. I think it was the worst mistake in American foreign-policy history, with the exception of Vietnam" (Olsen 2008).

He also has written *The Great Awakening: Reviving Faith and Politics in a Post-Religious Right America* (2008) and *Rediscovering Values: On Wall Street, Main Street, and Your Street* (2010). His earlier titles include *The Call to Conversion: Why Faith Is Always Personal But Never Private* (1981, revised 2005); *The Soul of Politics: Beyond "Religious Right" and "Secular Left"* (1995); *Faith Works: How Faith Based Organizations Are Changing Lives, Neighborhoods, and America* (2000); and *Faith Works: How to Live Your Beliefs and Ignite Positive Social Change* (2005).

In addition to his many books, Wallis has written numerous opinion pieces for major newspapers and magazines regarding the need for social change, which he believes is beginning to take place. For example, in an article for *Time* magazine in 2007, he wrote: "In the churches, a combination of deeper compassion and better theology has moved many pastors and congregations away from the partisan politics of the religious right. In politics, we are beginning to see a leveling of the playing field between the two parties on religion and 'moral values,' and the media are finally beginning to cover the many and diverse voices of faith.... People know now that God is neither a Republican nor Democrat, and we are all learning that religion should not be in the pocket of any political party; it calls all of us to moral accountability" (Wallis 2007).

Along with his prolific writing, Wallis also has been a guest on a variety of television news channels and is in demand nationwide as a speaker. In addition, he continues to work with the Sojourners community, which merged with Call to Renewal in 2006 and became known as simply Sojourners. The combined advocacy group brings together people of diverse Christian faiths and political persuasions to address social justice issues. His work has been honored by the Catholic Pacem in Terris Peace and Freedom Award presented in 1995, the Peace Abbey Courage of Conscience awarded in 2002, and appointment in 2009 to President Barack Obama's White House Office of Faith-Based and Neighborhood Partnerships. He has served as Obama's spiritual adviser as well.

See also Berrigan, Daniel, and Berrigan, Phillip; Day, Dorothy; Horowitz, David; King, Martin Luther, Jr.; Malcolm X

References

Barrick, Audrey. "Christian Music Fest Draws Fire Over Jim Wallis Invitation." *Christian Post*, July 1, 2010. http://www.christianpost.com/article/20100701/christian-music-fest-draws-fire-over-jim-wallis-invitation/ (accessed January 1, 2011).

Dalrymple, Timothy. "The Legacy of an Activist Career: An Interview with Jim Wallis." August 9, 2010. http://www.patheos.com/Resources/Additional-Resources/The-Legacy-of-an-Activist-Career-An-Interview-with-Jim-Wallis?offset=3&max=1&showAll=1 (accessed January 4, 2011).

Laksin, Jacob. "Jim Wallis: Expanded Profile." *DiscoverTheNetworks*, 2005. http://www.discoverthenetworks.org/Articles/jimwallisexpanded.html (accessed January 4, 2011).

Olsen, Ted. "Where Jim Wallis Stands." *Christianity Today*, May 2008. http://www.christianitytoday.com/ct/2008/may/9.52.html (accessed January 4, 2011).

Tippett, Krista. "Speaking of Faith." American Public Media, November 29, 2007. http://being.publicradio.org/programs/jimwallis/transcript.shtml (accessed January 3, 2011).

Wallis, Jim. *God's Politics: Why the Right Gets It Wrong and the Left Doesn't Get It*. San Francisco: HarperSanFrancisco, 2005.

Wallis, Jim. "Put Your Faith into Action for Social Justice." Change.org, January 16,

2010. http://uspoverty.change.org/blog/view/put_your_faith_into_action_for_social_justice (accessed January 3, 2011).

Wallis, Jim. "The Religious Right's Era Is Over." *Time*, February 16, 2007. http://www.time.com/time/nation/article/0,8599,1590782,00.html (accessed January 5, 2011).

Wallis, Jim. "What Glenn Beck Doesn't Understand about Biblical Social Justice." *Huffington Post*, March 24, 2010. http://www.huffingtonpost.com/jim-wallis/what-glenn-beck-doesnt-un_b_511362.html (accessed January 1, 2011).

Wiesel, Elie (1928–)

Holocaust survivor Elie Wiesel wrote that "the Nazis in Germany set out to build a society in which there would be no room for Jews. Toward the end of their reign, their goal changed: they decided to leave a world in ruins in which Jews would seem to have never existed . . . It is obvious that the war that Hitler and his accomplices waged was a war not only against the Jewish men, women, and children, but also against Jewish religion, Jewish culture, Jewish tradition, therefore Jewish memory" (Wiesel 2006, viii). Wiesel is a political activist and advocate for peace who has been an impassioned spokesperson against "the dark shadow of humanity" that includes world wars, civil wars, assassinations, and other forms of violence" (Wiesel 1999).

In 1933, more than nine million Jews were living in Europe. In January, the Nazis rose to power in Germany. They believed the German race was "superior" and Jews were not only "inferior," but also posed a threat to them. Additional groups—such as the Roma (Gypsies), the disabled, and some Slavic peoples such as Poles and Russians—also were deemed substandard and dangerous. Those holding different beliefs—such as communists and socialists, or people who were "unconventional" (for example, Jehovah's Witnesses or homosexuals)—were persecuted, too. Early in the Nazi regime, the government established "concentration camps." Initially, these places detained ideological and political opponents. As time passed, they came to be warehouses for all "undesirables." From 1941 to 1944, millions of Jews from Germany, occupied territories, and Germany's allies were deported to ghettos and killing centers and mass executed in gas chambers. The Nazis' policy, called the "Final Solution," resulted in the deaths of nearly two out of every three European Jews and hundreds of thousands of others by 1945. The term "Holocaust" (the original Greek meaning is "sacrifice by fire") evolved to define this "systematic, bureaucratic, state-sponsored persecution and murder of approximately six million Jews by the Nazi regime and its collaborators" (U.S. Holocaust Memorial Museum web site).

Wiesel was named Elieser but affectionately called "Leizer" by his family. He was born on September 30, 1928, in Sighet, Transylvania, in the Kingdom of Romania, in the Carpathian Mountains. The only son, he was the third of four children; his older sisters were Hilda and Beatrice; the youngest was Tsiporah. The family primarily spoke Yiddish, but also German, Hungarian, and Romanian. In part, this was due to his mother, Sarah Feig, being more highly educated than most local women. Wiesel's father, Schlomo, was a well-regarded businessman—the family ran a grocery—and community leader. Wiesel "lived entirely in the world of books, stories and prayers that was brought forth by that 'religious humanism' [of the Hassidic movement]" (Bochert-Kimmig 1999, 59–65). As a Hassidic Jew, he believed that God was everywhere; through prayer and trust in Him, daily problems would be overcome (Stern 1996, 3).

Wiesel was extreme in his religious beliefs and practices. However, both his well-ordered life and his reassuring faith would be upended. On May 16, 1944, the German Army deported Wiesel, along with his family and the entire Jewish community of Sighet, to the Auschwitz-Birkenau concentration camp complex in Auschwitz, Poland. Upon arrival, he and his father were separated from the women. Sarah and Tsiporah likely perished immediately in the Auschwitz gas chambers. Wiesel and his father lived through what he later termed the "kingdom of night" (Bochert-Kimmig 1999, 60). As Wiesel wrote: "Never shall I forget that night the first night in camp... Never shall I forget that smoke... Never shall I forget those flames that consumed my faith forever... Never shall I forget those moments that murdered my God and my soul and turned my dreams to ashes, Never shall I forget those things... Never" (Wiesel 2006, xix).

Young Wiesel had inmate number A-7713 tattooed on his arm, a permanent reminder of all that he was to endure in the year ahead. He and his father were sent to an attached work camp, Buna, and managed to stay together for over eight months, enduring and witnessing all manner of unspeakable horrors. As the war wound down, they were shuffled between camps, undergoing a brutal enforced march to Buchenwald in Germany. The elder Wiesel, ill from dysentery, starvation, and beatings by guards, ultimately succumbed and died shortly before the camp was liberated by the U.S. Army on April 11, 1945.

Much to his surprise, Wiesel learned his older sisters had survived and reunited with them; both sisters immigrated to North America. He ultimately moved to France,

Writer and Holocaust survivor Elie Wiesel speaks after receiving the Nobel Peace Prize in Oslo, Norway, on December 10, 1986. (AP Photo/Bjoern Sigurdsoen)

where he learned the language and completed his education, studying literature, philosophy, and psychology; he also resumed his studies of the Hebrew scriptures (Bochert-Kimmig 1999, 60). The authors of *Hope against Hope* (1999) recounted that during this time, Wiesel was attempting to (in the words of one of his future semiautobiographical characters), "grasp the meaning of the events of which I had become a victim." They added, "Everything had changed, however. His naïve access to God was closed to him; his faith in human beings was shattered. Barely able to form relationships, he lived distantly, plagued by memories... For ten years he was unable to speak about his experiences. Not a word about Auschwitz. After ten years he passed through the door of silence into literature" (Bochert-Kimmig 1999, 60).

During this time, Wiesel stayed in Paris, working as a journalist for Israeli and

French newspapers. He came to the realization that he had to bear witness. "having lived through this experience, one could not keep silent no matter how difficult, if not impossible, it was to speak. And so I persevered.... my manuscript... was rejected by every major publisher" (Wiesel 2006, x). The initial result was a 900-page tome, written in Yiddish. It was published, in abridged form, in Buenos Aires. Wiesel had difficulty finding a publisher for the subsequent 127-page French version. Few copies sold. He met Georges Borchardt, a literary agent, who became and remains his lifelong agent. Borchardt eventually found a small publishing company, Hill and Wang, to agree to publish Wiesel's book *Night* (1960) in English. It sold just over 1,000 copies in 18 months. The first printing of 3,000 copies took three years to sell. However, to date, the book has been translated into more than 30 languages; millions have sold, and it was chosen the January 2006 Oprah Winfrey Book Club Selection, adding to its popularity with the American public. *Night* describes the Nazi death camp—"that damned, inhuman realm where death was mass-produced the way other factories make toothpaste"—and recounts the deaths of Wiesel's family members (Bochert-Kimmig 1999, 60).

"If in my lifetime, I was to write only one book, this would be the one," Wiesel stated. "I only know that without this testimony.... my life would not have become what it is: that of a witness who believes he has a moral obligation to try to prevent the enemy from enjoying one last victory by erasing his crimes from human memory (Wiesel 2006, vii–viii).

Wiesel's first book was followed up by *Dawn* (1961) and *The Accident* (1962). With the exception of his two books of memoirs, only in his first book does Wiesel address the Holocaust directly and detail the experience that shattered his faith in both God and humanity. However, in all of Wiesel's works (of which there are close to five dozen, both fiction and nonfiction), "it is always a question to God: Where were you when your children needed you most?... And yet... One of the most important phrases in Wiesel's work is 'And yet.' Despite the despair from that event, in that despair, he finds a source of trust in God and in human beings which lies not in forgetting the horror, but precisely in remembering it" (Bochert-Kimmig 1999, 60).

Wiesel, his wife, Marion, and their son, Schlomo Elisha, made New York City their home. He became an American citizen in 1963. From 1972 to 1976, Wiesel was a distinguished professor at the City University of New York. In 1976, he began teaching at Boston University, being made Andrew Mellon Professor of Humanities in the mid-1980s. In 1982, he served as the first Henry Luce Visiting Scholar in Humanities and Social Thought at Yale University. From 1997 to 1999, he was Ingeborg Rennert Visiting Professor of Judaic Studies at Barnard College.

Perhaps his greatest honor came in 1986 when he received the Nobel Peace Prize. In his Oslo acceptance speech, Wiesel said, "No one may speak for the dead, no one may interpret their mutilated dreams and visions. And yet, I sense their presence. I always do—and at this moment more than ever. The presence of my parents, that of my little sister... This honor belongs to all the survivors and their children and, through us, to the Jewish people with whose destiny I have always identified" (Wiesel 2006, 117–18). After winning the Nobel Prize, Wiesel and his wife started the Elie Wiesel Foundation for Humanity, whose "mission is to combat indifference, intolerance and injustice through international dialogues and youth-focused programs that promote acceptance, understanding and equality (Elie Wiesel Foundation web site).

President Jimmy Carter's 1979 Commission on the Holocaust, which Wiesel chaired, recommended creation of a Washington, D.C., memorial museum and educational center. Wiesel was appointed initial chair of the council charged with building the museum, which was dedicated on April 22, 1993. Wiesel, President Bill Clinton, and then council chair Harvey M. Meyerhoff jointly lit the eternal flame outside the museum. From 1993 to 2011, more than 31.8 million have visited the Museum, with another 38 million visiting its online site.

Wiesel has received numerous literary accolades, such as the Remembrance Award, the Jewish Heritage Award, France's *Prix Medicis*, the French Academy *Prix Bordin*, the Jewish Book Council Frank and Ethel S. Cohen Award, the *Prix Livre-International* and *Prix des Bibliothecaires*. Some of his other honors include the Eleanor Roosevelt Memorial Award, Israel's Jabotinsky Medal, the International League for Human Rights Humanitarian Award, the B'nai B'rith Profiles in Courage Award, the International Human Rights Law Group Award, the Human Rights Campaign Fund Humanitarian Award, the Ellis Island Medal of Honor, the Interfaith Council on the Holocaust Humanitarian Award, the Humanitarian of the Century by the Council of Jewish Organizations, a U.S. Congressional Gold Medal, an honorary knighthood in the United Kingdom, and named a commander of the Legion of Honor in France. Many academic titles have been bestowed upon him; similarly, several scholastic chairs been established in his name.

In addition to being a literary voice for those who died in the Holocaust, Wiesel has spoken more broadly for all who are abused. "Human rights are being violated on every continent. More people are oppressed than free. How can one not be sensitive to their plight? Human suffering anywhere concerns men and women everywhere" (Wiesel 2006, 119). He has advocated for causes ranging from apartheid in South Africa and genocide in Bosnia to the crisis in Darfur and the troubles in the Middle East. But he remains unflagging in his efforts to ensure that those who were brutalized and murdered in the Holocaust are not forgotten. "To forget would be not only dangerous but offensive; to forget the dead is akin to killing them a second time" (Wiesel 2006, xv). In his words, "My message is a very simple one: never fight against memory. Even if it is painful, it will help you; it will give you something; it will enrich you ... One cannot live without it. One cannot exist without remembrance" (Bochert-Kimmig 1999, 67).

In his 2006 introduction to his wife's updated translation of *Night*, Wiesel reflected, "Sometimes I am asked if I know 'the response to Auschwitz?' I don't even know if a tragedy of such magnitude *has* a response. What I do know is there is a 'response' in responsibility. When we speak of this era of evil and darkness, so close and yet so distant, 'responsibility' is the key word. The witness has forced himself to testify. For the youth of today, for the children who will be born tomorrow. He does not want his past to become their future" (Wiesel 2006, xv).

Margaret Gay

References

Bochert-Kimmig, Reinhold, and Ekkehard Schuster. *Hope against Hope: Johann Baptist Metz and Elie Wiesel Speak Out on the Holocaust*. Edited by J. Matthew Ashley. Mahwah, NJ: Paulist Press, 1999.

Elie Wiesel Foundation web site. http://www.eliewieselfoundation.org (accessed April 11, 2011).

Nomberg-Przytyk, Sara, and Eli Pfefferkorn, eds. *Auschwitz: True Tales from a Grotesque Land*. Translated by Roslyn Hirsch. Chapel Hill: University of North Carolina Press, 1985.

Stern, Ellen Norman. *Elie Wiesel: A Voice for Humanity*. Philadelphia: Jewish Publication Society, 1996.

United States Holocaust Memorial Museum web site. "Holocaust History: Introduction to the Holocaust." http://www.ushmm.org/wlc/en/article.php?ModuleId=10005143 (accessed April 11, 2011).

Wiesel, Elie. *All Rivers Run to the Sea: Memoirs*. New York: Schocken Books, 1995.

Wiesel, Elie. *Legends of Our Time*. New York: Rinehart and Winston, 1968.

Wiesel, Elie. *Night*. Translated by Marion Wiesel. New York: Hill and Wang, 2006. (Originally published in 1958 by Les Editions de Minuit, France, as *La Nuit*.)

Wiesel, Elie. "Remarks at Millennium Evening: The Perils of Indifference: Lessons Learned from a Violent Century." White House Official Transcript, April 12, 1999. http://www.historyplace.com/speeches/wiesel-transcript.htm (accessed April 16, 2011).

Wolf, Hazel (1898–2000)

Originally from British Columbia, Canada, Hazel Wolf lived most of her life as a citizen of the United States. But because she had been a member of the Communist Party, as were many other citizens during the Great Depression of the 1930s, the U.S. government tried to deport Wolf to Canada. With a little persuasion from Wolf's friends, the Canadian government refused to accept her, so the U.S. Immigration and Naturalization Service (INS) tried to exile her to Great Britain, but that effort failed also.

Wolf left the party in 1947, but for more than a decade, the U.S. government tracked her activities, harassed her, and attempted to deport her. She became a U.S. citizen in 1974, according to her biographer and the King County, Washington, historical web site. From then on, she was a civil rights advocate, especially protesting the abusive treatment of the foreign born by the INS. She also became an avid environmental activist, working from Seattle, Washington, where she made her home.

When she was born in Victoria, British Columbia, on March 10, 1898, she was named Hazel Anna Cummings Anderson. She often declared that it seemed as if she had been named after a nut—the hazelnut. Her father, George William Anderson, was a Scottish-born Canadian and a seaman in the merchant marines; her mother, Nellie Frayne Anderson, was American born. She and George met while he was stationed in Tacoma, Washington, where she was a waitress; they married in 1894. She lost her citizenship, however, when she married George. As Hazel explained, "Both in Canada and in the United States, women lost their citizenship if they married foreigners, and that law prevailed right up until 1922." When Nellie was about to give birth to Hazel, George was at sea, so Nellie went to Victoria to stay with her husband's parents. Thus Hazel was born a Canadian citizen (Starbuck 2002, 13).

In 1903, Hazel's father was injured in a shipboard accident and was an invalid for the rest of his life. He died in 1908. Hazel's mother took a variety of menial jobs to support her family, which included Hazel and two younger siblings, brother George and sister Dorothy. They grew up in Victoria in what Hazel called a "tough neighborhood" with prostitutes and "rough elements." Some of the prostitutes paid "walloping good money" to rent rooms in the Anderson home, but, as Hazel noted, "They went to hotels when they had their clients" (Starbuck 2002, 24).

During her childhood, Hazel was rebellious, stubborn, mischievous, and adventurous. She loved playing in the streets with a gang of boys. Although some of them were in trouble with the police, Hazel never was caught breaking the law. Her favorite activities were connected with the sea and an inlet called the Gorge. She spent as much time as possible swimming, boating, fishing, and camping on the beach, and dreamed of being a sailor. In addition, she loved to play basketball and ride her bicycle. She was an outdoor person, who early in her life appreciated the natural world and the living things she found and studied.

Hazel's schooling shifted between a parochial school and public school for the elementary grades. She attended a private Catholic school when her mother could afford the tuition. When there was little money, Hazel went to public school. She did not attend high school because she had to get a job to help support the family. She completed a secretarial course and found a job with a law firm.

In 1913, Hazel's mother married again, and Hazel spent most of her teenage years filled with hate for her stepfather Jacob Hughes, although as she wrote, "Jacob didn't abuse me. I abused him.... He was a really good man.... He financed my stenography training, and he found me jobs." She finally reconciled with him when she was 18 or 19 years old. "I realized what a creep I had been!" she said (Starbuck 2000, 47).

When she was nearly 20 years old, Hazel fell in love. She told her biographer: "I married the first guy who kissed me, and that was Ted Dalziel," a member of a family she had known most of her life. The couple's daughter, Nydia, was born in December 1918. But by 1920, the marriage was over. "Marriage was a custom I couldn't stay with," she said. "It had nothing to do with my husband, his personality, or any of those things, because he was a truly fine person, but we had hardly anything in common" (Starbuck 2000, 59, 62).

Hazel needed to find a job, but as was common practice at that time, employers would not hire married women. So, according to her biographer, in 1921, Hazel left her daughter with her mother in Victoria and went to the United States to search for a job in Seattle, Washington. Only menial work was available, but she finally found a secretarial job and in 1923 was able to make a home with her daughter at a Catholic boarding house in Seattle. Hazel's mother, brother, and sister moved to Port Angeles, Washington, in 1925 and with her family nearby, Hazel felt she had two homes—Port Angeles and Seattle. She frequently traveled back and forth between the two cities.

By 1928, Hazel was married again—to Herbert Wolf. They lived near Port Angeles for a time. But that marriage also was brief, and after her divorce, Hazel Wolf returned to Seattle.

Seattle in the 1930s was like most U.S. cities that suffered from the Great Depression, with tens of thousands out of work. Many of Seattle's unemployed had worked either in the shipbuilding and shipping industries, or in the Northwest lumber mills that had closed. According to a news report, "Hundreds of men lived in a shantytown known as 'Hooverville,' a few blocks south of [downtown], where the unemployed picked their own mayor, enforced their own rules and tweaked the establishment. The climate was ripe for radical politics" (Anderson 2001). "Hooverville" was a common name for homeless settlements at the time; they were named derisively for President Herbert Hoover, who some believed was responsible for the Depression. In this type of setting, the Communist Party of the United States of America (CPUSA) flourished as it attempted to help the unemployed. By then, Wolf had no job and received relief aid (welfare checks) through the Federal Emergency Relief Act that provided funds to the states. In 1934, while she was in line for her welfare check, she met a member of the CPUSA, who invited her to a meeting. She was impressed with the CPUSA's advocacy for social justice and emphasis on education, and joined the party.

During the 1930s, President Franklin D. Roosevelt's administration established more than a dozen "New Deal" programs or laws. Along with the Federal Emergency Relief Act were the Public Works Administration that provided federal funds for public works nationwide; the Agricultural Administration Act that provided aid to farmers; the Civil Works Administration that provided public works jobs; the Civilian Conservation Corps that hired young men for conservation and reforestation projects; and the Works Progress Administration, better known by its acronym WPA. The WPA employed workers to construct bridges and buildings such as libraries and in the arts, music, theater, photography, and writing projects. Wolf was hired for several WPA jobs, one of which was secretary for the Federal Theater Project in Seattle, Washington.

After World War II began in Europe, jobs became more plentiful in the United States, and Wolf began to lose interest in the Communist Party. The U.S. Congress passed legislation in 1940 to establish a military draft, and thousands became part of the military. Jobs increased in industries, especially those manufacturing war supplies.

Wolf left the Communist Party in 1947 and that same year attempted for the third time to gain U.S. citizenship. Her two earlier attempts had ended in denial. In her first application she missed the INS hearing because she was in the hospital; the INS denied her second application on the grounds that she was immoral. However, she was allowed to live in the United States as a legal resident alien.

Wolf's third application for citizenship came at a time when State Representative Albert Canwell from Spokane was heading a Fact-Finding Committee on Un-American Activities that held hearings regarding what Canwell declared were communists in "the Washington Pension Union [WPU], an advocacy group that had won increased social security benefits for seniors and pensions for single mothers. In carefully orchestrated testimony, a parade of friendly witnesses claimed that the WPU served as a front-group for the Communist Party. Next, the committee took aim at the University of Washington, where one politician claimed there were over 100 Communists on the university faculty" (Gregory). The Washington committee helped set the stage for the U.S. congressional hearings chaired by Senator Joseph McCarthy, who falsely claimed communists had infiltrated the U.S. Army and other institutions. During the "Red Scare," as the anticommunist period was called, the INS attacked numerous aliens. Wolf was among those the INS labeled "foreign born subversives."

In 1949, the INS began another attempt to deport Wolf. At the time, she was working as a secretary in the law office of John Caughlan, who defended her throughout the next 14 years that the INS sought her deportation. By the end of 1963, the INS finally dismissed charges, and more than a decade later, in 1974, she became an American citizen, although she called herself "a citizen of the world" (Starbuck 2002, 163–64).

Before gaining citizenship, Wolf took another direction in her life. A friend, who was a member of the Audubon Society, had been urging Wolf to join the group. But, Wolf said, "I didn't want to belong to that group of bird-watchers" (Starbuck 2002, 173). Nevertheless, she went on a field trip to Seattle's Lincoln Park and observed the activities of birds among the Douglas Fir trees. Her friend urged her to attend a meeting of the Seattle Audubon Society, and once there, Wolf decided to join the group. She retired from her job with Caughlan in 1965, and became active in the Seattle Audubon as secretary, helping to organize 21 Audubon state chapters. The organizations went beyond bird-watching to become environmental lobbyists.

Wolf's environmental concerns were underscored with Rachel Carson's book *Silent Spring* (1962), which pointed out that the overuse of pesticides killed birds and other wildlife. Carson posited the argument that nothing exists in nature alone, and that people had the right to live in a safe environment.

Advocating for environmental conservation and preservation, Wolf was a member of numerous organizations that campaigned for environmental protection such as Greenpeace, the Earth Island Institute, and the Sierra Club. She was president of the Federation of Western Outdoor Clubs and editor of the federation's magazine.

"In 1979, Hazel became one of the nation's first forest advocates to ally with Native Americans," according to Bill Donahue writing for the conservation magazine *American Forests*. "She visited most of Washington's 24 tribes to speak about logging and salmon. The result: a conference of representatives from most tribes and from Sierra Club and Greenpeace." The tribal groups called "Hazel 'el lobo loco' (Spanish for 'crazy wolf,').... She is fearless and peerless ... [and] played a key role in protecting native fishing rights and in saving Indian sacred forests, such as a 7,000-acre grove of cedar on Whidbey Island in Puget Sound," according to a "treaty rights specialist for Washington's Lummi Indian Nation," Donahue wrote (1996, 48).

Some of her other activities included work with environmental justice groups such as those articulated by Professor Robert Bullard in his book *Dumping on Dixie* (1990). Bullard's studies found that toxic landfills, incinerators, petrochemical plants, and nuclear dumps were located in communities made up predominately of people of color who had little power to resist. Wolf helped organize a Community Coalition for Environmental Justice in Seattle. She also was convinced that the revolutionary Sandinistas in Nicaragua would lead the way in a worldwide environmental justice movement. In this Central American country, the Sandinistas "connected stewardship for the land with democratic socialism for the people" (Starbuck 2002, 125).

During her lifetime, Wolf received many awards from environmental groups, government officials, and socialist publications. She remained active in her advocacy for the causes she championed, and physically active in the outdoors—snowboarding, kayaking, hiking, and bird watching—into her 90s. She was recovering from hip replacement surgery in a Port Angeles, Washington, nursing home, when she died on January 19, 2000.

See also Bullard, Robert; Carson, Rachel; McCarthy, Joseph

References

Anderson, Ross. "Gritty 'Old Seattle's' Last Stand: The 1930s." *Seattle Times*, July 29, 2001. http://seattletimes.nwsource.com/

news/local/seattle_history/articles/story6.html (accessed December 18, 2010).

Cushman, John H., Jr. "Hazel Wolf, 101; Fought for the Environment." *New York Times*, January 24, 2000. http://www.nytimes.com/2000/01/24/us/hazel-wolf-101-fought-for-the-environment.html (accessed December 16, 2010).

Donahue, Bill. " 'El lobo loco.' (Hazel Wolf's Campaigns for the Conservation of Forests and the Environment)." *American Forests*, Summer 1996.

Gregory, James (project director). "The 1948 Canwell Un-American Activities Hearings." Communism in Washington State History and Memory Project, n.d. http://depts.washington.edu/labhist/cpproject/canwell_hearings.shtml (accessed December 19, 2010).

Tate, Cassandra. "Wolf, Hazel (1898–2000)." HistoryLink: The Free Online Encyclopedia of Washington State History, n.d. http://www.historylink.org/index.cfm?DisplayPage=output.cfm&file_id=8794 (accessed December 18, 2010).

Starbuck, Susan. *Hazel Wolf: Fighting the Establishment*. Seattle and London: University of Washington Press, 2002.

Woodhull, Victoria (1838–1927)

While others of my sex devoted themselves to a crusade against the laws that shackle the women of the country, I asserted my individual independence; while others prayed for the good time coming, I worked for it; while others argued the equality of woman with man, I proved it by successfully engaging in business; while others sought to show that there was no valid reason why women should not be treated, socially and politically, as being inferior to man, I boldly entered the arena of politics and business and exercised the rights I already possessed. I therefore claim the right to speak for the unenfranchised women of the country, and believing as I do that the prejudices which still exist in the popular mind against women will soon disappear, I now announce myself as candidate for the Presidency. (Woodhull and Carpenter 2010, 1–2)

The above comments from Victoria Woodhull appeared in the *New York Herald* on April 2, 1870. Woodhull was—to put it mildly—one of the more contentious activists of the nineteenth and early twentieth centuries. A feminist, socialist, spiritualist, and political figure, she was notable not only for her outspokenness in a time when women were traditionally "seen and not heard," but also for the flamboyant fashion in which she chose to make her case. She patently refused to honor conventional boundaries of public behavior, challenging gender roles, questioning sexual mores, and demanding equal rights for women.

Life was much more restrictive for women during the time in which Woodhull lived. They had little to limited rights regarding property and their person. Married women who worked had their wages given directly to their spouses. Women were unable to dispose of their property upon death. Divorcees automatically gave up custody of their children. Women were not allowed to attend universities, law schools, or medical schools, nor could they serve on juries, nor exercise the right to vote. Women had similarly little to limited control and protection over their bodies and physical well-being. Laws did not exist to prohibit abuse from their mates (although in some states, laws stipulated the size of objects used to inflict discipline). Wives could not legally deny their husbands sexual congress.

Career choices were limited to domestic positions, factory work, teaching, writing, and prostitution. While men could and were expected to exercise all manner of sexual freedoms, women who strayed from their marital vows faced imprisonment (Goldsmith 2010).

Born on September 23, 1838, in Homer, Ohio, and named Victoria California Claflin, Victoria had an unusual upbringing that had much to do with the adult person she became. Her childhood, such as it was, instilled in her both deeply held convictions and an unparallel free spirit. She was the seventh of 10 children (three did not survive) and was named after the queen of England. Her mother, Roxanna, was zealously religious, a "spiritualist" before the movement existed, according to her daughter. "Victoria's biographer, Theodore Tilton, later wrote that Mama Roxy, 'tormented and harried her children until they would be thrown into spasms, whereat she would hysterically laugh, clap her hands, and look as fiercely delighted as a cat in playing with a mouse ... This lady, compounded in equal parts of Heaven and Hell will pray till her eyes are full of tears and in the same hour curse till her lips are white with foam'" (Goldsmith 1998, 19).

The youngest member of the Claflin family, Tennessee Celeste, was seven years younger than Victoria. Both girls were considered quite attractive, as well as somewhat eccentric. From an early age, they seemed to follow in Roxanna's footsteps, claiming to be clairvoyant. "Tennie" was even believed to possess healing abilities.

Not many kind words can be found about Victoria's father, Reuben Buck Claflin. Most often, he is described as a con man of the snake-oil salesman variety. He was deemed a jack-of-all-trades in that he would try just about anything if it might possibly offer a

American feminist reformer Victoria Woodhull was one of the more contentious activists of the 19th and early 20th centuries. A feminist, socialist, spiritualist, and political figure, she was notable not only for her outspokenness, but also for the flamboyant fashion in which she chose to make her case. (Hulton Archive/Getty Images)

sliver of easy financial reward. He recognized that Victoria possessed great oratory abilities and, from the age of eight, took her on the revival circuit to preach redemption to sinners and put coins in the family's coffers. In time, Claflin created a traveling spiritualist show, which featured folk medicine and fortune telling. The family profited from Victoria's and Tennie's talents, but the girls suffered greatly, both physically and mentally.

Exhausted from so many years of continuous abuse and manipulation, Victoria eagerly escaped into marriage by eloping when she was just 15 years old. Her choice was unfortunate: Dr. Canning Woodhull, who was more than 12 years her senior and a reputed alcoholic and womanizer. After they married, Victoria often had to work a variety of jobs to support herself, Canning, and their two children—a daughter, Zula, and a son, Byron, who was born with a mental disability. The couple divorced in 1864.

It is quite possible that Victoria developed her belief in the idea of "free love" during and because of her experience with Canning. In the United States at that period in time, social convention dictated that women remain in their marriages—period. Divorce was considered a great scandal. A divorcee was beyond the pale for interaction in proper society and a stigma most women could not endure. Victoria believed that a woman should have the right to leave an unbearable marriage. She thought it was hypocritical when married men could have mistresses on the side and visit prostitutes, in blatant disregard of their marital vows. She summed up her position on the subject as follows:

> Yes, I am a Free Lover. I have an *inalienable*, *constitutional*, and *natural* right to love whom I may, to love as long or as short a period as I care; to *change* that love *every day* if I please, and with *that* right neither *you* nor any *law* you can frame have *any right to interfere*. And I have the further right to demand a free and unrestricted exercise of that right, and it is *your duty* not only to *accord* it, but as a community, to see that I am protected in it. I trust that I am fully understood, for I mean *just* that, and nothing less! (Woodhull 2010, 52)

Regardless of her adamant advocacy for "free love," Victoria also believed in monogamous relationships—stipulating that each woman should be able to choose which type of lifestyle was appropriate for her. Victoria once again did so when she married her second husband, Colonel James Blood, in 1866.

In 1868, Victoria and her sister made their way to New York City, gaining access to its social circles via their talents for fortune telling and spiritualism. Their beauty and charms did much to ease their entry, as well. The girls caught the attention of elderly, wealthy, railroad magnate and industrialist Cornelius Vanderbilt, who is said to have romanced—and possibly proposed—to the younger sister. Vanderbilt gave the women financial advice and assistance in starting up Woodhull, Claflin & Co., the first ever female-owned brokerage company on Wall Street. When the business opened in 1870, Victoria and Tennessee were heralded as "the Queens of Finance" and "the Bewitching Brokers." At the time, articles ran that portrayed the women in suggestive ways; all the same, the venture proved to be a success.

Two years later, with some of the capital they had accrued from the profits from their firm, Victoria and Tennessee founded *Woodhull and Claflin's Weekly*, a newspaper that would eventually grow to have 20,000 subscribers. The *Weekly* became a mouthpiece for the women to espouse their views on equal rights for women, a single standard of morality for both sexes and, of course, for free love. Victoria was not only interested in issues concerning the female gender, however; the newspaper also covered other subjects about which she was passionate, such as various labor reform issues of the day.

Her very vocal and visible position on women's rights would, one would think, endear her to those in suffragette movement of the day—that is, those advocating for women's right to vote. However, her radical ways (translation: personal promiscuity and advocacy for free love) polarized the movement. The conservative and moderate suffragettes wanted nothing to do with Victoria, while others looked on her "no holds barred" attitude with awe and admiration. It was with just such chutzpah that the two sisters, U.S. Constitution in hand, valiantly tried to cast their votes in the 1871 elections. That unsuccessful effort resulted in a drawing that ran nationally in *Harper's Weekly*, entitled, "Mrs. Woodhull Asserting Her Right to Vote."

Woodhull also achieved two other notable "firsts" in 1871. She made an impassioned speech on women's rights to the U.S. House Judiciary Committee—the first such appearance by a female before such a highly regarded congressional committee; she favorably impressed the legislators and even won over many of her suffragette critics.

Also, toward the end of that year, in the December 13, 1871, edition of the *Weekly*, she and her sister published the first English translation of Karl Marx's *Communist Manifesto*. This 1848 pamphlet called for an overthrow of capitalism, the abolition of private property, and a takeover of the means of production. Ironically, Victoria eventually lost her party membership because of her radical feminist positions.

A year later, on February 17, 1872, another illustration appeared in *Harper's*. This time, in the background, a frazzled, unkempt young woman is shown traversing a rocky cliff, one child in arms, another child and drunken husband toted on her back. A horned and winged Victoria Woodhull stands in the foreground with a sign, "BE SAVED BY FREE LOVE." The caption reads: "Get thee behind me, (Mrs.) Satan!" (Woodhull 2010, xxiii).

Although not embraced wholeheartedly by the suffragette movement, Victoria was more the liking of the minor National Reform Party or the Equal Rights Party (a splinter group of more radical feminists). It supported women's right to vote, work, and love freely; the nationalization of land; cost-based pricing; labor rights; reduction of interest rates; free speech; and free press. At its convention at the Apollo Hall in New York City in 1872, the party chose Victoria Woodhull as its presidential nominee, with abolitionist and former slave Frederick Douglass as her vice presidential running mate. Douglass did not accept this nomination and, instead, served as a presidential elector in the U.S. Electoral College for the state of New York. Woodhull became a footnote in history for being the first woman ever to run for the U.S. presidency, even though she was never considered to be a serious threat to incumbent Ulysses S. Grant or his opponent, newspaperman Horace Greeley.

After Victoria's presidential run, she and Tennessee continued to be a source of gossip and innuendo. Author Harriet Beecher Stowe and her sister Catharine Beecher were two of their more vociferous critics. Dually motivated by revenge and to expose hypocrisy, the sisters published an expose in the *Weekly* on February 2, 1872, accusing Henry Ward Beecher of Brooklyn's Plymouth Church, Harriet and Catharine's brother, of adultery. They ran another expose about stockbroker Luther Challis's self-proclaimed scandalous exploits involving young girls. Both women, along with Victoria's husband, the colonel, were arrested and jailed. They were charged with libel with regard to the first article and under the Comstock Law—for the distribution of obscene material via the mail—for the second. They spent considerable time in jail and considerable funds before the charges were dropped in 1873 and 1874, respectively. The ordeal took its toll on Victoria's health as well as on her reputation. She was never able to regain the credibility she once had with preexisting supporters. In October 1876, Victoria divorced for the second time.

The sisters decided to make a fresh start and moved to England in 1877. Each married Englishmen: in 1883, Victoria married her third and final husband, a wealthy banker named John Biddulph Martin; Tennessee wed Francis Cook, an English art collector, who became a baronet.

The women lectured as well as published books and pamphlets. Victoria's writings include *Stiripculture or the Propagation of the Human Race*, *The Human Body, the Temple of God* (cowritten with Tennessee), and *Humanitarian Money*. With her daughter Zulu, from 1892 to 1910, she also copublished a eugenics journal entitled, *Humanitarian*, about the study of hereditary improvement of the human race by controlled selective breeding. Tennessee died in 1923; Victoria died on June 10, 1927, while living as a widow at her country estate in Norton Park, Bremons, Worcestershire, England.

In 2003, in honor of Victoria's life and accomplishments, the Woodhull Freedom Foundation was established to promote sexual freedom as a fundamental human right.

Margaret Gay

References

Goldsmith, Barbara. *Other Powers: The Age of Suffrage, Spiritualism and the Scandalous Victoria Woodhull*. New York: Alfred S. Knopf, Inc., 1998.

Goldsmith, Barbara. "About Victoria Woodhull." Woodhull Sexual Freedom Alliance.org, 2011. http://www.woodhullalliance.org/about-us/about-victoria-woodhull/ (accessed September 5, 2011).

Tilton, Theodore. "Victoria C. Woodhull, a Biographical Sketch." New York: Office of *The Golden Age*, 1871. http://www.victoria-woodhull.com/tiltonbio.htm (accessed March 12, 2011).

Woodhull, Victoria, and Cari M. Carpenter, eds. *Selected Writings of Victoria Woodhull: Suffrage, Free Love, and Eugenics*. Lincoln: Board of Regents of the University of Nebraska, 2010.

Wright, Ann (1947–)

"I believe the Administration's policies are making the world a more dangerous, not a safer, place. I feel obligated morally and professionally to set out my very deep and firm concerns on these policies and to resign from government service as I cannot defend or implement them" (Wright 2003). So wrote retired colonel Ann Wright to U.S. Secretary of State Colin Powell on March 19, 2003. After serving 13 years in the U.S. Army, followed by 16 years in the U.S. Army Reserves, several years serving in the Foreign Service and as U.S. deputy ambassador, Wright resigned her post in public protest of U.S. government policy under the administration of President George W. Bush.

"It was hard. I liked representing America," Wright explained in a 2005 interview (Engelhardt 2005). Her stance became even more difficult when three years after her resignation, she was charged with sedition because of her antiwar activities.

Born in 1947, Mary Ann Wright experienced a "normal childhood" while growing up in Bentonville, Arkansas. Her father worked as a banker. In fact, her father gave Sam Walton a loan that helped launch the Wal-Mart Corporation (Sizemore 2008). She was a member of the Girl Scouts, which helped to provide the foundation for her career in the military. Working on the Girl Scout badges, she had the opportunity to travel and learned to create and achieve goals. The Girl Scouts reflected those organizations she would later work in, including state departments and the military. "It's kind of interesting, the militarization of our society, how we don't really think of some things, and yet when I look back, there was a little Girl Scout in my green uniform," she explains (Engelhardt 2005). Wright even learned to salute while in the Girl Scouts.

During the mid-1960s, as the Vietnam War raged in Southeast Asia, Wright attended the University of Arkansas initially as an education major. In her junior year, she saw the film, *Join the Army, See the World*, and listened to an army recruiter speak about opportunities for women. She became intrigued with the idea of joining the army. This was a time when career opportunities for women were limited. Not wanting a career as a teacher or a nurse, Wright signed up for the three-week training program. She found the program challenging, and the experience helped her to decide to join the army. Wright went on to earn both a master's degree and her law degree. Eventually, Wright would earn a master's degree in national security affairs from the U.S. Naval War College in Newport, Rhode Island.

Wright enlisted into the army reserves from May 27, 1967, to May 31, 1968. On June 1, 1968, Wright became active duty in the army and served for 13 years. On October 1, 1984, she joined the reserves, and served another 16 years in the service of her country. She also became airborne qualified.

While in the army, Wright's responsibility concerned the law of warfare and included special operations in civil affairs. From 1982 to 1984, she was based in Fort Bragg, North Carolina, home of the 82nd Airborne, which was one of the first forces used in rapid deployment. During this time, the army was planning contingency operations in what would become Central Command should the United States attack foreign countries, including the Middle East. As Wright explains, she helped to develop "plans about how to interact with the civilian population, how you protect the facilities—sewage, water, electrical grids, libraries." Wright helped to develop such plans "for every country in the world, or virtually. So we did one on Iraq; we did one on Syria; on Jordan, Egypt. All of them." According to Wright, such plans were their obligation under the law of land welfare (Engelhardt 2005).

During the 1980s, Wright became part of a group of women who challenged the army's Direct Combat Probability Coding for army units. As the army tried to reduce the career potential of military women, she became "a bit of a rabble-rouser" (Engelhardt 2005). On November 19, 1987, Martin M. Ferber, senior associate director of national security and international affairs, began his testimony to the U.S. House of Representatives, reassessing the roles of women in the services.

Achieving the rank of colonel, Wright retired from active duty. In October 1984, she was placed in Retired Ready Reserves. This meant that the president could call her back to active duty during a time of need. In 1987, Wright joined the Foreign Service within the U.S. State Department to work as a diplomat. For 16 years, she traveled the world. Coauthoring an article with fellow diplomats John Brown and Brady Kiesling, Wright and her colleagues defined their responsibilities: "Our job was to build effective relationships with key figures outside the United States. We used our language skills, respectful curiosity, and understanding of local politics to promote U.S. national interests as our president and secretary of state directed" (Wright, Brown, and

Kiesling 2008). Because of her military background, she often served in combat environments. She was deputy chief of mission of U.S. Embassies in war-torn countries such as Grenada, Uzbekistan, Nicaragua, and Somalia.

While serving in Sierra Leone, she helped evacuate 2,500 persons as the country exploded in civil war. As a result of her actions, she received the State Department's Award for Heroism. When she was assigned to Somalia, she worked on loan to the United Nations' operations. She witnessed the UN military actions, including the bombing of buildings, as they hunted down rebel leader Mohamed Farrah Addid, who was not found. Wright wrote a legal opinion to the special representative of the secretary general, detailing her concerns over these military tactics. The memo was leaked to the *Washington Post*. While initially Wright was disciplined for her memo, her analysis eventually proved accurate.

When assigned in Grenada, she was part of the team who discovered many U.S. troops looting private homes. These soldiers were eventually court-martialed for a violation of the law of land warfare. Wright and her team used this example when they rewrote how the code of conduct and the Geneva Convention on the responsibility of occupiers are taught.

Retired army colonel Ann Wright is removed by police on Capitol Hill in Washington, September 11, 2007, as General David Petraeus and U.S. ambassador to Iraq Ryan Crocker testified on the future course of the war in Iraq before the Senate Foreign Relations Committee. Wright resigned from the military in public protest of U.S. government policy under the administration of President George W. Bush. (AP Photo/Gerald Herbert)

In December 2001, three months after the September 11 attacks on the World Trade Center, Wright felt the need to respond to the attacks and volunteered to be part of the first State Department team to go to Kabul, Afghanistan, after the evacuation of the Taliban. Their job was to reopen the U.S. embassy, which had been closed for 12 years. Wright knew it was going to be a tough assignment.

During this time, the Islamist guerrilla warriors, the Taliban, continued battling each other for control of Afghanistan. Wright and her team had taken the interim president of the Afghan Transitional Administration, Hamid Karzai, to the air base, where he was safely sent to the United States. He had been invited to hear President Bush's State of the Union address.

On January 29, 2002, as rockets fired over their heads, Wright and her team hid in a bunker in Kabul. They listened to President Bush's State of the Union address on a television powered by a satellite dish made of pounded-out Coke cans and a computer chip sent from Islamabad. Waiting to hear news about what would happen in Afghanistan, she instead listened to a speech that to her resounded like a war cry, labeling Iran, Iraq, and North Korea as the axis of evil. Wright grew concerned about the future of the United States in Afghanistan. Her concern grew as 100,000 troops were stationed in the Middle East. She suspected that the Bush administration had ulterior motives. The administration was asking for UN inspectors to return to Iraq to investigate evidence of weapons of destruction, but the military buildup seemed well underway. "I was hoping against hope that our government would not go into what really is an illegal war of aggression that meets no criteria of international law" (Engelhardt 2005).

In March 2003, Wright was reassigned to Mongolia as deputy ambassador. She continued to follow developments in Afghanistan and Iraq. By this time, war was apparent. As Wright explains in the prologue of her book, *Dissent: Voices of Conscience* (2008), "This was the first time I ever thought about resigning. I loved my job and serving my country, and wanted to continue. But a foreign service officer's assignment is to implement the policies of the administration in power, and if one disagrees strongly with an administration's policy and wants to speak out publicly, the only option is to resign" (Wright 2008, xi).

On March 13, 2003, the eve of the U.S. invasion of Iraq, Colonel Ann Wright sent a letter of resignation to then secretary of state Colin Powel. She cited four reasons for her resignation: (1) her disagreement with the administration's policy on Iraq; (2) the administration's lack of effort in resolving the Israeli-Palestinian conflict; (3) the administration's lack of policy on North Korea; (4) her disagreement with the administration's policies on the curtailment of civil liberties within the United States.

After her resignation, Wright began to speak publicly in protest of the war in Iraq and other policies. As Wright describes in a 2005 interview, "I slowly but surely have been moving towards the need for civil disobedience" (*Revolution* 2005). Since then, Wright has become a prominent figure in social activism.

In August 2005, Wright demonstrated with antiwar activist Cindy Sheehan outside George W. Bush's ranch in Crawford, Texas. She worked again with Sheehan in September 2005 on the antiwar protest and rally, Bring Them Home Now bus tour. On September 26, 2005, Wright was arrested while demonstrating in front of the White House. Wright explains the irony of her arrest, "[A]s a representative of the United States . . . I always encouraged other countries to look at the United States and the strength we had, in our government and in our citizens. That we could protest and challenge our government. . . . Now I am doing the acts that I encouraged in other countries, you know?" (*Revolution* 2005).

In January 2006, Wright served as one of five judges at the International Commission of Inquiry on Crimes against Humanity Committed by the Bush Administration. In a January 2010 interview with Jacob Shafer, Wright details why she believes members of the Bush administration should be tried for war crimes. "If the Bush administration is not held accountable for creating a war of choice, not for the defense of our country, then future administrations may be tempted to put our nation at war for equally illegal purposes" (Shafer 2010).

In 2006, Wright was charged with sedition for passing out flyers on the film, *Sir, No Sir: The Suppressed Story of the GI Movement to End the War In Vietnam*, on a military base. According to the army spokesperson, Wright was charged because "Col. Wright was inappropriately distributing literature in violation of Army Regulations 210-7 and 360-1, Section 3-8, which prohibit distribution of any non-DoD material on an Army installation without prior permission from the installation commander" (Goodman 2006). She has been banned from two military bases for placing postcards on the grounds about the documentary. She is also banned permanently from the National Press Club.

Critics, including such conservative organizations as Free Republic and Protest Warriors, claim that Wright's activism is insulting and undermines support for the troops. Responds Wright, "Military personnel and their families do not make the decisions to go to war. Elected politicians make those decisions. Dissent against the decision is toward the politicians, not toward the military" (Shafer 2010).

Wright is a member of Code Pink: Women for Peace, founded in 2002 by a group of women, including antiwar activist Medea Benjamin. The group has been criticized for vigorous publicity tactics, including the 2005 demonstration at Walter Reed Medical Hospital Center in Washington, D.C., in which the group displayed coffins and chanted aggressive slogans.

In December 2008, Wright and a handful of pro-Palestinian activists demonstrated outside the Kailua compound in Hawaii of then president-elect Barack Obama. Obama's chief national security spokesperson, Brooke Anderson, said, "The president-elect values citizen participation in our nation's foreign policy, but there is one president at a time, and we intend to respect that" (Rucker 2008).

In response to Israel's 22-day war in the Gaza Strip in December 2008, Wright became a leading member of the steering committee for the Gaza Freedom March. In 2009, Wright traveled to Gaza three times. In December 2009, the Gaza effort brought together 1,300 people from more than 40 countries in a nonviolent political march to end the blockade of the Gaza Strip. Endorsers of the march included such notables as Pulitzer Prize–winning novelist Alice Walker and Holocaust survivor Hedy Epstein, among others.

Wright has been honored with the first annual Truthout and Democracy Award, which she received in 2007. In May 2010, the Montana Peace Seekers named Wright the Peace Seeker of the Year 2010.

Bobbi Miller

See also Benjamin, Medea; Sheehan, Cindy; Walker, Alice

References

Bush State of the Union Address (transcript). CNN.com/Inside Politics, January 29, 2002. http://archives.cnn.com/2002/ALLPOLITICS/01/29/bush.speech.txt/ (accessed August 5, 2010).

Engelhardt, Tom. "Tomdispatch Interview: Ann Wright on Service to Country." *TomDispatch.com*. November 2005. http://www.tomdispatch.com/post/35448/ (accessed August 5, 2010).

Goodman, Amy. "Retired Army Cl. Charged with Sedition For Handing Flyer on Anti-War Vietnam Vets." *Democracy Now!* May 24, 2006. http://www.democracynow.org/2006/5/24/retired_army_col_charged_with_sedition (accessed August 17, 2010).

"The *Revolution* Interview: Ann Wright, Former U.S. Diplomat. Revolution #020," October 30, 2005. Revcom.us. http://revcom.us/a/020/ann-wright-interview.htm (accessed August 18, 2010).

Rucker, Philip. "Pro-Palestinian Activists Picket Obama Compound in Hawaii." *Washington Post*, December 30, 2008. http://voices.washingtonpost.com/44/2008/12/30/pro-palestinian_protesters_pic.html (accessed August 17, 2010).

Shafer, Jacob. "Interview with Retired Colonel Ann Wright. U.S. Labor against the War, January 21, 2010. http://www.uslaboragainstwar.org/article.php?id=21337 (accessed August 5, 2010).

Sizemore, Bill. "Retired Soldier Now in Fight against War in Iraq." U.S. Labor against the War, September 2008. http://uslaboragainstwar.org/article.php?id=17129 (accessed September 5, 2011).

"Truthout 2007: Freedom and Democracy Awards." *Truthout*, February 2007. http://www.democraticunderground.com/discuss/duboard.php?az=view_all&address=389x106194 (accessed November 4, 2011).

Wright, Ann, John Brown, and Brady Kiesling. "Why We Said No: Three Diplomats' Duty." *Huffington Post*, March 20, 2008. http://www.huffingtonpost.com/john-brady-kiesling/why-we-said-no-three-dipl_b_92488.html (accessed August 5, 2010).

Wright, Ann, and Susan Dixon. *Dissent: Voices of Conscience*. Maui, HI: Koa Books, 2008.

Wright, Mary Ann. "Mary A. Wright's Resignation Letter." Government Executive.com, March 21, 2003. http://www.govexec.com/dailyfed/0303/032103wright.htm (accessed August 5, 2010).

Yasui, Minoru (1916–1986)

When Minoru Yasui of Japanese descent was sent to a concentration camp (euphemistically called internment center) during World War II (1939–1945), he declared:

> It was my feeling and belief, then and now, that no military authority had the right to subject any United States citizen to any requirement that does not equally apply to all other U.S. citizens. Moreover, if a citizen believes that the sovereign state is committing an illegal act, it is incumbent upon that citizen to take measures to rectify that error, or so, at least, I believed. Finally, it seemed to me then and now that if the government unlawfully curtails the rights of any person, the damage is done not only to that individual person but to the whole society. If we believe in America, if we believe in equality and democracy, if we believe in law and justice, then each of us, when we see or believe errors are being made, has an obligation to make every effort to correct them. (Tateishi 1984, 70–71)

The government errors that Yasui referenced were the result of the Japanese attack on the U.S. naval base in Pearl Harbor on December 7, 1941, which resulted in the United States declaring war on its attacker. Americans feared another attack, and many believed that people of Japanese descent would be disloyal and be spies for Japan. On February 19, 1942, President Franklin D. Roosevelt signed an executive order mandating that tens of thousands of people of Japanese descent be forcefully removed from their U.S. homes and placed in internment camps where they lived in barracks or horse stables, surrounded by barbed wire and guarded by the military. Yasui was one of 120,000 people of Japanese descent relocated to a prison camp. Another was Yuri Kochiyama, whose experience radicalized her as it did Yasui. She became an avid civil rights activist and close friend of Malcolm X.

According to HistoryontheNet.com, "More than two thirds of those interned were American citizens and half of them were children. None had ever shown disloyalty to the nation. In some cases family members were separated and put in different camps. During the entire war only ten people were convicted of spying for Japan and these were all Caucasian."

Yasui's father, Masuo Minoru, immigrated to the United States from Japan in 1902 when he was only 16 years of age. Like many other Asians new to the country, he first found employment on a railway gang and then moved on to work as a houseboy for a family in Portland, Oregon. He was eager to assimilate in his new land. He studied Christianity at the local Methodist Church and attended night classes at the English Couch School, where he grew proficient in the native tongue. In time, his increasing familiarity with the English language enabled him to act as a go-between with Caucasian orchard owners and fellow immigrants (Tamura 1993, 75).

By 1908, Yasui co-owned a store—the Yasui Brothers Store—in Hood River, Oregon, a town located about 60 miles east of Portland, on the Columbia River Gorge. He also maintained a small fruit farm of his own. He married a Japanese immigrant named Shidzuyo, with whom he had many children (conflicting records report between seven and nine children). Their second child, Minoru, was born into this close-knit family on October 19, 1916. He was raised as a Methodist, attended the local public schools, and grew up in a world where his father was regarded as a respected and prominent leader in the Japanese American community (Ng 2002, 78).

After graduating from high school in 1933, Minoru attended the University of Oregon in Eugene. While in college, he participated in the U.S. Army's Reserve Officer's Training Corps (ROTC). Upon graduation in 1937, he was commissioned on December 8 of that same year as a second lieutenant in the reserves.

Minoru immediately enrolled in law school, choosing to stay at the University of Oregon. He graduated two years later, sat for the state bar, and passed. Of note, he was the first Japanese American citizen to do so (Tamura 1993, xiv). This significant feat aside, Minoru's attempts to earn a living practicing law in Portland proved unsuccessful. It was a particularly difficult time for anyone to find employment, let alone for someone of Japanese ancestry. So, with the assistance of his father's connections, Minoru managed to obtain a position in Chicago, Illinois, at the Japanese consulate. He was hired as one of several consular attaches. The United States required all citizens working for a foreign government to complete the appropriate paperwork, registering as an agent employed by a foreign nation. Minoru complied. In doing so, he

American lawyer Minoru Yasui in 1983 visiting the detainment camp where he was held during World War II because of his "Japanese ancestry." (Carl Iwasaki/Time Life Pictures/Getty Images)

described his day-to-day duties as mostly clerical—which they were—but indicated that he also occasionally gave speeches about Japan and its policies to American service clubs and other organizations as part of his responsibilities.

The day after the December 7, 1941, attack by Japan on Pearl Harbor, Minoru resigned from his employment with the Japanese consulate. He then made plans to return to Oregon. His first attempt to travel home by train was thwarted when the agent refused to sell a ticket to him. However, after he received written orders from the U.S. Army to report for duty, that paperwork enabled him to secure a ticket, and he was finally able to arrange transportation to the West Coast. Once there, when he initially tried to report for duty, he was told that he was unacceptable for service and ordered off base—despite the fact that he had the prerequisite military training and was a commissioned U.S. Army reserve officer. Although he had not been told so directly, Minoru suspected that he had been sent away because of his Japanese ancestry.

Shortly thereafter, his father Maruo was arrested and sent to a Department of Justice (DOJ) camp in Missoula, Montana, for a loyalty hearing. He was not allowed to have a lawyer represent him, although his son did travel to Missoula to observe the proceedings that he found farcical. Among the things the elder Yasui was questioned about were children's drawings of the Panama Canal that had been found in his home; it was asserted that the pictures might represent a potential bomb plot. Eventually, the hearing concluded with a determination that Masuo Yasui was potentially "disloyal," largely due to the fact that he had once received an award from the emperor of Japan prior to the start of the war. He remained jailed in Montana until being transferred to another DOJ camp located in Santa Fe, New Mexico (Ng 2002, 78–79).

This incident, coupled with the army's refusal to allow him to serve, caused Minoru to question various government actions with regard to Japanese American citizens. Over a matter of decades, some of the most significant of these included the following:

- 1922: The Supreme Court ruled in *Takeo v. Ozawa* that citizenship was limited to free white persons and aliens of African ancestry, banning those of Japanese ancestry from becoming naturalized citizens on the basis of race.
- 1923: The Immigration Act of 1924, which included the Natural Origins Act and the Asian Exclusion Act, barred all immigration from Japan.
- December 27, 1941: The U.S. attorney general ordered all suspected enemy aliens on the West Coast to turn in short-wave radios and cameras.
- January 14, 1942: the U.S. president ordered re-registration of all suspected enemy aliens in Western states.
- January 29, 1942: The U.S. attorney general issued orders removing all suspected enemy aliens from newly established "strategic military areas" on the West Coast.
- February 4, 1943: The U.S. attorney general established curfew zones in California.
- February 14, 1943: Lieutenant General John DeWitt, commander of the Western Defense Command, recommended removal of all Japanese and other subversive persons from West Coast areas.
- February 19, 1943: President Franklin Roosevelt signed Executive Order 9066 authorizing establishment of "military areas" that would exclude any and all persons as needed.

Minoru questioned the legality of the evacuations and the curfews that the military was enforcing. In fact, he questioned whether the entire Executive Order 9066 issued by the president was constitutional. He consulted with local Portland attorney Earl F. Bernard, who advised that challenging the law would be pointless unless and until there were criminal penalties associated with disobeying them—and, to date, there had not been any put in place. However, on March 21, President Roosevelt signed Public Law 503, making it a federal offense to violate any order by a military commander under the authority of Executive Order 9066. Minoru now had the elements he had been advised he needed for his challenge. He was prepared to take his stand against the curfew that had been imposed on all enemy aliens and Japanese American citizens, requiring them to be in their homes between 8:00 p.m. and 6:00 a.m., and restricting them to a five-mile radius from their homes to their places of work during non-curfew hours. In his mind, Minoru saw this as violating the "equal protection" clause of the U.S. Constitution, since it made a distinction between citizens based on their ancestry.

So, on March 28, 1942, Minoru deliberately broke the curfew by walking around downtown Portland late at night. When no one questioned his being out on the streets, he finally tracked down a police officer and asked to be arrested—showing him a copy of the military order and his birth certificate to verify his Japanese ancestry. However, the officer just told him to go home. Minoru then went to a police station and basically "argued himself into jail" (Ng 2002, 79).

While in jail, Minoru announced his further intent to disobey the newly issued proclamation forbidding voluntary migration by people of Japanese descent from the West Coast to areas outside the military zone. After his release on bail for the curfew charge and return home to Hood River, he was soon arrested again for a second charge of disobeying the evacuation charge.

He was held initially at the North Portland Livestock Pavilion, then later moved to the Minidoka Relocation Center in Idaho. However, his trial was held in federal court in Portland. The attorney he had initially consulted, Earl Bernard, provided his defense, and he chose to waive his rights to a jury trial, leaving his fate in the hands of a sole person—Judge James Alger Fee. After a lengthy deliberation, Judge Fee determined on November 16, 1942, that: (1) Public Law 503 was—as Minoru contended—not constitutional as it applied to U.S. citizens (that is, the curfew law was not legal) and (2) Minoru had forfeited his U.S. citizenship because he had worked for the Japanese consulate shortly after his graduation from law school and, therefore, the curfew order was legal as it applied to him at the time he disobeyed it (Ng 2002, 80–81).

Fee handed down a one-year sentence along with a fine of $5,000. Minoru filed an immediate appeal but, in the meantime, he was incarcerated in Multnomah County Jail in Portland, where he was kept in solitary confinement for nine months. His isolated living arrangements had been deemed necessary because he was declared an "enemy alien." Finally, his appeal was argued before the U.S. Supreme Court on May 10, 1943. On June 21, the highest court in the land handed down a split decision. The Supreme Court determined that Minoru still retained his U.S. citizenship; the Court reversed Judge Fee's earlier decision on this issue. However, the Court ruled unanimously that the government did have the authority to restrict the lives of civilian citizens during wartime and, thus, remanded Minoru's case to the lower court for resentencing on that charge. Judge Fee then removed the $5,000 fine and reduced Minoru's sentence to time served.

Released from jail, Minoru was moved to an internment camp, where he remained through the summer of 1944. He then went to Chicago, Illinois, for a brief period before making Denver, Colorado, his home for the remainder of his life. He faced another legal challenge in that state: once he had passed the bar there, he had to appeal the Colorado Supreme Court for permission to practice law.

In November 1945, he married fellow camp internee True Shibata, and they went on to have three daughters, Iris, Holly, and Laurel. In time, Minoru became quite involved in Denver community affairs and, similar to his father, became a well-respected and prominent community leader. In 1954, he was named chair of the Japanese-American Citizens League's (JACL) district that covered Colorado, Wyoming, Texas, Nebraska, New Mexico, and Montana. He also was a member of the Committee of Community Relations from 1959 to 1983, a group that dealt with race relations and other social issues; he served as its executive director from 1967 to 1983. In 1974, the annual Minoru Yasui Community Service Award was created in his honor to recognize members of the Denver volunteer community.

For nearly a decade, Minoru was active on a JACL committee devoted to the redress of World War II Japanese American internees' grievances, serving as chair in 1981. On a more personal note, in 1984, he filed a "coram nobis" (a writ addressed to a court, calling attention to errors of fact that would invalidate a judgment already given) in the federal court in Portland to have his conviction overturned. Unfortunately, he died in Hood River on November 12, 1986, never having had his record expunged. His widow attempted to complete Minoru's quest to clear his name; however, on October 5, 1987, the Supreme Court denied her petition to continue the case (Tamura 1993, xli).

Margaret Gay

See also Kochiyama, Yuri; Malcolm X

References

Ng, Wendy. *Japanese American Internment during World War II: A History and Reference Guide*. Westport, CT: Greenwood Press, 2002.

Tamura, Linda. *The Hood River Issei: An Oral History of Japanese Settlers in Oregon's Hood River Valley*. Champaign-Urbana: Board of Trustees of the University of Illinois, 1993.

Tateishi, John. *And Justice for All: An Oral History of the Japanese American Detention Camps*. New York: Random House, 1984.

"World War Two—Japanese Internment Camps in the USA." HistoryontheNet.com, updated February 1, 2011. http://www.historyonthenet.com/WW2/japan_internment_camps.htm (accessed March 6, 2011).

Yeshitela, Omali (1941–)

"A revolution that goes beyond reform is necessary. Reform serves only to perfect the process of expropriating value from people's labor and resources. A total transformation, a total overturning of the existing social system is absolutely necessary if Africans and other people here and all over the world are ever to know freedom" (Yeshitela 2005). Omali Yeshitela, whose given name at birth was Joseph Waller, is often called "the last man standing," because many of his allies in the Black Panther Party and related organizations during the 1960s and 1970s were killed in confrontations with law enforcement, including the Federal Bureau of Investigation.

Joseph Waller was born in St. Petersburg, Florida, on October 9, 1941, and was raised by his single mother and his grandmother Della Thomas. As a child, Joe was encouraged to learn how to read when he was only two years old, his grandmother beside him with the *St. Petersburg Times* spread out on the floor, the little boy working his way down through the stories, paragraph by paragraph, with his grandmother's help.

St. Petersburg is a city that long has prided itself on its tourist trade and as a retirement community where the elderly could live out their days in perpetual sunshine. One of the easily recognized symbols for the good life in St. Petersburg are the numerous green benches downtown; but in the past, an African American could be arrested for sitting on them. For Joe Waller and other African Americans, St. Petersburg was a typical southern city, where they were welcome to dirt-poor jobs with little prospects of a living wage or advancement, and where they were expected to stay in the shadows, allowing those of the white race to enjoy themselves.

In 1951 at the age of 10, Joe took a job helping at a shoeshine stand. When the owner told him to dance to attract more white customers, Joe refused, and after some heated words, walked away.

After joining the army in 1960, Joe looked forward to basic training, convinced that whites and blacks would live together, work together, and, if necessary, fight together for a common purpose, to protect the United States. That likelihood was tarnished when a fellow recruit, who was white, casually turned to Joe and complained about a black recruit who was having a casual conversation with a white woman at a railway station on the way to their training camp. "That young white recruit soon paid a price for his racism. When I saw him next he was black and blue from some black soldier he insulted face to face," Yeshitela recounted in a speech at University of South Florida on January 21, 2010.

Waller served in the U.S. Army, at one point as part of a tank team facing the Soviet troops in their tanks in the city of Berlin, Germany. He quickly realized that despite his willingness to serve, and his ability, that to many of the whites he served with, he was just a nigger.

In 1966, Waller joined the Student Nonviolent Coordinating Committee (SNCC) headed by Stokely Carmichael. Unlike the black leadership of people like Dr. Martin Luther King Jr., Carmichael through SNCC sought confrontation to push for civil rights, through activities such as sitting at restaurant counters, expecting and demanding to be served. One of the defining moments for Joe Waller becoming Omali Yeshitela came when he and a small group of blacks spoke up about a large mural hanging in the City Hall of St. Petersburg that depicted white tourists as normal human beings but showed all the blacks serving them as caricatures with exaggerated physical features. Repeatedly, the group asked the City Council to remove the offensive mural, but no action was taken. So Waller and several friends walked into City Hall and removed the mural, and Waller walked out with it under his arm. As photographs show, in a short time, St. Petersburg police arrived, surrounded Waller in the street, and placed him under arrest. For removing the racist art, Waller was convicted of several felonies, including grand theft, and was sentenced to five years in state prison, serving two years.

While in prison, Waller formed the Junta of Militant Organizations (JOMO). Four years later, in the wake of the U.S. government's attack on the Black Power movement, he organized the African People's Socialist Party, from which the Uhuru Movement derived. *Uhuru* means freedom in the African language Swahili. In fact, members of the movement greet each other with "Uhuru" when they meet. Waller took the name Omali Yeshitela and became Uhuru chairman.

In 1976, the party formed the African People's Solidarity Committee, an organization of white people who work under the party's leadership. What is unique about Yeshitela's vision is that he sees socialism as the answer to black freedom. All Africans, regardless of where they are in the world, including Africa itself, have been the continual victims of colonial and imperialistic forces, which have deprived them of their lands, their resources, and their freedom. In Yeshitela's view, only through solidarity with each other, will Africans worldwide have the freedom and the decent lives they deserve. He offers a worldview of Africans that calls for self-determination, not slavery of the mind and body and spirit through charity or paternalism, or anything else that keeps the African from fulfilling his or her own destiny.

The Uhuru Movement is active in several large American cities: St. Petersburg, Florida; Philadelphia, Pennsylvania; and Oakland, California. Uhuru runs a number of businesses including a bakery, a record studio, a restaurant, a furniture store, a graphics store and a fitness center, among others. With this base, Yeshitela, who also heads the African Socialist International, is establishing Socialist parties in Africa and elsewhere as well. In 2009, he and a contingent from the Uhuru Movement traveled to Sierra Leone, Kenya, and South Africa, not just to begin socialist organizations, but also to establish self-help programs, including the training of midwives and outfitting boats with motors to allow fishing in the deeper ocean waters. His Uhuru organization also publishes the *Burning Spear*, a weekly newspaper.

Yeshitela has been called an agitator, quick to put people in the streets when a black person is shot by law enforcement officials, and demanding that such shootings be investigated and that the officers be held accountable. In St. Petersburg alone, there have been more than 80 such shootings of African Americans. He has also been called a racist, but he has a strong supporting organization of whites and others who assist the Uhuru Movement. He welcomes any and all to his Uhuru headquarters in St. Petersburg, treating everyone with the same respect, and kindness.

Yeshitela has called for black reparations—payments to American blacks for their years

Omali Yeshitela, of the Florida Alliance for Peace and Social Justice, speaks in support of jailed professor Sami Al-Arian during a Muslim Student Association news conference at the University of South Florida in Tampa on February 21, 2003. (AP Photo/Chris O'Meara)

in slavery and economic deprivation. A recent study estimated that black slaves and those kept in economic slavery in the years following the Civil War are owed a staggering $200 billion in wages never paid. In addition, the promise of 40 acres and a mule to freed blacks was never fulfilled, so there is a way to estimate the actual costs of slavery. It is now known that the White House, for instance, was built with slave labor. It is difficult to imagine working hard, hour by hour, day after day, for years and years, knowing that slavery means one will never have any reward for one's labor.

Chairman Yeshitela is considered a passionate, inspired speaker, and many say he has inherited the mantle of Marcus Garvey, the "Back to Africa" leader during the 1920s who owned oceangoing ships and sought to put blacks in charge of their own destiny. According to Yeshitela, Garvey's success resulted in false criminal charges that destroyed his efforts and led to his imprisonment and eventual deportation. He is compared as well to Malcolm X, who urged blacks to fight for what was rightfully theirs, to be a free citizen of the United States, not relying on the largesse or paternalism of the whites who would be unlikely to give up their hold on power.

What distinguishes Yeshitela's worldview is that he does not limit his criticism to white power, but he also criticizes the well-meaning but ill-informed progressive whites as well as the black middle class. As the recent global conference regarding global climate change in Copenhagen has shown, there is a new vision of a rapacious global north of the equator exploiting the natural resources of the global south below the equator, resulting in most countries north being wealthy and south being poor. Though Africa is the new target for exploiting its mineral resources of diamonds, uranium, lithium, and other potential riches, this pattern began with the European nations invading and conquering North, Central, and South America where the native populations were enslaved and forced to dig out their gold and silver, to surrender their lands, and left in poverty. Imperialism and capitalism are two sides of the same coin; where there is one, there is the other.

In his writing and speeches, Yeshitela emphasizes he is not simply analyzing a historic reality. Rather, he is putting light on a continuing, ongoing parasitic imperialism that motivated the U.S. attack on Iraq, the so-called blood diamonds in many African countries including Sierra Leone, the child labor employed to export chocolate from Ivory Coast to supply Hershey's and Nestle's, as the white world in its wealthy excesses thrives on the poverty and subjugation of people of color. He sees most people of wealth, blacks and whites, as so well off and powerful for so long that they no longer question how that came to be, or why it needs to change. Yeshitela believes such wealthy people are inclined to blame people of color for being lazy, or without discipline or drive.

Yeshitela is highly critical of President Barack Obama and his administration, seeing him as continuing the system of exploiting people of color and continuing the status quo that preserves a permanent lower class ruled by whites. When candidate Obama visited St. Petersburg during his presidential campaign, young members of Uhuru heckled him. Despite shouting and critical comments from those attending toward the Uhurus, Obama asked them to allow the Uhuru members to voice their concerns and responded to them, but not in a way that satisfied Yeshitela or the Uhuru Movement.

In early 2010, Yeshitela was honored by the Poynter Institute and the University of South Florida in St. Petersburg by having his collected works placed in a permanent display in the library. The chairman spoke of the personal sacrifices he has paid for his beliefs. He apologized to his adult children in the audience for the poverty they endured, and for his many absences from home. He spoke of the St. Petersburg police killing 18-year-old Tyron Lewis on October 24, 1996, and how three weeks afterward, a grand jury exonerated the cops responsible for the killing. In addition, 300 police attacked a meeting at the Uhuru House, teargasing the 100 people, young and old, attending. As a result, the black community of St. Petersburg erupted in a full-blown riot in which a police helicopter was destroyed and two policemen were wounded.

Yeshitela remains active in his organizations and his causes. He exercises caution during his public appearances, however, flanked on his left and right by loyal security men as he speaks, even when he was speaking at the Unitarian Universalist Church of Tarpon Springs, Florida, in the summer of 2009. On that occasion, he spoke to a congregation that is 100 percent white, though a number of African Americans visited that day. His message was uncompromising and brutally honest, but respectful and with moments of humor. Those attending were impressed by a man they expected to be something short of a terrorist, and a hater of whites, and someone to be feared or hated. Without exception, all those who heard him speak were impressed with his knowledge of politics and history, his commitment to his cause, and his ability to distinguish between the goodness of individuals regardless of race, and the evil of groups seeking to retain their centuries-old grip of power over others.

Daniel Callaghan

See also Carmichael, Stokely/Ture, Kwame; King, Martin Luther, Jr.; Malcolm X

References

Omali Yeshitela Historical Calendar 2010. St. Petersburg, FL: Burning Spear Publications, 2009.

Yeshitela, Omali. *Yeshitela Speaks: Articles, Interviews, Presentations*. St. Petersburg, FL: Burning Spear Publications, 2005.

Yeshitela, Omali. *One Africa, One Nation: The African Socialist International and the Movement to United and Liberate Africa and African People Worldwide*. St. Petersburg, FL: Burning Spear Publications, 2006.

Zappa, Frank (1941–1993)

Frank Zappa was vocal—in song and musical compositions and spoken word—in his critiques of society, political processes, organized religion, and mainstream education while being a passionate advocate for free speech, First Amendment rights, and the abolition of censorship. Highly intelligent and articulate, his music was the medium by which he championed his controversial positions. But, in turn, he relied on the uproar his music generated to create a platform for him to give interviews on topics he wanted to promote. "Provocateur" is an apt description of the man, someone commonly defined as a writer, artist, political activist, etc., whose works, ideas, or activities are regarded as a threat to accepted values or practices. Zappa was certainly all of those. He was a self-taught eclectic and experimental composer and performer, whose recordings rarely earned significant airplay or sales, although he did have a dedicated core of cult-like fans. Over time, and since his death, he has attained respect. He penned lyrics to all of his songs, oftentimes humorous and almost always satirical and mocking of the American establishment, as well as the hippies and counterculture with which he was frequently and mistakenly associated.

Frank Vincent Zappa was born on December 21, 1941, in Baltimore, Maryland. He was the oldest of four siblings. His mother, Rose Marie Colimore Zappa, was of Italian and French descent. His father emigrated from Sicily as a boy and was a chemist and mathematician. Soon after his first child was born, he went to work at a chemical warfare facility (Zappa 1999, 15–21) and, for the rest of his career, he would work in the defense industry. Because they lived so close to stored mustard gas, every family member had a gas mask—"just in case." He was a sickly child, but his health improved after the family moved to Florida, worsening when they returned to Baltimore. They next moved to California, where Zappa's father taught metallurgy at the Navy postgraduate school. The family continued to move frequently and Zappa attended a half-dozen or more high schools (Zappa 1999, 22–25).

"Around the age of twelve (1951 or '52) I started getting interested in the drums," Zappa recalled, "I guess a lot of young boys think the drums are exciting, but it wasn't my idea to be a rock and roll drummer or anything like that, because rock and roll hadn't been invented yet. I was just interested in the sounds of things a person could beat on" (Zappa 1999, 29). By 1956, he was playing the snare drum in a high school rhythm and blues band, the Ramblers. It was then that he first became influenced by the works of Edgard Varese and Igor Stravinsky—hardly what a typical teenager was playing on a turntable (Zappa 1999, 31). Zappa recounted his gratitude to an Antelope Valley High School music teacher for being "the first person to tell me about twelve-tone music" and "He let me conduct orchestra a couple of times, he let me write music on the blackboard, and had the orchestra play it" and "Mr. Ballard threw me out of marching band for smoking in uniform—and for that I will be *eternally grateful*" (Zappa 1999, 35). He also discovered the guitar and formed his own group, the Blackouts.

After high school, Zappa attended junior college for a while, met and married his first wife, Kay Sherman, in December 1960, and worked at a variety of jobs. He pursued music in any way possible, playing in cocktail lounges, scoring movie tracks, and recording other artists' albums. Eventually, he got a job at tiny but state-of-the-art Pal Studio in Cucamonga, California, working for other people but still able to follow his own dreams. He staged and broadcast a concert of orchestral music in 1963 (Miles 2004, 74) and, that same year, appeared on Steve Allen's late-night show, playing a bicycle as a musical instrument (Lyons 1987).

By 1964, Zappa had saved enough to buy Pal Studio, renaming it "Studio Z." He supplemented the under-booked business with film recording, earning the nickname "Movie King of Cucamonga" and making police suspect him of filming pornography. An entrapment sting ensued, and Zappa was charged with "conspiracy to commit pornography." Ultimately, the felony charge was reduced to a misdemeanor; his sentence was reduced, with all but 10 days suspended. The experience solidified Zappa's already antiauthoritarian streak (Miles 2004, xv, 85–87). He closed the studio in 1965, moved to Los Angeles, and joined the Soul Giants as guitarist and co-lead singer. Soon, they

Frank Zappa, shown here in concert on February 5, 1978, was a passionate advocate for free speech, First Amendment rights, and the abolition of censorship. Music was the medium by which he championed his controversial positions. (AP/Wide World Photos)

were playing his compositions and going by the name of the Mothers, eventually the Mothers of Invention.

The group gained national popularity in the mid-1960s, signing with the Verve/MGM label and releasing their first album, *Freak Out!* (1966). They established themselves as one of the most outrageous bands of the era. He explained, "Hardly anybody outside of L.A. and San Francisco had long hair. We were all ugly guys with weird clothes and long hair" (Zappa 1999, 79). Ironically, Zappa's music often parodied popular music and the counterculture; although he had long hair and wore jeans, he belittled hippies and drugs. The album only had moderate success.

In July 1966, a now-divorced Zappa met Gail Sloatman. They married in September 1967, just before she gave birth to the first of the four children they would have: Moon Unit, Dweezil, Ahmet Emmuukha Rodan, and Diva.

Zappa's group produced other albums, but none were commercial hits. Their fan base grew, however, as did criticism of their work for being vulgar and tasteless. The band roster changed frequently as Zappa explored new musical arenas. In August 1969, the Mothers of Invention gave their final performance in their original form. A week later, Zappa announced he was breaking up the band.

In 1970, Zappa collaborated with Los Angeles Philharmonic conductor Zubin Mehta, arranging a concert augmented by a rock band. He then formed a reincarnation of the Mothers, producing and performing with and without an ever-changing group, also forming other bands, for the rest of his career.

Zappa and his wife formed their own recording company and developed other business ventures. He was finally able to produce music the way he wanted, releasing it prodigiously. Ardent fans bought everything, but some songs achieved wider popularity, most notably "Valley Girl." In the early 1980s, he focused on classical music, recording orchestral compositions with the London Symphony Orchestra and performing live with the Berkeley Symphony Orchestra.

In the mid-1980s, Frank Zappa became a household name when he took on the Parents Music Resource Center (PMRC) founded by Tipper Gore, wife of Tennessee senator Al Gore, and other wives of politically connected spouses. These women called for a mandatory records rating system, with labels on "offensive" albums. They suggested that stores put albums with explicit covers under counters and that TV stations be pressured not to broadcast explicit songs or videos. They also wanted a standards panel, and created a classification for offensive songs.

In late 1984, the National Parent-Teacher Association (PTA) wrote the Recording Industry Association of America (RIAA), proposing the industry label records with "explicit lyrics or content." At first, RIAA and record companies resisted, citing wide industry variations. However, 19 companies agreed to print the warning "Parental Guidance: Explicit Lyrics" on records. Before labeling could begin, the Senate announced a hearing on "the subject of the content of certain sound recordings and suggestions that recording packages be labeled to provide a warning to prospective purchasers of sexually explicit or other potentially offensive content." The five-hour media circus hearing began on September 15, 1985. Congressman Hollings, whose wife was one of the wives protesting, said, "If I could do away with all of this music constitutionally, I would" (Miles 2004, 335–36).

Up until that point, "Zappa was quick to give an opinion on almost any subject—from education to TV evangelism—but he rarely ventured into politics.... During the Vietnam War, for instance, unlike many of his contemporaries, Zappa refused to be drawn into antiwar protests or demonstrations" (Miles 2004, 334). In contrast, the popular folk singer Pete Seeger was an antiwar activist ready to stir up protests whenever he had the opportunity.

At the hearing, Zappa surprised people with his articulateness and eloquence but, true to form, could not resist mocking the senators and their wives. He received wide press coverage. His well-researched and factually accurate speech gave Zappa "a solid base from which to stray into flights of rhetoric to please the media and ensure that his views were reported: 'Ladies, please be advised: the $8.98 purchase price does not entitle you to a kiss on the foot from the composer or performer in exchange for a spin on the family Victrola.'" He noted country music was exempt from labeling, pointing out that the genre was full of "songs about sex, violence, alcohol and the devil... sung for you by people who have been to prison and are proud of it" (Miles 2004, 336–37). Zappa was especially critical of the wives' imposing their morals on others. "It seems to enforce a set of implied religious values on its victims. Iran has a religious government. Good for them... Fundamentalism is not a state religion. How a person worships is a private matter, and should not be inflicted upon or exploited by others" (Miles 2004, 337).

Before the hearings ended, the record companies agreed to put stickers on albums, but they would only state "parental advisory" instead of including the added warning about explicit lyrics. Consequently, Wal-Mart, J. C. Penney, Sears, and Fred Meyer refused to sell labeled records, while others limited sales to minors. Today, independent, non-RIAA releases do not have to carry the labels. Some suggest that labeling has backfired and that labels actually increase sales. Zappa promptly released an album, *Frank Zappa Meets the Mothers of Prevention*, containing excerpts from the hearings.

While he lost the PMRC battle, Zappa continued to speak out against censorship and government suppression. Politics became a more prominent passion in his later years. He had always encouraged fans to register to vote on album covers; through 1988, he staffed registration booths at his concerts (Miles 2004, 364). Through the 1980s, he continued his eclectic musical pursuits, releasing albums in the classical, rock, and jazz genres. He won his first Grammy for Best Rock Instrumental Performance with "Jazz from Hell" in 1987; the track itself won a Grammy for Best Instrumental Composition. The instrumental album (without lyrics) received a "RIAA" warning label.

In February 1988, Zappa launched his final tour, playing in North America and Europe. The following year he published his coauthored autobiography, *The Real Frank Zappa Book* (1989). He also began traveling to Russia as a business liaison, then went to Czechoslovakia, meeting with Czech president and Zappa fan Václav Havel, who asked him to become a trade representative. Zappa, an underground Czech hero, agreed, but the offer was downgraded to that of unofficial cultural attaché due to pressure from the United States (Miles 2004, 357–61). In January 1990, Zappa was diagnosed with prostate cancer. Still he pursued his musical, business, and political interests, traveling to Czechoslovakia and Hungary the following year. Upon his return to the United States, he tackled as many unfinished projects as he could in the days remaining. Zappa passed away on December 4, 1993.

He was posthumously inducted into the Rock and Roll Hall of Fame in 1995 with these words: "Frank Zappa was rock and roll's sharpest musical mind and most astute social critic." He received the Lifetime Grammy Achievement Award in 1997. He has had an asteroid, a mollusk, a fish, a jellyfish, a spider, a bacterium's gene, and a fossil named after him. In 1995, a bust of Zappa was installed in the Lithuanian capital Vilnius. On the 25th anniversary of Zappa's testimony to the U.S. Senate, a dedication ceremony was held for a replica of that bust, presented as a gift to the city of Baltimore. The city also holds an annual "Frank Zappa Day" in honor of his musical accomplishments and his defense of the First Amendment.

Margaret Gay

See also Seeger, Pete

References

Lyons, Steve, and Batya Friedman (interviewers). "Winter in America, It's 1987. Do You Know Where Your Culture Is?" *Option*, January–February 1987. http://www.afka.net/articles/1987-01_Option.htm (accessed April 16, 2011).

MacDonald, Ian. *Revolution in the Head: The Beatles Records*. Chicago: Chicago Review Press, Inc., 2007.

Miles, Barry. *Zappa: A Biography*. Broadway, New York: Grove/Atlantic Books, 2004.

Zappa, Frank, with Peter Occhiogrosso. *The Real Frank Zappa Book*. New York: Touchstone, 1989, 1999.

Zinn, Howard (1922–2010)

Howard Zinn once described himself as "Something of an anarchist, something of a socialist. Maybe a democratic socialist" (Glavin 2003). He was an American dissident, author, historian, intellectual, playwright, and veteran. When asked in 2009, the year before his death, about today's prospects for radical politics, Zinn said,

> Let's talk about socialism. I think it's very important to bring back the idea of socialism into the national discussion to where it was... before the Soviet Union gave it a bad name. Socialism had a good name in this country. Socialism had Eugene Debs. It had Clarence Darrow. It had Mother Jones. It had Emma Goldman. It had several million people reading socialist newspapers around the country. Socialism basically said, hey, let's have a kinder, gentler society. Let's share things. Let's have an economic system that produces things not because they're profitable for some corporation, but produces things that people need. People should not be retreating from the word socialism because you have to go beyond capitalism. (Zirin 2010)

Howard Zinn is probably best known for his left-wing views and the unapologetic positions he took in expressing those views whenever he put pen to paper—whether it be in writing his master's thesis on the Colorado coal strikes of 1914 or for his seminal professional work, *A People's History of the United States* (1980).

Both of Zinn's parents were Jewish immigrants. Howard's father Eddie came to the United States shortly before World War I, traveling from Austria-Hungary. His mother Jenny was from Irkutsk, a city in eastern Siberia. Like many others new to the United States, both found factory work and, subsequently, each other. Jenny gave birth to Howard on August 24, 1922, in Brooklyn, New York. Although their financial resources were limited, the Zinns placed a premium on education and did what they could to foster Howard's education from an early age. However, his studies were interrupted by the country's entry into World War II.

From 1943 through 1945, Howard served with distinction as a second lieutenant in the Army Air Force, flying bombing missions in Europe. In the final year of his service, he participated in the first military use of napalm in Royan, France, which he would write about later in two books, *The Politics of History* (1970) and *The Zinn Reader* (1997).

Returning home after the war, Howard took advantage of the GI Bill and, in 1951, earned a BA degree from New York University. A year later, he earned his master's at Columbia University, studying history and political science. He taught at Upsala College in East Orange, New Jersey, from 1953 to 1956 and, in 1958, got his PhD. "LaGuardia in Congress" was the title of Zinn's doctoral dissertation on New York mayor Fiorello LaGuardia's congressional career. In it, Zinn lionized the mayor as a champion who fought for pro-labor legislation and rubbed against the grain of fellow Republicans and their elitist economic policies. When published in 1959, it was nominated for the American Historical Association's Beveridge Prize as the best English-language book on American history.

Zinn spent seven years of his life, from 1956 until 1963, as history and social science chair at an all-girls African American college. Located in Atlanta, Georgia, Spelman College provided Zinn with the opportunity not only to witness, but also to take on an activist role in the burgeoning civil rights movement. He grew increasingly upset with the government's unwillingness to proactively protect its citizens and their rights, as well as its failure to secure the physical safety of citizens in their quest for racial equality. Zinn was arrested on more than one occasion and acted as adviser to the Student Nonviolent Coordinating Committee. His book about its activities, *SNCC: The New Abolitionists* (1964), placed the era's struggles in context with that of pre–Civil War activists. Ultimately fired from his position at Spelman for his activism, Zinn joined the faculty at Boston University, where he was a member of the staff throughout the remainder of his career. He later became a visiting professor at the University of Paris and the University of Bologna and, in 1960–1961, was a postdoctoral fellow in East Asian Studies at Harvard University. True to form, his tenure there was controversial because of his activities on and off campus.

Like many others at the time, Zinn was strongly opposed to the involvement of the United States in Vietnam. Along with Noam Chomsky, he was one of the most vocal antiwar scholars of that era. He also participated in the American Mobilization Committee's national drive to bring an end to the U.S. intervention. He was one of David Dellinger's recruits, traveling with David Berrigan to Hanoi during the Tet offensive in February 1968. The Vietnamese agreed to release the very first American prisoners of war, and Zinn wrote firsthand accounts of the experience.

Zinn played a role in the case of the Pentagon Papers, in which Daniel Ellsberg had secretly copied government policy documents concerning the Vietnam War. Zinn and Chomsky wrote an analysis that accompanied a version of these papers that Zinn's editor at Beacon Press released. When Ellsberg was put on trial for his crimes, Zinn testified as an expert witness for the defense, providing the jury with a history of the United States' involvement in Vietnam from World War II until 1963. Ellsberg was acquitted, due to inappropriate conduct by the Nixon administration. Zinn's critics largely found fault with his partisan stance, but Zinn defended himself in an early collection of essays, *The Politics of History* (1970), arguing that all political writing was inherently political and biased. "[T]he historian is a participant in history by his writing. Even when he claims neutrality he has an effect—if only with his voluminous production of irrelevant data, to clog the social passages. So it is now a matter of consciously recognizing his participation, and deciding on which direction his energies can be expended" (Zinn 1970, 31). He fervently believed that historians had a moral imperative to take a stand against the evils of their day, thus acting not just as recorders of history, but also as shapers of it.

Nowhere was Zinn's personal slant on history more evident than in *A People's History of the United States* (1980). A finalist for the National Book Award in 1981, a year after its publication, Zinn's book generated a great deal of controversy. Fellow historian Eric Foner, in a *New York Times* book review, wrote that "historians may well view it as a step toward a coherent new version of American history." Many others, even liberal historians, were more skeptical. Sean Wilentz, a professor of history at Princeton University, noted, "he's a popularizer, and his view of history is topsy-turvy, turning old villains into heroes, and after a while the glow gets unreal" (Powell 2010).

Zinn also published numerous scholarly works as well as articles for a variety of periodicals, from the *Saturday Review* to the *Nation*. In 1990, he published *Declarations of Independence*, a continuation of his populist approach to American history. Zinn also authored three plays over the course of his lifetime, all of which celebrated radical political figures: *Marx in Soho*, *Emma*, and *Daughter of Venus*.

You Can't Be Neutral on a Moving Train (1994) was made into a documentary about Zinn in 2004. That same year, *Voices of A People's History of the United States* was released, a sourcebook of speeches, articles, essays, poetry, and song lyrics by the people whose stories are told in *A People's History of the United States*. In 2005, Zinn was invited back to Spelman, the school from which he had been fired for insubordination over 40 years prior; now he was the commencement speaker and awarded an honorary doctorate of humane letters.

For all of the criticism that Zinn received, he achieved ample accolades as well. He received the Peace Abbey Courage of Conscience Award in 1996 and, in 1998, the Eugene V. Debs Award, the Thomas Merton Award, and the Lannan Literary Award for nonfiction. In 1999, he won the Upton Sinclair Award for social activism. The *Prix des Amis du Monde diplomatique* was bestowed upon him for the French version of his seminal work, *Une histoire populaire des Etats-Unis*. In 2006, Zinn received the Haven's Center Award for Lifetime Contribution to Critical Scholarship.

A People's History of the United States has established a solid niche in pop culture. It has inspired several musicians in their artistic pursuits—Bruce Springsteen's acclaimed album *Nebraska*, Pearl Jam's song "Down," and the opening song, "Blues for Howard," on the award-nominated 2007 CD by Watermelon Slim, to name a few. Matt Damon and Ben Affleck worked *A People's History* into their movie, *Good Will Hunting*; and, in a flashback scene of when she was in college, in an episode of *The Simpsons*, Marge is seen reading an upside-down copy of the book. *The People Speak*, a 2010 DVD release, is a documentary inspired by the lives of ordinary people who fought back against oppressive conditions over the course of the history of the United States and includes performances by Zinn, Damon, Morgan Freeman, Bob Dylan, Springsteen, Eddie Vedder, Viggo Mortensen, Josh Brolin, Danny Glover, Marisa Tomei, Don Cheadle, Sandra Oh, and others.

Zinn died of a heart attack on January 27, 2010, in Santa Monica, California. His daughter Myla Kabat-Zinn, son Jeff Zinn, and five grandchildren survive him. His wife Roslyn had passed away in 2008. In an obituary, the progressive periodical *The Week* wrote about Zinn's take on history: "the story of the United States was hardly a majestic tale of enlightened Founding Fathers and liberty for all. Rather, it was a 200-year exercise in oppression by slaveholders, robber barons, and white men in general against minorities, women, and the powerless" (*The Week* 2010, 43).

Yet Zinn did not see just the negative and dark side of man. He wrote:

> To be hopeful in bad times is not just foolishly romantic. It is based on the fact that human history is a history not only of cruelty, but also of compassion, sacrifice, courage, kindness. What we choose to emphasize in this complex history will determine our lives. If we see only the worst, it destroys our capacity to do something. If we remember those times and places—and there are so many—where people have behaved magnificently, this gives us the energy to act, and at least the possibility of sending this spinning top of a world in a different direction. And if we do act, in however small a way, we don't have to wait for some grand utopian future. The future is an infinite succession of presents, and to live now as we think human beings should live, in defiance of all that is bad around us, is itself a marvelous victory. (Zinn 2004).

Margaret Gay

See also Berrigan, Daniel, and Berrigan, Philip; Chomsky, Noam; Darrow, Clarence; Debs, Eugene V.; Dellinger, David; Ellsberg, Daniel; Goldman, Emma; Jones, Mary Harris

References

Engelhardt, Tom. "Tomgram: Graduation Day with Howard Zinn." TomDispatch, May 24, 2005. http://www.tomdispatch.com/post/2728/graduation_day_with_howard_zinn (accessed April 24, 2010).

"Experts, Howard Zinn, Historian: The Legacy of Howard Zinn." BigThink, n.d. http://bigthink.com/howardzinn (accessed April 24, 2010).

"The Historian Who Championed the Masses." *The Week*, February 12, 2010.

Kreisler, Harry. "Howard Zinn Interview: Conversations with History." Berkeley: University of California, Berkeley, Institute of International Studies, April 20, 2001. http://globetrotter.berkeley.edu/people/Zinn/zinn-con1.html (accessed April 24, 2010).

Powell, Michael. "Howard Zinn, Historian, Is Dead at 87." *New York Times*, January 28, 2010. http://www.nytimes.com/2010/01/29/us/29zinn.html (accessed May 12, 2010).

Zinn, Howard. "The Optimism of Uncertainty." *Nation*, September 20, 2004. http://www.thenation.com/article/optimism-uncertainty/ (accessed May 12, 2010).

Zinn, Howard. *A People's History of the United States: 1942–Present*. New York: Harper-Collins, 2003.

Zinn, Howard. *The Politics of History*. Boston: Beacon Press, 1970.

Zinn, Howard. *You Can't Be Neutral on a Moving Train: A Personal History of Our Times*. Boston: Beacon Press. 2002.

Zirin, Dave. "Howard Zinn: The Historian Who Made History." *Huffington Post*, January 28, 2010. http://www.huffingtonpost.com/dave-zirin/howard-zinn-the-historian_b_439757.html (accessed April 27, 2010).

Selected Bibliography

Most of the print selections in this bibliography are autobiographies or biographies of subjects profiled in this encyclopedia. For example, there are autobiographical or biographical accounts of such diverse individuals as boxing great Muhammad Ali, settlement house founder Jane Addams, author Zora Neale Hurston, former Alaska governor and vice presidential candidate Sarah Palin, comedian and dissident George Carlin, death row prisoner Mumia Abu-Jamal, and self-styled undercover journalist James O'Keefe. Other books have been written by profiled individuals, and their publications focus on their specific interests or causes. In a few instances, books by or about early twentieth-century activists are in the public domain and are available on the web site of Gutenberg.org (as indicated in the listing) and can be downloaded or read online. (They may also be available at libraries or for sale in print.) Other print sources include major magazine and newspaper articles that cover important aspects of subjects' lives. Some electronic sources contain transcripts of interviews with such activists as David Horowitz, Mary McLeod Bethune, Dan Choi, and Louis Farrakhan. In addition, this bibliography includes YouTube videos, documentaries, and movies that dramatize the lives of various activists and their causes.

Abbey, Edward, and David Peterson, eds. *Confession of a Barbarian: Selections from the Journals of Edward Abbey, 1951–1989*. Boston: Little, Brown & Co., 1994.

Abu-Jamal, Mumia. "Mumia Abu-Jamal: Essays from Death Row." International Action Center, n.d. http://www.iacenter.org/polprisoners/majessay.htm (accessed September 8, 2010).

Adams, Katherine H., and Michael L. Keene. *Alice Paul and the American Suffrage Campaign*. Urbana and Chicago: University of Illinois Press, 2008.

Addams, Jane. *Twenty Years at Hull House*. New York: The Macmillan Company, 1912.

Ali. Directed by Michael Mann. A film biography of Muhammad Ali, played by Will Smith. Sony DVD, 2001.

Ali, Muhammad. *The Greatest: My Own Story*. New York: Ballantine Books, 1979.

Ali, Muhammad, and Hana Yasmeen Ali. *The Soul of a Butterfly: Reflections on Life's Journey*. New York: Simon and Schuster, 2004.

Alperovitz, Gar. *The Decision to Use the Atomic Bomb*. New York: Vintage Books/Random House, 1996.

Ambinder, Marc. "The Town Halls, Independents, and Lyndon LaRouche." *Atlantic*, August 13, 2009.

"America: Meet Sarah Palin." YouTube video, 19:20, posted by CBS, August 29, 2009. http://www.youtube.com/watch?

v=Gg0darQB7r4 (accessed November 7, 2010).

Andersen, Jervis. *A. Philip Randolph: A Biographical Portrait*. Berkeley: University of California Press, 1986.

Anderson, S. E., and Tony Medina. *In Defense of Mumia*. New York: Writers and Readers, 1996.

Appenzell Daily Bell with Scott Smith. "Lyndon LaRouche Explains the Collapsing Western Economy and How the World Really Works." *Gold Speculator*, June 20, 2010. http://www.gold-speculator.com/appenzell-daily-bell/31907-lyndon-larouche-explains-collapsing-western-economy-how-world-really-works.html (accessed August 14, 2010).

Aptheker, Bettina. *The Morning Breaks: The Trial of Angela Davis*. New York: International Publishers, 1975.

Asner, Ed, and Burt Hall. *Misuse of Power: How the Far Right Gained and Misuses Power*. Mahomet, IL: Mayhaven Publishing, 2005.

Avrich, Paul. *Sacco and Vanzetti: The Anarchist Background*. Princeton, NJ: Princeton University Press, 1991.

Ayers, William. *Fugitive Days: A Memoir*. Boston: Beacon Press, 2001.

Azikiwe, Abayomi. "Remembering Fred Hampton and Mark Clark." *Workers World*, December 11, 2009.

Balaji, Murali. *The Professor and the Pupil: The Politics and Friendship of W. E. B. Du Bois and Paul Robeson*. New York: Nation Books, 2007.

Baldwin, Chuck. "Interview with David Horowitz" (transcript). *Chuck Baldwin Live*, June 6, 1997. http://www.chuckbaldwinlive.com/horowitz.html (accessed December 8, 2010).

Baldwin, James. *The Fire Next Time*. New York: Dial Press, 1963.

Banks, Dennis, with Richard Erdoes. *Ojibwa Warrior: Dennis Banks and the Rise of the American Indian Movement*. Norman: University of Oklahoma Press, 2004.

Bari, Judi. *Timber Wars*. Monroe, ME: Common Courage Press, 1994.

Barsky, Robert F. *Noam Chomsky: A Life of Dissent*. Cambridge: MIT Press, 1998.

Barstow, David. "An Abortion Battle, Fought to the Death." *New York Times*, July 26, 2009. http://www.nytimes.com/2009/07/26/us/26tiller.html?_r=2&pagewanted=1&ref=global-home (accessed November 26, 2010).

Baxandall, Rosalyn Fraad. *Words on Fire: The Life and Writings of Elizabeth Gurley Flynn*. New Brunswick, NJ: Rutgers University Press, 1989.

Beckerman, Marty. "The Cunning Linguist: George Carlin's Literary Genius." *Reason*, October 2008.

Bellafante, Ginia. "At Home with Phyllis Schlafly: A Feminine Mystique All Her Own." *New York Times*, March 30, 2006. http://www.nytimes.com/2006/03/30/garden/30phyllis.html?_r=1&pagewanted=all (accessed February 24, 2011).

Benet, Lorenzo. *Trailblazer: An Intimate Biography of Sarah Palin*. New York: Threshold Editions, 2009.

Benjamin, Medea. "When Will US Women Demand Peace?" *Conscience*, Summer 2006.

Berlet, Chip, and Matthew N. Lyons. *Right-Wing Populism in America: Too Close for Comfort*. New York: Guilford Press, 2000.

Berton, Justin. "Catching Up with Julia Butterfly Hill." *San Francisco Chronicle*, April 16, 2009.

Betzold, Michael. *Appointment with Dr. Death*. Royal Oak, MI: Momentum Books, 1993.

Bird, Kai, and Martin J. Sherwin. *American Prometheus, the Triumph and Tragedy of J. Robert Oppenheimer*. New York: Vintage Books/Random House, 2006.

Birney, Angelina Perri. "Waging Peace: Medea Benjamin of CODEPINK." *Pure Vision*, September 15, 2010. http://perribirney.wordpress.com/ (accessed November 29, 2010).

Bishop, James, Jr. *Epitaph, for a Desert Anarchist: The Life and Legacy of Edward Abbey*. New York: Touchstone, 1995.

Bisson, Terry. *On the Move: The Story of Mumia Abu-Jamal*. Farmington, PA: Litmus Books, 2001.

Bloodworth, William A. *Upton Sinclair*. Boston: Twayne Publishers, 1978.

Bochert-Kimmig, Reinhold, and Ekkehard Schuster. *Hope against Hope: Johann Baptist Metz and Elie Wiesel Speak Out on the Holocaust*. Translated by J. Matthew Ashley. Mahwah, NJ: Paulist Press, 1999.

Boehlert, Eric. "The Prime-Time Smearing of Sami Al-Arian." *Salon*, January 19, 2002. http://www.salon.com/technology/feature/2002/01/19/bubba/index.html (accessed November 13, 2010).

Boggs, Grace Lee. *Living for Change: An Autobiography*. Minneapolis and London: University of Minnesota Press, 1998.

Bollen, Peter D. *Frank Talk: The Wit and Wisdom of Barney Frank*. Lincoln, NE: iUniverse, 2006.

Botsch, Carol Sears. *Modjeska Monteith Simkins*. South Caroliniana Library, University of South Carolina–Aiken, December 14, 2007. http://www.usca.edu/aasc/simkins.htm (accessed March 23, 2011).

Bowe, Frank. *Rehabilitating America: Toward Independence for Disabled and Elderly People*. New York: Harper & Row, 1980.

Bowser, Kenneth (writer). *Phil Ochs: There but for Fortune*. A documentary, 2010.

Boyd, Valerie. *Wrapped in Rainbows: The Life of Zora Neale Hurston*. New York: Scribner, 2003.

Braun Levine, Suzanne, and Mary Thom, eds. *Bella Abzug: How One Tough Broad from the Bronx Fought Jim Crow and Joe McCarthy, Pissed Off Jimmy Carter, Battled for the Rights of Women and Workers, Rallied Against War and for the Planet, and Shook Up Politics along the Way*. New York: Farrar, Straus and Giroux, 2007.

Brinkley, Alan. *Voices of Protest: Huey Long, Father Coughlin, and the Great Depression*. New York: Vintage Books, 1983.

Brown, David Jay. *Mavericks of Medicine: Exploring the Future of Medicine with Andrew Weil, Jack Kevorkian, Bernie Siegel, Ray Kurzweil, and Others*. Petaluma, CA: Smart Publications, 2007.

Brown, Dee. *Bury My Heart At Wounded Knee: An American History of the West*. New York: Henry Holt and Company, 1970.

Brownmiller, Susan. *Against Our Will: Men, Women, and Rape*. New York: Bantam/Simon and Schuster, 1986. First published 1975.

Brownmiller, Susan. *In Our Time: Memoir of a Revolution*. New York: Dial Press, 1999.

Bullard, Robert. *Dumping in Dixie: Race, Class, and Environmental Quality*. Boulder, CO: Westview Press, 1990.

Bullard, Robert. *The Quest for Environmental Justice: Human Rights and the Politics of Pollution*. San Francisco: Sierra Club Books, 2005.

Burnett, Constance (Buel). *Five for Freedom: Lucretia Mott, Elizabeth Cady Stanton, Lucy Stone, Susan B. Anthony, Carrie Chapman Catt*. New York: Abelard Press, 1953.

Burns, Stewart, ed. *Daybreak of Freedom: The Montgomery Bus Boycott*. Chapel Hill: University of North Carolina Press, 1997.

Butler, Amy E. *Two Paths to Equality: Alice Paul and Ethel M. Smith in the ERA Debate, 1921–1929*. Albany: State University of New York Press, 2002.

Bynum, Cornelius L. *A. Philip Randolph and the Struggle for Civil Rights*. Urbana: University of Illinois Press, 2010.

Byrd, Rudolph, ed. *The World Has Changed: Conversations with Alice Walker*. New York: New Press, 2010.

Cahalan, James M., *Edward Abbey: A Life*. Tucson: University of Arizona Press, 2001.

Cammermeyer, Grethe, with Chris Fisher. *Serving in Silence*. Bloomington, IN: Author House, 2005. First published 1994.

Campbell, James. *Talking at the Gates: A Life of James Baldwin*. New York: Viking, 1991.

Capitalism: A Love Story. Directed by Michael Moore. Documentary film focusing on corporate America. 2009.

Carlin, George, with Tony Hendra. *Last Words*. New York and London: Free Press/Simon and Schuster, 2009.

Carmichael, Stokely, and Charles V. Hamilton. *Black Power: The Politics of Liberation in America*. New York: Random House, 1992.

Carmichael, Stokely. *Stokely Speaks: Black Power to Pan-Africanism*. Chicago: Chicago Review Press, 2007. First published 1965.

Carson, Clayborne. *Malcolm X: The FBI Files*. New York: Ballantine Books, 1995.

Catt, Carrie Chapman, compiler. *Woman Suffrage by Federal Constitutional Amendment*. New York: National Woman Suffrage Publishing Co., 1917. http://www.gutenberg.org/files/13568/13568.txt (accessed May 31, 2010).

Center for Defense Information. "Modern American Patriot: William Sloane Coffin, Jr." (video transcript). Washington, DC: America's Defense Monitor, February 6, 1995.

Chafets, Zev. *Rush Limbaugh: An Army of One*. New York: Centinel HC/Penguin, 2010.

Chalberg, John. *Emma Goldman: American Individualist*. New York: HarperCollins, 1991.

Chall, Malca, and Hannah Josephson (interviewers). "Jeannette Rankin: Activist for World Peace, Women's Rights, and Democratic Government." *Suffragists Oral History Project*. Berkeley: Regents of the University of California, 1974. http://content.cdlib.org/view?docId=kt758005dx&brand=calisphere&doc.view=entire_text (accessed May 21, 2010).

Choi, Daniel. "Lt. Daniel Choi Begs to Keep His Job in National Guard: Open Letter to President Obama and Every Member of Congress." ABC News/U.S., May 11, 2009. http://abcnews.go.com/US/story?id=7569476 (accessed April 23, 2011).

Chomsky, Noam. *Failed States: The Abuse of Power and the Assault on Democracy*. New York: Metropolitan Books/Henry Holt, 2006.

Chomsky, Noam. *Hopes and Prospects*. Chicago: Haymarket Books, 2010.

Clark, Brooke (interview summary). "Walter Hubbard Interview Conducted by Trevor Griffey and Brooke Clark," February 17, 2005. http://depts.washington.edu/civilr/Hubbard%20interview%20summary.htm (accessed April 11, 2011).

Clayborne, Clarence, ed. *The Autobiography of Martin Luther King, Jr*. New York: Warner Books, 1998.

Cockburn, Alexander. "The Ongoing Persecution of al-Arian." *Counterpunch*, August 2–3, 2008. http://www.counterpunch.org/cockburn08022008.html (accessed November 13, 2010).

Coffin, William Sloane, Jr. *Once to Every Man: A Memoir*. New York: Atheneum, 1977.

Cohn, Roy. *McCarthy*. New York: New American Library, 1968.

Cole, Luke, and Sheila Foster. *From the Ground Up: Environmental Racism and the Rise of the Environmental Justice Movement*. New York: New York University Press, 2001.

Coleman, Kate. *The Secret Wars of Judi Bari: A Car Bomb, the Fight for the Redwoods and the End of Earth First!* San Francisco: Encounter Books, 2005.

Colford, Paul D. *The Rush Limbaugh Story: Talent on Loan from God: An Unauthorized Biography*. New York: St. Martin's Press, 1993.

Commoner, Barry. *The Closing Circle: Nature, Man, and Technology*. New York: Alfred A. Knopf, 1971.

Commoner, Barry. *Making Peace with the Planet*. New York: New Press, 1992.

Commonwealth v. Mumia Abu-Jamal aka Wesley Cook. Court of Common Pleas, First Judicial District of Pennsylvania, Criminal Trial Division, August 11, 1995. http://www.justice4danielfaulkner.com/pcra/95-08-11.html#singletary (accessed September 8, 2010).

Communist Party USA, n.d. http://www.cpusa.org/about-us/ (accessed December 7, 2010).

Cook, Philip L. *Zion City, Illinois: Twentieth-Century Utopia.* Syracuse, NY: Syracuse University Press, 1996.

Cooke, Stephanie. *In Mortal Hands: A Cautionary History of the Nuclear Age.* New York: Bloomsbury, USA, 2009.

Corbett, James. *Goatwalking: A Guide to Wildland Living.* New York: Viking Penguin Press, 1991.

Corrie, Craig, and Cindy Corrie, eds. *Let Me Stand Alone: The Journals of Rachel Corrie.* New York and London: W. W. Norton, 2008.

Coughlin, Charles Edward. *A Series of Lectures on Social Justice.* Royal Oak, MI: Radio League of the Little Flower, 1935.

Cowan, Geoffrey. *The People v. Clarence Darrow: The Bribery Trial of America's Greatest Lawyer.* New York: Random House, 1993.

Craig, John M. " 'The Sex Side of Life': The Obscenity Case of Mary Ware Dennett." *Frontiers: A Journal of Women Studies*, September 1995.

Critchlow, Donald T. *Phyllis Schlafly and Grassroots Conservatism: A Woman's Crusade.* Princeton, NJ: Princeton University Press, 2005.

Crittenden, Ann. *Sanctuary: A Story of American Conscience and the Law in Collision.* New York: Weidenfeld & Nicolson, 1988.

D'Emilio, John. *Lost Prophet: The Life and Times of Bayard Rustin.* New York: Free Press, 2003.

Dalrymple, Timothy. "The Legacy of an Activist Career: An Interview with Jim Wallis." August 9, 2010 http://www.patheos.com/Resources/Additional-Resources/The-Legacy-of-an-Activist-Career-An-Interview-with-Jim-Wallis?offset=3&max=1&showAll=1 (accessed January 4, 2011).

Darrow (1991). Directed by John David Coles. Starring Kevin Spacey. TV and DVD film about famous lawyer Clarence Darrow. Atlantis Films, 1991.

Darrow, Clarence. *The Story of My Life.* New York: Charles Scribner's Sons, 1932.

Dart, Justin, Jr. "Statement by Justin Dart, Jr., Commissioner, Rehabilitation Services Administration, to the oversight hearing on the Rehabilitation Services Administration held by the Select Education Subcommittee of the House Committee on Education and Labor, November 18, 1987." http://www.bcm.edu/ilru/html/about/Dart/statement_of_conscience.htm (accessed December 14, 2010).

Dart, Mari Carlin. "The Resurrection of Justin Dart, Jr.: A Quest for Truth and Love." *Ability Magazine*, http://www.abilitymagazine.com/carroll_dart.html (accessed December 12, 2010).

Davidson, Miriam. *Convictions of the Heart: Jim Corbett and the Sanctuary Movement.* Tucson: University of Arizona Press, 1988.

Davis, Allen Freeman. *American Heroine: The Life and Legend of Jane Addams.* New York: Oxford University Press, 1973.

Davis, Angela. *Women, Race, and Class.* New York: Random House/Vintage Books, 1981.

Davis, Angela Y. *Angela Davis: An Autobiography.* New York: Bernard Geis Associates Book/Random House, 1974.

Davis, Cynthia J. *Charlotte Perkins Gilman: A Biography.* Stanford, CA: Stanford University Press, 2010.

Day, Dorothy. *The Long Loneliness: The Autobiography of Dorothy Day.* San Francisco: HarperCollins, 1980. Reprint of 1952 edition.

Dees, Morris, and Steve Fiffer. *A Season for Justice: The Life and Times of Civil Rights Lawyer Morris Dees.* New York: Macmillan, 1991.

DeFreitas, Gregory. "Human Rights, Foreign Workers, and American Unions: A Conversation with Charles Kernaghan." *Regional Labor Review*, Fall 1999.

Deloria, Vine, Jr. *Custer Died for Your Sins: An Indian Manifesto.* Norman: University of Oklahoma Press, 1988.

Deloria, Vine, Jr. *God Is Red: A Native View of Religion.* Golden, CO: Fulcrum Publishing, 2003. First published 1972.

Deparle, Jason. "Washington at Work; Eclipsed in the Reagan Decade, Ralph Nader Again Feels Glare of the Public." *New York Times*, September 21, 1990.

Dicum, Gregory. "Justice in Time, Meet Robert Bullard: The Father of Environmental Justice." *Grist*, March 14, 2006. http://www.grist.org/article/dicum (accessed October 25, 2010).

Diliberto, Gioia. *A Useful Woman: The Early Life of Jane Addams*. New York: Scribner, 1999.

Dobbs, Jean. "And Justin for All." *New Mobility*, March 1998. http://www.newmobility.com/articleView.cfm?id=84 (accessed December 13, 2010).

Donahue, Bill. " 'El lobo loco.' (Hazel Wolf's Campaigns for the Conservation of Forests and the Environment)." *American Forests*, Summer 1996.

Dowbiggin, Ian. *Merciful End: The Euthanasia Movement in Modern America*. New York: Oxford University Press, 2003.

Dowie, Mark, and David Talbot. "Asner: Too Hot for Medium Cool." *Mother Jones*, August 1982.

Downey, Kirstin. *The Woman behind the New Deal: The Life of Frances Perkins, FDR's Secretary of Labor and His Moral Conscience*. New York: Nan A. Talese/Doubleday, 2009.

Doyle, Kevin (interviewer). "Noam Chomsky on Anarchism, Marxism and Hope for the Future." First published in *Red and Black Revolution*, May 1995. http://flag.blackened.net/revolt/rbr/noamrbr2.html (accessed September 9, 2010).

Drinnon, Richard. *Rebel in Paradise: A Biography of Emma Goldman*. Chicago: University of Chicago Press, 1961.

Du Bois, W. E. B. *The Autobiography of W. E. B. Du Bois: A Soliloquy on Viewing My Life from the Last Decade of Its First Century*. New York: International Publishers, 1968 (published posthumously).

Du Bois, W. E. B. *Darkwater: Voices from within the Veil*. New York: Harcourt Brace, 1920. A Project Gutenberg E-book, released February 28, 2005.

Du Bois, W. E. B. *The Souls of Black Folk*. 1903. A Project Gutenberg E-book, released January 29, 2008.

Dubofsky, Melvyn. *We Shall Be All: A History of the Industrial Workers of the World*. New York: Quadrangle Books, 1969. (An abridged edition edited by Joseph A. McCartin was published in 2000 by the University of Illinois Press.)

Dunaway, David King. *How Can I Keep from Singing? The Ballad of Pete Seeger*. New York: Villard Books, 1982, 2008.

Edmonds, Anthony O. *Muhammad Ali: A Biography*. Westport, CT: Greenwood Press, 2006.

Edwin, Ed (interviewer). "The First Freedom Ride: Bayard Rustin on His Work with CORE." Columbia University Oral History Collection, September 1985. http://historymatters.gmu.edu/d/6909 (accessed March 20, 2011).

Egan, Michael. *Barry Commoner and the Science of Survival*. Cambridge, MA: MIT Press, 2007.

Egerton, John. "Oral History Interview with Modjeska Simkins," May 11, 1990. Southern Oral History Program Collection, Wilson Library, University of North Carolina at Chapel Hill http://docsouth.unc.edu/sohp/A-0356/ (accessed March 24, 2011).

Eliot, Marc. *Death of a Rebel: A Biography of Phil Ochs*. New York: Franklin Watts, 1989. First published 1979.

Ellsberg, Daniel. *Secrets: A Memoir of Vietnam and the Pentagon Papers*. New York: Penguin Books, 2003.

Ellsberg, Robert, ed. *By Little and by Little: The Selected Writings of Dorothy Day*. New York: Knopf, 1988.

Engelhardt, Tom. "Tomdispatch Interview: Ann Wright on Service to Country." TomDispatch.com, November 2005. http://www.tomdispatch.com/post/35448/ (accessed August 5, 2010).

Engelhardt, Tom. "TomGram: Graduation Day with Howard Zinn." TomDispatch.com, May 24, 2005. http://www.tomdispatch

.com/post/2728/graduation_day_with_howard_zinn (accessed April 24, 2010).

Ervin, Mike. "Person of the Year. Harriet McBryde Johnson: A Life Well Lived." *New Mobility*, January 2004. http://newmobility.com/articleView.cfm?id=811&srch=harriet%20mcbryde (accessed March 7, 2011).

Fabros, Alex S. "A Short History of the 1st and 2nd Filipino Infantry Regiments of the U.S. Army in World War II." California State Military Museum, n.d. http://www.militarymuseum.org/Filipino.html (accessed March 4, 2011).

Falk, Candace. *Love, Anarchy, and Emma Goldman*. New Brunswick, NJ: Rutgers University Press, 1990.

Farrakhan, Louis. "Minister Farrakhan Challenges Black Men." Transcripts from Minister Louis Farrakhan's Remarks at the Million Man March. CNN Interactive, October 17, 1995. http://www-cgi.cnn.com/US/9510/megamarch/10-16/transcript/index.html (accessed April 8, 2011).

Faulkner, Maureen, and Michael A. Smerconish. *Murdered by Mumia: A Life Sentence of Loss, Pain and Injustice*. Guilford, CT: Lyons Press/Globe Pequot, 2008.

Feklisov, Alexander. *The Man behind the Rosenbergs*. New York: Enigma Books, 2003.

Fetherling, Dale. *Mother Jones: The Miners' Angel*. Carbondale: Southern Illinois University Press, 1974.

Fields, Suzanne. "A Radical Who Wasn't Completely Wrong: Reconsidering Betty Friedan." *Jewish World Review*, February 9, 2006. http://www.jewishworldreview.com/cols/fields020906.php3 (accessed February 26, 2011).

The Fight in the Fields: Cesar Chavez and the Farmworkers' Struggle. Directed by Rick Tejada-Flores and Ray Telles. Documentary film that covers César Chávez's life and organization of farmworkers. ITVS, 1997.

Fike, Rupert, ed. *Voices from the Farm: Adventures in Community Living*. Summertown, TN: 1998.

Fitzgerald, John. "Paul Goodman Biography." *Anarchy Archives*, n.d. http://dwardmac.pitzer.edu/Anarchist_Archives/bright/goodman/goodman-bio.html (accessed January 9, 2011).

Flexner, Eleanor. *Century of Struggle: The Woman's Rights Movement in the United States*. New York: Atheneum, 1974. Reprint of 1959 edition by Harvard University Press.

Flynn, Elizabeth Gurley, *The Rebel Girl: An Autobiography, My First Life (1906–1926)*. Rev. ed. Lincolnwood, IL: Publications International, 1976.

Foner, Philip S., ed. *Mother Jones Speaks: Collected Writings and Speeches*. New York: Monad Press, 1983.

Fowler, Virginia C., and Nikki Giovanni. *Conversations with Nikki Giovanni*. Jackson, MS: University Press of Mississippi, 1992.

Franken, Al. *Lies and the Lying Liars Who Tell Them: A Fair and Balanced Look at the Right*. New York: Penguin, 2003.

Franken, Al. *Rush Limbaugh Is a Big Fat Idiot and Other Observations*. New York: Delacorte, 1996.

Frankfurter, Felix. "The Case of Sacco and Vanzetti." *Atlantic*, March 1927. http://www.theatlantic.com/past/docs/unbound/flashbks/oj/frankff.htm (accessed June 10, 2010).

Friedan, Betty. *The Feminine Mystique*. 20th Anniversary ed. New York: W. W. Norton, 1983. First published 1963.

Friedan, Betty. *Life So Far: A Memoir*. New York: Simon and Schuster, 2000.

Fujino, Diane. *The Revolutionary Life of Yuri Kochiyama: Heartbeat of Struggle*. Minneapolis: University of Minnesota Press, 2005.

Gardell, Mattias. *The Name of Elijah Mohammad: Louis Farrakhan and the Nation of Islam*. Durham, NC: Duke University Press, 1996.

Garlin, Sender. *Three American Radicals: John Swinton, Crusading Editor; Charles P. Steinmetz, Scientist and Socialist; William Dean Howells and the Haymarket Era*. Boulder, CO: Westview Press, 1991.

Gaskin, Stephen. *An Outlaw in My Heart: A Political Activist's Users Manual*. Philadelphia: Camino Books, 2000.

Gaskin, Stephen. *The Caravan*. Rev. ed. Summertown, TN: Book Publishing Co., 2000. First published 1972.

Gibbs, Lois. *Love Canal: The Story Continues*. Gabriola Island, BC, Canada: New Society Publishers, 1998.

Gibbs, Nancy. "Tiller's Murder: The Logic of Extremism on Abortion." *Time*, June 2, 2009. http://www.time.com/time/nation/article/0,8599,1902120,00.html (accessed November 27, 2010).

Gilman, Charlotte Perkins. *Our Androcentric Culture, or the Man Made World*. 1911. Project Gutenberg E-book released January 15, 2009.

Gilman, Charlotte Perkins. *The Living of Charlotte Perkins Gilman: An Autobiography*. Madison: University of Wisconsin Press, 1991. First published 1935.

Giovanni, Nikki. *Gemini: An Extended Autobiographical Statement My First Twenty-five Years Being a Black Poet*. New York: Penguin, 1976.

Gitlin, Todd. *The Sixties: Years of Hope, Days of Rage*. New York: Bantam Books, 1993.

Glavin, Paul, and Chuck Morse. "War is the Health of the State: An Interview with Howard Zinn." *Perspectives on Anarchist Theory*, Spring 2003. http://flag.blackened.net/ias/13zinn.htm (accessed April 27, 2010).

Goldman, Emma. *Anarchism and Other Essays*. New York: Dover, 1969. Reprint of 1910 ed.

Goldman, Emma. *Living My Life*. New York: Knopf, 1970. Reprint of 1931 ed.

Goldmark, Josephine. *Impatient Crusader: Florence Kelley's Life Story*. Urbana: University of Illinois Press, 1953.

Goldsmith, Barbara. "About Victoria Woodhull." Woodhull Sexual Freedom Alliance.org, n.d. http://www.woodhullalliance.org/about-us/about-victoria-woodhull/ (accessed September 9, 2011).

Goldsmith, Barbara. *Other Powers: The Age of Suffrage, Spiritualism and the Scandalous Victoria Woodhull*. New York: Alfred S. Knopf, Inc., 1998.

Goldstein, Warren. *William Sloane Coffin, Jr.: A Holy Impatience*. New Haven, CT: Yale University Press, 2006.

Goodman, Amy (interviewer). "Leonard Peltier Speaks from Prison." *Democracy Now!* June 12, 2000. http://www.democracynow.org/2000/6/12/leonard_peltier_speaks_from_prison (accessed March 20, 2011).

Goodman, Paul. *Growing Up Absurd: Problems of Youth in Organized Society*. New York: Vintage, 1960.

Goodman, Paul. *New Reformation: Notes of Neolithic Conservative*. New York: Vintage Books, 1971. First published 1969.

Goodwin, Doris Kearns. *No Ordinary Time: Franklin and Eleanor Roosevelt*. New York: Simon and Schuster, 1994.

Gorn, Elliott J. *Mother Jones: The Most Dangerous Woman in America*. New York: Hill and Wang/Farrar, Straus and Giroux, 2001.

Green, Ben. *Before His Time: The Untold Story of Harry T. Moore, America's First Civil Rights Martyr*. Gainesville: University Press of Florida, 2005. First published 1999 by Free Press.

Gregory, Dick, with Robert Lipsyte. *Nigger: An Autobiography*. New York: Pocket Books, 1969. First published by E. P. Dutton, 1964.

Gregory, Dick. *Up from Nigger*. New York: Stein and Day, 1976.

Gregory, James. "Seattle Civil Rights and History Project." University of Washington, n.d. http://depts.washington.edu/civilr/segregated.htm (accessed April 9, 2011).

Grinde, Donald A. *Ecocide of Native America: Environmental Destruction of Indian Lands and Peoples*. Santa Fe, NM: Clear Light Books, 1994.

Grossberger, Lewis. "The Rush Hours." *New York Times Magazine*, December 16, 1990.

Grossman, Mark. *The ABC-CLIO Companion to The Native American Rights Movement*. Santa Barbara, CA: ABC-CLIO, 1996.

Gwinn, Kristen E. *Emily Greene Balch: The Long Road to Internationalism*. Urbana and Chicago: University of Illinois Press, 2010.

Haas, Jeffrey. *The Assassination of Fred Hampton: How the FBI and the Chicago Police Murdered a Black Panther*. Chicago: Lawrence Hill Books, 2009.

Haas, Jeffrey. "Fred Hampton's Legacy." *Nation*, December 14, 2009.

Haley, Alex, and Malcolm X. *The Autobiography of Malcolm X*. New York: Ballantine Books, 1987.

Hall, Gus. *Fighting Racism: Selected Writings*. New York: International Publishers, 1985.

Hall, Jacquelyn. "Oral History Interview with Modjeska Simkins, July 28, 1976." Southern Oral History Program Collection, Wilson Library, University of North Carolina at Chapel Hill. http://docsouth.unc.edu/sohp/G-0056-2/menu.html (accessed March 23, 2011).

Hamill, Pete. "What Does Lou Grant Know about El Salvador?" *New York Magazine*, March 15, 1982.

Hammond, John Winthrop. *Charles Proteus Steinmetz: A Biography*. Reprint ed. Kennsinger Publishing, 2006. First published by the Century Company, 1924.

Hardy, David, and Jason Clarke. *Michael Moore Is A Big Fat Stupid White Man*. New York: HarperCollins, 2004.

Harper, Will. "The Unsolved Mysteries of Judi Bari." *East Bay Express*, September 12, 2001. http://www.eastbayexpress.com/eastbay/the-unsolved-mysteries-of-judi-bari/Content?oid=1066036 (accessed July 11, 2010).

Harris, Leon A. *Upton Sinclair, American Rebel*. New York: Crowell, 1975.

Hawxhurst, Joan C. *Mother Jones: Labor Crusader*. Austin, TX: Steck-Vaughn Company, 1994.

Hayden, Tom. *Ending the War in Iraq*. New York: Akashik Books, 2007.

Hayden, Tom. *Reunion: A Memoir*. New York: Collier Books/Macmillan, 1988.

Height, Dorothy. *Open Wide the Freedom Gates: A Memoir*. New York: Public Affairs, Perseus Book Group, 2003.

Height, Dorothy I., and Jacqueline Trescott. "Remembering Mary McLeod Bethune." *Essence*, February 1994.

Heller, Ann Conover. *Ayn Rand and the World She Made*. New York: Anchor Books, 2009.

Hemenway, Robert E. *Zora Neale Hurston: A Literary Biography*. Urbana: University of Illinois Press, 1977.

Hennessee, Judith Adler. *Betty Friedan: Her Life*. New York: Random House, 1999.

Herman, Arthur. *Joseph McCarthy: Reexamining the Life and Legacy of America's Most Hated Senator*. New York: Free Press/Simon and Schuster, 2000.

Herrick, William. *Jumping the Line: The Adventures and Misadventures of an American Radical*. Edinburgh, London, and Oakland, CA: AK Press, 2001. First published by University of Wisconsin Press, 1998.

Hessel, Dieter T., ed. and Margaret E. Kuhn. *Maggie Kuhn on Aging*. Philadelphia: Westminster Press, 1977.

Hill, Julia Butterfly. *The Legacy of Luna: The Story of a Tree, a Woman, and the Struggle to Save the Redwoods*. San Francisco: HarperSanFrancisco, 2000.

Hill, Mary A. *Charlotte Perkins Gilman: The Making of a Radical Feminist 1860–1896*. Philadelphia: Temple University Press, 1980.

Hirsh, Michael. "Al Franken Gets Serious." *Newsweek*, July 5, 2010. http://www.newsweek.com/2010/07/05/al-franken-gets-serious.html (accessed August 29, 2010).

Hitchens, Christopher. "Assassins of the Mind." *Vanity Fair*, February 2009. http://www.vanityfair.com/politics/features/2009/02/hitchens200902 (accessed January 9, 2011).

Hoffman, Abbie, and Norman Mailer. *The Autobiography of Abbie Hoffman*. New York: Four Walls Eight Windows, 1980; revised 2000.

Hoffman, Abbie. *Revolution for the Hell of It.* New York: Thunder's Mouth Press, 2005. First published 1968.

Holland, Bernard. "Sending a Message, Louis Farrakhan Plays Mendelssohn." *New York Times*, April 19, 1993. http://www.nytimes.com/1993/04/19/arts/sending-a-message-louis-farrakhan-plays-mendelssohn.html?pagewanted=all (accessed April 8, 2011).

Holt, Rackham. *Mary McLeod Bethune: A Biography.* Garden City, NY: Doubleday, 1964.

Honeywell, Carissa. "Paul Goodman: Finding an Audience for Anarchism in 20th Century America." *Political Studies Association*, May 2010. http://www.psa.ac.uk/journals/pdf/5/2010/397_543.pdf (accessed January 9, 2011).

Horne, Gerald. *W. E. B. Du Bois: A Biography.* Santa Barbara, CA: Greenwood Press/ABC-CLIO, 2010.

Horowitz, David. *Radical Son: A Generational Odyssey.* New York: Touchstone, 1997.

Humphry, Derek. *Final Exit: The Practicalities of Self-Deliverance and Assisted Suicide for the Dying.* Eugene, OR: The Hemlock Society, 1991.

Humphry, Derek, and Ann Wickett. *Jean's Way, 2003 Edition.* Junction City, OR: ERGO/Norris Lane Press, 2003.

Hung, Melissa. "Yuri Kochiyama: The Last Revolutionary." ModelMinority.com, March 13, 2002. http://www.modelminority.com/joomla/index.php?option=com_content&view=article&id=390:yuri-kochiyama-the-last-revolutionary-&catid=43:leaders&Itemid=56 (accessed March 10, 2011).

Hurston, Zora Neale. *Their Eyes Were Watching God.* New York: HarperPerennial, 1990. Reprint of 1939 publication.

Ida M. Tarbell web site. http://www.tarbell.allegheny.edu (accessed November 3, 2010).

Industrial Workers of the World. "Preamble to the IWW Constitution." http://www.iww.org/culture/official/preamble.shtml (accessed January 8, 2011).

James, G. Robert. *Sarah Palin: The Real Deal.* Lakeland, FL: White Stone Books, 2008.

James, Joy, ed. *The Angela Y. Davis Reader.* Oxford, UK, and Malden, MA: Blackwell Publishers, 1998.

Jamieson, Kathleen Hall, and Joseph N. Cappella. *Echo Chamber: Rush Limbaugh and the Conservative Media Establishment.* New York: Oxford University Press, 2008.

Johnson, Anne Janette. *The Scopes "Monkey Trial."* Detroit, MI: Omnigraphics, 2004.

Johnson, Charles Spurgeon. "Interview with Mary McLeod Bethune." 1939 or 1940. http://www.floridamemory.com/OnlineClassroom/MaryBethune/interview.cfm (accessed May 22, 2010).

Johnson, Harriet McBryde. "Alas for Tiny Tim, He Became a Christmas Cliché." *New York Times*, December 25, 2006. http://www.nytimes.com/2006/12/25/opinion/25johnson.html?_r=3&scp=2&sq=harriet+mcbryde+johnson&st=nyt&oref=login (accessed March 7, 2011).

Johnson, Harriet McBryde. *Too Late to Die Young: Nearly True Tales from a Life.* New York: Henry Holt, 2005.

Johnson, Haynes. *Age of Anxiety: McCarthyism to Terrorism.* Orlando, FL: Harcourt, Inc., 2005.

Johnson, Kaylene, *Sarah: How a Hockey Mom Turned Alaska's Political Establishment Upside Down.* Kenmore, WA: Epicenter Press, 2008.

Jones, Mother. *The Autobiography of Mother Jones.* Edited by Mary Field Parton. Mineola, NY: Dover Publications, 1980. Republication of the work originally published in 1925 by Charles H. Kerr & Company, Chicago.

Josephson, Hannah. *Jeannette Rankin, First Lady in Congress: A Biography.* Indianapolis, IN: Bobbs-Merrill, 1974.

Josephy, Alvin M., Jr. *Red Power: The American Indians' Fight for Freedom.* New York: McGraw-Hill, 1971.

Kaplan, Carla. *Zora Neale Hurston: A Life in Letters*. New York: Doubleday, 2002.

Katz, William Loren. *Eyewitness: A Living Documentary of the African American Contribution to American History*. Revised and updated. New York: Touchstone/Simon and Schuster, 1995.

Kaye, Roger. "Celebrating a Wilderness Legacy: The Arctic National Wildlife Refuge." *International Wildlife Journal*, April 2010.

Kelley, David. "The Capitalist Ideal: The Moral Vision of Atlas Shrugged." The Atlas Society, March 2009. http://ayn-rand.info/cth—2165-Capitalist_ideal.aspx (accessed December 27, 2010).

Kelly, Kathy. "Witnessing against Torture: Why We Must Act!" *Huffington Post*, June 22, 2010. http://www.huffingtonpost.com/kathy-kelly/witnessing-against-tortur_b_621038.html (accessed November 19, 2010).

Kelly, Kathy. *Other Lands Have Dreams: From Baghdad to Pekin Prison*. Petrolia, CA: Counterpunch Press, 2005.

Kennedy, David. "The Man, The Martyr, The Mystery: Harry T. Moore." *Florida Monthly*, 2004.

Kernaghan, Charles. "Children Exploited by Kathie Lee/Wal-Mart." Testimony before Democratic Policy Committee Congressional Hearings, April 29, 1996. http://www.nlcnet.org/alerts?id=0246 (accessed December 4, 2010).

Kersten, Andrew Edmund. *A. Philip Randolph: A Life in the Vanguard*. Lanham, MD: Rowman and Littlefield Publishers, 2006.

Kilbane, Doris. "Charles Proteus Steinmetz: Genius, Freethinker." *Electronic Design*, October 20, 2006.

King, Dennis. *Lyndon LaRouche and the New American Fascism*. New York: Doubleday, 1989.

Knight, Richard. "Silent No More: Interview with Col. Margarethe Cammermeyer." *Windy City Times*, September 20, 2006. http://outlineschicago.com/gay/lesbian/news/ARTICLE.php?AID=12658 (accessed February 14, 2011).

Kochersberger, Robert C., Jr., ed. *More than a Muckraker: Ida Tarbell's Lifetime in Journalism*. Knoxville: University of Tennessee Press, 1996.

Kochiyama, Yuri. *Passing It On*. Los Angeles: UCLA Asian American Studies Center Press, 2004.

Kolbert, Elizabeth. "Firebrand: Phyllis and the Conservative Revolution." *New Yorker*, November 7, 2005.

Kovic, Ron. *Born on the Fourth of July*. New York: Akashic Books, 1976, 2005.

Krakow, Kari. *The Harvey Milk Story*. Ridley Park, PA: Two Lives Publishers, 2002.

Krupa, Stephen J., S.J. "Celebrating Dorothy Day." *America Magazine—the National Catholic Weekly*, August 27, 2001.

Kuhn, Maggie. *Get Out There and Do Something about Injustice*. New York: Friendship Press, 1972.

Kuhn, Maggie, with Christina Long and Laura Quinn. *No Stone Unturned: The Life and Times of Maggie Kuhn*. New York: Ballantine Books, 1991.

Kunstler, William M., with Sheila Isenberg. *My Life as a Radical Lawyer*. New York: Birch Lane Press, 1994.

Kupfer, David. "Martin Sheen Interview." *Progressive*, July 2003. http://www.progressive.org/mag_intvsheen (accessed January 23, 2011).

LaDuke, Winona. "The Indigenous Women's Network: Our Future, Our Responsibility: Statement of Winona LaDuke." *The Indigenous Women's Network Our Future, Our Responsibility*. Presented at the United Nations Fourth World Conference on Women, Beijing, China, August 31, 1995. http://www.ratical.org/co-globalize/WinonaLaDuke/Beijing95.html (accessed April 4, 2011).

Lane, Ann J. *To Herland and Beyond: The Life and Work of Charlotte Perkins Gilman*. New York: Pantheon Books, 1990.

Langum, David J. *William M. Kunstler: The Most Hated Lawyer in America*. New York: New York University Press, 1999.

LaRouche, Lyndon, Jr. *The Power of Reason: A Kind of an Autobiography*. New York:

The New Benjamin Franklin House Publishing Company, 1979.

Lash, Joseph P. *Eleanor and Franklin: The Story of Their Relationship, Based on Eleanor Roosevelt's Private Papers.* New York: W. W. Norton & Co., 1971.

Lazarus, Catie. "A Fair and Balanced Look at Al Franken." *Forward*, February 4, 2005. http://www.forward.com/articles/2877/ (accessed August 31, 2010).

Le Beau, Bryan F. *The Atheist: Madalyn Murray O'Hair.* New York and London: New York University Press, 2003.

Leeming, David. *James Baldwin: A Biography.* New York: Alfred A. Knopf, 1994.

Leibovich, Mark. "Being Glenn Beck." *New York Times Magazine*, October 3, 2010.

Leigh, David, and Luke Harding. *WikiLeaks: Inside Julian Assange's War on Secrecy.* New York: Public Affairs, 2011.

Lenin, V. I. *Lenin Collected Works*. Moscow: Progress Publishers, 1976 (first published in *Pravda*, April 19, 1922). http://www.marxists.org/archive/lenin/works/1922/apr/10cps.htm (accessed March 29, 2011).

Leopold, Aldo. *A Sand Country Almanac, with Essays on Conservation.* New York: Oxford University Press, 2001.

Levy, Jacques E. *Cesar Chávez: Autobiography of La Causa.* Minneapolis: University of Minnesota Press, 2007.

Lewis, David Levering. *W. E. B. Du Bois, 1868–1919: Biography of a Race 1868–1919.* New York: Henry Holt and Company, 1994.

Limbaugh, Rush. *See, I Told You So.* New York: Pocket Books, 1993.

Limbaugh, Rush. *The Way Things Ought to Be.* New York: Simon and Schuster, 1992.

Linn, James Weber. *Jane Addams: A Biography.* New York: Greenwood Press, 1968.

Lomax, Louis E. *When the Word Is Given a Report on Elijah Muhammad, Malcolm X and the Black Muslim World.* New York: New American Library, 1963.

Long, Priscilla. *Mother Jones: Woman Organizer.* Boston: South End Press, 1976.

Lorbiecki, Marybeth. *Aldo Leopold: A Fierce Green Fire.* Helena, MT: Falcon Press, 2005.

Lynch, Dan. "Dorothy Day's Pro-Life Memories." *Catholic Exchange*, September 24, 2002. http://www.catholiceducation.org/articles/abortion/ab0063.html (accessed March 8, 2010).

Malcolm X. Directed by Spike Lee. A biographical film of the black leader, played by Denzel Washington. 1992.

Malcolm X and George Breitman, ed. *Malcolm X Speaks: Selected Speeches and Statements.* New York: Grove Press, 1994.

Mankiller, Wilma, and Michael Wallis. *Mankiller: A Chief and Her People.* New York: St. Martin's Griffin, 1999.

Mankiller, Wilma P. *Every Day Is a Good Day: Reflections by Contemporary Indigenous Women.* Golden, CO: Fulcrum Publishing, 2004.

Marcus, Eric. *Making History: The Struggle for Gay and Lesbian Equal Rights.* New York: HarperCollins, 1992.

Margaret Sanger Papers. "Birth Control or Race Control? Sanger and the Negro Project," *Margaret Sanger Papers Project #28*, Fall 2001. http://www.nyu.edu/projects/sanger/secure/newsletter/articles/bc_or_race_control.html (accessed October 28, 2010).

Matthiessen, Peter. *In the Spirit of Crazy Horse.* New York: Viking Penguin, 1991. First published by Viking, 1983.

May, Lee. "Dart's Defiance." *Los Angeles Times*, December 10, 1987. http://articles.latimes.com/print/1987-12-10/news/vw-27981_1_justin-dart-jr (accessed December 13, 2010).

McCabe, Scott. "Crime History—Attica Prison Riot Begins, Ending With 39 Killed." *Washington Examiner*, September 9, 2009. http://washingtonexaminer.com/crime-and-punishment/2009/09/crime-history-attica-prison-riot-begin sending-39-killed (accessed February 21, 2011).

McCarthy, Tim. "Light of Day Shines Yet at Catholic Worker." *National Catholic Reporter*, May 21, 1993.

McCartney, David. "FBI Kept a Close Eye on Chapman Catt." *Charles City Press*, July 10, 1999. http://www.catt.org/ccabout4.html (accessed June 3, 2010).

McCorvey, Norma, and Gary Thomas. *Won by Love*. Nashville, TN: Thomas Nelson Publishers, 1997.

McCorvey, Norma, with Andy Meisler. *I Am Roe: My Life*, Roe v. Wade, *and Freedom of Choice*. New York: HarperCollins, 1994.

McMahon, Brian T., and Linda R. Shaw, eds. *Enabling Lives: Biographies of Six Prominent Americans with Disabilities*. Boca Raton, FL: CRC Press, 1999.

McMichael, William H. "West Point Grads Form Support Group." *Navy Times*, March 16, 2009. http://www.navytimes.com/news/2009/03/military_westpoint_knightsout_031609w/ (accessed April 21, 2011).

McMillan, Priscilla J. *The Ruin of J. Robert Oppenheimer and the Birth of the Modern Arms Race*. New York: Viking, 2005.

Means, Russell, with Marvin J. Wolf. *Where White Men Fear to Tread: The Autobiography of Russell Means*. New York: St. Martin's Press, 1995.

Meigs, Cornelia. *Jane Addams: Pioneer for Social Justice*. Boston: Little, Brown and Company, 1970.

Meine, Curt D. *Aldo Leopold: His Life and Work*. Madison: University of Wisconsin Press, 1988.

Michelman, Kate. *With Liberty and Justice for All: A Life Spent Protecting the Right to Choose*. New York: Hudson Street Press, 2005.

Michelman, Kate. "A System from Hell: How Medical Crises Have Taken My Family to Financial Ruin." *Huffington Post*, April 13, 2009. http://www.huffingtonpost.com/kate-michelman/a-system-from-hell-how-me_b_186177.htm (accessed September 14, 2010).

Miles, Barry. *Zappa: A Biography*. Broadway, NY: Grove/Atlantic Books, 2004.

Milk. Directed by Gus Van Sant. The Harvey Milk story on film, with Sean Penn as Milk. Focus Features, 2008.

Miller, Calvin Craig. *A. Philip Randolph and the African-American Labor Movement*. Greensboro, NC: Morgan Reynolds, 2005.

Moon, Margo. "Grethe Cammermeyer Interview." Our Big Gayborhood, September 12, 2009. http://www.ourbiggayborhood.com/2009/09/grethe-cammermeyer-interview/ (accessed February 12, 2011).

Moore, Michael. *Stupid White Men . . . and Other Sorry Excuses for the State of the Nation*. New York: HarperCollins, 2001.

Murie, Margaret E. *Two in the Far North*. 2nd ed. Anchorage, AK: Northwest Publishing Company, 1978.

Myers, Jim. "J. Edgar Hoover Irked by George Carlin." *Newsmax*, January 30, 2009.

NAACP. "NAACP History: Harry T. and Harriette Moore." n.d. http://www.naacp.org/pages/naacp-history-Harry-T.-and-Harriette-Moore/ (accessed February 10, 2011).

Nadelson, Regina. *Who Is Angela Davis?* New York: Peter H. Wyden, 1972.

Nader, Ralph. *Unsafe at Any Speed: The Designed-in Dangers of the American Automobile*. New York: Grossman Publishers, 1965.

Nader, Ralph, and Theodore Jacobs. "Do Third Parties Have a Chance? Ballot Access and Minority Parties." *Harvard Law Record*, October 9, 1958. http://www.facebook.com/topic.php?uid=2208102184&topic=1948 (accessed April 22, 2011).

Nagel, Joane. *American Indian Ethnic Renewal: Red Power and the Resurgence of Identity and Culture*. New York: Oxford University Press, 1997.

National Association for the Deaf (NAD). "Frank G. Bowe, Advocate for Hearing Impaired and Deaf." *Hearing Review* http://www.hearingreview.com/insider/2007-11-15_05.asp (accessed October 20, 2010).

Ng, Wendy. *Japanese American Internment during World War II: A History and Reference Guide.* Westport, CT: Greenwood Press, 2002.

Nies, Judith. *Nine Women: Portraits from the American Radical Tradition.* Berkeley, Los Angeles, and London: University of California Press, 2002.

Nollen, Scott Allen. *Paul Robeson: Film Pioneer.* Jefferson, NC: McFarland Publishing, 2010.

Nomberg-Przytyk, Sara, and Eli Pfefferkorn, eds. *Auschwitz: True Tales from a Grotesque Land.* Translated by Roslyn Hirsch. Chapel Hill: University of North Carolina Press, 1985.

Obama, Barack. "Equality Is a Moral Imperative: Open Letter Concerning LGBT Equality in America, Reaffirming His Steadfast Commitment to Equal Rights for All Americans." 2012 BarackObama.com, February, 28, 2008. http://my.barackobama.com/page/community/post/alexokrent/gGggJS (accessed April 23, 2011).

Obama, Barack. "Remarks by the President in State of the Union Address, U.S. Capitol." January 27, 2010 http://www.whitehouse.gov/the-press-office/remarks-president-state-union-address (accessed April 23, 2011).

Ochs, Phil. Album Notes for *I Ain't Marching Anymore.* Elektra, 1965.

Oklahoma Library Association. "Oklahoma Library Legends, An OKL Centennial Project: Ruth Brown." n.d. http://www.library.okstate.edu/dean/jpaust/legends/people/brown.htm (accessed May 4, 2010).

Oldenburg, Don. "Julia Butterfly Hill, from Treetop to Grass Roots." *Washington Post,* September 22, 2004.

Oliver, Myrna. "Gus Hall; Communist Party Leader in the U.S. for 40 Years." *Los Angeles Times,* October 17, 2000.

Olsen, Ted. "Where Jim Wallis Stands." *Christianity Today,* May 2008. http://www.christianitytoday.com/ct/2008/may/9.52.html (accessed January 4, 2011).

Othow, Helen Chavis. *John Chavis: African American Patriot, Preacher, Teacher, and Mentor (1783–1838).* Jefferson, NC: McFarland & Co., Inc., 2001.

Ott, Chris. "Seattle School Boycott (1966)." BlackPast.org, n.d. http://www.blackpast.org/?q=aaw/seattle-school-boycott-1966 (accessed April 11, 2011).

Ouellette, Alicia. "Disability and the End of Life." *Oregon Law Review,* November 30, 2006.

Palin, Sarah. *Going Rogue: An American Life.* New York: HarperCollins, 2009.

Parks, Rosa, and Gregory J. Reed, *Quiet Strength.* Grand Rapids, MI: Zondervan Publishing House, 1994.

Parks, Rosa, with James Haskins. *Rosa Parks: My Story.* New York: Penguin Group, 1999. First published by Dial, 1992.

Pasachoff, Naomi E. *Frances Perkins: Champion of the New Deal.* Oxford and New York: Oxford University Press, 1999.

Paul, Sonia, and Robert Perkinson. "Winona LaDuke." Chap. 4 of *No Middle Ground: Women and Radical Protest,* edited by Kathleen M. Blee. New York: New York University Press, 1998.

Peare, Owen. *Mary McLeod Bethune.* New York: Vanguard Press, 1951.

Peck, James. *The Chomsky Reader.* New York: Pantheon Books, 1987.

Peck, Mary Gray. *Carrie Chapman Catt: A Biography.* New York: H. W. Wilson Co., 1944.

"Phil Ochs: The Life and Legacy of a Legendary American Folk Singer" (interview transcript) *Democracy Now!* January 6, 2011. http://www.democracynow.org/2011/1/6/phil_ochs_the_life_and_legacy (accessed March 10, 2011).

Polner, Murray, and Jim O'Grady. *Disarmed and Dangerous: The Radical Life and Times of Daniel and Philip Berrigan, Brothers in Religious Faith and Civil Disobedience.* New York: Westview Press/Perseus Books Group, 1998.

Prazniak, Roxann, and Arif Dirlik. *Places and Politics in an Age of Globalization.* Oxford: Rowman and Littlefield, Publishers, 2001.

Public Broadcasting Service. "Freedom Never Dies: The Legacy of Harry T. Moore." PBS.org, 2001. http://www.pbs.org/harrymoore/harry/mbio.html (accessed February 10, 2011).

Public Broadcasting Service. "RFK American Experience, People and Events: Cesar Chávez (1927–1993)." PBS.org, July 1, 2004. http://www.pbs.org/wgbh/amex/rfk/peopleevents/p_chavez.html (accessed September 8, 2011).

Public Broadcasting Service. "William Kunstler: Disturbing the Universe." PBS.org, June 10, 2010; updated June 20, 2010. http://www.pbs.org/pov/disturbingtheuniverse/background.php (accessed February 18, 2011).

"*The Rachel Maddow Show* for Friday, March 20, 2009" (transcript). MSNBC.com, March 20, 2009. http://www.msnbc.msn.com/id/29836340 (accessed April 23, 2011).

Radosh, Ronald, and Joyce Milton. *The Rosenberg File*. 2nd ed. With a new introduction containing revelations from National Security Agency and Soviet sources. New Haven, CT: Yale University Press, 1997.

Rains, Scott. "Dr. Frank Bowe: Longtime Professor and Renowned Champion of People with Disabilities." *Rolling Rains Report: Precipitating Dialogue on Travel, Disability, and Universal Design*, August 24, 2007. http://www.rollingrains.com/archives/001784.html (accessed October 20, 2010).

Rand, Ayn. *Capitalism: The Unknown Ideal*. New York: Signet/Penguin Group, 1967.

Rand, Ayn. "Man's Rights." Ayn Rand Center for Individual Rights, April 1963. http://www.aynrand.org/site/PageServer?pagename=arc_ayn_rand_man_rights (accessed December 26, 2010).

Randall, Margaret. "Deporting Dissent." *Nation*, April 19, 1986.

Randolph, A. Philip. "The March on Washington Movement." *Survey Graphic*, November 1942. http://www.bsos.umd.edu/aasp/chateauvert/mowmcall.htm (accessed June 6, 2010).

Rashke, Richard L. *The Killing of Karen Silkwood: The Story behind the Kerr-McGee Plutonium Case*. 2nd ed. New York: Cornell Paperbacks, 2000.

Reeves, Thomas C. *The Life and Times of Joe McCarthy: A Biography*. Briarcliff Manor, NY: Stein and Day, 1982.

Reinhardt, Akim D. *Ruling Pine Ridge: Oglala Lakota Politics from the IRA to Wounded Knee (Plains Histories)*. Lubbock: Texas Tech University Press, 2007.

Robbins, Louise S. *The Dismissal of Miss Ruth Brown: Civil Rights, Censorship, and the American Library*. Norman: University of Oklahoma Press, 2000.

Roberts, Sam. *The Brother: The Untold Story of the Rosenberg Case*. New York: Random House, 2003.

Robeson, Paul. *Here I Stand*. Boston: Beacon Press, 1958.

Robeson, Paul, Jr. *Paul Robeson: Quest for Freedom, 1939–1976*. New York: John Wiley & Sons, 2010.

Roosevelt, Eleanor. *The Autobiography of Eleanor Roosevelt*. New York: First Da Capo, 1992.

Rosemont, Franklin. *Joe Hill: The IWW and the Making of a Revolutionary Workingclass Counter Culture*. Chicago: Charles H. Kerr Publishing Company, 2002.

Rosen, Marjorie. "Friend of the Earth: Indian Activist Winona LaDuke Fights to Return Tribal Lands to Her People" *People*, November 28, 1994. http://www.people.com/people/archive/article/0,,20104531,00.html (accessed March 31, 2011).

Rovzar, Chris. "The Inevitable Backlash against James O'Keefe's Heavily Edited NPR 'Sting' Begins." *New York Magazine*, March 14, 2011. http://nymag.com/daily/intel/2011/03/the_inevitable_backlash_agains.html (accessed April 28, 2011).

Rudd, Mark. *Underground: My Life with SDS and the Weathermen*. New York: HarperCollins, 2009.

Rudd, Mark. "Underground with Mark Rudd." YouTube video, 3:02, posted by "William Morrow1," April 6, 2009. http://www.youtube.com/watch?v=pxrL9iiDcSg (accessed March 11, 2011).

Russert, Tim. "Farrakhan Meets the Press (Interview with Tim Russert)." *Final Call*, online edition, April 13, 1997. http://www.finalcall.com/national/mlf-mtp5-13-97.html (accessed April 11, 2011).

Rustin, Bayard. *Down the Line: The Collected Writings of Bayard Rustin*. Chicago: Quadrangle Books, 1971.

Rustin, Bayard. "From Protest to Politics: The Future of the Civil Rights Movement." *Commentary Magazine*, February 1965. http://www.commentarymagazine.com/article/from-protest-to-politics-the-future-of-the-civil-rights-movement/ (accessed March 18, 2011).

Sacco, Nicola, and Bartolomeo Vanzetti. *The Letters of Sacco and Vanzetti*. New York: Penguin Group, 1997. First published by Viking, 1928.

Sacco and Vanzetti. Directed by Peter Miller. A documentary film about anarchists Nicola Sacco and Bartolomeo Vanzetti and their trial. Willow Pond Films, 2006.

Sanger, Margaret. *Margaret Sanger: An Autobiography*. New York: W. W. Norton, 1938.

Sanjek, Roger. *Gray Panthers*. Philadelphia: University of Pennsylvania Press, 2009.

Saunders, Robert W., Sr. *Bridging the Gap: Continuing the Florida NAACP Legacy of Harry T. Moore*. Tampa, FL: University of Tampa Press, 2000.

Scharlin, Craig, and Lilia Villanueva. *Philip Vera Cruz: A Personal History of Filipino Immigrants and the Farmworker Movement*. Seattle: University of Washington Press, 2000.

Schultz, Emily. *Michael Moore: A Biography*. Toronto, Ontario, Canada: ECW Press, 2005.

Schumacher, Michael. *There but for Fortune: The Life of Phil Ochs*. New York: Hyperion Books, 1997.

Schutzman, Mady, and Michael David Korolenko (writers). *Chords of Fame*. 1984. A documentary about the life of folk singer Phil Ochs.

Scott, Ivan. *Upton Sinclair: The Forgotten Socialist*. Lanham, MD: University Press of America, 1996.

Seid, Roberta E. "Rachel Corrie's Dreams: The (Self) Deceit of Rachel Corrie." *Commentary*, January 1970. http://www.commentarymagazine.com/viewarticle.cfm/the—self—deceit-of-rachel-corrie-11453?page=all (accessed January 18, 2011).

Shafer, Jacob. "Interview with Retired Colonel Ann Wright. *U.S. Labor against the War*. January 21, 2010. http://www.uslaboragainstwar.org/article.php?id=21337 (accessed August 5, 2010).

Shapiro, Mark. "The Salon Interview: Al Franken." *Salon*, n.d. http://www.salon.com/07/features/franken.html (accessed August 29, 2010).

Shaw, Bill. "Morris Dees: A Wily Alabamian Uses the Courts to Wipe Out Hate Groups and Racial Violence." *People*, July 22, 1991.

Shilts, Randy. *The Mayor of Castro Street* (Harvey Milk). New York: St. Martin's Press, 1982.

Shulman, Alix. *Red Emma Speaks: Selected Writings and Speeches by Emma Goldman*. New York: Random House, 1972.

Sinclair, Upton. *Autobiography*. New York: Harcourt, Brace, & World, 1962.

Sinclair, Upton. *Boston: A Documentary Novel*. Cambridge, MA: Robert Bentley, Inc., 1978.

Sinclair, Upton. *The Jungle*, 2006. Project Gutenberg E-book, released March 11, 2006.

Sklar, Kathryn Kish, and Beverly Wilson Palmer, eds. *The Selected Letters of Florence Kelley, 1869–1931*. Urbana: University of Illinois Press, 2009.

Sklar, Kathryn Kish. *Florence Kelley and the Nation's Work*. New Haven, CT: Yale University Press, 1995.

Smiley, Tavis (interviewer). "Ed Asner." PBS.org, May 21, 2009. http://www.pbs

.org/wnet/tavissmiley/archive/200905/20090521_asner.html (accessed April 8, 2011).

Smith, Gibbs M. *Joe Hill*. Layton, UT: Gibbs M. Smith, Inc., Peregrine Smith Books, 1969.

Smith, Norma. *Jeannette Rankin: America's Conscience*. Helena: Montana Historical Society Press, 2002.

Solomon, Martha. *Emma Goldman*. Boston: Twayne, Macmillan, 1987.

Sontag, Susan. *Against Interpretation and Other Essays*. New York: Farrar, Straus and Giroux, 1966.

Sontag, Susan. *Under the Sign of Saturn: Essays*. New York: Picador USA/Farrar, Straus, and Giroux, 2002. First published 1972.

Standley, Fred L., and Nancy V. Burt. *Critical Essays on James Baldwin*. Boston: G. K. Hall & Co., 1988.

Starbuck, Susan. *Hazel Wolf: Fighting the Establishment*. Seattle and London: University of Washington Press, 2002.

Stebner, Eleanor. *The Women of Hull House: A Study in Spirituality, Vocation, and Friendship*. Albany: State University of New York Press, 1997.

Stein, Leon, ed. *Out of the Sweatshop: The Struggle for Industrial Democracy*. New York: Quadrangle/The New York Times Book Company, 1977.

Stein, Leon. *The Triangle Fire*. New York: J. B. Lippincott Company, 1962.

Stern, Ellen Norman. *Elie Wiesel: A Voice for Humanity*. Philadelphia: Jewish Publication Society, 1996.

Stoehr, Taylor. *Decentralizing Power: Paul Goodman's Social Criticism*. New York: Black Rose Books, 1994.

Stone, Irving. *Clarence Darrow for the Defense: A Biography*. New York: Doubleday, 1941, 1989.

Strong, Tracy B., and Helene Keyssar. *Right in Her Soul: Life of Anna Louise Strong*. New York: Random House, 1983.

Sugg, John F. "Sami Al-Arian Speaks." *Counterpunch*, November 16, 2005. http://www.counterpunch.org/sugg11162 005.html (accessed November 12, 2010).

Tall, JoAnn. "Indian Boarding School Abuse." YouTube video, 4:02, posted by "robertleokelly," July 24, 2007. http://www.youtube.com/watch?v=p1tiQB8gt5g (accessed October 24, 2010).

Tamura, Linda. *The Hood River Issei: An Oral History of Japanese Settlers in Oregon's Hood River Valley*. Champaign-Urbana: Board of Trustees of the University of Illinois, 1993.

Tarbell, Ida M. *All in the Day's Work*. Urbana and Chicago: University of Illinois Press, 2003.

Tarbell, Ida M. *The History of the Standard Oil Company*. 2 vols. Gloucester, MA: Peter Smith, 1963.

Tateishi, John. *And Justice for All: An Oral History of the Japanese American Detention Camps*. New York: Random House, 1984.

Tierney, Kevin. *Darrow: A Biography*. New York: Thomas Y. Crowell, Publishers, 1979.

Tims, Margaret. *Jane Addams of Hull House, 1860–1935*. New York: Macmillan, 1961.

Toffler, Alvin. "Playboy Interview: Ayn Rand: A Candid Conversation with the Fountainhead of 'Objectivism.'" *Playboy*, March 1964. http://www.playboy.com/articles/ayn-rand-playboy-interview/ (accessed November 30, 2010).

Tóibín, Cohn. "The Henry James of Harlem: James Baldwin's Struggles." *Guardian*, September 14, 2001. http://www.guardian.co.uk/books/2001/sep/14/jamesbaldwin (accessed June 16, 2010).

Troupe, Quincy, ed. *James Baldwin: The Legacy*. New York: Simon and Schuster/Touchstone, 1989.

Tuhus-Dubrow, Rebecca. "Self-Portrait: Susan Sontag's Early Years." *Dissent*, February 5, 2009. http://www.dissentmagazine.org/online.php?id=203 (accessed January 9, 2011).

U.S. Congress. Senate. Select Committee to Study Governmental Operations with Respect to Intelligence Activities. *Final*

Report of the Select Committee to Study Governmental Operations with Respect to Intelligence Activities. The FBI's Covert Action Program to Destroy the Black Panther Party. April 23, 1976. http://www.archive.org/details/finalreportofsel06unit (accessed April 26, 2010).

Valledor, Sid Amores. *Americans with a Philippine Heritage: The Original Writings of Philip Vera Cruz.* Indianapolis, IN: Dog Ear Publishing, 2006.

Van Gelder, Sarah. "An Interview with Winona LaDuke." *Yes! Magazine*, Summer 2008. http://www.yesmagazine.org/issues/a-just-foreign-policy/an-interview-with-winona-laduke (accessed April 5, 2011).

Verdoia, Ken (producer/director). " 'We'll Scrape Gold Off the Streets!' " Public Broadcasting Service, 2000. http://www.kued.org/productions/joehill/story/biography/scrape_gold.html (accessed January 6, 2011).

Vesely-Flad, Ethan. "Leading Creative Action for Social Change: Medea Benjamin." Forusa.org, September 23, 2010. http://forusa.org/blogs/ethan-vesely-flad/leading-creative-action-social-change-medea-benjamin (accessed November 28, 2010).

Vine, Phyllis. *One Man's Castle: Clarence Darrow in Defense of the American Dream.* New York: HarperCollins/Amistad, 2004.

Vogel, Virgil J. *This Country Was Ours: a Documentary History of the American Indian.* New York: Harper & Row, 1972.

Walker, Alice, ed. *I Love Myself When I Am Laughing and Then Again When I Am Looking Mean and Impressive: A Zora Neale Hurston Reader.* New York: The Feminist Press at the City University of New York, 1979.

Walker, Alice. "Alice Walker—an Open Letter to Barack Obama." *NowPublic.com.* November 7, 2008. http://www.nowpublic.com/world/alice-walker-open-letter-barack-obama-1 (accessed August 30, 2010).

Walker, Alice. *We Are the Ones We Have Been Waiting For.* New York: New Press, 2006.

Wall, Richard. "The Radical Individualism of Paul Goodman." LewRockwell.com, n.d. http://www.lewrockwell.com/orig3/wall10.html (accessed January 9, 2011).

Wallis, Jim. *God's Politics: Why the Right Gets It Wrong and the Left Doesn't Get It.* San Francisco: HarperSanFrancisco, 2005.

Wallis, Jim. "Put Your Faith into Action for Social Justice." Change.org, January 16, 2010. http://uspoverty.change.org/blog/view/put_your_faith_into_action_for_social_justice (accessed January 3, 2011).

Wallis, Jim. "The Religious Right's Era Is Over." *Time*, February 16, 2007. http://www.time.com/time/nation/article/0,8599,1590782,00.html (accessed January 5, 2011).

Walton, Mary. *A Woman's Crusade: Alice Paul and the Battle for the Ballot.* New York: Palgrave Macmillan, 2010.

Warren, Donald. *Radio Priest: Charles Coughlin, the Father of Hate Radio.* New York: Free Press, 1996.

Warren, Patricia Neil. "Bayard Rustin: Offensive Lineman for Freedom." Outsports.com, February 15, 2009. http://www.outsports.com/os/index.php/component/content/article/45-2009/170-bayard-rustin-offensive-lineman-for-freedom%20 (accessed March 19, 2011).

Watson, Bruce. *Sacco and Vanzetti: The Men, the Murders, and the Judgment of Mankind.* New York: Viking, 2007.

Weinberg, Steve. *Taking on the Trust: How Ida Tarbell Brought Down John D. Rockefeller and Standard Oil.* New York: W. W. Norton & Company, 2009.

Weisenberg, Stuart. *Barney Frank: The Story of America's Only Left-Handed, Gay, Jewish Congressman.* Amherst: University of Massachusetts Press, 2009.

Weiss, Mike. *Double Play: The San Francisco City Hall Killings.* Reading, MA: Addison-Wesley, 1984.

Wicker, Tom. *Shooting Star: The Brief Arc of Joe McCarthy.* Orlando, FL: Houghton Mifflin Harcourt, 2006.

Widmer, Kingsley. *Paul Goodman*. Boston: Twayne Publishers, 1980.

Wiesel, Elie. *All Rivers Run to the Sea: Memoirs*. New York: Schocken Books, 1995.

Wiesel, Elie. "Remarks at Millennium Evening: The Perils of Indifference: Lessons Learned from a Violent Century." White House Official Transcript, April 12, 1999. http://www.historyplace.com/speeches/wiesel-transcript.htm (accessed April 16, 2011).

Wilkins, Roy, and Ramsey Clark, chairmen. *Search and Destroy: A Report by the Commission of Inquiry into the Black Panthers and the Police*. New York: Metropolitan Applied Research Center, Inc., 1973.

Wilkinson, Alec. *The Protest Singer: An Intimate Portrait of Pete Seeger*. New York: Vintage Books, 2010.

Williams, Juan, with the Eyes on the Prize Production Team. *Eyes on the Prize: America's Civil Rights Years, 1954–1965*. New York: Viking Penguin, 1987.

Woodhull, Victoria, and Cari M. Carpenter, eds. *Selected Writings of Victoria Woodhull: Suffrage, Free Love, and Eugenics*. Lincoln: Board of Regents of the University of Nebraska, 2010.

Wright, Ann, and Susan Dixon. *Dissent: Voices of Conscience*. Maui, HI: Koa Books, 2008.

Wright, Mary Ann. "Mary A Wright's Resignation Letter." GovernmentExecutive.com. March 21, 2003. http://www.govexec.com/dailyfed/0303/032103wright.htm (accessed August 5, 2010).

Young, William, and David E. Kaiser. *Postmortem: New Evidence in the Case of Sacco and Vanzetti*. Amherst: University of Massachusetts Press, 1985.

Zaitchik, Alexander. *Common Nonsense: Glenn Beck and the Triumph of Ignorance*. New York: Wiley, 2010.

Zappa, Frank, with Peter Occhiogrosso. *The Real Frank Zappa Book*. New York: Touchstone, 1989, 1999.

Zinn, Howard. "The Optimism of Uncertainty." *Nation*, September 20, 2004. http://www.thenation.com/article/optimism-uncertainty/ (accessed May 12, 2010).

Zinn, Howard. *A People's History of the United States: 1942–Present*. New York: HarperCollins, 2003.

Zinn, Howard. *You Can't Be Neutral on a Moving Train: A Personal History of Our Times*. Boston: Beacon Press. 2002.

Zora Neale Hurston: Their Eyes Were Watching God. (2008) Hurston's life story, which includes reenactments of a 1941 interview with Hurston at a New York radio station.

About the Editor and Contributors

Editor

Kathlyn Gay is the author of more than 100 nonfiction books on a variety of topics such as social issues, environmental preservation, history (American, Russian, Chinese), health, religious and cultural diversity, food security, and eating disorders. She has also written teacher manuals, ESL programs, portions of textbooks, and reference works such as *Rainforests of the World* (2001), *Encyclopedia of Women's Health Issues* (2002), and *African-American Holidays, Festivals, and Celebrations* (2007). She has been featured in *World's Who's Who of Authors; Contemporary Authors; About the Author;* and *Junior Authors and Illustrators.*

Contributors

Anni Margrethe Callaghan was formerly an educator and social worker and has been a longtime peace activist, especially concerned with U.S. involvement in Iraq and Afghanistan.

Daniel Callaghan is a retired U.S. Marine and former teacher who is owner of a used-and-rare-book store. He is actively involved—speaking, marching, writing—in numerous peace and justice movements, especially those involving Native American, civil rights, Muslim, and Mexican American issues.

Margaret Gay was a public relations writer and researcher for national and state (Illinois) professional medical organizations. She has written and edited material for numerous professional newsletters and other publications as well as worked as a paralegal in general practice law.

Martin K. Gay is a writer and consultant with several nonfiction titles to his credit, including *Encyclopedia of Political Anarchy* (1999), *Encyclopedia of North American Eating and Drinking Traditions, Customs and Rituals* (1996), and *Heroes of Conscience: A Biographical Dictionary* (1996).

Karen L. Hamilton is a legal assistant for a Florida attorney. She also has been a researcher for nonfiction young adult titles on a variety of topics.

Eric A. Kimmel is an award-winning author of dozens of children's books. He has been a literature professor at Indiana University, South Bend, Indiana, and at Portland State University in Portland, Oregon. He retired from college teaching in 1993 and is Professor Emeritus of Education at Portland State.

Bobbi Miller earned her Master of Fine Arts in Writing for Children from Vermont College of Fine Arts and her Master of Arts in Children's Literature from the Center for the Study of Children's Literature, Simmons College. Her books, *One Fine Trade* (2009) and *Davy Crockett Gets Hitched* (2009), made the "Bank Street College of Education List for Best Children's Books of the Year 2010." She is an adjunct professor of college reading and writing and English literature.

Index

Abbey, Edward, **1–4**, 48
Abernathy, Ralph, 65
Abolitionists, xix
Abortion, 84, 234, 406–9, 414–19, 457, 530, 537, 593–97
Abu-Jamal, Mumia, **4–9**, 26, 108, 136
Abzug, Bella, **9–13**, 65, 234, 450
Abzug, Martin, 10
Academic Bill of Rights, 305–6
ACORN. *See* Association of Community Organizations for Reform Now (ACORN)
Adams, Joan Vollmer, 93–94
Addams, Jane, **13–17**, 36, 247, 334–35, 487, 569
Addams, John, 13, 14, 15, 115
Afghanistan, 630
African Americans: discrimination against, 208; equal employment opportunity for, 498–99; Great Migration by, 208; involuntary sterilization of, 272; in military, 311–12; police brutality and, 276, 277; reparations for, 306, 639. *See also* Civil rights movement
Ageism, 234–35, 363–66
Agricultural Workers Organizing Committee (AWOC), 118, 601
AIDS, 574
Al-Arian, Sami, **17–22**
Alaska Independent Party (AIP), 602–5
Alaska Lands Act, 431–32

Alaska National Interest Lands Conservation Act (ANILCA), 605
Alcatraz occupation, 190–91, 395–96
Ali, Muhammad, **22–26**, 391
Alien Registration Act, 269
All-African People's Revolutionary Party (AAPRP), 108
American Birth Control League (ABCL), 532
American Civil Liberties Union (ACLU), 183, 221, 369
American Coalition of Citizens with Disabilities (ACCD), 76–77
American Enterprise Association (AEA), 534–35
American Friends Service Committee (AFSC), 378
American Indian Movement (AIM), 43–47, 191, 370, 411–13, 482, 586
American Railroad Union (ARU), 178–79, 332
Americans with Disabilities Act (ADA), 167–68, 326
American Veterans Movement (AVM), 361
Anarchism/anarchists, 16, 132, 254–56, 257–58, 474, 476–77, 525–28
Antinuclear movement, 10, 47, 65–66, 145–47, 439, 559–63
Anti-Semitism, 158–60, 217–18, 253, 289
Anti-sweatshop movement, 60–61
Antiwar activism, 29–30; Iraq War, 61–62, 339, 362, 550–55, 610, 613, 627–31; Vietnam War, 60, 63–66, 131, 135,

187–88, 280–81, 360–63, 420–21, 448–50; World War I, 36–37, 115, 174, 179–80, 255, 336, 500, 502, 583; World War II, 186–87, 257–58, 503
Arctic National Wildlife Refuge (ANWR), 432, 435
Ashcroft, John, 19–20
Asmussen, Oscar, 577–78
Asner, Ed, **26–29**
Assange, Julian, 399–400
Assisted suicide, 315–18, 345–49
Association of Community Organizations for Reform Now (ACORN), 457–58
Atlas Shrugged (Rand), 491, 493, 494
Atomic bomb, 460, 462–63
Atomic Energy Commission (AEC), 146–47, 463, 559, 562
Audubon Society, 622
Ayers, William, **29–34**, 519

Bagley, Sarah, xxi
Balch, Emily Greene, **35–39**
Baldwin, James, **39–43**
Ballut, Ghassan Zayed, 19
Banks, Dennis, **43–47**
Bari, Judi, 3, **47–50**, 296
Bari v. Held (1991), 49–50
Batterham, Forster, 175
Bean v. Southwestern Waste Management, Inc. (1979), 86–87
Beat Generation, 90–95
Beck, Glenn, **51–55**, 495, 611
Beck, Julian, 556
Bella Abzug Leadership Institute (BALI), 13
Bellecourt, Clyde, 44
Benitez, Lucas, **55–59**
Benjamin, Medea, **59–63**, 610
Berrigan, Daniel, **63–67**, 136
Berrigan, Philip, **63–67**, 136, 558
Bethune, Albertus, 68
Bethune, Mary McLeod, **67–71**
Beverly, Arnold, 7
Birth control, 193, 195–97, 529–33

Black, Jack, 93
Black Arts movement, 250
Black Hills Alliance (BHA), 586–87
Black Panther Party, 5, 108, 276–78, 304, 542–46, 637
Black Power, 73, 105–9, 250, 299, 353, 390–91
Blackwell, Henry, xxi
Blue Spring Community, xx
Boggs, Grace Lee, **71–75**
Boggs, James, 73, 74
Boudin, Kathy, 33
Bowe, Frank G., **75–78**
Bowling for Columbine (film), 429
Brandeis Brief, 336
Branden, Nathanial, 494
Brown, Jerry, 46, 281–82
Brown, Ruth, **78–82**
Brownmiller, Susan, **82–86**
Brown v. Board of Education (1954), 565
Bruce, Lenny, 102
Bryant, Anita, 422
Bullard, Linda McKeever, 86–87
Bullard, Robert, **86–90**
Bureau of Indian Affairs (BIA), 43, 45, 142, 144, 370, 396–97, 482, 586
Burns, Jack, 102
Burroughs, William, **90–95**
Bush, George W., 28, 136–37, 380, 440, 552–53, 630, 631
Byrne, Ethyl, 532

Cammermeyer, Grethe, **97–100**
Cancer, 573–74
Capitalism, 179, 269
Carlin, George, **100–105**
Carmichael, Stokely, 42, **105–9**, 300, 353, 390, 638
Carroll, Joy, 613
Carson, Rachel, **109–13**, 622
Carter, Jimmy, 12, 242–43
Catholic Church, 175–76, 313
Catholic Interracial Council (CIC), 313
Catholic Worker movement, 176, 556, 613

Catt, Carrie Chapman, 36, **113–17**, 501–2
Center for Constitutional Rights (CCR), 369
Central American refugees, 150–52
Central Area Motivation Project (CAMP), 314
Chávez, César, **117–21**, 558, 602
Chavis, Benjamin Franklin, **121–25**
Che-Lumumba Club, 172
Cherney, Darryl, 48–49, 50
Chernobyl, 562
Cherokees, xviii–xix
Chicago, 330–31
Chicago Eight, 187–88, 281, 300–301, 369, 545–46
Chicago Garment Workers strike, 16
Chicago Seven, 29, 281, 300–301, 369–70, 546
Child labor, 61, 332, 333, 336
Chinese workers, xx
Choi, Daniel, **125–29**
Chomsky, Carol, 130–31
Chomsky, Noam, **129–34**
Christian communism, 173
Christian Science, 202
Citizen's Clearinghouse for Hazardous Waste (CHEJ), 243–44
City Lights Books, 91–92
Civil disobedience, xix–xx
Civil Rights Act (1964), 42, 353, 480
Civil rights activists, xix–xx. *See also specific activists*
Civil rights movement, 41–42, 73–74, 84, 263; Black Power and, 73, 105–9, 250, 299, 353, 390–91; segregation and, 122, 139, 311–13, 353; voter registration and, 273–74, 310, 425
Clark, Mark, 544
Clark, Ramsey, **134–37**
Clay, Cassius. *See* Ali, Muhammad
Cline, Wilma, 387
Clinton, Bill, 89, 225, 417
Clinton, Hillary, 12–13
Coalition of Immokalee Workers (CIW), 55–58

CODEPINK (CP), 59, 61–62, 609–10, 631
Coffin, William Sloane, **137–41**
COINTELPRO, 277, 543–44
Cold War, 506, 511–16, 535
Coler, Jack, 483
Collier, John, **141–45**
Colonial America, dissenters in, xviii
Colvin, Claudette, 471
Commission on the Status of Women, 285
Committee on the Practice of Democracy (COPD), 79
Commoner, Barry, **145–49**, 297
Common Sense (Paine), xviii
Communism, 173, 267–70, 287–89, 333, 378, 535–36
Communist Party, 47, 209, 477, 513–14, 579–80, 619, 621
Communist Party of the United States of American (CPUSA), 222–23, 267–70, 287, 289
Communists, 80, 170, 209
Communitarian experiments, xx, 237–40, 288
Comstock Law, 193, 195, 197, 530, 531, 626
Conformity, 258
Congress of Racial Equality (CORE), 79–80, 84, 106, 122, 353, 521
Conservation movement, 432
Consumer movement, 335–36, 437–38
Contraception, 195–96, 529–33
Cook, Wesley. *See* Abu-Jamal, Mumia
Corbett, Jim, **149–52**
Corrie, Rachel, **152–56**
Coughlin, Charles E., **156–60**, 405
Craig, Mary, 570
Crisis (magazine), 207–8
Crusade of the Mill Children, 332
Cuba, 60, 170, 259, 327, 448
Czolgosz, Leon, 255

Daley, Richard J., 300
Danaher, Kevin, 60
Darrow, Clarence, **161–65**, 453
Dart, Justin, Jr., **165–69**

Darwin, Charles, 15
Davis, Angela, 42, 83, **169–73**, 269
Dawes Act, 142–43
Day, Dorothy, **173–77**, 556, 569, 612–13
Days of Rage, 29, 31, 519
Dean, James, 258
Debs, Eugene V., 162–63, 174, **177–81**, 207, 292, 332, 579, 583
Declaration of Rights and Sentiments, xxi–xxii
Dees, Morris, **181–85**
Defense spending, 11
Dellinger, Daniel, 64, 281
Dellinger, David, **185–89**
Deloria, Vine, Jr., **189–93**
DeMille, Cecil B., 493
Democratic National Convention (1968), 187–88, 281, 300, 369, 450, 545
Democratic Socialists of America (DSA), 28
Denison House, 36
Dennett, Mary Ware, **193–97**, 532
Dennett, William Hartley, 194
Desert Solitaire (Abbey), 2–3
Detroit Summer, 74
Dioxin, 148
Disability rights movement, 75–78, 165–68, 325–28
Disarmament, 140
Dissent: separation as, xx; tradition of, xviii–xxii
Divelbess, Diane, 99
Divorce, 625
Dohrn, Bernardine, 30, 32, 33, 519
Donald v. United Klans of America (1987), 183–84
Don't Ask, Don't Tell policy, 99–100, 125–28, 226
Douglas, Marjory Stoneman, **197–201**
Douglass, Frederick, xix
Dowie, John Alexander, **201–5**
Draft resistance, 64, 139, 187, 255, 259
Du Bois, W. E. B., **205–10**, 269, 506–7, 579
Durham, Priscilla, 7

Earth First!, 3, 47, 48, 49, 296
Eddy, Mary Baker, 202
Edison, Thomas, 578
Eickenmeyer, Rudolph, 578
Eisenhower, Dwight, 536
Ellsberg, Daniel, 65, **211–14**, 400, 648–49
El Salvador, 27, 342–43
Emerson, Steve, 20–21
End Poverty in California (EPIC), 570
Engels, Friedrich, 333, 334, 474
Environmental Justice Movement (EJM), 74, 86–90, 622
Environmental Justice Resource Center, 88–89
Environmental movement: Aldo Leopold and, 380–84; Barry Commoner and, 145–49; Hazel Wolf and, 622; JoAnn Tall and, 585–88; Julia Hill and, 294–98; Marjory Stoneman Douglas and, 197–200; Rachel Carson and, 109–13
Environmental Protection Agency (EPA), 87, 88, 438
Environmental racism, 86–90, 123
Equal Employment Opportunity Commission (EEOC), 233
Equality Act, 12
Equal Rights Amendment (ERA), 12, 234, 480, 481, 534, 536–37
Equity, xx
Espionage Act, 180, 213, 400
Euthanasia, 315–18, 345–49
Everglades, 199–200
The Everglades: River of Grass (Douglas), 197, 199
Evers, Medgar, 42

Factory workers, xxi
Fahrenheit 9/11 (film), 429–30
Fair Labor Standards Act, 488
Faith healing, 202, 204
Fariz, Hatim Naji, 19
The Farm, 237, 238–40

Farmworkers, 55–58, 117–21, 601–2
Farrakhan, Louis, **215–19**
Fascism, 288
Faulkner, Daniel, 4, 6–8
Faulkner, Maureen, 8
Fechter, Michael, 20
Federal Communications Commission (FCC), 103–4
Federal Trade Commission (FTC), 438
Fellowship of Reconciliation, 37, 521
The Feminine Mystique (Friedan), 84, 231, 233, 480
Fife, John, 150, 151
Final Exit (Humphry), 317–18
Final Exit Network, 318
Fiorito, Eunice, 76
Fish-ins, 191
Flores, Miguel, 57
Florida, 423–24
Florida Tomato Growers Exchange (FTGE), 57, 58
Flynn, Elizabeth Gurley, **219–23**, 292
Fonda, Jane, 281
Food First, 60
Forced labor, by farmworkers, 55–58
Ford, Gerald, 12
Foreman, George, 25
Foreman, James, 73–74
The Fountainhead (Rand), 493
Fox News, 54
Frank, Barney, **223–27**, 380
Franken, Al, **227–31**, 409
Frazier, Joe, 25
Freedom of Access to Clinic Entrances (FACE), 595–96
Freedom of Information Act, 12, 438
Freedom Riders, 280, 521
Freedom Summer, 84
Free love, 625, 626
Freire, Paulo, 310–11
Friedan, Betty, 84, **231–35**, 480
Fugitive Slave Law, xix
Fukushima Nuclear Power Plant, 562–63
Fuller, Millard, 182

Gandhi, Mahatma, 118
Garvey, Marcus, 640
Gaskin, Stephen, **237–40**
Gay rights, 12, 99–100, 224, 226, 419–23
General Electric (GE), 578, 579
General Motors (GM), 428
Genetic engineering, 148
Gibbs, Lois, 89, **240–44**
Gifford, Kathie Lee, 343–44
Gilman, Charlotte Perkins, **244–48**
Ginsberg, Allen, 91–92, 94, 450
Giovanni, Nikki, **248–53**
Global Exchange, 59–61
Global Fashion, 343–44
Globalization, 343
Glover, Jim, 448
Gold, Harry, 514
Gold, Ted, 32–33
Goldman, Emma, **253–56**, 530, 583
Goldwater, Barry, 536, 583
Gomez, Sebastian, 57
Goodman, Paul, **256–60**, 573
GOONS (Guardians of Our Oglala Nation), 45, 482
Gore, Al, 440
Gray Panthers, 365
Great Chicago Fire, 330
Great Depression, 488, 564–65, 620–21
Great Migration, 208
Greenglass, David, 514, 515
Green Party, 440
Greenwich Village, 195
Gregory, Dick, **260–65**, 586
Grimké, Sarah, xix
Growing Up Absurd (Goodman), 256, 258
Guardians of the Oglala Nation, 45, 482
Guevara, Che, 517
Gulf Peace Team (GPT), 338–39
Guma, Greg, 185–86
Gunn, David, 595

Haldeman, George, 14
Hall, Gus, **267–71**
Hamer, Fannie Lou, 84, **271–75**

Hammoudeh, Sameeh, 19
Hampton, Fred, 135, **275–78**, 544
Hannity, Sean, 54
Happersberger, Lucien, 41
Harding, Warren, 177, 180
Harmonie, xx
Harris, Zellig, 131
Hawken, Harvey, 98–99
Hayden, Casey, 280
Hayden, Joseph L., 578
Hayden, Tom, **278–82**
Haymarket Square riot, 331, 476
Haywood, William "Big Bill", 163, 174, 179
Health care, 418
Height, Dorothy, **282–86**
Helms-Burton Bill, 609
Hemlock Society, 316, 317–18
Henry, Patrick, xviii
Herrick, William, **286–90**
Highlander Folk School, 309–11
Hill, Joe, 49, **290–94**
Hill, John, 370
Hill, Julia "Butterfly," **294–98**
Hiltzik, George, 53
Hip-Hop Summit Action Network (HSAN), 124
Hitler, Adolf, 37, 116, 217, 289, 521
Hoffman, Abbie, 281, **298–302**
Holmes, John Clellon, 91
Holmes, Larry, 25
Holocaust, 615–18
Homestead Act, 500
Homosexuals: discrimination against, 225; in military, 97–100, 125–28, 226
Hoover, Herbert, 37
Hoover, J. Edgar, 267, 276, 354, 463, 543
Horowitz, David, 20, **302–7**
Horton, Myles, **307–11**
House Un-American Activities Committee (HUAC), 82, 494, 535–36, 549, 566
Housing discrimination, 312–13
Hubbard, Walter, Jr., **311–15**
Hull, Cornell, 488

Hull House, 13, 15, 16, 36, 247, 334–35, 486–87, 569
Human Rights Watch, 338
Humphry, Derek, **315–19**
Huncke, Herbert, 93
Hurricane Katrina, 90
Hurston, Zora Neale, 68, 70, **319–23**
Hussein, Saddam, 134
Hutchinson, Anne Marbury, xviii
Hutton, Bobby, 544

Ickes, Harold, 142
Immokalee, Florida, 55–58
Indian Removal Act, xviii
Indian Reorganization Act, 43, 44, 141, 142–44
Indian schools, 43–44
Indian Wars, xviii
Industrial Workers of the World (IWW), 47, 174, 179, 220–21, 290, 292–94, 476, 497, 582, 583
International Labor Defense (ILD), 221–22
International Solidarity Movement (ISM), 152–55
International Woman Suffrage Alliance (IWSA), 114–15
International Working People's Association (IWPA), 475
Iraq, 136
Iraq War, 28, 61–62, 153–54, 339, 362, 550–55, 610, 613, 627–31
Islamic Committee for Palestine (ICP), 18
Israel-Palestinian conflict, 62, 133, 152–55, 339–40, 574, 610, 631

Jackson, Andrew, xviii–xix
Jackson, Anthony, 6–7
Jackson, George, 172
Jackson, Jesse, 120, 123, 276
James, C. L. R., 73
Japanese American internment, 354–58, 633–37
John Birch Society, 536
Johnson, Harriet McBryde, **325–28**
Johnson, Lyndon, 135, 139, 285, 353, 499

Johnson, Zilphia, 309–10
Johnson-Forest Tendency, 73
Jones, Mary Harris, 292, **329–32**
The Jungle (Sinclair), 174, 487, 567, 568–69

Kapashesit, Randy, 374
Kelley, Florence, **333–37**
Kelly, Kathy, **337–41**
Kennedy, Edward M., 12
Kennedy, John F., 139, 259, 263, 281, 391
Kennedy, Robert, 42, 119, 135, 259, 281, 395
Kent State, 281
Kernaghan, Charles, **341–45**
Kerouac, Jack, 90, 92, 93, 94
Kevorkian, Jack, **345–50**
Keys v Carolina Coach (1955), 471
King, Martin Luther, Jr., xix, 42, 73, 106, 118, 121–22, 250, 259, 310, **350–54**; assassination of, 350, 354; "I Have a Dream" speech, 285, 520; "Let Freedom Ring" speech, 353; Montgomery bus boycott and, 352, 471–72, 522
Kirshner, Jacob, 255
Knights of Labor, 331
Kochiyama, Yuri, **354–58**
Kolata, Gina, 47
Kovic, Ron, **358–63**
Kropotkin, Peter, 16
Kuhn, Margaret, **363–66**
Kunstler, William, 46, 281, **366–71**

Labor movements, xx–xxi, 16–17, 36, 331–32, 341, 343–45, 475–76; farmworkers and, 55–58, 117–21, 601–2; IWW and, 47, 174, 179, 220–21, 290, 292–94
Labor unions, 177–80, 268, 292–94, 331–32, 538–41
LaDuke, Winona, **373–77**, 440
Lakota Tribe, 585–88
Lamo, Adrian, 399, 400
Landrieu, Mary, 458

LaRouche, Lyndon, 136, **377–80**
LaRouche Youth Movement, 379
League of Women Voters (LWV), 116
Lenin, Vladimir, 255, 492, 579–80
Leopold, Aldo, 375, **380–84**
Leopold, Nathan, 163
Lesbian, gay, bisexual, and transgender (LGBT) rights, 12, 99–100, 224, 226, 419–23
Leslie, Miriam, 115
Lewis, Jerry, 326–27
Libya, 218
Limbaugh, Rush, 53, 54, 160, 229, **384–88**, 495
Lincoln, Abraham, 14
Liston, Sonny, 24
Loeb, Richard, 163
Los Alamos, 462
Love Canal, 240–44
Lovejoy, Elijah, xix
Lowell Female Labor Reform Association, xxi
Lowell textile mills, xxi
Lucas, Robert, 276
Lynchings, 506, 565

Mailer, Norman, 10
Malcolm X, 23–26, 42, 73, 106, 124, 217, 250, 264, 353, **389–93**, 543, 640
Manifesto for a Black Revolutionary Party (1969), 73–74
Mankiller, Wilma, **393–97**
Manning, Bradley, 214, **397–401**
March on Washington Movement, 72–73, 498, 520, 521
Marshall, John, xviii
Marshall, Thurgood, 425
Martin, Joe, 23
Marx, Karl, 207, 268, 269, 333, 334, 474, 612–13, 626
Massachusetts colony, xviii
Maurin, Peter, 176
Maxwell, xx
Maxwell, Bill, 57

Mayday March, 188
Mazzocchi, Tony, 560
McAlister, Elizabeth, 65
McCain, John, 33, 465
McCarthy, Eugene, 450
McCarthy, Joseph, 10, 20, 80, 85, 102, 209, 269, 289–90, 378, **401–6**, 443, 463
McCorvey, Norma, **406–9**
McGovern, George, 183
McKinley, William, 16, 255, 599
Means, Russell, 191, **409–14**, 586
Meat Inspection Act, 569
Merton, Thomas, 64
Michelman, Kate, 414, **414–19**
Military: homosexuals in, 97–100, 125–28, 226; segregation in, 311–12, 497–98
Milk, Harvey, **419–23**
Million Man March, 124, 215, 218
Minimum wage, 488
Mississippi, 272–73
Mississippi Freedom Democratic Party (MFDP), 274
Modern Times, xx
The Monkey Wrench Gang (Abbey), 3
Montgomery bus boycott, 469–72, 522
Montgomery Improvement Association (MIA), 352, 471–72, 522
Mooney, Edward, 159–60
Moore, Harry, **423–27**
Moore, Michael, 28, **427–31**
Morgan, Irene, 521
Most, Johann, 254
Mother Jones. *See* Jones, Mary Harris
Mothers of Invention, 645
Motion Picture Alliance for the Preservation of American Ideals (MPA), 494
Mott, John R., 38
Mott, Lucretia, xxi
MOVE, 6
Moynihan, Daniel Patrick, 12
Muckrakers, 567–71, 589–92
Muhammad, Elijah, 23, 216, 217, 389, 390, 391
Muller v. Oregon (1908), 336

Murie, Margaret, **431–36**
Murray v. Curtlett (1963), 451, 454
Muscular Dystrophy Association (MDA), 326–27
Muste, A. J., 521

Nader, Ralph, 61, 376, **437–41**
The Naked Lunch (Burroughs), 94
NARAL Pro-Choice America, 416–18
National Abortion Rights Action League (NARAL), 234
National American Woman Suffrage Association (NAWSA), 114–15, 194–95, 478, 501
National Association for the Advancement of Colored People (NAACP), 84, 121, 124, 164, 169, 207–9, 273, 310, 336, 424–26, 470, 564–66
National Association of Colored Women (NACW), 70
National Birth Control League (NBLC), 195
National Congress of American Indians (NCAI), 190
National Consumers League (NCL), 335–36
National Council of Negro Women (NCNW), 70, 284–86
National Environmental Justice Advisory Council (NEJAC), 89
National Labor Committee (NLC), 343–45
National Labor Relations Act, 488
National Office for Black Catholics (NOBC), 313–14
National Organization for Women (NOW), 84, 233–34, 596
National Public Radio (NPR), 458–59
National Traffic Safety Administration (NTSA), 438
National Urban Indian Movement (NUIO), 411
National Woman's Party, 478–79
National Women's Political Caucus, 12
Nation of Islam (NOI), 23–26, 124, 216–18, 250, 389–92
Native American dissent, xviii–xix

Native Americans: activism by, 189–92, 373–76, 393–97, 409–14, 481–85, 585–88; American Indian Movement (AIM), 43–47, 411–13, 482, 586; environmental movement and, 622; Indian Reorganization Act and, 141–44; rights of, 141–44; voting rights of, 565–66
Native Resource Coalition (NRC), 586
Native Son (Wright), 41
Navarette, Cesar, 57
Navarette, Geovanni, 57
Nazi-Soviet Pact, 289
New Deal, 158, 488, 533, 534, 564, 621
New Harmony, xx
Newton, Huey, 42, 304, 543, 544
New York Radical Feminists, 84, 85
New York Radical Women, 84
Niagara Movement, 207
Nichols, Kamook, 46
Niebuhr, Reinhold, 138
Night (Wiesel), 617, 618
9-11 Visibility Project, 28–29
Nineteenth Amendment, 116, 480
Nixon, Richard, 213, 214, 281, 420–21, 536
Nonviolence, 118, 119–20, 352
Norman, Mildred, **441–45**
Nuclear power, 559–63
Nuclear Test Ban Treaty, 10
Nuclear weapons, 146–47, 209, 536

Obama, Barack, 33, 126, 127, 218, 286, 380, 400–401, 418, 610, 640
Objectivism, 494
Occupational Safety and Health Administration (OSHA), 438
Ochs, Phil, **447–51**
O'Hair, Madalyn Murray, **451–55**
Oil, Chemical and Atomic Workers (OCAW) Union, 559
O'Keefe, James, **455–60**
On Civil Disobedience (Thoreau), xix
Oppenheimer, J. Robert, **460–64**
O'Reilly, Bill, 20, 54, 226–27, 229

Oughton, Diana, 32–33
Owen, Changler, 496–97
Owen, Robert, xx

Pacific Tomato Growers (PTG), 58
Pacifists, 17, 35, 173, 500–503
Paine, Thomas, xviii
Palestinian Islamic Jihad, 19–20, 21
Palestinians, 18, 62, 152–53
Palin, Sarah, **465–69**, 603
Pan-Africanism, 208
Parents Music Resource Center (PMRC), 645–46
Parks, Rosa, 80, 310, 352, **469–73**, 521, 522
Parson, Albert, 473–75, 476
Parsons, Lucy, 292, **473–77**
Pate, Kenneth, 7
Paterson, Isabel, 494
Patriot Act, 19
Paul, Alice, 115, **477–81**, 501–2, 536, 537
Peace movement, 337–40, 362, 443–44. *See also* Antiwar activism
Peace Pilgrim, 443–44
Peace Planting, 338
Peltier, Leonard, 8, 26, 46, 136, **481–85**
Penn, William, xviii, 13
Pentagon Papers, 131, 212–14, 400, 648
A People's History of the United States (Zinn), 649–50
Perkins, Frances, **485–89**, 541
Pine Ridge Reservation, 45, 586
Planned Parenthood, 456–57
Pledge of Resistance, 47–48
Plowshares Movement, 65–66, 136
Police brutality, 276, 277
Pornography, 85–86
Port Huron Statement, 280
Potter, Paul, 30
Potts disease, 14–15
Powderly, Terrence, 476
Powell, Adam Clayton, 522
Prairie Fire, 31–32
Privacy Act, 12
Progressive Party, 209

Prostitution, 487
Public Citizen, 439, 440
Puget Sound Co-Operative Colony, xx
Pullman strike, 16, 162–63, 178–79, 497
Pure Food and Drug Act, 569
Puritans, xviii
PVC campaign, 243–44

Quakers, xviii, 37

Racial discrimination, 23, 39–41, 67, 68, 73, 80, 124, 169, 182, 424
Racism, environmental, 86–87
Radosh, Daniel, 431
Rand, Ayn, **491–95**
Randolph, A. Philip, 73, **496–500**
Rankin, Jeannette, 115, **500–503**
Rape, 82–83, 85
Rapp, George, xx
Reagan, Ronald, 27, 170, 558
Red Scare, 209, 463, 535
Redwoods, 294, 296–97
Redwood Summer project, 48–49
Refugees, 150–52
Rehabilitation Act (1973), 76
Religion, 451–55
Religious dissenters, in colonial times, xviii
Religious freedom, xviii
Religious Society of Friends (Quakers), xviii, 37
Reparations, 306, 639
Reproductive rights, 414–19, 529–33
Reudrich, Randy, 468
Revolutionary Youth Movement (RYM), 518–19
Rhode Island, xviii
Ridge, Tom, 7
Right-to-die movement, 318
Riis, Jacob A., 486
Robbins, Terry, 33
Robeson, Paul, **503–7**
Roe v. Wade (1973), 406, 407–9, 537
Roger and Me (film), 28, 429

Roosevelt, Eleanor, 70, 284, 310, 356, 488, **507–11**, 565
Roosevelt, Franklin D., 70, 73, 142, 158, 380, 488, 497–98, 508–10, 534, 541, 621
Roosevelt, Theodore, 567, 569
Rose, Lila, 456–57
Rosenberg, Ethel and Julius, 28, 47, 303, 369, **511–16**
Rudd, Mark, 30, **516–20**
Rumsfeld, Donald, 552
Rushdie, Salman, 575
Russian Revolution, 255, 492
Russo, Anthony, 213
Rustin, Bayard, **520–23**
Rutgers Centurion (newspaper), 455–56

Sacco, Ferdinando Nicola, 222, 515, **525–29**, 570
Sachs, Sadie, 530
Same-sex marriage, 99, 399, 537
Sanctuary movement, 150–52
A Sand Country Almanac (Leopold), 383–84
Sanger, Margaret, 195, 196, **529–33**
Saunders, Ed, 450
Schiavo, Terri, 328
Schiller, Friedrich, 378–79
Schlafly, Phyllis, **534–38**
Schlessinger, Laura, 54
Schneiderman, Rose, **538–42**
School of the Americas Watch (SOA), 337–38
School prayer, 451–55
Scopes trial, 161, 163–64
Screen Actors Guild (SAG), 27
Seale, Bobby, 281, 300–301, 369, **542–46**
Seattle Black Catholic Lay Caucus (SBLCC), 314
Seeger, Pete, **546–50**
Segregation, 84, 122, 139, 169, 311–12, 353, 497–98
Seneca Falls Convention, xxi–xxii

Separation, as dissent, xx
September 11, 2001, 28–29, 571–72, 630
Settlement house movement, 13, 15, 16, 36, 115, 501
Sex education, 193, 195, 196–97
Sex trafficking, 86
Shaw, Anna Howard, xxi
Sheehan, Cindy, **550–55**, 630
Sheen, Martin, **555–59**
Silent Spring (Carson), 109, 111–12, 622
Silkwood, Karen Gay, 48, **559–63**
Simkins, Andrew, 564
Simkins, Modjeska Monteith, **563–67**
Sinclair, Upton, 174, 487, **567–71**
Singletary, William "Dales," 7
Sirhan, Sirhan, 32
Skinner, Alice, 448–49
Slavery, 306, 423, 639
Sloatman, Gail, 645
Smith, Mary Rozet, 15
Smith Act, 223
Smith v. Allwright (1944), 425
Sobell, Morton, 47, 369, 515
Social Democratic Party, 179, 207, 474
Socialism, 179, 267, 269, 270, 333–34, 506
Socialist Labor Party (SLP), 475
Socialist Party, 269, 579
Socialist Workers Party (SWP), 378
Soledad Brothers, 171–72
Solidarity movement, 574
Sontag, Susan, 258, **571–76**
Sotomayor, Sonia, 409
The Souls of Black Folks (Du Bois), 207
Southern Christian Leadership Council (SCLC), 106, 121–22, 352–53, 522
Southern Poverty Law Center (SPLC), 183–84
Soviet Union, 579–80, 583
Spanish Civil War, 288–89
Spry, William, 293
Stalin, Joseph, 289
Standard Oil, 589, 591–92
Stanton, Elizabeth Cady, xxi

Starr, Ellen Gates, 15, 16
Steel Workers Organizing Committee (SWOC), 268
Steinmetz, Charles, **576–80**
Sterilization, 272
Stetson, Walter, 246
Stone, Lucy, xxi
Stoner, Fred, 23
Strikes, xx–xxi
Strong, Anna Louise, **581–84**
Student movements, 29–30
Student Nonviolence Coordinating Committee (SNCC), 84, 105–8, 263, 273, 279–80, 638
Students for Academic Freedom, 305
Students for a Democratic Society (SDS), 30, 280, 517–18
Suffragist movement, 194–95, 198, 501, 626
Suffragists, xxi–xxii, 36; Alice Paul, 477–81; Carrie Chapman Catt, 113–17; Jane Addams, 13–17; Mary Ware Dennett, 194–95
Sugg, John, 21
Sumpter, Jim, 52
Survival Programs, 545
Sweatshops, 343–44
Sweeney, Mike, 47, 48
Swimmer, Ross, 396–97

Taliban, 630
Talk show hosts, 51–55, 384–88
Tall, JoAnn, **585–89**
Tarbell, Ida, 567, **589–93**
Teamsters union, 268
Tea Party Movement, 51, 54, 459, 468
Tell, David, 20
Terrorism, 18–19
Terrorist organizations, 19–20
Textile mills, xxi
Thoreau, Henry David, xix
Three Mile Island, 562
Till, Emmett, 275
Tiller, George, **593–97**
Title VII, 480–81

Tomato pickers, 55–58
Torture, 400–401, 575
Townsend, Jim, 271, 272
Trade unionism, 292–94, 331–32, 538, 539–41. *See also* Labor movements
Trail of Broken Treaties, 45
Trail of Tears, xix
Tree spiking, 48
Tresca, Carlo, 221
Triangle Shirtwaist factory fire, 487, 540
Trotsky, Leon, 288
Truman, Harry, 380, 488–89, 498
Truth, Sojourner, xix
Ture, Kwame. *See* Carmichael, Stokely
Tydings-McDuffie Act, 600

Uhuru Movement, 639, 640
United Church of Christ's Commission for Racial Justice (UCC-CRJ), 122, 123
United Farm Workers (UFW), 119, 120, 599, 601–2
United Mine Workers (UMW), 331–32
United States, tradition of dissent in, xviii–xxii
U.S. foreign policy, 132–33, 134, 136–37
U.S. Social Forum (USSF), 74
U.S.v. David Dellinger et al. (1968), 188
U.S. v. Flores (1997), 57–58
U.S. v. Navarette (2008), 57
U.S. v. Ramos (2004), 58
U.S. v. Tecum (2001), 58
Utopia, xx
Utopian communities, xx

Van Patter, Betty, 304
Vanzetti, Bartolomeo, 222, 515, **525–29**, 570
Vera Cruz, Philip, **599–602**
Veterans, 358–62, 503
Vietnam War, 11, 24–25; draft resistance, 64, 139, 187, 259; Pentagon Papers, 212–14; protests against, 29–30, 60, 63–66, 131, 135, 187–88, 280–81, 360–63, 420–21, 448–50; veterans, 358–62

Violence, against women, 82–83
Vogler, Joe, **602–6**
Voices for Creative Nonviolence (VCNV), 339–40
Voices in the Wilderness (VITW), 339
Voter registration, 273–74, 310, 425
Voting rights, 565–66
Voting Rights Act (1965), 183, 274, 353–54, 566

Wade, Sally, 104
Walker, Alice, **607–11**
Walker, David, xix
"Walker's Appeal" (Walker), xix
Wallis, Jim, **611–15**
War crimes, 136–37
Warren, Josiah, xx
Washington, Booker T., 207
Watergate scandal, 213
Watts Riots, 263, 354
Weather Underground Organization (WUO), 29–31, 516, 518–19
Weavers, 548–49
Weld, Angelina Grimké, xix
"We Shall Overcome" (Johnson), 309–10
White, Dan, 422
White Earth Reservation, 374–75
Wickett, Ann, 316–17
Wiesel, Elie, **615–19**
WikiLeaks, 214, 398, 399–400
Wilkerson, Cathy, 33
Wilkins, Roy, 135, 566
Williams, Roger, xviii
Williams, Ronald, 483
Willkie, Wendell, 493
Wilmington 10, 122–23
Wilson, Caldwell, 487–88
Wilson, Richard, 45
Wilson, Woodrow, 116, 180, 293, 478, 479, 496, 502
Wobblies. *See* Industrial Workers of the World (IWW)
Wolf, Hazel, **619–23**

Woman's Christian Temperance Union (WCTU), 334
Woman's Peace Party, 17, 36
Women, violence against, 82–83
Women Against Pornography (WAP), 85–86
Women and Economics (Gilman), 247
Women's International League for Peace and Freedom (WILPF), 17, 37, 38, 502
Women's Liberation movement, 82–86
Women's Peace Party (WPP), 115, 195, 336
Women's rights movement, xxi–xxii, 13, 231–35, 244–45, 625–26. *See also* Suffragist movement
Women's Trade Union League (WTUL), 487, 539–41
Woodhull, Victoria, **623–27**
Workers Party, 73
Workingmen's Party of the United States (WPUSA), 474–75
Works Progress Administration (WPA), 621
World War I, 17, 36–37, 115, 174, 179–80, 255, 336, 500, 502, 583
World War II, 37–38, 116, 138, 158–59, 186–87, 257–58, 311–13, 503; Japanese-American internment during, 354–58, 633–37
World Women's Party (WWP), 480
Worth, Eugene, 41
Worthy, Bill, 369
Wounded Knee, 370, 395, 586–87
Wright, Ann, 62, **627–32**
Wright, Richard, 41, 80

Yasui, Minoru, **633–37**
Yeshitela, Omali, **637–41**
Young Women's Christian Association (YWCA), 282–83, 284, 285
Youth Communist League (YCL), 521
Youth International Party (Yippies), 299, 300, 450

Zappa, Frank, **643–47**
Zepp, Helga, 378
Zinn, Howard, xx, 131, 302, **647–50**
Zion City, 203–4, 205
Zion Home, 202
Zionism, 9
Zitek, Terry, 21